About Island Press

Island Press is the only nonprofit organization in the United States whose principal purpose is the publication of books on environmental issues and natural resource management. We provide solutions-oriented information to professionals, public officials, business and community leaders, and concerned citizens who are shaping responses to environmental problems.

In 1999, Island Press celebrates its fifteenth anniversary as the leading provider of timely and practical books that take a multidisciplinary approach to critical environmental concerns. Our growing list of titles reflects our commitment to bringing the best of an expanding body of literature to the environmental community throughout North America and the world.

Support for Island Press is provided by The Jenifer Altman Foundation, The Bullitt Foundation, The Mary Flagler Cary Charitable Trust, The Nathan Cummings Foundation, The Geraldine R. Dodge Foundation, The Charles Engelhard Foundation, The Ford Foundation, The Vira I. Heinz Endowment, The W. Alton Jones Foundation, The John D. and Catherine T. MacArthur Foundation, The Andrew W. Mellon Foundation, The Charles Stewart Mott Foundation, The Curtis and Edith Munson Foundation, The National Fish and Wildlife Foundation, The National Science Foundation, The New-Land Foundation, The David and Lucile Packard Foundation, The Pew Charitable Trusts, The Surdna Foundation, The Winslow Foundation, and individual donors.

Natural Hazard Mitigation

Natural Hazard Mitigation

Recasting Disaster Policy and Planning

DAVID R. GODSCHALK

TIMOTHY BEATLEY

PHILIP BERKE

DAVID J. BROWER

EDWARD J. KAISER

CHARLES C. BOHL

R. MATTHEW GOEBEL

Island Press

WASHINGTON, D.C.

COVELO, CALIFORNIA

Natural hazard mitigation : recasting disaster policy and planning /
David Godschalk . . . [et al.].

    p. cm.

    Includes bibliographical references and index.

    ISBN 1-55963-602-5 (pbk)

    1. Disaster relief—Law and legislation—United States.

2. Natural disasters—Law and legislation—United States. 3. United States. Federal Emergency Management Agency. 4. Assistance in emergencies—United States.   I. Godschalk, David R.

KF3750.N38 1999

344.73′05348—dc21   98-34884

                                                    CIP

Contents

Part I
Coping with Floods, Earthquakes, and Hurricanes: U.S. Hazard Mitigation Policy

Part II
Mitigation in Action: Six Disaster Cases

Part III
Assessing the National Mitigation System

Part IV
Recasting the National Mitigation System

List of Figures and Tables

Figures

Tables

Preface

This book is the outcome of a collaborative study by the authors and members of our project advisory panel. These practitioners and experts brought the real world of day-to-day mitigation into our deliberations, ensuring that this would not be simply an ivory tower research project. We are deeply indebted to the panel members:

Donna Dannels, Chief, Program Delivery Branch, Mitigation Directorate, Federal Emergency Management Agency, Washington, D.C.

Steven French, Professor and Director, Graduate City Planning Program, Georgia Institute of Technology, Atlanta, Georgia

Maureen Gregg, Principal Planner, Metropolitan Dade County Planning Department, Miami, Florida

Clancy Philipsborn, President, Mitigation Assistance Corporation, Boulder, Colorado

Paula Schulz, State Hazard Mitigation Officer, Governor's Office of Emergency Services, Oakland, California

Richard Thibedeau, State Hazard Mitigation Officer, Massachusetts Department of Environmental Management, Boston, Massachusetts

In addition, we are indebted to mitigation practitioners across the country who freely shared their knowledge, data, and experience with us. We learned a great deal from them. Many are acknowledged by name in the chapters describing our case studies. But many others contributed by responding to our telephone surveys and our requests to FEMA headquarters and regions for information, as well as by offering valuable suggestions regarding our preliminary presentations of research findings. We specifically appreciate the continued support and feedback from FEMA's Mitigation Directorate.

This study could not have been carried out without the support of Dr. William Anderson of the National Science Foundation. His dedication to improving natural hazards research has been critical in raising the level of knowledge in this field.

Study coinvestigators David R. Godschalk, Philip Berke, David J. Brower, and Edward J. Kaiser are faculty members of the Department of City and Regional Planning at the University of North Carolina at Chapel Hill. They constitute the Natural Hazards Working Group of the University's Center for Urban and Regional Studies. They were joined on this project by Timothy Beatley, a faculty member of the Department of Urban and Environmental Planning at the University of Virginia at Charlottesville. This team has worked together on hazard mitigation planning and research during the past two decades.

A number of capable research assistants from the graduate program in City and Regional Planning at the University of North Carolina contributed to this study. Charles C. Bohl, R. Matthew Goebel, Mark Healey, and Kevin Young coauthored chapters of the original project report. Karl Fulmer and Susan Hass, along with other team members, worked on the evaluation of the state hazard mitigation plans. Sara Hinkley assisted in editing the book manuscript, and Junko Peterson helped edit the project report.

We appreciate the logistical support of the staff of the Center for Urban and Regional Studies at the University of North Carolina at Chapel Hill, including Carroll Cyphert, David Hardt, Carolyn Jones, Holly McBane, Mary Beth Powell, and Bill Rohe. We were fortunate in being able to draw on the long-standing contributions to knowledge of natural hazards generated by the center's past research projects.

Assessing the state of the art in hazard mitigation planning and implementation and its evolution over some eight years since enactment of the Stafford Act has been an ambitious undertaking. If our findings and recommendations help to strengthen natural hazard mitigation policy and practice, we will be well rewarded.

Acknowledgment

This report is based on work supported by the National Science Foundation under Grant No. CMS-9408322, "Assessing Planning and Implementation of Hazard Mitigation Under the Stafford Act" and Grant No. SBR-9312161, "Ethical Issues in Natural Hazard Management." Any opinions, findings, and conclusions or recommendations expressed in this report are those of the authors and do not necessarily reflect the views of the National Science Foundation.

Coping with Floods Earthquakes, and Hurricanes: U.S. Hazard Mitigation Policy

CHAPTER 1

Mitigating Natural Hazards: A National Challenge

Screaming headlines announce another presidential declaration of disaster as the latest flood, hurricane, or earthquake strikes a populated area. Television airs images of devastated homes and freeways. Governors demand federal disaster relief funds. Hearts go out to unfortunate victims huddled in shelters. The Federal Emergency Management Agency rushes in with recovery and rebuilding programs. This frenzied scenario has been repeated many times, with each new disaster seemingly bigger than the last. In fact, the first half of the 1990s saw the largest and most costly floods, hurricanes, and earthquakes in U.S. history.

Why are these disaster damages growing so large? Do we simply have to bite the bullet and keep rebuilding our disaster-stricken communities? Is something wrong with our national disaster policy? Could some of the damage and suffering from natural disasters be prevented?

To answer these questions, this book digs into the decisions and programs behind the headlines. It is the first complete analysis of the outcomes of the Stafford Act, the basic U.S. disaster law, to examine how natural hazard mitigation—the technical term for prevention of future harm from disasters—has worked over time and how it can be made to work more effectively in the future. Its authors are the first to study how federal hazard mitigation funds have actually been spent since the Stafford Act was adopted in 1988, what is actually contained in state hazard mitigation plans required by the Stafford Act, what goes on in mitigation decision making following a major disaster, how government mitigation officials rate the effectiveness of the mitigation system, and what changes are

being considered to solve the widely recognized problems with the present way of coping with natural disasters.

Importance of Natural Hazard Mitigation

Disasters happen when nature's extreme forces strike exposed people and property. These recurring natural phenomena, such as floods, hurricanes, and earthquakes, are known as natural hazard events. When natural hazard events take place in unpopulated areas, no disaster occurs, when they take place in developed areas, damaging life and property, they are called natural disasters. The magnitude of a disaster depends on the intensity of the natural hazard event, the number of people and structures exposed to it, and the effectiveness of pre-event mitigation actions in protecting people and property from hazard forces.

Natural disasters have grown larger as more people and property have become exposed to natural hazards. Unfortunately, the places where hazards occur are often the same places where people want to live—along ocean shores and riverfronts or near earthquake faults. As more urban development takes place in such high-hazard areas, the risk of damage and injury from disasters multiplies. During the first half of the 1990s, the United States suffered unparalleled damage from natural disasters. Hurricanes, floods, earthquakes, and other natural disasters caused billions of dollars in damage, destroyed homes and businesses, and cut off roads, bridges, water systems, and other public infrastructure.

Yet much of the damage and suffering from natural disasters can be prevented. Natural hazard events cannot be prevented from occurring, but their impacts on people and property can be reduced if advance action is taken to mitigate risks and minimize vulnerability to natural disasters. Following disasters in the early 1990s, the U.S. Congress directed the Federal Emergency Management Agency to place its highest priority on natural hazard mitigation, shifting its emphasis from responding to, and recovering from, disasters once they have occurred to mitigating future hazard events. This marked a fundamental change, moving from reactive to proactive national emergency management policy.

This book describes and analyzes the way hazard mitigation has been carried out in the United States under the national disaster law—the Robert T. Stafford Disaster Relief and Emergency Assistance Act, enacted in 1988. We seek to answer questions about how the requirements of this

law, establishing a national system for hazard mitigation, have worked in practice and how they might be made to work better. Our goal is a sound system of natural hazard mitigation, which we believe is a prerequisite to a safe future for the nation and its communities.

The Concept of Natural Hazard Mitigation

Natural hazard mitigation is advance action taken to reduce or eliminate the long-term risk to human life and property from natural hazards. Typically carried out as part of a coordinated mitigation strategy or plan, such actions, usually termed either structural or nonstructural, depending on whether they affect buildings or land use, include the following:

• Strengthening buildings and infrastructure exposed to hazards by means of building codes, engineering design, and construction practices to increase the resilience and damage resistance of the structures, as well as building protective structures such as dams, levees, and seawalls (structural mitigation)

• Avoiding hazard areas by directing new development away from known hazard locations through land use plans and regulations and by relocating damaged existing development to safe areas following a disaster (nonstructural mitigation)

• Maintaining protective features of the natural environment by protecting sand dunes, wetlands, forests and vegetated areas, and other ecological elements that absorb and reduce hazard impacts, helping to protect exposed buildings and people (nonstructural mitigation)

Of the four stages of disaster response—mitigation, preparedness, response, and recovery—*mitigation* is the only one that takes place well before the disaster event. The other stages all occur just before or after the disaster. The *preparedness* stage includes short-term activities, such as evacuation and temporary property protection, undertaken when a disaster warning is received. The *response* stage includes short-term emergency aid and assistance, such as search-and-rescue operations and debris clearance, following the disaster. And the *recovery* stage includes postdisaster actions, such as rebuilding of damaged structures, to restore normal community operations (Godschalk, Brower, and Beatley 1989).

Natural hazard mitigation is an important national policy issue because monetary damages from natural disasters are reaching catastrophic

proportions. Fueled by increasing urbanization in areas exposed to natural hazards, disaster costs have skyrocketed. Insurance companies can no longer continue insuring property in high-hazard areas. The federal Treasury is called on to pay huge sums for postdisaster relief, rebuilding, and recovery. And the personal monetary and psychic costs in lost homes and businesses and disrupted lives are staggering (see Box 1.1).

Disaster Costs

Disaster relief is a large and increasing public expenditure. Between the Stafford Act's passage in 1988 and May 1996, a total of 295 disaster declarations have been made by the president, resulting in disaster relief expenditures of more than $12.6 billion by the Federal Emergency Management Agency for public and individual assistance and hazard mitigation grants. (Public assistance grants are made to state or local governments or nonprofit agencies for repair or restoration of disaster-damaged facilities.

Box 1.1. Record Natural Disasters of the 1990s

Hurricane Andrew

In 1992, Hurricane Andrew resulted in the highest total damage costs of any natural disaster in U.S. history, estimated at more than $25 billion.[1] More than 36 million people live in the counties fronting the Gulf of Mexico and the Atlantic Ocean, the area most susceptible to hurricanes and with the highest growth rates and rising property values (FEMA 1997). The next major hurricane there could be even more disastrous than Andrew, depending on where and when it strikes.

Midwest Floods

The costliest flood disaster in U.S. history was the 1993 flood in the upper Mississippi River basin, which affected nine midwestern states and resulted in an estimated $12–$16 billion in damage. In the United States, more than 9 million households and $390 billion in property are at risk from flooding. Property damage from flooding has averaged more than $2 billion per year in recent years (FEMA 1997).

Northridge Earthquake

The 1994 earthquake in Northridge, California, caused $20 billion in damage costs. Nationwide, more than 109 million people and 4.3 million businesses are exposed to some degree of seismic risk. The average annual loss from earthquakes is estimated at $1 billion (FEMA 1997a).

Individual assistance grants are made to individuals or families to meet disaster-related expenses not otherwise covered. Hazard mitigation grants are made to state or local governments to reduce future hazard risks.) As shown in table 1.1, about 82 percent of this relief funding has gone to disasters involving hurricanes, typhoons, and coastal storms ($4.1 billion), flooding ($2.1 billion), and earthquakes ($4.1 billion).

Disaster relief costs will certainly increase. Petak and Atkisson (1982) estimated that the real value of losses from nine common natural hazards in the United States will increase by a factor of 69 percent between 1980 and 2000. Between 1995 and 2010, costs of natural disasters are projected to be in the range of 5,000 lives and $90 billion (Engi 1995). Table 1.2 shows the total public and individual assistance and hazard mitigation grant funding for some recent large-scale disasters. Stafford Act expenditures for Hurricane Hugo were $1.27 billion, and expenditures for Hurricane Andrew were $1.64 billion. Expenditures for the 1994 Northridge earthquake alone were $3.32 billion, and expenditures for the 1993 Midwest floods approached $900 million. The geographic spread of these disasters is vast. The eleven disasters listed in table 1.2 affected some 822

Photo 1.1. Grand Forks, North Dakota, April 1997. Courtesy of the American Red Cross.

Table 1.1. Summary of Declared Disasters, 1988–1996

Type of Disaster	Number of Declarations	% of Total Declarations	Total FEMA Funding (IA, PA, HMGP)[a]	% of Total FEMA Funding	Average Funding per Declaration	FEMA Regions Affected	States and Territories Affected	Counties Affected
Flood or tornado	32	10.85	$522,901,063	4.14	$16,340,658	5	16	877
Coastal storm	5	1.69	$38,067,314	0.30	$7,613,463	2	4	23
Earthquake	6	2.03	$4,118,292,700	32.61	$686,382,117	2	2	23
Flood	98	33.22	$2,133,068,366	16.89	$21,766,004	10	42	1,747
Hurricane	21	7.12	$3,679,768,771	29.14	$175,227,084	5	15	326
Typhoon	12	4.07	$350,021,651	2.77	$29,168,471	2	8	47
Fishing losses	3	1.02	$10,863,000	0.09	$3,621,000	2	3	18
Fire	6	2.03	$334,054,048	2.65	$55,675,675	2	2	20
Snow or ice storm	34	11.53	$280,014,577	2.22	$8,235,723	10	26	984
Tornado	22	7.46	$70,294,189	0.56	$3,195,190	5	13	179
Volcano	1	0.34	$12,454,712	0.10	$12,454,712	1	1	1
Severe storm	52	17.63	$1,065,193,657	8.44	$20,484,493	10	31	857
Human cause	2	0.68	$10,471,721	0.08	$5,235,861	2	2	2
Other	1	0.34	$2,303,463	0.02	$2,303,463	1	1	1
Totals[b]	295	100.00	$12,627,769,232	100.00	$42,805,997			

Source: Federal Emergency Management Agency for period from 11/24/88 to 5/6/96.

[a] IA = Individual Assistance Program; PA = Public Assistance Program; HMGP = Hazard Mitigation Grant Program.

[b] Percentage totals rounded to 100%.

Table 1.2. Selected Hurricanes, Floods, and Earthquakes, 1988–1996

Disaster Number	FEMA Region	State or Territory	Date Declared	FEMA Program Obligations to Date (IA, PA, HMGP)[a]	Counties Affected	Disaster Name
841	II	VI[b]	9/20/89	$318,119,849	3	Hurricane Hugo
842	II	PR[c]	9/21/89	$520,243,465	57	Hurricane Hugo
843	IV	SC	9/22/89	$364,827,404	24	Hurricane Hugo
844	IV	NC	9/25/89	$61,816,707	29	Hurricane Hugo
				$1,265,007,425	113	
845	IX	CA	10/18/89	$761,545,597	12	Loma Prieta earthquake
913	I	RI	8/26/91	$10,373,949	5	Hurricane Bob
914	I	MA	8/26/91	$29,886,472	11	Hurricane Bob
915	I	ME	8/28/91	$4,469,384	9	Hurricane Bob
916	I	CT	8/30/91	$6,167,495	6	Hurricane Bob
917	I	NH	9/9/91	$1,973,102	4	Hurricane Bob
918	II	NY	9/16/91	$12,686,413	1	Hurricane Bob
				$65,556,815	36	
955	IV	FL	8/24/92	$1,497,444,929	4	Hurricane Andrew
956	VI	LA	8/26/92	$138,178,415	36	Hurricane Andrew
				$1,635,623,344	40	
961	IX	HI	9/12/92	$238,165,574	7	Hurricane Iniki
995	VII	MO	7/9/93	$237,307,814	105	Midwest floods
996	VII	IA	7/9/93	$229,465,905	99	Midwest floods
997	V	IL	7/9/93	$219,486,907	39	Midwest floods
998	VII	NE	7/19/93	$53,229,345	52	Midwest floods
999	VIII	SD	7/19/93	$30,340,297	39	Midwest floods
1000	VII	KS	7/22/93	$78,910,359	57	Midwest floods
1001	VIII	ND	7/26/93	$26,629,270	39	Midwest floods
				$875,369,897	430	
1008	IX	CA	1/17/94	$3,316,583,693	3	Northridge earthquake
1033	IV	GA	7/7/94	$197,502,825	55	Tropical Storm Alberto
1062	IV	FL	8/10/95	$21,754,442	6	Hurricane Erin
1067	II	VI[b]	9/16/95	$415,783,112	3	Hurricane Marilyn
1068	II	PR[c]	9/16/95	$38,662,961	14	Hurricane Marilyn
				$454,446,073	17	
1069	IV	FL	10/4/95	$77,254,887	15	Hurricane Opal
1070	IV	AL	10/4/95	$38,269,472	38	Hurricane Opal
1071	IV	GA	10/10/95	$14,717,750	50	Hurricane Opal
				$130,242,109	103	

Source: Federal Emergency Management Agency, for a period from 11/24/88 to 5/6/96.

[a] IA = Individual Assistance program; PA = Public Assistance program; HMGP = Hazard Mitigation Grant Program

[b] Virgin Islands of the United States.

[c] Puerto Rico.

counties in twenty-three states, with the Midwest floods alone hitting 430 counties.

Total insured losses caused by major natural disasters between 1989 and 1995 reached $45 billion (FEMA 1997a). Led by Hurricane Andrew's insured losses of $15.5 billion in 1992 and the Northridge earthquake's losses of $12.5 billion in 1994, these damages put serious strain on the nation's private insurance system (See table 1.3). A number of small insurance companies went out of business, and several companies in particularly hazard-prone states discontinued hazard insurance.

Natural Hazard Mitigation Policy Framework

To counter the increasing damages from natural disasters, Congress created a mitigation policy framework consisting of a set of basic laws establishing goals, planning and implementation program tools to achieve the goals, and an intergovernmental system linking federal, state, and local government agencies responsible for operating the programs.

Table 1.3. Total Insured Losses from Major Natural Disasters, 1989–1995

DISASTER	DATES	INSURED LOSSES (BILLIONS)
Hurricane Andrew	8/92	$15.5
Northridge earthquake	1/94	$12.5
Hurricane Hugo	9/89	$4.2
Hurricane Opal	10/95	$2.1
Severe winter storms	3/93	$1.7
Firestorm, Oakland, CA	10/91	$1.7
Severe winter storms	1/94–2/94	$1.6
Hurricane Iniki	9/92	$1.6
Hailstorms, TX and NM	5/95	$1.135
Loma Prieta earthquake	10/89	$0.96
Fires, southern CA	10/93–11/93	$0.725
Wind, hail, and tornadoes Denver, CO	7/90	$0.625
Midwest floods	6/93–8/93	$0.6
Total	9/89–10/95	$44.995

Source: FEMAa 1997a, p. xx.

Mitigation Policy Under the Stafford Act

In the United States, natural hazard mitigation policy is set forth in the Robert T. Stafford Disaster Relief and Emergency Assistance Act (42 U.S.C. 5121) and its accompanying regulations in Title 44 of the Code of Federal Regulations, Part 206 (44 C.F.R. 206). In the Stafford Act, Congress declares that because disasters cause loss of life, human suffering, loss of income, and property loss and damage; disrupt the normal functioning of governments and communities; and adversely affect individuals and families, special measures are necessary to assist states in rendering aid, assistance, emergency services, and reconstruction and rehabilitation of devastated areas. The intent of the act is to provide orderly and continuing federal assistance to state and local governments in carrying out their responsibilities to alleviate the suffering and damage caused by disasters. Among the means listed are comprehensive disaster preparedness plans and hazard mitigation measures to reduce losses.

The Stafford Act creates a procedure for a *presidential declaration* that a major disaster has occured. The governor of the affected state requests such a declaration on the basis of a finding that the disaster is of such severity and magnitude that effective response is beyond the capability of the state and its local governments and that federal assistance is necessary. If the request is approved, the president of the United States declares a disaster, and federal disaster assistance is provided.

Stafford Act regulations define *hazard mitigation* as any action taken to reduce or eliminate the long-term risk to human life and property from natural hazards (44 C.F.R. 206.401). Implementing hazard mitigation under the Stafford Act is the responsibility of the Federal Emergency Management Agency, commonly known as FEMA, which prepared a National Mitigation Strategy in 1995 (box 1.2). Operating through its ten regional offices, FEMA assists state emergency management agencies in planning and carrying out their hazard mitigation strategies. Each state is encouraged to formulate a mitigation plan based on the hazards it faces and its institutional capabilities.

Mitigation Tools

Between 1988 and 1996, mitigation under the Stafford Act was carried out through three primary postdisaster activities, which may be thought of as the primary tools of the mitigation planner during that period:

- Section 409 mitigation plans

- Section 404 mitigation grants

Box 1.2. The National Mitigation Strategy: Partnerships for Building Safer Communities

The National Mitigation Goal sets two strategic targets to be achieved by the year 2010:

1. *To substantially increase public awareness* of risk from natural hazards so that the public demands safer communities in which to live and work

2. *To significantly reduce the risk* of loss of life, injuries, economic costs, and destruction of natural and cultural resources that result from natural hazards

To achieve the National Mitigation Goal and to guide state and local mitigation planning and implementation, ten principles are proposed:

1. Risk reduction measures ensure long-term economic success for the community as a whole rather than short-term benefits for special interests.

2. Risk reduction measures for one natural hazard must be compatible with risk reduction measures for other natural hazards.

3. Risk reduction measures must be evaluated to achieve the best mix for a given location.

4. Risk reduction measures for natural hazards must be compatible with risk reduction measures for technological hazards and vice versa.

5. All mitigation is local.

6. Disaster costs and the impacts of natural hazards can be reduced by emphasizing proactive mitigation before emergency response is required; both predisaster (preventive) and postdisaster (corrective) mitigation are needed.

7. Hazard identification and risk assessment are the cornerstones of mitigation.

8. Building new federal-state-local partnerships and public-private partnerships is the most effective means of implementing measures to reduce the impacts of natural hazards.

9. Those who knowingly choose to assume greater risk must accept responsibility for that choice.

10. Risk reduction measures for natural hazards must be compatible with protection of natural and cultural resources.

Source: FEMA 1995.

- Hazard Mitigation Survey Teams and Interagency Hazard Mitigation Teams

Section 409 of the Stafford Act requires the preparation of state disaster mitigation plans as a condition of receiving federal disaster assistance. These plans require states and their localities to identify and adopt programs and policies to reduce future risks from natural hazards. FEMA can condition disaster assistance funds on the implementation of state hazard mitigation plans.

A *hazard mitigation* plan is defined as the plan resulting from a systematic evaluation of the nature and extent of vulnerability to the effects of natural hazards present in society; it includes the actions needed to minimize future vulnerability to hazards. At a minimum, the state hazard mitigation plan must contain the following:

- An evaluation of the natural hazards in the designated area

- A description and analysis of the state and local hazard management policies, programs, and capabilities to mitigate the hazards in the area

- Hazard mitigation goals and objectives and proposed strategies, programs, and actions to reduce or prevent long-term vulnerability to hazards

- A method of implementing, monitoring, evaluating, and updating the mitigation plan on at least an annual basis, to ensure that implementation occurs as planned and that the plan remains current (44 C.F.R. 206.405[a])

States are encouraged to develop a mitigation plan prior to a disaster so that the basic plan can be revised to address specific issues arising from the disaster (44 C.F.R. 206.405 [b]). However, in practice FEMA has assumed that most mitigation plans will be developed in a postdisaster situation (FEMA 1990, p. 6). Following a presidentially declared disaster, the state must submit a hazard mitigation plan or plan update to FEMA within 180 days of the date of the declaration. The FEMA regional director may grant extensions as long as to 365 days (44 C.F.R. 206.405[d]).

A sound planning process is essential to the development and implementation of an effective hazard mitigation plan. Involvement of key state agencies, local governments, and other public- or private-sector bodies that influence hazard management or development policies is critical (44 C.F.R. 206.406 [a]). Although the primary responsibility for preparing the plan is assigned to one state agency, any state agency that influences development within hazardous areas through ongoing activities should be

involved in developing and implementing hazard mitigation plans (44 C.F.R. 206.406 [c]). Local participation is essential because regulation and control of development within hazardous areas normally occur at the local level. It is the responsibility of the state to ensure that appropriate local participation is obtained during development and implementation of hazard mitigation plans (44 C.F.R. 206.406 [d]).

A *hazard mitigation project* is any mitigation measure, project, or action proposed to reduce risk of future damage, hardship, loss, or suffering from disasters. For example, hazard mitigation projects carried out after the Midwest floods included public acquisition of damaged properties and relocation of residents to safe locations, and those after Hurricane Andrew included installation of steel storm shutters on public buildings to prevent future wind damage.

Section 404 of the Stafford Act creates the Hazard Mitigation Grant Program (HMGP), which provides federal matching funds for state and local mitigation projects. These grant funds are tied to disaster declarations and are limited to a percentage of the federal disaster assistance monies made available. Between 1988 and the end of 1995, FEMA approved 876 applications for hazard mitigation grant projects, obligating some $215 million, with another $271 million in pending applications.

A *Hazard Mitigation Survey Team* (called an *Interagency Hazard Mitigation Team* for flood disasters) is a FEMA-state-local team that is activated after disasters to identify immediate mitigation activities and issues to be addressed in the Section 409 hazard mitigation plan. Following every declared disaster, a Hazard Mitigation Survey Team or an Interagency Hazard Mitigation Team is called into action. The team reports to the disaster scene, reviews the damage, and quickly formulates a report on hazard mitigation opportunities and actions to guide preparation of the state's Section 409 hazard mitigation plan and its Section 404 hazard mitigation grant application. For example, the Interagency Hazard Mitigation Team report for Hurricane Andrew (FEMA 1992) identified 53 mitigation issues and 115 recommended actions to reduce the loss of life and property in future disasters.

Intergovernmental Mitigation System

Hazard mitigation under the Stafford Act is envisioned as a process carried out over time through an *intergovernmental system for natural hazard mitigation planning and implementation.* This federal-state-local institutional system is not unlike the system created for implementation of national coastal zone management policy (Godschalk 1992).

As depicted in figure 1.1, the intergovernmental mitigation system consists of six related components:[2]

1. *Federal policy.* The national policies in effect for hazard mitigation, including Stafford Act policies and implementing regulations for state Section 409 plan preparation and Section 404 grant approval, as well as national mitigation priorities, procedures, and programs

2. *FEMA regional implementation.* Actions of FEMA regional offices that convert federal policy to practice, including efforts to build state mitigation commitment and capacity and review of Section 409 plans and Section 404 projects

3. *State commitment and capacity.* State (1) political and organizational commitment (willingness) to support and pursue hazard mitigation goals and policies—the institutional value placed on mitigation relative to that placed on other state goals and policies—and (2) available funding, staff, information, and authority and other capacity to plan and carry out mitigation efforts—the institutional resources at hand for mitigation

4. *State Section 409 plan.* A state's formal document prepared under Stafford Act regulations that defines its mitigation needs, goals, and policies; the quality, purpose, and content of the plan reflect the scope and vision of state mitigation policy

5. *State implementation actions.* Approved and executed Section 404 projects and other mitigation actions (executive orders, technical assistance, development of hazard awareness programs, etc.) that make up the tangible outcomes of state efforts to reduce the impact of future disasters

6. *Risk reduction.* Effectiveness of mitigation actions in reducing risks from natural hazards at both the state and local levels through both struc-

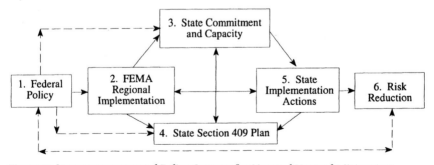

Figure 1.1. Intergovernmental Policy System for Natural Hazard Mitigation.

tural techniques (dams, seawalls and levees, building strengthening, etc.) and nonstructural techniques (relocation, land acquisition, density reduction, etc.)

To understand how the intergovernmental mitigation system works, it is helpful to "walk through" the process it illustrates and examine its assumptions (see figure 1.1). Initially, the federal government, as represented by FEMA headquarters in Washington, D.C., adopts *federal mitigation policy*—the Stafford Act and its regulations plus any further policy decisions. Next, *FEMA regional implementation* converts federal policy to practice through efforts by the regional offices to build state mitigation commitment and capacity and through review and approval of state Section 409 plans and Section 404 project proposals.

The level of *mitigation commitment and capacity* achieved by individual states then influences *state Section 409 plan* quality, purpose, and content and *state implementation actions*. Implementation includes actions taken under Section 404 projects as well as other mitigation actions. Implementation actions are determined both by state mitigation commitment and capacity and by the quality of state mitigation plans. Next, state implementation actions influence the effectiveness of *risk reduction* at the state and local levels through structural and nonstructural mitigation actions. Finally, as indicated by the *feedback* loop, changes in risk levels can modify federal policy and the intergovernmental policy system.

As originally designed, the Stafford Act envisions continuous mitigation planning and implementation process, but it has resulted in a *disaster-driven* process in which state Section 409 hazard mitigation plans have been prepared and approved following presidentially declared disasters primarily to be eligible to receive Section 404 hazard mitigation grant funds. Even though this does not prevent a state from completing its Section 409 plan in advance of a disaster, in practice disaster events have been the catalyst for plan preparation. Thus, Section 409 plans and Section 404 grants have responded to the last disaster rather than anticipating the next disaster. The process depicted in figure 1.1 shows the Stafford Act's theory. To correspond to practice, figure 1.1 should include a presidentially declared disaster following the federal policy and FEMA regional implementation components, since the disaster event activates much of the state planning and implementation activity.

The future challenge is to activate the intergovernmental hazard mitigation policy system ahead of disasters—to convert it to a *threat-driven* process that anticipates disasters in order to carry out advance mitigation activities. In order to turn the process from reactive to proactive, it is important first to understand how the existing system has worked over time—the focus of our study.

Assessing the Effectiveness of Hazard Mitigation

Mitigation is arguably the most critical activity of the four phases of emergency management, which include mitigation, preparedness, response, and recovery. Particularly for recurrent natural hazards whose general locations are predictable, such as hurricanes, floods, and earthquakes, advance actions to lessen property damage and human injury are much more cost-effective than after-the-fact reconstruction. By reducing the magnitude of future disasters, effective mitigation can substantially reduce the cost of disaster response and recovery.

Surprisingly, given its importance, mitigation has been the least understood and least implemented emergency management activity. Although the Stafford Act contains explicit mitigation requirements, a 1991 report by the U.S. General Accounting Office on federal disaster assistance following Hurricane Hugo and the Loma Prieta earthquake does not even recognize the existence of mitigation, citing only three phases of emergency management—preparedness, response, and recovery (GAO 1991, p. 13). However, there is a growing body of literature on mitigation.

One of the newest mitigation books is *Confronting Natural Hazards: Land-Use Planning for Sustainable Communities* (Burby 1998). A product of the second National Assessment of Research and Applications on Natural Hazards, this book, written by a number of national mitigation experts, focuses on the potential of nonstructural measures, such as local land use planning and growth management, to achieve communities that are safe and sustainable. A second volume from the National Assessment, *Designing Future Disasters: An Assessment and Bolder Course for the Nation* (Mileti forthcoming), reports on a broad set of findings and conclusions from this ambitious national review of hazard policy. *Designing Future Disasters* strongly argues for a new "sustainability paradigm" for hazard mitigation, a view similar to the one proposed in the final chapter of this book.

Other authors have identified obstacles to improving the implementation of mitigation, including the perception of disaster assistance as a social entitlement, concern about imposing limitations on the use of private property, the costs of mitigation programs (such as public acquisition of hazard-prone lands), and the organizational fragmentation of mitigation efforts (Godschalk, Brower, and Beatley, 1989; Beatley 1993; Burby et al. 1988; NAPA 1993; Platt 1978; Berke and Beatley 1992; Brenner 1997). A joint task force of the National Emergency Management Association, the Association of State Floodplain Managers, and FEMA evaluated some aspects of the Section 404 Hazard Mitigation Grant Program (Joint Task Force 1992).

Several studies have examined the process of coping with individual natural hazards, including earthquakes (Berke and Beatley 1992; Palm and Hodgson 1992), hurricanes and coastal storms (Mittler 1993; Godschalk, Brower, and Beatley 1989; Godschalk et al. 1998), riverine flooding (Mittler 1997; Burby et al. 1988), and tornadoes and severe storms (Fuller 1987). Other studies (e.g., May and Williams 1986; Mittler 1989) have addressed elements of emergency management common to several types of hazards. Commentators on both right and left have criticized the present disaster relief system (e.g., Bovard 1996; Solomon 1996). FEMA (1997a) has published an analysis of the costs and benefits of natural hazard mitigation, defending its mitigation measures as cost-effective.

Despite this body of work, little is known overall about the actual content of mitigation plans, the ways in which mitigation grants have been spent, the outcomes of these plans and expenditures, and the processes by which plans and programs have been formulated since enactment of the Stafford Act. Prior to the study reported in this book, no comprehensive empirical analysis of the products and operations of the intergovernmental system responsible for carrying out hazard mitigation under the Stafford Act had been published.

Ours is the first systematic study of the complete intergovernmental system for natural hazard mitigation, including its major elements and the linkages among them.[3] The lack of a prior holistic analysis of this complex and dynamic policy implementation system made it difficult for us to evaluate the success of the national hazard mitigation policy. The lack of such knowledge has also hindered the formulation of more effective mitigation efforts to handle increasingly expensive disasters.

Study Purpose

The purpose of our study is to describe and analyze the hazard mitigation efforts carried out under the Stafford Act since its inception, with a focus on the three major types of recurrent natural disasters—floods, earthquakes, and hurricanes. We assess the *content* of state Section 409 mitigation plans, mitigation grant program *expenditures* under Section 404, and the *outcomes* of implementing these plans and programs. We describe and analyze the planning and decision-making *processes* used in formulating the Interagency Hazard Mitigation Team reports and the state mitigation plans for a selected set of disasters. Finally, we offer *recommendations* for improved hazard mitigation policy.

Our study has five major research objectives:

1. To describe the process by which state-level hazard mitigation planning is done and to relate the characteristics of the setting, the actors involved in the process, the timing of activities relative to windows of opportunity, and the planning process itself to planning outcomes

2. To conduct a systematic assessment of existing hazard mitigation plans prepared in compliance with Stafford Act provisions

3. To examine expenditure patterns for mitigation grants funded under Section 404 and to analyze these patterns for systematic relationships between expenditures and Stafford Act goals, types of disasters, and state Section 409 plans

4. To describe and assess the outcomes of implementing Section 409 plans and Section 404 grants, using systematic criteria that relate actions to anticipated mitigation effectiveness

5. To assess the current state of hazard mitigation planning under the Stafford Act and to recommend measures to enhance the effectiveness of Section 409 mitigation plans and Section 404 mitigation grants

Policy Trends Review

Instead of conducting a traditional review of literature, we reviewed the recent hazard mitigation policy documents and proposals. Our findings include the recommendations of recent mitigation policy analyses and proposals, such as those of the Galloway Report following the Midwest floods of 1993 and a number of congressional studies of this policy area. (See chapter 2 for a summary of the evolution of mitigation policy.)

Process Evaluation

To gain an understanding of postdisaster mitigation decision making, we conducted intensive case studies of individual mitigation efforts. After consulting with our project advisory committee, we chose six cases representative of disaster mitigation planning under the Stafford Act but with enough difference to allow for variation: Florida following Hurricane Andrew, Missouri and Iowa following the Midwest floods of 1993, California following the Loma Prieta and Northridge earthquakes, Massachusetts following Hurricane Bob and other storms, and Tennessee following floods and other disasters. During field visits, we interviewed state, local, and regional mitigation officials. Summary lessons learned from these case

studies are outlined in the introduction to part II; individual case studies are described in detail in chapters 3–8.

Because most mitigation planning and implementation are carried out in the postdisaster period, the cases focus on that time frame. The salience of mitigation is high in the wake of a disaster. Moreover, the reconstruction process presents an opportunity to implement mitigation measures. However, in the case studies we also looked for evidence of the influence of predisaster mitigation efforts, and we recognized that postdisaster mitigation for one event becomes predisaster mitigation for the next.

We asked the following questions during our process evaluation research: What are the context and process of mitigation plan preparation? What agencies play the major roles? What is the decision-making process for preparation of the Interagency Hazard Mitigation Team's report? To what extent are the recommendations of that report incorporated into the state Section 409 plan? What is the decision-making process for preparing the state Section 409 plan? What is the role of the state Section 409 plan in postdisaster mitigation? What is the timing of mitigation decisions? Are they limited to narrow windows of opportunity? How are mitigation project applications formulated, reviewed, and approved? How do institutional capacity and commitment affect decision making?

Plan Content

No complete national archive of state Section 409 plans existed in 1994. We collected all available state Section 409 mitigation plans from individual state emergency management and hazard mitigation agencies. This was not a trivial task, since plans were not widely published and were in various stages of drafting or revision, and states were sometimes reluctant to furnish copies of their plans for outside scrutiny.

Next, we performed a systematic content analysis of the collected Section 409 plans. We checked the degree to which the statutory requirements of the Stafford Act were met and compared the content of each plan with a standardized list of potential mitigation actions. This analysis allowed us to evaluate the breadth and quality of each plan component. (See chapter 9 for the outcome of this evaluation.)

We asked the following questions during our plan content research: Do the states have current hazard mitigation plans, as required by the Stafford Act? Do the plans contain the main components called for in the act: hazards assessment, capability assessment, goals and objectives, proposed strategies and actions, and sections on implementation, monitoring and

updating, and evaluation? What is the quality of individual plan elements? Are the plans focused on a single type of hazard, or are they multihazard in orientation? Do they cover only the disaster area or the entire state? Do their proposals follow best mitigation practice? Is plan implementation linked to the Section 404 Hazard Mitigation Grant Program? How comprehensive and internally consistent are the plans?

Expenditure Patterns

To identify mitigation expenditure patterns, we reviewed Section 404 mitigation grant data. Again, no complete national archive of Section 404 expenditure data existed in 1994; we collected this data from the FEMA regional offices. This also was not a trivial task, since the data were maintained in a variety of formats, ranging from computer spreadsheets to paper files, and provision of the data by the regional offices sometimes was a burden for FEMA staff. Transfer of the nondigital data sets into spreadsheet format required a major effort.

Next, we categorized expenditures by overall type of mitigation action, using a standard classification system. We then described and analyzed the expenditures by time period, type of disaster, and changes in national disaster policy, such as the shift to acquisition of flood-damaged property following the 1993 Midwest floods. This enabled us to display the change over time in emphasis on types of disaster mitigation grant expenditures (e.g., from an initial structural emphasis to a later acquisition and relocation emphasis). (See chapter 10 for the outcome of this evaluation.)

We asked the following questions during our mitigation expenditure research: What types of expenditures are funded by Section 404 grants? What is the frequency distribution of these types? How do they vary by type of disaster? How have they changed over time? What is their timing relative to the disaster? What is the relationship of expenditures to Stafford Act goals?

Linkages Analysis

To study the effects of the intergovernmental mitigation system on mitigation capacity and commitment, state Section 409 plans, and implementation actions, we looked for linkages among system components. We conducted telephone surveys of state hazard mitigation officers and federal hazard mitigation officers in FEMA regional offices to learn how they rated capacity and commitment. We searched for linkages between these factors

and plan quality ratings and implementation actions, which could help to explain why certain outcomes occurred. (See chapter 11 for the outcome of this evaluation.)

We asked the following questions during our linkages research: What are the variations in commitment and capacity among state and federal mitigation planners and decision makers? What is the relationship between commitment and capacity and plan quality? Between commitment and capacity and implementation actions? What is the relationship between state mitigation context and plan quality? Between state mitigation context and implementation actions? What is the relationship between plan quality and implementation actions?

Mitigation Policy Recommendations

Finally, we identified important ethical issues that arise during hazard mitigation (chapter 12) and, on the basis of our assessment of critical implementation gaps within the present mitigation system, made recommendations for strengthening future mitigation policy and practice (chapter 13).

We asked the following questions during our mitigation policy research: How fairly are mitigation burdens and benefits spread? Who is responsible for mitigation? What can be done to implement a new mitigation ethic? What are the policy and practice implications of the new paradigm linking mitigation with sustainable communities? How can Stafford Act assumptions of a reactive, disaster-driven mitigation system be transformed to create a proactive, policy-driven system? How can mitigation commitment and capacity be increased? How can mitigation plan quality be improved? How can mitigation implementation actions be made more effective?

Structure of the Book

This book consists of thirteen chapters organized into four parts. Part I, "Coping with Floods, Earthquakes, and Hurricanes: U.S. Hazard Mitigation Policy," contains this introductory chapter and a chapter on the evolution of disaster assistance policy. Part II, "Mitigation in Action: Six Disaster Cases," includes six chapters describing the findings of our individual state case studies, preceded by a comparative overview of case study lessons. Part III, "National Mitigation System Assessment," comprises three chapters that analyze state Section 409 mitigation plans, Section 404 hazard mitigation grant expenditures, and linkages among mitigation system components. Part IV, "Recasting the Mitigation System," has two chapters, one setting forth ethical guidelines for mitigation and one offering recom-

mendations for strengthening mitigation policy and practice. References follow each chapter.

Notes

1. Disaster damage estimates often vary, depending on the time and assumptions of the estimate. Pielke and Landsea (1998) review the different estimation techniques. They cite current estimates of $30 billion in damage cost directly related to Hurricane Andrew and note that if normalized to 1995 dollars by inflation, increases in value of personal property, and changes in population of coastal counties, the estimate would rise to $33 billion, However, they point out, had the great 1926 Florida hurricane happened in 1995, it would have been even more costly, causing $72 billion in damage.
2. This system concept, the conceptual framework for our analysis, builds on and extends work done in prior studies of land use and environmental plans and state mandates (Berke 1994; Berke and French 1994; Burby and Dalton 1994; Dalton and Burby 1994; Berke, Roenigk, and Kaiser 1995).
3. Our complete study findings are contained in our project report, *Making Mitigation Work* (Godschalk et al. 1997), and in a series of fifteen Natural Hazard Working Papers on Assessing Planning and Implementation of Hazard Mitigation Under the Stafford Act, available from the Center for Urban and Regional Studies at the University of North Carolina at Chapel Hill.

References

Beatley, Timothy. 1993. *Risk Allocation Policy in the Coastal Zone: The Current Framework and Future Directions.* Washington, D.C.: Office of Technology Assessment.

Berke, Philip. 1994. "Evaluating Environmental Plan Quality: The Case of Planning for Sustainable Development in New Zealand." *Journal of Environmental Planning and Management* 37 (2): 155–170.

Berke, Philip R., and Timothy Beatley. 1992. *Planning for Earthquakes: Risk, Politics, and Policy.* Baltimore: Johns Hopkins University Press.

Berke, Philip, and Steven French. 1994. "The Influence of State Planning Mandates on Local Plan Quality." *Journal of Planning Education and Research* 13: 237–250.

Berke, Philip, Dale Roenigk, and Edward Kaiser. 1995. *Enhancing Plan Quality: Evaluating the Role of State Planning Mandates.* Chapel Hill: University of North Carolina, Department of City and Regional Planning.

Bovard, J. 1996. "FEMA Money! Come and Get It." *American Spectator,* September, 25–31.

Brenner, Eric. 1997. *Reducing the Impacts of Natural Disasters: Governors' Advisors Talk About Mitigation.* Washington, D.C.: Council of Governors' Policy Advisors.

Burby, Raymond J., ed. 1998. *Confronting Natural Hazards: Land-Use Planning for Sustainable Communities.* Washington, D.C.: National Academy Press, Joseph Henry Press.

Burby, Raymond J., and Linda Dalton. 1994. "Plans Can Matter! The Role of Land

Use and State Planning Mandates in Limiting Development of Hazardous Areas." *Public Administration Review* 54 (3): 229–238.

Burby, Raymond J., Scott A. Bollens, James Holway, Edward J. Kaiser, David Mullan, and John R. Sheaffer. 1988. *Cities Under Water: A Comparative Evaluation of Ten Cities' Efforts to Manage Floodplain Land Use.* Institute of Behavioral Science Monograph No. 47. Boulder: University of Colorado.

Dalton, Linda, and Raymond J. Burby. 1994. "Mandates, Plans, and Planners: Building Local Commitment to Development Management." *Journal of the American Planning Association* 60 (4): 444–461.

Engi, Dennis. 1995. *Historical and Projected Costs of Natural Disasters.* Albuquerque, N.M.: Sandia National Laboratories.

FEMA (Federal Emergency Management Agency). 1990. *Post-Disaster Hazard Mitigation Planning Guidance for State and Local Governments.* DAP-12. Washington, D.C.: FEMA.

———. 1992. *Interagency Hazard Mitigation Team Report, Hurricane Andrew.* Atlanta: FEMA, Region IV.

———. 1995. *National Mitigation Strategy: Partnerships for Building Safer Communities.* Washington, D.C.: FEMA.

———. 1997a. *Multi Hazard Identification and Risk Assessment.* Washington, D.C.: FEMA.

———. 1997b. *Report on Costs and Benefits of Natural Hazard Mitigation.* Washington, D.C.: FEMA.

Fuller, John G. 1987. *Tornado Watch Number 211.* New York: Morrow.

GAO (General Accounting Office). 1991. *Disaster Assistance: Federal, State, and Local Responses to Natural Disasters Need Improvement.* Washington, D.C.: GAO.

Godschalk, David R. 1992. "Implementing Coastal Zone Management: 1972–1990." *Coastal Management* 20 (2): 93–116.

Godschalk, David R., David J. Brower, and Timothy Beatley. 1989. *Catastrophic Coastal Storms: Hazard Mitigation and Development Management.* Durham, N.C.: Duke University Press.

Godschalk, David R., Timothy Beatley, Philip Berke, David J. Brower, Edward J. Kaiser, Charles C. Bohl, R. Matthew Goebel, Mark Healey, and Kevin Young. 1997. *Making Mitigation Work: Recasting Natural Hazards Planning and Implementation.* Final Report, National Science Foundation Grant No. CMS-9408322. Chapel Hill: University of North Carolina, Center for Urban and Regional Studies.

Godschalk, David R., Richard Norton, Craig Richardson, David Salvesen, and Junko Peterson. 1998. *Coastal Hazards Mitigation: Public Notification, Expenditure Limitations, and Hazard Areas Acquisition.* Chapel Hill: University of North Carolina, Center for Urban and Regional Studies.

Joint Task Force (National Emergency Management Association, Association of State Floodplain Managers, and Federal Emergency Management Agency). 1992. *Mitigation Grant Program: An Evaluation Report.* Washington, D.C.: National Emergency Management Association.

May, Peter J., and Walter Williams. 1986. *Disaster Policy Implementation: Managing Programs Under Shared Governance.* New York: Plenum Press.

Mileti, Dennis, ed. Forthcoming. *Designing Future Disasters: An Assessment and Bolder Course for the Nation.* Washington D.C.: National Academy Press, Joseph Henry Press.

Mittler, Elliott. 1989. *Natural Hazard Policy Setting: Identifying Supporters and Opponents of Nonstructural Hazard Mitigation.* Program on Environment and Behavior Monograph No. 48. Boulder: University of Colorado.

———. 1993. *The Public Policy Response to Hurricane Hugo in South Carolina.* Natural Hazards Research and Applications Information Center Working Paper No. 84. Boulder: University of Colorado.

———. 1997. *An Assessment of Floodplain Management in Georgia's Flint River Basin.* Natural Hazards Research and Applications Information Center Monograph No. 59. Boulder: University of Colorado.

NAPA (National Academy of Public Administration). 1993. *Coping with Catastrophe: Building an Emergency Management System to Meet People's Needs in Natural and Manmade Disasters.* Washington, D.C.: NAPA.

Palm, Risa, and Michael Hodgson. 1992. *After a California Earthquake: Attitude and Behavior Change.* University of Chicago Geography Research Paper No. 233. Chicago: University of Chicago Press.

Petak, William, and Arthur Atkisson. 1982. *Natural Hazard Risk Assessment and Public Policy.* New York: Springer-Verlag.

Pielke, Roger A., Jr., and Christopher Landsea. 1998. *Normalized Hurricane Damages in the United States: 1925–1995.* Boulder, Colo: National Center for Atmospheric Research, Environmental and Societal Impacts Group.

Platt, Rutherford H. 1978. "Coastal Hazards and National Policy: A Jury-Rig Approach." *Journal of the American Institute of Planners* 44 (2): 170–180.

Solomon, J. 1996. "Flirting with Disaster: Calamities Like Hurricane Fran Make Great Footage, but They Don't Make Great Relief Policy." *Washington Monthly,* October, 9–11.

CHAPTER 2

Evolving Mitigation Policy Directions

This is an unprecedented time in the evolution of natural hazard mitigation in the United States. As chapter 1 indicates, the 1990s have seen a series of devastating and costly natural disasters, with much of their costs absorbed at the federal level. Consensus is growing that the current approach to natural disasters is not working and that fundamentally new approaches are necessary. An unusual number of studies, reports, and legislative initiatives mark this period as people and organizations look at what is broken with the current system and how it might be fixed.

This chapter reviews the history and evolution of mitigation and disaster assistance policy. It then summarizes recent studies, critical literature, and legislative and executive initiatives. Finally, it identifies key trends and emerging directions in U.S. mitigation policy.

History and Evolution of Mitigation and Disaster Assistance Policy

The current disaster policy framework has evolved slowly and incrementally. Although there is now an extensive federal system for assisting state and local governments in recovering from disasters, this framework is relatively recent. Prior to the 1930s, there was little federal involvement in natural disaster management. And prior to 1950, there was no ongoing framework for the provision of federal disaster assistance to states and localities, though Congress did provide occasional assistance in response to specific disaster events.[1] The current disaster assistance framework came into existence in 1950 with the passage of the first Disaster Relief Act.

Subsequent versions of the act were introduced in 1953 (authorizing assistance for individual victims as well as state and local governments), 1970, 1974, and, most recently, 1988, with passage of the Robert T. Stafford Disaster Relief and Emergency Assistance Act.

This gradual expansion of the federal role has been accompanied by a growing sense of entitlement to federal disaster assistance on the part of state and local governments and individual disaster victims. At the same time, there has been increasing politicization and nationalization of natural disasters, fueled by the virtually instant national media attention given to disaster events. This media attention makes it hard for state and local officials not to seek the maximum amount of aid from the federal government and makes it equally difficult for federal officials to deny such requests (see NAPA 1993 for a discussion of the "CNN syndrome").

The federal bureaucratic structure responsible for disaster management policy has also evolved dramatically since the 1950s (see table 2.1). Perhaps the most significant development was President Jimmy Carter's creation in 1979 of the Federal Emergency Management Agency (FEMA)—a single federal agency with responsibility for coordinating federal disaster policy. FEMA was created by consolidating five agencies: the Defense Civil Preparedness Agency (from the Pentagon), the Federal Insurance Administrator and the Federal Disaster Assistance Administration (from the Department of Housing and Urban Development, or HUD), the Federal Preparedness Agency (from the General Services Administration, or GSA), and the National Fire Prevention and Control Administration (from the Department of Commerce). This consolidation sowed some seeds of confusion about FEMA's mission. Is it primarily a civil defense agency or an agency concerned with natural disasters? Is it an agency concerned primarily with predisaster mitigation and planning or with postdisaster response and recovery? These tensions have remained, though recent shifts in the direction of the agency have made its mission somewhat clearer.

Despite the existence of FEMA, contemporary federal disaster policy can be characterized as highly fragmented and uncoordinated, still suffering from conflicting goals and (until recently) the lack of a cohesive national strategy or plan. Disaster assistance is actually provided by a host of different federal agencies and programs, including FEMA, HUD, the Departments of Transportation and Education, and Small Business Administration. Moreover, vulnerability of people and property is influenced by numerous public investments made by many of the same federal agencies (e.g., see Beatley 1992).

Table 2.1. Significant Disasters and Major Mitigation Policy Initiatives

Year	Disaster Events	Mitigation Policy Initiatives
1917		Flood Control Act of 1917
1928		Flood Control Act of 1928
1936		Flood Control Act of 1936
1965	Hurricane Betsy	
1968		National Flood Insurance Act of 1968 (creation of the NFIP)
1969	Hurricane Camille	Commission on Marine Science, Engineering and Resources (Stratton Commission)
1972	Tropical Storm Agnes	Coastal Zone Management Act (CZMA)
1973		Flood Disaster Protection Act of 1973
1977		Earthquake Hazards Reduction Act; Executive Order 11988, "Floodplain Management" Executive Order 11990, "Protection of Wetlands"
1979		Federal Emergency Management Agency (FEMA) is created
1982		Coastal Barrier Resources Act (CoBRA)
1988		Robert T. Stafford Disaster Relief and Emergency Assistance Act
1989	Hurricane Hugo Loma Prieta earthquake	
1991	Oakland (CA) firestorm	
1992	Hurricane Andrew	Interagency Floodplain Management Task Force assessment report
1993	Mississippi–Missouri valley floods	Creation of Mitigation Directorate within FEMA
1994	Northridge earthquake	Interagency Floodplain Management Review Committee report (Galloway Report) National Flood Insurance Reform Act of 1994 *Unified National Program for Floodplain Management* Executive Order 12941, "Seismic Safety of Existing Federally Owned or Leased Buildings"
1995		First National Mitigation Conference (December) *National Mitigation Strategy*
1996	Hurricane Fran	National Earthquake Loss Reduction Program *Natural Disaster Reduction: A Plan for the Nation* Performance Partnership Agreements
1997	Red River floods	Disaster-Resistant Communities Program

Source: Modeled after Platt 1994, Table 2, p. 273 and "Project Impact: Disaster Resistant Communities."

The Robert T. Stafford Disaster Relief and Emergency Assistance Act of 1988 was an important overhaul of the nation's disaster relief system and a major watershed in the history of disaster management. It is the primary legislation governing the provision of federal disaster assistance and determining the nature of the federal-state disaster assistance framework. Its provisions have implications for all phases of disaster management. The act provides funding for state disaster preparedness (through its Comprehensive Cooperative Agreements), and following a presidential declaration of disaster, the act makes available extensive monies for both public and individual or family disaster assistance.

Mitigation is an important goal of the Stafford Act. The Hazard Mitigation Grant Program (HGMP) provides monies for hazard mitigation measures and projects following disasters. Under the original 1988 act, the federal government could assume as much as 50 percent of the costs of these projects, for a total not to exceed 10 percent of the total public assistance costs for a particular disaster declaration. Under the Hazard Mitigation and Relocation Assistance Act of 1993 (P.L. 103-181, the so-called Volkmer bill, after its chief sponsor in the House), these funding limits were increased to 75 percent for the federal share, with total funds not to exceed 15 percent of all disaster assistance provided. These changes have substantially increased the amount of funding available for mitigation. Mitigation planning requirements are also included as a condition for states receiving disaster assistance under the Stafford Act. Under Section 409 (formerly 406), states must prepare a state hazard mitigation plan within six months of a presidential declaration of disaster.

The latest stage in the evolution of national disaster policy might be described as the "mitigation era." It represents a period, especially in the mid-1990s, in which the importance of mitigation—both before and after disasters—has received unprecedented political support and emphasis. A significant milestone was the creation, on November 28, 1993, of the Mitigation Directorate within FEMA. This represented a fundamental change in the approach taken to disaster and emergency management. "For the first time in the history of federal disaster assistance, mitigation—sustained action taken to reduce or eliminate long-term risk to people and their property from hazards and their effects—has become the cornerstone of emergency management" (FEMA 1995b, p. vii). Other milestones include publication of the *National Mitigation Strategy* (FEMA 1995c), and the convening of the first National Mitigation Conference in December 1995.

The history of mitigation planning and policy can also be described for different types of hazards. Mitigation policy differs somewhat from one type of hazard to the next, though clearly there are parallel trends in policy

evolution. It is instructive to compare the history of mitigation policy for the three major types of disasters: floods, hurricanes, and earthquakes.

Flood Mitigation Policy

Flooding along the nation's rivers is a significant and costly natural disaster, most dramatically illustrated by the Midwest floods of 1993. It has been estimated that flooding is involved in some 80 percent of all presidentially declared disasters (FEMA 1995c).

Flood hazard policy has evolved substantially over the past fifty years. Early efforts at flood control focused on structural approaches, with a heavy reliance in the Mississippi basin on the construction of levees. As with disaster assistance, federal involvement in flood control emerged incrementally. Federal involvement dates to the mid-1800s, when Congress authorized the U.S. Army Corps of Engineers to study flood control alternatives for the lower Mississippi. A series of federal flood control acts, beginning in 1917, instituted federal cost sharing for flood control projects, and gradually federal involvement expanded. The period 1930–1950 was a time of massive construction of flood control works, with some $11 billion in federal monies expended (Wright 1996). Until the late 1960s, structural measures, such as the building of levees and flood walls, were the dominant approach to riverine flood management.

However, levees, seawalls, diversions, and other structural measures are extremely costly and can disrupt or destroy the natural environment. Structural projects may also create a false sense of security, increasing the amount of property at risk of flooding as people and businesses locate behind levees and flood walls (Clark 1993). Platt (1982), for instance, described the experience of Jackson, Mississippi, where the Army Corps of Engineers had constructed levees in the 1960s to protect the town from flooding along the Pearl River. The levees were overtopped, however, in the 1979 "Easter flood," with some 40 percent of the damage being inflicted on new construction behind the levee.

A major shift in flood policy emerged in the 1960s following a series of expensive flood disasters. Two separate national studies examined federal flood policy in the aftermath of these events: Congress directed the secretary of HUD to examine the feasibility of federal flood insurance (under the Southeast Hurricane Disaster Relief Act of 1965), and a Presidential Task Force on Federal Flood Control was formed by the Bureau of the Budget (Platt 1991b). Gilbert White directed the Flood Control Task Force, which was influential in arguing for alternatives to structural approaches. The White Report proposed a more balanced approach using a number of

mitigation measures, including land use management and flood insurance (see U.S. House 1966a, 1966b).

These studies, along with concerns about the costs of recent flooding events, ushered in a new era of nonstructural approaches to floodplain management. One of the most significant outcomes was the creation of the National Flood Insurance Program (NFIP) in 1968 (and the addition of strong incentives for participation in 1973). About 18,600 communities currently participate in the NFIP (FEMA 1995b).

Over time, appreciation of the importance of naturally functioning river systems and of the environmental benefits and ecosystem functions provided by floodplains has grown (Interagency Floodplain Management Task Force 1992a). Also receiving greater attention in the 1970s and 1980s was the strategy of relocating structures and communities outside floodplains and thus out of harm's way. The relocation approach is a dramatic repudiation of the structural or engineering ethic. Prior to the 1993 Midwest floods, few relocations had been undertaken, though several large and successful projects had been carried out. Tulsa, Oklahoma, is one notable example, with efforts to clear development out of its floodplain dating back to the 1970s. Since that time, some 875 buildings have been acquired (Patton 1993). Another notable example is Soldier's Grove, Wisconsin, a town that chose to relocate entirely outside the floodplain, turning down a proposed $3.5 million Army Corps of Engineers levee (Clark 1993; Becker 1994).

Modest relocation has also been done under Section 1362, the Flooded Properties Purchase Program, of the NFIP. This program historically has been underfunded and has resulted in only a small number of properties (about 100) being purchased and relocated each year. Since its creation, Section 1362 has resulted in the acquisition of approximately 1,400 properties (FEMA 1995b). One large and notable Section 1362 project was carried out in Baytown, Texas, following Hurricane Alicia in 1983. Here, instead of a repeatedly flooded 300-home neighborhood being redeveloped, the homes were purchased and demolished (Godschalk, Brower, and Beatley 1989). From the federal view, this type of action is much more cost-effective than payment of flood insurance claims in every future flood event.

The most extensive use of relocation occurred after the 1993 Midwest floods. The administration of President Bill Clinton took a longer view, deciding to move people and property out of harm's way rather than continually fund reconstruction and recovery. At completion of the program, more than 9,000 properties will have been acquired, representing 156 buyout projects in nine states (FEMA 1995b). Notable examples of relo-

cated communities include Valmeyer, Illinois, and Pattonsburg, Missouri (Becker 1994).

Following the Midwest floods, a special Interagency Floodplain Management Review Committee was charged with recommending improvements to the current flood management framework. The Galloway Report, named for the committee's chair, Brigadier General Gerald Galloway, represents a significant point in national floodplain policy—it further endorses the gradual move away from structural measures, embraces land use and relocation strategies, and emphasizes protecting and restoring the natural functioning of river systems (Interagency Floodplain Management Review Committee 1994).

Hurricane and Coastal Storm Mitigation Policy

The history of coastal hazard mitigation policy largely parallels the history of riverine floodplain management. Early coastal policy focused on structural measures and armoring of the coastline against hurricanes, coastal storms, and long-term shoreline erosion. The Army Corps of Engineers played an influential role in advocating and implementing "hard" structural solutions. Seawalls, revetments, groins, jetties, and offshore breakwaters have all been extensively used along the American coastline, often through substantial federal subsidy.

Like flood policy, coastal management of the late 1960s and early 1970s shifted away from exclusive reliance on shore hardening to "softer" approaches. Concerns about the negative effects of shore-hardening structures led several states, notably North Carolina and Maine, to ban permanent shore-hardening structures (Beatley, Brower, and Schwab 1994).

One increasingly important alternative is beach replenishment (or renourishment), used by a number of coastal cities, notably Miami Beach, Florida; Virginia Beach, Virginia; and Ocean City, Maryland. Facilitated by the Army Corps of Engineers, such programs have received heavy federal subsidies. The Corps spent approximately $328 million, in 1993 dollars, on beach replenishment, between 1950 and 1993; FEMA has also provided funding for replenishment (NRC 1995). Critics such as coastal geologist Orrin Pilkey have questioned the growing reliance on replenishment and its cost (almost always more than originally estimated) and project duration (the Corps often overestimates how long such projects will stay in place). A substantial body of literature, both critical and supportive, has developed on beach replenishment, (Pilkey and Dixon 1996; U.S. Army Corps of Engineers 1996; NRC 1995). A recent report by the Marine Board of the National Research Council (NRC 1995) supports increased beach

replenishment, declaring it "a viable engineering alternative for shore protection" (p. 3). Moreover, the board believes that recreational and other benefits from beach replenishment are often greater than thought and recommends that benefit-cost analyses be adjusted to account for these benefits. However, even for its supporters, beach replenishment poses a number of policy and design questions.[2]

The 1970s also saw a new concern for coastal planning and management, fueled by growing developmental pressures on coasts, a belief in protecting the national interest in coastal resources, and a perception that states were not adequately protecting their coasts. This resulted in the groundbreaking federal Coastal Zone Management Act (CZMA), enacted in 1972. Recognizing that coastal land use and development issues are fundamentally a matter of state and local control, the act created positive incentives for states to develop and implement comprehensive coastal management programs. The primary incentives included provision of federal monies and, through Section 307 of the act, a provision requiring that future federal actions be consistent with approved state coastal programs (see Godschalk 1992 for a history of the CZMA). Even though the CZMA is a voluntary, incentives-based program, by almost all measures it has been a success. State participation has been high, and many states now have planning and management capabilities that did not exist before the CZMA. Although each state program is different, many include strong regulatory and other provisions aimed at reducing the hazardous aspects of coastal development patterns, such as minimum coastal setbacks, land acquisition, local hazard mitigation plans, and restrictions on wetlands development (see Platt et al. 1992; Godschalk, Brower, and Beatley 1989).

The past twenty years have also witnessed a growing concern about sea level rise and the implications of global warming for the hazardousness of coastal areas. Predictions have varied, but it is generally believed that average global sea level may rise by as much as three feet by the year 2100. The Environmental Protection Agency sponsored research on the likely effects of different scenarios involving sea level rise, and there has been a great deal of literature and commentary about how coastal states and localities can and should prepare for these changes (e.g., Kana et al. 1984; Titus 1986, 1991; Klarin and Hershman 1990; Edgerton 1991; Platt 1991a; OTA 1993).

To many, the only sensible policy response to sea level rise, and indeed to the dynamic and hazardous nature of coastal areas generally, is long-term "strategic retreat." Retreat implies that instead of further reinforcing and armoring the coastlines, settlements are moved back from high-risk locations (Pilkey et al. 1980; Platt et al. 1992). A number of state and local

coastal management programs attempt to implement, at least partially, long-term shoreline retreat. Such measures include coastal setbacks, as required under North Carolina's Coastal Area Management Act; restrictions on rebuilding after a major hurricane or storm, as under the original South Carolina Beachfront Management Act; and prohibitions on building nonmovable shoreline structures, as under New York's coastal erosion law (see Platt et al. 1992). Moreover, federal programs have provided funds for coastal relocation (e.g., the Upton-Jones Act, Section 1362, Flooded Properties Purchase Program), and some states adopted similar programs to facilitate shoreline relocation (e.g., Michigan's Emergency Home Moving Program; see Platt et al. 1992; Beatley, Brower, and Schwab 1994). As with riverine floodplain management, there has been a gradual realization that often the most effective coastal mitigation strategy is protection of the natural mitigative features of the environment—dune systems, wetlands, forests, and natural vegetation (e.g., Thieler and Bush 1991; Phillippi 1994).

A related mitigation tack has reassessed the role of government subsidies in promoting dangerous coastal development patterns. Federal and state governments provide a host of financial incentives for hazardous coastal development, including subsidized flood insurance under the NFIP, disaster assistance, a variety of development monies for highways and infrastructure, and tax benefits such as the casualty loss deduction under the U.S. tax code. An innovative federal law, the Coastal Barrier Resources Act (CoBRA), enacted in 1982, removes subsidies for development on designated undeveloped barrier island units. The area covered by the act was substantially expanded under the Coastal Barrier Improvement Act of 1990 and now includes some 600 barrier island units and 1,200 miles of shoreline. Several national studies have attempted to examine its effectiveness at discouraging barrier island development, and considerable debate has occurred about the actual effects of CoBRA (GAO 1992; Beatley 1992; Godschalk 1987). Although CoBRA has slowed development in some coastal areas, economic pressures often overcome the withdrawal of these public subsidies.

The functioning of the NFIP in coastal environments has been debated in recent years. A significant criticism is that the NFIP does not adequately account for erosion risks and does not require coastal communities to adopt even minimal coastal setbacks. Several congressional proposals in the early 1990s sought to reform the NFIP in this regard, but they were controversial and did not succeed. H.R.1236, or the National Flood Insurance, Mitigation and Erosion Management Act, introduced in 1991, encouraged coastal localities to adopt an erosion setback system like North

Carolina's to prohibit new development or redevelopment seaward of the thirty-year erosion line and to limit development seaward of the sixty-year line to low-density, readily movable structures (Beatley 1992). Localities choosing not to adopt the erosion standards would be ineligible for certain mitigation assistance, and future flood insurance claims for existing structures would be limited. Although many of the provisions of H.R. 1236 and its Senate counterpart, S.R. 2907, were later incorporated into the National Flood Insurance Reform Act of 1994, the erosion management standards were opposed by many local governments and even some FEMA administrators, most notably the director of the Flood Insurance Administration at that time. Instead, the 1994 act only requires FEMA to study the coastal erosion problem.

Overlaid on the evolution of coastal mitigation policy is a history of devastating hurricanes and storms (see table 2.1). However, over the past thirty years, while the coastal population has soared, the nation has experienced a relative lull in hurricane activity (Catalamo 1995). But experts believe that the late 1990s mark the beginning of a period of unusually high hurricane activity (Pendick 1996). It may be in coastal areas especially that the inadequacies of the current mitigation system will become most evident.

Earthquake Mitigation Policy

Seismic mitigation policy developed somewhat differently, though some parallels with floodplain and coastal hazards policy can be noted. Until recently, the federal role in mitigating seismic hazards has been limited. Even though a number of states and metropolitan population centers face major seismic threats, serious mitigation has been undertaken primarily in California. Most of the damaging earthquakes have occurred there (e.g., the Northridge and Loma Prieta earthquakes; see table 2.1 and chapter 6), and California has led the nation and other seismically prone states in mitigation. The state's mitigation initiatives have included adoption and gradual strengthening over time of seismic building standards such as the Unified Building Code, mapping of fault systems and restrictions on building in fault zones, real estate hazard disclosure, seismic elements for local general plans (now through a general safety element), and a requirement for the development of local retrofit programs (Berke and Beatley 1992).

The primary federal initiative is the National Earthquake Hazards Reduction Program (NEHRP), created by the Earthquake Hazards Reduction Act of 1977. NEHRP emphasizes the funding of research, under-

standing and mapping of seismic hazards, and education and technical assistance. It facilitates state and local mitigation efforts with funds from FEMA, the U.S. Geological Survey (USGS), the National Science Foundation (NSF), and the National Institute for Standards and Technology. NEHRP has funded several regional seismic mitigation initiatives, notably the Southern California Earthquake Preparedness Program (SCEPP) and the San Francisco Bay Area Regional Earthquake Preparedness Program (BAREPP). These are regional collaborative programs seeking to foster an understanding of seismic risks and to develop local capabilities for mitigating seismic threats. Through USGS leadership, substantial research has been conducted into the nature of seismic threats and major efforts have been undertaken to map these hazards.

Much of the focus of NEHRP has been on carrying out public education and getting private organizations to adopt seismic mitigation standards. Recent reports of the Office of Technology Assessment (OTA) and the Advisory Committee of NEHRP are critical of this information dissemination approach and suggest ways in which the federal government could be more effective (OTA 1995). In response, a Strategy for National Earthquake Loss Reduction was unveiled in April 1996. Under this strategy, FEMA will coordinate the activities of different federal agencies and will emphasize adoption of mitigation measures and application of mitigation technologies (National Earthquake Strategy Working Group 1996).

A more direct federal mitigation role is evident in Executive Order 12699, issued in January 1990. The order establishes minimum seismic standards for new federal buildings. A more recent executive order (E.O. 12941, issued in December 1994) requires that certain mitigation retrofit standards be applied to existing federal buildings (OTA 1995). Many have observed that the most effective role for the federal government is to lead by example. These executive orders reflect this sentiment.

An important issue in the seismic mitigation debate is reform of the seismic insurance system. In the aftermath of record damages from the Northridge earthquake, insurance companies in California have substantially curtailed availability of earthquake insurance (Appleby 1995). Those continuing to offer earthquake insurance raised deductibles and premiums. What to do about this has been a contentious issue in California. (There are proposals to issue insurance through a new state entity, the California Earthquake Authority.) Many believe that these problems would be solved by creating a national all-hazards insurance system, based on the model of the NFIP, which would extend federal insurance to earthquakes and other hazards as well as floods. Such proposals have been controversial, and at present, their passage by Congress appears unlikely.

Critically Assessing the Current Framework

The early to mid-1990s were marked by a strong sense that the current disaster management framework was not working, in the face of unprecedented costs of disasters such as Hurricane Andrew, the Midwest floods, and the Northridge earthquake. Major studies and critiques of the system undertaken since 1992 (the post-Andrew period) are summarized here to illustrate the range of findings and recommendations.

National Academy of Public Administration Study

In 1992, in the aftermath of Hurricanes Andrew and Iniki, Congress commissioned the National Academy of Public Administration (NAPA) to study the country's ability to respond to natural disasters. NAPA's 1993 report, *Coping with Catastrophe: Building an Emergency Management System to Meet People's Needs in Natural and Manmade Disasters*, assesses the state of emergency management at that time, including obstacles to effectiveness and opportunities created by the post–cold war environment.

The report documents the rise in federal involvement in disaster response as well as several "enduring problems" that make effective emergency management difficult in the United States. These problems include American resistance to long-range planning, the short-term perspective of American politics, the difficulty of coordinating many organizations and agencies, and the lack of a "natural constituency base" for emergency management, at least prior to a disaster. It highlights the unique historical context of the 1990s, including a "new world order" and a diminished threat of nuclear war; the greater "intrusiveness and influence" of the media (what the panel calls the "CNN syndrome," whereby disaster management becomes susceptible to "soundbite politics"); and the rising expectations of the public, particularly with respect to the federal government (NAPA 1993, p. 18).

NAPA's report concludes that the country needs, but does not yet have, a "well-organized, effective emergency management system." It recommends establishing within the Executive Office of the President a Domestic Crisis Monitoring Unit, the use of joint assessment teams to be rapidly deployed following a disaster, development of a graduated scale for disasters, and improvements to the federal response plan (NAPA 1993, chap. 3). Such improvements would ensure an appropriate federal role as provider of coordination and intelligence, not as the "911 first responder" (p. 28).

The report is particularly critical of FEMA, which it describes as "an institution not yet built," and even suggests the possibility of its dissolution if it fails to reform or reorganize. It calls on FEMA to create a "coherent sense of mission," with primary emphasis on civil emergencies and disas-

ters and on all functions of disaster management (mitigation, preparedness, response, and recovery) (NAPA 1993, p. 63, chap. 4).

NAPA's 1993 report emphasizes the importance of disaster management capability at the state and local levels of government (chap. 6). The report asserts that FEMA must do more to help build this capability and offers a number of specific recommendations for this.[3] One recommendation is for increased financial incentives to encourage state and local governments to do more mitigation. Postdisaster funding can be a disincentive, especially if the federal government assumes 100 percent of the disaster costs. "For some states and localities that have neglected to develop and maintain an adequate emergency management capacity, 100 percent federal money is a windfall that can be seen as a reward for their neglect. The negligent governments may receive as much money as those that made significant efforts at emergency management prior to the disaster" (NAPA 1993, p. 91). A system of incentives is recommended that would encourage more responsible state and local behavior (p. 92).

Finally, the report expresses concern about the rising nationalization and politicization of emergencies and disasters. The growing number of federal declarations, combined with expectations that the federal government will handle, and absorb much of the cost of, both large and "routine" emergencies and disasters, is alarming. "In the panel's judgment, however, the federal government can never be the government of first response" (NAPA 1993, p. 1010). What is needed is a "cooperative intergovernmental system" with "shared governance" whereby the federal government primarily works to enhance and build state and local capacity, stepping in only when emergencies or disasters overwhelm state and local capabilities.

NAPA conducted a follow-up study to evaluate policy changes made in response to the 1993 report. Although the authors of the follow-up report are encouraged by a number of the changes made by FEMA's director, James Lee Witt, they found that many recommendations had not been addressed. Few political appointee slots had been eliminated (all presidentially appointed, senate-confirmed positions had been retained); little progress in declassifying positions had been made; no effort had been made to create a Domestic Crisis Monitoring Unit in the White House, although the report does acknowledge the director's unusual access to the president; no new charter for FEMA had been enacted; and, although FEMA had been considering doing so, no joint assessment teams or graduated response system had been created. The report did note progress in recognizing "the need for creating a vision, redefining the mission, or choosing a few strategic goals and objectives for FEMA" (NAPA 1994, p. 3).[4]

National Performance Review

One of the priorities of the Clinton administration has been to "reinvent" government to be more effective and responsive. Spearheaded by Vice President Al Gore, the National Performance Review (NPR) critically examined the way the federal government operates and identified a variety of actions to improve and streamline its performance.

A specific study focused on FEMA (NPR 1993). Many of its conclusions are similar to those of the NAPA panel. The report calls on FEMA to create a "more anticipatory and customer-driven response" to natural disasters. Suggestions to improve the agency's performance include the establishment of rapid-response teams, prepositioning of staff and resources in anticipation of a disaster event, reexamination of FEMA's regional office structure, and, possibly, creation of "regional centers of excellence," whereby each regional office would specialize in a particular kind of disaster. The report also calls for a shift in emphasis away from national security and nuclear preparedness functions and toward preparedness for all hazards. To this end, it suggests reducing the number of security clearances given, as these have been found to impede communication and collaboration within FEMA.

The NPR study also focuses on mitigation and on ways to reduce the long-term costs of natural disasters. Overall, the report is critical of the current system of disaster preparedness incentives (NPR 1993, p. 13):

> This country's response to catastrophic events relies to a great extent on federal assistance to state and local governments, whether or not those governments have tried to reduce the effects, including the costs, of such disasters. The ready availability of federal funds may actually contribute to disaster losses by reducing incentives for hazard mitigation and preparedness.

The report criticizes the lack of objective federal criteria for issuing a presidential disaster declaration. Declarations are often issued for small events, and state and local governments seek the maximum amount of aid available. Objective criteria would help to depoliticize the disaster assistance system. Reform of the incentive system would also mean more adequate insurance coverage by individuals and communities at risk and more concerted efforts at predisaster mitigation. The report endorses shifting the costs of disasters to those who bear the risks, and it recommends that FEMA examine several proposals for this, including increasing federal matching funds for states that have effective mitigation and preparedness programs, distinguishing among different levels of disaster for purposes of

providing aid, and relying to a greater degree on insurance and loans to cover state and local disaster costs.

Congressional Natural Disaster Task Forces

Several important studies have been undertaken by Congress itself. A Bipartisan Task Force on Disasters in the U.S. House of Representatives, cochaired by Representatives Dick Durbin (D-Illinois) and Bill Emerson (R-Missouri), issued its report in 1994. The report calls for reducing the cost of disasters to the federal taxpayer and emphasizing the supplemental role of the federal government, whereby individuals assume greater personal responsibility and state and local governments assume more active roles in disaster mitigation, preparedness, response, and recovery. Recommended means of strengthening state and local roles include encouraging states to create disaster relief funds (e.g., by increasing the federal share of disaster costs for states that have such funds and by requiring a two-fifths majority vote for Congress to provide disaster monies to states without such funds); encouraging state and local governments to adopt and enforce model building and development codes; requiring FEMA-approved disaster preparedness and mitigation plans, and building code enforcement as conditions of federal funds (U.S. House 1994).

The U.S. Senate conducted its own analysis of federal disaster funding and management through the Senate Task Force on Funding Disaster Relief, cochaired by Senators John Glenn (D-Ohio) and Christopher S. Bond (R-Missouri). The 1995 report of the task force analyzes existing laws and programs and identifies options for reform. The report does not recommend specific policy changes but does identify a range of alternatives and the relative advantages of each. One of the task force's most important activities was to tabulate the extent of federal funds expended on disaster relief—the federal disaster accounting system is very rudimentary, and this study may represent the first comprehensive tabulation of these costs. The task force found that nearly $120 billion (in constant dollars) had been spent between fiscal years 1977 and 1993 (U.S. Senate 1995). The report notes that supplemental appropriation acts have increasingly been used as a way of providing federal assistance for large disaster events. Such "supplementals" totaled more than $22 billion in the three-year period 1992–1994 alone. Moreover, there is every reason to believe that supplementals will continue to be used, as the amounts appropriated to the Disaster Relief Fund do not appear to reflect realistic federal disaster

expenditures; for example, only $320 million was requested by the president for fiscal year 1995 (U.S. Senate 1995).

FEMA Inspector General's Report

How well does the mitigation planning framework stipulated in the Stafford Act actually work? In 1994, analysts from FEMA's Office of Inspector General visited thirteen states and reviewed some ten state Section 409 plans, finding that many of the plans were inadequate. Four of the plans did not contain all the required elements. Although six of the plans met the minimum Stafford Act criteria, many of these plans were found to be of low quality, in large part a result of the tendency for states to prepare Section 409 plans primarily to qualify them to receive mitigation funds following a disaster. The hurried preparation of plans following disasters has meant that the plans are not very useful to states. This is perhaps the most disturbing conclusion of the inspector general's report (FEMA 1994, p. 14):

> Although some plans were state-wide and did include all hazards, the major problem was that most were not used by the States. State mitigation managers generally agreed that because the plans were prepared hurriedly in the post-disaster environment to meet FEMA requirements, they were of little value to anyone. Several said that once FEMA approved their plan, they put it on the shelf until the next disaster. FEMA regional mitigation managers told us that the plans, even complete ones, did not help evaluate mitigation projects because the plan objectives were so general that they covered any project.

The report also points to a lack of full-time staff as a major problem. In eleven of the thirteen states visited for the study, the state mitigation officer was employed part-time. Coordination among state agencies was difficult for similar reasons, as such agencies were unlikely to allocate staff time and resources to mitigation.

A key issue is the relationship between predisaster and postdisaster mitigation funding. The current system for funding mitigation makes the bulk of these monies available *after* a disaster event rather than *in advance* of it. The report notes, for instance, that in fiscal year 1993, FEMA earmarked only $10 million for mitigation and planning to be provided to states through their Comprehensive Cooperative Agreements (CCAs), whereas in the same year it provided some $153 million through the Hazard Mitigation Grant Program (HMGP). The study strongly questions the logic of providing so much of this mitigation funding after disasters.

Overall, the study shows that mitigation planning is not a high priority

for most states and that efforts need to be made to elevate its importance at the state level. FEMA was also implicated. The study found that FEMA did not generally withhold disaster aid from states with inadequate plans, though it does withhold HMGP funds. The report also criticizes the lengthy application process involved with the HMGP, finding that FEMA takes an average of two years after a disaster to obligate funding for a specific project.

The report recommends streamlining the provision of postdisaster grants; providing states with more mitigation funding up front (i.e., not attached to specific disasters or geographic areas); providing states with greater flexibility in using mitigation funds; helping state and local governments expand their mitigation capabilities through greater technical assistance; developing a marketing plan to expand public awareness of the benefits of mitigation; and improving the federal interagency hazard mitigation team process (FEMA 1994).

Joint Task Force on the Hazard Mitigation Grant Program

The Joint Task Force on the Hazard Mitigation Grant Program was a cooperative effort of the National Emergency Management Association (NEMA), the Association of State Floodplain Managers (ASFPM), and FEMA (Joint Task Force 1992b). Its report addressed administrative problems with the HMGP and recommended improvements. As part of the evaluation, a questionnaire was mailed to the memberships of NEMA and ASFPM and to FEMA regional mitigation staff. A survey of projects submitted to FEMA was also conducted (Joint Task Force 1992a).

The study provided one of the first summaries of HMGP mitigation projects and the ways in which HMGP monies have been used. The task force found that $43 million had been obligated for HMGP projects between January 1989 and August 1992. By far the largest category of projects was "public/private facilities," which constituted 58 percent of the funded projects (seismic retrofits, floodproofing of sewage treatment facilities, etc.). Drainage projects accounted for 14 percent of the projects, equipment purchases 12 percent, relocation of structures 11 percent, and planning products 3 percent; education/training and land improvements each accounted for 1 percent (Joint Task Force 1992a).

The task force found that in its first four years, the HMGP had been implemented "cautiously," for three reasons: confusion about the definition of mitigation and the time required to convey its meaning; high degrees of technical assistance, coordination, and time required to identify

and select projects; and the fact that many states did not have active mitigation programs, requiring time to be spent on this after disasters occurred,
rather than beforehand (Joint Task Force 1992a, p. 6).

To address these deficiencies and to advance the HMGP beyond its "cau-
tious" implementation, the Joint Task Force recommended developing a
federal-state mitigation strategy after each disaster declaration; strengthening state mitigation plans through the federal-state agreement; and
improving the HMGP process (Joint Task Force 1992a, pp. 7–8). For each
recommendation, the report lays out a series of "support tasks." Many call
for more training and education programs, technical assistance (especially
to local governments), and written guidance. Other recommendations are
for permanent full-time state hazard mitigation officers "who are devoted
to hazard mitigation" (Joint Task Force 1992b, p. 15); predisaster mitigation plans that include mitigation strategies and projects; marketing strategies to educate and sell the public on mitigation; and clear criteria for evaluating long-term results of mitigation. The latter is particularly important
because neither the HMGP nor the Public Assistance program has the "systematic means or criteria for evaluating the long term impact of funded
hazard mitigation projects" (Joint Task Force 1992b, p. 24). The report also
stresses the need for states to develop an ongoing mitigation capability, not
just to implement projects after disasters.

Council of State Governments–
NEMA Study of State Expenditures

Many state and local governments are also absorbing greater costs associated with nonfederally declared emergencies and disasters. A recent study
by the Council of State Governments (CSG) and NEMA estimated these
costs and how states were paying for these events (NEMA and CSG 1996).
The study, described as the first "comprehensive overview of state structures, authorities and spending for disaster preparedness and response,"
found that in fiscal year 1994 states spent about $1.6 billion in emergency
management (about $32 million per state) and spending rose by 37.5 per-
cent between fiscal years 1992 and 1994. Because states were not able to
collect data from all agencies, these estimates are thought to be low. The
postdisaster part of this funding, including response and recovery expenditures was found to have risen at a much higher rate, growing by 56 percent between fiscal year 1992 and fiscal year 1994, compared with a 10
percent increase in predisaster spending. This is consistent with the study's
findings that whereas the number of federal declarations went down from
fifty-five in fiscal year 1992 to thirty-seven in fiscal year 1994, the number

of state disaster events and declarations rose markedly during this period. Recovery costs rose by 108 percent.

Concerning mitigation expenditures, the survey contains both positive and negative findings. On the positive side, the majority of the increase in pre-event state expenditures is in mitigation. Although total state expenditures in preparedness went up by only 5 percent between fiscal year 1992 and fiscal year 1994, mitigation expenditures went up by 58 percent, a substantial increase over this three-year period (NEMA and CSG 1996; Cabot 1996). The mitigation increase is second only to the increase in state recovery expenditures. On the negative side, mitigation expenditures as a percentage of total state expenditures for comprehensive emergency management remain low. In 1994, states spent an average of about $4.5 million on mitigation, or about 12.7 percent of total emergency management costs (up from 11 percent in 1992, down from 15.8 percent in 1993; see NEMA and CSG 1996, p. 9). These findings do suggest that state and local governments absorb significant, and increasing, disaster-related costs.

The survey also examined the mechanisms states use to pay for emergency and disaster assistance. Whereas in about half the states, legislatures provide appropriations for specific disaster events, some eighteen states have a separate disaster fund, with appropriations for the fund as needed. A number of states have more than one fund. Three states have funds for which revenues are specifically dedicated from a specific source, such as a tax on insurance policies.

Advisory Committee of the National Earthquake Hazards Reduction Program

As described earlier, the National Earthquake Hazards Reduction Program (NEHRP), originally created by Congress in 1977, has been the primary federal effort addressing seismic hazards. The Advisory Committee to NEHRP issued a report in 1993 that recommended a major reformulation of national earthquake policy (FEMA 1993). Although the committee acknowledged considerable progress in mitigation efforts, it criticized the current framework and concluded "that progress in earthquake risk reduction is not proceeding as rapidly as society has a right to expect or as Congress, in enacting the NEHRP, contemplated" (FEMA 1993, p. 4). The report pointed to the lack of "prioritized goals" and incentives for individuals and state and local governments to adopt seismic mitigation measures.

The committee recommended fundamentally changing the structure of NEHRP and creating a single entity "that has the authority and responsibility to direct implementation of the goals of the program on a

strategic basis, integrating priorities and focusing the budgeting and expenditure of funds so as to maximize the impact of program resources" (FEMA 1993, p. 10). Otherwise, each of the four primary agencies funded through NEHRP acts on its own, with its own budget and with little ability to strategically pursue crosscutting goals and priorities. This single entity must have authority to submit a single budget to Congress, manage and direct NEHRP agencies in implementing priorities and a strategic plan, evaluate and monitor effectiveness, and serve as the primary NEHRP advocate.

The committee was also critical of the fact that more progress had not been made in implementation of mitigation measures. "Although some jurisdictions have made important advances in earthquake risk mitigation, many areas at significant risk have done little or nothing to address the problem" (FEMA 1993, p. 11). Little had been done at the local level and by the private sector to mitigate seismic risks. Although the program had enhanced public awareness and knowledge among those concerned with earthquake mitigation, it had not led to the "creation of a sufficient institutionalized structure for marketing and applying earthquake risk-reduction measures." The committee recommended an accelerated program of implementation and a system of incentives and marketing to encourage adoption of mitigation measures. Suggested financial incentives included federal income tax credits to encourage businesses to make mitigation investments; tax-exempt status for private bonds used to finance retrofitting of private facilities; creation of a federal matching grant for retrofitting critical state and local government facilities; and establishment of a federal disaster insurance program with strong mitigation requirements (p. 14). The report also contains several subcommittee reports (e.g., on implementation, earth sciences, engineering, and socioeconomic research) and a working paper on development of a national earthquake hazards Mitigation Plan.

Office of Technology Assessment's Study

A recent study by the Office of Technology Assessment (OTA), *Reducing Earthquake Losses* (OTA 1995), builds on the themes addressed by the NEHRP Advisory Committee and provides an even more comprehensive assessment of the adequacy of the current seismic mitigation framework. The OTA is critical of the limited federal role in NEHRP, though it finds that the program has contributed to a more widespread understanding of seismic hazards. NEHRP is characterized as essentially a "research program"; 75 percent of NEHRP funds are used for research. Although these

efforts to generate knowledge about earthquake hazards are important, they fail to address the "implementation gap," or the failure to implement "known technologies and practices" (OTA 1995, p. 17). Other problems with the current program stem from the lack of "clear and workable goals and strategies." Without an overall set of goals and strategies, each of the four federal units receiving funds under NEHRP will tend to pursue its own priorities, and overall performance will be difficult to evaluate.

The OTA attributes the failure to address the implementation gap to the inherent limitations of a federal approach that relies primarily on distribution of information (OTA 1995, pp. 19–20): "NEHRP's approach to reducing earthquake losses can be thought of as supplying information on earthquake risks and possible countermeasures to those who may wish to mitigate. . . . However, the frequent lack of mitigation activity often reflects not a lack of information, but a lack of interest or incentive to take action. *Information alone will not result in widespread implementation*" (emphasis in original).

The study identifies policy options, including operational changes that could help NEHRP move beyond its current "loosely coordinated confederation of agencies." It recommends that Congress consider an increased federal role beyond simply information distribution. The policy options include insurance, regulation, and financial incentives. The report is neutral on all-hazards insurance proposals but does suggest that strong consideration be given to the insurance options: "Clearly insurance can be a strong incentive for earthquake mitigation—if the cost of insurance reflects the risk" (OTA 1995, p. 29). Concerning regulation, the federal government could play a more aggressive role by requiring states and localities to meet certain minimum building code standards for seismic safety, or minimum code enforcement, as a condition of federal aid (p. 30). Financial incentives might also be used (p. 31); "these could take the form of rewards for greater mitigation (e.g., tax credits or low-interest loans) or punishments for insufficient mitigation (e.g., taxing buildings not meeting codes, or reducing disaster assistance to those who did not mitigate)."

Federal Interagency Floodplain Management Task Force Assessment

A major assessment of floodplain management, commissioned and prepared before the 1993 floods, provides one of the most complete evaluations of the U.S. experience to date. The report of the Federal Interagency Floodplain Management Task Force, *Floodplain Management*

in the United States: An Assessment Report, is presented in two volumes
(Federal Interagency Floodplain Management Task Force 1992a, 1992b).
It is self-described as "the first comprehensive assessment in over 25
years" of floodplain management (1992a, p. 65). The findings of this
study, in combination with the later experiences of the Midwest floods,
were important inputs to the *Unified National Program for Floodplain
Management* and the Galloway Report, both described later in this
chapter.

The report of the task force describes the present nature of floodplains,
their uses and value, and trends in flood losses. It concludes that whereas
there is no indication that loss of life from floods has been rising (there
were an average of 101 flood-related deaths per year between 1916 and
1985), property losses have clearly been increasing. For instance, the
report notes that between 1916 and 1950, per capita property losses rose
by a factor of almost 2.5, though as a proportion of national gross
domestic product, losses have remained fairly constant (Federal Interagency Floodplain Management Task Force 1992a, p. 18).

The report reviews current and past programs to manage floodplains, noting the evolution of floodplain management from a structural emphasis (1900–1960) to a broader perspective in the 1960s and
1970s, with more attention to flood insurance and environmental
protection. The 1980s are characterized as a period when even greater
attention was given to the natural and cultural values of floodplains
and state and local governments assumed greater roles in hazard
mitigation.

Overall, the report concludes that accomplishments to date have been
"impressive" but that "a considerable distance remains between the status
quo and the ideal that can be envisioned" (Federal Interagency Floodplain
Management Task Force 1992a, p. 60). Achievements include more public
recognition of flood hazards, judicial decisions supportive of floodplain
management, prevention of losses in many localities through floodplain
mapping and development regulations, improvements in the institutional
framework, and preservation of considerable floodplain land, especially
wetlands. The management framework has "matured and expanded significantly since the 1960s," gradually shifting away from reliance on structural control measures. Two major deficiencies remaining in the current
framework are that there are "few clearly stated, measurable goals" and
that "there is not enough consistent, reliable data about program activities
and their impacts to tell how much progress is being made in a given direction" (p. 60).

Floodplain Management Reform;
Post–Midwest Flood Policy Critiques

The Midwest floods of 1993 accelerated the national debate about the adequacy of current approaches to floodplain management. They stimulated extensive commentary about the failings of federal, state, and local floodplain management policy. Several major national studies were prepared.

Many commentators advocated preventing the exposure of people and property to flood hazards, adjusting the incentive structure that encourages such exposure, and breaking the repeated cycle of damage-rebuild-damage (e.g., see Burby et al. 1988; Patton 1993; Schwab 1996; Platt, Beatley, and Miller 1991). Kusler and Larson (1993) argued for "a new approach" to U.S. floodplain management, emphasizing broader multiobjective, watershed-based plans and extending floodplain management beyond simply reducing property losses to consider the broader national and cultural values of floodplains. Ideally, such efforts should be community based, with the federal government helping to facilitate and creating incentives for planning (see also Myers and White 1993).

The Lincoln Institute of Land Policy sponsored a national conference in 1994 titled "Community Land Policy and River Flooding: The Great Flood of 1993," which brought together floodplain management experts and representatives of thirty-three flooded communities to discuss flood policy. The conference report, *On Borrowed Land: Public Policies for Floodplains* (Faber 1996; see also Glavan 1995), concluded that the federal government and other levels of government providing postdisaster aid must begin to practice "tough love." Conference participants "compared federal, state and even private disaster assistance to an addiction from which floodplain communities and residents would not recover if it was always easier to ask for help after a flood than to get out of harm's way ahead of time" (Faber 1996, p. 10). Participants acknowledged the difficulties of implementing such a policy, such as the need for elected officials to resist pressure from constituents and the issue of fairness that might be raised regarding the loss of affordable housing in riverfront communities. The report notes the dilemmas of moving people out of floodplains in the face of "deep-seated respect for property" and of "outpourings of empathy and neighborliness" following a flood disaster (p. 27).

The Lincoln report identifies flood mitigation options, including minimum building codes, land use controls, and incentives to discourage dangerous development patterns. The Community Rating System under the NFIP is cited as an example of positive incentives. Other possibilities include provision of tax benefits for landowners who maintain their

floodplain land in natural use and penalties for risky actions and behavior. For example, the city of Des Plaines, Illinois, imposes a $200 surcharge on development in the floodplain (Faber 1996, p. 26). Regional, watershed-scale planning is cited as an effective mitigation strategy, as opposed to the current uncoordinated system of flood hazard reduction. The report discusses floodplain management techniques and provides case analyses of some successful watershed planning initiatives, including those carried out in the Charles River basin in Massachusetts and Bucks County, Pennsylvania, and the initiative carried out by Upper Mississippi River Basin Association.

Although the Lincoln report accepts the need for some structural flood control, it concludes that structural approaches can no longer be the primary focus of floodplain management. It notes that often the construction of a levee or floodwall creates a false sense of security and induces greater risk as a result. It also raises questions of fairness: "Taxpayers of whole states or the nation pay to build or maintain some flood control structures, without clear evidence that the entire state or nation benefits from these structures in proportion to their costs" (Faber 1996, p. 22). The report reccomends relocation, curtailing of development in the floodplain, use of incentives and public education, and regional watershed planning as more effective and sustainable ways to reduce flood hazards.

A major conclusion from the Lincoln conference was the need to "invert the pyramid" in floodplain management—that is, to give more emphasis and responsibility to local decision making. Federal and state governments should provide "consistent standards" and technical assistance and should link postdisaster assistance to predisaster local planning. "Communities that allow floodplain development should be prepared to pay the costs, as long as federal and state officials have made those costs clear from the start" (Faber 1996, p. 25). Technical assistance would include help in undertaking regional watershed planning and providing up-to-date floodplain maps. In the end, the "tough love" approach would mean severely limiting the extent to which the public bails out or subsidizes risky development, with a raft of political difficulties attached. Even with supportive elected officials, the public must be convinced to accept this change (Faber 1996, p. 27).

Other commentators have noted problems with the National Flood Insurance Program. Kusler and Larson (1993) recommend extending mapping and management efforts to smaller rivers and streams (31 percent of flood payments go to properties located outside mapped 100-year floodplains; 100 million acres, or one-half of the nation's floodplains, are currently not mapped, mostly along smaller streams and creeks); giving

greater attention to the needs of special high-risk hazard areas; and making a more concerted effort to deal with repetitive loss properties (2 percent of the flood policies under the NFIP account for 30 percent of the claims) and substantially damaged structures.

Interagency Floodplain Management Review Committee Report (Galloway Report)

Following the Midwest floods, a special Interagency Floodplain Management Review Committee was appointed to analyze causes of the flooding, effectiveness of existing floodplain management measures, and ways to improve floodplain management. The committee, chaired by Brigadier General Gerald E. Galloway, submitted its report to the administration Floodplain Management Task Force in 1994. The report, titled *Sharing the Challenge: Floodplain Management into the 21st Century,* commonly referred to as the Galloway Report, is the most comprehensive analysis of the existing floodplain management framework, and it is quite critical of existing approaches. It puts forth both a different philosophy for floodplain management and a tangible set of policy recommendations for bringing this philosophy about. The report lays out a "vision for the floodplain" (Interagency Floodplain Management Review Committee 1994, chap. 4) that is substantially at odds with the historical view of floodplains. This vision does not preclude human use of floodplains but seeks a more sensible balance between use and conservation. The vision is defined in the report by two strategic goals:

1. Reduce the nation's vulnerability to the dangers that result from floods.

   Reduce the vulnerability to urban areas, industry and agriculture, when such reduction is justified and reasonable; avoid new development when reduction is not appropriate. As appropriate, move those currently at risk from the floodplain. Strive to eliminate threats to life, property, and the environment, and to the mental health and well being of floodplain occupants. Ensure the viability of critical infrastructure and the regional economy. (p. 66)

2. Preserve and enhance the natural resources and functions of floodplains.

   Treat the floodplain as part of a physical and biological system that includes the floodplain within the larger context of its watershed. Seek to identify and enhance the cultural, historic, and aesthetic values of floodplains. Where appropriate, restore and enhance bottomland and related upland habitat and flood storage. Use existing government and private programs to acquire, over

time, environmental interest in these lands from willing sellers. Ensure the consideration of social and environmental factors in all actions relating to the floodplain. (p. 67)

The vision emphasizes the natural and ecological functions of rivers and foucuses on actions to reduce future vulnerability. Consistent with these goals is the advocacy of a more "balanced" perspective on how floodplains are used. The report favors moving away from reliance on structural approaches to flood control and toward nonstructural strategies, and recommends avoidance of floodplains as a first priority and minimizing and mitigating impacts when floodplains cannot be avoided. And, again, any approach should happen in a manner that "concurrently protects and enhances the natural environment" (p. 68).

The Galloway Report recommends actions for advancing this vision of floodplain management. Many involve modifying the organizational structure through which floodplain management occurs. It recommends enactment of a national floodplain management act that would articulate a national floodplain policy (emphasizing nonstructural approaches) and provide funding and support for the development of state and local floodplain management plans. Such state programs would have to meet certain minimum federal standards, and if they did not, monies not tied to disaster mitigation could be withheld. Perhaps the most interesting proposal would be a requirement, similar to provisions under the federal Coastal Zone Management Act (CZMA), that subsequent federal projects and actions be consistent ("to the maximum extent practicable") with approved state programs. Other proposals in the report include reestablishing river basin commissions; limiting the federal cost share of postflood disaster assistance to no more than 75 percent and seeking a consistent standard among federal agencies; strengthening and improving the NFIP; improving management and operation of the existing levee system; and expanding floodplain buyouts and the use of other nonstructural measures.

In advocating a more balanced approach to floodplain management, the report acknowledges that many environmental and other benefits of floodplains are often difficult to quantify in strict economic analyses. The report recommends readjusting priorities to give more weight to these benefits and functions, including changes to the Principles and Guidelines—the federal rules governing water resource development projects—to better take into account environmental and social values. Enhancement of environmental quality would become a coequal objective with economic development, and the standard benefit-cost analysis required would be supplemented by a "system of accounts" that would track a variety of potential benefits and impacts, including those that are non-

quantifiable. Other proposed environmental enhancement actions include establishing a lead agency for coordinating floodplain land acquisitions and focusing on acquiring land that has significant habitat value.

A collaborative approach to floodplain management, within an eco-system framework, is endorsed. Federal, state, and local agencies as well as private organizations would work together in partnerships. At the federal level, efforts would be made to move away from the project-by-project and agency-by-agency focus that has characterized much decision making in the past.

Unified National Program for Floodplain Management

Similar policy recommendations are contained in the most recent version of the *Unified National Program for Floodplain Management* (Federal Interagency Floodplain Management Task Force 1994). Required by Congress under the National Flood Insurance Act of 1968, the *Unified National Program* sets forth national floodplain management goals, along with objectives and strategies for achieving them. The Galloway Report draws from and cites the 1994 *Unified National Program*, and the two reports generally parallel each other.

The *Unified National Program* argues for "wise use" of floodplains and consideration of risks both to humans and to the natural environment (Federal Interagency Floodplain Management Task Force 1994):

> The definition of *wise use* provides its own self-test. In theory, floodplain decision makers can ask themselves, "If this development (or other activity) is located in a floodplain, is it possible to minimize the loss of life and damage from flooding?" If the answer to this is "No," then the activity may not be a wise use of the floodplain land. If the risk to life and property can be mitigated, there is a second question, "Does locating this development in the floodplain allow for maintaining the floodplain's natural functions?" If it does not, then the activity may not be a wise use of the floodplain, even if the first test was met. In other words, the answer to both questions must be "yes." (p. 9)

> *Wise use* of floodplains means enjoying the benefits of floodplain lands and waters *while still* minimizing the loss of life and damage from flooding *and at the same time* preserving and restoring the natural resources of floodplains as much as possible. Wise use thus is any activity or set of activities that is compatible with both the risks to the natural resources of floodplains and the risks to human resources (life and property). (p. 9)

The *Unified National Program* reiterates the Galloway Report's caution about developing the floodplain and its emphasis on protecting and

restoring the natural functions of floodplains. It recommends that flood-plain managers choose "the best mixture of strategies and tools, balancing competing uses, weighing costs and benefits, and evaluating various alter-natives—always keeping in mind the physical characteristics of the flood-plain in question, the needs and desires of the people who have an interest in it, and the potential impact proposed uses will have on the future" (Fed-eral Interagency Floodplain Management Task Force 1994, p. viii).

The *Unified National Program* sets forth national goals, including estab-lishment of a national goal-setting and monitoring system' and reduction by at least one-half of the risk to life, property, and natural resources by the year 2020. (The latter is quite similar to the goal in the original version of the *National Mitigation Strategy*.) Other goals address the need to increase public awareness about floodplains and to establish floodplain manage-ment capability "in every state and locality throughout the nation." A detailed action agenda is also provided for accomplishing each goal, including such objectives as completing a national inventory of structures in floodplains and establishing training programs.

Recent Legislative and Policy Development Activity

In response to many of the perceived problems and limitations of the cur-rent mitigation framework, a flurry of legislative proposals before Congress and a host of other policy initiatives appeared in the mid-1990s. The most significant of these initiatives are summarized in the sections that follow.

National Flood Insurance Reform Act of 1994

Major reforms of the NFIP were enacted as part of the Riegle Community Development and Regulatory Improvement Act of 1994. Specifically, the National Flood Insurance Reform Act of 1994 seeks to correct deficiencies in the program. Among other things, the act mandates new lender com-pliance requirements, including a requirement that all regulated lending institutions not issue new loans for properties within the floodplain without insurance, a requirement that lenders notify borrowers when flood insurance is required and actually purchase it for borrowers if bor-rowers do not do so within a certain time period, and requirements for the escrowing of flood insurance premiums. The act extends the waiting period for new flood insurance policies to thirty days (a problem in the Midwest floods) and extends the maximum amounts of insurance cov-

erage for residential and commercial structures (as much as $250,000 for residential structures and $500,000 for commercial structures) and their contents.

The act reorganizes mitigation programs under the NFIP. It eliminates the flooded properties purchase program (Section 1362) and the erosion-threatened structures program (Upton-Jones) and creates a new mitigation assistance program, including a new National Flood Mitigation Fund and a program of mitigation grants for state and local governments. Grants are to be available on a matching basis (25 percent state or local, 75 percent federal), both for planning assistance and for carrying out mitigation measures. To be eligible for grant monies, a state or locality must have prepared (and have approved by FEMA) a "flood risk mitigation plan." Under the act, "[t]he mitigation plan shall be consistent with a comprehensive strategy for mitigation activities for the area affected by the mitigation plan, that has been adopted by the state or community following a public hearing (Section 1366[a])." Mitigation activities eligible for funding include demolition or relocation of structures, elevation and flood-proofing, acquisition of floodplain properties, "minor physical mitigation efforts," beach nourishment, and state provision of technical assistance to localities. Mitigation activities funded under the Section 1362 and Upton-Jones programs thus will remain eligible. FEMA is to give priority to mitigation activities addressing repetitive loss structures and substantially damaged structures.

One of the more interesting changes under the act is a provision that permits property owners additional flood insurance coverage for the cost of complying with land use and floodplain management requirements. This provision applies only to repetitive loss structures and structures that have been substantially damaged (where the cost of repair is 50 percent or more of the value of the structure), and it allows for the assessment of a $75 insurance surcharge to cover these compliance costs.

Proposed Implementation Rules for the Flood Mitigation Assistance Program and the Hazard Mitigation Grant Program

FEMA recently promulgated interim final rules for the new Flood Mitigation Assistance Program (FMAP), created under the National Flood Insurance Reform Act of 1994, and for the Hazard Mitigation Grant Program (HMGP), created under the Stafford Act.

The proposed interim rule for the FMAP specifies types of eligible projects, program requirements, and the process for funding and implementing

projects (FEMA 1996a). Three types of grants are to be provided under the program: planning assistance grants, project implementation grants, and technical assistance grants. To receive funding for project implementation, a locality or state must have prepared a Flood Mitigation Plan. The preparation of these plans is itself eligible for funding under the first type of grant, and some jurisdictions may be deemed to already have a qualifying plan (e.g., a state's Section 409 plan or a local plan prepared under the Community Rating System). The rule also stipulates what must be included in a Flood Mitigation Plan.

The proposed interim rule for the HMGP, which was subsequently withdrawn, would have created a "dual management system" to give states an incentive for building mitigation capability. States would have been designated either "managing" or "coordinating" states, depending on their mitigation capability. Those given the management designation would have final authority for dispersal of project funds, whereas coordinating states would require a FEMA sign-off on projects. Criteria for determining whether a state could assume a managing role included the presence of a full-time permanent hazard mitigation officer, the existance of an approved state mitigation planning process and documentation, and the ability to provide technical assistance on mitigation techniques (FEMA 1996b, pp. 18–19).

Proposals for National All-Hazards Insurance

Much recent congressional activity has focused on expanding the NFIP's insurance approach to cover other hazards.[5] Several legislative proposals have been submitted to create an "all-hazards" insurance system, but none has been successful so far (e.g., H.R. 2873 and S.R. 2350 in the 103rd Congress; see Stalberg 1995 for a brief summary).

If passed, the Natural Disaster Protection and Insurance Act of 1995 (S.R. 1043) would create a Natural Disaster Insurance Corporation to provide insurance and reinsurance for hurricanes, earthquakes, volcanic eruptions, and tsunamis. It would be governed by an independent Natural Disaster Insurance Board of Actuaries, which would review and approve the corporation's plan of operation, including its proposed rates. The system would include incentives for purchase of disaster insurance (modeled after the NFIP). Coverage would be required for federally related mortgages in states prone to earthquakes, volcanic eruptions, tsunamis, and hurricanes, and owners of residential property in these disaster-prone states would not be eligible for future disaster assistance unless insured. Each disaster-prone state would be required to have in place minimum multihazard building codes and a state mitigation plan. A state's failure to

meet these mitigation requirements would result in a 50 percent reduction in the federal share of disaster assistance under the Stafford Act. A Mitigation Account would be established, and mitigation grants would be allocated to states on the basis of a pro rata formula.

Proposals to create a national disaster insurance system remain controversial in Congress. Despite provisions in the bills to ensure premiums that are actuarially sound, there is fear that national disaster insurance would amount to a major new federal subsidy program. The GAO has expressed concern that such a framework would expose the federal government to large financial liabilities (McCool testimony, cited in U.S. House 1994).

National Mitigation Strategy

The years 1994 and 1995 also saw the preparation and publication of FEMA's *National Mitigation Strategy.* The strategy is the result of eleven regional mitigation forums held around the country, attended by some 1,800 people. It consists of basic principles, a "vision for the future," a national mitigation goal, and specific mitigation objectives, many with time frames attached. The basic principles underlying the strategy are as follows (FEMA 1995c, pp. 9–11):

- Risk reduction measures ensure long-term economic success for the community as a whole rather than short-term benefit for special interests.

- Risk reduction measures for one natural hazard must be compatible with risk reduction measures for other natural hazards.

- Risk reduction measures must be evaluated to achieve the best mix for a given location.

- Risk reduction measures for natural hazards must be compatible with risk reduction measures for technological hazards, and vice versa.

- All mitigation is local.

- Disaster costs and the impacts of natural hazards can be reduced by emphasizing proactive mitigation before emergency response; both predisaster (preventive) and postdisaster (corrective) mitigation are needed.

- Hazard identification and risk assessment are the cornerstones of mitigation.

- Building new federal-state-local partnerships and public-private partnerships is the most effective means of implementing measures to reduce the impacts of natural hazards.

- Those who knowingly choose to assume greater risk must accept responsibility for that choice.

- Risk reduction measures for natural hazards must be compatible with the protection of natural and cultural resources.

The strategy's "vision for safer communities," emphasizes the need for mitigation. The vision is elaborated by eight objectives to be accomplished by the year 2020, as follows: (1) society will make choices using comprehensive hazard identification and risk assessment processes; (2) the United States will become a model for balancing economic development and preservation of natural and cultural resources; (3) the United States will promote public awareness and provide early warning and preparation for natural hazards for all populations; (4) funding and incentives will ensure continued development and application of mitigation; (5) mitigation will be incorporated into all federal actions, and state and local governments will have similar capabilities; (6) all new structures will be built to national multihazard building standards; (7) upgrade and retrofit programs will be implemented; and (8) disaster recovery will be carried out with minimal economic disruption (FEMA 1995c, p. 13).

The final version of the mitigation strategy presents a 2010 National Mitigation Goal with two parts: "(1) to substantially increase public awareness of natural hazard risk so that the public demands safer communities in which to live and work; and (2) to significantly reduce the risk of loss of life, injuries, economic costs, and destruction of natural and cultural resources that result from natural hazards" (FEMA 1995c, p. 15). Interestingly, the 1994 draft of the strategy contained a more specific goal: to "reduce by at least half the loss of life, injuries, economic costs (1994 dollars), and destruction of natural and cultural resources that result from the occurrence of natural hazards" (FEMA 1994b, p. 8). Although these goals would be difficult to achieve, it was unfortunate that FEMA backed away from attempting to set measurable targets.

The *National Mitigation Strategy* is a major accomplishment and a watershed document in the history of U.S. mitigation policy. However, many of its goals and objectives are broad, subject to substantial interpretation ("adopt incentives . . . promote awareness"), and not overly ambitious. The vision presented is neither clear nor compelling. Since the plan's completion, it is not clear that many of the shorter-term objectives have been accomplished. Nevertheless, it is the first attempt at the federal level to think strategically about mitigation and to begin to put forth a systematic agenda for advancing mitigation in the United States. Moreover, some major steps toward implementing the plan can already be noted, such as the convening of a federal Interagency Hazard Mitigation Task Force.

FEMA Strategic Plan

1994 also saw the preparation of FEMA's first strategic plan. A revised and updated version of the plan was adopted in 1997. The plan, titled *Partnership for a Safer Future* (FEMA 1997), describes the mission of FEMA and presents an overall vision for the agency. Three strategic goals are presented:

1. Protect lives and prevent loss of property from all hazards.

2. Reduce human suffering and enhance the recovery of communities after disaster strikes.

3. Ensure that the public is served in a timely and efficient manner.

For each goal, objectives and measures for judging performance are stated. Mitigation is emphasized as a strategy for achieving goal (1), and a specific target is set of reducing by 15 percent the risk of property loss and economic disruption from natural hazards by fiscal year 2007, as measured by a national loss estimation model and by improvements in state and local emergency management capability (FEMA 1997). Five-year objectives are also given. Within five years, for instance, expected annual losses from flood disasters should be reduced by $1 billion and state emergency management capability should be improved by 10 percent.

The strategic plan is strong in delineating clear targets and objectives and how they are to be measured, but it is less detailed about how the goals and objectives are to be accomplished. A four-pronged mitigation strategy is specified: federal mitigation, state mitigation, community mitigation, and a private-public mitigation partnership. The foreword to the plan emphasizes FEMA's intention to shift its emphasis from reacting to natural disasters to one of preventing them. The concept of disaster-resistant communities, the subject of a FEMA initiative described later, in the section on Project Impact, is identified as a key element in this new emphasis.

Public-Private Partnership 2000

An alliance of public- and private-sector organizations has recently begun a joint initiative to identify and examine new strategies for mitigating natural disasters. The initative is called Public-Private Partnership 2000 (PPP 2000); key sponsors include the National Science and Technology Council's Subcommittee on Natural Disaster Reduction and the Institute for Business and Home Safety (IBHS, formerly the Institute for Natural Hazard Loss Reduction). The main activity of PPP 2000 is to promote dialogue on new mitigation strategies. The first in a series of forums was held in September 1997, focusing specifically on initiatives of the insurance

sector. The primary goals of the forum were "to bring all of the stake-holders together to break through traditional patterns of thinking" (IBHS 1997, p. 1). More than a dozen forums are planned, addressing a variety of mitigation topics.

A report summarizing the first forum and the nature of the discussions carried out during the forum presented several proposed actions. One of the most interesting was to make disaster reduction "a public value" through the preparation of "disaster impact statements" before major decisions are made or actions taken (analogous to environmental impact statements under the National Environmental Policy Act) (IBHS 1997, p. 3).

National Science and Technology Council

The Subcommittee on Natural Disaster Reduction of the National Science and Technology Council (NSTC) recently issued recommendations for addressing natural disasters. The subcommittee, with representatives from nineteen federal agencies and offices (e.g., FEMA, HUD, USGS), published its final report, *Natural Disaster Reduction: A Plan for the Nation*, in 1996. The plan is composed of two main parts: a *Strategic Plan* and an *Implementation Plan*.

Although many of its recommendations build on existing initiatives, the plan is unique in its philosophical tone. It argues for the creation of a more "sustainable society" and strongly endorses the idea of sustainable development. It views a sustainable society as one that strives to be more resilient to the variations of nature and natural forces. It discusses the need to address natural disasters in terms of loftier philosophical and ethical imperatives, asserting that disaster reduction is a matter of environmental justice (noting that effects of natural disasters often fall disproportionately on minority groups and the poor), and a matter of considering future generations. It advocates "fundamental new approaches" to natural disasters, including a shift from reactive to anticipatory policies, a shift from "resistant" to more "resilient" strategies, and more comprehensive and coordinated community-wide approaches. The plan also calls for individuals to assume greater responsibility for insuring against risks, for creation of federal-state-local and private-sector partnerships, and for the United States to assume greater leadership in promoting hazard reduction internationally. The *Implementation Plan* states the need for enhanced coordination among the federal agencies represented on the subcommittee. It highlights several recommendations, including development of a National Risk Assessment and an Integrated Natural Disaster Mitigation Information Network.

Performance Partnership Agreements

In 1996, FEMA began a new strategic process—Performance Partnership Agreements (PPAs)—by which it provides federal emergency management funds to states. PPAs are a direct outgrowth of the National Performance Review, and although they do not yet replace the annual cooperative agreement approach, they do impose on it a new goal-oriented, performance-based framework. They are intended to provide states with greater flexibility in using federal emergency management funds and to impose greater accountability on states to ensure performance from the use of these funds.

Under the PPA system, states negotiate and enter into five-year agreements with FEMA. Each PPA identifies a set of national partnership goals, and each state develops a more specific set of measurable objectives for the five-year period, ideally based on a strategic planning process. The state also stipulates specific annual outcomes (FEMA 1995a). Each year's cooperative agreement between FEMA and the state is intended to provide the financial and technical assistance to implement the state's performance objectives. States are required to evaluate and report their annual progress at meeting objectives.

Fiscal year 1996 was the first year PPAs were used, and about half of the states entered into them. Although it is too early to judge its success, the PPA approach is promising. It responds to concerns of recent evaluative studies by encouraging establishment of goals and objectives, focusing on performance and the ability to measure success in achieving mitigation and providing state and local governments with greater flexibility in expending federal monies. It also formalizes a process of interaction and dialogue between FEMA and the states and provides a mechanism for them to agree on a national and state program of hazard mitigation. The PPA process has the potential of creating, as the name implies, real partnerships between federal and state (and local) governments.

Advantages of this system to states include substantially greater flexibility achieved through the following means (FEMA n.d., *Performance Partnership Agreement Template*):

- Consolidation of programs and funding streams
- Elimination of micromanagement
- Devolution of decision making (there should be established national goals and outcomes with more flexibility for state and local partners to determine how to achieve them—performance partnerships should accommodate different state program strategies)
- Reduction of wasteful paperwork and barriers to success

Annual assessments of state achievement would provide accountability. FEMA intends to reward states, financially and otherwise, for their progress in meeting agreed-on objectives. For example, FEMA funding, through its annual cooperative agreement, will be based in part on performance. Other possible incentives include giving states greater flexibility and more favorable cost shares for disaster assistance monies.

Disaster-Resistant Communities: Project Impact and the Showcase Communities Initiative

Two recent initiatives focus on encouraging and helping localities to become more "disaster resistant," one through FEMA and the other through the Institute for Business and Home Safety. FEMA's Project Impact provides financial resources and technical assistance to communities designated as disaster resistant. Communities enter into a formal agreement with FEMA to undertake a host of predisaster actions to mitigate and minimize hazard vulnerability. Under the agreement, FEMA provides $1 million in seed money to fund disaster reduction actions. Deerfield Beach, Florida, is the first disaster-resistant community under this initiative, and six other cities and counties are to participate as pilot communities: Allegheny County, Maryland; Oakland, California; Pascagoula, Mississippi; Seattle, Washington; Tucker and Randolph Counties, West Virginia; and Wilmington, North Carolina.

Project Impact develops partnerships and involves the broader community in reducing vulnerability to hazards. Other nongovernmental entities participating in the Deerfield Beach program include Florida Power and Light, the Promus Hotel Corporation, and the Fort Lauderdale *Sun-Sentinel*. Home Depot, an early participant, will be providing educational displays and offering product knowledge courses for interested homeowners. FEMA's Project Impact guidebook suggests that communities designate a "community CEO," someone in the community who will assume responsibility for the program; create a "Disaster-Resistant Community Planning Committee"; and develop a strategic plan for accomplishing mitigation (FEMA n.d., *Project Impact*). Project Impact also involves a national awareness campaign and an outreach effort aimed at alerting businesses and communities to the economic benefits of mitigation.

A similar initiative has been undertaken by the Institute for Business and Home Safety (IBHS). Called Showcase Communities, its goal is to encourage disaster-prone communities to adopt mitigation strategies to make them more disaster resistant. Communities agree to develop comprehensive hazards programs, which include, at a minimum, incorporating education and

hazard awareness into school curriculums, developing and maintaining up-to-date emergency response and recovery plans, and modifying local land use practices and policies to reduce vulnerability. Showcase communities are expected to appoint a single local official as coordinator and must satisfy fourteen criteria set forth by IBHS.[6]

Participating communities are encouraged to create disaster recovery business alliances. Evansville, Illinois, and Vanderburgh County, of which Evansville is the county seat, constitutes the first showcase community; plans are under way to add additional communities. The Showcase Communities program is working in close cooperation with Project Impact, and it is likely that Deerfield Beach, Florida, will be the second community designated as a showcase community. IBHS does not have additional funding to offer participating communities but stresses the benefits of designation as a showcase community. IBHS is working with its insurance company members on possible reductions of insurance rates in showcase communities, similar to the Community Rating System under the NFIP.

U.S. Army Corps of Engineers Reform Proposals

In 1995 and 1996, the Clinton administration proposed changes in the way U.S. Army Corps of Engineers flood control projects are evaluated and funded. The most significant changes were proposed in 1995 as part of the administration's fiscal year 1996 budget proposals. The proposed changes would have substantially scaled back the circumstances under which the Corps is involved in flood control and stipulated new, more stringent criteria for determining eligible projects. They would have restricted involvement and funding of the Corps to only those flood control projects that are national and interstate in nature, raised the required benefit-cost ratio, and changed the cost-sharing requirements, substantially reducing the federal share in flood control projects.

The proposed changes met with considerable resistance (under the criteria, politically powerful states such as California would have been excluded from flood control projects), and Congress instead reaffirmed the cost-sharing and funding criteria contained in the Water Resources Development Act of 1986. In the proposed budget for fiscal year 1997, the administration again proposed changes. However, these were primarily restricted to cost sharing, such as the proposed 50-50 cost share between federal and nonfederal levels. The administration also announced its intention not to fund any new Army Corps of Engineers Shore Protection Projects, though it intends to honor commitments already made, such as that of carrying out periodic replenishment of beaches. These are essentially

local projects, with primarily local, regional, and state benefits, and thus should be funded at nonfederal levels.

National Earthquake Loss Reduction Program

Following a review of the National Earthquake Hazards Reduction Program by the president's National Science and Technology Council and findings of the NEHRP Advisory Committee and other reports, an extensive new strategy, the National Earthquake Loss Reduction Program (NEP), was unveiled in 1996 (National Earthquake Strategy Working Group 1996). The NEP does not propose any increase in funding levels but seeks to substantially enhance coordination and "interagency strategic planning" to reduce duplication and to focus on priority goals (p. 7). The plan lays out a series of specific targets and timelines, organized around nine major goals.[7]

Under the goal of providing leadership and coordination, the strategy proposes developing a balanced national prioritized research and mitigation agenda and a nationwide strategic plan to integrate and coordinate existing research and mitigation programs into a unified, needs-driven, goal-oriented program. Under the goal of expanding technology transfer and outreach, targets include assessing the costs and benefits of mitigation techniques and disseminating state-of-the-art information on mitigation to design-professionals. Targets also include developing seismic design standards (e.g., for lifelines such as major roads and water mains and rehabilitation of existing structures) and introducing multihazard standards by the year 2000. A number of the targets promote better understanding of obstacles to implementation of mitigation and better understanding of mitigation's social, political, and economic dimensions.

It is not clear how the NEP will change the current federal approach to seismic policy. Although the NEP strategy does include some specific recommendations, many of the target activities are quite general (e.g., "develop a nationwide strategic plan"). As much as anything, the NEP appears to create a new process and structure for coordinating and prioritizing seismic policies, with a much stronger emphasis on mitigation and application of technology.

Other Recent Legislative and Policy Activities

A number of other legislative proposals and policy initiatives have been undertaken since 1992. Following Hurricane Andrew, there was heated debate in Congress about the need for FEMA reform (e.g., see GAO 1993). Several reform bills were drafted, with the most comprehensive

introduced in May 1993 by Senator Barbara Mikulski of Maryland. S.R. 995, the Disaster Preparedness and Response Act of 1993, would have reorganized FEMA around a risk-based, all-hazards strategy; overhauled the federal response plan; created disaster strike teams; reduced to five the number of political appointees in FEMA; reduced the number of regional offices and located them in areas of high risk; and created a stronger role for the White House in disasters (including creation of a Domestic Crisis Monitoring Unit, to be headed by the vice president; see NAPA 1994 for a discussion).

In 1994, in response to the Midwest floods, Congress enacted the Federal Crop Insurance Reform Act of 1994 (P.L. 103-354), which requires farmers to take out, at the minimum, catastrophic risk protection insurance as a condition of receiving crop support payments, direct loans, or loan guarantees (Wright 1996). The Hazard Mitigation and Relocation Assistance Act of 1993 (the Volkmer bill) increased the federal funds available for hazard mitigation, raising the federal share from 50 percent to 75 percent for mitigation projects and raising the overall amount available from 10 percent of public assistance to 15 percent of all disaster assistance provided for an event. Other relevant legislation with hazard mitigation implications includes the Coastal Zone Protection Act of 1996 (reauthorization of the Coastal Zone Management Program) and the 1996 Federal Agriculture Improvement and Reform Act. Mitigation of coastal hazards is a CZMA goal, and the farm bill extends the wetlands reserve program, which in turn can have important flood control benefits. The sixteen-state Southern Regional Emergency Management Compact, signed in 1993, formalizes mutual aid arrangements.

Major Trends in Mitigation Policy; Common Themes in the Debate

The attention given in recent years to critiquing and reforming the disaster management framework is unprecedented. Congressional task forces, special study groups, and others have critically examined the system, and legislation has been proposed and, in some cases, enacted. From this national debate, certain key themes can be distilled.

New Importance Given to Mitigation

One of the clearest trends is the new importance given to mitigation. Historically, disaster management has focused on the other three phases of disaster policy—preparedness, response, and recovery. Increasingly it is

recognized that mitigation is the most cost-effective approach in the long run, ultimately minimizing the need for expenditures in the other phases. Recent national studies have emphasized mitigation (e.g., NPR 1993; NAPA 1993), and recent national initiatives and legislative proposals strengthen mitigation. FEMA elevated mitigation within its organizational mission by creating a Mitigation Directorate, preparing the *National Mitigation Strategy* (FEMA 1995c), forming a federal Interagency Mitigation Task Force, and convening the first National Mitigation Conference. FEMA is shifting from a reactive approach to natural disasters to one that is fundamentally preventive (FEMA 1997).

Several recent federal acts expand the resources available for mitigation, notably the National Flood Insurance Reform Act of 1994 and the Stafford Act. The Hurricane Program, formerly called the Hurricane Preparedness Grant Program, has taken on mitigation as a new area of emphasis. (U.S. Senate 1995). State governments are also spending more money on mitigation. The recent survey of states by the National Emergency Management Association and the Council of State Governments documented a 58 percent increase in mitigation spending between fiscal years 1992 and 1994 (see Cabot 1996; NEMA and CSG 1996).

Increasing Favor of Nonstructural Mitigation

Much recent mitigation literature supports deemphasizing structural approaches, including levees and floodwalls in riverine environments and seawalls, revetments, groins, and other similar structures in coastal environments. The new consensus is that the structural approach can no longer be the primary mitigation strategy (Interagency Floodplain Management Review Committee 1994; Faber 1996; Federal Interagency Floodplain Management Task Force 1992a). Negative aspects of structural measures include their cost, environmental impacts, and effects in inducing further exposure of people and property. The Clinton administration's decision following the Midwest floods to focus mitigation efforts on acquisition and relocation marked a new era in floodplain management and mitigation policy—one in which nonstructural measures, especially proactive measures such as avoidance, gained unprecedented endorsement.

Nonstructural mitigation measures supported include building codes and construction standards, though their effectiveness was questioned in the aftermath of Hurricane Andrew (OTA 1993; FEMA 1995c). Acquisition and relocation has become an important mitigation strategy in the Midwest floods recovery program. Despite implementation problems, the

economic logic of clearing out high-risk floodplains has been seen in more recent flooding events (for a discussion of the economic savings experienced during subsequent floods as a result of the 1993 buyouts, see FEMA 1995c). Land use planning and regulation mitigate hazards through avoidance—keeping people and property out of harm's way in the first place (FEMA 1995c, p. 26). Insurance remains popular, and notwithstanding the controversy surrounding recent congressional proposals, much literature supports national all-hazards insurance. Moreover, although the NFIP has been criticized, it is still seen as a positive way to ask those exposed to flooding risks to help meet flood recovery costs. Disagreement exists regarding beach replenishment as a mitigation measure, with support from the Marine Board of the National Research Council and opposition from critics (e.g., Pilkey and Dixon 1996). The proposed implementation rules for the new Flood Mitigation Assistance Program state that beach nourishment will not qualify for mitigation funding and in fact serves to induce further development and growth in high-risk locations (FEMA 1996a).

Personal Responsibility and Overcoming the Victim Mentality

Many recent policy initiatives hold that individuals and communities ought to assume greater responsibility for the consequences of their actions and decisions relative to natural hazards. The *National Mitigation Strategy* emphasizes personal responsibility, making it clear that "those who knowingly choose to assume greater risk must accept responsibility for that choice" (FEMA 1995c, p. 11). Much of the cost of recent disasters, for example, has resulted from foolish decisions to locate homes in high-risk velocity zones or on barrier islands or from decisions to locate highways, roads, or other public investments in 100-year floodplains. As discussed earlier, participants, including local officials, in a national conference examining the 1993 Midwest floods argued for a policy of "tough love"—withdrawing government subsidies and bailouts for risky behaviors, and expecting individuals and communities to educate themselves about risks and to assume greater responsibility and accountability for their actions (Faber 1996).

A related theme is the need to enhance public awareness of the desirability of mitigation and of the mitigation measures available to individuals and communities. Much greater public education and public awareness are essential prerequisites to responsible decision making. The *National Mitigation Strategy* calls for promoting "widespread public awareness" and

targeting education toward a wide range of individuals and segments of the public, including planning and design professionals; state and local elected and appointed officials; business owners, employees, and customers; and the general public (see FEMA 1995c, p. 11).

Adjusting the Incentive Structure

Adjustments to the incentive structure are necessary to encourage more responsible decisions and to ensure that these decisions reflect their true costs (NPR 1993; NAPA 1993; NSTC 1996; OTA 1995; National Earthquake Strategy Working Group 1996). The House Bipartisan Task Force on Disasters is critical of the expectations that have developed and the incentive structure that serves to exacerbate risk patterns (U.S. House 1994, pp. 7–8).

Controversy continues to surround the National Flood Insurance Program (NFIP), even under current reforms, with many believing it encourages hazardous development. One recurring theme is the need to expand the number of property owners who purchase hazard insurance, in order to encourage responsible personal behavior and reduce the public costs of disasters. Participation rates in the NFIP have been low—only 13 percent of property owners within flood hazard areas hold flood insurance policies. Administration of the NFIP has been described as irresponsible, for having allowed downriver property owners to sign up for flood insurance in advance of the oncoming Midwest floods—an inequity to property owners who had been paying flood insurance premiums for many years. Following the floods, federal disaster assistance, including buyout and relocation benefits, was provided to many property owners who had not purchased flood insurance or who had let their policies lapse. A conservative commentator noted that those who don't buy aren't stupid; "they know that the government will step in with disaster relief, including low-cost loans for rebuilding" (Richman 1993).

Recent proposals for all-hazards insurance and reinsurance have been supported as a strategy for encouraging greater personal responsibility. Again, there is a strong belief that individuals making decisions that place their homes and property at risk should be asked to contribute to or fully assume the costs of these decisions. The report of the National Science and Technology Council, for instance, states as one of its recommendations: "Reliance on federal bailouts must give way to increased individual responsibility for insuring against unacceptable risk" (NSTC 1996, p. 5).

Wright (1996) suggests the need to eliminate many forms of federal disaster assistance and to install in their stead a "contract with all Americans" (p. 272). Wright's proposed contract (pp. 272–273) includes the following:

1. An inventory of all properties located in known flood hazard areas

2. Full disclosure of flood risk to individuals through personal contact and in terms and ways they can understand (e.g., expected depths of floodwater on properties or around or in structures and expected frequency and duration of floods)

3. Provision of information about options individuals should consider to reduce their exposure to flood risk (e.g., structural modification) or to reduce their losses when a flood does occur (e.g., flood insurance)

4. Further disclosure to individuals, perhaps included in step (3), that most forms of existing disaster assistance (particularly grants) will be eliminated

In Wright's view, such a contract would "send a loud, clear message—hereafter only individuals, not government, will be held responsible for their decisions regarding occupancy or use of flood hazard areas and lack of action to reduce their existing exposure or potential economic losses" (Wright 1996, p. 273).

Other incentives could be created to encourage individuals and communities to adopt and implement mitigation measures (FEMA 1993). These could take the form of tax credits or low-interest loans (OTA 1995; Beatley 1992). The Community Rating System (CRS), which reduces flood insurance premiums in communities where flood reduction measures have been undertaken, exemplifies another role that positive incentives can play.[8]

Greater State and Local Responsibility

Much recent policy discussion has criticized the growing role of the federal government in assuming greater responsibility, especially financial responsibility, for natural disasters. Critics emphasize the need to reestablish the role of the federal government as the "government of last resort," placing primary responsibility for disaster mitigation on state and local governments (NAPA 1993; Interagency Floodplain Management Review Committee 1994). The NAPA study concludes that what is needed is a cooperative intergovernmental system with shared governance, in which one of FEMA's central missions is to enhance and help build state and local capacity.

At the same time, more flexibility for state and local governments in their use of disaster assistance monies is advocated. FEMA is replacing its Comprehensive Cooperative Agreements (CCAs) with states with Performance Partnership Agreements (PPAs), whereby states have discretion in utilizing preparedness funds if they agree to achieve mitigation targets.

Others emphasize local actions. The Lincoln Institute of Land Policy's *On Borrowed Land* (Faber 1996) advocates inverting the government pyramid— leaving most floodplain management decisions to local governments but ensuring that federal and state governments provide "consistent standards" and technical assistance (see also Glavan 1995). The *National Mitigation Strategy* places considerable emphasis on the local level as well, stating as one of its principles that "all mitigation is local" (FEMA 1995c, p. 10).

Building New Partnerships

In recognition of the fact that no single agency, organization, or individual will be able to address the growing cost of natural disasters, partnerships are often advocated (NPR 1993; Interagency Floodplain Management Review Committee 1994; Moore 1995). The *National Mitigation Strategy* states: "Building new State-local partnerships and public-private partnerships is the most effective means of implementing measures to reduce the impacts of natural hazards" (FEMA 1995c, p. 11). FEMA's Project Impact and the Showcase Communities initiative of the Institute for Business and Home Safety stress the development of local partnerships to build disaster-resistant communities (FEMA n.d., *Project Impact*; IBHS 1997).

A report by the American Insurance Association and the Alliance of American Insurers titled *New Partnerships for Catastrophe Response* identifies actions that can be taken by businesses, insurers, and consumers to reduce risks and to leverage limited resources (AIA and AAI 1995). The report states: "There is a need for a spirit of partnership between government and the insurance industry to enable each to better assist the consumers that fund both of our salaries" (p. 15). Recent political alliances between the insurance industry and the environmental community on climate change issues and between the insurance industry and state and local governments on code enforcement are further examples of the power of partnerships.

Bearing a "Fair Share" of the Costs of Disasters and Mitigation

Much debate has centered on the fairness of the present distribution of the costs of disasters. The House Bipartisan Task Force on Disasters called for a return to a "supplemental" role for the federal government in disaster assistance and for a national disaster policy that will "encourage all members of society to bear their fair share of the costs of disasters" (U.S. House 1994, p. 8). Bearing a fair share of the costs implies a number of possible

changes. At the individual level, it may mean shouldering the responsibility for purchasing and maintaining insurance (NPR 1993). All-hazards insurance, as recommended by the House task force, is also seen as a way to distribute the costs of disasters equitably.

One issue is what the federal share of disaster assistance should be. This raises the questions of whether the federal share is too high and whether the federal share should be fixed and certain rather than determined on a case-by-case basis, in response to politics and circumstances. The Stafford Act stipulates only that the federal share shall be "not less than 75 percent." In recent events the federal share has been raised, leaving state and local officials uncertain about the current rules of the game. Following Hurricane Andrew, the federal share was 100 percent (after the state spent $33 million), and it was 90 percent for the Northridge earthquake. Again, many believe that the current system discourages state and local governments from undertaking mitigation (NPR 1993; NAPA 1993). The NAPA study suggests lowering the standard federal cost share to 50 percent but allowing a higher federal share when states can show that they have developed at least minimal emergency management capacity (NAPA 1993, p. 92).

Other proposals to readjust the costs of disasters include adopting objective criteria for declaring a federal disaster and distinguishing among different magnitudes of disasters (for example, it may not be appropriate to reimburse state and local governments for the modest and predictable burden of snow removal); requiring state and local governments to rely more heavily on insurance and loans; and raising matching funds and creating other incentives to promote state and local mitigation that reduces the long-term costs of disasters (e.g., see NPR 1993). The "fair-share" issue has also arisen with respect to flood control projects of the Army Corps of Engineers. Unsuccessful proposals by the Clinton administration would have lowered the federal cost share for such projects and restricted Corps participation to projects with clear national significance.

The fair-share theme also emphasizes the importance of local and state governments finding their own sources of mitigation and disaster funding, derived from those who benefit from risky behavior or who contribute to the costs. Some local governments have enacted special taxing districts to address hazard mitigation or emergency management. For example, Oakland, California, established benefit assessment districts to fund vegetation management and other fire control activities in the aftermath of the 1991 firestorm; Lee County, Florida, proposed an emergency management taxing district; and beach replenishment districts are becoming increasingly common. Florida funds its new emergency management trust fund

through an annual surcharge on residential and commercial casualty insurance policies (chapter 3).

All-Hazards Codes and Strategies

Recent studies of disaster preparedness echo the theme of comprehensive, all-hazards planning. The NAPA and NPR studies support a move from the civil defense and nuclear defense functions of FEMA toward the full range of emergencies and disasters faced by the nation: "The time has come to shift the emphasis from national security to domestic emergency management using an all-hazards approach" (NAPA 1993, p. viii). NAPA also recommends a statutory charter for FEMA "centered on integrated mitigation, preparation, response and recovery from emergencies and disasters of all types" (p. ix). There is considerable evidence that FEMA is moving in the direction of a comprehensive, all-hazards approach.

There is recognition that homes and businesses should be constructed to standards that offer protection from all significant hazards. All-hazards codes are proposed in the *National Mitigation Strategy* goal that by the year 2010, "all new structures, including critical facilities and infrastructure, will be built to national multi-hazard standards that are incorporated into building codes that have been adopted and enforced by all municipalities, counties and states" (FEMA 1995c, p. 13). The *Strategy for National Earthquake Loss Reduction* contains similar wording (National Earthquake Strategy Working Group 1996).

Sustainability and Sustainable Communities

Sustainability, the new watchword in environmental policy, is increasingly pursued in natural disaster mitigation. Sustainability implies living within fundamental ecological limits. The Brundtland Commission defined it as development that "meets the needs of the present without compromising the ability of future generations to meet their own needs" (World Commission on Environment and Development 1987, p. 8). Sustainable development implies patterns of development that keep people and property out of harm's way and that also create resilient communities (Beatley 1995, 1996; Berke 1995). *Agenda 21*, the action agenda adopted at the 1992 United Nations Conference on Environment and Development (Rio Summit), advocates "redirecting inappropriate new development and human settlements to areas not prone to hazards" and supporting efforts in "contingency planning, with participation of affected communities for

post-disaster reconstruction and rehabilitation" (United Nations 1992, pp. 61–62). Worldwide, sustainable development reduces the vulnerability of populations to natural disasters while working to reduce poverty, provide jobs and economic opportunity, and improve living conditions (Berke 1995; Munasinghe and Clarke 1995).

The 1996 report of the National Science and Technology Council states that sustainable development requires, in addition to economic growth, environmental protection, and sustainable use of ecological systems, "a fourth criterion, of equal importance: Sustainable development must be resilient with respect to the natural variability of the earth and the solar system" (NSTC 1996, p. 2). This variability includes hurricanes, floods, volcanic eruptions, and other natural forces, which "reveal that our economic development is unacceptably brittle and fragile" (p. 2).

The term *sustainable communities* connotes the minimization of exposure of people and property to natural disasters (Beatley and Brower 1993; Beatley, Brower, and Schwab 1994; Geis and Kutzmark 1995). The disasters that result when communities and developments are located in high-risk areas suggest the ultimate definition of an "unsustainable" community. There is evidence that sustainable communities are carrying out hazard reduction projects (Topping 1996; Becker 1994). Several communities seeking to relocate outside the floodplain following the Midwest floods, for example, have described their efforts as attempts to become sustainable communities, and the Midwest Working Group on Sustainable Redevelopment organized a conference, with funding from the Department of Energy, to help midwestern communities explore ways to rebuild more sustainably (Becker 1994). Valmeyer, Illinois, and Pattonsburg, Missouri, are the two best examples. Pattonsburg has even adopted a set of principles of sustainability to guide its redevelopment. Following Hurricane Andrew in 1992, redevelopment design charrettes explored sustainable place designs. One example of a sustainable community project that has reached fruition is Jordan Commons in South Florida, a forty-acre, 187-unit project being built by Habitat for Humanity with energy and resource efficiency features, use of solar energy, strategic tree plantings, and steel frame building designed to withstand the region's hurricanes (Habitat for Humanity n.d.).

Building Disaster-Resistant Communities

Another recent theme, as discussed earlier, is creating "disaster-resistant" communities through FEMA's Project Impact and IBHS's Showcase

Communities Initiative. In exchange for additional financial resources (in FEMA's case), technical assistance, and designation as disaster-resistant communities, localities agree to adopt comprehensive measures in order to become less vulnerable to future disasters. These measures include standard mitigation efforts, education and outreach, up-to-date response and recovery plans, and collaboration with businesses and other nongovernmental actors in the community. Insurance companies are also exploring the possibility of lowering premiums in disaster-resistant communities.

Protecting and Restoring Natural Functions

Recent policy documents, such as the Galloway Report and the 1994 *Unified National Program for Floodplain Management,* emphasize protecting the natural functions of floodplains, and these environmental goals now appear coequal to protecting property and preventing loss of life (e.g., see Interagency Floodplain Management Task Force 1994). Floodplain management studies reach similar conclusions (Faber 1996; Faber and Hunt 1994; Federal Interagency Floodplain Management Task Force 1992a). Meanwhile, structural mitigation measures, such as seawalls and revetments to protect communities from coastal storms or flood walls and levees to guard against riverine flooding, are now perceived negatively because of their adverse effects on the natural environment (Pilkey et al. 1980; Pilkey and Dixon 1996).

Not only are environmental values worthy of protecting, but also protecting natural functions and processes may be the most effective and efficient way to safeguard people and property. Coastal dunes and beaches serve as natural seawalls protecting the people and property located behind them. Natural wetlands mitigate flood losses (e.g., see Phillippi 1994). Recent flooding and mudslides in the Pacific Northwest, the most severe flooding there in thirty years, appear to be the result of clear-cutting of forests and road building that have dramatically increased peak flows (Seideman 1996).

Restoration of natural environmental functions is a related recommendation. The National Academy of Sciences recommends restoration of some 4 million miles of streams and rivers (NRC 1992). There have been recommendations to restore 1–2 million acres of wetlands in the Mississippi basin (Tripp, cited in Wright 1996; Phillippi 1994). Programs such as the California Urban Stream Restoration Program (Kusler and Larson 1993) promote ecological restoration, but more could be done. Mitigation must increasingly mean restoration.

Multiobjective Planning and Management

Because of scarce mitigation staff and funding, most states and localities must combine hazard mitigation with other goals. "Multiobjective planning" can promote economic development, environmental restoration, water quality enhancement, and recreation along with hazard mitigation, especially land use and nonstructural strategies (FEMA 1994b). Advantages include expansion of funding sources and increased political and popular support for mitigation. Zahn (1994, p. 5) notes: "Hazard mitigation is a low priority in most local budgets but when the mitigation activity is combined with creating a greenway or preserving an historic district, for example, assistance from the state, federal, and private entities that support those projects suddenly becomes potentially available. By the same token, some funds that are available only after disasters can be obtained and applied to other purposes if the other purpose is related to hazard mitigation and the two are packaged into one project."

Multiobjective planning has a long history in riverine floodplain management. Multiobjective river corridor management is under way in a number of basins and is advocated by the Association of State Floodplain Managers, the Association of State Wetland Managers, and the National Park Service. Successful cases include the Charles River in Massachusetts, the South Platte River and Boulder Creek in Colorado, the Chattahoochee River in Georgia, and the Kickapoo River in Wisconsin (National Park Service 1991). After the Midwest floods, the National Park Service's Rivers, Trails, and Conservation Assistance Program helped communities develop open space plans for floodplain areas where federal and state buyouts were occurring. In the largest residential buyout program, 187 parcels are being acquired in the town of Cherokee, Iowa, along the Little Sioux River. Here, the Park Service has helped the locality in planning for the resulting sixty-seven acres of floodplain open space and furthering the town's goal of creating a floodplain greenbelt (Hanson and Lemanski 1995).

Regional, Multijurisdictional Strategies

Regional strategies are necessary to plan transportation, growth management, solid waste management, and hazard mitigation. Planning for hurricane evacuation and sheltering needs is difficult, if not impossible, at the level of individual localities. Many mitigation activities and functions, such as mapping of hazards using geographic information systems (GIS), will be more economical at a regional level. A study by NAPA recommends that FEMA promote regional approaches to disaster preparedness and planning

(NAPA 1993), and a 1994 follow-up study notes the importance of regional strategies "as concern mounts about large population concentrations in areas highly vulnerable to hurricanes (i.e., the Sunbelt states) and earthquakes (i.e., the Mississippi Valley and San Andreas fault zones)" (NAPA 1994, p. 29). Advantages include "(1) more cost effectiveness; (2) hazards and disasters do not occur within discrete political boundaries—either county, state or national; (3) ability to capitalize on specific knowledge of local needs, preferences for service delivery, lifestyle, etc.; (4) pre-arranged mutual aid arrangements may exist; and (5) formal interstate compacts may be in place that would expedite large scale response and recovery activities" (p. 29). The *Strategy for National Earthquake Loss Reduction* also contains the target "Encourage and assist regional consortia" (National Earthquake Strategy Working Group 1996, p. 9).

   Examples of regional efforts include the Southern Regional Emergency Management Compact, earthquake preparedness efforts carried out in California by the San Francisco Association of Bay Area Governments, evacuation plans formulated by regional planning councils in Florida, and regional plans aimed at steering development away from high-risk areas in Florida (South Florida Regional Planning Council 1996).

Ecosystem Management

Ecosystem management, an effort to use a geographic scale of analysis defined by ecological or environmental parameters (often watersheds), seeks an understanding of ecological systems and adopts a long time perspective. A report by the federal Interagency Ecosystem Management Task Force advocates ecosystem management, and the National Performance Review endorsed it as a way to coordinate federal land management planning and decisions (Interagency Ecosystem Management Task Force 1995; NPR 1993). In environmental policy areas from wetlands restoration to protection of endangered species and conservation of urban open spaces, there is a growing consensus that ecosystem management is required.[9]

   The mitigation application is clearest in floodplain management, in which an ecosystem framework is necessary to understand the numerous discrete decisions that contribute to flooding. Distant actions can influence the severity of local flooding, and individual actions, such as filling of wetlands, creation of impervious surfaces, and construction of levees and flood walls, have cumulative effects. Moreover, local programs and actions are typically fragmented and uncoordinated. Ecosystem manage-

ment takes into account the entire watershed, including its hydrological and ecological processes and functions, in order to monitor change and establish ecosystem-wide goals to guide management decisions.

The Galloway Report and the Lincoln Institute's floodplain management study endorse ecosystem or watershed management as the appropriate direction for future floodplain management (Interagency Floodplain Management Review Committee 1994; Faber 1996). Other recent literature on floodplain management reaches similar conclusions (e.g., Kusler and Larson 1993; federal Interagency Floodplain Management Task Force 1992a).

Experience with large-scale ecosystem management is limited, though significant experience exists with smaller-scale watershed planning and estuarine management (e.g., Doppelt et al. 1993). Experience with regional habitat conservation and regional open space protection is also growing. These experiences demonstrate the benefits of organizing mitigation at such broader levels. Several practical issues must be confronted, including how an ecosystem's boundaries will be defined and how large or small an area will be included. Another issue concerns planning and decision-making authority and whether or not new regional or ecosystem planning units are needed. The Galloway Report recommends the reestablishment of river basin commissions as one possible planning mechanism, at least for floodplain management.

From Resistance to Resilience

Common societal responses to natural disasters have taken the form of resistance. In coastal areas, shoreline armoring has been a traditional approach to dealing with hurricanes, coastal storms, and shoreline erosion (Godschalk, Brower, and Beatley 1989; Pilkey and Dixon 1996). In riverine environments, resistance has taken the form of flood walls, levees, and river-straightening projects, techniques that are costly and environmentally destructive and may increase exposure to disaster (Faber 1996). Nonstructural approaches, including land use planning, national flood insurance, building elevation, and beach replenishment, seek resilience, instead. A report by the National Science and Technology Council (NSTC 1996) endorses policies designed to build resilience: "After-the-fact retrofits must give way to societal planning and ways of doing business that build in resilience to natural hazards from the beginning and from the ground up" (p. 5).

International Disaster Mitigation

Although most of the mitigation trends discussed in this book relate to domestic disasters, concern about disasters on an international level is also increasing (Munasinghe and Clarke 1995). This is to be expected during an era of growing concern about global environmental problems and in light of the realization that many of these problems, including climate change, stratospheric ozone depletion, and biodiversity loss, are indeed global and extranational in nature, with solutions that require multinational responses, such as the Montreal Protocol, an international treaty setting limits on ozone-producing activities. The United Nations declared the 1990s as the International Decade for Natural Disaster Reduction (NRC 1994). The *National Mitigation Strategy* states that within a year a "Federal focal point for collaborative international mitigation activities" will be designated (FEMA 1995c, p. 21).

There is little question about the seriousness of the threat of global natural disaster, especially in developing countries. Degg's (1992) analysis of regional vulnerability found much higher loss of life in developing countries and greater exposure and vulnerability in the world's largest and fastest-growing cities, which are located in the developing world. The combination of higher exposure and lower socioeconomic status does not bode well for the future. Many developing countries, Degg argues, are currently in a "state of limbo" when it comes to mitigation: "Traditional forms of adjustment are no longer applicable or viable, yet adverse socio-economic pressures have prevented them from successfully implementing the types of hazard response strategy employed by developed societies" (p. 209).

The report of the National Science and Technology Council (NSTC 1996) makes a case for U.S. leadership on an international level, largely on the self-interested grounds that the United States is directly affected by disasters in other countries. The report cites the eruption of Mount Pinatubo, which forced the closure of a U.S. Air Force base and caused $1 billion in U.S. damages. The report also argues that natural disasters, particularly in developing countries, serve as tremendous "triggers for geopolitical instability" and recommends diverting a portion of U.S. foreign disaster monies to natural hazard reduction programs in developing countries. The *Strategy for National Earthquake Loss Reduction* emphasizes the importance of international collaboration as a way to share research and knowledge about mitigation and to leverage limited resources. Moreover, the report points out, such collaboration can reduce long-term costs: "Transferring technology and providing training and expertise to earthquake-prone developing countries so that they can implement hazard mitigation practices is

much cheaper than providing disaster relief after a devastating earthquake" (National Earthquake Strategy Working Group 1996, p. 17).

Conclusions

The 1990s have been an active period of debate about the appropriate course of mitigation policy. Prompted by unprecedented disaster damage and the prospect of even greater damage and loss of life in the future, many observers call for a fundamentally different mitigation approach. The reports, literature, and legislative activity described here suggest some of the elements of a new approach to address these challenges. In chapter 13 we propose a new mitigation vision that includes many of these new themes and planning directions.

Notes

1. Occasional disaster relief bills were enacted by Congress, as early as 1811 in response to the New Madrid earthquake, which struck the seven state area surrounding New Madrid in southern Missouri (Wright 1996).
2. One question is whether shore-hardening structures should be permitted. The Marine Board of the NRC concludes that permanent shore-hardening structures may be desirable in conjunction with beach replenishment projects. Other questions include whether beach replenishment justifies the redrawing of flood maps under the NFIP (the Marine Board believes it does not) and whether replenishment projects should remain eligible for disaster assistance following a storm (the Marine Board believes they should).
3. The more important of these include preparing a strategic plan to develop state and local capabilities and adjusting the mission and vision of the state and local program directorate to reflect this emphasis; assessing current state capabilities and establishing baselines; establishing performance standards as part of the Comprehensive Cooperative Agreement (CCAs are the annual state/FEMA agreements or state work plans for the coming year) funding process and conditioning future state funding on meeting these standards; using financial incentives to encourage state and local efforts; streamlining postdisaster procedures and reimbursement of state and local governments; improving training and education programs (e.g., retooling the Emergency Management Institute [EMI] and developing regional training centers); developing a plan to more effectively utilize research (the report notes that most disaster research is funded by other organizations, such as the NSF and the USGS, though FEMA has the most direct operational responsibility in this area); encouraging the use of peer

exchanges (e.g., developing closer relationships with professional organizations) and mutual aid agreements; and encouraging regional planning for disasters and hazards (NAPA 1993, pp. 98–99).

4. Witt's key themes are an all-hazards, risk-based orientation; a proactive stance
in disaster response; an emphasis on mitigation; better service to customers;
forging a partnership with other federal agencies and with state and local governments as well as private organizations; and strengthening state and local
emergency management programs (NAPA 1994, p. 3). In the end, the report
appears guardedly optimistic that FEMA is making progress and moving in the
right direction (p. 32).

5. Another approach was considered by Congress in 1998. The Homeowners
Insurance Availability Act is designed to backstop private market and state government coverage of massive property damage claims following major hurricanes and earthquakes. It creates a federal fail-safe claims payment mechanism
to be used if state-chartered reinsurance organizations are unable to cover
claims following large natural disasters, in order to protect homeowners who
face nonrenewal of their private insurance.

6. A showcase community must (1) formally commit to participation by adopting a
formal resolution to that effect; (2) adopt or agree to adopt the latest version of one
of the model building codes as the minimum code and enforce it; (3) participate
in the National Flood Insurance Program (NFIP) if in a floodplain and participate
in the NFIP's Community Rating System; (4) receive a suitable fire suppression
rating system grade from the Insurance Services Office; (5) complete a risk assessment of its natural hazards or agree to do so; (6) offer mitigation training to
building design and construction professionals; (7) support IBHS and its partners
in nonstructural retrofitting of nonprofit child care centers; (8) develop programs
to increase public awareness of natural hazards and ways to reduce or prevent
damage; (9) incorporate natural hazard awareness and reduction programs into
its school curriculums; (10) complete a land use plan that delineates the relevant
hazards and incorporates them as factors in all land use decisions; (11) maintain
emergency response and postdisaster recovery plans; (12) develop public-sector
incentives for mitigation to complement private-sector financial incentives developed by IBHS and its partners; (13) develop inspection and certification procedures for incorporating mitigation into new construction and retrofitting of existing buildings; and (14) develop a Disaster Recovery Business Alliance.

7. The nine major goals are to (1) provide leadership and coordination for federal
earthquake research; (2) continue and expand technology transfer and outreach; (3) improve engineering of the built environment; (4) improve data for
construction standards and codes; (5) continue development of seismic hazard
and risk assessment tools; (6) analyze seismic hazard mitigation incentives;
(7) develop an understanding of the societal and institutional issues related to
earthquake hazard mitigation; (8) analyze the medical and public health consequences of earthquakes; and (9) continue documenting earthquakes and
their effects.

8. A recent OTA study, *Reducing Earthquake Losses,* notes the advantages of an in-

centives-based strategy: it maintains flexibility and freedom of choice, can be structured to require no additional federal funding, and can serve to adjust prices to reflect the true costs of hazardous development or decisions. Disadvantages noted include possible high administrative costs, uncertain market responses, and difficulty in quantifying mitigation benefits, whereby "incentives for increased mitigation may mean more money poorly spent" (OTA 1995, p. 31).

9. Several prominent examples include efforts to plan for the Yellowstone National Park ecosystem, the Everglades ecosystem, and the Chesapeake Bay ecosystem. Other ecosystem management or landscape-level planning programs are under way in the New Jersey Pinelands, at Lake Tahoe, and at the Adirondack Park. For a discussion of ecosystem management, see Gunderson, Holling, and Light 1995 and Lincoln Institute of Land Policy 1995.

References

AIA and AAI (American Insurance Association and Alliance of American Insurers). 1995. *New Partnerships for Catastrophe Response.* Washington, D.C.: American Insurance Association.

Appleby, Julie. 1995. "Where the Fault Lies." *Washington Post,* July 20.

Beatley, Timothy. 1992. *Risk Allocation Policy in the Coastal Zone: The Current Framework and Future Directions.* Washington, D.C.: Office of Technology Assessment.

———. 1994. "Promoting Sustainable Land Use: Mitigating Natural Hazards Through Land Use Planning." In *Natural Disasters: Local and Global Perspectives.* Boston: Insurance Institute for Property Loss Reduction.

———. 1995. "Planning and Sustainability: A New (Improved?) Paradigm." *Journal of Planning Literature* 9:383–395.

———. 1996. "The Vision of Sustainability." Unpublished manuscript.

Beatley, Timothy, and David J. Brower. 1993. "Sustainability Comes to Mainstreet." *Planning,* May, 16–19.

Beatley, Timothy, David J. Brower, and Anna Schwab. 1994. *An Introduction to Coastal Zone Management.* Washington, D.C.: Island Press.

Becker, William S. 1994. "The Case for Sustainable Redevelopment." *Environment and Development* (American Planning Association), November, 1–4.

Berke, Philip. 1995. "Natural Hazard Reduction and Sustainable Development: A Global Assessment." *Journal of Planning Literature* 9:370–382.

Berke, Philip, and Timothy Beatley. 1992. *Planning for Earthquakes: Risk, Politics, and Policy.* Baltimore: Johns Hopkins University Press.

Bullard, Robert. 1990. *Dumping in Dixie: Race, Class, and Environmental Quality.* Boulder, Colo.: Westview Press.

Burby, Raymond J., Scott A. Bollens, James Hollway, Edward J. Kaiser, David Mullan, and John R. Sheaffer. 1988. *Cities Under Water: A Comparative Evaluation of Ten Cities' Efforts to Manage Floodplain Land Use.* Institute of Behavioral Science Monograph No. 47. Boulder: University of Colorado.

Cabot, Sandra. 1996. "The Art of Readiness: Results of a National Survey Reveal

That Many Disaster Costs Are Absorbed at the State and Local Levels." *State Government News*, January, 18–21.

Catalamo, Peter. 1995. "Hurricane Alert." *Popular Science*, September, 65–70.

Clark, Charles S. 1993. "Disaster Response." *CQ Research* 3 (38):889–912.

Clary, Bruce B. 1985. "The Evolution and Structure of Natural Hazard Policies." *Public Administration Review* 45 (January): 20–28.

Colden, Anne. 1995. "Regulators Address Disaster Insurance: Recent Natural Catastrophes Have Created Havoc in the Industry." *Washington Post*, September 16, F6.

Degg, Martin. 1992. "Natural Disasters: Recent Trends and Future Prospects." *Geography* 77 (336): 198–209.

Doppelt, Bob, Mary Scurlock, Chris Frissell, and James Karr. 1993. *Entering the Watershed: A New Approach to Save America's River Ecosystems*. Washington, D.C.: Island Press.

Edgerton, Lynne T. 1991. *The Rising Tide: Global Warming and World Sea Levels*. Washington, D.C.: Island Press.

Engi, Dennis. 1995. "Historical and Projected Costs of Natural Disasters." *Sandia Report*. Albuquerque: Sandia National Laboratories. Available from National Technical Information Service, Springfield, Va.

Faber, Scott. 1996. *On Borrowed Land: Public Policies for Floodplains*. Cambridge, Mass.: Lincoln Institute of Land Policy.

Faber, Scott, and Constance Hunt. 1994. "River Management Post-1993: The Choice Is Ours." *Water Resources Update*, No. 95, 21–23.

FEMA (Federal Emergency Management Agency). 1993. *Report of the Advisory Committee of the National Earthquake Hazards Reduction Program*. January. Washington, D.C.: FEMA, Office of Earthquakes and Natural Hazards.

———. 1994a. *Audit of FEMA's Mitigation Programs*. September. Washington, D.C.: FEMA, Office of Inspector General, Audit Division.

———. 1994b. *A Multi-Objective Planning Process for Mitigating Natural Hazards*. Denver: FEMA, Region VIII.

———. 1995a. *Federal Emergency Management Agency Fiscal Year 1996 Cooperative Agreement Guidance*. July 19. Washington, D.C.: FEMA.

———. 1995b. *Mitigation: Cornerstone for Building Safer Communities*. Report of the Mitigation Directorate for Fiscal Year 1995. Washington, D.C.: FEMA.

———. 1995c. *National Mitigation Strategy*. January. Washington, D.C.: FEMA.

———. 1996a. *Proposed Rule for Flood Mitigation Assistance Program, 44 C.F.R. Part 78, RIN 3067-AC45*. April 1. Washington, D.C.: FEMA.

———. 1996b. *Proposed Rule for Hazard Mitigation Grant Program, 44 C.F.R. Part 206, RIN Disaster Assistance, Hazard Mitigation*. April 1. Washington, D.C.: FEMA.

———. 1997. *Partnership for a Safer Future*. Strategic Plan, Fiscal Year 1998–Fiscal Year 2007. Washington, D.C.: FEMA.

———. n.d. *Performance Partnership Agreement Template*. Washington, D.C.: FEMA.

———. n.d. *Project Impact: Building a Disaster Resistant Community*. Washington, D.C.: FEMA.

Federal Interagency Floodplain Management Task Force. 1992a. *Floodplain Management in the United States: An Assessment Report.* Vol. 1, *Summary Report.* Washington, D.C.: Federal Emergency Management Agency.

———. 1992b. *Floodplain Management in the United States: An Assessment Report.* Vol. 2. Washington, D.C.: Federal Emergency Management Agency.

———. 1994. A *Unified National Program for Floodplain Management.* Washington, D.C.: Federal Emergency Management Agency.

GAO (General Accounting Office). 1992. *Coastal Barriers: Development Occurring Despite Prohibition Against Federal Assistance.* Report No. GAO/RCED-92-115. July. Washington, D.C.: GAO.

———. 1993. "Recent Disasters Demonstrate the Need to Improve the Nation's Response Strategy." Testimony of J. Dexter Peach, Assistant Comptroller General, before the Committee on Armed Forces, Subcommittee on Nuclear Deterrence, Arms Control and Defense Intelligence, U.S. Senate, May 25. Washington D.C.: GAO.

Geis, Don, and Tommy Kutzmark. 1995. "Developing Sustainable Communities: The Future Is Now." *Public Management,* August, 4–13.

Glavan, Harrison. 1995. "Land Policy and River Flooding: Tough Love, Not Bailouts." *Landlines* 7 (1): 6–7.

Godschalk, David R. 1987. "The 1982 Coastal Barrier Resources Act: A New Federal Policy Tack." In *Cities on the Beach,* ed. Rutherford H. Platt. Chicago: University of Chicago, Department of Geography.

———. 1992. "Implementing Coastal Zone Management: 1972–1990," *Coastal Management* 20:93–116.

Godschalk, David R., David J. Brower, and Timothy Beatley. 1989. *Catastrophic Coastal Storms: Hazard Mitigation and Development Management.* Durham, N.C.: Duke University Press.

Governor's Committee (Governor's Disaster Planning and Response Review Committee). 1993. *Final Report.* January. Tallahassee, Fla.

Gunderson, Lance H., E. S. Holling, and Stephen S. Light, eds. 1995. *Barriers and Bridges to the Renewal of Ecosystems and Institutions.* New York: Columbia University Press.

Habitat for Humanity. n.d. *Jordan Commons: A Homestead Habitat for Humanity Neighborhood.* Homestead, Fla.: Habitat for Humanity.

Hanson, Kate, and Ursula Lemanski. 1995. "Hard-Earned Lessons from the Midwest Floods: Floodplain Open Space Makes Economic Sense." *River Voices* 6 (1): 16–17.

Houlahan, John. 1989. "Comparison of State Coastal Setbacks to Manage Development on Coastal Hazard Areas." *Coastal Management* 17:219–228.

IBHS (Institute for Business and Home Safety). 1997. *Natural Disaster Initiatives of the Insurance Sector.* Public-Private Partnership 2000 Report on First Forum. September 10. Cosponsored by the National Science and Technology Council's Subcommittee on Natural Disaster Reduction. Boston, Mass.: Institute for Business and Home Safety.

Interagency Ecosystem Management Task Force. 1995. *The Ecosystem Approach: Healthy Ecosystems and Sustainable Economies.* June. Washington, D.C.: U.S. Department of Interior.

Interagency Floodplain Management Review Committee. 1994. *Sharing the Challenge: Floodplain Management into the Twenty-First Century.* (Galloway Report.) Washington, D.C.: Government Printing Office.

Joint Task Force (National Emergency Management Association, Association of State Floodplain Managers, and Feederal Emergency Management Agency). 1992a. *The Hazard Mitigation Grant Program: Summary.* Washington, D.C.: National Emergency Management Association.

————. 1992b. *Mitigation Grant Program: An Evaluation Report.* Washington, D.C.: National Emergency Management Association.

Kana, Timothy W., Jacqueline Michel, Miles O. Hayes, and John R. Jensen. 1984. "The Physical Impact of Sea Level Rise in the Area of Charleston, South Carolina." In *Greenhouse Effect and Sea Level Rise: A Challenge for This Generation,* ed. Michael C. Barth and James G. Titus. New York: Van Nostrand Reinhold.

Klarin, Paul, and March Hershman. 1990. "Response of Coastal Zone Management Programs to Sea Level Rise in the United States." *Coastal Management* 18 (summer): 143–165.

Kusler, Jon, and Larry Larson. 1993. "Beyond the Ark: A New Approach to U.S. Floodplain Management." *Environment* 35 (5): 6–11, 31–34.

Lincoln Institute of Land Policy. 1995. *Managing Land as Ecosystem and Economy.* Cambridge, Mass.: Lincoln Institute of Land Policy.

Lynch, Colum F. 1996. "Global Warming: Warm Up to the Idea: Global Warming Is Here." *Amicus Journal* 18 (spring): 20–25.

McKibben, Bill. 1995. *Hope, Human and Wild.* Boston: Little, Brown.

Moore, Richard T. 1995. "Partnerships for Building Safer Communities." *Natural Hazards Observer* 19 (6): 1–3.

Munasinghe, Mohan, and Caroline Clarke, eds. 1995. *Disaster Prevention for Sustainable Development.* Washington, D.C.: International Decade for Natural Disaster Reduction and World Bank.

Myers, Mary Fran, and Gilbert F. White. 1993. "The Challenge of the Mississippi Flood." *Environment,* December, 6–9, 25–35.

NAPA (National Academy of Public Administration). 1993. *Coping with Catastrophe: Building an Emergency Management System to Meet People's Needs in Natural and Manmade Disasters.* Washington, D.C.: NAPA.

————. 1994. *Review of Actions Taken to Strengthen the Nation's Emergency Management System.* March. Washington, D.C.: NAPA.

National Earthquake Strategy Working Group. 1996. *Strategy for National Earthquake Loss Reduction.* Report prepared for the National Science and Technology Council. April. Washington, D.C.: NSTC.

National Park Service. 1991. *A Casebook in Managing Rivers for Multiple Uses.* October. Washington, D.C.: U.S. Department of the Interior, National Park Service.

NEMA and CSG (National Emergency Management Association and Council of

State Governments). 1996. *NEMA/CSG Report on State Emergency Management Funding and Structures.* Lexington, Ky.: NEMA and CSG.

NPR (National Performance Review). 1993. *Federal Emergency Management Agency.* September. Washington, D.C.: Office of the Vice President of the United States.

NRC (National Research Council). 1990. *Managing Coastal Erosion.* Washington, D.C.: National Academy Press.

————. 1992. *Restoration of Aquatic Ecosystems.* Washington, D.C.: National Academy Press.

————. 1994. *Facing the Challenge: The U.S. National Report to the IDNDR World Conference on Natural Disaster Reduction.* Washington, D.C.: National Academy Press.

————. 1995. *Beach Nourishment and Protection.* Washington, D.C.: National Academy Press.

NSTC (National Science and Technology Council). Subcommittee on Natural Disaster Reduction. 1996. *Natural Disaster Reduction: A Plan for the Nation.* February 26. Doc. 1, *Strategic Plan.* Doc. 2, *Implementation Plan.* Washington, D.C.: National Science and Technology Council.

OTA (Office of Technology Assessment). 1993. *Preparing for an Uncertain Climate.* Washington, D.C.: Government Printing Office.

————. 1995. *Reducing Earthquake Losses.* Washington, D.C.: OTA.

Patton, Ann. 1993. *From Harm's Way: Flood-Hazard Mitigation in Tulsa, Oklahoma.* Tulsa Okla.: Public Works Department.

Pendick, Daniel. 1996. "Mean Season: Last Year's Wild Atlantic Storm Season May Have Been a Preview of Things to Come. If So, Hurricane Researchers Want to Be Ready," *Earth,* June, 24.

Phillippi, Nancy. 1994. "Plugging the Gaps in Flood Control Policy." *Issues in Science and Technology,* winter, 71–78.

Pilkey, Orrin, and Katharine Dixon. 1996. *The Corps and the Shore.* Washington, D.C.: Island Press.

Pilkey, Orrin, H., Jr., William J. Neal, Orrin H. Pilkey, Sr. 1980. *From Currituck to Calabash: Living with North Carolina's Barrier Islands.* Durham, N.C.: Duke University Press.

Platt, Rutherford H. 1982. "The Jackson Flood of 1979: A Public Policy Disaster." *Journal of the American Planning Association* 48 (2): 219–231.

————. 1991a. "Coastal Erosion: Retreat Is Often the Best Course." *Cosmos* 18:38–43.

————. 1991b. *Land Use Control: Geography, Law, and Public Policy.* Englewood Cliffs, N.J.: Prentice Hall.

————. 1994. "Evolution of Coastal Hazards Policies in the United States." *Coastal Management* 22:265–284.

————. 1996. *Land Use and Society: Geography, Law, and Public Policy.* Washington, D.C.: Island Press.

Platt, Rutherford H., Timothy Beatley, and H. Crane Miller. 1991. "The Folly at Folly Beach and Other Failings of U.S. Coastal Erosion Policy." *Environment* 33:7–9, 26–32.

Platt, Rutherford H., H. Crane Miller, Timothy Beatley, Jennifer Melville, and Brenda G. Mathenia. 1992. *Coastal Erosion: Has Retreat Sounded?* Boulder, Colo.: University of Colorado, Institute of Behavioral Science.

Rabinovitch, Jonas, and Josef Leitman. 1996. "Urban Planning in Curitiba." *Scientific American*, March, 46–53.

Richman, Sheldon. 1993. "Disaster Relief—Flooded with Errors." *Wall Street Journal*, July 8.

Schwab, Jim. 1996. "'Nature Bats Last': The Politics of Floodplain Management." *Environment and Development*, January–February, 1–4.

Seideman, David. 1996. "Out of the Woods." *Sierra*, July–August, 66–75.

Showalter, Pamela, William Riebsane, and Mary Fran Myers. 1993. *Natural Hazard Trends: A Preliminary Review for the 1990s.* Natural Hazards Research and Applications Information Center Working Paper No. 83. February. Boulder: University of Colorado.

South Florida Regional Planning Council. 1996. *Strategic Regional Policy Plan for South Florida.* August. Hollywood, Fla.: South Florida Regional Planning Council.

Stalberg, Christian. 1995. "Disaster Patrol." *Planning*, February, 18–21.

Thieler, Robert, and David Bush. 1991. "Hurricanes Gilbert and Hugo Send Powerful Messages for Coastal Development." *Journal of Geological Education* 39:291–299.

Titus, James G. 1986. "Greenhouse Effect, Sea Level Rise, and Coastal Zone Management." *Coastal Zone Management Journal* 14:147–171.

———. 1991. "Greenhouse Effect and Coastal Wetland Policy." *Environment Management* 15:39–58.

Topping, Ken. 1996. "Mitigation from the Ground Up. Sustainable Cities in California: An Invited Comment." *Natural Hazards Observer* 20 (G): 1–2.

United Nations. 1992. *Agenda 21.* New York: United Nations.

Unnewehr, David. 1995. *Coastal Exposure and Community Protection: Hurricane Andrew's Legacy.* Boston, Mass.: Insurance Institute for Property Loss Reduction and Insurance Research Council.

U.S. Army Corps of Engineers. 1996. *Shoreline Protection and Beach Erosion Control Study, Final Report: An Analysis of the U.S. Army Corps of Engineers Shore Protection Program.* June. Alexandria, Va.: Institute for Water Resources.

U.S. House. 1966a. *Insurance and Other Programs for Financial Assistance to Flood Victims.* 89th Congress, 2nd Session. Committee Print 43.

———. 1966b. *A Unified National Program for Managing Flood Losses.* 89th Congress, 2nd Session. House Document 465.

———. 1994. *Report of the Bipartisan Task Force on Disasters.* 103rd Congress. December 14 (not printed).

U.S. Senate. 1995. *Report on the Senate Task Force on Funding Disaster Relief.* 104th Congress, 1st Session. March 15. Document S. 104-4.

World Commission on Environment and Development. 1987. *Our Common Future.* Oxford, England: Oxford University Press.

Wright, James M. 1996. "Effects of the Flood on National Policy; Some Achieve-

ments; Major Challenges Remain." In *The Great Flood of 1993: Causes, Impacts, and Responses,* ed. Stanley A. Changnon. Boulder, Colo.: Westview Press.

Zahn, Sheryl. 1994. "Multi-Objective Planning for Natural Hazard Mitigation." In *A Multi-Objective Planning Process for Mitigating Natural Hazards.* Denver, Colo.: Federal Emergency Management Agency, Region VII.

Zirschky, John H. 1995. *Complete Statement of John Zirschky, Acting Secretary of the Army (Civil Works), Before the Subcommittee on Appropriations, U.S. House of Representatives, on Fiscal Year 1996 Civil Works Budget.* 104th Congress, 1st Session. February 21. Item No. 1011; 1011A.

PART II

Mitigation in Action: Six Disaster Cases

One way to test a national policy is to see if its objectives are achieved in practice. If it's not broke, then don't fix it, as the saying goes. But if the policy fails to achieve its objectives in the real world, then the policy implementation system fails the test, and changes are called for. We put the effectiveness of the national hazard mitigation system to several tests. One test format consisted of case studies of mitigation programs following disasters in six states. Although the system had some successes, it also had some troubling faults.

The six case studies, conducted during 1995, looked back at hazard mitigation following some very large disasters, such as Hurricane Andrew in South Florida in 1992, the 1993 Midwest floods in Iowa and Missouri, and the 1989 Loma Prieta and 1994 Northridge earthquakes in California, as well as some medium-sized disasters, such as Hurricane Bob and some northeasters in Massachusetts in 1991 and 1992 and a series of floods, winter storms, and tornadoes in Tennessee between 1990 and 1995. In each instance, two-member research teams visited the site of the disaster; interviewed federal, state, and local mitigation agency staff members; and collected data from records and published sources.

Detailed findings of each case study are laid out in chapters 3–8. Before going into the details of each state's experience, however, it is enlightening to look at the bigger picture. Part II of this book summarizes and compares the disasters and mitigation contexts in the six case study states. Then it compares the postdisaster mitigation actions required under the Stafford Act with what actually happened in the case study states in terms of the following:

- Mitigation planning under Section 409 of the Stafford Act

- Mitigation project funding under Section 404 of the Stafford Act

- Strategy alternatives for mitigating specific hazards

- Institutional arrangements linking federal, state, and local mitigation efforts

An Overview of the Six Disaster Cases

The six cases were chosen to provide a sample of contemporary hazard mitigation experience in various regions following earthquake, flood, and hurricane disasters that ranged in severity from moderate to extreme. Table II.1 summarizes the disasters and mitigation contexts in the six case study states.

Table 11.1. Summary of Case Study Disasters and Mitigation Contexts

State	Disaster	Damage Estimate	Role of Section 409 Plan	Major Mitigation Strategy	State Planning Mandate
FL	Hurricane Andrew (Category 4), 1992	$25 billion	Limited	Abate wind damage	Yes
MO	Midwest floods, 1993	$3 billion	None	Buy out flooded areas	No
IA	Midwest floods, 1993	$3.4–$5.7 billion	None	Buy out flooded areas	No
CA	Loma Prieta earthquake (7.1 magnitude), 1989	$6 billion	Limited	Retrofit damaged facilities	Yes
CA	Northridge earthquake (6.7 magnitude), 1994	$20 billion	Limited	Retrofit damaged buildings	Yes
MA	Hurricane Bob (Category 2), 1991, and other storms, 1991–1992	$1.5 billion (from Hurricane Bob)	Limited	Retrofit and floodproof	No
TN	Winter storms and spring floods, 1994	Not available	None	Miscellaneous	No

Estimated damage costs from the disasters in the case study states, all except one declared in one four-year period during the first half of the 1990s, amounted to about $60 billion. Top individual state damage totals were Hurricane Andrew's $25 billion, the Northridge earthquake's $20 billion, and the Loma Prieta earthquake's $6 billion. Next highest were the damage estimates from the Midwest floods in Iowa and Missouri; their individual totals were part of the regional damage estimate of $12–$16 billion for all nine states that experienced major damage from the Midwest floods, the largest on record for the United States.

Required under Section 409 of the Stafford Act, the state hazard mitigation plan is the primary blueprint for mitigation action following a disaster. It should play an important role in postdisaster mitigation decisions. Yet in no case study state did the Section 409 hazard mitigation plan play a major role in guiding the hazard mitigation projects proposed after the disaster. Even in California, which had adopted the most specific state hazard mitigation plan in the country, the plan was not a major influence in formation of the mitigation strategy following the Loma Prieta and Northridge earthquakes. The case study chapters explain this unexpected finding.

Hazard mitigation plans are expected to deal with all hazards faced by a state, not simply to respond to the most recent disaster. According to FEMA regulations, a hazard mitigation plan is "the plan resulting from a systematic evaluation of the nature and extent of vulnerability to the effects of natural hazards *present in society* and includes the actions needed to minimize future vulnerability to hazards" (44 C.F.R. 206.401) (emphasis added). However, the mitigation strategies employed after a disaster tend to concentrate on the types of damage suffered during that particular disaster rather than dealing with all hazards faced by the state. Thus, Florida concentrated on mitigating future wind damage after experiencing the high winds of Hurricane Andrew, Missouri and Iowa concentrated on buying out flooded property after the Midwest floods, and California concentrated on retrofitting damaged public buildings after the Loma Prieta and Northridge earthquakes. Tennessee, on the other hand, concentrated on potential flooding and earthquake hazards almost completely unrelated to the 1994 storms and floods that qualified the state for FEMA funds.

A number of states require their local governments to prepare comprehensive plans to manage growth, including development of land subject to natural hazards (May et al. 1997). Among our case study states, Florida has such a comprehensive plan mandate, which includes a component dealing with coastal hazards, and California has a state mandate for preparation of

an earthquake hazards plan. Thus, an unexpected finding from our case studies was the lack of influence of the state planning mandate on decision making during the postdisaster mitigation process. Even in Florida, which has the country's most rigorous state mandate for local and regional growth management, the required local and regional comprehensive plans were not major influences on mitigation decision making, and the state itself lacked an effective Section 409 plan. The case study chapters explain why the planning context at the time of the disaster failed the test of effectiveness in these two states.

Some clear lessons emerged from the case studies. These are discussed more comprehensively in chapter 13, along with lessons from other parts of the study, but we summarize them here to illustrate consistent themes from the cases.

Mitigation Planning Lessons

Mitigation planning is guided by Section 409 of the Stafford Act, which directs states to prepare or update mitigation plans following a declared disaster in order to qualify for Section 404 Hazard Mitigation Grant Program funding for that disaster. If states fail to submit an updated Section 409 plan to FEMA within a specified time after the disaster declaration, they lose their eligibility for Section 404 grants. The mitigation projects are presumed to be carrying out, or implementing, the mitigation strategies and objectives of the plans.

If this process is compared to the construction of a building, Section 409 mitigation plans would be like architects' plans and Section 404 mitigation projects would be like building elements such as walls and floors. In building construction, no contractor would erect walls or lay floors before the building plan is drawn. However, the analogy breaks down in hazard mitigation, since it was common practice in the case study states to request and receive funds for Section 404 projects before the Section 409 plans were prepared.

Plan content is specified by FEMA regulations. A state hazard mitigation plan must start with an analysis of the problem faced and the way in which existing government policies and capabilities cope with that problem. Then it must set targets for action in the form of goals and objectives. Next, it must propose actions to achieve its targets in the form of strategies, programs, and implementation activities. Finally, it must recommend ways to monitor, update, and evaluate the plan in order to improve it and keep it current in light of new information and conditions (44 C.F.R. 206.405).

Each state hazard mitigation plan must contain the following components:

- Assessment of natural hazards faced by the state
- Analysis of existing state hazard mitigation policies and state and local capabilities to mitigate hazards
- Hazard mitigation goals and objectives to be achieved by the plan
- Proposed hazard mitigation strategies, programs, and actions
- Proposed approach to plan implementation
- Proposed approach to monitoring of implementation and hazard conditions
- Proposed approach to updating of the plan
- Proposed approach to evaluation and implementation of the plan

If the case study plans had taken all the required components seriously, they would have been very useful guides to postdisaster hazard mitigation. Unfortunately, some did not have all the components, and many did not do a thorough job on each component.

In the case study states, the process for preparing mitigation plans during the heat of the disaster recovery period was deeply flawed. The plans came out too late to guide postdisaster mitigation actions. They were often poorly prepared and not taken seriously by the states in terms of formal adoption, funding, and follow-up actions. They were usually too general to allow measurable performance evaluations and thus accountability. And they tended to be too disaster specific, looking back at the most recent event rather than forward to the next event or to different types of disasters.

During the postdisaster period in the six case studies, state hazard mitigation plans played virtually no role in the formation and choice of a mitigation strategy or in strategy implementation through the choice of hazard mitigation grant projects. In several cases, plans prepared before the disaster were not even consulted during recovery. In other cases, no previously approved plan existed. Few federal, state, or local officials interviewed during the case studies saw any relevance to Section 409 plans as currently defined and executed. They saw more relevance in the Section 404 administrative plans, which affected the selection and funding of hazard mitigation grant projects.

In Iowa and Missouri after the 1993 Midwest floods, for example, mitigation officials did not rely on either their state's predisaster Section 409

plan or its postdisaster Section 409 plan in making recommendations for mitigation actions. Instead, these recommendations for mitigation projects proceeded independently of the plans, on separate tracks.

Advance planning was rarely seen as guiding action. It was more likely to be viewed as one more onerous administrative requirement to be completed on the way to securing FEMA disaster grants. The concept of advance mitigation was given lip service, but the practice was dictated by postdisaster grant chasing, in which "paper" plans were completed in order to qualify for Section 404 hazard mitigation grants.

If Section 409 plans are to guide mitigation effectively, they must be products of an ongoing, serious emergency management planning process. Federal, state, and local plans must be consistent with one another. All plans must be formally reviewed and approved by top state officials. Plans must contain measurable objectives, and their implementation must be regularly reviewed against these standards. Plans must be prepared *before* the disaster event, deal with all potential hazards, and be tied to funded implementation schedules. At the same time, requirements must allow enough flexibility to meet individual state organizational structures, hazard configurations, political conditions, and unforeseen disaster contingencies.

Every state should have a full-time mitigation planning officer, properly placed and supported to carry out necessary technical and coordination activities to ensure disaster readiness and to integrate mitigation into public and private decision making. The state hazard mitigation plan should be a forward-looking document that guides an ongoing implementation effort, incorporating hazard and risk assessments as well as priorities for pre- and postdisaster projects. To encourage serious mitigation planning, FEMA could provide incentives, in the form of block grants for hazard mitigation projects, to states whose plans have been approved by FEMA. Rather than being bureaucratic roadblocks, plans might become avenues to cutting red tape.

Lessons in Mitigation Project Implementation

Mitigation projects are funded under the guidance of the Hazard Mitigation Grant Program (HMGP), as defined by Section 404 of the Stafford Act. The program provides matching federal funds for state and local mitigation projects that are deemed consistent with a state's Section 409 plan (44 C.F.R. 206.435). Projects are generally initiated and implemented at the

local community level, but they must be reviewed (and sometimes approved or at least prioritized) by the state and then reviewed by FEMA, which determines which projects receive funding. Section 406 of the Stafford Act, applied to rebuilding of damaged public facilities, also allows the extra cost of mitigation improvements to be incorporated into public-sector reconstruction grants (44 C.F.R. 206.220).

We found the procedures for preparing, reviewing, and approving HMGP (Section 404) grants to be flawed and a source of dissatisfaction to almost all state, local, and FEMA regional officials. They were dissatisfied with an application and review process perceived as frustrating, myste-rious, and time-consuming; application requirements beyond the capacity of some local governments; unexplainable and inordinately long delays in funding even approved projects; an irrational review process that some-times approved projects simply on the basis of their being the first to apply; and lack of flexibility in the application process and mitigation project design.

The success of mitigation project applications was influenced by the varying availability of able and entrepreneurial local government staff persons, the uneven informal information network by which local offi-cials learned of the Hazard Mitigation Grant Program, and the existing backlog of unfunded local or state projects. That is, the types of projects, their locations, and the amount of funding they received through FEMA were largely determined not so much by the availability of federal funding and/or the content of a state mitigation strategy as by the capability of state and local governments to collaborate in formulating compelling pro-ject applications and by their capacity to provide matching funds. Mitiga-tion thus tended to be a piecemeal collection of separate projects rather than implementation of a comprehensive, prioritized, and technically grounded mitigation strategy developed through an advance planning process.

Because of the cumbersome and uncertain application process; the absence of matching monies, particularly at the local level; the drawn-out project approval process; and delays in follow-up funding of approved pro-jects, total Section 404 project expenditures were much smaller than allowed by the Stafford Act and even much less than had been approved by the states and FEMA. This was less so in states that experienced very large disasters, such as California, Florida, Missouri, and Iowa.

The case study findings suggest the need for clearer, more consistent guidelines for project applications, with greater flexibility and simplicity in application format and project design. FEMA could utilize state or regional planning agencies, or even FEMA regional offices, to assist local commu-nities in writing grant applications and implementing projects.

Lessons in Mitigation Strategy

Two strategy lessons are highlighted by the case studies. First, more attention must be paid to defining and implementing effective, best practice mitigation strategies. Second, existing strategies must be broadened to include more holistic hazard mitigation approaches.

What is "effective" hazard mitigation practice? FEMA, the states, and local communities disagree about what constitutes appropriate mitigation. There are also inconsistencies within FEMA even during a single disaster recovery period, particularly if FEMA officials from several regions become involved. Thus, the definition of what qualifies as mitigation under the Stafford Act varies over time and across space. States and localities want a flexible definition; FEMA wants a narrow definition. In some cases, such as the Midwest floods, FEMA virtually limited mitigation to buyouts, and FEMA normally declares ineligible any project that "can be plugged in" or that requires one "to push a button," and it excludes warning systems and training programs.

The definitional debate involves both content and process issues. Should mitigation incorporate multiple objectives? For example, should mitigation include local economic development, as when flood protection is combined with promotion of an employment center or a commercial center? Should it include protection of public open space, wildlife, and ecological systems, as when wildlife habitats or greenway networks are acquired or wetlands are allowed to flood naturally? Should mitigation include protection or provision of affordable housing in conjunction with buyouts of dwellings of lower-income families?

The buyout experience suggests lessons for mitigation best practice. FEMA actions help determine effectiveness. For example, FEMA facilitated the buyout strategy following the Midwest floods by categorically determining that buyout is cost-effective, exempting buyouts from environmental impact assessment, streamlining the requirement to assess impacts on cultural resources, authorizing a five-year kickback of NFIP premiums, allowing Section 406 grants to be used for demolition costs of buyouts, allowing use of Community Development Block Grant (CDBG) monies as matching funds for Section 404 grants and allowing the match at the state level (rather than requiring each community to have CDBG funds), establishing payment levels on the basis of the property's "replacement value" rather than its preflood market price, and taking a positive attitude toward resolving issues in implementing the strategy.

Buyout was also promoted by FEMA regional office policies facilitating administration and coordination of grant application, review, and implementation. For example, a regional office published a guidebook for states and local communities and a book of standard operating procedures; held

workshops; allocated funds quickly to demonstrate success; and postponed some checklist criteria. It wrote contracts with regional planning agencies to help local communities with plans and applications; established a process at the regional level to deal with the complex "duplication of benefits" issue; let state and local governments establish their own priorities among different types of properties, and allowed state and local governments to establish their own administrative procedures and criteria for governing the program, within the boundaries of the region's own "blue book" of policies.

States facilitated the buyout strategy by setting up a streamlined process and panel to review and approve applications, appointing a state hazard mitigation officer (SHMO) with sufficient authority to implement the program, and delaying site visits to project areas until later, on a spot auditing basis.

How broad should a mitigation strategy be? The case studies illustrate the need for more holistic hazard mitigation, addressing multiple objectives and hazards. Such mitigation would take a larger geographic perspective, addressing an ecological region, such as a river basin, and it would take a longer-range perspective. The notion of sustainable development has been suggested as an appropriate concept to incorporate such a hazard mitigation vision.

A sustainable development strategy would link mitigation to open space for recreation, preservation of habitats, wetland preservation, and affordable housing as well as to long-term economic development. It would connect elements in the natural and built environments and assess the cumulative effects of discrete actions, such as alteration of agricultural and urban lands in a river basin or watershed or construction or repair of a levee system. Such an approach would incorporate long-range land use planning and growth management to achieve growth patterns that minimize development in higher-risk locations.

Lessons in Institutional Arrangements for Mitigation

Mitigation planning is carried out within an intergovernmental framework linking FEMA headquarters, FEMA regional offices, and state and local governments. Mitigation policies, grants, and technical assistance are exchanged within this framework, which on paper is a top-down decision-making structure but actually allows considerable discretion. This structure and the actors within it determine the success of mitigation planning

and implementation. Results were mixed in the case studies. In some places, the structure facilitated mitigation effectiveness; in others, it frustrated mitigation effectiveness. Much dissatisfaction with the workings of institutional arrangements was expressed by states, localities, and FEMA regional offices .

The predisaster phase places different demands on institutional arrangements from those of the postdisaster phase. During the period between disasters, it is important to maintain the mitigation commitment and capability of states and local governments. In some of the case study locations, this was done fairly well. However, in other places there was a severe drop in mitigation planning, education, and activity between disasters. This drop resulted from a lack of ongoing funding for state hazard mitigation officers (SHMOs), from a lack of state laws and programs guiding mitigation, from a lack of FEMA incentives for pre-event mitigation planning, and from delays in funding and carrying out mitigation projects from the last disaster. Even those states that maintained their commitment to mitigation often functioned on a relative shoestring budget. Thus, they were hard pressed to maintain active mitigation coordination between the SHMO and other state agencies, local governments, and the FEMA regional office, resulting in organizational tension, poor communication, and weakened commitment.

Different tensions arise during the postdisaster phase. In large disasters, the FEMA regional staff becomes overwhelmed and must call in reinforcements from other FEMA regional officers to lead the interagency hazard mitigation teams. Not only does this introduce unfamiliar actors and perspectives into the already stressed state scene, but it also causes the FEMA regional offices to lay aside their mitigation project work in progress elsewhere in the region, further delaying ongoing projects from previous events. With each turnover in postdisaster FEMA personnel, state and local emergency management personnel encounter new interpretations of federal regulations and new beliefs of how to carry out effective mitigation. State staffs report feeling overwhelmed by the numbers of FEMA staff and frustrated at having to educate new people about state conditions and needs. Uncertainty about rule interpretation delays the formulation and submission of mitigation project applications. Further delays and uncertainty result when FEMA headquarters overturns project approvals by regional offices. Personality clashes add to the tension.

Future institutional reforms need to improve basic institutional arrangements beyond strengthening predisaster mitigation commitment and capability at the state level. One possibility would be for FEMA to create predisaster mitigation planning teams that would work with states

on an ongoing basis. FEMA mitigation planning teams might travel regularly to states to conduct training, provide technical assistance, create risk assessment databases, review mitigation plans, evaluate performance in state mitigation strategy implementation, and the like. This would allow them to develop a collaborative working relationship with state and local mitigation planners. Then, in the postdisaster period, the same teams would come in to help in the recovery phase and to develop and process hazard mitigation grant applications. They would have the advantage of previous knowledge about the states and their hazard mitigation plans and implementation programs as well as previous experience in working with state and local mitigation personnel.

Another institutional reform might aim at developing a broader public and private sense of responsibility for mitigation—a new mitigation ethic. At present, there is confusion about whose job it is to conduct advance hazard mitigation. Partly this is a result of the Stafford Act's focus on postdisaster planning and project funding. Partly it is a result of the belief that the federal government will come in and fix all the problems after a disaster. And partly it is a result of an inherent human drive to "put things back the way they were" after a disaster rather than question whether the status quo would continue to put people and property at risk. These are powerful perceptions, and it will take a concerted effort to replace them with a mitigation ethic that those in hazard-prone localities must not wait for a disaster to happen before taking all possible mitigation actions and that postdisaster thinking must not focus simply on restoring the status quo but must also aim to avert damage from future disasters.

Implementing the new mitigation ethic will be a broad social learning task requiring a number of mitigation champions to help carry the torch. Some promising experience has taken place within private firms and government agencies and at the individual level. But a much more concerted effort is needed.

Conclusions

The review of lessons from six case studies presented in chapters 3–8 highlights both problems and opportunities within the present mitigation system. FEMA is addressing some of the problems with new approaches such as Mitigation Strategy Papers, which streamline postdisaster planning, and Performance Partnership Agreements, which focus on predisaster planning, and Project Impact, which designates disaster-resistant communities. However, other problems must be addressed as well. The

goal should be to build a coordinated mitigation system in which predisaster state and local planning sets goals, objectives, and priorities to be carried out by coordinated mitigation projects, using proven strategies for all risks faced and supported by collaborative institutional arrangements. Recommendations for developing such a system are presented in the final chapter of this book.

Reference

May, Peter, R. J . Burby, N. J. Ericksen, J. W. Handmer, J. Dixon, S. Michaels, and D. I. Smith. 1997. *Making Governments Plan: State Experiments in Managing Land Use.* Baltimore: Johns Hopkins University Press.

CHAPTER 3

Florida After Hurricane Andrew

This chapter examines the impacts on Florida of Hurricane Andrew in 1992, recovery activities, and lessons learned. It begins with the physical storm forces, the damage that occurred, and the vulnerability of South Florida to hurricanes. It then describes the planning and mitigation framework that existed before Andrew. Next, the chapter documents post-storm recovery and reconstruction activities, including mitigation projects, changes to building codes, and design charrettes on alternative rebuilding strategies. Finally, it identifies mitigation policy issues, describes recent policy initiatives, and makes recommendations based on the case study conclusions.[1]

Hurricane Andrew and, indeed, the state of Florida represent a laboratory for understanding mitigation. The large numbers of people and property holdings at risk, the extremely vulnerable environment, and the likelihood of future Andrew-like events pose a daunting mitigation challenge. The Florida case raises questions about the role of the state mitigation plan, the mitigation choices made following Andrew and the limited mitigation options in South Florida, and the strengths and limitations of Florida's system of comprehensive planning and growth management.

The Hurricane Event

Hurricane Andrew was a Category 4 storm when it struck in the early morning hours of August 24, 1992. It came ashore just east of Homestead Air Force Base, with maximum sustained winds of 140 miles per hour and gusts of as much as 175 miles per hour. Surges were nearly seventeen feet at their highest point, setting a record for the state of Florida.

Because Andrew was not a wide-radius storm and moved ashore quickly, the extent of surge impact was minimized. Since it struck an undeveloped shoreline area south of Miami and north of the Florida Keys, property damage from surges was relatively small. As a relatively dry storm, it caused little inland flooding and did not exceed the capacity of Dade County's flood control canals (more than 600 miles of them), designed to control a ten-year flood. Most damage was caused by the storm's heavy winds.

A major evacuation was undertaken in advance of Andrew, with 650,000 people moved out. Although evacuation generally went well, a high percentage of residents of some communities in the evacuation zone chose not to evacuate, (including approximately half of the residents of Homestead and Florida City, which sustained severe damage.) It is surprising, then, that loss of life was limited to fifty-two people.

Damage Costs from Andrew

Hurricane Andrew was the most costly hurricane in U.S. history. Estimates of property damage exceed $25 billion; some sources have placed the estimate as high as $30 billion (Pielke 1995). With $15.5 billion in insured damages, it was also the most costly insured disaster in U.S. history (Colden 1995). Most of the damage occurred in southern Dade County, but four counties were declared federal disaster areas: Dade, Broward, Monroe, and Collier. More than 107,000 homes were damaged and some 28,000 were destroyed; 8,000 businesses were damaged or destroyed; 180,000 residents were left homeless; and 1.4 million residents were left without electricity (see table 3.1). Some 90 percent of the mobile homes in the county were destroyed.

In southern Dade County, both Homestead and Florida City (the only two incorporated communities affected) were decimated. Most of the buildings on Homestead Air Force Base, one of the largest employers in southern Florida, were also destroyed. There was extensive damage to parks, destruction of four libraries, and damage to Miami International Airport and Kendall Tamiami Executive Airport, public school buildings, hospitals, wastewater treatment plants, and public utilities. Tremendous debris was left by the storm. Impacts on agriculture were severe, with damage to more than 3,600 farms in Dade County (about 80 percent) and losses in excess of $1 billion, with $350 million in crop damage and $580 million in damage to physical plant and equipment (FEMA 1993).

Significant damage to the natural environment occurred. An estimated

Table 3.1. Impacts of Hurricane Andrew in Florida

Type of Impact	Magnitude (Number Affected)
Homes destroyed	28,066
Homes damaged	107,380
Persons left homeless	180,000
Businesses destroyed or damaged	8,000
Acres of farmland damaged	32,000
Public schools destroyed or damaged	31
Health facilities and hospitals damaged	59
Traffic signs and signals damaged	9,500
Miles of power line destroyed	3,300
Water mains damaged	3,000
Residents losing electricity	1.4 million
Residents losing telephone service	150,000

Source: Governor's Committee 1993.

Photo 3.1. Hurricane Andrew. Courtesy of the American Red Cross.

Photo 3.2. Houses Flattened by Hurricane Andrew. Courtesy of the American Red Cross.

10,112 acres of mangrove forest were damaged, and 2,800 mangrove trees were killed (Metro-Dade County Planning Department 1993b). Both national parks in the region (Everglades and Biscayne) incurred serious damage.

A Vulnerable South Florida

Hurricane Andrew should not have been a surprise. South Florida has an extensive history of hurricane activity, though most of it occurred prior to the extensive growth of the past several decades. Between 1900 and 1989, Southeast Florida experienced twenty-four hurricanes, including ten major hurricanes (Category 4 or 5; Metro-Dade County Planning Department 1993a). The area leads the nation in the number of hurricane hits, ahead of Louisiana and North Carolina. Major hurricanes occurred in 1919, killing 600–900 people, and in 1926, 1935, and 1947. Prior to Hurricane Andrew, however, the area had not experienced a hurricane since 1965.

The location and topography of South Florida make the region extremely vulnerable to natural hazards. Much of the land is low-lying and within the floodplain. Some 85 percent of Dade County lies within the

100-year flood zone (Metro-Dade County Planning Department 1993a). A large number of people live in storm surge areas; it is estimated that during the hurricane season, more than 224,000 people live within the Category 1 surge zone (see figure 3.1), the area most vulnerable to storm surge effects. Some 30 percent of the population of South Florida's four counties—nearly 1 million people—live within a Category 5 storm surge area (South Florida Regional Planning Council 1995).

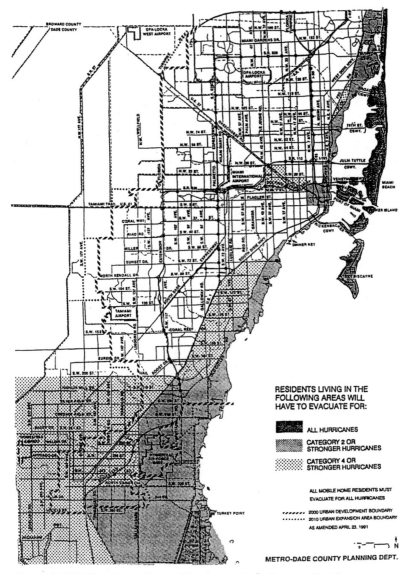

Figure 3.1. 1992 Hurricane Evacuation Areas, Dade County, Florida.

The damage costs resulting from Hurricane Andrew were astounding to many, reaching some $30 billion and making Andrew one of the nation's costliest natural disasters. Actual costs far exceeded even the worst-case scenario considered in a 1987 study sponsored by the South Florida Regional Planning Council, which predicted that a Category 5 hurricane would cause $8.9 billion in damage, less than a third of the cost of Andrew.

As it happened, the path Andrew took actually minimized the hurricane's destruction. With landfall of the eye of the storm around Homestead Air Force Base, no coastal community experienced a major storm surge. Had the storm gone north and hit Miami, the resulting damage and loss of life would have been catastrophic. Bob Sheets, former director of the National Hurricane Center, estimated that had Andrew tracked thirty miles to the north, damage costs could have exceeded $100 billion (Catalano 1995).

Population growth in South Florida has been substantial and will most likely continue. The population of the Metropolitan Miami area has grown to about 2 million, with approximately 9 million annual visitors, and is projected to reach some 2.7 million by the year 2015. The population of the South Florida region as a whole (Dade, Broward, and Monroe Counties) has grown from about 2 million in 1970 to 3.4 million in 1994 and will probably reach 4.3 million by 2015. In less than fifty years, then, the population of the region will have more than doubled (South Florida Regional Planning Council 1995).

The fact that it had been some seventeen years since a hurricane struck South Florida meant that much of this growth and development had occurred during a period of relative complacency. Massive development, much of it in the form of urban sprawl, had taken place in an atmosphere of relatively low public awareness of the hurricane hazard.

The region's steady growth and sprawling development pattern make it vulnerable in many ways. Increased population and development necessitate longer evacuation times. In South Florida, evacuation clearance times already range from a low of more than fourteen hours for Category 1–2 storms in Dade County to a high of more than forty-one hours for Category 3–5 storms in Broward County (see table 3.2). These evacuation times are expected to rise by 40 percent in Dade County by the year 2000, with clearance times estimated at thirty-three to thirty-five hours for a Category 4–5 storm (see Dade County Metropolitan Planning Organization 1995).

Much of the development and population in Dade County is located in the riskiest locations (figure 3.1). More than 300,000 people live in the coastal area, with more than 135,000 permanently living in the Coastal

Table 3.2. Evacuation Clearance Times for South Florida

COUNTY	CATEGORY 1–2 STORMS (HOURS)	CATEGORY 3–5 STORMS (HOURS)
Monroe	23.75	37.00
Dade	14.50	27.75
Broward	19.75	41.75

Source: Florida Department of Community Affairs 1996a, Table IIIA.

High Hazard Area, the area to be evacuated in a Category 1 hurricane. Of special concern are the critical facilities (e.g. hospitals, nursing homes, and police and fire stations) located in this high-risk area. In 1988, the county began prohibiting, under state law, the siting of critical facilities within Coastal High Hazard Areas. However, the numerous facilities built prior to 1988 remain especially vulnerable to storm hazards.

Evacuation and sheltering are major concerns in South Florida and, indeed, in the state as a whole. A recently released evaluation of state shelter needs is particularly sobering. The study found in 1995 a statewide shelter deficit of 360,903 spaces for Category 4 and 5 shelters, predicted to grow to some 513,418 spaces by the year 2000 (Florida Division of Emergency Management 1995). In Dade County, the deficit of shelter spaces was estimated to exceed 51,000 and had grown by about 19 percent between 1992 and 1995.

The Pre-Andrew Planning and Mitigation Framework

Prior to Hurricane Andrew, Dade County had been engaged in a number of planning and mitigation activities. Florida has an extensive and vertically integrated planning and growth management system. Under Florida law, the county was required to prepare a Comprehensive Development Master Plan (CDMP), and this plan was to be consistent with both the State Comprehensive Plan and the *Strategic Regional Policy Plan for South Florida* (South Florida Regional Planning Council 1995; for a discussion of the general planning framework in Florida, see Godschalk, Brower, and Beatley 1989, chap. 5).

The county's plan must include several elements relevant to coastal hazard mitigation. One of the most important is the coastal element. The coastal element of the county's 1988 CDMP contained goals of mitigating coastal hazards and specifically prohibited the development and redevelopment of certain facilities in the designated Coastal High Hazard Area,

including critical facilities, public facilities, mobile homes, and facilities that use or generate hazardous materials or waste (Metro-Dade County Planning Department 1988).

Under the state's growth management system prior to Andrew, localities were to discourage development in Coastal High Hazard Areas (CHHAs). When the 1988 coastal element was prepared, the CHHA included the velocity zone (V-zone) under the National Flood Insurance Program (NFIP) as well as the area seaward of the Coastal Construction Control Line (CCCL), delineated by the state since the 1970s.

After Hurricane Andrew, the state changed these definitions. The CHHA was redefined to encompass the Category 1 hurricane evacuation zone (under the regional hurricane evacuation plan) and a Hurricane Vulnerability Zone was defined as the Category 3 hurricane evacuation zone (Metro-Dade County Planning Department 1996). Also, the Strategic Regional Policy Plan for South Florida established policy for Category 4 and 5 hurricane evaluation zones (South Florida Regional Planning Council 1995).

Each objective in the 1988 coastal element was to be implemented through a series of policies. Together, these objectives and policies described a county committed to discouraging development and redevelopment in areas of high hurricane risk. For example, in Coastal High Hazard Areas, the policies prohibited public expenditures that subsidize additional development; construction of public facilities, except for beach access improvements and hurricane evacuation facilities; critical facilities; and mobile home parks. Structures that incurred damage costs exceeding 50 percent of their prestorm value had to be rebuilt to meet all current code requirements, and potential sea level rise had to be considered in the design and location of public facilities in the CHHA (Metro-Dade County Planning Department 1988).

Metro-Dade County's CDMP also reflected concern about wasteful urban sprawl and discouraged development outside a designated Urban Development Boundary (UDB). Areas within the UDB were to receive first priority in provision of public facilities and services, with second priority given to areas within the designated Urban Expansion Area (UEA). The plan sought to concentrate growth and development around designated centers of activity, to promote contiguous growth patterns and infill, and to facilitate growth in blighted and already developed areas. At the same time, it sought to protect sensitive natural lands and productive farmland to the west.

By 1992, the county also was to have prepared a postdisaster redevelopment plan. These plans were required by Florida state law (Rule 9J-5),

but few had actually been prepared when Hurricane Andrew struck. (Only a handful have been prepared to date.) Components of such a plan were included in the county's Hazard Mitigation Plan adopted in 1993.

Since 1992, the county's Comprehensive Development Master Plan has been substantially changed. Proposed changes in 1996 further strengthen the plan's provisions on natural hazards. Under the new policy, development proposals within the redefined CHHA and the Hurricane Vulnerability Zone (HVZ) must contain provisions to achieve the following:

1. Discourage development on barrier islands and in shoreline areas susceptible to destructive storm surge.

2. Direct new development and redevelopment to high ground along the Atlantic Coastal Ridge and to environmentally suitable lands inland.

3. Maintain or reduce densities and intensities of new urban development and redevelopment within the CHHA to that of surrounding existing development and zoning, and include new residential units—whether year-round or seasonal—in density and intensity totals, unless it is certified by recorded covenant that the units will not be occupied during hurricane season.

4. Prohibit construction of new mobile home parks and critical facilities in the CHHA.

5. Prohibit amendments to land use plan maps or rezoning actions that would increase allowable residential density in the FEMA V-zone or on land seaward of the Coastal Construction Control Line (CCCL).

6. Continue to closely monitor new development and redevelopment in areas subject to coastal flooding in order to implement requirements of the National Flood Insurance Program.

The county was participating in the National Flood Insurance Program, and it had taken steps to join the Community Rating System. Other mitigation efforts included beach replenishment along 15.4 miles of beachfront (Miami Beach and Sunny Isles) and adoption of the South Florida Building Code (SFBC). The SFBC, in force since 1957, required structures to be able to resist minimum wind pressures of 120 miles per hour at a height of thirty feet; additional safety factors were also mandated for specific building components (see FEMA 1992a). A "high wind speed pressure standard" and "fastest mile wind speed standard" were also enforced in the coastal zones, as required by state law.

Land acquisition has also been an important planning strategy for

Metro-Dade County. Natural lands serve important mitigative functions, and in South Florida they often represent especially dangerous places, in which people and property should not be located. Dade County's Environmentally Endangered Lands (EEL) program, initiated in 1990, is funded through a $90 million bond measure that was approved by voters. As of December 1994, five sites, totaling 104 acres had been purchased and fourteen coastal sites, totaling more than 50,000 acres, had been listed for acquisition.

Despite the commitment to mitigation reflected in Metro-Dade County's CDMP, a number of implementation problems appeared in the aftermath of Hurricane Andrew. The county had not prepared the mandatory postdisaster redevelopment plan, for instance, and some development in the Coastal High Hazard Area had been approved despite policy discouraging it. Moreover, owners of many homes destroyed or heavily damaged by Andrew were permitted to rebuild without having to adhere to elevation standards. Each of these planning issues is described in greater detail in later sections of this chapter.

Within Florida's planning and growth management system, regional strategic plans, prepared by the regional planning councils, are also very important. Local plans must be consistent with regional plans, and the *Strategic Regional Policy Plan for South Florida*, adopted in August 1995, contains specific and extensive guidance on natural hazard reduction (South Florida Regional Planning Council 1995). The plan presents an overall vision for South Florida that emphasizes achieving a "livable, sustainable and competitive regional community" (p. 30).

The regional plan is explicitly strategic. It focuses on "high priority, strategic issues facing the region over a 20-year time horizon" (South Florida Regional Planning Council 1995, p. 8). One of the plan's six strategy areas is disaster preparedness, and six strategic regional goals are presented. For each of these goals, benchmarks and indicators are provided as well as specific regional policies (pp. 147–154). The plan is impressive in its identification of measurable risk reduction benchmarks; these, along with the strategic goals, are presented in table 3.3. Policies direct local governments to reduce allowable densities on barrier islands and in Category 1 hurricane evacuation zones; to place high priority on acquiring these areas and restoring them to a natural condition; to reduce allowable densities in Category 3 hurricane evacuation zones "to no greater than the current use of the property if developed"; to ensure that development adheres to the requirements of the NFIP, the SFBC, and shelter policies in the strategic regional plan; and to give priority to acquiring property in areas destroyed by hurricanes.

Table 3.3. Regional Goals and Benchmarks/Indicators for Emergency Preparedness from Strategic Regional Policy Plan for South Florida

GOAL	BENCHMARKS/INDICATORS
Direct future development away from areas most vulnerable to storm surges	Average annual rate of population growth in Category 3 hurricane evacuation area to be no more than 0.5% for the decade 1990–2000
	Development densities in local comprehensive plans to reflect the policies listed in the Strategic Plan by the end of the Evaluation and Appraisal Report process
	Priority land acquisition list for post-hurricane redevelopment to result in an increase of 25% in dedicated open space acreage in hurricane evacuation areas by 2000
No increased risk to hospital patients and special needs population due to an emergency	25% of vulnerable health care facilities to be wind-hardened by 2000; 100% by 2015
	100% of vulnerable health care facilities to have emergency plan for licensing by 2000
Encourage all levels of government and the private sector to work together to ensure adequate and timely shelter within the region for those residing in hurricane evacuation areas	Regional sheltering capacity to be established for 25% of vulnerable regional population by 2000; for 75% by 2015
	Regional evacuation clearance times greater than twelve hours to be reduced by 25% by 2000; 75% by 2015
	Population evacuating out of the region to be reduced by 25% by 2000; 75% by 2015
	25% of residences in nonvulnerable locations to be converted to home shelters by 2000; 100% by 2015
Achieve consistency between goals and objectives of agency plans and emergency plans	Emergency preparedness consistency in state statutes to be achieved by 2000
	Standing regional emergency planning committee to be established by 2000
Minimize future risk to lives and property, partly through timely completion of postdisaster redevelopment plans	Number of repetitive loss properties to be reduced
	Public facilities and infrastructure exposed to risk from emergencies to be reduced
	Number of lives lost to disasters to be reduced
Achieve flexible and comprehensive emergency planning for a variety of emergencies	List of basic necessities to sustain life and corresponding supplies to be identified and agreed to by 2000

Source: South Florida Regional Planning Council 1995, pp. 147–154.

Response and Recovery from the Storm

Hurricane Andrew had an immense impact on South Florida, and immediate and short-term recovery decisions and activities were numerous and complex. More than 107,000 homes were damaged and more than 180,000 people were dislocated; local economies were devastated; and a 300-square-mile area was affected.

A number of recovery activities were undertaken by public agencies and private organizations. Activities in the first few months were aimed at restoring basic functions. Some 2,200 traffic lights were repaired and 150,000 street signs replaced, and more than 40,000 trees were planted. Debris clearance was a major task; as of October 1993 some 20 million cubic yards of debris had been disposed of and nearly 3,000 miles of roads cleared (Metro-Dade County Planning Department 1993b). FEMA funded a free jitney service for residents.

Because of the heavy damage to housing stock, a housing shortage in the aftermath of the storm was a major problem. Dade County instituted a "clean and secure" program requiring unsafe structures to be either secured or demolished. Temporary housing, including mobile homes and trailers, was installed, public housing units were renovated, and temporary and permanent housing for migrant farmworkers was constructed.

The county made special efforts to assist residents in receiving postdisaster assistance and in taking advantage of county services and other programs. In March 1993, Project CHART (Coordinated Hurricane Andrew Recovery Team) was created to facilitate and expedite recovery. Located in the county manager's office and headed by an assistant county manager, CHART created a central clearinghouse for information about county and other services and coordinated recovery activities. A nonprofit corporation, We Will Rebuild, also was formed to bring national attention to the disaster and to generate rebuilding funds.

The federal government provided more than $10 billion in grants and loans through several different agencies. Much of the funding focused on restoring and rebuilding the economy of southern Dade County. A major grant from the U.S. Department of Commerce's Economic Development Administration (EDA) provided funding for a study of short- and long-term strategies for economic recovery (Metro-Dade County Planning Department 1993b). Several of the projects the EDA funded, in combination with Community Development Block Grants (CDBGs) and other federal and state monies, led to a number of major economic development and community development projects and improvements in southern Dade County. These included community development plans for affected

communities (generally referred to as the "Moss plan," described later in this chapter); upgrading of public facilities, such as increased sewage treatment capacity for the Highway 1 corridor; funding for economic ventures, including the Miami-Dade Homestead Motor sports complex; and planning for realignment of Homestead Air Force Base, among others.

Mitigation Activities and Opportunities

Some of the redevelopment and recovery activities in the aftermath of Hurricane Andrew involved efforts to mitigate hazards, but others were oriented primarily toward getting neighborhoods and communities "back on their feet" and restoring and strengthening local economies (see table 3.4 for a chronology of events).

Table 3.4. Florida Mitigation Chronology Following Hurricane Andrew

DATE	EVENT
August 24, 1992, 4:52 A.M.	Hurricane Andrew makes landfall
September 1992	Governor Lawton Chiles Disaster Planning and Response Review Committee
January 1993	Disaster Planning and Response Review Committee issues its final report
March 1993	Project CHART is formed in Dade County manager's office
	Winter storm strikes (FEMA-982-DR-FL, March 13)
	Dade County adopts significant changes to South Florida Building Code
	H.B. 911 is enacted, strengthening emergency management in Florida
May 1993	Dade County hazard mitigation plan is completed
May 1994	FEMA approves state's hazard mitigation plan
	Winter Storm Task Force issues its report
August 10, 1995	State and FEMA sign Performance Partnership Agreement (PPA)
	Academic Task Force on Hurricane Catastrophic Insurance issues its final report
November 1995	Dade County Comprehensive Development Master Plan (CDMP) is updated
October 1996	CDMP objectives and policies are updated

Hazard Mitigation Grant Program

Following Hurricane Andrew, approximately $15 million became available for the Hazard Mitigation Grant Program (HMGP) under Section 404 of the Stafford Act. The process for generating grant proposals and for gaining FEMA approval for mitigation projects was long and complicated. Although funds had been dispensed in earlier disasters, there was no previous experience comparable to Andrew.

The first step in the HMGP process was a series of preapplication meetings organized by the state and conducted in and around Dade County with local officials. It is estimated that approximately 486 preapplications totaling $90 million were developed and submitted to the state and by the state to FEMA.

Following Andrew, each of the four counties with disaster declarations prepared its own hazard mitigation plan (roughly during the period when the state was preparing its Section 409 plan). Dade County's plan was adopted in May 1993, before the state completed its plan. The preparation of these plans was mandated by the state as part of the state-local disaster agreement, to guide localities in submitting hazard mitigation grant proposals to the state. During the interviews we conducted for our case studies, it became apparent that these plans did not have a very clear purpose. State mitigation personnel said that there was little relationship between these plans and Section 404 mitigation grant applications or other postdisaster mitigation actions. Local officials, however, indicated that the plans were useful in prioritizing mitigation projects.

How the local governments developed and submitted their applications is an interesting process. In Dade County, a special review committee was established to collect and review mitigation proposals. Each county department generated its own proposals and submitted them to the review committee. The review committee ultimately conducted its own cost-effectiveness analysis (FEMA does this as well) and evaluated the proposals primarily against the county hazard mitigation plan.

Some preapplications were filtered out in the initial months, and the final number of completed applications was just fewer than 500. At first, FEMA officials directed that all applications be submitted to them for an extensive sufficiency review. At a certain point, however, according to state officials FEMA began to appreciate the magnitude of the burden this was creating and proposed a modified approach. The state had in fact passed along applications totaling $90 million, even though eligible funding amounted to only $15 million. Therefore, FEMA asked the state to prioritize the applications.

By this point (May 1993), the state had completed its own Section 409 plan and used the plan to prioritize projects. In addition, some local pro-

jects fell by the wayside as a result of the information requirements of the sufficiency review.

The entire process took many months. As of 1996, four years after Andrew's landfall, only a small percentage of approved projects had received reimbursement from FEMA. The HMGP does permit retroactive funding of projects, so if local governments had received approval letters from FEMA by late spring of 1994, they could generally be confident that federal money would be forthcoming. Local governments can also expend their own funds even before receiving formal approval letters (the state does not recommend this), but such a practice represents a greater risk.

A large proportion of the HMGP funding has gone toward shutters and other building improvements intended to protect the outer envelope of buildings. Of the 120 projects approved as of March 1996, 72 were solely for shutter installations, comprising about 28 percent of the total funds allocated. Thirty-four of the projects were for retrofitting of water management district or storm water control facilities (reinforcement of telemetry control buildings). Other large HMGP projects included major improvements in the state's emergency management and communications center in Tallahassee (Recovery Management Project), strengthening of the Dade County Youth Fair building so that it can be used as a hurricane shelter ("various structural mitigation measures"), and Dade County's Home Inspection and Retrofit Program. Table 3.5 lists these funded projects.

The heavy emphasis on storm shutters has met with some criticism. Some believe that the mitigation funds could have been more effectively spent. Supporters argue, however, that installation of storm shutters is in keeping with the findings of the Interagency Hazard Mitigation Team and mitigates the wind-related damage of storms such as Andrew. Mitigation responses in this case were strongly influenced by Hurricane Andrew's dryness and high wind speed.

An interesting program that met with disappointing results was Dade County's Home Inspection and Retrofit Program. Under this program, 800 homeowners were eligible for retrofits to their homes for as little as one-half the cost, not to exceed $1,500 per home. The homeowner was to pay for the initial inspection. Retrofit improvements could include installation of shutters, structural bracing, and elevation of electrical boxes, among others. Local participation in the program, however, was very low, estimated at around fifty. One reason for this may have been a fear that the initial inspection would identify code violations, necessitating major additional repairs or renovation work.

One state mitigation planner commented that the HMGP proposals following Hurricane Andrew were very "piecemeal"—that is, they were submitted for a number of discrete, separate projects and did not appear to be

Table 3.5. HMGP Projects and Expenditures for Hurricane Andrew

TYPE OF PROJECT	NUMBER OF PROJECTS	TOTAL COST (THOUSANDS)	% OF TOTAL COST
Recovery Management Project (Florida Department of Community Affairs)	1	$1,600	16.4
Relocation of Emergency Operations Center (Coral Springs)	1	$638	6.5
Architectural and engineering fees	1	$79	0.8
Shutters	72	$2,711	27.8
Metal overhead doors for fire station; supplement for fire station	2	$67	0.6
Automated flood control gate	1	$82	0.8
Roll-up doors	1	$45	0.4
Retrofitting of facilities	1	$230	2.3
Home Inspection and Retrofit Program (Dade County)	1	$1,641	16.8
Replacement of culvert entrance	3	$99	1.0
Reinforcement of walls and roof of telemetry control building	34	$272	2.7
Strengthening of Emergency Operations Center, South Florida Water Management District	1	$202	2.2
Various structural mitigation measures (Dade County Youth Fair)	1	$2,077	21.3
Total	120[a]	$9,743	100[b]

Source: Florida Department of Community Affairs 1996b.

[a] Includes only funded projects; another twenty projects recommended for funding are not included here.

[b] Percentage total rounded to 100%.

implementing a broader mitigation strategy. The Florida Division of Emergency Management (DEM) now encourages local governments to submit applications that contain more comprehensive, coordinated strategies. One recent example is the local buyout program in Volusia County following Tropical Storm Gordon. This HMGP project proposed a regional strategy for storm water retention, coordinated by the area's Council of Governments (COG).

Changes to the South Florida Building Code and Regulation of the Construction Industry

Given the reputation of South Florida's coastal building code as one of the strongest in the country, the severity of structural damage following Hurricane Andrew was surprising to many. However, Andrew uncovered

serious flaws in current assumptions about building codes and construction standards and raised serious questions about the extent to which even strong codes can be relied on to protect people and property.

Much of the focus of the Interagency Hazard Mitigation Team's report was on improving the current building code and compliance system. Several special task forces were also created to explore these issues, including a County Building and Zoning Code Review Task Force and a FEMA Building Performance Assessment Team (FEMA 1992a, 1992b). Two grand juries were also convened in Dade County to examine issues (Dade County Grand Jury 1992, 1993).

A number of critical problems were identified, including unlicensed contractors; serious understaffing of inspection offices; an ineffective building inspection process; inadequate design of structural elements and design wind standards (and the need to adopt ASCE 7-88 as the state wind speed standard); and problems in standards for manufactured and mobile homes and window design.

Ironically, many older structures fared better than newer buildings in the winds of Andrew. A *Miami Herald* study of inspection data from 50,000 homes found that homes built since 1980 experienced much greater damage than did those built earlier; for example, in Country Walk, 33 percent of the homes built after 1980 were uninhabitable, compared with 10 percent of older homes (Metro Dade County Planning Department 1993a).

The findings of the two grand juries were particularly damning of the process by which homes were built before Andrew. The reports describe a terribly flawed building construction and regulation system and point the blame in a number of directions. A theme in the reports is the failure of the building-related professions to assume responsibility. In the words of the first grand jury (Dade County Grand Jury 1992, p. 10):

> The effectiveness of this community's building inspection process has been questionable for decades. The process has remained vulnerable to innuendoes of corruption, at worst, and apathy, at best. We have been advised that once upon a time, the construction professionals, such as architects and engineers, were held more accountable for their final products. But this is no longer so. Certifications and assurances of code compliance have been replaced over the years by a system relying primarily upon building inspections. Even functioning at its best, the inspection process for residential homes cannot fully insure code compliance. Essentially, we have foolishly been a community dependent upon the building industry to police itself.

Members of the grand juries found it hard to believe that architects and engineers were not required to certify that the structures they designed

would ultimately comply with plans or with the building code. Building inspections were inadequate and infrequent, and building inspectors were inadequately trained. Construction practices were deficient and workmanship shoddy. "In short, what has evolved is a building profession that no longer is held to a standard of professionalism. This lackadaisical approach to regulation and professionalism by the industry itself, and by the government which regulates it, is no longer tolerable" (Dade County Grand Jury 1992, p. 14).

In response to the grand jury findings and the recommendations of the building code evaluation task force, in March 1993 the Board of County Commissioners made a number of changes to the SFBC, including (Metro-Dade County Planning Department 1993a, p. 19):

• Using the 116-mile-per-hour national wind speed standard that takes into account wind gusts and the rise of wind pressures on building edges and corners (the ASCE 7-88 code)

• Requiring protection for windows and doors of all new homes

• Requiring that all structural plans be reviewed by a structural engineer

• Requiring concrete columns in single-story homes

• Mandating gable ends to be built from concrete block when the home is built of block

• Increasing the number of required roofing inspections, including a mandatory final inspection

Further improvements were made. Dade County significantly increased the number of building inspectors (from sixteen to forty-three a year after Andrew) and roofing inspectors (from four to thirty-one a year later; Dade County Grand Jury 1993). HUD also strengthened the wind speed standard for mobile homes, instituting the ASCE 7-88 standard.

Rethinking Settlement Patterns: Post-Andrew Design Charrettes

Following the storm, there were a number of efforts to reconsider neighborhood and community development patterns and to take advantage of the opportunity to redesign and rebuild in more desirable ways. Shortly after Andrew, the South Dade Planning and Design Work Group was established by the Florida Atlantic University/Florida International University Joint Center for Environmental and Urban Problems to consider alternative redevelopment options and directions. This group and the Uni-

versity of Miami School of Architecture, with funding from We Shall Rebuild, organized a major design charrette called Design for a New South Dade. Rather than creating a specific design plan for the region, the planning charrette aimed to produce a series of case study models and general principles.

A number of smaller design charrettes were also conducted, in particular for Homestead, Florida City, and the unincorporated areas of southern Dade County. In both Florida City and Homestead, specific design plans proposed that neighborhoods be organized around a main street to promote walkability and that each have its own park and community center. Also proposed in each case was a Pioneer Village in which shops, civic buildings, and a visitor's center would be located (Dash, Peacock, and Morrow 1997).

The Florida City charrette was criticized by community members as not responsive to immediate local needs, especially for housing, and as possibly displacing poor and longtime residents. For these reasons, the charrette's plan was eventually scrapped. The Homestead plan met with similar opposition from the minority community there, primarily because of plans to demolish a farmworkers' neighborhood in order to build the Pioneer Village. The Enterprise Foundation, a national nonprofit development company that funded the Homestead charrette, also eventually withdrew its support for the plan, calling it "urban removal" (Dash, Peacock, and Morrow 1997). Despite these complaints, the city of Homestead is moving forward to implement the plan.

Although the post-Andrew charrettes were an admirable effort to take advantage of rebuilding and redevelopment opportunities, they were generally unsuccessful. The charrettes focused on overcoming the problems of traditional suburban development and embraced neotraditional design principles rather than focusing primarily on hazard mitigation (Brower and Hass 1995). The experience confirmed the difficulty of recasting an already developed landscape, despite a major disaster. To some critics, the charrettes seemed not to take into account the fixed nature of existing streets and roads, utility lines, and property lines. Even though a few of the recommendations eventually were implemented or made their way into other plans (a proposed bikeway-greenway was included in the transportation improvements plan for the Metropolitan Planning Organization), the charrettes did not result in dramatic rebuilding changes.

One successful post-Andrew charrette prepared a plan for a new Habitat for Humanity development on a forty-acre site in southern Dade County. Jordan Commons is an integrated neotraditional village of 200 homes that will be pedestrian friendly and will include ball fields, green space, and a

community center. Perhaps most impressive are the project's sustainability features. The homes will incorporate solar energy for water heating and outside lighting; minimize cooling requirements by use of ceiling fans, highly reflective rooftops, window tinting, and tree shading; and feature energy-efficient appliances. Water will be recycled and used to irrigate vegetation. Construction wastes will also be recycled. Finally, the buildings are designed to be stronger and more resistant to hurricanes and storm forces, incorporating steel frame construction.

Financing Recovery and Mitigation

Mitigation financing was one of the more interesting dimensions of the Hurricane Andrew recovery. The state created a special hurricane trust fund specifically for Dade County to fund postdisaster recovery needs not funded through FEMA, insurance, or other means. The state Hurricane Andrew Recovery and Rebuilding Trust Fund was used for economic recovery, natural area restoration, and hazard mitigation projects, such as elevating homes affected by the 50 percent rule to meet current code. Monies were provided by additional sales taxes generated in the county following the storm; the county was allowed to retain the extra sales taxes generated from recovery-related sales and economic activities rather than distributing them to other Florida jurisdictions. The trust fund was used in part to fund a number of local economic development projects, such as the Miami-Dade Homestead Motorsports Complex.

Two additional funding mechanisms created after Andrew were the Florida Hurricane Catastrophe Fund (CAT), which provides reinsurance coverage in the event of catastrophic storm events, and the state Emergency Management Preparedness and Assistance Trust Fund (EMPATF) created in 1993 and funded through an annual surcharge on insurance policies for residential ($2) and commercial ($4) buildings. The latter supports local emergency management, planning activities, and mitigation projects. Both of these funding mechanisms are discussed in more detail later in this chapter.

Planning Community Development

Hurricane Andrew set in motion a great deal of community development and redevelopment activity, much of it in direct response to the hurricane but relatively little of it focused on mitigation. Substantial federal development and redevelopment monies were provided following the storm, including significant HUD and EDA grants.

One of the largest redevelopment efforts was the so-called Moss plan, named after Dennis Moss, commissioner from southern Dade County. This was a plan for using HUD Community Development Block Grant (CDBG) monies in nine communities (eight in southern Dade County that were affected by the hurricane). In each community, workshops were held to identify community needs and priorities. What resulted were wish lists of community improvements, typically including a range of items from affordable housing to new libraries, day care centers, and other community facilities and services. About half the projects funded involved rebuilding damaged or destroyed property, but the other half were for entirely new facilities and improvements. A number of Community Development Corporations (CDCs) were also created to facilitate community redevelopment.

In addition to CDBG funding, other community development monies flowed into the region. A sizable grant from the EDA and the Department of Commerce was provided to fund a major sewer improvement project along the Highway 1 corridor.

A considerable amount of economic development planning occurred following the storm. A South Dade Regional Development Plan was prepared, for instance, which focused on strengthening the business base of damaged areas of southern Dade County. As another example, the Greater Miami Visitors and Convention Association prepared a tourism plan for the region.

Enforcing Floodplain Management Standards

One of the most controversial facets of the recovery process was the relaxing of FEMA's NFIP standards concerning substantial improvement. Under most earlier interpretations of FEMA requirements, structures damaged beyond 50 percent of their value would need to conform to current flood standards if rebuilt, including elevating the structure to the current base flood elevation. In some areas of Dade County, this amounted to elevating structures an additional twelve feet above their original elevation.

An estimated 3,000–4,000 residents of Dade County were affected by the 50 percent rule. Elevations typically cost $30,000–$40,000 per structure. Resistance to the elevation requirement was especially strong in the Saga Bay neighborhood, where the requirements were seen as burdensome and leading to inconsistent building elevations.

FEMA eventually gave permission to relax the substantial improvement standard. Specifically, FEMA allowed Dade County to calculate the 50 percent value based on replacement cost of damaged structures rather than

on the usual fair market value approach. Under this rule, structures would not be required to be elevated unless their damage exceeded 50 percent of their replacement cost. Because replacement costs are typically higher than fair market value, the net effect was to reduce the number of homes considered 50 percent damaged and to relieve a number of property owners of the elevation requirement. FEMA also allowed the county to apply a special variance waiving the elevation requirement for structures within six inches of the mandated base flood elevation.

Interestingly, these looser standards were applied only to buildings damaged by Hurricane Andrew. The 50 percent of current market value rule has since been reinstated, raising questions about uniformity and fairness. And others question the value of reinstating the tougher market value standard when a similar waiver request will probably be sought and granted after the next major disaster.

Responding to the Insurance Crisis

The massive amount of property damage caused by Hurricane Andrew precipitated a major insurance crisis. More than $15 billion in insurance claims was paid. By January 1993, eight small insurance companies had gone out of business; the number eventually reached ten. Some eleven other companies, including Allstate, stopped writing policies for South Florida. About 16,000 residents were left without homeowners' insurance following Andrew (Metro-Dade County Planning Department 1993a). Florida did have a state system in place, however, to cover insurance claims of failed companies. The Florida Insurance Guaranty Association (FIGA) provided millions of dollars to cover such claims, assuming, up to a certain amount, the liability of the companies that failed (Colden 1995).

Stopping the withdrawal of coverage by private insurance companies following Andrew became a major public policy focus. The state prohibited companies doing business in Florida from canceling more than 5 percent of their policies in any year and later, in June 1996, extended this moratorium on mass cancellation of policies for another three years, through S.B. 2314.

The state also created a mechanism to insure homeowners who were unable to find insurance elsewhere, called the Florida Residential Property and Casualty Joint Underwriting Association. There are now more than 800,000 policyholders in this system, and it has become the third largest insurer in Florida (Colden 1995).

In December 1993, the state legislature created a unique state reinsurance fund—the Florida Hurricane Catastrophe Fund (CAT)—to cover

future hurricane-related claims. The fund covers insurance losses after a certain "trigger" level is reached (and, unlike FIGA, before companies become bankrupt); it is financed through an assessment on all property and casualty insurance. The CAT fund grew from about $422 million in the first year to about $1 billion in the spring of 1996, and it has a borrowing capacity of about $5 billion. The CAT legislation has also advanced mitigation in several ways. First, beginning in 1997, the fund will provide $10 million annually for mitigation projects. Second, insurers are now required by law to offer homeowners premium discounts of 7–18 percent when they install approved impact-tested windows and doors or when they install shutters on windows.

A major remaining challenge is to find ways to coax the private insurance market to maintain and expand its coverage in the state. The report of the Academic Task Force on Hurricane Catastrophic Insurance (1995) proposes strengthening the private insurance system rather than relying on a state-sponsored insurer. However, to create a viable insurance system for Florida, the report calls for "drastic changes," including capping private insurance losses, increasing the Florida CAT fund, and providing new mitigation incentives.

The task force's report offers sensible recommendations for addressing Florida's insurance crisis. Particularly promising is its focus on mitigative and preventive actions, individualized risk assessments, and other financial incentives for mitigation. It recommends actively involving mortgage bankers and creating a role for strategic partnerships in solving the insurance crisis.

However, the plan would leave in place a strong government underwriting function through an expansion of the Florida Hurricane Catastrophe Fund, which the report candidly notes will accumulate sufficient reserves only if the state is able to escape major hurricane landfalls in the next decade.

Governor's Disaster Planning and Response Review Committee

Hurricane Andrew prompted a reassessment of Florida's emergency management system at several levels. In September 1992, Governor Lawton Chiles appointed (through Executive Order 92-291) a special Disaster Planning and Response Review Committee, with a mandate to "evaluate the response to Hurricane Andrew and develop recommendations for improving Florida's emergency preparedness and recovery programs" (Governor's Committee 1993, p. 1). The committee, also known as the

Lewis Committee, after its chairman, Philip D. Lewis, issued its final report in January 1993. The report recommends taking action before storms (communications, evacuation, sheltering) as well as following storms (postdisaster communications and public information programs; postdisaster response and recovery operations; compilation of damage assessment data; medical care and relief; coordination of volunteers, donations, and supplies) (Governor's Committee 1993).

The report outlines four "key solutions": (1) improve communications at and among all levels of government; (2) strengthen plans for evacuation, sheltering, and postdisaster response and recovery; (3) enhance intergovernmental coordination; and (4) improve training (Governor's Committee 1993, p. 3). Some ninety-four specific recommendations are made, ranging from amending the state's comprehensive emergency management plan to improving the evacuation system (e.g., widening roads and suspending toll collection) and expanding sheltering capability (e.g., incorporating shelter design criteria into state building standards for public buildings and erecting hurricane shelters in mobile home parks).

The report concludes that the state currently does not devote enough funding to emergency management programs and recommends the creation of an Emergency Management Preparedness and Disaster Assistance Trust Fund, to be administered by the Department of Community Affairs. Possible sources of money for this fund include surcharges on property and casualty insurance policies, marina and docking fees, building permit fees, and fees on other transactions or activities in high-risk areas (Governor's Committee 1993, pp. 63–64).

A number of the committee's recommendations have been adopted. The report led to the enactment of H.B. 911, which brought about a major overhaul in Florida's disaster preparedness system and specifically mandated many of the mitigation recommendations of the study (described in the following section).

H.B. 911 and Other Actions Strengthening Florida's Disaster Preparedness Framework

Substantial changes in the disaster preparedness framework in Florida were brought about through the enactment of H.B. 911 in March 1993. A direct response to the Governor's Committee report, this legislation incorporated many of the committee's recommendations.

H.B. 911 created new requirements for sheltering in the state, intended to address the growing shelter deficit. It required the Florida Division of Emergency Management (DEM) to add a shelter component to the state

Comprehensive Emergency Management Plan that addresses how the state will meet future sheltering needs, imposes a requirement that no region in the state have a shelter deficit by 1998, and requires that all new educational facilities be built to stronger wind and storm standards.

The latter requirement has been controversial, as the state Department of Education is responsible for modifying school design standards to incorporate safe shelters. An initial draft of design criteria (to be incorporated into Rule 6A-2 (of the Florida Administrative Code) was objected to by many local school administrators because of estimates that it would add 10 percent to the cost of new school buildings. As a consequence, a less stringent version was prepared (though it has not yet been adopted) to create in school buildings "a wind and debris resistant storm pod" rather than applying the strengthening standards to the entire building. These "pods," or Enhanced Hurricane Protection Areas (EHPAs), are predicted to raise building costs by only 2 percent.

Other key features of the H.B. 911 expand and extend the system for mutual aid between localities and provide for state coordination of mutual aid; require that new state university buildings be constructed so that they can be used as hurricane shelters; mandate emergency management standards and structural requirements for hospitals and nursing facilities; require localities to compile a registry of disabled persons; authorize emergency refilling of prescriptions; extend immunity from civil liability for provision of medical care during declared emergencies; and implement new restrictions to prevent marinas from requiring removal of vessels.

The legislation also mandates an expanded role and increased capability for local emergency management. It requires each county to prepare an emergency management plan and program, consistent with the state plan, and to appoint a director. The legislation lays out the powers and authorities of such agencies.

Provisions of the state Comprehensive Emergency Management Plan are also specified in the legislation. The evacuation component of the plan must include "specific regional and interregional planning provisions" and promote intergovernmental coordination of evacuation activities. It must, at a minimum, "contain guidelines for lifting tolls on state highways; ensure coordination pertaining to evacuees crossing county lines; set forth procedures for directing people caught on evacuation routes to safe shelter; establish strategies for ensuring sufficient, reasonably priced fueling locations along evacuation routes; and establish policies and strategies for emergency medical evacuation" (H.B. 911, 2nd engrossed, p. 20). The legislation gives similar guidance about what must be included in the sheltering and postdisaster response and recovery components.

One of the important tasks under the postdisaster response and recovery component was the establishment of Rapid Impact Assessment Teams (RIATs). The state has established such teams, each consisting of ten to twelve subject matter experts. Teams will be self-sufficient and able to enter damaged areas and quickly determine the immediate needs of residents (e.g., food, water, shelter) and impacts on infrastructure.

A major new funding source for many of the local emergency management activities specified in H.B. 911 was created by Senate Bill 1858, a companion bill also enacted in 1993. Specifically, it created the EMPATF, funded by a surcharge on residential ($2 per year) and commercial ($4 per year) property insurance. Grants are than made to local governments for emergency management purposes, and these governments are given considerable discretion on how they can use the funds.

State Hazard Mitigation Plan

When Hurricane Andrew struck Florida, the state did not have in place a Section 409 hazard mitigation plan. It later prepared one, and the plan was approved by FEMA on May 24, 1994, a full twenty-one months after the disaster event.

Although the state had not undertaken adequate mitigation planning before Andrew, the current (1994) plan is, in many respects, a strong one. The plan was prepared in response to four disaster declarations. In addition to Andrew (FEMA-955-DR-FL), there were declarations for major floods in June 1992 (FEMA-952-DR-FL), tornadoes and flooding in October 1992 (FEMA-966-DR-FL), and a major winter storm in March 1993 resulting in coastal flooding, high winds, and tornadoes (FEMA-966-DR-FL).

The plan is clearly organized to satisfy the requirements of the Stafford Act. An introductory section defines hazard mitigation and summarizes previous disaster declarations. An extensive "Natural Hazards" section describes the natural disasters Florida is exposed to but does not relate the hazards to one another or provide a quantitative, all-hazards risk assessment. Indeed, the plan states that "it is not intended as a quantitative risk analysis," nor is it "intended to take the place of the kind of in-depth hazards analysis that can be done at the local level in the local government comprehensive plans, the local emergency management plan and the local mitigation and redevelopment plan." It proposes continued development of a statewide geographic information system (GIS) to make it possible to "'paint a picture' in increasing detail of Florida's existing and future vul-

nerability and risk" (Florida Division of Emergency Management 1994, p. 23). Similarly, the plan does not prioritize the hazards identified. However, the first hazards described in the "Natural Hazards" section (and those discussed at greatest length) are hurricanes and coastal storms, and the plan states that they are the "most serious catastrophic threat to Florida's population" (p. 25).

The "State Capabilities" section is thorough and comprehensive but not evaluative or analytic. It is a descriptive listing of the many state agencies with some relationship to hazard mitigation. The reader gets the impression of a fragmented and piecemeal policy framework. Little attempt is made, at least in the "State Capabilities" section, to assess the overall effectiveness and functioning of this diffuse system in planning for and reducing the impacts of the natural hazards.

The plan's "Goals and Objectives" section provides an overall sense of direction and guidance to the plan, although the goals are not prioritized or ordered. The real heart of the plan, however, lies in the "Issues and Recommendations" section. Drawn largely from the earlier Interagency Hazard Mitigation Team reports, the plan also references the Governor's Disaster Planning and Response Review Committee report as useful in identifying issues and recommendations. Altogether, 105 specific recommendations are presented, organized around forty issue areas and nine broad mitigation subjects: Florida's hazard mitigation program; emergency management; public education and awareness; land use planning and growth management; rebuilding, recovery, and redevelopment; coastal and floodplain management; infrastructure; building codes and ordinances; and natural resources and the environment. For each recommendation, the plan designates a lead agency and support agencies.

The plan does lay out criteria for prioritizing its many recommendations. Priority is given to an issue, for instance, if it is part of the "911" legislation, if it flows from the recommendations of the Lewis Commission's report or the IMC Winter Storm Task Force report, or if it is recommended in the Interagency Hazard Mitigation Team report, among other criteria. Table 3.6 lists the plan's immediate and highest priorities. Among the immediate priorities are recommendations to address mitigation for critical systems and critical infrastructure, sheltering needs, repairs and retrofitting for hazard mitigation, protection of the outside envelope of buildings, and intergovernmental coordination. Highest-priority recommendations are in the areas of manufactured and mobile homes, building code enforcement and inspection, common building code, standards for state buildings, local comprehensive planning, relocation and land acquisition,

and the permitting process. The detail and depth of the plan's issues and recommendations are impressive. The plan, moreover, does present fairly clear mitigation priorities, and these are nicely clustered around issue areas (see table 3.6). The recommendations are also clear and specific enough to enable the state to evaluate their implementation. However, no cost estimates or time frames are provided for completing the recommendations.

The plan includes an implementation element that stipulates a process and a timetable for revising and updating the plan every two years. In addition, the plan calls for the State Hazard Mitigation and Recovery Team to meet and evaluate the plan every six months and provides for yearly updates, to be submitted by the state hazard mitigation officer.

Table 3.6. Priorities in Florida's Hazard Mitigation Plan

Issue	Recommendation Numbers[a]	Timing	Disaster Number				Costs Included
			952	955	966	982	
Immediate Priority							
Predisaster mitigation for critical systems	II: 8–11	X	X	X	X	X	X
Mitigating loss of critical infrastructure	VII: 75–78	X	X	X	X	X	X
Shelter strategy	II: 17–21	X		X			X
Repairs and retrofitting for hazard mitigation	VIII: 80–83	X	X	X	X	X	X
Protection of outside envelope of buildings	VIII: 85–87	X		X		X	X
Intergovernmental coordination/State Hazard Mitigation and Recovery Team	I: 1–6	X		X	X	X	
Highest Priority							
Manufactured and mobile homes	VIII: 88–90			X		X	
Building code enforcement and inspection	VIII: 93–95		X	X		X	
Common building code	VIII: 96			X			
Standards for state buildings	VIII: 97			X		X	
Local government comprehensive planning	V: 49–51		X	X	X	X	X
Relocation and land acquisition	V: 55–57				X	X	X
Permitting process	V: 59–60		X	X	X	X	

Source: Florida Division of Emergency Management 1994.

[a]Objectives grouped by plan subject areas.

Key Policy Issues Emerging After the Storm

Hurricane Andrew redefined disaster policy in the state of Florida. Its immense impacts highlighted a number of critical weaknesses in the previous approach to mitigation in the Sunshine State.

Role of the State Mitigation Plan

Prior to Hurricane Andrew, the state of Florida had prepared several hazard mitigation plans in response to specific disaster events. The state did not, however, have in place a comprehensive mitigation plan to guide the recovery and reconstruction process and decision making concerning hazard mitigation grants and proposals. Moreover, as mentioned earlier, the plan required under the Stafford Act was not completed until twenty-one months after Andrew hit. State mitigation plans and policies, then, had little influence on short-term decisions following Andrew.

Instead, much of the early mitigation guidance in Andrew came from the report of the Interagency Hazard Mitigation Team. Dade County also prepared its own postdisaster mitigation plan, which drew heavily on the recommendations of the team's report. The county plan guided decision making concerning hazard mitigation grant proposals (e.g., it was used by the Building and Zoning Department and DERM Floodplain Management to evaluate development proposals, by the Office of Emergency Management in response planning, and by the county in its comprehensive master plan update and code amendments), but its overall utility and extent of use are uncertain.

Once completed, Florida's Section 409 plan was eventually used by the state in prioritizing HMGP applications. The plan became useful in the latter stages of the mitigation process, but the lack of a plan undoubtedly slowed the approval of eligible mitigation projects in Florida. Florida has in many ways learned its lesson, and now the state has not only implemented a meaningful mitigation plan but also developed several levels of mitigation planning and guidance.

Role of Hurricane Characteristics in Shaping Mitigation

Hurricane Andrew was a relatively dry hurricane; most of the damage came from high winds. Storm surges, though high, caused relatively little damage in contrast with the massive destruction elsewhere. As a conse-

quence, the heavy wind damage shaped the types of mitigation strategies pursued. The most striking example is the large proportion of mitigation funding directed toward installation of shutters.

The controversy over elevation of damaged structures in Saga Bay mentioned earlier was in part exacerbated by the perception of hurricane winds as the primary threat. Several officials interviewed indicated that homeowners could not understand why they should be required to elevate—and thus to mitigate from floods—when the problem was wind. The heavy reliance on shutters has been questioned by some who believe that this measure does not constitute long-term mitigation and is not the most effective use of mitigation funds, although FEMA has defended it as cost-effective (FEMA 1997, pp. 23–25).

Mitigation Options in Heavily Developed Areas

The storm also raised questions about which mitigation options are appropriate in a heavily developed region such as South Florida. Possibilities for avoiding high-hazard areas and for directing development and growth away from high-hazard zones are limited there. It is estimated that Dade County is 83 percent built out (within its Urban Development Boundary). The highly vulnerable barrier islands of Miami Beach and Key Biscayne also are almost completely built out.

Long-term shoreline retreat or relocation is not likely to be an option in this area, though it is frequently advocated in the coastal management literature. In part, this is a reflection of the tremendous economic investment in, and benefits derived from, these coastal locations. Coastal development is worth billions of dollars in Dade County and contributes substantial economic benefits to the private sector and to government through taxes and tourism. Dade County documents clearly state that retreat or relocation is not a realistic or desirable alternative. However, there is an opportunity to maintain and possibly reduce population density and intensity by regulating parcel-specific new development and redevelopment (Metro-Dade County Planning Department 1995, p. IX-219).

The charrette experiences described earlier in this chapter further highlight the difficulties of redesigning or fundamentally changing land use and development patterns. Only a few ideas from the charrettes were implemented, including a proposed bikeway-greenway that was endorsed in the southern Dade County charrette and is found in a transportation plan prepared by the Metropolitan Planning Organization, as well as some other environmental proposals.

Growth Containment and Risk Reduction: Conflicting Goals?

Planners in South Florida pointed out that sometimes the objectives of growth containment and compact growth were at odds with keeping population density and development low in high-risk locations. In South Florida, there are very real limits to growth. Ideally, and according to the Metro-Dade County's plan, development should be kept away from farmland and wetlands to the west. Yet to do this means funneling more growth into hurricane evacuation zones. These are areas where, under the policies of the *Strategic Regional Policy Plan, for South Florida* (South Florida Regional Planning Council 1995), densities should not be allowed to increase. These two sometimes conflicting policy directives make Dade County planners feel squeezed.

It will be a significant challenge for southern Dade County to balance these goals of curtailing sprawl and directing growth away from hurricane vulnerability zones. This will require directing much of the region's future growth into corridors outside high-risk hurricane zones yet within designated urban development boundaries. Infill, reurbanization, and increased density in these "safer" locations could be encouraged (or mandated), along with transit and other public investments to serve them.

Emphasis on Economic Development

Much development and redevelopment following Hurricane Andrew clearly had little to do with hazard mitigation and instead appears to have been aimed at economic development and improvement of the general quality of life. The extensive economic development activities in Homestead, for instance, are impressive. Projects include the Miami-Dade Homestead Motorsports Complex (home to the Miami Grand Prix), the Homestead Sports Complex, and realignment plans for Homestead Air Force Base. Substantial investments in improving local infrastructure have also been made.

In these instances, planning for the next hurricane does not seem to be a high priority. Moreover, in touring some of the facilities and projects (e.g., the motor speedway), one wonders whether disaster assistance funds are justified for such large economic development projects. These projects seem to go well beyond helping communities restore or rebuild and give an impression of pork barrel politics. However, economic recovery and improvement in quality of life are a significant part of postdisaster recovery. In fact, the Economic Development Administration of the U.S. Department

of Commerce was one of the first federal agencies to arrive in Dade County after Hurricane Andrew. And several economic recovery projects contributed to hazard mitigation, even though that was not their main purpose. In the future, however, postdisaster economic recovery projects should be evaluated primarily for their contribution to hazard mitigation.

Strengths and Limitations of Florida's Planning System

Florida has been active in mandating local and regional planning and growth management. Hurricane Andrew highlighted both the strengths and the limitations of this approach. Local governments must prepare postdisaster mitigation plans as part of their coastal elements. Most local governments, however, have not prepared these plans, and pushing local governments to do so has not been a high priority for the state's Department of Community Affairs (DCA).

Under state standards, coastal localities are not to allow increases in density in the Coastal High Hazard Areas (CHHAs). Planning officials in Dade County indicate that in the past, new development has been approved in these areas because developers claim it is seasonal development—that is, it will not contribute to the number of people at risk during the hurricane season. Many of these so-called seasonal units, however, end up serving as year-round residences. Proposed changes in the county's development plan would correct this loophole.

Another problem noted by planners is confusion over the definition of zones. The Florida growth management system involves a number of different management and planning zones, many of which appear to be very similar. Moreover, the meaning of these zones has changed over time. In 1993, the definition of the Coastal High Hazard Zone was changed and the Coastal High Hazard Area was replaced by the Hurricane Vulnerability Zone (and its definition was changed as well). In addition to the general confusion they created, such changes have also complicated the data collection and analysis required of local governments (for a discussion of the implications for Dade County, see Metro-Dade County Planning Department 1995, p. ix-81).

There are many positive features, however, of the state planning framework. Some of the most impressive actions that can be undertaken to reduce risk have been put in place through the state's coastal program. One important strategy is the coastal setback, and Florida has adopted a thirty-year erosion setback standard. This standard prohibits construction of new buildings seaward of a point that is likely to erode within the next

thirty years. Although Florida's Department of Environmental Protection (DEP) is in charge of enforcement, these determinations are made on a case-by-case basis, usually by private consultants. In addition, some localities have adopted their own setback standards.

Localities have considerable power, moreover, to implement creative mitigation programs within the state's framework. Sanibel Island, which has for many years controlled development on the basis of protecting ecological carrying capacity and hurricane evacuation capability, is but one example. Localities across the state, such as Lee County, are utilizing a variety of creative planning tools, including transfer of development rights and special assessment districts, among many others. Monroe County has been utilizing a rate-of-growth ordinance, largely keyed to evacuation capacity. Florida localities have both the legal tools and the state planning support to pursue natural hazard reduction.

Relaxation of Flood Standards

Hurricane Andrew raised significant questions not only about Metro-Dade County's commitment to enforce its floodplain management ordinance but also about the federal government's commitment to ensure that the substantial improvements standard under the NFIP is enforced in good faith. Allowing the use of the replacement value standard appears to be a response to political pressure following Andrew, and FEMA's actions could be described as "buckling" under such pressure. These actions raise serious questions about whether flood hazards can be reduced over the long term when FEMA backs away from stringent enforcement of such flood hazard mitigation standards. Also of concern are the uniformity and fairness of construction standards applied during rebuilding. Some homeowners were expected to elevate their homes at great expense, but other similarly situated homeowners were able, under the relaxed rule, to rebuild without elevating.

In the long run, South Florida may become significantly safer only if events such as Hurricane Andrew are seen as opportunities to strengthen and improve the existing housing stock. The issue of substantial improvement following a hurricane will probably be significant in Dade County in the years ahead. Estimates that the county contains some 150,000 structures built before 1974 (thus probably unelevated) and lying within the 100-year floodplain (Metro-Dade County Planning Department 1993a) indicate the magnitude of the problem.

The Andrew experience suggests not only that a single, meaningful elevation standard should be applied in the case of substantially damaged

structures but also that some form of expeditious financial assistance must be provided. The latter would enhance the acceptability and perceived fairness of elevation requirements. The 1993 *Dade County Hazard Mitigation Addendum* includes the stated goal of identifying in advance structures subject to the substantial improvement standard and creating "a permanent source of funding to assist those who will face this requirement in the future" (Metro-Dade County Planning Department 1993a, p. 43). The state's Hurricane Andrew Recovery and Rebuilding Fund did provide grants to cover as much as 25 percent of the cost of elevation, but the percentage was considered too low and the funds were not made available in a timely fashion.

The Insurance Crisis and the Collectivization of Natural Disaster Risks

Hurricane Andrew was an abrupt awakening for the insurance industry, to the extent of insurance companies' exposure in coastal areas, and to homeowners, who believed insurance would always be available. An insurance crisis developed after Andrew, which resulted in some $15.5 billion in insured losses—the largest insured losses from a natural disaster. Some ten companies went out of business, and many others, including large companies such as Allstate Insurance Companies, announced plans to curtail coverage in Florida. Some companies, including State Farm Insurance Companies, will not be writing new homeowners policies in Florida. What this has meant is a greater reliance on the state as the insurer of last resort, namely through the Florida Residential Property and Casualty Joint Underwriting Association. The association now has more than 800,000 policy holders and is the third largest insurer in the state. The insurance problems faced in Florida are similar to those experienced in California, where insurance companies either are not writing new policies or are adding substantial restrictions that make purchase of insurance difficult.

These trends raise several public policy issues. One concern is that state government is increasingly assuming an insurance role and that the general public is increasingly asked to underwrite these risks. In this sense, there is a trend toward "collectivizing" hurricane risks. A second, and clearly related, concern is that many homeowners may simply be left with no coverage at all (now or after the next event). This may in turn increase the future need for postdisaster assistance, in effect leading again to a greater collectivizing of risk. In either case, the need for effective long-term mitigation measures becomes that much greater and more defen-

sible; that is, if the state is underwriting citizens' risk, it is entirely fair for the state to request adherence to stricter codes and mitigation provisions.

The recommendations of the Academic Task Force on Hurricane Catastrophic Insurance (1995) are encouraging and probably will, if adopted, strengthen the insurance system in Florida. Particularly encouraging is the emphasis the recommendations give to individualized risk assessment and mitigation. Florida's Hurricane Catastrophe Fund (CAT) is a key element in the task force's recommendations, yet the long-term viability of this fund remains uncertain. The report of the task force notes that the fund is projected to grow to $18 billion within ten years but also notes, very disturbingly, that this projection is based on the absence of major hurricane strikes in the state during that period.

Inadequate Construction Standards and the Question of Responsibility

The South Florida Building Code was considered one of the strongest in the country, so the tremendous level of damage caused by Hurricane Andrew surprised many. The impact of Andrew gave rise to questions about the safety of South Florida's construction practices and the adequacy of its regulations. The Andrew experience demonstrated clearly that simply adopting a strong building code is not sufficient to prevent serious damage.

More fundamentally, the Andrew experience raises serious questions about who is responsible for ensuring the safety of structures. Does responsibility lie primarily with those who construct the buildings or with the architects and engineers who design them? Is it primarily the responsibility of government to ensure the safety of structures and to adequately enforce building code standards and conduct the inspections needed to ensure compliance with the code? Or do homeowners and housing consumers bear some of the responsibility as well? Should they either be better educated to understand and demand better-designed and better-constructed homes or be prepared to accept the consequences when another Andrew occurs? Although this issue remains unresolved, responsibility seems to lie at a number of levels and be shared among a number of parties involved in the construction and building process; indeed, the post-Andrew evaluations and commentaries demonstrate this (see Dade County Grand Jury 1992, 1993).

Hurricane Andrew uncovered a number of deficiencies in construction standards, each of which has substantial implications for future mitigation actions and policy. First, deficiencies were discovered in the building code itself, and a number of key areas were identified in which the code needed

to be stronger. The code has been strengthened, with changes to increase the design wind standard, new requirements for windows and doors, and requirements that all structural plans be reviewed by structural engineers.

One key finding of the post-Andrew evaluations was that there was considerable variation in the quality of construction and that higher-quality workmanship resulted in less hurricane damage (e.g., see FEMA 1992a). This finding suggests that even though a building may be designed properly and built with the correct materials, its safety will be determined primarily at the point at which "hammer meets nail." It suggests, perhaps, that builders must accept a greater sense of personal responsibility but also highlights the importance of education programs, such as those suggested by the FEMA post-Andrew building performance study. Concerted efforts at education might also help create a more informed housing consumer. The FEMA study recommends the development of community outreach programs for precisely this purpose (FEMA 1992a).

Serious deficiencies in enforcement of the county's building standards were also uncovered. These included an understaffed building code department (too few inspectors and inspector supervisors) and inadequate training of staff. The experience of Hurricane Andrew supports the recent move by the insurance industry to rate communities according to their code enforcement capabilities and the qualifications and training of code enforcement personnel. Florida also has approved a plan for rating cities and counties according to building code enforcement; the first round of grading was to have been completed by the end of 1996.

Sustainable Development and Ecosystem Management

Hurricane Andrew highlighted the vulnerability of development in South Florida and the need to rethink mindless patterns of urban sprawl and development. To many, Andrew highlighted both the unsustainability of current building and development practices and potential opportunities to promote more sustainable patterns and practices.

The concept of sustainability is beginning to be taken seriously in South Florida. Notably, the Jordan Commons project illustrates how sustainable development can lead to a different type of development and redevelopment. Jordan Commons represents an effort to create homes and a neighborhood more resilient to the natural forces of South Florida (incorporating steel frame designs) while recognizing the resource and other ecological limits of the regional environment. As described earlier, these

homes minimize resource and energy consumption, recycle water, and incorporate solar energy. The homes are also affordable and are designed around a traditional, walkable neighborhood with open space and community buildings, implementing many of the principles advocated by the "new urbanists." Had the 26,000 homes destroyed by Hurricane Andrew been rebuilt to these sustainable building and design principles, the region would have taken a significant step in the direction of greater sustainability. Furthermore, the strategic plan of Florida's Department of Community Affairs gives important attention to reducing energy consumption in the state and increasing the use of solar and renewable energy (Florida Department of Community Affairs 1996a, Chap. IV).

The theme of sustainability appears in the 1995 *Strategic Regional Policy Plan for South Florida,* prepared by the South Florida Regional Planning Council (see figure 3.2). Its "overall regional vision" statement gives prominence to sustainability (South Florida Regional Planning Council 1995, p. 30):

> The South Florida region will strive to become a livable, sustainable and competitive regional community, a community which provides opportunities to all residents to grow, prosper and enjoy life. The region is committed to economic prosperity, balanced with environmental protection and restoration.

The plan identifies six strategic areas in which efforts to achieve the stated vision are to be focused: land use and public facilities, natural resources of regional significance, economic development, regional transportation, affordable housing, and emergency preparedness. As figure 3.2 indicates, each of these strategic elements is tied to livability, sustainability, and competitiveness. For each strategic area, the plan identifies trends and conditions, strategic regional goals, benchmarks and indicators, regional policies, and implementation strategies.

One strategic regional goal views sustainable land use patterns as those that reduce exposure to natural hazards (South Florida Regional Planning Council 1995, p. 47):

> Achieve long term efficient and sustainable development patterns by guiding new development and redevelopment within the region to areas which are most intrinsically suited for development, including areas (1) which are least exposed to coastal storm surges; (2) where negative impacts on the natural environment will be minimal; and (3) where public facilities and services already exist, are programmed or, on an aggregate basis, can be provided most economically.

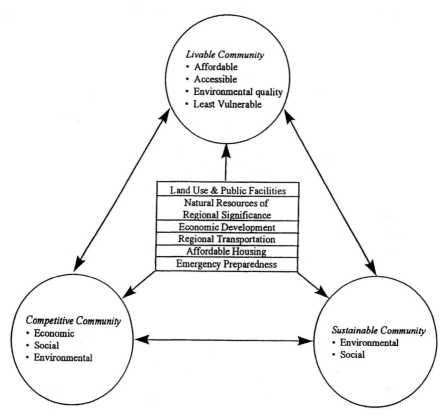

Figure 3.2. Overall Regional Vision and Strategic Subject Areas. *Source:* South Florida Regional Planning Council 1995.

To assess success at achieving this goal, a specific benchmark or indicator is provided: "Increase the proportion of the region's population growth which occurs outside the category 3 hurricane evacuation area away from Natural Resources of Regional Significance, and in proximity to designated transportation corridors or within Transportation Concurrency Exception Areas" (p. 47).

In support of this goal, a number of policies are put forth recommending that local governments reduce densities on barrier islands and in Category 1 hurricane evacuation areas; reduce densities in Category 3 evacuation areas to no greater than the current densities; restrict development of environmentally sensitive lands; and divert future development and redevelopment to areas where infrastructure already exists.

Other strategic regional goals and policies seek, for example, to revi-

talize deteriorating urban areas, protect and restore the Everglades and natural resources of regional significance, develop more efficient and sustainable allocation of water, and achieve a coordinated transportation system in the region. These are many of the strategies typically discussed under the heading of sustainable communities. As noted earlier, emergency preparedness is one of the six strategic areas addressed in the plan, and a number of regional goals and specific benchmarks and policies address various aspects of preparedness in South Florida, further giving form to the vision of a livable, sustainable, and competitive South Florida (South Florida Regional Planning Council 1995, pp. 137–153).

Several other long-range planning projects have potential for influencing the safety of residents in South Florida and for realizing the interconnectedness of the issues of growth management, sustainability, and ecosystem management. One such initiative is the Governor's Commission for a Sustainable South Florida (created by Executive Order 94-54), which recently issued its initial report (1996). In the words of the report: "We are confident that working together to build on South Florida's tremendous assets—its human, natural, and economic resources—we can reverse the negative trends and create sustainable communities that are safe, prosperous and beautiful. Sustainable communities are those that believe today's growth must not be achieved at tomorrow's expense" (pp. 21–22). The report's objectives focus on sustainably managing water, preventing pollution, controlling the spread of exotic species, containing urban development and promoting urban infill, and enhancing quality of life (e.g., education and affordable housing).

Many of the commission's recommendations involve understanding, protecting, and restoring key South Florida ecosystems, including the Everglades. Several other federal and state initiatives have similarly sought to improve ecosystem restoration and management in South Florida, notably the South Florida Ecosystem Restoration (Federal Interagency) Task Force and the state's ten-year Save Our Everglades program. These efforts have proposed actions to restore the hydrological and other functions of the region's ecosystem and to protect (e.g., through accelerated land acquisition) remaining undeveloped lands (see Metzger, Regalado, and Schneider 1995; South Florida Ecosystem Restoration Working Group 1994). Restoring the integrity of the Everglades ecosystem will help preserve South Florida's resilience to hurricanes and coastal storms as well as achieve a number of other important goals, such as protecting the natural capital on which the tourist economy increasingly relies. Mangrove die-off and wetlands loss, for instance, are indicative of an environment less able to mitigate naturally the forces of a hurricane.

Recovery and Mitigation in a
Multicultural, Multilingual Environment

South Florida is a complex mosaic of different cultures, with different cultural reference points and populations speaking different languages. Hurricane Andrew demonstrated that efforts to plan for and respond to such major disaster events must be sensitive to these cultural and linguistic differences. The implications are most obvious in preparedness and response (e.g., the need to communicate evacuation notices in multiple languages through multiple media), but they are important in recovery and mitigation as well.

Serious questions of fairness and equity also emerge in this multicultural environment. Studies by Walter Peacock and his colleagues suggest that members of minority groups and the poor are less likely to succeed in gaining access to the disaster assistance system and receiving needed benefits after a disaster. They found that in Florida City, a predominantly black and Hispanic community, the percentage of applicants for individual and family grant programs was extremely low in comparison with that in other communities. The researchers speculate that the poor and members of minority groups may harbor little hope of receiving aid, believe that the system does not work for them, and, at least for some respondents, be afraid of drawing attention to themselves, as in the case of migratory farmworkers with questionable documentation. The researchers also point to a confusing and complex application process and the need for "a considerable amount of savvy and perseverance to successfully work through the bureaucracy to obtain a grant," as with the confusing requirement that one must apply to the Small Business Administration before qualifying for FEMA grants. Transportation to disaster assistance centers probably was also a problem for many members of disadvantaged communities. For all these reasons, poor and minority communities are less likely to be able to take advantage of disaster assistance programs (Dash, Peacock, and Morrow 1997).

Peacock's research also found discrepancies at the community level. For example, Florida City received less aid than did its more affluent neighbor, Homestead. Even though Florida City was more severely affected by Hurricane Andrew, it was less able to deal effectively with recovery issues and less able to push for recovery and redevelopment monies. The community's lower capability to "mobilize" for recovery resulted in its receiving much less redevelopment aid than Homestead.

Taken together, these differences in household and community recovery lead Peacock and his colleagues to suggest changes in the way aid is distributed following disasters, including the need to target low-income

and socially vulnerable neighborhoods for mitigation assistance and to use special methods to reach these groups, such as door-to-door canvassing or a community-based center (Dash, Peacock, and Morrow 1997).

Federal Versus State Allocation of Disaster Aid

One striking aspect of the Hurricane Andrew experience is the length of FEMA's delays in providing funding for state and local mitigation projects. As of our interview with Dade County's hazard mitigation coordinator in the fall of 1995, the county had received only a small fraction of the approved funding. Of Section 404 funds, only an estimated $1.4 million, out of the approximately $15 million available, had been dispensed. For Section 406 projects, only $1.6 million of an allowable $350 million had been dispensed. Local officials were critical of the way mitigation monies were distributed and believed there must be a more effective method. What are the implications of these delays from a mitigation perspective? In some cases mitigation opportunities are probably lost. In other cases, mitigation projects (e.g., retrofitting of airport hangars) can indeed be carried out productively many months after the storm.

Another issue involved disagreements about projects' eligibility under Section 404. State officials expressed frustration that FEMA chose not to fund or approve some projects that, in their view, clearly met the Section 404 funding criteria. They were also critical of the fact that FEMA did not more clearly indicate, at least following Hurricane Andrew, which specific types of projects were eligible. Several state officials interviewed cited the example of warning systems and communications projects. FEMA chose not to fund these projects even though they appear to be eligible under Section 404 regulations.

A related issue involved the state's flexibility to creatively combine different sources of funding. Florida needs an immense amount of funding for current and future mitigation as well as the capacity to leverage and maximize existing funds and find other sources of funding. State officials indicate recent Hurricane Opal as a case in point. Twenty million dollars was available in funds from the Hazard Mitigation Grant Program (HMGP), but the buyout program along the flooded Imperial River alone will cost $11 million. The state cannot afford to expend such a large proportion of its mitigation monies on one project, so other sources must be found.

Federal officials are not always sensitive to the states' needs to mix and match program funding. First, programs such as the HMGP and the Community Development Block Grant (CDBG) program have quite different regulations and program requirements, which creates obstacles to

combining funding from the two sources. In addition, discretionary decisions by federal officials are sometimes unsupportive. Florida mitigation staff cited an example of a CDBG-funded buyout program (following the flooding associated with Tropical Storm Alberto) for which the state had hoped to be able to fund demolition through the HMGP. However, FEMA disapproved the use of Section 404 funds because the project was not considered to be an HMGP project.

The Immensity of Managing Postdisaster Reconstruction

When we asked officials from the Metro-Dade County Building and Zoning Department whether the building stock was safer and stronger than before Hurricane Andrew, we were surprised that they indicated it was not. Indeed, we heard from several people that many of the construction mistakes made before Andrew had largely been repeated in rebuilding. The size and magnitude of recovery and rebuilding in Andrew meant that the county was faced with a Herculean task in inspecting and monitoring reconstruction to ensure that it was up to code and to police against unlicensed contractors. But the challenges of regulating and managing the massive rebuilding—some 107,000 homes damaged; more than 200,000 building permits issued by the county in the first year—were clearly daunting (Metro-Dade County Planning Department 1993b).

The county did establish satellite permitting offices after the storm, and it has adopted other measures to strengthen its enforcement and inspection process. For instance, it has substantially increased the number of inspectors on staff.

One lesson learned from the experience of Hurricane Andrew, however, is that future disasters will very likely dwarf the building control and inspection system and the county and other jurisdictions will need to develop more effective strategies and procedures for ensuring code compliance. If not, rather than working to gradually strengthen the housing stock, hurricanes and coastal storm events may actually serve to diminish its strength and resilience.

Growing Fragmentation of Local Government

Hurricane Andrew had an emotional and psychological effect on people, influencing their feelings about whether public officials were listening to them and looking out for their interests. Many perceived that their voices were not heard and their needs were not adequately considered in the recovery process.

Although the situation is difficult to evaluate empirically, many believe that these feelings have accelerated efforts to incorporate new cities in South Florida, further fracturing and fragmenting local government there. There are currently twenty-seven municipalities in Dade County, but several communities have begun the process of incorporation. The push for incorporation is a result of a number of factors, including the belief by many residents that they are not getting sufficient services for the taxes they pay and a desire for greater local autonomy. However, many disaster preparedness and mitigation issues, such as evacuation and sheltering, are clearly regional in nature, requiring regional strategies. The proliferation of local governments will make it more difficult to plan for and reduce risks associated with hurricanes and coastal storms.

Evacuation and Sheltering Issues

Florida has a serious problem in protecting people from future storm events. The combination of dramatic population growth and the concentration of development along high-risk coastlines means that the state must increasingly look for ways to get people out of harm's way.

The state is also faced with the difficult task of sheltering people during storms and is seriously addressing the issue. As noted earlier, recent studies show significant and growing shelter deficits in the state. The 1993 report of the Governor's Disaster Planning and Response Review Committee included a number of recommendations concerning evacuation and sheltering and led to the passage of House Bill 911, in turn imposing new mitigation requirements on many state agencies. Recall that among the shelter-related provisions of H.B. 911 were a requirement that the Florida Division of Emergency Management add a shelter component to the state Comprehensive Emergency Management Plan to address sheltering needs in the state; a requirement that no region in the state have a shelter deficit by 1998; and a requirement that all new educational facilities be built to stronger wind and storm standards.

The state Department of Education has proposed school design standards that would require each new school to have an Enhanced Hurricane Protection Area or hurricane protection pod within it. More stringent strengthening requirements were resisted by local education officials because of the likely effect on the cost of new schools (the requirements were originally estimated to add about 10 percent to the cost). This issue pitted two important public values against each other—safety of children versus necessary expenditures for other aspects of a quality education, such as books and educational equipment. In a period of fiscal austerity, such choices are especially difficult. The more limited requirement for

hurricane safety pods represented a compromise—hurricane shelters would still be provided in schools but at a significantly lower cost; the pods are estimated to raise the cost of new schools by only 2 percent.

It is likely that a similar debate will occur over design standards that create sheltering capability for residential structures. The *Strategic Regional Policy Plan for South Florida* directs local governments to revise their building codes to require a "safe room" in all new structures outside storm surge areas and to provide incentives to encourage retrofitting of existing structures (South Florida Regional Planning Council 1995).

Evacuation is a related concern in Florida, and as populations increase, evacuation clearance times rise. As indicated by table 3.2, clearance times are very high in South Florida, especially for larger hurricane events. For Category 3–5 storms, evacuation clearance times range from 27.75 hours in Dade County to 41.75 hours in Monroe County. One approach is to accept the fact that not enough roads can be built to keep up with growth and development, especially in Florida's coastal counties (between 1990 and 1993 alone, the population of Florida coastal counties grew by more than 350,000); and thus alternatives, namely sheltering, are essential. The state has been exploring ways to improve evacuation, however, and the Department of Community Affairs has initiated a five-year phased process to develop a statewide evacuation management strategy (Florida Department of Community Affairs 1996a).

Property Rights and Hazard Mitigation

Mitigation planners in Florida must confront concerns by some citizens that government actions unduly restrict private property rights. Local planners cited a recent state law as a potential obstacle to implementing more stringent hazard reduction measures, especially land use and local planning requirements. The Florida Property Rights Act of 1995, commonly known as the Harris Act, is one of a number of state laws around the country intended to address the perceived inequities of overzealous land use and environmental regulators (for a discussion and review of the Harris Act, see Powell, Rhodes, and Stengle 1995). Although it is not a "takings" law per se, the act provides a process by which landowners may seek relief if they believe that a new law creates an "inordinate burden" for them. To be eligible for relief, a landowner must have a vested development right and be proposing a land use activity that is compatible with surrounding uses. A judge must also find that the proposed use is in the public interest. If the judge finds that the threshold conditions are met and the restriction represents an inordinate burden, two outcomes can occur: the judge may

either direct that the proposed use be allowed or order that the landowner be compensated.

At first blush, this law appears to represent a significant obstacle to hazard mitigation. If local governments, such as that of Metro-Dade County, wish to modify their land use regulations to reduce permissible densities in high-risk locations such as coastal high-hazard areas, it is conceivable that such actions could be deemed an inordinate burden and compensation (or allowance of the use) would be ordered. The obstacles posed by this law, however, may be less real than thought. Jim Murley, secretary of the Florida Department of Community Affairs, believes that the process is reasonable and one in which a finding of inordinate burden will be unusual. Indeed, so far the provision has not been used, and there have been no cases of landowners seeking relief.

More significant, however, may be the symbolic and perceptual effects of this law. However unlikely adverse determinations may be, we found local planners uneasy about the law, and it could lessen the stringency of mitigation efforts in Florida.

Recent Initiatives and Future Directions in Florida

Much changed in Florida following Hurricane Andrew. Andrew was a stiff wake-up call that highlighted the inherent vulnerability of the state and the inadequacies of the existing disaster planning and mitigation system. Since Andrew, the state has experienced additional coastal disasters, including the winter storm of 1993 and Hurricane Opal, which struck the Florida Panhandle in October 1995. These disasters, along with Andrew, have further stimulated the state to change the way it plans for and responds to hurricanes and storms. These changes suggest that Florida not only is moving in the right direction but also is on the cutting edge in state efforts to plan for and mitigate natural hazards.

One change involves the method of establishing postdisaster mitigation priorities. Florida has followed FEMA's lead in replacing the Interagency Hazard Mitigation Team process, an often cumbersome process involving a number of different agencies, with a more streamlined postdisaster process. The new process involves a much smaller team and preparation of a "strategy paper." This allows the state to focus on a limited number of strategic mitigation actions following a disaster and to act on them more expeditiously. The old approach was seen as involving too many people and generating long recommendation wish lists, many of which were

either infeasible or technically flawed. Moreover, participants in the old process often represented a narrow range of interests.

Florida also now has a meaningful Section 409 plan, and the strategy papers are viewed as flowing from and giving more precise meaning to this plan. In this way, the state is moving in the direction of a more effective and integrated system of mitigation policy whereby strategy papers and other, more specific disaster-related decisions implement the broader state mitigation plan. So far, two strategy papers have been prepared and the state has gone through the new process twice—for Hurricane Opal and for Tropical Storm Erin. With Hurricane Opal, the strategy paper was influential in setting the major mitigation priorities for the event, giving priority, for example, to land acquisition and elevation.

Another significant reform is the development of a Performance Partnership Agreement (PPA) with FEMA. The state signed its PPA on August 10, 1995; it covers a five-year period, continuing through September 30, 2000. The PPA, which gives the state greater flexibility in using its federal monies, contains a series of pre- and postevent goals and state-specific objectives. Regarding mitigation, for example, the state agrees to "update and maintain an all-hazards multi-objective strategic mitigation plan" and to "develop and maintain . . . a comprehensive program of education, awareness and outreach on mitigation for public and private sectors to reduce risks" (FEMA 1995, p. 4). Under the agreement, performance by the state could mean greater financial resources and technical support and more flexibility in the way it uses these monies. The agreement states that following a disaster event, if it is determined that the state has made progress toward its objectives, FEMA "will reward the state with incentives that might include increased flexibility and more favorable cost-shares" (FEMA 1995, p. 11).

There is also substantial support at the upper levels of state government to extend these reforms even further. During the interviews we conducted for this case study, the current director of the Division of Emergency Management (DEM), Joe Myers, described with great enthusiasm how the state's future mitigation efforts will be more creative and effective. In the near future, Myers said, Florida's Section 409 plan "will become radically different." Among the ideas Myers spoke of are finding more flexible ways to combine federal funding for mitigation (e.g., combining CDBG, EDA, FEMA, and other funds); exploring more effective ways to leverage state funds; and employing ideas such as the "global match," which would allow the state (with FEMA's approval) to apply mitigation expenditures toward the match required in subsequent disaster events.

Upcoming regulatory changes in the mitigation grants program were

greeted with enthusiasm by Myers and other state officials. Again, they saw these as giving states greater flexibility in crafting their own mitigation programs and strategies. Among the changes seen as positive are those allowing the use of mitigation monies in nondeclared communities, permitting a set-aside for special projects, and allowing funds to be shifted from one disaster to another.

Florida has expanded its emergency management capacity at both the state and local levels. There are currently 185 employees in the Division of Emergency Management (DEM), and most counties now have three or four emergency management staff members. In part, this is a result of the funding mechanisms the state has put in place. The state's Emergency Management Preparedness and Assistance Trust Fund (EMPATF), for instance, generates about $14 million per year, of which 60 percent was to fund state and local emergency management personnel. Despite this expanded workforce, however, major problems still exist, such as the perennial difficulty of coordinating local emergency management and growth management.

Since Hurricane Andrew, state and local governments in Florida have improved their ability to respond to disaster events. Major improvements have been made in emergency communication and geographic information systems. The DEM has also instituted Rapid Impact Assessment Teams, which should significantly enhance the response to future disasters.

The state is also attempting to create incentives for local governments to reduce the costs of disasters. Counties, for instance, can obtain additional base grant funding from the EMPATF if they maintain a full-time emergency management program, and funding is also available to municipalities that establish programs (FEMA 1995). Moreover, local governments are eligible for additional emergency management funds if they sign the statewide mutual aid agreement. If localities choose not to participate in such agreements there will be major financial ramifications; for example, they will have to contribute a greater share of matching funds in the event of a disaster. The state has served as coordinator and broker for these local agreements. All but six counties have agreed to participate, and the resulting system of mutual aid agreements should both enhance the effectiveness of disaster response and reduce the long-term cost of disasters.

The Florida Department of Community Affairs has prepared a five-year strategic plan that gives high priority to disaster planning. Titled *Building Partnerships for Successful Communities,* the plan describes trends and conditions as well as existing and future vulnerabilities and lays out goals, objectives, and implementation strategies for addressing disasters. The plan indicates the state's intention to move toward an all-hazards approach and to place high priority on integrated mitigation management (IMM), which

"recognizes that hazard mitigation is a process that must cross all areas of traditional and nontraditional emergency management if it is to be effective in reducing our vulnerability to all hazards" (Florida Department of Community Affairs 1996a, p. 37). Its implementation targets are pegged to specific years: "By October 1996, 100 percent of counties will develop procedures to perform rapid needs and damage assessments . . . by December 1998, increase the number of identified county shelter spaces by 225,000 in order to eliminate the statewide shelter deficit" (p. 39). Implementation strategies relate to goals and objectives, have dates attached, and are largely quantifiable and measurable. Whether the plan is actually utilized is unclear, but the content suggests both a commitment to disaster planning by this important agency and strategic thinking and guidance about what needs to be done.

Florida has been a leader in other important areas of long-term loss reduction as well. Especially impressive are its efforts in acquiring and setting aside land. Florida's tradition of land acquisition dates back to the 1972 Environmental Land and Water Management Act. Most acquisition funding is now provided through the Preservation 2000 program in a series of state bond measures that result in approximately $300 million for land acquisition each year. These bonds are financed through a state real estate documentary stamp fee. Of the acquisition funds available each year, 50 percent go to the Conservation and Recreation Lands program (CARL), 30 percent go to Save Our Rivers, 10 percent go to the Florida Communities Trust, and the remainder goes to assorted other local and state programs. By law, 20 percent of CARL's funds must be used to purchase coastal properties. Although hazard mitigation is not a key objective of these programs, Florida residents and property are clearly safer as a result. One particularly impressive acquisition project involved the purchase of some sixty miles of coastline and coastal wetlands in the Big Bend area of the state (Dixie and Taylor Counties). Here, substantial coastal development in a very hazardous area has essentially been precluded through the program.

The effectiveness of these acquisition efforts can be expanded by leveraging and coordination with other acquisition "partners." The CARL program, for example, provides local governments with a 50 percent match for acquisition of environmental land (CARL will provide 50 percent of the cost of acquiring land under an approved program). So far, some eighteen localities have passed bond referenda to fund such acquisitions. Dade County has raised as much as $90 million, and Palm Beach County has raised $100 million. This illustrates the ability of local governments to make the sacrifices necessary to acquire land and habitat. Acquisition of land, these localities are finding, is politically feasible and popular with the public.

The state has also taken the lead in planning for a connected and integrated system of protected lands—a system that could simultaneously achieve a number of state and local objectives, including reduction in vulnerability to natural disasters. Two notable recent examples include preparation of a statewide "gap analysis" and a proposal for a state greenways system. The former, prepared by the Florida Game and Fresh Water Fish Commission, involved the use of a statewide geographic information system (GIS) to identify areas important for habitat and biodiversity conservation but not currently protected by the current system of parks and conservation areas (thus the identification of "gaps"). The result of the study is a statewide map showing existing conservation areas and identifying "strategic habitat conservation areas" to be given acquisition priority in the future (Cox et al. 1994). Similarly, a statewide greenways system has been proposed, to build on existing parks and protected lands and provide a statewide system of green spaces. In 1995, the state legislature created the Florida Greenways Coordinating Council to coordinate greenway projects and to prepare a five-year greenways implementation plan (Henderson, Drake, and Ross 1995). These efforts extend Florida's reputation as a leader in the area of land acquisition. They also suggest the promise of integrating hazard vulnerability into such statewide plans and of securing a statewide pattern of land use and settlement that at once protects biological and ecological integrity and reduces vulnerability and exposure to natural disasters.

Conclusions and Recommendations

Prior to Hurricane Andrew in 1992, South Florida had been living on borrowed time. The region had not suffered a major hurricane strike in almost thirty years. During this period, population growth had ballooned and the amount of development at risk had risen dramatically. Andrew exposed significant deficiencies in the ways South Florida had protected itself and revealed a population much more vulnerable to hurricane and storm forces than previously thought. This chapter highlighted a number of these deficiencies, most notably limitations in the South Florida Building Code and the procedures and mechanisms through which the code was enforced. Andrew focused attention on a number of important issues, including, among many others, the state's sheltering and evacuation capability, insurance system, mitigation assistance framework, and efforts to manage growth and redevelopment to reduce exposure to hazards.

Much can be learned from the rebuilding and recovery process following Hurricane Andrew, as well as from an understanding of the ways in

which the entire mitigation context in Florida has evolved and improved since Andrew. A number of important conclusions and recommendations can be offered:

- *Accelerate the HMGP process.* The state of Florida did not have a usable Section 409 hazard mitigation plan until some twenty-one months after Hurricane Andrew. FEMA must ensure that future plans are completed in a more timely fashion and be prepared to impose financial and other penalties for failure to do so. The process for funding hazard mitigation grant projects must be substantially expedited. Even though Andrew struck in August 1992, formal approval letters for projects did not go out until May 1994, and as late as 1996 FEMA had disbursed only a relatively small amount of HMGP funds. Having an approved state Section 409 plan certainly would have helped, but the Andrew case demonstrates a strong need to streamline the HMGP process.

- *Encourage more coordinated local approaches.* Rather than responding to a wish list of possible mitigation activities and projects, the state's recent effort at preparing a strategy paper after disaster events should be followed in the future.

- *Provide continuing flexible funding.* The Florida case study illustrates the importance of steady sources of funding for recovery as well as for long-term mitigation and emergency management. Florida's H.B. 911 legislation, creating a dedicated source of emergency management funding, is commendable and should be emulated by other states. Additionally, the magnitude of mitigation expenses often requires states to mix and match funding from different federal programs. States should be given greater flexibility to do this, and the federal government should make program requirements consistent or at least eliminate unnecessary obstacles to combining funds.

- *Develop incentives for local government participation.* Florida provides clear monetary incentives to local governments to develop permanent emergency management and mitigation capability and to participate in the statewide system of mutual aid (and provides disincentives for not participating). The state should continue to develop this system of incentives, and other states should consider emulating Florida's creative approach.

- *Strengthen building code standards and enforcement.* South Florida jurisdictions should continue to improve South Florida Building Code standards and their enforcement. The state should help localities develop enforcement capabilities and should consider a building code certifica-

tion process. The Hurricane Andrew experience supports the concept, in experimental use by the insurance industry, of tying insurance premiums to enforcement certification. All parties involved in the construction process, including the ultimate housing consumer, should be encouraged to accept responsibility for structural safety. Targeted education programs will be important in achieving this objective.

- *Bolster state hazard insurance provisions.* Florida's insurance system remains vulnerable in the aftermath of Hurricane Andrew, and the state must continue to take actions to strengthen it. Many recommendations of the Academic Task Force on Hurricane Catastrophic Insurance are sound and sensible and should be acted on.

- *Build mitigation into land use plans.* Florida's system of state-regional-local planning and growth management has the potential to prevent or minimize development in high-risk locations. Yet to strengthen implementation, the state should take steps to improve the system. It should require preparation of postdisaster redevelopment plans as part of the local coastal element. It should clarify the system of regulatory and planning boundaries it employs. It should help localities find ways to promote compact growth patterns while reducing or halting development in high-risk hazard zones.

- *Acquire land in high-risk locations.* Florida illustrates the comprehensive benefits of land acquisition through its greenways and habitat conservation programs, including the potential of a statewide system of protected lands to incorporate floodplains and other high-risk locations. Both pre- and postdisaster acquisition are endorsed as a mitigation strategy in a number of documents, including the state Section 409 hazard mitigation plan. Florida is unusually well positioned to extend its exemplary efforts in land acquisition to address hazard mitigation, and it should do so.

- *Keep high-density development and critical facilities out of hazard areas.* Metro-Dade County should continue to hold the line on increases in density and intensity of development in the Coastal High Hazard Area and other high-risk locations. Its proposed changes to the Comprehensive Development Master Plan should help by eliminating the seasonal occupancy loophole. The county should also continue to prohibit the siting of critical facilities in high-risk locations, especially the CHHA.

- *Prevent reconstruction in hazard areas.* Local governments should enforce the substantial improvement provisions of their floodplain ordinances, and FEMA should nullify its more lenient "replacement value" stan-

dard. This standard permits reconstruction of homes that remain vulnerable to future flooding and fails to take advantage of the opportunity to strengthen the building stock. New mechanisms and strategies are needed to fund elevation or financially assist in elevation when the substantial improvement standard is enforced.

- *Focus mitigation funding on sustainable development.* Much of the funding after Hurricane Andrew promoted long-term economic development. It is questionable whether this should be a primary role of government, especially the federal government, following such an event. A greater effort should be made to link these economic development projects to hazard mitigation and to the creation of a safer, more sustainable pattern of development.

- *Explore alternative mitigation strategies.* The situation of South Florida, where a large and growing urban population lies in one of the country's most dangerous and hazard-prone areas, shows the need for creative mitigation strategies. Conventional evacuation remains an important strategy, but in the future it will not be possible to evacuate all or even most residents. Localities and states should explore reinforced "shelter pods" in schools and public buildings and reinforced "safe rooms" in individual houses.

- *Seek resiliency through ecosystem management.* Ecosystem management initiatives offer promise in maintaining a resilient natural environment in South Florida. Projects such as Jordan Commons also demonstrate that future development and redevelopment can be made more resilient in the face of hurricane forces while reducing other environmental demands and impacts (e.g., reducing energy and water consumption and utilizing solar energy).

- *Ensure equity in applying mitigation programs.* Special mitigation strategies are necessary to reach all groups and communities in a multicultural, multilingual region such as South Florida. Certain groups—minorities and the poor especially—may be at a serious disadvantage in gaining access to postdisaster assistance and mitigation programs. Special sensitivity to equity in disaster assistance and mitigation is needed, and special strategies, such as mitigation targeted to certain neighborhoods and based in the community, may also be necessary.

Florida Update

As of the summer of 1998, the Florida mitigation framework continues to evolve, with several new programs and initiatives started since our orig-

inal case study was prepared. A major new strategy called "Breaking the Cycle," also called Florida Long-Term Redevelopment, has been developed within the Department of Community Affairs (DCA), representing a collaboration between the Divisions of Housing/Community Development and Emergency Management. It reflects the recognition that too often Florida localities simply allow the same buildings to be rebuilt, in the same hazardous locations, equally vulnerable to the next event.

To implement this new agenda, several major programs have been developed, with the most important being a new Local Mitigation Strategy Initiative. Growing out of a recognition that many Florida localities are not prepared to effectively take advantage of postdisaster mitigation opportunities, including Section 404 funding, it is an effort to build this capacity in advance. According to Eric Poole, the Florida SHMO, the heart of the initiative is the provision of mitigation planning grants to all counties in the state (and to cities through the counties). Funds amounting to $8.2 million have already been made available through a combination of federal Section 404 funds (FEMA approved a special policy allowing the state to apply unused funds from previous disasters) and U.S. Department of Energy funds. Localities are provided technical assistance and Florida DEM has prepared a local mitigation manual to guide them in this mitigation planning. (The entire manual can be found at the Florida DEM web site: http://www.state.fl.us/comaff/DEM/.)

Another element of the Breaking the Cycle initiative is the Residential Construction Mitigation Program, which provides technical assistance and forgivable state loans for wind retrofits to homes. Three counties are participating under the pilot program: Monroe, Dade, and Palm Beach. Under the program, a "retrofit audit" is prepared for interested homeowners (much like an energy audit), evaluating the wind resistance of one's home and indicating needed improvements and their cost. Loans to cover the cost of these improvements are then offered by the state, and they become grants if the residents have not moved or sold their homes within a certain number of years.

The state is also participating in both FEMA's Project Impact and the Showcase Communities program of the Institute for Business and Home Safety (described in chapter 2). One pilot location in the state, involving a city and a county (Deerfield Beach and Broward County), has been designated under both programs and is serving as a laboratory for experimenting with a variety of new mitigation initiatives. DCA has one staff person dedicated solely to working on this project.

Many of the state-level plans and documents described in our original case study have been revised or updated. A new Section 409 state hazard mitigation plan was prepared in the fall of 1997 (called the State Hazard

Mitigation Strategy) and submitted to FEMA in December of that year. As of mid-1998, it had not yet been approved by FEMA. Major changes in the plan include more emphasis given to local vulnerability assessment and mitigation planning, reflecting the new local mitigation planning initiative.

Other recent updated documents include a revised five-year DCA Agency Strategic Plan: 1997–1998, a 1998 Florida Comprehensive Emergency Management Plan, and a 1997–1998 Performance Partnership Agreement with FEMA (with no significant changes, however, from the previous PPA). Also, the Florida Governor's Building Codes Study Commission issued their report in 1997 suggesting ways to improve the state's building code system. These documents are available and can be accessed through the DEM web site.

Recent state progress on a number of other disaster and mitigation planning fronts is documented in a DCA report (Florida Department of Community Affairs 1997). This report reviews progress made toward achieving the recommendations of the original Lewis Commission report following Hurricane Andrew. The report notes a number of areas of progress, including a major hurricane public awareness campaign; extensive evacuation planning by hospitals, nursing homes, and residential care facilities; improvements in evacuation planning and coordination at a number of governmental levels; promulgation of a new rule to implement shelter design requirements for public schools; and progress in implementing a building code enforcement rating system by the insurance industry.

The state of Florida continues to promote the notion of sustainability, especially at the local level. One important and unique initiative is the Florida Sustainable Communities Demonstration Project, a program emerging out of the Governor's Commission for Sustainable South Florida. Under the program, designated pilot communities develop programs and initiatives for becoming more sustainable. They specifically agree to pursue a set of six sustainability principles and enter into a written agreement with DCA indicating the specific initiatives or programs they will focus on. An incentive for communities is that once an agreement is signed they will be relieved of certain state and regional permitting review.

The program has already been very popular. Twenty-eight localities applied for designation under the first round, from which five were chosen: Boca Raton, Martin County, Ocala, Orlando, and Tampa/Hillsborough County (as joint applicant). Two of these five pilot communities, Martin County and the city of Boca Raton, specifically plan to address hazard mitigation as part of their sustainability initiatives. Also, many of the other community initiatives have potential implications for reducing

natural hazards (e.g., those in the areas of environmental protection and conservation, ecosystem management, and containment of sprawl).

In addition, to take advantage of the interest of those communities not chosen in the first round, DCA has established the Florida Sustainable Communities Network. Participation in the network occurs through the adoption of a local resolution indicating the intention to strive to become a sustainable community. Activities of the network include intensive workshops and the sharing of information and experiences among localities. A Florida Sustainable Communities Center has been established on the Internet to facilitate this (http://sustainable.state.fl.us/).

Note

1. This chapter is based on a case study conducted by Timothy Beatley and David Brower, who interviewed state and local mitigation officials concerning mitigation after Hurricane Andrew.

References

Academic Task Force on Hurricane Catastrophic Insurance. 1995. *Final Report: Restoring Florida's Paradise.* Tallahassee, Fla.: Collins Center for Public Policy.

Brower, David J., and Susan E. Hass. 1995. "Pre-Event Planning for Post-Disaster Recovery and Reconstruction: The Hurricane Andrew Experience in South Dade County." August. Chapel Hill: Center for Urban and Regional Studies, University of North Carolina.

Catalano, Peter. 1995. "Hurricane Alert." *Popular Science,* September, 65–70.

Citizens' Advisory Committee on Coastal Resources Management. 1993. *1993 Annual Report: Report to the Governor on the Florida Coastal Management Programs.* Tallahassee, Fla.: Citizens' Advisory Committee on Coastal Resoures Management.

Colden, Ann. 1995. "Regulators Address Disaster Insurance: Recent Natural Catastrophes Have Created Havoc in the Industry." *Washington Post,* September 16, F6.

Cox, James, Randy Kautz, Maureen MacLaughlin, and Terry Gilbert. 1994. *Closing the Gaps in Florida's Wildlife Habitat Conservation System.* Tallahassee, Fla.: Florida Game and Fresh Water Fish Commission.

Dade County Grand Jury. 1992. *Final Report of the Dade County Grand Jury, Circuit Court of the Eleventh Judicial Circuit of Florida in and for the County of Dade, Spring Term A.D. 1992.* December 14.

———. 1993. *Final Report of the Dade County Grand Jury, Circuit Court of the Eleventh Judicial Circuit of Florida in and for the County of Dade, Fall Term A.D. 1992.* August 4.

Dade County Metropolitan Planning Organization. 1995. *Transportation System Hurricane Emergency Preparedness Study.* July. Report prepared for Dade County Metropolitan Planning Organization and Office of Emergency Management by Post, Buckley, Schuh, and Jernigan, Inc. Miami: Dade County MPO.

Dash, Nicole, Walter Gillis Peacock, and Betty Hearn Morrow. 1997. "And the Poor Get Poorer: A Neglected Black Community." In *Hurricane Andrew: Ethnicity, Gender, and the Sociology of Disasters,* ed. Walter Gillis Peacock, Betty Hearn Morrow, and Hugh Gladwin. New York: Routledge.

FAU/FIU (Florida Atlantic University/Florida International University Joint Center for Environmental and Urban Problems). 1996. "Excerpts from the Initial Report of the Governor's Commission for a Sustainable South Florida." *Environment and Urban Affairs* 23 (winter): 19–30.

FEMA (Federal Emergency Management Agency). 1992a. *Building Performance: Hurricane Andrew in Florida.* December 21. Washington, D.C.: FEMA.

———. 1992b. *Report of the Hurricane Andrew Interagency Hazard Mitigation Team.* Washington, D.C.: FEMA

———. 1993. *Interagency Hazard Mitigation Team Report.* Washington, D.C.: FEMA

———. 1995. *Performance Partnership Agreement for Emergency Management Between the State of Florida and the United States of America.* August 10. Washington, D.C.: FEMA.

———. 1997. *Report on Costs and Benefits of Natural Hazard Mitigation.* Washington, D.C.: FEMA.

Florida Department of Community Affairs. 1996a. *Building Partnerships for Successful Communities: Agency Strategic Plan for Fiscal Years 1995–96 Through 2000–01.* Tallahassee.: Florida Department of Community Affairs.

———. 1996b. *State Hazard Mitigation Grant Program 404 Current Status for 952-DR-FL, 955-DR-FL, 966-DR-FL, and 982-DR-FL, as of March 29.* Tallahassee: Florida Department of Community Affairs.

———. 1997. *Final Update—Governor's Committee on Disaster Planning and Response Review.* July. Tallahassee: Florida Department of Community Affairs.

Florida Division of Emergency Management. 1994. *State of Florida Hazard Mitigation Plan.* July 20 (approved May 12). Tallahassee: Florida Department of Community Affairs.

———. 1995. *Shelter Study.* Tallahassee: Florida Department of Community Affairs.

Godschalk, David R., David J. Brower, and Timothy Beatley. 1989. *Catastrophic Coastal Storms: Hazard Mitigation and Development Management.* Durham, N.C.: Duke University Press.

Governor's Committee (Governor's Disaster Planning and Response Review Committee). 1993. *Final Report.* January. Tallahassee, Fla.: Governor's Office.

Henderson, Clay, Debbie Drake, and Jamie Ross. 1995. "1995 Legislative Session Update." *Environmental and Urban Affairs,* fall, 1–6.

Metro-Dade County Planning Department. 1988. *Comprehensive Development Master Plan.* Miami: Metro-Dade County Planning Department.

———.1993a. *Dade County Hazard Mitigation Addendum.* May. Miami: Metro-Dade County Planning Department.

———. 1993b. *Economic Recovery Strategies. Phase II: Long-Term Strategies.* October. Report prepared by Management and Consulting Services. Miami: Metro-Dade County Planning Department.

———. 1995. *Evaluation and Appraisal Report for the Coastal Management Element.* Miami: Metro-Dade County Planning Department.

———. 1996. *November 1995–1996 Cycle Applications to Amend the Comprehensive Development Master Plan.* March. Miami: Metro-Dade County Planning Department.

Metzger, Patricia, Nanciann Regalado, and Martin A. Schneider. 1995. "Spotlight on the Everglades." *Environmental and Urban Affairs* 22 (2): 9–12.

Pielke, Roger A., Jr. 1995. *Hurricane Andrew in South Florida: Mesoscale Weather and Societal Responses.* Boulder, Colo.: National Center for Atmospheric Research.

Powell, David L., Robert M. Rhodes, and Dan R. Stengle. 1995. "Florida's New Law to Protect Private Property Rights." *Environmental and Urban Affairs,* fall, 10–19.

South Florida Ecosystem Restoration Working Group. 1994. *Annual Report.* December 2. Miami: Florida International University, South Florida Ecosystem Restoration Task Force.

South Florida Regional Planning Council. 1995. *Strategic Regional Policy Plan for South Florida.* August. Hollywood, Fla.: South Florida Regional Planning Council.

Persons Interviewed

State of Florida

Greg Brock, director, Conservation and Recreation Lands program
Dan Evans, Hazard Mitigation Grant Program manager
Charles Lanza, Division of Emergency Management
Mike Loehr, Hurricane Planning Division
James Murley, secretary, Florida Department of Community Affairs
Joe Myers, director, Florida Division of Emergency Management
Eric Poole, state hazard mitigation officer
Marc Roger, Hazard Mitigation Grant Program
Dennis Smith, mitigation planner
Leroy Thomas, mitigation planner

Local Government and Private Sector

Bert Castro, Team Metro
Debbie Curtain, Team Metro
Charlie Danger, Building Code Compliance Office, Dade County
Teresita Garcia, Bermello Ajamilas Partners, Inc.
Maureen Gregg, Metro-Dade County Planning Department
Patricia Metzger, assistant director of research, Florida Atlantic University/Florida International University Joint Center for Environmental and Urban Problems
Elizabeth Ogden, FEMA grants contract coordination officer, Dade County
Gil Scott, planning director, City of Homestead
Charles Speight, director, Flood Program
Ron Szep, Metro-Dade County Building and Zoning Department

CHAPTER 4

Missouri After the Midwest Floods of 1993

This chapter examines hazard mitigation influences, planning, procedures, and effectiveness in Missouri following the Midwest floods of 1993. It describes the disaster, evaluates Missouri's Section 409 hazard mitigation plan, and assesses the state's hazard mitigation planning and implementation process as well as results of its mitigation efforts, principally its buyout program. Finally, the chapter identifies key issues of the Missouri case study and offers some conclusions and recommendations.[1]

The Disaster Events

The Midwest floods of 1993 were a series of prolonged flood events that occurred from early 1993 through the spring of the following year (SEMA 1994a). Unusual weather patterns produced unprecedented rainfall and runoff throughout the midwestern United States. Nine states were principally affected: Illinois, Iowa, Kansas, Minnesota, Missouri, Nebraska, North Dakota, South Dakota, and Wisconsin. Missouri alone received four presidential disaster declarations within twelve months. As the site of the convergence of two of the largest river systems in the country—the upper Mississippi and the Missouri—the state experienced some of the Midwest's heaviest and most damaging flooding.

The flooding in Missouri began after several extended periods of heavy rainfall, first in July, September, and November 1992 and later from January through July 1993. The first disaster declaration covered the period of April 15 through May 29, 1993, and provided individual assistance for eight Mississippi River counties in the eastern part of the state, centered on the St. Louis–St. Charles area (disaster designation FEMA-989-DR-MO).

Photo 4.1. House Surrounded by Floodwaters (Missouri). Courtesy of the American Red Cross.

A second disaster declaration came in the summer of 1993, covering the period of June 10 through October 25 (FEMA-995-DR-MO). Because of saturated ground and extremely heavy rainfall during this long-term flood event, 102 Missouri counties and 3 cities were declared federal disaster areas eligible for individual assistance, and 88 counties and 3 cities were declared eligible for public assistance. The heaviest devastation occurred in communities along the Mississippi and Missouri Rivers. More than 30,000 state residents were evacuated during the summer of 1993 as nightly television news reports focused the entire country's attention on the crisis in Missouri and the rest of the Midwest. Twenty-one deaths in Missouri were attributed to this round of flooding.

Another major wave of flooding in November, prompted by heavy rains and saturated soils, triggered a third disaster declaration covering the period of November 13–19, 1993 (FEMA-1006-DR-MO). Confined primarily to the south-central and southeastern part of the state, this declaration provided individual assistance for 24 counties and public assistance for 14 counties. The state's crisis continued the following spring, when severe rains and flash flooding in April and May 1994 prompted a fourth disaster declaration, this time making 17 counties and the city of St. Louis eligible for individual assistance (FEMA-1023-DR-MO).

Overall, the floods of 1993 (and into 1994) in Missouri constituted the longest sustained disaster in the history of the state. Of Missouri's 114 counties, 112 were declared disaster areas at some point during the flooding. There were forty-nine deaths and damage costs of approximately $3 billion, in addition to $1.8 billion in agricultural losses caused by the flooding of 3.1 million acres of farmland. The Missouri Department of Agriculture estimated that one-half million acres of Missouri River bottomland were destroyed by washouts and sand scouring. Although the state's extensive levee system was considered a success, there was serious damage to more than half of the state's almost 1,500 public and private levees.

The human costs of the disaster were tremendous. Between 15,000 and 17,000 residents were left homeless for some period because of the flooding, and $7.8 million in disaster unemployment insurance benefits was disbursed. Fewer than one in ten floodplain residents in Missouri carried flood insurance. More than 37,000 Missourians applied for disaster assistance. They obtained financial relief from a variety of sources, including the Small Business Administration (SBA), the Federal Emergency Management Agency (FEMA), and the Missouri State Emergency Management Agency (SEMA). An extensive network of charities, religious organizations, and state agencies addressed the emotional and psychological repercussions of the disaster.

Missouri's 1994 Section 409 Plan

The Missouri State Emergency Management Agency (SEMA) prepared the *State of Missouri Hazard Mitigation Plan* in July 1994 in response to the four federally declared disasters that constituted the Midwest floods of 1993. Although numerous state and federal agencies are credited with contributing to the plan, SEMA was the principal author. The Governor's Office approved the plan in August 1994, and FEMA's Region VII did likewise in October 1994.

The plan covers all 114 counties in the state and deals with several different hazards: flooding, tornadoes, earthquakes, droughts, dam failures, severe winter weather, and wildfires. The flooding threat receives the most attention. Nineteen proposed mitigation initiatives are presented under the subheadings of mitigation coordination; acquisition, relocation, and retrofitting; floodplain management; public safety; emergency preparedness; earthquakes; drought; and wildfires.

Strengths of the Plan

The primary strengths of the 1994 version of Missouri's Section 409 plan are its straightforward organization and its readability. All major plan elements required by federal regulations are present and clearly identified. The nineteen mitigation initiatives are usefully grouped under subheadings, with individual initiatives presented in a consistent format. Each initiative includes an introductory paragraph or two providing background information that describes the need for the initiative; an identification of lead and support agencies; a list of general funding sources; and a schedule for completion. Although the categories are a bit of a mix, overall the initiatives add up to a fairly coherent mitigation program.

Weaknesses of the Plan

Although it is usefully organized, the plan provides little substantive information to support its proposed initiatives. Each section fulfills its general requirements but fails to go into the analytical depth characteristic of a useful Section 409 plan. For example, the assessment of natural hazards facing Missouri is brief and cursory. For each hazard, a few paragraphs describe the nature and magnitude of the hazard, citing past damage and loss of life. No systematic or thorough risk delineation or assessment is provided. No maps or tables illustrate the number of people, the amount of property, or the nature of critical facilities at risk. Despite Missouri's high susceptibility to a major earthquake along the New Madrid Fault, earthquakes are addressed in only two brief paragraphs of the seven-page hazard assessment.

Similarly, the capability assessment is mostly descriptive rather than evaluative or analytic. Most of the section describes the federal framework for disaster preparation and response, with some attention also paid to state agencies. Local capability is hardly addressed at all. This section provides no discussion of coordination or interaction among different jurisdictional levels and among different agencies and programs on the same levels (some discussion of this does come later in the plan, as part of the mitigation initiatives). Such an omission is noteworthy given SEMA's support of the FEMA regional office's Duplication of Benefits Program, which is premised on the assumption that a number of federal agencies have overlapping disaster relief responsibilities.

The goals and objectives seem to relate more to the purposes of the Section 409 plan document than to the ultimate purposes of hazard mitigation. Rather than summarizing the direction in which the state is attempting to head with its mitigation, the list of goals largely restates the

required steps of the Section 409 planning process (e.g., "Identify the types of natural hazards that affect the state and develop a brief history of each").

Use of the Plan

Officials at both SEMA and FEMA's Region VII office stated that Missouri's Section 409 plan was prepared solely to meet federal funding requirements, and they confirmed that the plan was not used in SEMA's decision-making process following the 1993 floods or subsequent disaster events. Indeed, in his letter approving the plan, Region VII's mitigation director, Stephen Harrell, suggested that one area for improvement of the plan would be to orient it "more toward helping the state and local governments to develop hazard management capabilities and programs as part of normal governmental functions." In its current form, the plan is a useful introduction to Missouri's hazard mitigation efforts and certainly meets federal requirements, but given the complexity and sophistication of the buyout efforts under way in the state since the 1993 floods, the Section 409 plan fails to provide the level of detail needed to guide the state's future mitigation planning.

Missouri's Hazard Mitigation Planning and Implementation Process

This section includes a listing of key players in the mitigation planning and implementation process, a description of FEMA's federal and regional (Region VII) activities, a description of activities at the state level in Missouri, and a description of the Hazard Mitigation Grant Program (Section 404 of the Stafford Act) as it operated in that state.

Key Players

Table 4.1 lists the key players and their roles in the hazard mitigation planning and Section 404 program implementation in Missouri at the time of the 1993 flooding.

FEMA Regional Activities

Federal officials appear to have made a unilateral decision to pursue a single mitigation strategy in the Midwest following the floods of 1993. The situation was unique in two respects. First, FEMA headquarters initially

Table 4.1. Key Players in the Missouri Mitigation Process

TITLE	NAME	ROLE
FEMA		
FEMA headquarters representative	Larry Zensinger	"Flood czar"; coordinated federal buyout policy
Mitigation director, Region VII	Stephen Harrell	Oversaw Region VII mitigation policy selection and implementation
Federal hazard mitigation officer (FHMO), Region VII	Jodi E. Broida	Was responsible for hazard mitigation efforts in KA, IA, MO, NE; set and coordinated policy for Region VII mitigation activities; directed St. Louis Region Disaster Field Office
Director, Duplication of Benefits Office, Region VII	Phil Dolan	Administered Region VII "duplication of benefits" activities for KA, IA, MO, NE
Missouri Staff		
Governor	Mel Carnahan	Directed policy selection and coordination
Director, Missouri State Emergency Management Agency (SEMA)	Jerry B. Uhlmann	Directed all state emergency management activities
State hazard mitigation officer (SHMO), SEMA	Buck Katt	Oversaw all hazard mitigation activities statewide (Section 409 planning and workshops, Section 404 projects); acted as intermediary between locals and FEMA Region VII
Staff auditor, SEMA	Destin Frost (later appointed SHMO)	Assisted SHMO in oversight of all statewide hazard mitigation activities
Chief, Disaster Recovery Branch, SEMA	David Williams	Directed activities of Disaster Recovery Branch

selected a single strategy: a systematic buyout of houses located in the floodplain that had experienced repetitive losses due to flooding. Second, the states agreed to pursue this strategy as their chief means of mitigating future flood damages. Both decisions set the stage for the way hazard mitigation occurred in the aftermath of the flooding.

A specially appointed "flood czar," Larry Zensinger, coordinated the buyout program at the federal level, emphasizing that acquisition of flood-damaged properties should take precedence over other mitigation strategies such as elevation, retrofitting, and structural projects. Zensinger and other top FEMA policy makers held several meetings in the Midwest to announce the federal buyout policy and iron out the details. The new policy had implications for several federal agencies, beginning with the Small Business Administration (SBA). Traditionally the first agency to which disaster victims applied for disaster relief (in the form of loans), the SBA had usually approved loans quickly and with little concern about

what was done with the money. With the new federal emphasis on buy-outs, however, the SBA now emphasized relocation loans.

FEMA's regional offices were responsible for implementing the new federal buyout policy and coordinating the programs of individual states. Jodi E. Broida, Region VII's federal hazard mitigation officer (FHMO), prepared a standard operating procedure booklet to establish uniformity in the regional office's operations. One important innovation in policy administration made in the Region VII office was the creation of a Duplication of Benefits (DOB) task force. Since disaster victims usually receive financial relief from other agencies (e.g., the SBA) before their property is purchased, FEMA established the DOB task force to ensure that no one received more money than was appropriate. For example, if a homeowner had already received $5,000 in individual assistance, the DOB office made sure to subtract that amount from the final buyout check the homeowner received from sale of the property. The DOB office keeps track of disaster relief from six different funding sources, including the Small Business Administration, the National Flood Insurance Program (NFIP), the Community Development Block Grant (CDBG) program, FEMA Individual Assistance and Public Assistance programs, insurance payments, and other sources.

The state hazard mitigation officers (SHMOs) from each of the nine flood-impacted states implemented their states' buyout programs differently, utilizing various levels of assistance from federal hazard mitigation officers at the FEMA regional offices. Within Region VII, for instance, Missouri utilized the region's DOB program, whereas Iowa did not. Buck Katt, Missouri's SHMO, principally oversaw that state's buyout program, in collaboration with Jodi Broida, the Region VII FHMO, and with assistance from Destin Frost, SEMA's staff auditor.

State Hazard Mitigation Planning

Immediately after the first two disaster declarations, FEMA and SEMA convened two meetings of the Interagency Hazard Mitigation Team (IHMT) in June and September 1993, fulfilling the federal regulations implementing the Stafford Act. Since the third and fourth disaster declarations came so quickly after the first two, no additional IHMT meetings were held for the later declarations in November 1993 and May 1994. The team's members included representatives from eighteen federal departments and agencies, twelve state offices and agencies, seven local governments, and one private relief organization. The IHMT developed recommendations related to eight

issues: statewide floodplain management; levee construction and repair; acquisition, relocation, and retrofitting; flood risk behind levees; National Flood Insurance Program mapping; National Flood Insurance Program training; hazardous materials; and preparedness.

These recommendations, published in the IHMT's report in April 1994 (FEMA 1994), served as the basis for preparation of the statewide hazard mitigation plan (Section 409 plan). SEMA took the maximum allowable time (one year) to prepare its plan, finally submitting it to FEMA in August 1994 after obtaining a 180-day extension to the basic 180-day time limit. The plan was regarded as a necessary requirement for the state to receive federal disaster relief, but it did not play an active role in SEMA's hazard mitigation effort following the flood, much of which was already well under way before the plan was submitted.

Instead, SEMA's mitigation program revolved solely around the Missouri Community Buyout Program and efforts to streamline the buyout procedure. The SHMO and SEMA staff worked with FEMA Region VII staff to develop a uniform system of documentation and document processing to guide the huge number of buyout projects in the state. For example, SEMA developed a standard buyout application form for local communities, and Broida, the FHMO, developed a blue book to brief communities on procedures to follow after their approval for participation in the buyout program.

Implementation of the Hazard Mitigation Grant Program

Most of the activity at SEMA centered on disbursement of Hazard Mitigation Grant Program (HMGP) funds, authorized by Section 404 of the Stafford Act. As explained earlier, HMGP funds provide as much as 75 percent federal funding for cost-effective mitigation projects (except that only 50 percent federal funding was allowed for projects funded on the basis of the spring 1993 flooding; FEMA-989-DR-MO). Projects undertaken must therefore have 25 percent state and/or local funding to be completed.

In Missouri, these matching funds almost always came from Community Development Block Grant (CDBG) funds, administered by the U.S. Department of Housing and Urban Development and/or in-kind services, equipment, or materials. A strong advocate of hazard mitigation, Missouri's governor, Mel Carnahan, declared that Section 404 funds would be matched dollar for dollar with CDBG funds. Thus, the $30 million available to Missouri in Section 404 monies was matched by $30 million in

CDBG funds, giving the state $60 million to spend on buyout projects in the aftermath of the floods.

The SHMO is responsible for preparing an administrative plan outlining priorities for the expenditure of HMGP funds. Working with the governor's office, which actively promoted the buyout program as the most effective way to minimize future flood damage, SEMA assigned buyout priority to primary residences, vacant residential lots, and mobile home pads in the floodplain; rehabilitation and elevation of floodplain houses were not to be funded.

SEMA solicited Section 404 project applications from all flood-stricken communities and received applications for HMGP funding from fifty-seven of those communities. The governor appointed a four-person panel to review all applications, listen to oral presentations by applicants, and select applicants who best fit the criteria outlined in federal regulations and federal and state priorities. Panel members represented SEMA, the Department of Economic Development, the Missouri Housing Development Commission, and the Governor's Office. The panel selected forty-nine communities to participate in the HMGP program.

Results

Virtually all mitigation implementation in Missouri following the Midwest floods of 1993 resulted from the buyout program. Simply in terms of the number of properties purchased within the floodplain thus far, the program appears to have been a huge success. The summer 1993 floods resulted in the provision of $60 million in CDBG and Section 404 funds for buyouts in forty-two communities.[2] This money funded the purchase of approximately 2,400 primary residences, more than 1,100 mobile home pads, 4 apartment buildings, and 385 vacant lots. The November 1993 floods resulted in money for two communities, targeted toward the purchase of 20 primary residences, 1 vacant lot, 10 mobile home pads, and 12 rental properties. In addition, CDBG funds for the spring 1994 floods provided $7 million for purchase of 435 floodplain primary residences in thirteen communities and $8.7 million for buyouts of commercial businesses in thirteen communities. An additional $3.7 million in extra CDBG funds was spent in 1993 to purchase 225 houses.

FEMA and SEMA consider each property available for buyout to be a "development opportunity" (i.e., one homesite per household—either a developed homesite, a mobile home pad, or a vacant lot available for

future development). At the time of our study, of a total of 4,483 development opportunities in Missouri floodplains, 2,678 had been closed. The state had thus completed 60 percent of all feasible buyout projects by midsummer 1995.

Following are descriptions of the buyout programs in several communities that the researchers personally visited or discussed in detail with SEMA staff.

City of Arnold

The researchers met with Eric Knoll, city administrator, to discuss the city of Arnold's buyout program. Arnold is one of the few municipalities in the country to have been practicing hazard mitigation for decades, buying up floodplain property well in advance of FEMA's emphasis on acquisition following the 1993 flooding. Arnold has traditionally relied on funding from various sources to purchase houses: Section 404 funds, CDBG funds, Section 1362 funds (one of the earliest available federal grants for buyouts, which requires 50 percent damage and flood insurance for eligibility), tax waivers from local taxing authorities, and tax-related foreclosures, as well as donations of privately owned land. Another proposed funding mechanism is a local tax on catalog sales, which provides funds for acquisition and maintenance activities (the use of the tax for acquisition is currently being challenged in court).

Arnold is located about fifteen miles south of St. Louis on the Mississippi River. Its flood hazard comes from the relatively small Meramec River, a tributary of the Mississippi. Approximately 20 percent of the city, or about 11.5 square miles, lies in the Meramec's floodplain. Because of a history of flood problems, the city has been acquiring repetitively damaged properties for at least two decades, with the stated goal of owning the entire floodplain.

Hit hard by the 1993 floods, Arnold was the site of a flood summit on July 17, 1993, attended by state and local officials, federal and regional officials, and President Bill Clinton. Arnold received a Section 404 grant of $2.33 million in June 1994.

Following the floods, Knoll mailed a survey to flood victims asking how they would most like to see the city expend its disaster relief funds. The vast majority, Knoll said, responded that they wanted to see the money go to acquisition. The city eventually acquired 85 residential structures, 2 commercial structures, and 143 mobile home pads. Ten of the structures were at least 50 percent damaged and qualified for Section 1362 funds; the other buyouts were funded by Section 404 and/or CDBG funds. At the

time of our survey, all of the 172 development opportunities funded jointly by Section 404 and CDBG funds had been closed, and all but two of the 19 development opportunities funded solely by CDBG funds had been closed.

The effect of the buyout had been "tremendous," according to Knoll. Although the 1995 flood was the fourth largest in the city's history, by then most of the flooded areas had been bought out, and therefore far fewer homeowners had been required to cope with sandbagging, evacuation, and the like, and far fewer qualified for disaster relief. Knoll estimated that 40–60 houses remained to be purchased before the city owned its entire floodplain.

A FEMA analysis claims that the Arnold mitigation was highly cost-effective. It points out that the total amount of federal assistance granted after the 1993 floods was over $2 million. However, after the ensuing 1995 flood, the damage was less than $40,000 as a result of the previous non-structural mitigation (FEMA 1997, pp. 25–30).

A variety of uses were proposed for the city's vast new tracts of open space, depending on the individual parcels and their surroundings. For example, if a purchased parcel was surrounded by woods, the city would allow it to return to its natural state. If the parcel was large enough, it might become a city park or recreational field. A consultant was preparing a master land use plan for the entire floodplain area.

Knoll noted that some key policy decisions were crucial to the success of Arnold's buyout program. One was his decision to make the appraisals public so that citizens could make a fair evaluation of the offers made for their houses. He did not negotiate appraisal values. The policy established a climate of trust, and only five or six homeowners obtained private appraisals. Moreover, to ensure consistency and fairness, Knoll used the same appraisers and same appraisal methodology for all buyout properties. He noted that the use of a professional appraiser is essential to a successful buyout program.

City of Festus

Located about thirty miles south of St. Louis, Festus is close to the Mississippi River, though its main flood threat appears to come from a stream channel that feeds into the river. The researchers met with Rick Turley, city administrator. He explained the general features of the city's buyout program, which involved far fewer properties than did Arnold's program. Of a total of thirty-three development opportunities in Festus funded jointly by CDBG and Section 404 funds, eight buyout offers had been refused, leaving twenty-five net buyout opportunities. At the time of our

interviews, fifteen of these projects had been completed. FEMA's share of the project was $144,000, which was disbursed in June 1994. Five additional development opportunities, funded solely by the CDBG program, had been completed. On completion of the buyout, the city's new open space, about three acres, was to be seeded and perhaps used as a linear park running along the stream channel.

Turley believed the Section 404 program had worked well in Festus, though he was disappointed that it did not fund the relocation of churches and public buildings. For example, even though the town had selected an elevated site suitable for relocation of a repetitively damaged church building and was willing to donate the land to the church, the buyout and relocation project fell through for lack of funding.

Lincoln County

Lincoln County's buyout program was unique in the state. Although it was not the largest in terms of numbers of houses purchased or amount of money received from FEMA, the program was the most aggressive in addressing the issue of disposal of solid waste generated by the demolition of hundreds of government-purchased dwellings. The county's highly sophisticated recycling program demonstrates how innovative hazard mitigation efforts can flourish under the leadership of creative, resourceful individuals.

Located north of St. Charles County along the Mississippi River, Lincoln County is mostly rural, with an agriculturally based economy and a 1990 population of about 30,000. The researchers met with Chuck Freidrichs, county engineer, for a tour of the county and a detailed discussion of the buyout program. Following the 1993 floods, there was a total of 409 buyout opportunities in the county. Of those, 11 buyout offers were later withdrawn and 42 were refused by the property owners, leaving a net of 356 buyout opportunities. Two hundred eighteen buyouts had been completed by midsummer 1995, giving the county a project completion rate of 61 percent.

Freidrichs's involvement was critical to the success of the buyout and the recycling program. A manufacturing engineer from California, he came to Lincoln County as an independent contractor for a consulting firm hired to conduct damage assessments, to administer individual assistance funds, and to prepare the county's Section 404 grant application. When the grant was approved, Freidrichs's job was done. However, recognizing the lack of local technical knowledge to guide the buyout and seeing an opportunity to apply his managerial and engineering skills to a project that

could have a long-lasting, positive effect on the community, he accepted an offer to become county engineer and officially oversee the buyout.

One of Freidrich's first actions was to develop an accurate, fair system for appraising flood-damaged houses, utilizing the county's tax database to obtain a preflood appraisal value for each house. He used that value as a basis for determining a dollar amount of damage for each home. As was done in Arnold, Freidrichs followed the same appraisal methodology for all buyout properties to ensure consistency and fairness. The damage assessment team conducted 1,100 damage assessments in six weeks.

First priority for buyout was given to primary residences with at least 50 percent damage; second priority was given to primary residences with less than 50 percent damage; third priority was given to secondary residences, such as vacation homes and investor-owned dwellings; and the lowest priority was given to all other buildings, including homes bought after the buyout had begun.

Immediately after the floods, Freidrichs mailed a survey and a letter describing the buyout program to all homeowners with at least 50 percent damage. He also held informal meetings every morning for several weeks at a local restaurant to provide information about buyout procedures and to allow citizens to meet with members of the damage assessment team.

Concurrently, Freidrichs sought bids from demolition contractors. Since the area did not have many contractors qualified to handle demolition of all the buyout properties, the contract was broken into three parts: homes smaller than 1,200 square feet, homes 1,200 square feet and larger, and manufactured homes. Freidrichs expected to have three sets of bids and fair competition between smaller and larger firms. Unexpectedly, however, the same small company, Miller-Dozig, was the low bidder on all three contracts and thus was awarded all the demolition work in Lincoln County. Although Freidrichs was required by federal regulations to award the work to Miller-Dozig, he did not believe the company had sufficient staff and resources to complete the contracts on time and within budget. The dilemma triggered the idea of instituting a recycling program: if most of the materials from the buyout properties could be salvaged and sold, the amount of demolition work would decrease dramatically and Miller-Dozig would be able to fulfill its contractual obligations.

Freidrichs seems to have implemented much of the county's recycling program himself. His first problem was the prevailing wage rate for laborers in the area: at $19 per hour, the county could not afford to hire additional workers to extract salvageable materials, since the resulting price of the salvaged materials would be much too high to be competitive with new materials. Thus, Freidrichs formed a separate company, King's

Lake Wholesale Company, which was actually a three-person not-for-profit partnership made up of himself, Donald Miller of Miller-Dozig, and Miller's accountant. The company first taught local laborers to be independent contractors and then bought the salvageable materials these independent contractors removed from the buyout properties. In this way, the costs of payroll and benefits (e.g., worker's compensation) for additional county staff were avoided.

A $30,000 house could be expected to provide as much as $1,500 in recyclable materials, most of which would be dimensional lumber, plus some fixtures. Each two-man demolition crew received 50 percent of every dollar it made selling recyclable materials from the houses. Another 20 percent went to a crew that transported the materials from the buyout site to the county's sales yard. The remaining money went to the partnership to pay taxes, maintain the sales yard, and cover other administrative costs. The houses were much easier to demolish after scavenging, since the asbestos and insulation and all salvageable materials had been removed. Thus, the demolition became financially feasible for Miller-Dozig. Hazardous materials were disposed of according to state and Environmental Protection Agency (EPA) regulations; other materials were burned in a specially constructed pit and the ashes buried. Freidrichs was especially proud of his clean burning and ash disposal operation, noting that everything buried in Lincoln County's floodplain would eventually end up in St. Louis's water supply.

The county had one sales yard where all salvageable materials from the buyout properties, including dimensional lumber, roof materials, appliances, and fixtures, were sold to the public. Buyers were contractors or homeowners simply wanting to fix up or enlarge their homes.

Every Monday morning, all participants in this complex recycling process met to go over the project schedule for the week. With more than 200 properties demolished by midsummer 1995, the county seemed to have the recycling of flood-damaged houses down to a science. Freidrichs expected the buyout to be completed by April 1996.

Lincoln County's new open space was to be managed in a variety of ways: some was to be leased to owners of adjacent land, with the provision that no vehicles could be parked on the land between October 15 and April 15, ensuring that no structures would be built. Regular lots were to be leased for $50 per year; waterfront lots would bring in as much as $300 per year. The county's goal was to generate enough revenue from the leases to pay the salary of a floodplain manager and, perhaps, fund future buyouts. Freidrichs was also arranging a lease-type partnership with the Missouri Department of Conservation (MDC) for wetlands properties

whereby the county would continue to own the property but the MDC would manage the wetlands.

Freidrichs offered many suggestions for improving the response of state and federal emergency management officials after the next big flood. Immediately after the disaster, for example, trained disaster assessment teams should salvage plywood and other materials from damaged homes and use these to board up windows and doors to deter vandals. Disaster victims themselves should be put to work, perhaps in a salvage operation, to keep their minds busy and distract them from their troubles. Freidrichs noted that his hardest task had been figuring out ways to "legally circumvent the system to make it work here [in Lincoln County]," as exemplified by the training of local workers to be independent contractors.

Freidrichs commented that FEMA and SEMA should have made greater efforts immediately after the flooding to coordinate buyout efforts of neighboring localities. Lack of communication among county officials often led to citizens on opposite sides of a county line being treated quite differently by officials, leading to frustration and anger on the part of those who perceived that they were getting an unfair deal. He also noted that state and federal officials should have done more to explain key methodological details of the buyout process. The few postflood conferences the state did hold, according to Freidrichs, were ineffective because they involved too much talk about the "big picture" of hazard mitigation and not enough "nitty-gritty" details about how to actually implement a buyout.

Perhaps because of the complexity of Lincoln County's recycling program, or maybe because of a lack of innovators like Chuck Freidrichs, large-scale recycling of buyout properties is not being practiced anywhere else in Missouri. Most acquisition programs seem to focus primarily on the buyout itself (e.g., assembling the matching funds and convincing homeowners to participate in the buyout) rather than on the subsequent phases of demolition and open-space property management; thus, demolition is often delayed and costly.

The City of St. Charles

The city of St. Charles, the original capital of Missouri, is located on the northwestern outskirts of the St. Louis metropolitan area, just across the Missouri River. The researchers toured the city with Patrick M. Owens, an associate with the St. Louis–based Community Program Development Corporation (CPDC). This private consulting firm provided various types of service to St. Charles, St. Louis, and St. Louis County following the

floods of 1993. In St. Charles, the firm was contracted to administer the entire buyout program so that additional permanent city staff would not have to be hired.

As an "entitlement community," St. Charles received most of its money for the buyout directly from the Department of Housing and Urban Development (HUD), rather than by application to the Section 404 program. This arrangement expedited the buyout, as it removed an entire level of government—the state—from the administration of most of the money. Some HMGP funds were used, however; the city received about one-half ($133,000) of the Section 404 funds requested. Of the 111 development opportunities funded jointly by the HMGP and the CDBG program, nine buyout offers were refused, leaving a net total of 102 development opportunities. At the time of our interviews, sixteen of these had been closed, giving the CPDC a project completion rate of approximately 16 percent. Of the 61 development opportunities funded solely by the CDBG program, only three had been closed. The entire St. Charles buyout covered about seventy-seven acres in the historic Frenchtown and North End areas and was expected to cost approximately $9.2 million at completion.

The CPDC adopted a "risk management" strategy in deciding which houses to purchase: first priority was given to owner-occupied dwellings in the floodplain; next came investor-owned residential floodplain properties; third priority was given to all other properties closest to the river at the lowest elevations; and the lowest priority was given to all other properties extending westward from the river.

St. Charles, unfortunately, had to engage in some buyout competition with a local casino. To prevent other casinos from acquiring prime river frontage in St. Charles, the casino paid top dollar for many houses on adjacent property that were being targeted for buyout by the CPDC. The casino's offers inflated the expectations of many property owners in the floodplain, frustrating the CPDC's efforts to purchase the remaining homes at fair market value.

Like Arnold, St. Charles has a buyout history predating the 1993 floods. After a severe flood in 1973, an entire riverfront subdivision was bought out with local funds. This area has subsequently reverted to a mostly natural state and is used as a park and boat-landing site. St. Charles officials hope to turn that land, along with much of the city's new open space, into a grand "eco-park" on the shores of the Missouri River. They envision a park with wildlife habitat and nature trails as the best use for land that has endured repetitive flooding over the past century. The city must acquire some of the casino's land to make the park a reality, however.

Although the St. Charles buyout appeared to be progressing relatively smoothly, Owens believed that the federal regulations implementing the Stafford Act were insufficient to guide a complicated mitigation effort such as Missouri's buyout program. He would like to see a "Stafford Act II" explicating certain policies and procedures related to acquisition and relocation of houses in high-hazard areas. Owens was also sharply critical of the National Flood Insurance Program; he saw it as an ineffective mechanism for controlling floodplain development along the Missouri. He said that many property owners were able to simply wait until the last minute to purchase flood insurance because of the relative ease of forecasting floods days in advance by tracking the flood peak as it moved down the long Missouri River.

Owens described a new regional floodplain management network in the St. Louis–St. Charles region. This informal organization of county and local officials, coordinated by the Department of Political Science at the University of Missouri at St. Louis, was still in the formative stages at the time of our interviews. Its members believe that the wisest, most efficient decisions concerning floodplain management are made from a regional perspective that includes the entire watershed area. Its members "don't like other jurisdictions making our decisions for us," according to Owens. Presumably, these other jurisdictions are state and federal agencies such as SEMA, the U.S. Army Corps of Engineers, and FEMA, which issue what local officials see as overly intrusive, ill-conceived regulations concerning floodplain management. Although Owens saw the new organization as having the potential to effect positive change, he cautioned that the group had yet to establish a clear list of priorities—an important first step toward ensuring that all group members are working for common goals and are not motivated by hidden agendas.

St. Charles County

The largest and one of the most ambitious buyout programs in Missouri was under way in St. Charles County, located at the intersection of the Missouri and Mississippi Rivers immediately north and northwest of St. Louis County. Although the city of St. Charles is located in St. Charles County, the two entities administered their hazard mitigation programs separately. Forty-three percent of the county is located in the floodplain of one or both of the rivers, and there are more than 100 miles of river frontage. The researchers met with Steven G. Lauer, county planning director, to discuss the county's buyout program.

At the time of our study, of a total of 1,557 buyout opportunities, 83 offers had been withdrawn by the county and 89 had been refused by property owners, leaving a net total of 1,385 buyout opportunities. Of this total, 1,366 had been closed, giving the county a project completion rate of almost 99 percent—one of the highest in the state. Slightly more than half of the buyout was funded by the CDBG program, with the rest funded by the Section 404 program. Primary residences and mobile home pads were given priority.

Some of the earliest buyouts, in the fall of 1993 and spring of 1994, were completed using Section 1362 funds. The county received a grant from its Economic Development Council to prepare a grant application for Section 404 and CDBG funds for its buyout program. This application, made in mid-December 1993, was approved and officially funded in June 1994. (The county also applied for funds to elevate one subdivision, but state officials rejected the application, as they were denying funding for almost all projects not related to acquisition and relocation.)

The county began buying properties in March 1994, even before its request for Section 404 and CDBG funding was officially approved. The county's planning department rented space for a buyout office and six other disaster service organizations, including mental health counselors and the Salvation Army. The office also housed an Unmet Needs Committee, which assisted disaster victims who "fell through the cracks" of other relief organizations. Lauer believed the physical consolidation of these offices to be an especially helpful service the county provided to its citizens after the floods.

Unlike the city of St. Charles, the county chose to make permanent additions to its planning staff to administer the buyout program, thus indicating a willingness to incorporate some type of ongoing buyout into its long-range plans. The planning staff held all-day meetings every day in the weeks following the floods to explain the buyout to residents and put victims in touch with the proper relief organizations. In addition, about twenty inspectors completed damage assessments for the county, evaluating more than 4,000 flood-damaged structures and agricultural properties. They divided all properties into three categories: 50 percent or more damaged, less than 50 percent damaged, and "borderline" damaged.

Demolition of buyout properties began in the summer of 1994. County officials entered into individual contracts with different contractors for each of more than ten subdivisions and mobile home parks—a decision that Lauer acknowledged was a mistake. He believed that for simplicity's sake and to avoid duplication of effort, the county should have entered

into one master demolition contract, much like the one operating in Lincoln County. Unlike their neighbors to the north in Lincoln County, the directors of the St. Charles County buyout did not aggressively advocate a recycling program to reduce the amount of solid waste created by the buyout.

The county's vast new tracts of open space were to remain in public ownership, according to Lauer, though the lands would be managed in different ways. Some isolated parcels would be leased to owners of adjacent land; this mutually beneficial arrangement would provide cheap land for the homeowner to use as a garden or an extended backyard and would relieve the county of responsibility for maintenance. Other, larger tracts might be transferred to state or federal agencies for recreational and/or conservation purposes. For example, the Missouri Department of Natural Resources was interested in some parcels for additions to its Katy Trail system of parks. Sometime in the near future, the county was to participate in a workshop with state and federal officials to discuss the long-term management of many important new county properties, such as those in St. Charles harbor. The county planned to complete the buyout by the end of 1995.

Lauer believed that the low level of flood damage from the 1995 floods demonstrates the effectiveness of the county's buyout program. He noted that the experience of the 1993 floods strengthened the county's commitment to hazard mitigation, as evidenced by new support from elected officials for the National Flood Insurance Program and stronger floodplain management regulations. The county had formed a "vision committee" to chart a course for the area's future land use policies; subcommittees were studying various aspects of floodplain management.

Lauer said he would like to see an ongoing buyout program in St. Charles County, one not necessarily tied to specific flood events as is the Section 404 program. For example, when a hypothetical couple was ready to retire and move out of the floodplain, Lauer wanted to have a fund in place to purchase that property for the county, regardless of whether there had been recent flood damage to the property. The proposal targets eventual, almost complete ownership of the floodplain by the county—just what Eric Knoll hoped to accomplish in the city of Arnold.

Towns of Rhineland and Pattonsburg

The researchers did not visit Rhineland and Pattonsburg, but the two communities were noted by SEMA officials as good examples of how the

buyout had operated in dramatically contrasting ways in different communities. The SHMO considered Rhineland to be one of the great mitigation success stories in Missouri. The town decided to finance a substantial part of its buyout without state and federal funds. A small town of only about fifty homes and with a 1990 population of approximately 150, Rhineland is located on the northern bank of the Missouri River midway between St. Louis and Jefferson City. Town residents met in the local tavern to allocate lots at a new location atop a hill and to determine how much money should be offered to induce residents to move out of the floodplain on their own. An upper limit of $10,000 per house was agreed on, and the town treasury paid as much as that amount to move individual homes up the nearby hillside. No Section 404 funds were used in the Rhineland buyout, although CDBG funds were being used for seventeen buyout projects. Much of Rhineland's business district remained in the floodplain; only the residences were relocated. Central to the buyout's success was the presence of infrastructure at the new site; thus, there was no need to build new schools, city hall, highways, sewer plants, and the like. The town's small scale, its homogeneous community values, and the townspeople's ability to reach consensus were also seen as key elements of the program's success.

Pattonsburg's buyout program, on the other hand, was considered by state officials to be likely to fail. Located just north of the Grand River, a tributary of the Missouri in the northeastern part of the state, Pattonsburg is a larger community than Rhineland (1990 population was approximately 400). The town was attempting to relocate itself entirely to a new location—businesses, residences, and industry alike. This "new town" concept was not cost-effective, requiring an estimated $10–$15 million for construction of new infrastructure, such as a post office, city hall, school, and sewer system. In addition, according to SEMA officials, there was no strong economic base to justify creating a town at the new location. At the time of our study, the buyout was not proceeding swiftly: of 332 net development opportunities, none had been closed. Two hundred parcels remained to be acquired. Although the town had received a huge FEMA grant ($3.15 million), only $415,000 had been spent.

Conclusions and Recommendations

A number of conclusions may be drawn from the opinions of the key participants interviewed during the case study and the research team's later assessment of the stories they told.

Window of Opportunity

In response to the Midwest floods of 1993, policy makers with FEMA and the state of Missouri took advantage of a "window of opportunity" to make the system work in a way that appears to be unmatched in our other case studies. The window of opportunity was created by the sense of crisis resulting from the sheer size of that disaster—a 500-year flood covering large parts of nine states—which made officials and the public more aware of the need for, and more receptive to, radical change from normal FEMA and state government policy. Both federal and state policy makers responded quickly by conducting working meetings to bring together federal and state officials at the highest levels. The meetings and follow-up sessions resulted in quick and decisive determination of an overall strategy. In this case, it was a buyout strategy promoted at the federal level but apparently arrived at jointly by state and federal officials. Just as important as determination of a strategy was the way the parties worked out radical changes in FEMA's operating policies and, to some extent, the state's policies in order to facilitate implementation. The innovations for facilitating the buyout strategy were instituted at FEMA's national headquarters, in FEMA's Region VII office, and at the state level in Missouri.

National Level

At the national level, FEMA set the tone in several ways. First, FEMA established that a buyout would be cost-effective, thereby eliminating the need to establish such a finding in a Section 404 application, a requirement normally necessitating much data collection and effort on the part of local applicants and the state. Moreover, FEMA allowed Section 406 (public assistance) grants to be used for demolition of buyout properties, thereby extending the leveraging of Section 404 funds that otherwise would have been devoted to demolition as well as buyout costs. In addition, FEMA established that buyouts were categorically exempted from the need for an environmental assessment, thereby eliminating another difficult and time-consuming step in the Section 404 application process and in the FEMA review process.

There were other ways in which the buyout was facilitated at the national level. Provisions of the Volkmer Act of 1993 increased the money available for Section 404 grants fivefold, from $6 million to $30 million. FEMA also set up a nine-state programmatic agreement to streamline and standardize the technical process for assessing impacts on cultural resources, namely historic structures; FEMA contracted at the Washington level to perform these assessments throughout the midwestern states.

FEMA also established the incentive of a five-year kickback of NFIP

premiums, funded from Section 404 grants and added to the buyout price. This feature created an extra reward for those property owners who had purchased flood insurance by paying them a bonus equal to the previous five years' premiums at the time of acquisition. Without this incentive, property owners who had maintained insurance were no better off than those who had avoided that cost, since insurance awards were deducted from acquisition payments. (We understand that other states penalized non–insurance holders, by imposing premium equivalents as a cost deduction from the buyout payment, rather than rewarding insurance holders.)

In addition, FEMA allowed the use of HUD CDBG monies as local-state matching funds for Section 404 grants and further allowed it by "global match." That is, the matching was, in effect, on the state level, not the local level, allowing some communities with insufficient CDBG funds to be subsidized by the excess CDBG monies of other communities (i.e., in excess of what was necessary to meet the 25 percent matching requirement).

FEMA allowed a departure from the NFIP policy of setting property appraisals at preflood market price, using instead a "replacement value" appraisal to make the buyout program, which is voluntary, more attractive to property owners. This same policy created problems, however, by raising the threshold level of "substantial damage," which triggers the need to floodproof a structure when repairing it, because 50 percent of replacement value was often much higher than 50 percent of preflood market value. Several of the communities visited in the case study stuck with appraisals of fair market value rather than replacement value of floodplain property in order to make their programs predictable and achieve the perception of consistent treatment among participating property owners.

Finally, FEMA appointed Larry Zenzinger as "flood czar," endowing a central figure with the authority to resolve issues and to approve and support the facilitating policies of FEMA at both the national and regional levels.

Regional Level

Region VII also took innovative steps, in some cases in conjunction with FEMA headquarters. First, the regional office placed a priority on facilitating administration and coordination of grant application and implementation procedures for local communities, the state of Missouri, and the FEMA region. For example, it promoted better understanding by all stakeholders in the procedures, streamlined procedures for local government and the state, and coordinated interaction among different agencies (the SBA, FEMA, and the CDBG program) by standardizing forms and procedures. The regional office also published a guidebook for the state

and communities, published a guidebook of standard operating procedures for Region VII, and held workshops. Officials at FEMA headquarters
collaborated by visiting the region and demonstrating how to "emphasize
getting results" (i.e., in approving projects). Furthermore, in collaboration
with headquarters, the regional office allocated monies quickly, both to
show Congress that FEMA really needed funds to meet the needs of the
nine affected states and to demonstrate to the states and local communities that FEMA could respond and achieve results within a reasonable
time. In addition, officials at the regional office decided to make buyout
grants and allow the money to be committed without an initial determination of compliance with the NFIP and other programs; they simply decided to deal with compliance later. They would also determine individual
payments and conduct an accounting of Duplication of Benefits later. All
these practices demonstrate the region's commitment to facilitating the
buyout program.

Second, FEMA's Region VII contracted with regional planning agencies
to conduct planning for local communities and help them write grant
applications. That process helped towns and counties that otherwise would
have had difficulty in preparing applications. The strategy might actually
work better in states such as North Carolina or Tennessee, where the
quality of the regional planning agencies is more dependable. In those
states, the regional agencies are actually state agencies with regional offices
offering community assistance, unlike the situation in Missouri, where
they are essentially voluntary councils of governments.

Third, Region VII established a Duplication of Benefits (DOB) process at
the regional office level instead of forcing the states and communities to
establish the necessary complex accounting procedure. DOB requires a
sophisticated database and accounting procedure cutting across several different federal programs. Region VII has a staff of sixteen people devoted to
that task for the four states in its jurisdiction. The process accounts for payments from several different sources—SBA loans, FEMA individual assistance payments, Section 406 public assistance payments, CDBG payments,
insurance payments, and other payments—that may have gone to a property owner. The process prevents "undue enrichment" by grant recipients,
avoids inconsistency in treatment of landowners in different communities
or states, and assumes the burden at a level best able to assemble the necessary expertise. Region VII personnel claimed that their DOB procedures
had already saved the federal government $30 million by reducing the
effective price of acquisition by the value of duplicated payments that
might not otherwise have been taken into account in arriving at buyout
value. FEMA also estimated that the buyout program reduced insurance

liability of floodplain property by $30 million, much of which, officials claimed, would have been paid just in damages for the post-buyout 1995 floods.

Fourth, Region VII allowed state and local governments to establish their own priorities among different types of properties and their own administrative procedures and criteria for governing the program. Missouri, for example, placed priority on developed residential property (primary residences, rental homes, mobile homes and pads) for Section 404 grants. Vacant residential property was given lower priority. Commercial, industrial, and agricultural property was generally not eligible. Furthermore, individual communities established their own priorities among types of properties, within overall state policy, and then used CDBG funds, Section 1362 funds, and other funds for buyouts outside the state policy (e.g., for commercial property or a second home).

Fifth, the regional office required individual communities to promise to adopt specific policies outlined by Region VII in its blue book within thirty days of receipt of the grant.

State Level

The state of Missouri also adapted its policies to facilitate the buyout strategy. It set up a streamlined four-person review panel to review and approve buyout applications and presentations by local governments beginning in January 1994. This group substituted for the larger, more cumbersome Interagency Hazard Mitigation Team and the Mitigation Task Force proposed in the Section 409 plan. The four panel members represented agencies directly involved in implementing the buyout strategy: SEMA, HUD (for the CDBG program), the Missouri Housing Development Commission, and the Governor's Office. The governor's representative served as facilitating chairperson; the CDBG program and the Missouri Housing Development Commission supplied matching funds. The state was able to review and approve grants to allocate approximately 95 percent of the available monies by the end of March.

Second, the state appointed a hard-driving and politically savvy administrator to the SHMO position in late summer 1993. The SHMO had the governor's confidence and hired a talented assistant. The SHMO then developed a project solicitation process and educated local community officials about the state's priorities and application procedures.

Third, to facilitate the process, the state eschewed site visits to the project areas prior to awarding grants. The state has since set up a program of visits by circuit riders to perform spot auditing and deliver details of the buyout program.

Redefining Working Relationships Among Agencies

Hazard mitigation is very much an intergovernmental process, requiring coordination and cooperation among agencies at every level of government as well as among different levels of government. At the federal level, the SBA, the NFIP, the Army Corps of Engineers, and HUD are all involved. There are important intergovernmental relationships within FEMA— between headquarters and the regional office and, in the case of the Midwest floods, among FEMA regions. There are also important relationships between FEMA (Washington and regional) and the state, among state agencies, and between all these and the local communities. In addition there is the need to coordinate several programs and sources of funds. All the parties and programs have their own missions, programs, and operating procedures. In addition, there are the personalities of the people involved and the legacies of past relationships.

The state level of government and the state-local interaction appear to be more political than the regional FEMA level. That situation indirectly interjects political considerations for FEMA at both the national and the regional level. This is especially true for grant approvals. Above the local level, much of the creativity involved in mitigation policy addresses intergovernmental coordination. For example, in Region VII, the federal agencies were able to standardize forms and procedures for different participating programs and agencies. In Missouri, the parties also were able to take advantage of nonstandard requirements of the different federal programs to meet the different aspects of the buyout strategy, depending on the extent of property damage and whether relocation or demolition was involved.

The roles of the FHMO and the SHMO are particularly critical. These officials need to be able to work together and have confidence in each other. The SHMO not only needs to be a good administrator but also needs to be supported by the governor and have solid relationships with local government officials.

The issue of centralization versus decentralization of mitigation programs is another important aspect of the intergovernmental problem. Within the state, for example, Missouri opted for a more centralized approach in the form of a small, four-person review board that represented only state-level agencies. There is very little local participation in formulation of state policy in Missouri, and the Interagency Hazard Mitigation Team is viewed by the SHMO as largely extraneous. Within FEMA, the distribution of authority between headquarters and the regional offices is still evolving. Officials with FEMA's regional offices believe the offices would operate more effectively if they had more authority, though state officials

seem to prefer that federal authority be more centralized. States also want the programs to offer more flexibility for state-level judgments (i.e., more of a block grant approach). Local governments, in turn, would like more flexibility within FEMA and state policies to set their own priorities and to establish rules that better fit their circumstances.

Role of the Section 409 Plan

Missouri's Section 409 plan played no role in the choice of a mitigation strategy, selection of projects, or other hazard mitigation in the state. The plan was not "pulled off the shelf" by FEMA, by state agencies, or by local governments. It served only to qualify the state for Section 404 grants. The submission date of July 1994 was a full year after the disaster declarations. The state purposefully used both the full 180-day submission period and the 180-day extension period to keep open the window of time for submission of Section 404 applications, which are cut off thirty days after submission of the Section 409 plan. Most decisions about Section 404 projects had already been made by the time the Section 409 plan was completed.

No key participant in the hazard mitigation process saw much relevance in the Section 409 plan. FEMA suggested the concept of a more focused strategy paper and in fact prepared a draft of that approach in response to the 1995 floods. The state SHMO would not sign off on it, however, and instead prepared his own Section 409 plan update. Participants saw more potential usefulness in the Section 404 administrative plan.

Dissemination of Successful Practices and Policies

Only a moderate degree of institutional dissemination and learning regarding disaster mitigation seemed to be taking place as a result of the Midwest floods of 1993. The local officials we interviewed in the St. Louis area did not typically communicate or learn from one another's experiences. Each community seemed to have gone its own way and developed its own approach. States also pursued separate strategies; Illinois and Texas apparently did not wish to replicate the priorities or implementation-facilitating approaches of Missouri. The Army Corps of Engineers, however, was studying the buyout strategy as an alternative to continued reliance on levee construction, maintenance, and repair.

Issues Surrounding the Buyout Strategy

It is difficult to measure the effectiveness of the Missouri buyout, although FEMA does claim that $30 million in potential flood losses was avoided in

1995 because so much less property was vulnerable to flooding. Nevertheless, a number of issues surround the implementation of the buyout strategy in Missouri. First, there is the principal issue of whether a truly effective and successful hazard mitigation program can rely on a single mitigation strategy—here, acquisition and relocation—to the exclusion of all others. It is not likely that the lowest-priority buyout project in the entire state is more effective and efficient than the best alternative type of project—repair and elevation, storm water drainage improvement, levee improvement, or some sort of more rigorous regulation and insurance program, for example. The rigid policy choice in Missouri closed the door on consideration of alternatives.

Second, Missouri chose to focus on owner-occupied homes (so-called primary residences), mobile homes, rental dwellings (other then apartment buildings), and vacant residential lots. The state would not approve purchase of industrial and commercial property or other institutions, such as churches, under Section 404 grants. The reason was partly political—helping people first—and partly economic: purchasing residential properties enables the state to purchase a greater number of properties. In addition, the state did not want to encourage the flight of any economic base. In some local communities, however, it would have been effective to purchase and relocate churches and some businesses because subsequent damage to those properties will necessitate humanitarian aid.

Third, Missouri chose to allow buyout of any damaged residence whether or not it was damaged beyond 50 percent of its value. On some of these properties, a less costly repair and floodproofing project might have been more cost-effective.

Fourth, the buyout program was totally voluntary. A program that allowed the application of eminent domain under specified conditions probably would have been more effective.

Fifth, buyout implies the need to include a parallel policy governing demolition or relocation. Some communities seemed to lag in implementing the demolition stage. Moreover, some communities did much more to salvage and recycle useful materials or relocate still-useful structures than did other communities. Lincoln County is an example of an exceptionally innovative and effective salvaging operation within an altogether aggressive and effective buyout program.

Sixth, Missouri requires local communities to retain ownership of the purchased property. That requirement ensures total control over the property, which otherwise might eventually revert to unsuitable private occupancy. But it also creates a property management challenge. Communities are taking a number of different approaches to this "life after demolition" issue. Solutions include leasing property to owners of adjacent land (to

mow or to farm), negotiating with state or federal park and open-space agencies, creating local parks, leasing to hunt clubs and other recreational users, and building golf courses. In any case, the community faces issues of maintenance and appropriate use as well as liability risks. Loss of tax base does not seem to be an issue, for several reasons. Floodplain properties generally do not generate high tax revenues, particularly in light of the high cost to local government of providing services and periodic flood relief. Moreover, people generally move to properties with better cost-revenue ratios. If they move out of the community, they take with them their demand for schools and other services.

Seventh, buyouts incorporate a maze of "duplication of benefits" issues. Property owners and residents obtain assistance payments from a number of different sources. For example, a property owner may receive an insurance payment for damage cost, an SBA loan for repairs, a grant from FEMA's Individual Assistance programs, and relocation assistance through the CDBG programs. All these payments must be deducted from the buyout payment in order to avoid undeserved duplication of benefits for the property owner. Proper accounting of all the various benefits requires a very sophisticated database and considerable management and analysis capability, but it makes the relief funding go further and helps prevent abuse.

Recommendations

A number of potential recommendations for mitigation policy may be inferred from the Missouri case study. Note that these recommendations are based on the Missouri case alone and must be compared with lessons drawn from other cases, surveys, and plan content analyses.

Be creative in devising mitigation strategies.

- FEMA and the states must find ways to facilitate the formulation and implementation of mitigation strategies in the way that was done in the Midwest in general and in Missouri in particular. However, the innovations must reach beyond the simple approach of selecting one easily expedited mitigation measure, such as buyouts.

  The Midwest flood mitigation experience demonstrates that FEMA, its regional offices, and the states are able to adapt their policies to facilitate the implementation of hazard mitigation. The sheer magnitude of the disaster created a "window of opportunity" in which everyone realized the benefits of appropriately streamlining procedures while protecting the mitigation program from abuse or perversion of its objectives. Mitigation policy makers must find ways to streamline

implementation while allowing states and localities to explore more complex mitigation strategies.

Among the adjustments to procedures and standards that seemed to be most effective in Missouri were the following:

- Focusing on a limited number of options (though they should be more diverse than the single-option strategy taken in the Midwest floods)

- Granting special status to a FEMA representative (i.e., designating a "hazard czar") to coordinate efforts and remove obstacles

- Preparing a guidebook of standard operating procedures

- Taking on some tasks at the regional office in service to the states, such as Region VII's operation of a Duplication of Benefits task force

- Allowing the state to explore creative ways to meet requirements for matching funds

- Holding working meetings of higher-level officials at the FEMA and state levels to make quick and decisive choices about mitigation strategy and innovations in procedures and to facilitate interagency coordination

- Providing assistance to local communities in preparing plans and applications for projects

Adapt procedures to local needs.

- Within the buyout strategy in particular, the approach taken by Missouri and FEMA's Region VII demonstrated a host of adaptations to procedures and standards that should be applicable to states and communities in other regions. Principles used in Missouri that might be considered elsewhere include the following:

- Making property appraisals systematically consistent and public

- Incorporating demolition, relocation, and materials recycling policy into the buyout program

- Streamlining the requirements of cost-benefit assessments and environmental impact assessments

- Returning portions of flood-prone properties to their fundamental ecological functions as wetlands and other lowland habitats

- Helping communities address the land management challenge that begins after acquisition of the properties

- Promoting intercommunity and interstate learning from successful programs

○ Allowing the buyout strategy to extend beyond specific hazard events, to which the present Section 404 program is limited

○ Incorporating a Duplication of Benefits operation into the regional office's responsibilities to deal with the maze of DOB issues

○ Incorporating some eminent domain (power to condemn property) into buyout strategies to avoid complete reliance on a voluntary program

Concentrate on building intergovernmental coordination.

• Hazard mitigation is very much an intergovernmental process, requiring coordination among agencies within and between every level of government: national, regional, state, and local. There are so many parties and programs with their own missions, programs, operating procedures, and particular strengths and limitations, that intergovernmental coordination becomes a difficult—indeed, a critical—challenge. Among the most important issues is the development of a strong working relationship between the FHMO and the SHMO. The merits of centralization versus decentralization must be considered with regard to this relationship. In the Missouri case, centralization at the federal, regional, and state levels facilitated the implementation process. On the other hand, local government officials felt constrained by a lack of flexibility to adapt programs to local circumstances. States can call for that flexibility in the form of block grant programs.

1997 Update

As of 1997, Missouri had not had a declared disaster since the 1995 spring flooding. The state hazard mitigation officer during the recovery from the 1993 and 1995 floods, Buck Katt, had been promoted out of that position by the governor. The assistant SHMO and staff auditor, Destin Frost, had become the SHMO.

The state's Section 409 plan had not been revised since 1995, although additional Section 404 projects had been completed. Although no new hazard mitigation legislation had been adopted since 1995, the SHMO was trying to secure matching funds for FEMA's new Flood Mitigation Assistance Program to fund buyouts, elevation projects, and land acquisition. The program provides $400,000 per year, on top of which the state must pay 25 percent. The SHMO had gone through the state budgetary process to request general revenue funds for the 25 percent match but was not confident that Missouri would appropriate the money. In the SHMO's

opinion, the political climate for hazard mitigation in Missouri is poor, with the state leery of spending money on predisaster mitigation efforts.

The SHMO believed that acquisition definitely remains the strategy of choice for mitigating flood hazards of the type experienced in Missouri. She would therefore continue to emphasize buyouts in a future flood disaster. Nevertheless, there are some adjustments to be made. One adjustment will be to rely on appraised market values determined before buyout offers are made rather than on postdisaster assessed values as estimates of fair market values. Second, although the post-1993 DOB program run by the state and FEMA was very successful, the SHMO recommended that FEMA adjust the program to make it more uniform from state to state and region to region.

The most problematic issue associated with the buyout program was the question of what to do with the resulting open space, now under local government jurisdiction. The buyout policy required that acquired land remain under public ownership to prevent it from reverting to residences or other uses that are vulnerable to flooding. However, during the hectic initial acquisition stages, there was no planning for the future of the acquired land and no guidance from FEMA on what would be appropriate uses of the land. Several Missouri communities have proposed uses for their properties that the SHMO believes are incompatible with the open-space requirement (e.g., development of a private recreational vehicle park, construction of a privately funded football complex, and leasing of space to an association for private recreational use). The SHMO has been unable to obtain guidance from FEMA on the issue of appropriate uses or on related issues, such as appropriate impervious surface standards. FEMA is now in the process of drafting a buyout manual, which the Missouri SHMO has reviewed and believes will contain helpful open-space definitions. She believes, however, that additional guidance is needed and that predisaster planning must be done to head off inappropriate community proposals for managing publicly owned flood-prone lands.

Notes

1. This chapter is based on interviews with state, local, and federal officials conducted by Edward J. Kaiser and R. Matthew Goebel during a case study visit in July 1995, two years after the Midwest floods of 1993.
2. All buyout program statistics are from a June 1995 FEMA printout provided by Jodi Broida; *FEMA Region VII HAZMIT Buy-Out Database: Missouri Development Opportunity Totals* (FEMA 1995), and from the "Community Buyout Report Card" in SEMA's summer 1995 *Buyout Bulletin*. (SEMA 1995).

References

FEMA (Federal Emergency Management Agency). 1994. *The Floods of '93, State of Missouri: Interagency Hazard Mitigation Team Report*. April. Kansas City, Mo.: FEMA, Region VII.

———. 1995. *FEMA Region VII HAZMIT Buy-Out Database: Missouri Development Opportunity Totals*. June. Kansas City, Mo.: FEMA, Region VII.

———. 1997. *Report on Costs and Benefits of Natural Hazard Mitigation*. Washington, D.C.: FEMA.

Governor's Task Force on Floodplain Management. 1994. *Report and Recommendations of the Governor's Task Force on Floodplain Management*. July. St. Louis: Missouri Governor's Office.

SEMA (Missouri State Emergency Management Agency). 1993. *State of Missouri Hazard Mitigation Plan in July*. May. Jefferson City, Mo.: SEMA.

———. 1994a. *The Response, Recovery, and Lessons Learned from the Missouri Floods of 1993 and 1994*. Jefferson City, Mo.: SEMA.

———. 1994b. *State of Missouri Hazard Mitigation Plan*. July. Jefferson City, Mo.: SEMA.

———. 1995. "Community Buyout Report Card." *Buyout Bulletin*. Summer. Jefferson City, Mo.: SEMA.

———. n.d. *Out of Harm's Way: The Missouri Buyout Program*. Jefferson City, Mo.: SEMA.

Persons Interviewed

FEMA Region VII Officials

Jodi E. Broida, federal hazard mitigation officer (The authors thank Ms. Broida for providing the general outline for the "Results" section of this chapter.)

Dorsey Hughes, Missouri team leader, Federal Hazard Mitigation Office

State of Missouri

Destin Frost, staff auditor, Missouri State Emergency Management Agency

Buck Katt, state hazard mitigation officer, Missouri State Emergency Management Agency

Local Government and Private Sector

Chuck Freidrichs, county engineer, Lincoln County, Missouri

Eric Knoll, city administrator, Arnold, Missouri

Steven G. Lauer, county planning director, St. Charles County, Missouri

Patrick M. Owens, associate, Community Program Development Corporation, St. Louis, Missouri

Rick Turley, city administrator, Festus, Missouri

CHAPTER 5

Iowa After the Midwest Floods of 1993

This chapter reports on mitigation during the disaster recovery process in Iowa after the 1993 Midwest floods. These floods were the largest on record in the United States in terms of amount of precipitation, river levels, flood duration, amount of land flooded, and economic losses (Interagency Floodplain Management Review Committee 1994). An estimated 6.6 million acres of land was flooded in the upper Mississippi River basin, causing an estimated $12–$16 billion in damage and costing thirty-eight lives. To assess the effectiveness of mitigation during this catastrophic regional flood, case studies were conducted in two of the stricken states—Iowa[1] and Missouri (reported in chapter 4)—each of which took a different approach to mitigation.

The Disaster Events

The flooding was the result of an unusual set of circumstances: persistent upper-level atmospheric summer patterns, resulting in record rainfalls, and antecedent wet conditions. Iowa experienced the wettest November–April period in 121 years (Interagency Floodplain Management Review Committee 1994). Between June and August, parts of the state received more than thirty-eight inches of rainfall. Flooding occurred in Iowa along several major rivers, primarily the Mississippi, Iowa, Des Moines, and Raccoon Rivers.

In Iowa, damage costs were estimated at $3.4–$5.7 billion. About half of the damage was to agricultural crops, livestock, buildings, and equipment. Of the more than 70,000 homes damaged in the basin, approximately

25,000 were located in Iowa. There was also substantial damage to the transportation system and other public facilities. The Des Moines Water Works, for example, sustained some $12 million in damage and was out of service for about twelve days.

Two separate presidential disaster declarations were issued in Iowa, one in April–May 1993 (FEMA-986-DR-IA) and one in July 1993 (FEMA-996-DR-IA). All ninety-nine counties in Iowa were included in the July declaration.

Iowa's Section 409 Plan

The *1994 Iowa Hazard Mitigation Plan* was issued by the Iowa Emergency Management Division (1994b) following the Midwest floods of 1993 and was approved by FEMA in October 1994. It is prefaced by a September 1994 letter from Iowa's governor, Terry E. Branstad.

The plan covers all ninety-nine counties and all hazards. It deals with the hazards posing the greatest risks—floods, tornadoes, winter storms, and hazardous materials—as well as the lesser threats of drought, commercial nuclear accident, and earthquake. Ten of its forty recommendations deal with floods, which had triggered six of the state's seven most recent presidentially declared disasters. The plan is a bulky document, about an inch and a half thick, containing all the elements required of a Section 409 plan as well as sixteen appendixes of background material. It was developed with extensive participation by local and state government agencies and trade and professional organizations, evidencing a comprehensive consensus-building process.

Strengths of the Plan

The Iowa plan is unique in several respects. First, it is one of the few Section 409 plans we reviewed that stresses a bottom-up approach to plan preparation, and it is the only one with such extensive local involvement and serious attention to the planning process.

Second, it is very readable. Its recommendations are presented in a clear and consistent framework, including rationale, activities (long- and short-term), outcomes (measurable results), time frame, lead agency, goals addressed, and general costs. An excellent executive summary provides an overview table of goals, objectives, and recommendations. The appendixes, which describe planning activities and inputs, are unusually detailed.

Finally, the plan is one of the few state Section 409 plans prepared by a consulting firm, the State Public Policy Group. This firm's knowledge of and experience in serving Iowa government contributed to the intergovernmental sensitivity and consensus-building approach of the planning process.

Two elements of the plan serve as models for other states to consider. First, the proposed strategies, programs, and actions contained in the recommendations section and the planning process rationale (appendix 1) describe an outstanding planning process. This process involved federal, state, and local officials and private-sector organizations. The strategies are aimed at building a strong statewide mitigation organization, with a full-time state hazard mitigation officer (SHMO) and state hazard mitigation grant administrator (SHMGA), backed up by active local mitigation programs. The recommendations are systematically designed and clearly articulated, constituting an ambitious agenda. The focus is not on mitigation projects but on improving mitigation policies, regulations, programs, and activities.

Second, the implementation and monitoring section and evaluation section are also exemplary. They are very sensitive to the intergovernmental dynamics of mitigation and seek to build a mitigation support and information network through SHMO visits, surveys, regional monitoring teams, and written reports. Evaluation is intended to assess mitigation recommendations as they relate to goals and expected outcomes. Both successes and problem areas are meant to be studied in detail.

Weaknesses of the Plan

The plan does have some weaknesses. Although its hazard assessment section is comprehensive, covering all ninety-nine counties and a variety of hazards, it sacrifices detail for broad coverage. Its hazard analysis is general and superficial and contains the surprising local perception that tornadoes are a more serious hazard than are floods in Iowa. The state recognizes these weaknesses, and its consultant has prepared a damage assessment manual to document hazard risks and to train local officials to conduct baseline surveys of damage (Iowa Emergency Management Division 1994a). If carried out as scheduled, this training effort could rectify the plan's failure to identify the areas of greatest vulnerability. For this purpose, Iowa also proposed to create an All Hazards Interactive Information System, using a geographic information system (GIS) and a fiber-optic network, but FEMA denied funding.

The plan's goals, objectives, and policies are centered on state actions,

primarily on building an institutional framework for hazard mitigation. Little attention is paid to local government mitigation actions. The proposed state actions are extensive and ambitious and, if carried out fully, would be very effective. However, the realities of state funding priorities have limited their implementation. For example, the plan proposes to fund a full-time state hazard mitigation officer (Action 25) and a full-time state hazard mitigation grant administrator (Action 26), but as of June 1996 these positions had not been funded by the Iowa legislature.

Finally, the plan does not specify priorities for mitigation in relation to specific hazards, detail a plan of action for postdisaster mitigation, or identify projects to be funded under the Hazard Mitigation Grant Program.

The implementation and monitoring section relies on the proposed SHMO position to serve as the "pivot point" for implementation with a demanding slate of activities, including chairing the state Hazard Mitigation Team, monitoring progress, training local officials, providing technical assistance, and visiting each of the ninety-nine counties on a three-year cycle. Unless the state fills the SHMO position, this agenda will be difficult to complete. Moreover, although the section includes a well-thought-out approach for monitoring and reporting, its plan evaluation and annual plan updates require action by a SHMO.

Iowa's Hazard Mitigation Planning and Implementation Process

Following the Midwest floods of 1993, Iowa initiated an active mitigation project review and long-term planning process. It added emergency management staff, coordinated state and local activities, and employed a consultant.

Chronology of Events

A review of the various activities during Iowa's mitigation process following the 1993 floods shows several stages over a two-year period, including initial gearing up and priority setting, responding to new federal policy, plan preparation and grant submissions, and project implemenation.

Immediate Aftermath: July–October 1993

In the first three months following the disaster declaration, the state geared up a mitigation team and procedures, established mitigation funding priorities and a regional grant application structure, and submitted two early Section 404 grant applications from Polk County (one for elevations by the

nonprofit organization Neighborhood Housing Services, Inc., and one for acquisitions by the city of Des Moines). It appeared that the most substantial mitigation funding would be available through HUD's Community Development Block Grant (CDBG) program instead of FEMA's Section 404 program. Meanwhile, FEMA headquarters sent the message via Larry Zensinger, the national-level FEMA official who became known as the "flood czar," that mitigation actions were to focus on acquisition of flood-damaged properties instead of elevation, floodproofing, and other structural projects. Given the scope and seriousness of the nine-state flooding disaster, the staff at FEMA's Region VII office were supplemented with personnel from Region X in Seattle, and all were headquartered in a Des Moines field office. The Interagency Hazard Mitigation Team report, due immediately after the disaster, was never completed in final form. A draft was written during this period, but there was controversy over its content and it was never finalized. During October, a second group of FEMA officials from Region I in Boston replaced Region X staff in the Des Moines field office.

Near-Term Recovery: November 1993–March 1994

In the next five months, the funding situation changed dramatically with passage of the Volkmer Act (Hazard Mitigation and Relocation Assistance Act of 1993) in December, which increased tenfold the Section 404 funds available to Iowa. Two more Section 404 projects were received: the Des Moines floodgate and the Ames acquisitions. A conference held in Davenport in January 1994 helped local officials understand the complexities of the recovery process and the mysteries of FEMA grant procedures.

Plan Preparation:
Major Mitigation Grant Submissions, April–August 1994

Working under contract as a consultant to the Iowa Emergency Management Division, the State Public Policy Group began preparing the Section 409 plan in April and delivered it to Region VII in August, following an extensive public participation and consensus-building effort. FEMA Region I officials departed in April, turning the Des Moines field office back over to Region VII, supplemented with Brenda Bruun, who was transferred in from FEMA headquarters in May. Twenty-two Section 404 projects, the bulk of the submissions, came in. Most were acquisitions, with some elevation projects and a few relocation projects.

Project Implementation: August 1994–June 1995

Three Section 404 projects (mostly acquisitions, with a few elevations and one relocation) were submitted. As of June 21, 1995, two years after the

disaster, $23,413,486 had been obligated for FEMA-996-DR-IA (the Section 404 federal share plus the grantee and subgrantee administrative funds for all projects), and another $9,924,907 was projected to make up the "lock-in" project total, plus estimated grantee and subgrantee administrative expenses, for an overall total of $33,338,393 for this disaster. Approved Section 404 projects (based on original applications, not including amendments) included 658 acquisitions, 37 elevations, and 1 floodgate (see figure 5.1 for location of projects).

State officials continued to submit Section 404 applications despite being advised that all available funding had been committed. Implementation of recommendations of the Section 409 plan proceeded slowly due to lack of state funding. A staff member of the Iowa Division of Emergency Management, Pat Hall, was appointed SHMO on a collateral duty basis. The National Flood Insurance Reform Act was signed in September 1994, tightening up flood insurance provisions and creating a $20 million Mitigation Assistance Fund to provide planning and mitigation grants to communities.

Key Players

Contrary to the usual perception of a stable group of officials playing the same roles throughout a disaster recovery, Iowa's two-year recovery process was marked by a number of changes in key players. Not only do these changes make it challenging to understand the decision-making process in retrospect, but they also made the process itself more complicated and difficult as turnover of FEMA officials responsible for the recovery brought confusing and frustrating changes in interpretation of the federal regulations and procedures. The key players in the Iowa mitigation process are listed in table 5.1.

Influence of the Stafford Act and National Priorities

Mitigation following the 1993 floods in Iowa was clearly influenced both by the predisaster procedures established by the Stafford Act and its implementing regulations and by a series of significant national mitigation priorities put in place after the disaster was declared.

The Stafford Act sets out the framework for postdisaster mitigation. Prior to the Volkmer Act in December 1993, mitigation grants were available to states under Section 404, in an amount based on 10 percent of assistance available under Categories C–G. The predisaster matching requirement was one state-provided dollar for every three federal grant

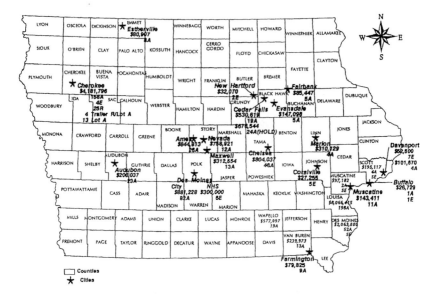

Figure 5.1. Approved Section 404 Housing Projects in Iowa as of June 14, 1995. *Source:* Iowa Emergency Management Division.

dollars. To be eligible for Section 404 grants, the state must prepare or revise its Section 409 plan, whose content is spelled out by regulations. The act does not specify mitigation priorities, leaving these to the state plan. Hazard mitigation options include floodproofing or elevation of damaged buildings (required under the NFIP where the cost of repair is 50 percent or more of the market value prior to the flood), structural flood protection, warning and awareness programs, and buyouts.

Following the 1993 disaster, a number of important national actions influenced Iowa's mitigation process. The three most important were a decision to emphasize acquisition as a mitigation strategy, a change in the Section 404 funding formula, and appropriation of supplemental funds from the Community Development Block Grant (CDBG) program, the HOME Investment Partnerships Program, and the Economic Development Administration (EDA). In addition, the National Flood Insurance Program (NFIP) was reformed.

The Clinton administration established buyouts (acquisition of flood-damaged properties) as the first priority for mitigation funds available for the Midwest floods. This was the cornerstone of the national buyout strategy established at FEMA headquarters shortly after the disaster and implemented through the appointment of a FEMA "flood czar" (Larry

Table 5.1. Key Players in the Iowa Mitigation Process

TITLE	NAME	ROLE	DATES
FEMA Staff			
FEMA headquarters representative	Larry Zensinger	"Flood czar"	July 1993–June 1995
Director, Mitigation Division, Region VII	Steve Harrell	Review and approval of Section 409 and Section 404 applications	July 1993–June 1995
Federal hazard mitigation officer (FHMO), Region VII	Jodi E. Broida	Current FHMO	
Temporary FHMO (from Region X)	Bob Freitag	First Iowa FHMO	July–October 1993
Temporary federal coordinating officer (FCO) (from Region X)	Dick Buck	First Iowa FCO	July–October 1993
Temporary FHMO (from Region I)	Paul White	Second Iowa FHMO	October 1993–April 1994
Temporary FCO (from Region I)	John Carleton	Second Iowa FCO	October 1993–April 1994
Lead hazard mitigation specialist, Region VII	Brenda Bruun	Iowa Field Office	May 1994–June 1995
Iowa Staff			
Director, Iowa Emergency Management Division (EMD)	Ellen Gordon	Top Iowa official	
State hazard mitigation officer (SHMO), EMD	Dick Bartell	Part-time duty	Left October 1993

Position	Name	Function	Dates
Emergency management specialist, EMD (Contract)	Chris Finch	Nonstructural (SHMO, August 1993–February 1995)	July 1993–June 1995
Emergency management specialist, EMD (Contract)	John Cavanaugh	Structural	July 1993–June 1995
National Floodplain Insurance coordinator, Iowa Department of Natural Resources	Bill Cappuccio	Permit approval	July 1993–June 1995
Field representative, Iowa Department of Economic Development (DED)	Michelle Guericke	CDBG projects	
Field representative (DED)	Henry Manning	CDBG projects	
Section 409 plan project director, State Public Policy Group (Consultant to EMD)	Arlinda McKeen	Section 409 plan consultant	April 1994–August 1994
SHMO	Pat Hall	Collateral duty	March 1995–June 1995

Zensinger) assigned to the Midwest. Attention initially focused on buying flooded property in wetlands because of the role played by wetlands in reducing flooding levels, but the strategy soon expanded to include acquisition and clearance of buildings in floodplains as a way to reduce future recovery costs (Morrish, Swenson, and Baltus 1994). In December 1993, President Clinton signed the Hazard Mitigation and Relocation Assistance Act of 1993 (Volkmer Act), which, along with the $130 million earmarked for the Midwest, became the force propelling the buyout.

Buyouts were expected to reduce flood damage, protect people and property, improve the quality of affordable housing, increase recreation opportunities and wildlife values, and add to community betterment (Interagency Floodplain Management Review Committee 1994, pp 118–120). However, the implementation of buyouts—never before attempted on this scale—was plagued by confusion among multiple federal programs, applications, and eligibility requirements.

Four types of buyouts can be identified (Morrish, Swenson, and Baltus 1994, pp. 23–26):

- *Basic buyout*, in which communities simply made the buyout program available to residents, without a community-sponsored relocation program. This left a remnant community of scattered houses, many elevated or floodproofed, and vacant lots, as in the city of Des Moines and Louisa County

- *Buyout and infill*, in which flood survivors were encouraged to move to empty lots in neighborhoods outside the flood hazard zone

- *Buyout and reorganization*, in which communities proactively relocated houses, residents, and businesses into existing and new subdivisions incorporating planning for utilities, open space, and other needs, as in Ames, Cherokee, Nevada, and Audubon

- *Buyout and complete relocation*, in which communities either built a new town from the ground up or moved structures from the old site to a new location, as initially proposed in Chelsea

Passage of the Volkmer Act in December 1993 changed the Section 404 funding formula, increasing mitigation grants to 15 percent of all categories and reducing state cost sharing from 50 percent to 25 percent. This resulted in a tenfold increase in hazard mitigation grant funds available to Iowa and caused a major change in Iowa's mitigation strategy when substantial Section 404 funds became available for buyouts. The change was also a source of confusion, however, due to inconsistent and overlapping

application requirements for Section 404, CDBG, HOME, and EDA mitigation funds.

Congressional supplemental appropriations for flood relief gave Iowa an additional $64.2 million in CDBG funds and nearly $10 million in HOME funds. Eight of the state's largest cities also received additional CDBG and HOME funds. More than $35 million of the CDBG funds and all the HOME funds were used for housing. Iowa used these funds for three housing activities: (1) repair (about $13 million for 1,100 homes); (2) hazard mitigation, including elevation, removal, or demolition (about $20 million to remove or elevate some 1,400 homes, in combination with FEMA funds); and (3) replacement of affordable housing. Applications for these funds, administered by the Iowa Department of Economic Development, were channeled through ten Housing Recovery Zones created after the floods (see figure 5.2).

In 1995, when our case studies were conducted, reforms in the National Flood Insurance Program had not been felt in Iowa. However, the NFIP coordinator reported that purchase of flood insurance policies went up sharply after the 1993 floods but subsequently declined, as shown in Table 5.2.

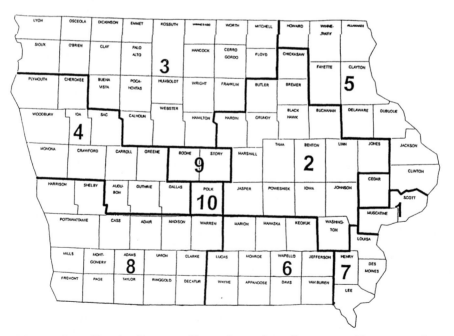

Figure 5.2. Iowa Housing Recovery Zones. *Source:* Iowa Emergency Management Division.

Table 5.2. National Flood Insurance Program Policies in Effect in Iowa, 1992–1994

Date	Number of Policies
12/31/92	6,440
9/30/93	7,707
1/31/94	8,689
6/30/94	9,406
9/30/94	8,888
11/30/94	8,718

Source: Bill Cappuccio, National Flood Insurance Program coordinator, Iowa Department of Natural Resources, 1995.

Results

After all mitigation decisions, plans, programs, and strategies are completed, the bottom line consists of the actual mitigation results. What was actually done as a result of the postdisaster mitigation effort in Iowa? This question requires an examination of the mitigation measures chosen, the way they were administered, and the outcomes that resulted.

Overview

The major mitigation strategy in Iowa, as in the other midwestern states affected by the 1993 floods, was purchase of flood-damaged properties and relocation of residents from these properties. Due to FEMA policy, other measures, such as elevating buildings and installing flood control structures, were used only in a minor way, despite state suggestions.

Mitigation Measures Used

Several types of mitigation measures were undertaken in Iowa following the 1993 floods. Acquisition and relocation of floodplain properties was the most significant of these strategies, a reflection of the mitigation priorities established by FEMA, the Clinton administration, and Congress. The major legislative changes that occurred after the disaster substantially shaped decisions regarding Iowa's postdisaster mitigation strategy.

The administration of the Section 404 buyout program was organizationally complex. After a review of the initial damage patterns, the state was grouped into ten Housing Recovery Zones. A lead county was chosen in each zone, which in turn contracted with a Council of Governments (COG) to manage the program. Because the boundaries of Housing

Recovery Zones did not match COG boundaries, as many as three COGs might be managing the program in a single recovery zone. To guide administration of the program, an administrative plan was prepared for each recovery zone. Among other things, these plans stipulated the conditions under which projects would be selected for purchase and the types and amounts of compensation to be offered to homeowners (e.g., different amounts for replacement housing and relocation assistance).

Acquisition and Relocation

It was estimated that some 9,000 structures would eventually be acquired and relocated in the states affected by the Midwest floods of 1993. In Iowa, the final number of structures purchased was 1,013. Exactly how the state went about its mitigation program was a matter of perception, depending on which individuals were interviewed. FEMA regional officials criticized the "first come, first served" aspect of the Iowa buyout program, as well as its slow start. They also argued that it resulted in the funding of less effective buyout projects, such as scattered properties. Iowa officials defended their approach as participatory and aligned with state and local needs as well as with federal policy.

Whether or not one agrees with the critics, the buyout program in Iowa does illustrate a number of potential problems with a buyout strategy. Particularly troubling is the uncertainty about whether buyout has in fact resulted in safer patterns of development. In many places the researchers visited, despite purchase and removal of numerous damaged structures, the basic development pattern remained unaltered even though the density of development had been reduced. This produced a "Swiss cheese" effect wherein the buyout resulted in a scattered pattern of vacant lots rather than in the setting aside of large, contiguous blocks of floodplain, as envisioned by buyout proponents. It is not clear what will become of these new scattered vacant lots, though they may present opportunities for creative neighborhood use (e.g., as community gardens). What effects, if any, these changes in housing and population will have on neighborhoods is an interesting sociological question. Setting aside of contiguous blocks of floodplain did occur in some places we visited, notably Ames. However, most of the areas we visited did not experience such a clear reduction in the overall risk of flooding or gain ecologically or recreationally valuable blocks of floodplain land.

In some cases, the buyout program simply shifted development from one part of a floodplain to another. Under the FEMA-approved Louisa County buyout program (the Reggie Meyers subdivision), homes purchased by the county under the program were resold (i.e., those that

incurred relatively little damage) to nonprofit organizations and others to be reused elsewhere. In the case of Louisa County, in the eastern part of the state, many of these homes were relocated only a few miles away from the buyout site. Such a process does not appear to be resulting in an overall reduction of flood risk.

A second troubling issue was whether the Iowa buyout program was being used primarily to address other local objectives unrelated to flood reduction. For instance, FEMA officials believed that once the new Army Corps of Engineers levee in Des Moines was certified to protect the community from 100-year floods, properties purchased in the Valley Junction area might be resold by the city in order to promote economic development. If this is true, the city would earn a profit on properties essentially purchased with federal monies. To FEMA observers, the acquisition effort appeared to be aimed primarily at local economic development rather than hazard reduction. Similarly, acquisition efforts in Louisa County appeared to be intended primarily to correct a sanitation and public health problem created by the combination of a high water table and heavy reliance on septic tanks and wells. Homes in the Reggie Meyers area, the main focus of the county's acquisition efforts, received relatively little direct damage from flooding and are protected by an Army Corps of Engineers levee designed to protect the area from 500-year floods; (the levee was not breached during the 1993 flood event). The buyout program here was clearly addressing an important local problem but not really advancing the goal of reducing risks from future flooding. Some observers believed that this lack of accountability for the use of buyout funds was in no small part a result of the "free" nature of these funds (i.e., with federal CDBG monies used even to cover the 25 percent required state match).

Another perceived problem with the buyout approach was its potential effect on the availability of affordable housing. Unlike the situation in coastal regions, homes and property in the riverine floodplain tend to be significantly less expensive than those in areas not subject to flooding. People who are relocating to areas outside floodplains will encounter higher housing prices and less affordable living conditions. This was the rationale behind the replacement housing payments, which provided funds ($9,000–$16,000 in Iowa) above and beyond the fair market value of the floodplain property being purchased. Additional relocation funds were also provided in some zones. Additionally, at least in the short term, the overall housing stock was reduced, raising further concerns about housing availability. This concern led several interviewees to note the importance of programs that build or facilitate the building of new structures in other, safer areas of the community. Several noted that there are

few federal sources of funds for providing essential infrastructure. Of course, in larger metropolitan areas, such as St. Louis, the effects of buyout on housing supply will probably be very small, but in smaller towns, this may be a serious concern.

Yet another problem encountered was difficulty in controlling and coordinating with volunteer and church groups helping to rebuild housing, especially those entering the state after a disaster. Sometimes these groups move quickly to rebuild homes without an understanding that permits are required, that new mitigation standards may apply (e.g., that the structure must be elevated), or that they may be rebuilding and repairing a structure that could or should be relocated. State mitigation officials believe there is a need to develop a better set of procedures for coordinating and managing these types of volunteer groups.

Selected Local Buyout Experiences

City of Des Moines

The city of Des Moines was the first in Iowa to receive Section 404 buyout money after the 1993 floods. There are several buyout areas in Des Moines. One of the most controversial is the Valley Junction area, where the U.S. Army Corps of Engineers has been building a new protective levee. As mentioned earlier, FEMA officials fear that once the levee is certified to protect the area from 100-year floods, the city will attempt to sell the acquired lots for subsequent development. FEMA officials have been vocal about their belief that such an action would violate the intentions behind the buyout program and that if the lots are resold, at the very least the city should be required to repay the federal government for the original acquisition costs. State officials point out that this project was approved under FEMA guidelines and meets all program requirements.

City of Davenport

Davenport's buyout program is an extension of a preexisting local effort to purchase floodplain properties. Davenport is unique among the localities we visited in that it had budgeted for acquisition each year since 1990. It began its acquisition program after two large flash floods occurred within a ten-day period. In the past, the acquisitions have been funded through a special sales tax. Following the 1993 floods, acquisition was concentrated in the Garden Addition area along Black Hawk Creek where the city had so far purchased twenty-one homes. City officials had attempted to interest homeowners in selling flood-prone properties along the Mississippi River, but to no avail. In the words of Suzanne Jordan of Davenport's

Building Inspections Department, "People like living along the river. . . . It's an escape." There was some interest in elevation along the river, however, and some seven elevation projects had been funded. The Garden Addition received emphasis in acquisition in part because limited funds would go further there. Average home values were $15,000–$25,000, much less than along the Mississippi. Davenport is also an interesting case because of its decision not to build a protective flood wall along the riverfront, in order to preserve its visual connection with the Mississippi River. Some expressed the view that because the city chose not to protect itself from flooding, others, such as federal and state taxpayers, should not have to pay for damages resulting from this decision.

Louisa County

Located on the eastern side of the state and along the Mississippi River, Louisa County had approximately 200 homes involved in its buyout program. One area where acquisition was concentrated is the Reggie Meyers subdivision. This is an area that lies behind and is protected by a 500-year levee (which was not breached during the floods) but yet where development probably should not have been permitted in the first place. The more significant problem here had been sanitation—houses rely on septic tanks and wells, and the water table is very high. Relatively little aboveground flooding occurred here, and the county was selling the homes to nonprofit organizations for $1 and to others on the open market. Major concerns were expressed about Louisa County's buyout program, which was recommended by Tennessee Valley Authority (TVA) experts brought in by FEMA. First, the program appeared to address general issues of community development and public health rather than flood hazards in particular, and second, many of the sold homes were apparently being relocated just a few miles away from their original sites. State and local officials believed there might have been more logical ways to address the area's problems with sanitation and high water table, including expansion of pumping capacity or installation of public water supply and sewage disposal systems.

City of Muscatine and Muscatine County

Muscatine County lies just north of Louisa County, on the eastern edge of the state and along the Mississippi River. During the 1993 floods, it experienced modest flooding along the Mississippi (its sand levee system held, though some seepage flooding was experienced) and along its interior creeks, which drain into the Cedar River. Both the city and the county participated in the federal buyout program, with about fifteen structures

purchased in each jurisdiction. The county's buyout structures were generally scattered throughout the county, whereas the city focused on acquiring properties in two flood-prone areas in the southern and eastern parts of the city. According to Jeff Carter, coordinator of the Muscatine County Emergency Management Agency, the county's strategy generally was not to try to clear out the floodplains but rather to ensure that homes there met zoning and elevation standards. Flooding is a normal part of life there, and it is unrealistic to expect that the floodplain will not be inhabited. Since the 1993 floods, then, the county's main strategy had been to "beef up" its zoning enforcement. Of particular concern were the more than 300 small recreational cabins located along the creeks in the county. These were once used only as summer fishing cabins, but many people had converted them into year-round homes, and because of a state court opinion, such use has been grandfathered. Over time, the county hoped to ensure that these cabins are elevated, have proper sewage, and meet basic zoning and floodplain standards.

Wapello Levee District

Located in Louisa County along the Iowa River, the Wapello levee system (Levee District 8) experienced eleven separate breaks and considerable resulting damage during the 1993 floods. With encouragement from the U.S. Department of Agriculture, officials of the levee district decided not to repair the levee but rather to seek a buyout of farmers there. The river at this particular stretch seeks to take a natural bend, and the buyout would help restore a more natural flow as well as help restore other natural features of the river. At the time of our interviews, the buyout was complete. In total, 2,600 acres were purchased from ten different landowners at a cost of $2.2 million. The purchases were negotiated by the Iowa Natural Heritage Foundation, with funding primarily from the Department of Agriculture under the Emergency Wetlands Reserve Program, funded in October 1993. The land had been added to the Mark Twain National Wildlife Refuge, and a management plan for the land was under way. It is expected that the land will be returned to a natural use; preliminary management ideas include restoring prairie habitat and planting trees and other native vegetation.

In addition to the Wapello district buyout, the Iowa Natural Heritage Foundation was working on farmland buyouts along nine other rivers in the state. Some $70 million was made available following the 1993 floods through the Emergency Wetlands Reserve Program and the regular Wetlands Reserve Program. As a result, several thousand additional acres of

agricultural land in the floodplain were to be permanently owned by the federal government and returned to wetlands and natural habitat.

Cities of Cherokee, Nevada, and Audubon

The buyout projects in the cities of Cherokee, Nevada, and Audubon were unique in part because they were being used by the communities as springboards for accomplishing other local goals. Assisting in the planning process was the National Park Service's (NPS's) Rivers, Trails, and Conservation Assistance Program, under a mission assignment to FEMA (Hanson and Lemanski 1995). After the floods, NPS staff members contacted each buyout community and offered help, and Cherokee, Nevada, and Audubon responded.

The philosophy behind the NPS involvement was that the local planning process should be grassroots and bottom-up. In each case, an initial step was to identify or help establish a community group to take the lead in planning. In Cherokee, for instance, a "green space" committee was formed. An important step in planning for local floodplain use was the undertaking of a public workshop and the preparation of a "concept plan." NPS staff then assisted in evaluating the technical merits of the ideas generated from the workshop and helped link up local design ideas with potential funding sources. For example, Nevada was working on an application to the Iowa Department of Natural Resources for funding for trail development and additional floodplain acquisition. In each community, the buyout program was seen as an opportunity to restore the floodplain to a more natural state and to create recreational and other benefits for local residents.

Cherokee also took an interesting approach in addressing the effect of the buyouts on housing availability. This was the largest buyout community in the state, acquiring some 187 residential properties in the floodplain and relocating 25 businesses as well. It was to set aside a contiguous riverfront area eventually to encompass about 160 acres along the Little Sioux River. City officials envisioned this area as a natural park, with trails and restored prairies and wetlands. Some streambank restoration was also to be undertaken.

Perhaps the most interesting aspect of the Cherokee program was the attempt to ensure that buyout families had adequate opportunities for relocation and replacement housing. Under the Cherokee program, homeowners had several options. They could sell their property and buy or build a home somewhere else. Or, if the structure survived the flood and was repairable, they could sell only the land and relocate the structure. About

fourteen homeowners chose the latter option. An additional thirty-six homes were purchased by the city and then resold to the general public for relocation. To provide a place for these relocated structures, the city designed and platted a new twenty-two-lot subdivision. Other structures were relocated to rural sites or placed on infill sites within the city. Using state CDBG monies, the city also implemented a down payment assistance program for low-income residents that provided as much as $22,000 for a down payment on a new home.

City of Ames

Located north of Des Moines, the city of Ames experienced significant flooding along the Skunk River and Squaw Creek in 1993. Altogether, twenty-eight homes were purchased and demolished in the South Russell–South Riverside neighborhood. Most were located in one area, where their removal created a contiguous area of open-space floodplain along Squaw Creek (see figure 5.3). A connecting street was removed and vegetation reestablished. The Ames project was clearly resulting in a less vulnerable settlement pattern—all the homes had been within the 100-year floodplain, and the area is to remain in permanent open space. The project was funded 50 percent with CDBG funds and 50 percent with Section 404 funds. To determine what to offer homeowners, the city used an assessed value approach and added 10 percent. In addition, an $8,500 relocation assistance grant (the approximate amount believed necessary for a down payment on a new home) was given to homeowners who agreed to relocate somewhere within the city but outside the floodplain. Moving expenses also were paid.

Chelsea

The town of Chelsea, located along the Iowa River in the central part of the state, is the only case in Iowa of an entire community seeking relocation, as did several communities in other flood-damaged states, such as Valmeyer, Illinois, and Rhineland, Missouri. Chelsea is an interesting case that highlights the difficulties in a relocation strategy.

According to Morrish, Swenson, and Baltus (1994), this community of 336 residents decided, by a narrow margin, to relocate the entire town to the hills above the original floodplain town site. The relocation was intended to accommodate residences and businesses; there was no major industry in the town. Some residents decided not to remain. Issues included repeated problems with securing the new town site due to concerns regarding the environmental impact on cultural resources and an

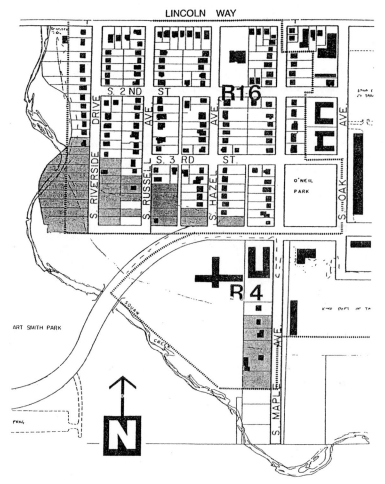

Figure 5.3. Ames, Iowa, Flood Buyout Area After Demolition. *Source:* City of Ames, Iowa.

endangered turtle species, as well as the owner's refusal to sell the land, which made FEMA's regional office reluctant to commit funds. Moreover, there was a gap between the financing needed and that available to move or build houses and businesses, and there were difficulties in securing funding for all aspects of a new town, such as parks, a business district, and the like. As a consequence, the relocation had been delayed.

Other Mitigation Measures

Although buyout was the dominant mitigation strategy employed in Iowa, other measures were used on a limited basis.

Elevation

Section 404 funding for elevation of damaged structures was provided on a limited basis. Compared with acquisition and relocation, elevation was not a very widely used form of mitigation in Iowa. Eleven communities were approved for elevation projects, for a total of forty-three houses. Unlike Missouri, which made the decision to fund only acquisition and relocation and not elevation, Iowa emphasized all three. Some observers were critical of the low number of elevation projects and the failure to use this mitigation strategy more effectively. They noted that there were many locations where the risk of future flooding was relatively low, given the low probability of another 1993 event, and where elevation would be the more cost-effective and appropriate form of mitigation. It is not entirely clear why so few communities and property owners in Iowa were interested in elevation. In many cases, the extent of devastation brought by the floods made people leery of rebuilding in their current locations. In some cases, however, communities did not give residents a choice. The greater flexibility given to the state in processing acquisition and relocation projects, as compared with elevation projects, may also have been a factor. In the case of acquisition and relocation projects, applicants were allowed to prepare benefit-cost analyses essentially after the fact. This was not generally the case with elevation projects, and as a result, there was an impression that funding for acquisition and relocation would be faster and easier.

The Des Moines Floodgate

The only major structural project funded after the floods was the Des Moines floodgates. Located west of downtown Des Moines, behind the central campus of Technical High School, the floodgate was constructed on a railyard and was designed to connect and complete a U.S. Army Corps of Engineers levee built in the 1960s along the Raccoon River. The floodgate is to be closed in the event of flooding but otherwise will allow the passage of railway traffic. (The project actually consists of fifty-three feet of flood-wall and two floodgates.) This railroad opening was the single most important point source of river flooding in Des Moines (in the Riverpoint-Dico area), resulting in more than $117 million in damage to the city. The cost of the floodgate was $484,000.

Flood Insurance

One mitigation measure used by a number of flood victims was insurance—flood insurance under the National Flood Insurance Program in the case of residential and commercial structures and crop insurance for agricultural losses. Significant problems were apparent in both programs. A major limitation of the NFIP was its low participation rate, both in Iowa

and in the nation as a whole. Although there were an estimated 50,000 flood-prone properties in the state, there were only 6,440 NFIP policies before the 1993 floods (see table 5.2). This low participation rate suggests the difficulty of relying on individual insurance to cover flood losses. Ironically, the buyout program created the impression for some that paying yearly flood insurance premiums was not necessary, since the federal government and/or the state would come along later and bail out a homeowner even if he or she did not have insurance.

The good news is that NFIP participation rose sharply following the floods, though it fell off a bit toward the end of 1994. Moreover, community participation was much higher—about two-thirds of eligible localities were participating in the program.

To its credit, the state of Iowa had been involved in floodplain management since 1957, and the state program enforced more stringent standards than those of the NFIP. For example, the state required elevation of structures one foot higher than the base flood elevation mandated under the NFIP.

One serious problem following the floods, noted by the state floodplain coordinators, was FEMA's undermining of the state's more stringent floodplain management regulations. A specific case in point was a letter from FEMA to localities participating in the NFIP telling them that in enforcing the "substantial damage" requirements, replacement value could be used (i.e., a property owner was required to rebuild to current flood standards only if damage exceeded 50 percent of the replacement value of the structure). However, the state used the more stringent market value standard, and the FEMA letter was viewed as confusing and undermining this stronger state position. In addition to these problems, the state floodplain coordinator indicated that reductions in state staff and funding had diminished the state's effectiveness in enforcing its (and FEMA's) floodplain management requirements.

Conclusions and Recommendations

The Iowa case raised a number of important questions about mitigation policy and procedures. Many of these involved heated disagreements among different levels of government, which need to be resolved if mitigation is to be effective in the future.

• *Define mitigation clearly.* Following the floods, great importance was clearly placed on promoting mitigation, yet it is also clear that there was

considerable disagreement about what mitigation encompasses. One FEMA official declared that anything requiring one "to push a button" is clearly not mitigation. FEMA's Region VII office viewed mitigation as measures that will reduce the long-term riskiness of development and human settlement patterns, such as relocation and floodplain land use controls. On the other hand, state mitigation officials sought much greater flexibility in using mitigation monies, including the funding of improvements to warning systems (such as Iowa's proposed all-hazards interactive information system), levees, and culvert replacements. As long as the net result is reduction of long-term risk, why shouldn't these be considered mitigation? Why shouldn't states be given the flexibility to determine which mixtures of measures will accomplish the greater mitigation result? Considerable disagreement, then, existed concerning what mitigation actually means, and standards and guidelines for administering funds under the Stafford Act are open to interpretation on this matter.

• ***Ensure a clear and consistent line of authority.*** The Iowa recovery effort was confused by changing federal bosses and uncoordinated federal agencies. Despite painfully detailed FEMA regulations, there remained ambiguous areas requiring individual interpretation. Having senior FEMA personnel from three different regions acting as FHMO highlighted the consequences of differences in interpretation of FEMA regulations. State officials reported that each successive FHMO took a different approach, requiring state and local officials to make adjustments with each changeover.

Several examples can be cited of the different ways in which the different regions and their federal coordinating officers and hazard mitigation officers interpreted regulations and policies after the floods. One example involved approval of an elevation program in the city of Des Moines (to be operated by a nonprofit organization). The Region X staff approved these elevation projects without requiring individual benefit-cost analyses. They apparently made this decision by assuming that if the elevation costs averaged $10,000 and the damage costs were at least $12,000, the projects would naturally be cost-effective. Region I took a different position, holding that benefit-cost analyses were essential and should be required. (As it turned out, the state suspended this particular elevation project at six homes out of a planned ninety because of their very high costs and other serious administrative problems.)

A second example involved interpretation of restrictions on duplication of benefits. FEMA is generally forbidden from duplicating disaster assistance benefits. Conflicting interpretations arose over what constituted duplicated benefits in the Des Moines program. Some Des Moines property

owners had been given as much as $10,000 in federal monies under the Emergency Minimal Repair (EMR) program. Region I held that the buyout and EMR benefits were not duplicative and so the city should not subtract the latter from the former in making awards to property owners. Region VII later made the opposite interpretation, holding that to the contrary, these were duplicative benefits and would have to be deducted. Individual homeowners, however, were never assessed this deduction. Instead, the city of Des Moines ended up absorbing the costs.

A third example involved a conflict over the mission assignment process. Region I staff believed that the services of the National Park Service's Rivers, Trails, and Conservation Assistance Program could and should be secured through the mission assignment mechanism, whereby the costs of NPS services would essentially be paid by federal disaster assistance funding. Region VII held a contrary view, believing that the activities of this NPS unit—namely working with communities to design open-space and recreational uses for buyout areas—were not legitimately part of FEMA's mission and thus should not be financed through a mission assignment. (In the end, a mission assignment was used.) These are three of the more prominent examples of the differing philosophies and policy interpretations of different FEMA regions and how they can sometimes confound and confuse postdisaster mitigation.

Confusion also arose from the necessity of dealing with multiple federal agencies, including FEMA, HUD, and the EDA. Each agency has its own rules and priorities, which are not coordinated among agencies. Had there been coordination, perhaps the use of funds from one federal program (CDBG funds) would have not been allowed to serve as the local match for another federal program (FEMA Section 404 grants). In Ames, for example, the city used $660,699 of its CDBG funds to buy out thirteen homes and to serve as the local match for FEMA Section 404 funds of about $700,000 (when the required match was still 50-50). But the Ames housing coordinator, in preparing the city's buyout program, was "too far ahead of FEMA." Lacking clear guidance as to what was permissible under the various federal regulations, she was forced to act before FEMA clarified and streamlined its restrictions on housing relocation and environmental review.

• *Clarify and simplify rules and procedures.* FEMA emphasized a uniform approach to mitigation funding, whereas states preferred having the flexibility to deal with their individual situations and needs. Yet even the uniform approach was subject to varying interpretation.

FEMA preferred a stable, continuing state mitigation organization and a state hazard mitigation officer to carry out an approved Section 409 plan. States, however, were confronted with unstable funding and lack of capacity to staff mitigation posts on a full-time basis. They emphasize the need to gear up after a disaster and to formulate a plan on the basis of the needs brought about by that disaster. Perhaps a solution to the staffing problem would be to create a state disaster mitigation reservist system, similar in concept to the FEMA reservist system. Updating of plans could be partially accomplished by incorporating a disaster mitigation element in all regional and local comprehensive plans.

• *Ensure administrative accountability.* Officials at FEMA's Region VII office were concerned because Iowa continued to forward Section 404 project applications in 1995, after the budget had been fully committed. They saw this as a continuation of a loosely organized, "first come, first served" grant review process by the state. They would have preferred a more organized screening process wherein the state set firm priorities, educated local governments as to what was possible, and guided and reviewed local government applications for Section 404 funds. This would have allowed communities to view mitigation funding as a community development opportunity, as in the Des Moines Valley Junction project. Many applications for structural projects were submitted in 1995, despite the national buyout priority. Of the eighty-two projects received by the region as of June 23, 1995, twenty-eight were "pending," and many of those were for structural projects such as flood walls and drainage improvements. Since twenty-seven of these projects would ultimately be rejected, FEMA believed that Iowa should withdraw them, but the state refused. FEMA also believed that the Section 409 plan should be used in state reviews of Section 404 applications.

Part of the problem was that some state and local governments tended to view Section 404 funds as similar to entitlements, particularly since the required local match could be taken from other federal funds, such as CDBG monies. Another part of the problem was FEMA officials' belief that the state and local governments did not adequately enforce the floodplain management program.

• *Strengthen intergovernmental coordination.* We discovered many instances of breakdown in communication between FEMA's regional office and the state of Iowa. Perhaps the most dramatic example was that FEMA's regional office staff did not know who occupied the Iowa SHMO position.

But this was only the most recent in what appears to have been a long line of breakdowns. FEMA personnel complained that the state was not responsible enough in screening Section 404 applications, meeting Section 409 plan preparation deadlines, setting priorities, and so forth. They said, "It's been a war in Iowa." State personnel complained that FEMA imposed unreasonable delays on project reviews and refused to put rule interpretations in writing. They said, "It's FEMA's problem."

• *Make the Section 409 plan relevant.* The Iowa case clearly shows the irrelevance of a postdisaster Section 409 plan. In this case, the plan was not completed until August 1994, more than a year after the disaster was declared. Its predecessor plan was not consulted during the postdisaster mitigation process. Although Iowa's 1994 plan undoubtedly includes decisions and policies forged in the preceding year, as a formal document it could not have affected those previous actions.

The Iowa case also demonstrates the vulnerability of state plan promises to the realities of the state budgeting process. Sound implementation recommendations made in the plan did not come to pass because of the state's failure to fund the necessary positions and programs.

More generally, the Iowa case raises major issues about what a "good" hazard mitigation plan should be:

○ Should it be a detailed blueprint or a statement of principles that can be adapted to various contingencies? In the Iowa case, the blueprint items never materialized.

○ Should it be a top-down, state-prepared plan or a bottom-up, locally derived plan? Iowa avoided the top-down approach by means of vigorous consensus building with localities and stakeholder groups. This created some anomalies in the plan, but it did build widespread support.

○ What is the relationship between the plan and the interagency hazard mitigation report? Interagency hazard mitigation teams tended to be scornful of Section 409 plans and instead derived their own recommendations, which often conflicted with state and local positions. How can these two mitigation elements be integrated? If the state has an effective Section 409 plan, should the interagency team be eliminated?

• *Use the cost-sharing match to encourage a sense of ownership.* The Iowa case also raised a number of questions about who ought to pay for, and in what proportion, the costs associated with disasters. FEMA officials

spoke with disdain of the sense of entitlement that had developed among individuals and communities affected by flooding.

One concern had to do with the way the hazard mitigation programs cost-sharing requirement was satisfied. The original 50 percent state-local cost share (now 25 percent) was intended to be covered through nonfederal sources, presumably as a legitimate and genuine contribution by the grant recipient—a fair distribution of cost and an actual and symbolic indication that the proposed project is believed in by the applicant. After the 1993 floods, however, the mitigation grant match was usually satisfied through supplemental CDBG funds—that is, federal funds were used to cover the match. The practical result was that in most cases, the federal government absorbed 100 percent of the cost of buyouts. Several individuals interviewed noted that this lack of a match tended to undermine any real "ownership" of the money—it was "free," so there was less reason to carefully scrutinize the merits of projects or ensure that the funded projects were carried out successfully. Requiring a sizable match, it is believed, creates a more equitable distribution of the costs of disasters and helps to build ownership of, and commitment to, the projects that are funded.

• *Build personal responsibility for safety.* An important issue raised throughout the Iowa case was the extent to which individuals and families were taking or being asked to take personal responsibility for their own safety and well-being. Some individuals believed that failure to take personal responsibility was indeed a major problem and that the provision of federal disaster assistance, in the degree to which it was provided and the manner in which it was provided, tended to undermine personal responsibility. Steve Harrell, director of the Mitigation Division at the FEMA regional office, for example, commented on the feeling that "everyone is a victim" and the prevalent belief that flood damage to one's home or possessions is "not my fault." The perception of oneself as a victim tends to lead to the expectation that government "owes it" to the person to replace or otherwise compensate for the damages incurred.

Jeff Carter, coordinator of the Muscatine County Emergency Management Agency, described what he saw as a change in the sense of who is responsible for the effects of disasters such as the 1993 floods. In his part of Iowa, flooding had always been a normal part of the environment; people were used to occasionally being "flooded out." Especially since the late 1980s, he observed, and with the increasing availability of federal disaster assistance, he had seen a change in the way people tended to look at things. People had begun to expect this assistance and to look to the federal government to help them cover costs for repairs and inconveniences that

they previously would have dealt with themselves. Carter and others spoke of the need to encourage personal responsibility in these matters and observed that the federal handouts tended to work against such responsibility. Carter described a couple who lived on a floodplain in Muscatine County and had been "washed out" a number of times in the past. After the 1990 floods, when they found out that financial assistance was available, they made the rounds of FEMA and the other aid agencies and received substantial family grant monies. In 1993, they were again flooded and expected the federal government to help. They received more than $11,000 in family grants and were lodged for two months in a hotel and for another three months in a rented house while repairs were made to their home. Although Carter and others agreed that the poor should be helped, they wondered about the expectations created by this system and whether riverfront residents should take greater personal responsibility for their plight.

Some observers believed that the buyout program played into these attitudes. Moreover, it compensated homeowners in excess of the fair market value of their structures, to address the fact that replacement cost may be much higher than fair market value, and many individuals were given funds to cover moving expenses and provided with temporary housing. In addition, homeowners were not required to have purchased flood insurance to receive buyout benefits, unlike the requirements of the Section 1362 Flooded Properties Purchase Program. The failure of many floodplain residents even to purchase flood insurance (the participation rate in Iowa was quite low, at less than 20 percent) is further indicative of people's failure to assume personal responsibility for their safety and the safety of their property.

• *Be sensitive to equity issues.* Several significant equity issues arose after the floods. One stemmed from the fact that unlike upper-income householders along the ocean coastline, residents of riverine floodplains often tended to be lower on the socioeconomic ladder. They were living in floodplains because property values and housing costs were lower there. These poorer residents were subject to repeated flooding disasters and yet were the least equipped and least prepared to deal with such events. The Galloway Report confirms this observation (Interagency Floodplain Management Review Committee 1994, p. 7):

> The Review Committee found during visits to over 60 communities in the flood affected region that the floodplain neighborhoods and subdivisions tended to be lower income neighborhoods of the community. These neighborhoods appear to have a higher percentage of rental properties, more elderly residents, more young families, more people on assistance, and lower

value housing. It is common to find houses in the floodplains of these communities that have market values of less than $25,000 and often as low as $10,000 or $5,000.

Another equity concern involved the effects of mitigation programs such as the floodplain buyout effort. Specifically in Iowa, there was concern that the buyout program might reduce the amount of affordable housing available. The buyout effort focused on clearing dangerous floodplain areas, with little emphasis given to developing nonfloodplain areas that might provide replacement housing. Did the postflood mitigation program, then, serve to reduce the availability of affordable housing and make richer communities more exclusive?

• *Incorporate multiple objectives in hazard mitigation project.* A recurrent theme in the Iowa case study was the potential to accomplish multiple objectives in undertaking postflood mitigation projects. The efforts in Nevada, Audubon, Cherokee, and other communities under the leadership of the National Park Service's Rivers, Trails, and Conservation Assistance Program are positive examples. Here, the goals of moving people and property out of the floodplain have dovetailed nicely with the goals of creating new recreational areas, such as biking and hiking trails, and of restoring wildlife habitat and other environmental qualities. The acquisition of 2,600 acres in the Wapello levee district in Louisa County and the addition of this land to a national wildlife refuge is another example of positive multiobjective planning and mitigation. These efforts are consistent with the recent interest in, and successful examples of, multiobjective river corridor management (National Park Service 1991).

On the other hand, some interviewees expressed concern over the fact that mitigation projects were being used primarily to fund and accomplish "other" local objectives, not primarily hazard mitigation. For example, the Louisa County buyout program, particularly in the area of the Reggie Meyers subdivision, appeared primarily to be addressing the health threats associated with septic tank contamination of groundwater and the more general objective of community development. The Des Moines program, particularly the buyout of properties in the Valley Junction area, was also criticized as being aimed primarily at economic development rather than hazard mitigation. Given the "free" nature of these federal funds, it is not surprising that local governments attempted to use them to address a variety of perceived local needs or problems.

• *Take an ecosystem approach.* The Iowa case raised a number of questions about the need for a broader, more holistic approach to managing flood hazards. One idea discussed by many, and included in the Galloway

Report, is the need to view the floodplain from a basin-wide, ecosystem management perspective. There is growing consensus nationally that ecosystem management is an effective strategy for resource protection and management (e.g., Interagency Ecosystem Management Task Force 1995), and the Midwest floods dramatically illustrate its potential role in providing a comprehensive framework for advancing hazard mitigation.

An ecosystem approach would require looking at the Mississippi basin more holistically, assuming a broader geographic scale of reference and establishing management goals and objectives over a much longer time frame. It would facilitate analysis of interconnections among elements in the natural (and human-made) system and of the cumulative effects of many discrete actions (e.g., construction and repair of levees, alteration of land and vegetation in the watershed). Further, it could serve as a framework to guide and coordinate the different management and mitigation policies and actions in the floodplain taken by different agencies and organizations. An ecosystem perspective would also encourage viewing the river system in its entirety and understanding the many different (though potentially complementary) environmental, economic, and social functions it serves. The north-south orientation of the river system, for instance, means that it represents an important migration corridor for waterbirds (Sparks 1995), a natural function that is sometimes overlooked.

Clearly related to this perspective is the perception that actions should be undertaken to restore, to the extent possible, the natural functioning of the river system. To some, this means removing or not rebuilding damaged levees. Perhaps the most effective comprehensive long-term strategy in the upper Mississippi basin would be to protect and restore its natural resilience—the ability of the natural system to absorb and naturally mitigate floodwater as well as to provide a host of other environmental and ecological benefits. Restoration of the basin's wetlands could be extremely important in this regard. Some 60 percent of midwestern wetlands have been destroyed since European settlement. Phillippi (1994, p. 77) argues for the need to take a certain amount of agricultural land out of production and allow it to revert to wetlands:

> Removing substantial portions of midwestern floodplain from production and restoring them to riverine wetland would appear to be a win-win national strategy: agricultural production reduced, wetlands restored. Restoring 2 million acres (less than one percent of total cropland and 10 percent of flood hazard areas) would be a nice first step—one that could have provided storage area for as much as 15 percent of the overbank floodwaters in 1993, reducing damages elsewhere. Restoring 2 million acres would cost about $2 billion, based on the typical $1000-per-acre value of land in the floodplain.

Recent research findings show that wetlands are able to absorb much greater amounts of floodwater than previously thought. Experimental wetlands constructed along the Des Plaines River in Illinois have recently shown dramatic results. A marsh only 5.7 acres in size has been found to absorb and retain the natural runoff of a 410-acre watershed (Stevens 1995). The conclusions suggest that a relatively small percentage of restored wetlands (an estimated 1.37–5.47 percent) would be needed to absorb runoff and prevent flooding. Extrapolated to the Mississippi River watershed, the Des Plaines study estimated that only 13 million acres of wetlands would have been needed to prevent flooding in 1993 (only 3 percent of the land area of the upper Mississippi watershed). And, of course, protecting and restoring wetlands also exemplifies multiobjective planning in that it not only controls flooding but also provides important habitat and environmental benefits.

Following the Midwest floods, there was considerable discussion about opportunities to restore the natural functioning of the river ecosystem and considerable advocacy of such an approach by outside commentators (Wright 1996). In Iowa, the one clear success story in this regard was the buyout of the Wapello levee district, which will return an additional 2,600 acres to natural land, in a spot along the Mississippi where the river naturally wants to bend and turn. This effort and other efforts around the state to purchase agricultural land under the Wetlands Reserve Program illustrate at once the desirability of a restorative philosophy of mitigation and the difficulty of undoing many years of human alteration and control.

• *Promote sustainable communities.* The Iowa case illustrates the potential importance of mitigation in promoting sustainable communities. The ultimate *unsustainable* community is one in which homes and businesses are repeatedly damaged and destroyed and people are repeatedly displaced by flood events. The Iowa buyout strategy can be seen as an effort (variously successful) to achieve land use and development patterns that are more sustainable in the long run. Fundamentally, the Midwest floods have raised a broader question: How should towns and communities relate to rivers and floodplains so as to allow for a *sustainable* relationship? Converting, where possible, floodplains to greenbelts and natural areas, as in the case of Nevada, is a positive step.

There is some indication that Iowa communities are beginning to think in terms of sustainability and to see the need to promote more sustainable land use and development patterns. For example, a very interesting collaborative regional planning initiative is under way in the Des Moines area. Called the Central Iowa Greenways Project, it is being coordinated by

the Iowa Natural Heritage Foundation. It is focused primarily on educating and bringing together local officials, business leaders, and developers to protect a regional system of open space. The project is based on the premise that open space is the basic environmental infrastructure of the region and significantly enhances the region's livability. Although open space is the project's focus, there is recognition of the need to address the broader issues of regional growth. One of the project's goals is to determine how much land would be consumed over the next twenty to thirty years under different growth assumptions and proposals. At the time of our interviews, an advisory committee had been meeting, and much of the initial effort had focused on education (slide presentations were planned for each of the local chambers of commerce) and on starting a regional dialogue about growth and open-space issues, especially within the business community. A greenways summit was planned, and it is hoped that the process eventually will result in a regional greenways plan, of which the floodplains of the Raccoon and Des Moines Rivers will be important elements.

• **Rethink the intergovernmental mitigation framework.** The Iowa case study well illustrates many of the tensions between federal mitigation goals and state and local mitigation goals. The emphasis placed on floodplain buyouts was clearly the result of a federal decision and federal priorities. In our discussions with state officials, it was evident that state officials would have preferred greater flexibility in spending disaster assistance and mitigation monies. Mitigation priorities in Iowa appeared to differ from the priorities of FEMA's regional and national offices. State officials believed that they were closer to the mitigation needs of the state and its localities and ought to have more authority in deciding how these funds should be spent—for example, on warning systems or geographic information systems, perhaps, rather than on floodplain buyouts. Indeed, Iowa was one of the first states to enter into a Performance Partnership Agreement (PPA) with FEMA, and this may give the state greater flexibility in making such decisions in the future. From a federal perspective, the Iowa case raised questions about relying too heavily on state block grants, which may result in the perceived wasting of funds and the failure to accomplish or promote any coherent mitigation strategy. Clearly, Iowa would have preferred to spend its funds differently from the way suggested by FEMA. But greater flexibility for Iowa would have meant greater loss of control at the federal level.

It is clear that even though many mitigation decisions made in Iowa related only to Iowa, there was a need for broader regional mitigation

strategies as well. Especially in the case of flooding, a basin-wide strategy seems necessary, even though it might constrain some state and local decisions. For example, protecting and restoring wetlands in one state may have little overall effect on flooding without similar efforts in other states; enlarging and reinforcing flood walls and levees in one state will have hydrological effects on downstream states. Perhaps what is needed is a nested mitigation framework for flood hazards in which a broad mitigation strategy is developed for the entire river basin or watershed, somewhat more detailed mitigation strategies and plans are prepared for subbasins, and specific mitigation measures and programs are adopted at the state and local levels.

1997 Update

To update the information collected during the 1995 case study, we conducted telephone interviews with Steve Zimmerman and Dennis Harper of the Iowa Emergency Management Division in 1997. They reported that Iowa had experienced three additional federally declared disasters: two floods (FEMA-1121-DR-IA and FEMA-1133-DR-IA) in 1996 and an ice storm (FEMA-1191-DR-IA) in 1997.

The Iowa's Section 409 plan was updated in 1996 to add mitigation priorities for the flooding, but no major changes were made. During a forthcoming update to set mitigation priorities for the ice storm, the plan was to be thoroughly rewritten, redefining the goals and objectives section. The list of some twenty goals included in the original plan had been unofficially whittled down to five by eliminating repetition and targeting local planning initiatives.

The emphasis on hazard mitigation for flooding has been twofold: acquisition of flood-prone properties and protection of critical facilities. (*Critical facility*, as defined by the state with FEMA guidance, includes water treatment plants, sewage treatment facilities, and power plants.) The focus of projects is on structural hazard protection (berms and dikes), safe construction, and retrofitting of existing critical facilities. These strategies have been deemed very successful: two communities that received significant buyout assistance in 1993 would have been overwhelmed by the 1996 flooding without the buyout program, and a power plant in Denison was successfully protected from disaster by berms created before the 1996 flooding.

There has been only one attempt at legislation: a bill was modeled after

Florida's legislation on insurance policies, imposing a surcharge on insurance policies to fund hazard mitigation activities. As of 1997, the bill was stalled in the legislature.

One new permanent posistion, that of hazard mitigation grants coordinating officer, was added to the formerly one-person hazard mitigation staff. There are three contract staff members working with Iowa's Hazard Mitigation Team in 1997; they are funded for the next year. Changes have also been made to the State Hazard Mitigation Team, which is established by the governor's executive order. Throughout 1997, state and private agencies worked to better define the roles played by the various members of the team. The team is now divided into a primary and secondary team: the primary team meets quarterly or as necessary, and the secondary team meets only annually but receives updates from primary team meetings. Four federal agencies are to be added to the list of team members, and two private agencies were taken off the governor's order for 1997. Essentially, the goal of this redefinition was to streamline the team and determine who were the key players in hazard mitigation in the state.

Iowa's current hazard mitigation focus is on encouraging local planning and conducting workshops to aid in local planning. Some local governments are frustrated by the fact that the only examples of successful community mitigation relate to flooding, a hazard that is not of concern in all areas of the state. The SHMO feels tension between trying to advocate a multihazard approach (which FEMA also encourages) and the lack of examples of nonflood mitigation. In our interviews, he also emphasized that most hazard mitigation money is for flooding mitigation.

Local hazard mitigation planning is now required by the state. This requirement is enforced by a FEMA-supported rule stating that communities awarded HMGP funds must use those funds to create a hazard mitigation plan if they don't have one already or must update their existing plan as appropriate. The state also requires communities to make new mitigation projects follow up on previous HMGP projects as well as to make them responsive to the state's overall mitigation goals.

Overall, the relationship between FEMA and state staff is very good—both agencies are very much in favor of buyout and local planning, and FEMA has given a lot of support to both initiatives. The Section 409 plan needs to be overhauled and made more focused, and everyone recognizes the need for a plan that will meaningfully prioritize and articulate mitigation goals so that local projects can conform with overall mitigation strategy for the state.

In summary, it appears that many of the problems identified during the Iowa case study have been effectively addressed. The state's Section 409 plan is being regularly updated, clear priorities for flood hazard mitigation have been identified, the permanent state mitigation staff has been doubled and the State Hazard Mitigation Team organization streamlined, the state emergency management staff is working well with the FEMA regional staff, and local government mitigation planning is proceeding. Still to be completed are a comprehensive update of the Section 409 plan and implementation of a multihazard mitigation strategy.

Acknowledgments

The authors appreciate the invaluable assistance of Steve Harrell and Chris Finch in carrying out the 1995 case study, including arranging interviews and obtaining information and data. However, they are not responsible for our reporting or our interpretations, which do not coincide with theirs on some of the issues.

Note

1. This chapter is based on interviews with state, local, and federal officials conducted by David R. Godschalk and Timothy Beatley in Kansas City, Des Moines, Davenport, Muscatine, Louisa County, and Ames in June 1995. Supplementary information was gathered during follow-up telephone calls in 1996 and 1997.

References

FEMA (Federal Emergency Management Agency) 1995. *Hazard Mitigation Project Flow-Chart.* June 23. Kansas City, Mo.: FEMA, Region VII.

Hanson, Kate, and Ursula Lemanski. 1995. "Hard-Earned Lesson from the Midwest Floods: Floodplain Open Space Makes Economic Sense," *River Voices* 6 (1) 16–17.

Interagency Ecosystem Management Task Force. 1995. *The Ecosystem Approach: Healthy Ecosystems and Sustainable Economies.* Vol. 1, *Overview.* June. Washington, D.C.: U.S. Department of Interior.

Interagency Floodplain Management Review Committee. 1994. *Sharing the Challenge: Floodplain Management into the Twenty-First Century.* (Galloway Report.) Washington, D.C.: Government Printing Office.

Iowa Emergency Management Division. 1994a. *The Book: A Guide to Local Damage Assessment*. October. Des Moines: Iowa Emergency Management Division.

————. 1994b. *1994 Iowa Hazard Mitigation Plan*. Des Moines: Iowa Emergency Management Division.

Morrish, William, Carol Swenson, and Michelle Baltus. 1994. "A First Look at Post-Flood Recovery Planning Issues in the Upper Mississippi River Valley." Minneapolis: University of Minnisota, College of Architecture and Landscape Architecture, Design Center for American Urban Landscape.

National Park Service. 1991. *A Casebook in Managing Rivers for Multiple Use*. Washington, D.C.: U.S. Department of the Interior, National Park Service.

Phillippi, Nancy. 1994. "Plugging the Gaps in Flood Control Policy." *Issues in Science and Technology*, winter, 71–78.

Sparks, Richard E. 1995. "Need for Ecosystem Management of Large Rivers and Their Floodplains" *BioScience* 45 (3): 168–182.

Stevens, William K. 1995. "Restored Wetlands Could Ease Threat of Mississippi Floods." *New York Times*, August 8, C1, C4.

Wright, James M. 1996. "Effects of the Flood on National Policy: Some Achievements; Major Challenges Remain." In *The Great Flood of 1993: Causes, Impacts, and Responses*, ed. Stanley A. Changnon. Boulder, Colo. Westview Press.

Persons Interviewed

FEMA Region VII

Brenda Bruun, lead hazard mitigation specialist, FEMA Field Office, Des Moines, Iowa

Steve Harrell, director, Mitigation Division

State of Iowa

Bill Cappuccio, National Flood Insurance Program coordinator, Iowa Department of Natural Resources

Chris Finch, emergency management specialist, Iowa Emergency Management Division

Michelle Guericke, field representative, Iowa Department of Economic Development

Dennis Harper, Hazard Mitigation Grant Program coordination officer, Iowa Emergency Management Division

Henry Manning, Community Development Block Grant program field representative, Iowa Department of Economic Development

Local Government and Private Sector

Vanessa Baker-Latimer, housing coordinator, city of Ames, Iowa

Jeff Carter, coordinator, Muscatine County Emergency Management Agency

Suzanne Jordan, Building Inspections Department, city of Davenport, Iowa

Arlinda McKeen, Section 409 plan project director, State Public Policy Group, Des Moines, Iowa (consultant to Iowa Emergency Management Division)

Betty Roudy-Bush, Louisa County, Iowa

U.S. Department of Interior

Kate Hanson, National Park Service Rivers, Trails, and Conservation Assistance Program, Disaster Field Office, Des Moines, Iowa

CHAPTER 6

California After the Loma Prieta and Northridge Earthquakes

This chapter documents and assesses the mitigation undertaken in California after the October 17, 1989, Loma Prieta earthquake in the San Francisco Bay Area and the January 17, 1994, Northridge earthquake in the Los Angeles area—the latter the most costly seismic disaster in the U.S. history. Initially, we planned to focus only on Northridge, but because the Loma Prieta experience so heavily influenced the Northridge postdisaster decisions, we also discuss that prior event, though necessarily briefly.[1]

California's emergency management program is sometimes characterized as the "Cadillac" of such programs because of the strength of its system of laws, planning, and institutional resources. Lessons from California's mitigation efforts illustrate the challenges faced by even top-of-the-line programs.

Two Earthquake Disasters

California is subject to numerous active earthquake faults throughout the state (see figure 6.1). It is not surprising that the damage profiles of the Loma Prieta and Northridge disasters are closely linked to the region's geophysical characteristics and its urban geography.

Loma Prieta Earthquake

The Loma Prieta earthquake struck along the San Andreas Fault in the San Francisco Bay Area on Tuesday, October 17, 1989. The epicenter was located about 10 miles east-northeast of Santa Cruz and 60 miles southeast of San Francisco. The earthquake was felt over a 400,000-square-mile

area. With a magnitude of 7.1, it remains the largest earthquake to strike
the Bay Area since the great 1906 earthquake. (Earthquakes of magnitude
7.0 or more are considered to be "major.") The 1906 earthquake ruptured
a 280-mile surface segment of the San Andreas Fault, compared with the
25-mile segment ruptured by the Loma Prieta event.

Losses sustained in this disaster were substantial: 62 people died, 3,750
were injured, and about 12,000 were left homeless (State and Federal
Hazard Mitigation Survey Team 1990). Earthquake damage was recorded
as far as 120 miles from the epicenter. Total damage costs exceeded $6 bil-

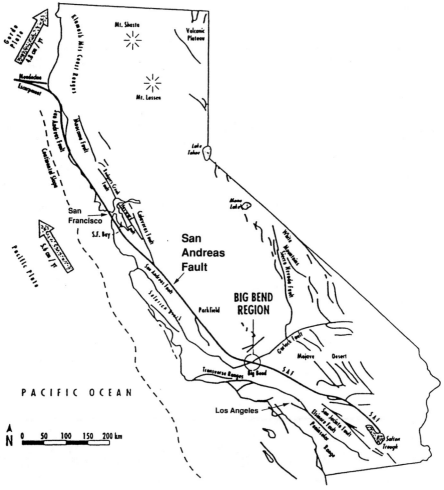

Figure 6.1. Earthquake Faults in California. *Source:* California Seismic Safety
Commission 1995.

lion, which included $1 billion in damage to highways and bridges. Indirect business losses were estimated to equal the physical damage estimates.

More than 22,000 residences, 1,567 commercial building, and 137 public buildings in the disaster impact area were damaged. Structural damage was primarily to unreinforced masonry commercial buildings, older wood frame homes and apartments, mobile homes, and unreinforced concrete frame structures. Almost all failed structures had not been built to current seismic standards.

As indicated in figure 6.2, the Loma Prieta earthquake dramatically

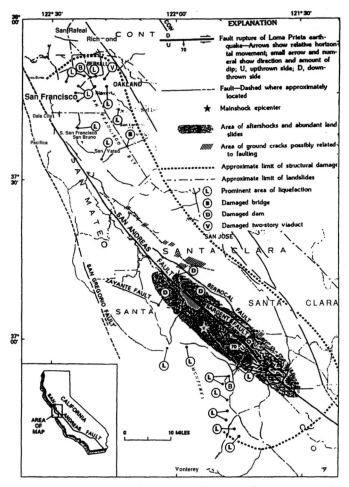

Figure 6.2. Approximate Limits of Damage Relative to the Epicenter of the Loma Prieta Earthquake. *Source:* State and Federal Hazard Mitigation Survey Team 1990.

Photo 6.1. Collapsed Freeway After the Loma Prieta Earthquake. Courtesy of the American Red Cross.

illustrated that ground shaking is related as much to surface geology and soil characteristics (including liquefaction, ground failure, and landslides) as to proximity to the fault rupture. Severe shaking and ground failure occurred in the epicenter region. Amplification of ground shaking occurred in water-saturated, loosely consolidated bay fill and riverbed soils. Sixty miles from the epicenter, fill underlying the Marina District of San Francisco suffered strong shaking relative to consolidated bedrock surfaces located only one mile away. In Oakland, the infamous collapse of a portion of the double-decked Interstate 880 freeway appeared to be directly related to surface geologic conditions of unconsolidated fill.

Northridge Earthquake

Losses incurred in the Northridge earthquake, which hit on January 17, 1994, were severe (California Seismic Safety Commission 1995). Fifty-seven people were killed, and nearly 9,000 were injured. The number of lives lost in the Northridge earthquake was remarkably low considering the intensity and location of this seismic event. Yet even though deaths and injuries were not as numerous as in other major U.S. disasters of the twentieth century, Northridge affected the lives of a tremendous number of

Photo 6.2. House in San Francisco After the Loma Prieta Earthquake. Courtesy of the American Red Cross.

people. More than 25,000 residential structures were destroyed, and more than 1,600 homes and apartment buildings were declared uninhabitable.

The Northridge earthquake was the most expensive seismic event in the history of the United States, with damage costs exceeding $20 billion. This figure represents only physical damage; it does not include many indirect losses incurred by businesses. About 50 percent of small businesses in heavily damaged residential areas remained closed nearly one year after the disaster.

The greatest loss in direct physical damage was incurred by older buildings—more than 112,000 of these structures were damaged (California Seismic Safety Commission 1995). Most structures built after adoption of the 1976 building codes performed significantly better. Despite this good performance, nonstructural damage was still a significant factor in newer buildings. Between 50 percent and 80 percent of the total repair cost was for nonstructural elements such as sprinklers, pipes, heating, lighting, air conditioning, and suspended ceilings. Indeed, a major lesson learned after Northridge was that sprinkler and piping systems in buildings were too rigid and susceptible to damage, even though the systems were designed to be flexible.

Lifelines (transportation and communications systems and water, gas, and electric utilities) also sustained significant damage. Despite the retrofits

and design improvements made after the 1971 San Fernando earthquake, several freeway overpasses collapsed and other major portions of highways failed. About 2 million customers in the Los Angeles area lost electric power.

The geologic characteristics of the Northridge impact area produced a moderate-sized earthquake of magnitude 6.7. Like the 1983 Coalinga and 1987 Whittier Narrows earthquakes, the Northridge earthquake resulted from a "blind" fault. Unlike many faults that break the surface of the earth, this type of fault is deeply buried anywhere in the earth's crust, from a few hundred feet to six miles or more under the surface. Blind faults are difficult to locate and map. Thus, they often are not mapped and accounted for under California's 1972 Alquist-Priolo Earthquake Fault Zoning Act, which stipulates building setback widths from earthquake faults. The Big Bend region of the San Andreas Fault system in southern California contains several known but not accurately mapped blind faults (see figure 6.1).

The Northridge earthquake caused strong ground motion and intense shaking. In particular, geologic features in the near-source area (the several-mile-diameter region around which the projection of the fault rupture plane meets the ground surface) of the Northridge earthquake caused ground velocities two to three times higher than those typically found outside these areas (see figure 6.3). Some observers suggested that the extraordinarily high velocities caused some steel frame buildings to sustain serious damage or even to collapse and caused some base-isolated buildings to sustain considerable damage (California Seismic Safety Commission 1995). Although these types of buildings were designed on the basis of building codes that ensured resistance to major earthquake forces, buildings complying with the codes were not expected to withstand high ground velocities in near-source areas.

Fortunately, the duration of intense shaking during the Northridge earthquake was relatively short, less than nine seconds—compared with several minutes in other seismic events. Had the magnitude been greater, the duration of strong shaking would have been longer and the damage would have been much more severe.

California's Section 409 Plan

Historically, California has approached hazard mitigation on the basis of individual hazard types, treating fires, floods, severe winter storms, and earthquakes separately rather than adopting a multihazard approach. Thus, it has produced separate mitigation plans for the major types of hazards encountered in the state, such as its *Flood Hazard Mitigation Plan*

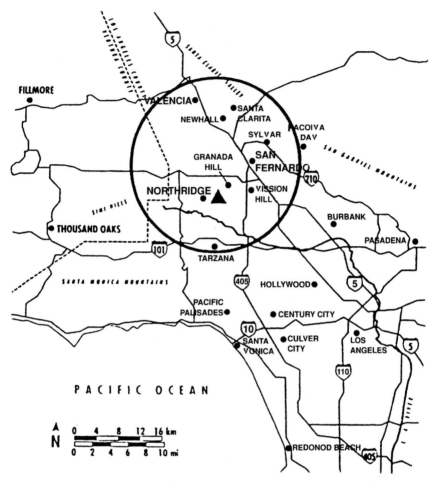

Figure 6.3. Preliminary Near-Source Area (in circle) for the Northridge Earthquake. *Source:* California Seismic Safety Commission 1995.

(Governor's Office of Emergency Services 1994a). This case study, however, focuses on earthquake mitigation, and therefore we discuss here the 1991 edition of the state's earthquake mitigation plan, *California at Risk: Reducing Earthquake Hazards 1992–1996* (California Seismic Safety Commission 1991). We evaluated this plan, along with the flood mitigation plan, during our overall assessment of state mitigation plans (Chapter 9).

California at Risk covers earthquake hazards on a statewide basis. It was prepared under a state law, the California Earthquake Hazards Reduction Act of 1986, which directs the California Seismic Safety Commission to establish a series of five-year programs to reduce statewide earthquake hazards significantly by the year 2000. Revised annually, this report lays

out the second five-year program aimed at meeting the year 2000 goal. It contains priorities, project schedules, funding sources and amounts, and forty-two hazard reduction initiatives organized into five categories:

- Reducing hazard vulnerability in existing facilities

- Encouraging hazard reduction in new facilities

- Encouraging improvements in emergency management

- Expediting the disaster recovery process

- Assisting research and education

Each initiative description contains a time-specific objective and milestones to measure progress, dollar-specific resources needed, a list of responsible agencies, status of the initiative, and relevant references.

California at Risk reflects on progress made since the first report, in 1986. It uses the lessons learned from the 1987 Whittier Narrows earthquake and the 1989 Loma Prieta earthquake as well as the results of continuing research to compile a comprehensive and integrated earthquake hazards reduction program. Implementation is scheduled through action plans that set forth activities for each calendar year of the five-year program and identify the responsible organizations and milestones for each year. Proposed legislation is outlined. An Interagency Earthquake Policy Coordinating Committee includes representatives from all the responsible agencies. However, the plan remains an "advisory document," not a directive for other state agencies or private organizations.

Unlike the typical state Section 409 plan, which is prepared by a state hazard mitigation officer (SHMO) in response to a disaster in accordance with the Stafford Act and Federal Emergency Management Agency (FEMA) guidelines, *California at Risk* is the product of a state-generated process. It is a detailed program plan with specific, measurable objectives, prepared by a specialized state agency with considerable depth of technical support. It also complies with the FEMA goal of an interagency, multiorganizational approach to risk assessment and planning.

Strengths of the Plan

The strong features of *California at Risk* include the following:

- Its analysis of the capability of state hazard mitigation programs, which contains a "hazard mitigation who's who" that describes twenty-five state, four federal, and three private agency responsibilities for hazard reduction, disaster support, and recovery support; a summary of

progress, experience, and learning since the previous (1987–1992) report; and a description of 198 earthquake mitigation bills signed into law during the previous five years, out of some 500 bills proposed

- Its description of proposed programs, based on the forty-two initiatives grouped into five coherent strategy categories discussed earlier

- Its clearly specified implementation approach, including cost estimates, measurable implementation milestones, responsible agencies, and present status for each initiative, along with commitments of state financial resources to carry out plan proposals

- Its internally consistent, clearly written, well-illustrated, and understandable executive summary and text, which include specific procedures for plan reevaluation and updating

Weaknesses of the Plan

The following are areas in which the plan could be strengthened:

- There is little discussion of local responsibilities and programs for earthquake hazard mitigation and no evidence of local participation in the plan's preparation; the focus is on state agencies and federal programs.

- The hazard assessment is very brief—two and a half pages plus one map of thirty-year earthquake probabilities for selected fault segments. This could be a result of the belief that widespread recognition of the California earthquake hazard rendered a more specific assessment unnecessary in the document, but it is somewhat surprising given the high level of hazard analysis knowledge in the state.

California's Earthquake Mitigation Planning and Implementation Process

California has developed an extensive earthquake hazard mitigation capability, with active cooperation with its FEMA region. Nevertheless, each earthquake poses new issues and challenges.

Chronology of Events

This section describes the sequence and nature of major actions taken following the 1989 Loma Prieta and 1994 Northridge earthquakes, up to mid-1995. California is atypical among states regarding emergency

management in several respects. First, earthquake hazard mitigation is driven by state law and implemented by an agency separate from, although coordinated with, the state emergency management agency. Second, California has relatively large institutional capacity for emergency management; as alluded to earlier, other state officials refer to it as the "Cadillac" of emergency management. Third, California has formulated a strong state mitigation philosophy and program, which do not always dovetail with FEMA policy and procedures, requiring sometimes extensive negotiation.

Prior to the Loma Prieta and Northridge earthquakes, the state of California had created an institutional structure for earthquake hazard mitigation. In 1986, its legislature enacted the California Earthquake Hazards Reduction Act, directing the California Seismic Safety Commission to prepare five-year hazard reduction programs aimed at significantly reducing earthquake hazards by the year 2000, as well as the Unreinforced Masonry Act, directing the preparation of a statewide hazard reduction plan. However, prior to Loma Prieta, the state did not have an approved Section 409 hazard mitigation plan, since the plan prepared after the 1987 Whittier Narrows earthquake had never been accepted by the state or by FEMA.

Loma Prieta Earthquake Activities

The Loma Prieta earthquake demonstrated the vulnerability of older urban areas to earthquake forces and stimulated mitigation planning and action in California. It also demonstrated the very high cost of mitigation.

Immediate Aftermath: October 1989–November 1990

During the immediate period following the October Loma Prieta disaster declaration, FEMA recommended, and the state adopted as its Section 409 plan, *California at Risk 1987–1992*, the first five-year program plan of the California Seismic Safety Commission (1989). FEMA initially estimated the available Hazard Mitigation Grant Program (HMGP) funding to be $20 million. The preface to the January 1990 report of the State and Federal Hazard Mitigation Survey Team for the Loma Prieta Earthquake, *Hazard Mitigation Opportunities for California*, stated that the lessons of previous earthquakes were relearned during Loma Prieta, when antiquated structures of unreinforced masonry and nonductile concrete took a devastating toll in death and injury (State and Federal Hazard Mitigation Survey Team 1990). It noted that the state needed the political will and economic commitment to match its capability to build an earthquake-safe environment. The report included fifty-seven recommendations, grouped into six categories: hazard identification and monitoring, land use planning and regu-

lation, repair and reconstruction, response planning, insurance, and funding.

Near-Term Recovery: December 1990–December 1991

The first HMGP applications were received by the FEMA regional office in 1991. Eighty-eight percent of these first fifty-one applications focused on either equipment purchases (twenty-three) or public and private facility improvements (twenty-two).

Midterm Recovery: January 1992–December 1994

The second group of HMGP project applications was received by the FEMA regional office in 1992. Two-thirds of these forty-five applications were for public and private facility improvements (thirty). In October 1992, FEMA officials raised the HMGP cost estimate to $30 million, and in December 1992 they raised it again to $43.4 million.

Late Recovery: January–July 1995

An additional group of thirty-one HMGP applications was received by the FEMA regional office during 1995. Of these, 74 percent (twenty-three) were for public and private facility improvements, and 26 percent (eight) were for equipment purchases. Three-quarters of these applications were left from original 1990 submissions, and one-quarter were new applications from San Francisco. In January 1995, FEMA raised the HMGP cost estimate to $56.6 million. In May, FEMA requested an explanation from the state concerning both the older applications and the new applications forwarded during 1995. As of July 1995, approximately $31 million of the $56.1 million in eligible project costs had been obligated to sixty-eight projects.

Northridge Earthquake Activities

The Northridge earthquake was even more damaging than the Loma Prieta earthquake. Its mitigation process was complex and slow to get under way.

Immediate Aftermath: January–April 1994

Immediately following the January 1994 Northridge earthquake, FEMA sent staff members from the Region X office in Seattle and elsewhere to assist the Region IX staff in San Francisco. The Earthquake Engineering Research Institute (EERI) set up a damage clearinghouse in Pasadena. On February 9, Governor Pete Wilson issued Executive Order W-78-94,

directing the California Seismic Safety Commission (SSC) to review the effects of the earthquake; coordinate a study of its policy implications, particularly regarding structural safety and land use planning; and present recommendations by September 1, 1994. In February 1994, the California Seismic Safety Commission issued an updated status report on *California at Risk* (1994) stating that thirty-five of the program's forty-two policy initiatives were moving ahead, but most were behind schedule. It observed that only about $5 million would be needed to complete the program and called on the state administration and legislature to provide leadership in strengthening state-owned buildings and state building practices; to speed identification of vulnerable services, hospitals, and schools; and to create a recovery plan.

Also in February 1994, the Governor's Office of Emergency Services and the FEMA Hazard Mitigation Team jointly issued the *Hazard Mitigation Early Implementation Strategy, Northridge Earthquake,* (OES 1994c), which served as the Interagency Hazard Mitigation Team report. The team included five staff members from the Governor's Office of Emergency Services and twenty-three FEMA staff members. The report recommended six major mitigation strategies:

1. Comply with the 1991 Uniform Building Code wherever possible.

2. Use temporary repairs to restore facility function promptly and to provide time to design long-term solutions.

3. Include mitigation considerations in damage analyses to reduce repetitive damage.

4. Encourage multihazard measures to mitigate risks.

5. Address structural and nonstructural recommendations.

6. Supplement existing community education with public information, voluntary organizations, and outreach efforts.

In March 1994, the Section 404 strategic planning committee developed an initial Section 404 strategy outline, though this was not published. In April 1994, the Governor's Office of Emergency Services issued the *Northridge Earthquake, January 17, 1994, Interim Report* (1994b), which noted the difficulty of creating a seismically safe environment for Californians and identified a number of issues to be addressed:

1. The number and severity of earthquakes are increasing.

2. Older structures continue to pose a great threat to life.

3. Retrofit programs have proved their effectiveness but are not complete.

4. Lifeline damage created widespread economic effects.

5. Some newer structures, including steel frame and precast parking structures, appear vulnerable to damage.

6. Schools and hospitals are vulnerable to disruption.

7. Housing and emergency sheltering continue to be a problem.

8. Nonstructural hazards are not addressed in the building code.

9. California's emergency management system has proved its effectiveness.

10. Geographic information systems (GIS) provided an invaluable tool for disaster data management.

11. California must continue and expand earthquake preparedness efforts.

Near-Term Recovery: May 1994–January 1995

In May 1994, the first Section 404 project application, Ground Acceleration Delineation for Seismic Hazard Zoning Maps, was submitted to deal with long-term land use.

The Governor's Office of Emergency Services (OES) held a hazard mitigation workshop in Pasadena, but attendance by local government officials was limited, as many were still busy with recovery and uncertain of benefits. In June 1994, voters rejected Measure 1A, a proposed $2 billion bond issue earmarked for earthquake relief, causing Governor Wilson to cancel a $575 million California Natural Disaster Assistance Program that was to have provided loans for housing reconstruction. FEMA hired twenty-five mitigation specialists and placed them in Earthquake Service Centers with local building officials to advise individuals on earthquake-safe building requirements and safe rebuilding practices. Funds to repair earthquake damage came from a variety of sources, including private insurance companies, FEMA's Minimum Home Repair Program, Small Business Administration (SBA) loans, and other resources. In September, FEMA and the OES (1994) issued the "Joint Section 406 Hazard Mitigation Policy Statement" stating that hazard mitigation under the Public Assistance program (Section 406 of the Stafford Act) was discretionary but inspectors would encourage hazard mitigation in permanent restoration projects and all proposals would be subject to benefit-cost analysis.

Mitigation Strategy Implemented: February–July 1995

In February 1995, OES (1995d) issued the "Section 404 Hazard Mitigation Grant Program Strategy," announcing five priority categories for grant disbursement:

1. Seismic hazard identification:

   a. Ground Acceleration Delineation for Seismic Hazard Zoning Maps

   b. Information transfer workshops and demonstration project

   c. Development/update of (local government general plan) safety elements

2. Educational institutions

   a. Nonstructural retrofits (K–14)

   b. Relocation of Castaic Elementary and Middle Schools

3. Medical facilities

4. Significant facilities

   a. Essential facilities

   b. Multifamily low-income housing

5. Technical information, research, education, and training

In May 1995, the OES and FEMA signed a "Hazard Mitigation Grant Program Memorandum of Understanding" identifying preapprovable types of projects, such as nonstructural retrofits, to streamline the program by making FEMA eligibility review unnecessary (though historic, environmental, and cost-effectiveness reviews would still be required). This memorandum of understanding was amended in July 1995 to apply to schools and to determine that suspended ceiling systems and pendant lighting fixtures in schools were cost-effective and eligible for funding. (See FEMA 1997, pp. 22–23 on cost-effectiveness of school lighting retrofitting.)

In July 1995, the California Seismic Safety Commission issued *Northridge Earthquake: Turning Loss to Gain*, the Northridge earthquake report responding to the governor's executive order. Funded through a project application to FEMA, it identified significant weaknesses in the exercise of land use planning laws and in the design and construction of buildings and lifeline facilities, calling for higher commitment, consistency, and priority for earthquake mitigation. The report set four goals: (1) make seismic safety a priority, (2) improve construction quality, (3) reduce risk from seismically vulnerable structures, and (4) improve lifeline performance. To achieve these goals, it defined seven broad tasks: (1) define acceptable risk, (2) provide risk reduction incentives, (3) improve the use of earth science knowledge to reduce risk, (4) improve the application of land use planning to manage risk, (5) improve the code development process, (6) support

focused research, and (7) improve state-level programs. It then made 168 recommendations for achieving these goals and tasks.

As of July 1995, when this case study was conducted, only one Section 404 project (Ground Acceleration Delineation for Seismic Hazard Zoning Maps; $9.4 million requested) had been approved. One other project (Castaic School replacement; $18.2 million requested) was pending. Since then, a number of Section 404 projects have been approved, with obligations of more than $129 million as of September 1996.

Key Players

The California hazard mitigation community includes a large number of players, some of whom served in multiple and sometimes overlapping roles during the period between the Loma Prieta and Northridge earthquakes. We have not attempted to include all those involved in both disasters. Instead, in table 6.1, we have listed the key federal and state players in the mitigation activities associated with the Northridge earthquake.

Table 6.1. Key Players in the Northridge Mitigation Process

TITLE	NAME	ROLE
FEMA Staff		
Federal hazard mitigation (FHMO) and acting chief, Mitigation Division, Region IX	Jack Eldridge	Deputy federal coordinating officer (FCO) for Mitigation
Senior mitigation specialist, Region IX	Helen DuBois	FHMO
Temporary FCO (from Region X)	Dick Buck	Temporary replacement FCO for mitigation
Temporary FHMO (from Region X)	Bob Freitag	Temporary FHMO
California Staff		
Director, Governor's Office of Emergency Services (OES)	Richard Andrews	State coordinating officer (SCO)
Deputy director, OES	Paul Flores	Section 404 Strategic Planning Committee
Assistant state hazard mitigation officer (SHMO), (OES)	Paula Schulz	Asstistant SHMO initally, then SHMO
Director, California Seismic Safety Commission (SSC)	Thomas Tobin	Section 404 Strategic Planning Committee
Acting director, SSC	Richard McCarthy	Section 404 Strategic Planning Committee
State geologist	Jim Davis	Section 404 Strategic Planning Committee

Influences on Recovery and Mitigation

The intergovernmental system was a major influence on recovery and mitigation following the Loma Prieta and Northridge earthquakes.

Federal Policy Initiatives

The federal government's commitment to mitigation policy increased considerably between the 1989 Loma Prieta earthquake and the 1994 Northridge earthquake. The heightened commitment is reflected by two key federal policy initiatives. One initiative was the strong advocacy position taken by FEMA's director, James Lee Witt, immediately after the Northridge event. According to a FEMA Region IX staffer, Witt told FEMA regional officials "to get mitigation grants out the door."

In response, FEMA placed high priority on establishing a public awareness program to educate people about the need for mitigation during rebuilding. The main thrust of this effort was in preparing educational materials and hiring mitigation advisors to staff newly created Earthquake Service Centers. These centers were intended to be similar to Disaster Assistance Centers (DACs), but their primary goal was to promote mitigation. The mitigation advisors were joined by an architect or a builder or both to ensure that recipients of SBA loans, temporary housing, minimal repairs, and insurance were well enough informed to consider mitigation in their rebuilding and repair efforts and knew how to apply mitigation standards correctly. This effort was expanded to include community education workshops and, with state support, a library of mitigation and preparedness information consisting of books, brochures, studies, videotapes, and an interactive CD-ROM program to teach residents and owners of small businesses how to integrate mitigation into reconstruction.

A second initiative involved congressional action (the Volkmer amendment to the Stafford Act, in response to the 1993 Midwest floods) that increased federal financial commitment to supporting postdisaster mitigation efforts. At the time of Loma Prieta, Section 404 mitigation funding under the Stafford Act required a 50 percent match from state or local government. Moreover, the maximum amount of Section 404 funds committed by FEMA could not exceed 10 percent of the total funding earmarked for public assistance. After June 1993, the federal portion of the match for Section 404 funds was substantially increased, from 50 percent to 75 percent, and the total Section 404 federal funding cap was raised to 15 percent of public assistance. In addition, after Northridge, Section 406 public assistance funding for mitigation under the Stafford Act was changed from a 75-25 federal-state match to 90-10.

A third initiative was not directly tied to promoting mitigation. Rather, it involved increased federal scrutiny of state and local use of federal mitigation funds by requiring review of certain Section 404 project applications at FEMA headquarters in Washington, D.C. This action had a major influence on decisions about Section 404 applications after the Loma Prieta earthquake.

These and other federal policy initiatives strongly influenced postdisaster reconstruction activities at the FEMA regional level and at state and local levels.

FEMA Regional Efforts

The work of FEMA regional staff during the Northridge recovery involved several key activities, including interorganizational coordination among FEMA regional agencies, expansion of mitigation staff, and setting up of public education programs through the creation of "mitigation tables."

Interregional Agency Coordination

Within days after the Northridge earthquake, staff from FEMA Region X (Seattle) arrived and joined forces with the FEMA Region IX (San Francisco) staff to help assess damage and needs within the impact area as well as to determine mitigation priorities. Because of the magnitude of the Northridge event, the FEMA Region IX staff needed substantial assistance to handle all the responsibilities associated with the federal mitigation and recovery assistance program.

After the Northridge event, officials from the Governor's Office of Emergency Services (OES) and FEMA Region IX agreed that the state was understaffed compared with FEMA. The imbalance was obvious, as there were about ten state staffers and thirty-five to forty staffers representing FEMA. Consequently, the OES staff became frustrated with the amount of time spent attempting to familiarize FEMA Region IX and X staff members with the local situation and policies.

FEMA Region X was viewed by the OES as taking a top-down approach in developing mitigation assistance programs. There was room for improvement in considering the particular needs and capabilities of state agencies and the disaster impact region, according to OES officials. As a result, OES staff perceived that too much time and effort were being devoted to educating FEMA staff about how mitigation was done in California. OES staff understood that some time would have to be spent in familiarizing FEMA Region X staff with state programs, and they indicated that FEMA personnel were receptive to change after being informed of

state programs and needs. Yet they also believed that the effort required was excessive and that more of their attention could have been directed toward meeting mitigation needs in the impact area.

Staffing for Mitigation

In response to FEMA headquarters' new emphasis on mitigation policy, all FEMA regions established new Mitigation Divisions, with one established in the FEMA Region IX office four months after the Northridge earthquake struck. Similar to the arrangement in all FEMA regions, the division's primary function was to oversee all mitigation activities at the regional office and to promote the renewed emphasis on mitigation initiatives. Another core function was to facilitate cooperation with state and local authorities. This latter function was critical, as FEMA Region IX staff consistently expressed a strong concern that federal mitigation initiatives would never get off the ground without cooperation among state and local authorities within the region.

FEMA Region IX staff members maintained that the idea of a new Mitigation Division was "forcefully pushed" by FEMA Region X staff during the immediate aftermath of the Northridge earthquake. It was clear, they said, that personnel of both Region IX and Region X were in agreement with this action as a signal of their commitment to promoting James Lee Witt's call for advancing mitigation.

Instituting the Mitigation Table Concept

As mentioned earlier, the FEMA regional office was charged with implementing mitigation tables. This effort involved the preparation of educational materials and the hiring of twenty-five mitigation specialists (almost all architects) to staff eleven informational tables in the three-county Northridge impact area. The mitigation tables were to be set up at each Earthquake Service Center to disseminate information about structural and nonstructural strengthening and rebuilding techniques. But institutional problems arose in the implementation of this project.

Initially, the OES strongly objected to the information provided at the mitigation tables, with staff members expressing liability concerns about the information to be disseminated. Information about building design and strengthening techniques was put together in a hurry and did not undergo the standard, rigorous technical review typical for new provisions in state building codes. OES officials were concerned that the information might not be accurate and that the state might be held liable for allowing potentially inappropriate information about building design to be used during reconstruction. Consequently, the OES requested that FEMA Region IX

staff agree not to provide drawings about building design for mitigation. FEMA Region IX staff also agreed that the mitigation specialists would conduct mitigation workshops (for residents, local contractors, and building inspectors) using only state-developed information.

The OES also objected to the placement of architects and builders at the mitigation tables. OES staff members were not sure that these mitigation specialists had the necessary training in highly technical aspects of structural mitigation and sufficient knowledge of seismic provisions of the California building code. In response, FEMA staff members assured the OES that every individual was highly professional and certified to practice in California. The OES also was assured that every individual was instructed to work closely with local building officials assigned to the DACs to ensure that no local codes were being overlooked. The group also met once each week for a coordination meeting that included a short workshop on some aspect of seismic design and application.

The OES soon accepted FEMA's strategy for mitigation table staffing. In fact, the OES considered the role taken by the architects and builders to be quite effective and even hired several staff members to handle the Hazard Mitigation Grant Program.

A third objection came from so-called traditionalists within both FEMA Region IX and the OES. They were concerned that the Earthquake Service Centers might detract from the main mission of the DACs, which is to provide immediate recovery assistance to households and small businesses. This issue was compounded by the initial placement of mitigation tables at DACs, since the Earthquake Service Centers were not operational during the first two or three months after the disaster. One FEMA Region IX official believed this placement could potentially cause "too much confusion and fear" on the part of victims. Another Region IX official maintained that "there was a big fight on the part of the traditionalists in recovery from FEMA IX staff and state OES. Traditionalists wanted only public assistance and individual assistance and fought tooth and nail against the mitigation tables."

Notwithstanding the controversy, four months after the Northridge event, the mitigation specialists and the mitigation tables were accepted by FEMA and the OES and allowed to operate at the Earthquake Service Centers. Throughout the initial stages of the recovery, FEMA Region IX convened the twenty-three specialists on a weekly basis so that they could share their experiences and receive mitigation training. Mitigation specialists were quick to point out that these meetings were crucial in upholding their morale and commitment to the program. The specialists used the meetings to share ideas about ways to educate the public about

mitigation as well as to exchange learning experiences and strategies for dealing with the intense pressure they were under at the Earthquake Service Centers.

The disaster recovery manager at the FEMA Field Office in Pasadena argued that given all the difficulties in placing the mitigation tables at DACs, perhaps it would be better to place them at Earthquake Service Centers and avoid dealing with DACs at all in the future. This individual further maintained that the new mitigation service at these centers generated some important benefits. One was the wide distribution of information on how to integrate mitigation into rebuilding and on grant eligibility for homeowners and owners of small businesses. Information on mitigation, for example, was sent to 200,000 homeowners. A videotape about mitigation was produced and disseminated to many communities and organizations throughout the impact area. A second benefit was that mitigation specialists played an important psychological role in helping people feel more in control of future earthquake risk. Staff members conducted regular workshops in many communities throughout the disaster area. In many respects, the community workshops were very effective in reaching out to citizens and were considered to be more effective than the one-on-one contact at the mitigation tables.

State Organizational Capability for Earthquake Recovery and Mitigation Planning

California has a high level of organizational capability for carrying out mitigation planning and implementation for earthquakes, but this capability is somewhat constrained by the delegation of seismic mitigation and planning responsibilities among state agencies. The California Seismic Safety Commission was established in 1979 and remains the lead state agency for earthquake mitigation planning. The commission is well staffed by professionals with expertise in geology, engineering, and planning. Although the Stafford Act requires that the state hazard mitigation officer (SHMO) be in charge of state mitigation planning, an exception is made for earthquake planning in California. Since the highest level of staff expertise and resources for addressing seismic safety planning issues has historically been lodged within the California Seismic Safety Commission and not the OES, the state considers the commission's plan—*California at Risk*—as its Section 409 plan for earthquakes.

This interorganizational arrangement raises an important concern. Two lead agencies play a role in mitigation planning—one charged with earthquake mitigation planning and the other charged with overall hazard mit-

igation leadership. There are potential coordination difficulties in advancing earthquake mitigation activities and plan implementation. Although this arrangement did not appear to constrain recovery and mitigation efforts after the 1989 and 1994 earthquakes in California, it may impede progress in future long-range mitigation planning. Dividing planning responsibility in this way increases the chances for fragmentation and duplication of effort.

State agencies in California have not been committed to hazard mitigation planning historically. Mitigation planning, especially for floods and other nonseismic hazards, has traditionally been weak due to reluctance of key agencies to become involved. This lack of commitment could be more effectively addressed if the OES had more resources to mobilize state agency interest and capability.

Several positive steps have been taken during the past several years to improve the OES's capacity as lead state mitigation agency. First, in the fall of 1993, the Risk Management Section of the OES was charged with integrating mitigation into the pre- and postevent phases of a disaster. This was the first time in California that a state agency created an organizational entity specifically charged with promoting mitigation from an "all-hazards" perspective during all relevant phases of a disaster. Second, the OES's staff was expanded. Prior to the Northridge event, OES staffing consisted of only two part-time positions. The OES's mitigation unit (the Risk Management Section of the Disaster Assistance Branch) has since been expanded to include seven full-time positions.

Another positive step was the hiring of the current SHMO following the Northridge event. Interviews revealed that this individual is generally considered highly capable throughout the mitigation community in California. One notable observer summed up the general sentiment toward the current SHMO: "This SHMO is highly respected by the OES hierarchy and has political punch compared to the previous SHMO . . . the mitigation program was broken when the current SHMO started at OES. There are still problems over there, but they would be a lot worse without that SHMO in charge."

A noteworthy state capacity-building activity was also undertaken after the Northridge earthquake, involving use of physical damage assessments to help the OES build a geographic information system (GIS) database on damage. The GIS has multiple functions including risk management modeling and automated mapping. The modeling involves a state-developed program known as RAMP (Regional Assessment of Mitigation Priorities). This investment will help improve the state's ability to identify high-priority mitigation activities, increasing the likelihood

that limited mitigation funds will be used effectively and efficiently. Moreover, OES staff members believe that RAMP will provide a stronger fact base to enable the state to prepare and update future Section 409 plans, prioritize mitigation needs, and provide an empirical basis for Section 404 project applications after future earthquakes.

Finally, the state received Section 404 grant funding to undertake a seismic mapping project in the three-county Northridge impact area. OES officials indicated that the seismic hazard maps produced from this project could be digitized and integrated into the RAMP risk management model. This joint state-FEMA initiative represents a collaborative effort to provide a tool needed by the state for mitigation policy making. It can be used to evaluate the extent to which losses might be reduced by changes in policy. OES officials envision that the RAMP model will gradually be extended throughout the state as funds become available.

Section 409 Mitigation Plan and Policies

Including responses from two disasters allowed us to compare mitigation strategies used after Loma Prieta with those used after Northridge.

Influence of Section 409 Plans on Seeking Section 404 Funding

The strategies pursued through the Section 409 planning processes after Northridge were considerably different from those pursued after Loma Prieta. Consequently, the two sets of strategies varied in their influence on mitigation initiatives during the recovery period for each disaster.

After the Loma Prieta event, the OES and FEMA agreed that local governments in the impact region of the San Francisco Bay Area should prepare individual local mitigation plans to serve as "annexes to the state hazard mitigation plan," which was adopted immediately after the earthquake (Governor's Office of Emergency Services 1989, p. 1). These local plans were to identify (1) potential vulnerability from future earthquakes (2) mitigation measures and priorities, and (3) funding sources for matching federal Section 404 funds. Two goals were set forth for the local plans. A short-term goal was to recommend policy actions for Section 404 funding requests based on community consensus and a sound fact base. The long-term goal was to integrate mitigation into day-to-day functions of local government.

Both local and state officials generally expressed satisfaction with this process. In particular, they believed that local governments were able to tailor specific Section 404 funding requests to meet local conditions and priorities. However, a key shortcoming of this process was the uneven

quality of the plans produced by different local governments. Some communities—such as Berkeley, San Jose, and San Francisco—had planning departments with considerable expertise and sufficient funds to prepare high-quality plans. Other, smaller communities were not in such a favorable position.

A general shortcoming of all local planning efforts in the impact area was a lack of technical rigor. This limitation could largely be traced to a general decline in local planning capability throughout California. The reasons for the decline include passage of the infamous statewide Proposition 13 legislation, which placed a tight cap on local tax revenues, and a severe downturn in the state economy that had started to become evident when the Loma Prieta earthquake struck in 1989. Local government budgets and staff positions for planning had experienced considerable cutbacks by the time of the earthquake. This significantly impaired the ability of local governments in the impact region to prepare high-quality mitigation plans (Bauman and Green 1995).

OES officials were concerned that the limited available federal Section 404 funds might not always be used for the most efficient and effective methods of reducing risk. Another concern indicated by OES staff members was that localities might not have a sound enough technical rationale for persuading FEMA to support local Section 404 applications. As discussed later in this chapter, this did become a major problem in some communities during the Loma Prieta recovery.

The strategy taken after the Northridge earthquake had a top-down emphasis, in contrast to the bottom-up, locally driven strategy pursued in the Loma Prieta recovery planning effort. After the Northridge earthquake, the OES issued a Hazard Mitigation Program Strategy paper in February 1995, that identified four priority areas for Section 404 funds: (1) nonstructural mitigation in schools; (2) strengthening of medical and hospital facilities; (3) strengthening of essential buildings (police and fire departments, Emergency Operations Centers, administrative buildings of local governments, public works facilities, and jails); and (4) education, training, and research (OES 1995). In addition, a fifth priority area was to be considered for statewide microzonation mapping. These priority areas were deemed consistent with policies set forth in the 1992–1996 plan document, which, as noted, serves as the state's Section 409 plan for earthquake hazards.

The first two priorities were particularly salient, according to OES staff, given the high degree of political and technical feasibility of achieving them. Schools and hospitals are controlled by the state, not by local governments. By targeting such facilities, the state would not have to deal

with facilities under the control of diverse local jurisdictions. Moreover, these priorities have high political and moral appeal.

Because of the enormous expense of carrying out these five priorities (the cost for undertaking the first priority alone was estimated to be $1.4 billion), OES officials decided that a systematic procedure was needed for identifying priority mitigation investments. As noted earlier, the RAMP computer model was used for this purpose. OES staff members were quick to point out to us that this model was needed to address the technical shortcomings of the approach to plan preparation used after the Loma Prieta earthquake. They also maintained that the model could eventually be used by local governments in mitigation decision making. However, as will be discussed, the top-down strategy taken by the state in using the model after the Northridge earthquake was criticized by local officials as time-consuming, inflexible, and lacking in local input.

Promotion of a Comprehensive Research Strategy Through Section 409 Planning

According to the acting director of the California Seismic Safety Commission, the current version of the state Section 409 plan for earthquakes, *California at Risk*, needs to be streamlined. The plan's forty-two policy initiatives are considered too detailed and too difficult to coordinate for successful implementation. The commission is currently working on paring the plan down to "a smaller, more realistic set of policies." The state has hired a well-respected engineering consultant who has considerable experience in working with local governments and state agencies to formulate seismic risk mitigation policies.

A key element of the *California at Risk* document is a comprehensive research strategy for earthquake mitigation in California. The strategy was intended to promote interdisciplinary research that would address the real-world earthquake problems the state faces. The strategy was to encompass a broad variety of research activities including the social, behavioral, geophysical, land use planning, and structural engineering fields.

In response to this policy, Senator Alquist, a longtime proponent of earthquake safety in California, ordered the California Seismic Safety Commission to generate legislative initiatives to produce a coordinated research plan for the state. The plan, completed in December 1994, is known informally as the Blue Report (California Seismic Safety Commission 1994b). The key component of the research plan is establishment of an interdisciplinary Earthquake Research Center, which is to act as a consortium for industry and for federal, state, and local government. The main

objective is to encourage the involvement of industry through demonstration of new technologies and their application to earthquake hazard mitigation. Interestingly, the Northridge earthquake has generated efforts by the declining defense industry to apply advanced technologies to hazard mitigation.

Implementation of the Hazard Mitigation Grant Program

The long delay in reviewing and approving Section 404 mitigation projects became a major issue after the Northridge earthquake struck. Eighteen months after this event received presidential declaration status, only two projects had been received by the FEMA regional office. In contrast, during a fourteen-month period after the Loma Prieta event, the state had forwarded forty-eight projects to FEMA.

Why was there such a dramatic difference in processing time? To answer this question, it is best to individually discuss state and federal actions associated with Section 404 funding for each disaster.

State Actions and Section 404 Mitigation Project Review

A major explanation for the delay was the OES's decision after Northridge to develop and apply the computerized RAMP model to conduct large-scale benefit-cost analyses. Although FEMA required that some type of benefit-cost analysis be undertaken to support Section 404 project selection, the analysis did not have to be based on such a technically advanced and complex model as RAMP. Further, the OES had only $5–$7 million in state monies to use as a match for Section 404 mitigation grants. Given this limited amount of funds, the OES did not want to take a "scattergun" approach to mitigation. Instead, OES officials wanted to spend mitigation funds in a targeted way by pursuing a strategy that prioritized actions based on cost-effectiveness.

Senior OES officials spent about one year after the Northridge disaster putting together the strategy that was driven by development of the RAMP model. During this period, reviews of Section 404 projects were delayed as the OES waited for RAMP results before deciding where to direct funding.

Ultimately, the RAMP model determined that hardening of suspended ceilings, pendant lighting, and sprinkler systems in schools should be the highest priority. The first wave of school applications for Section 404 funds was not expected until late 1995.

To some, the delays after Northridge tarnished the OES's already diminished reputation for processing Section 404 project applications. For

instance, seventy-eight applications from the winter storms of 1993 were submitted to the OES, but as of November 1994, the OES had reviewed only fifteen of these. No action was taken by the OES for more than a year on the remaining sixty-three applications. The slow turnaround was attributed largely to weak organizational capacity at the OES. As noted, however, OES mitigation staffing has been expanded from two part-time to seven full-time positions since the Northridge quake.

Moreover, some individual local planners in southern California believed that the entire RAMP-driven strategy for selecting Section 404 funding priorities was too inflexible. One local planner stated, "My community was left out of the loop after Northridge . . . this was due to how the RAMP modeling effort was conducted." Local planners believed that their communities would have spent the Section 404 funds in ways quite different from the RAMP-determined priorities.

Although the OES could legitimately be criticized for being too slow and for being inflexible in processing post-Northridge Section 404 applications, its approach had several positive outcomes. As noted, FEMA approved a seismic mapping project to cover the three counties included in the Northridge disaster declaration. At the time of our study, the California Department of Mines was planning to map seismic zones in four other metropolitan areas through use of state funds.

It is also evident that the RAMP model will become an integral part of long-range state mitigation planning. Local governments will also be able to use the RAMP model to argue for future Section 404 mitigation projects tailored to their own situations. These benefits extend far beyond the immediate recovery concerns after Northridge.

Although the review process for Loma Prieta was less time-consuming than that for Northridge, there were still some controversial issues. These centered on participation by FEMA and local governments in the mitigation decision-making process.

Another shortcoming of the Loma Prieta recovery was the considerable variation in quality of local mitigation plans. As a result, selection of Section 404–funded projects may not always have been based on the highest-priority mitigation needs but instead may have depended in part on the ability of local governments to prepare high-quality local mitigation plans that most rigorously demonstrated cost-effective mitigation projects. This shortcoming raises the question of how to build the capacity of local governments to prepare high-quality mitigation plans.

In sum, the contrasting approaches taken by the OES in the Loma Prieta and Northridge Section 404 decision-making processes offer some useful lessons. On the one hand, the top-down approach taken after the Northridge event had several advantages, including availability of a technically

advanced risk-modeling procedure and greater assurance that limited mitigation funds would be used for the highest-priority projects. The chief disadvantages were the long time delays required to apply the RAMP model and lack of local discretion in tailoring Section 404 funding decisions to local needs and priorities.

On the other hand, the bottom-up approach to Section 404 funding decisions taken after Loma Prieta had an obvious strength. It encouraged the involvement of local people, through planning, in controlling mitigation actions that would influence future community land use and development patterns. However, local governments were given limited guidance and financial support in preparing local mitigation plans. The quality of the plans thus varied considerably across localities. Consequently, the limited Section 404 mitigation funds may not always have been spent on the highest-priority needs in the San Francisco Bay Area.

Federal Actions and Section 404 Mitigation Project Review

Federal actions also influenced the extent of processing delays. First, continual changes in FEMA staffing caused inconsistency in decision making during the post-Northridge recovery. As discussed, FEMA headquarters in Washington, D.C., assigned staff members from different regions on a rotating basis in order to help FEMA Region IX staff in San Francisco manage the enormous demands of the recovery process.

A similar problem with rotating staff assignments occurred after the Loma Prieta event. An evaluation by the General Accounting Office (GAO 1992) indicated that at that time, FEMA's approach to postdisaster staffing "did not meet the requirements of a major earthquake . . . and lack of continuity among staff during the recovery led to disputes and delays" (p. 4). Given the recurring staff continuity problems after Northridge, it appears that FEMA did not take the necessary steps to provide more stable staffing arrangements. In its defense, FEMA has had to respond to an increasing number of disasters over the years. Consequently, the agency's limited staff has been stretched too thin to confront the competing demands. At the time of the Northridge recovery, for example, FEMA was also contending with intense recovery demands associated with Hurricane Andrew, which struck South Florida in the summer of 1994.

Changes in evaluation criteria for Section 404 projects also caused numerous difficulties. For example, a list of preapprovable categories of Section 404 projects was generated jointly by FEMA region IX and X mitigation teams to streamline the approval process. A project in one of the preapprovable categories required only limited formal review. Categories included, for example, basic retrofits (e.g., ceilings and light fixtures) that were eligible and cost-effective. The preapproval concept was coordinated

with the OES, but FEMA headquarters in Washington, D.C., rejected it on the basis of its decision to have each project individually run through a benefit-cost analysis approved by FEMA. This type of change generated considerable uncertainty and poor coordination, which resulted in further delays.

Subsequently, a mitigation memorandum of understanding (MOU) was approved by FEMA headquarters. The MOU identified four sets of criteria to be met at the start of the approval process: compatibility with (1) the list of preapprovable project categories, (2) the National Environmental Protection Act, (3) historic preservation requirements, and (4) FEMA's benefit-cost analysis model. Projects incompatible with any of the four criteria could not undergo an expedited review.

Another federal action that delayed Section 404 project reviews involved an additional step inserted into the review process. Specifically, during the summer of 1995, FEMA headquarters rescinded the authority of the regional office to review Section 404 projects in Northridge. As noted earlier, the shift in responsibility was a result of headquarters wanting more scrutiny over Section 404 funding, given the pending budget cuts being pushed by Congress.

The state's request for the microzonation mapping project fell victim to these stringent requirements. The intent of the project was to integrate the maps with RAMP modeling. The state requested $12 million in Section 404 funds for the mapping project. Currently, all Section 404 project requests exceeding $1 million are to be reviewed by FEMA headquarters in Washington, D.C., as well as FEMA Region IX. FEMA's Office of General Counsel and Policy Review Committee at headquarters review all such projects. In this case, the two entities decided that only the three counties within the Northridge disaster impact area were eligible; other high-priority but nonimpacted areas in the state were declared ineligible. Ultimately, FEMA allocated $7.2 million to the mapping project, but only after many months of debate. Indeed, FEMA held up the Section 404 mapping project request for nine months before approval. At the time of our interviews (July 1995), the state was appealing FEMA's decision.

Another obstacle in approval of Section 404 projects was the federal challenge to the state's authority to determine construction standards for hospital building. OES officials maintained that the state has such authority under the 1972 Hospital Safety Act. As of July 1995, FEMA was contesting the act's language, which, according to FEMA Region IX staff members, applies only to construction of new hospitals, not to repair of damaged ones.

Minimal Use of Section 404 Funding for Mitigation

An additional issue associated with both disasters involves the small amount of funds actually spent on mitigation in comparison with the total amount obligated by the federal government for recovery. As noted, the amount of funds obligated under Section 404 of the Stafford Act is based on a percentage of the total FEMA public assistance funds allocated to a given disaster. As of May 1996, FEMA Section 404 obligations for the Loma Prieta disaster were $56.6 million. This amount represents only about 2 percent of the $2.7 billion spent by all federal agencies on the entire recovery effort (Buika 1993).

Northridge funds were similarly underutilized. By September 1996, FEMA had allocated more than $129 million in Section 404 funds, or about twenty-two percent of the estimated $600 million available. There was also concern that state and local governments might be unable to match the 25 percent cost share for mitigation. A Los Angeles County official maintained that the underuse of funds might have been a result of the long delay in priority setting by the state: local governments had "lost so much momentum for mitigation after waiting so long." Another local official, from Ventura County, commented "We are going through very tight budgeting . . . other priorities on the county budget are moving ahead of mitigation." Thus, even with a substantial amount of federal funds available and with a higher matching payment by the federal government than was available with Loma Prieta, mitigation may have had too little political support and remained too expensive for subnational authorities.

Results

What was actually accomplished in postdisaster mitigation after the Loma Prieta and Northridge events? In the following discussion, we focus on the use of the HMGP Section 404 grant program, recognizing that there were substantial contributions from HUD's CDBG program and from the Department of Transportation. Table 6.2 summarizes the Section 404 obligations by project type.

The bulk of Section 404 project expenditures for Loma Prieta have been aimed at increasing the resistance of existing buildings and public facilities to future earthquake stresses. Improvements to public and private facilities include retrofits of fire stations, hospitals, city halls, schools, university buildings, libraries, water supply and wastewater treatment facilities, and the like. Most projects are structural in nature. Equipment purchases mainly include emergency power generators for fire and police departments,

hospitals, and schools. Table 6.2 shows that obligated HMGP funds as of July 1995 were $31,636,014 for the Loma Prieta disaster. This total increased to $34,928,940 in October 1996 (table 6.3).

As of July 1995, a year and a half after the Northridge earthquake, FEMA had received only two HMGP project applications (table 6.2). The statewide geohazards mapping project was in progress, though its scope remained under appeal. The Castaic School replacement project was pending environmental review. Since this case study was conducted, a number of additional project requests have been received, and as of September 1996, FEMA had approved more than $129 million in HMGP expenditures, most of it for school retrofits (table 6.3).

Table 6.2. Summary of HMGP Projects for Loma Prieta and Northridge Earthquakes as of July 1995

TYPE OF PROJECT (NUMBER RECEIVED)	TOTAL COST	FEMA SHARE	OBLIGATED
Loma Prieta			
Public/private facilities (76)	$95,166,166	$47,583,083	$27,346,930
Equipment purchase (37)	$16,705,690	$8,352,845	$3,761,924
Planning, legislation (8)	$1,191,150	$595,575	$443,575
Education, training (3)	$167,170	$83,585	$83,585
Total (124)[a]	$113,230,176	$56,615,088	$31,636,014
Northridge			
Public/private facilities (1)	$24,196,789	$18,147,592	—
Planning, legislation (1)	$12,500,000	$9,375,000	—
Total (2)	$36,696,789	$27,522,592	—

[a]Does not include one denied Land Improvement project, one withdrawn Unclassified project, and three Administrative Costs applications.

Table 6.3. Update of HMGP Projects for Northridge Earthquake as of September 1996

TYPE OF PROJECT	HMGP REQUESTS TO FEMA[a]	HMGP FUNDED BY FEMA[a]
Schools (K–14)	$107,720,046	$107,720,046
Medical facilities	$7,442,237	$5,197,299
Essential government facilities	$0	$0
State agencies	$39,950,360	$9,375,000
Other/Castaic School	$7,252,458	$7,252,458
Total	$162,365,101	$129,544,803

Source: Siavash Jay Jazayeri, hazard mitigation officer, FEMA-1008-DR-CA, Northridge Long-Term Recovery Area Office.

[a]Represents the 75 percent federal share of the project but does *not* include grantee and subgrantee administrative costs.

City of San Francisco

In October 1989, in response to the Loma Prieta earthquake, the city of San Francisco prepared and adopted the OES-required hazard mitigation plan (City and County of San Francisco 1990a). According to a city planner, however, this document was less a plan than a grant application. It has not guided the city in conducting hazard mitigation and was prepared primarily to obtain funds. The plan consists of four sections: (1) evaluation of potential losses from future earthquakes; (2) hazard mitigation policies in place (land use, zoning, redevelopment policy, building codes, and emergency response planning); (3) proposed hazard mitigation strategies and actions, including status and shortfalls in work and funding needed to complete each proposed action; and (4) a program for monitoring, evaluating, and updating the mitigation document.

San Francisco has undertaken several additional mitigation actions since the 1989 Loma Prieta earthquake. Between 1989 and 1992, the city administration successfully pushed four bond issues totaling about $783 million; in 1992, citizens voted for a $350 million bond, the biggest ever passed by the city. The city also received $6.1 million from FEMA and $4.48 million from a state bond after the earthquake event. In addition, the Mayor's Office has played a key role in assisting several organizations with Section 404 grant applications, including various city government agencies (housing, parks and recreation, and public works), the airport authority, public utilities, and private nonprofit organizations.

Several mitigation activities were spurred by Loma Prieta. One was a voluntary updating of the general plan's safety element. A draft version of *San Francisco's Community Safety Element* was prepared for the general plan of the City and County of San Francisco (City and County of San Francisco 1995). The safety element includes a hazard analysis section containing maps delineating hazard zones, overall hazard mitigation goals, and six categories of objectives, policies, and implementation actions. In addition, hazard mitigation policy is integrated throughout other parts of the general plan (e.g., transportation, capital improvements, land use) as well as other local plans and programs, such as the emergency operations plan and post-disaster hazard mitigation plan required by the state.

Another key mitigation action was to move the San Francisco Office of Emergency Services from the Fire Department to the Mayor's Office during the four years after Loma Prieta. This organization is now housed in the city administrator's office and has been directed to place greater priority on mitigation, augmenting its previous role as an emergency response agency. Both the preparation of a safety element for the general plan and the new organizational arrangement represent a considerable

improvement in mitigation policy in two respects: salience and access to key city decision makers.

A major point of contention between FEMA and the city, however, has been the use of Section 406 public assistance mitigation funding. An official from the city manager's office pointed out that "FEMA was supposed to let rebuilt buildings go beyond pre-disaster conditions primarily for mitigation. But FEMA was not accommodating in this regard." This staffer cited the controversy over upgrading the city hall building to support his contention that FEMA handled the Section 406 mitigation program poorly. FEMA did a benefit-cost analysis of a city-backed upgrade design that included base isolation technology for the city hall. The analysis estimated building upgrading costs for base isolation to be $185 million. FEMA was required to come up with a 75 percent match (about $138.6 million) under Section 406 funding, with state and local governments (primarily local) required to come up with the remaining funds. The city wanted to use base isolation technology because it was the best option to achieve safety and to retain the historic character of the building.

FEMA opposed this form of upgrade by arguing that it was too costly and that the limited mitigation funds should be more widely distributed rather than concentrated on a single facility. FEMA then hired a consultant to conduct a detailed review of the building. According to the lead official at the Mayor's Office, FEMA turned down the city's request one month before the study was completed. City staff believed that FEMA Region IX staff did not want to fund base isolation regardless of what the study results might suggest. Instead, FEMA wanted the building upgraded through installation of a shear wall. The city was vehemently opposed to this option because it would drastically compromise the historic integrity of the building. The Mayor's Office maintained that FEMA's position was particularly frustrating since a federal government building was undergoing a base isolation upgrade in San Francisco even though "the city has spent over five years haggling with FEMA over city hall." An editorial titled "FEMA Is a Disaster" in the *San Francisco Examiner* on September 2, 1992, stated: "FEMA is why City Hall is still a shambles with cracked ceilings and wooden bracing. FEMA constructed a neat Catch-22. If you fix up the building to withstand the next shake, we won't pay you for it. Unfortunately, that's the kind of FEMA double-speak people have come to expect."

A similar issue arose over the city's opera house, the third most historically important building in San Francisco. The city wanted to use Section 406 public assistance mitigation funds to install a base isolation system in this building, but again FEMA balked, arguing that the technique was too expensive.

City of Berkeley

Very little mitigation activity had taken place in Berkeley prior to the Loma Prieta earthquake. Although the city sustained only limited damage from Loma Prieta, the event heightened awareness and concern regarding the need for mitigation within the city.

Fortunately, two years before Loma Prieta, Berkeley had elected a council member who strongly advocated more mitigation efforts. When Loma Prieta struck, this council member was in a good position to push for action on several fronts. The assistant to the city manager was also concerned about seismic safety, particularly the hazards posed by schools built with unreinforced concrete.

These two individuals were instrumental in obtaining mitigation funds for Berkeley. Specifically, several actions were taken. The assistant to the city manager led an effort to prepare the OES-mandated mitigation plan and used the plan to apply for Section 404 funds. This effort brought $3.3 million for schools and $4 million to retrofit city hall. The city also acquired $8 million from a state bond to retrofit public buildings and campaigned to obtain a $17 million special appropriation for mitigation from the state legislature. The assistant to the city manager said that the "city fought hard for mitigation and was a leading advocate for mitigation. We did not make many friends in Sacramento." In addition, the city passed a $158 million bond in April 1992 to upgrade schools for seismic mitigation. It then passed another bond in November 1992 for $55 million to retrofit fire stations and install a redundant fire-fighting system.

The assistant to the city manager stated that several organizations provided helpful technical assistance to the city in preparing its mitigation plan for Section 404 project applications, including the now dissolved Bay Area Response and Earthquake Preparedness Program (BAREPP) and the California Seismic Safety Commission. She also indicated that the state Section 409 earthquake plan, *California at Risk* (California Seismic Safety Commission 1991), was especially useful in helping the city prepare Section 404 applications. In particular, the assistant to the city manager believed that *California at Risk* helped the city justify its requests for federal Section 404 and state grants. Overall, she believed that the Section 404 application process went quite well and was generally easy for the city staff to implement.

The city adopted several additional mitigation programs after Loma Prieta, waiving permit fees for private buildings undergoing retrofitting, enacting a 0.5 percent property transfer tax abatement for buildings that have been retrofitted, and adopting a new, more stringent building code for retrofitting unreinforced masonry buildings. In addition, the California

Seismic Safety Commission helped Berkeley set up a seismic mitigation education program for local contractors. The city plans to apply a model education program devised by the city of San Leandro. This program was to be up and running by fall 1995.

At the time this case study was completed, the city also had a Blue Ribbon Panel for Seismic Mitigation consisting of several experts from the University of California, Berkeley, and representatives of various interest groups from around the city. The panel was to help the city put together a comprehensive mitigation policy in 1995–1996. As of 1995, the panel was suggesting that the city push for another mitigation bond in 1996, for about $75–$100 million. The panel also encouraged the city administration to go forward on national policy issues regarding hazard mitigation. The city administration agreed with these recommendations and planned to place mitigation on the agenda of the National Council of Cities. A major issue will be to evaluate the distribution of funds under the National Earthquake Hazards Reduction Program. The assistant to the city manager stated that the city will press for answers to the central question, "Where is all that money going?" She maintained that "Berkeley and many other local governments at risk don't see how all the research funds in this program help them. Users don't use the research results. Why?"

City of Watsonville

The city of Watsonville (1990 population 31,099) was a prototypical case in earthquake hazard planning following the 1989 Loma Prieta disaster. After the earthquake, the city undertook three planning initiatives: (1) a stand-alone community disaster plan; (2) a safety element, as part of the local comprehensive plan; and (3) a stand-alone hazard mitigation plan for Section 404 projects. The quality of Watsonville's mitigation planning initiatives is a result of several factors, including state and federal policies and local needs and capabilities.

The 1992 *Community Based Disaster Plan* was prepared largely on the basis of lessons learned in emergency preparedness planning after the Loma Prieta event (City of Watsonville 1992). This plan is oriented primarily toward emergency preparedness and response actions immediately before and after a disaster event. It consists of nine elements, including, for example, organizational structure, communications, shelter management, volunteer management, and recovery. The recovery element focuses on organizational and resource acquisition needs for housing, family, and business recovery rather than on physical reconstruction.

The safety element of Watsonville's comprehensive plan, *Watsonville*

2005 General Plan, contains community-wide, rather than site-specific, policies for landslides, earthquakes, floods, fires, hazardous materials, and noise (City of Watsonville 1994). The policies rely on a variety of growth management tools, including land use and building design regulation, infrastructure location and design, and public education. Maps delineating flood, surface fault rupture, liquefaction, and flood hazards are included in the plan.

Finally, the 1990 *Hazard Mitigation Plan* was prepared to serve as a basis for submitting Section 404 applications during the aftermath of the Loma Prieta disaster (City of Watsonville 1990). As noted, this plan was prepared in response to a state requirement that local governments prepare a mitigation plan to be eligible for Section 404 mitigation funds. The document contains an evaluation of potential losses from future earthquakes affecting Watsonville and proposes twenty-eight hazard mitigation actions.

Overall, Watsonville's mitigation planning effort is quite comprehensive. The package of plans deals with both short- and long-term mitigation issues. The emergency plan links traditional emergency management actions with recovery, which is somewhat unusual. Such plans are typically narrowly focused on immediate disaster response demands. This emergency plan brings resources and organizations traditionally associated with the emergency response field into the long-term recovery arena.

Although Watsonville's effort is comparatively more comprehensive than those of the vast majority of U.S. communities, there is a key weakness. An examination of the three plan documents reveals a lack of integration. Most notably, the safety element, which was prepared after the other two plans, only briefly mentions the presence of the other plans and does not explain how the plans are interrelated. For example, the need for shelters in specific locations and sufficient evacuation route capacity are discussed in the emergency plan but are not dealt with in the safety element. Nor are they addressed in other elements (e.g., transportation, land use, capital improvements) of the comprehensive plan. It is obvious that shelters and evacuation routes are part of the built environment and should be dealt with in the comprehensive plan. Similarly, although the Section 404 plan mentions the twenty-eight mitigation projects, it does not make it clear how these projects relate to the goals, policies, and implementation actions set forth in the safety element.

Los Angeles and Ventura Counties

After the Northridge earthquake, local governments were to apply for Section 404 mitigation grants based on the OES's five funding priorities. As

noted earlier, the priorities took about a year to formulate, largely due to use of the computerized risk analysis model known as RAMP. The OES's initiative in setting priorities had two key implications from the perspective of two local governments (Los Angeles and Ventura Counties) in the Northridge impact area. One was that the long delay exacted a heavy toll in terms of loss of political support for mitigation. The other related to the inflexibility of the five priorities.

Planners from both Los Angeles and Ventura Counties indicated that during the first few months after the earthquake, local elected officials were highly supportive of funding mitigation projects. However, one local planner from Ventura County pointed out that "as the months tick by . . . politicians and the general public throughout the region are quickly losing interest in investing in problems associated with uncertain phenomena that may occur sometime in the unpredictable future." Indeed, the Northridge event was appearing increasingly distant. Officials from both counties maintained that as time passed, it became increasingly difficult to find local matching funds for Section 404 projects.

There was a general concern over the OES's inflexible stance. One local official viewed Los Angeles County's effort to organize local agencies along the state's funding priorities as working into the OES's "divide and conquer mentality" in getting its way with local governments. Specifically, once the OES priority list was released, Los Angeles County took an initial step of organizing three groups from thirteen county agencies. The groups represented education, hospitals, and public buildings, consistent with three of the OES's priority areas. Each group was charged with identifying specific evaluation criteria to reflect local needs and priorities. Although the county groups had some latitude in defining the criteria and in selecting the most appropriate projects, the range of choices was to be consistent with state Section 404 funding priorities.

Officials from both counties complained that the state-derived priorities were not necessarily consistent with local priorities. Ventura County officials, for example, wanted to apply for Section 404 funds to update the safety element of the county's general plan and to improve facilities at the county Emergency Operations center. Indeed, all ten cities in Ventura County pooled resources (staff and funds) and prepared Section 404 applications jointly in hopes that their effort would enhance technical rigor and demonstrate strong political appeal and thus encourage the OES to fund their requests, even if they did not fit exactly within the OES's three priorities.

Issues

Our review of mitigation after two major earthquakes in California raises several important issues that should be addressed to meet future disaster needs.

Insufficiency of Current Mitigation Policies to Cope with Future Earthquakes

Our evidence suggests that the present mitigation systems (policies and institutions) will not be adequate to mitigate the impact of a future large earthquake. Even though losses sustained in the Loma Prieta and Northridge earthquakes were severe, they could have been much worse; the geologic characteristics of both events produced earthquakes that could have been much more devastating. The Loma Prieta event was only a moderately severe earthquake but could have been equal in magnitude to the great 1906 earthquake. Fortunately, in the case of Northridge, the duration of intense shaking was relatively short and the magnitude of the earthquake was only moderate. Had the magnitude been greater, the duration of strong shaking would have been longer and the damage would have been much greater. Indeed, it is a matter of when, not if, great earthquakes will strike in northern and southern California. At issue is how effective federal, state, and local governments will be in reducing future damage, injury, and loss of life.

Institutional Issues

The California earthquake cases demonstrate well the problems that can arise within the U.S. intergovernmental hazard mitigation system.

FEMA Intra-agency Relationships

Many of the recovery problems after the Loma Prieta and Northridge earthquakes stemmed from changing procedural agreements among FEMA Regions IX (San Francisco) and X (Seattle) and national FEMA headquarters. Section 404 funding was delayed, for example, by midcourse changes in the review process for proposals. Recall that FEMA Regions IX and X closely coordinated their decision making by developing and supporting mitigation proposals during the Northridge earthquake aftermath. The plan this team developed to expedite mitigation projects was rejected because of benefit-cost and legal concerns raised by technical experts at

FEMA headquarters in Washington, D.C. The end product became FEMA policy but caused some delay and confusion over which mitigation projects were and were not eligible.

Another major reason for the long delays in distributing Section 404 funds was FEMA's lack of a workable staffing strategy for meeting the special challenges posed by both disasters. The OES maintained that numerous difficulties and inconsistent decisions were caused by continual changes in staff, which generated considerable uncertainty and poor coordination and resulted in disputes and delays.

FEMA Region X staff developed an effective method of promoting mitigation through the placement and staffing of mitigation tables. Tensions between the new mitigation staff and the more traditional Disaster Assistance Center (DAC) staff resulted in a refinement of the method whereby the tables were moved from DACs to separate Disaster Recovery Centers (similar to the Northridge Earthquake Service Centers but not disaster specific). These centers also have tables for the Small Business Administration and home improvement programs, among others.

Although the service centers are a positive step in assisting disaster-stricken communities, the effectiveness of the table concept needs to be evaluated. Initial experience after the Northridge earthquake suggests that the service centers and mitigation tables were reasonably successful in disseminating information. In fact, given the positive experience after Northridge, FEMA placed mitigation tables at DACs after the Houston, Texas, floods in 1994 and the widespread California floods in 1995. However, a follow-up evaluation would provide more detailed findings on the extent to which different types of information provided at the tables influence recovery and mitigation actions.

FEMA-State Relationships

After the Northridge disaster struck, FEMA staff overwhelmed state staff, both in number and by setting forth policy directions without state agency input. State agency staff spent valuable time acquainting FEMA staff with California mitigation policy. A key example of this issue involved the hastily prepared information about building design and structural strengthening to be distributed at the earthquake mitigation centers. OES staff had to explain to FEMA officials that this information must go through standard technical review procedures required by state building codes. They also were concerned that the mitigation specialists employed by FEMA might not have adequate technical training concerning seismic construction techniques in southern California.

On the positive side, FEMA Region IX staff did show a willingness to

adapt and respond to OES concerns. This was evidenced in the cooperation of the OES and FEMA regarding information dissemination. Specifically, the building design and earthquake retrofit materials used by the mitigation counselors at the Earthquake Service Centers were taken from the OES earthquake retrofit manual. This manual was jointly updated for the Northridge event, and all supplemental materials were jointly reviewed and approved by OES technical staff before they were used.

Institutional tension remains between the OES and FEMA Region IX, however. California is a leader in state mitigation policy, but at times FEMA seems to hinder state efforts to advance mitigation. After Northridge, even though the substantive ideas of FEMA Region X staff were appropriate, they were put forward in a top-down manner. The state, especially the OES, reacted against FEMA's top-down approach. Moreover, the OES expended time and effort in educating FEMA Region X staff about California mitigation programs and policies. More coordination is called for. The collaborative OES-FEMA effort to provide manuals on mitigation guidance at the tables and through public workshops represents a positive step in this regard.

FEMA-Local Relationships

After Loma Prieta, FEMA lacked specific guidance for determining the eligibility for funding of mitigation measures to protect buildings or to restore historic buildings that could be more economically replaced. The lack of specific guidance resulted in many disputes between FEMA and local jurisdictions such as San Francisco over the eligibility, scope, and cost of repairs as well as the type of mitigation measures to be used. The disputes led to delays in providing recovery and mitigation funds.

Relationships Among State Agencies

California has approached mitigation on the basis of individual hazards rather than through a more comprehensive multihazard approach. This orientation has led to a piecemeal and inconsistent mitigation response.

California must contend with the division of seismic mitigation responsibilities among its state agencies. By state law, the California Seismic Safety Commission is responsible for earthquake mitigation planning, while the OES is in charge of mitigation planning for all hazards except earthquakes. This arrangement poses coordination difficulties in advancing and coordinating earthquake mitigation activities and in implementing plans.

Although staff commitment and the leadership of the current SHMO in pursuing mitigation are very high at the OES, technical capacity is

somewhat low. Despite recent increases in staffing and budgeting for mitigation, the OES has inadequate resources to effectively carry out its mission.

State-Local Relationships

While the bottom-up approach to Section 404 funding decisions taken after Loma Prieta encouraged local governments to participate in the planning of mitigation actions, the lack of guidance and financial support resulted in plans and Section 404 projects of varying quality.

The delay in distributing Section 404 mitigation funds after the Northridge disaster resulted in loss of political support and enthusiasm for mitigation at the local level. Local government officials saw the entire risk-modeling strategy for selecting Section 404 funding priorities as too inflexible, despite its long-range benefit in identifying, analyzing, and prioritizing risk-generating characteristics of the built environment.

Inadequate Mitigation Funding

Mitigation funding after a disaster represents a very small proportion of federal funding targeted for recovery. As urban development in earthquake hazard areas continues in California, demands for public recovery funds will continue to rise. However, given the tightening federal purse strings and the trend toward devolution of responsibility to state and local governments, it is likely that the burden for disaster recovery assistance will fall increasingly on these subnational jurisdictions. Consequently, state and local governments will be increasingly called on to seek other funding sources, particularly from the insurance industry. Further, state and local governments will need to be more aggressive in pursuing risk mitigation strategies to reduce future costs of disaster recovery.

Conclusions and Recommendations

Clearly, the lessons from the Loma Prieta and Northridge earthquake recoveries are significant for mitigation policy, both in California and at the national level.

  • *Mitigation strategies need a research basis.* California needs to pursue a coordinated, interdisciplinary effort to further the understanding of earthquake prediction and earthquake impacts. There are numerous unknowns surrounding earthquakes, as evidenced by the presence of active blind faults and the effect of seismic forces in near-source areas. The

state plans to pursue a comprehensive and interdisciplinary research strategy through establishment of an Earthquake Research Center. Results from this effort should be incorporated into the state-level risk assessment and automated hazard-mapping effort.

• *Many state agencies need to cooperate in mitigation.* California also needs to increase support for the OES's capacity commensurate with its mission to pursue mitigation during the predisaster and recovery stages. Such capacity would probably encourage commitment by other key state agencies that have authority over issues related to hazard mitigation, such as coastal development, transportation, and building construction. These agencies have historically been reluctant to become involved in mitigation planning in California.

• *Build local mitigation planning.* California should reinvigorate efforts to mandate local multihazard mitigation planning before and after a disaster. Strong local land use and growth management programs should be instituted to limit future development in areas subject to catastrophic disasters. Emergency management and hazard mitigation planning initiatives should have mutually reinforcing goals and policies. Local jurisdictions with state-certified mitigation plans should be eligible for mitigation block grants to be spent in accordance with plan goals and policies. Similarly, FEMA and the OES should collarboratively pursue efforts to build mitigation into the safety elements of local general plans.

• *Avoid delays that let windows of opportunity close.* State and local government should take advantage of windows of opportunity in the aftermath of a disaster. Berkeley and San Francisco voters approved large bond measures for mitigation funding, and Watsonville created a comprehensive mitigation planning effort to guide short- and long-range mitigation actions within the community. A window may have closed after Northridge, however, as localities lost interest in supporting mitigation as a result of the state's long delay in administering Section 404 funds.

• *Encourage private sector participation.* State and local government should encourage the private sector to support mitigation efforts. Available federal funds for mitigation represent only a tiny portion of the total funds needed for adequate hazard mitigation. State and local government should pursue a dual strategy of reducing the long-term potential loss when an earthquake strikes and expanding the availability of insurance. Tax credits, development density bonuses, capital improvement programs, tax reduction schemes, and a variety of other land use planning measures should be used more aggressively to entice market involvement in mitigation funding. Such incentives should be used to encourage developers to avoid

high-hazard zones. Such incentives can also encourage private investment in retrofitting of existing development. The current state-mandated local planning legislation is already in place in California. What is lacking is strong state policy and enforcement to ensure that local governments adopt development management measures (incentives and regulations) consistent with local plan policies.

• *FEMA mitigation staffing should be stable.* FEMA needs to ensure that more stable staff arrangements are available for future disaster recovery efforts. Current FEMA policy is to return high-level disaster staff to their home regions within thirty to forty-five days. Although this policy recognizes the needs of the individuals involved, it can be disruptive of ongoing recovery management.

• *FEMA guidance should be specific.* FEMA also needs to develop more specific guidance about protecting buildings from future earthquakes and more specific regulations concerning eligibility of structures for federal mitigation funds. Cost containment policies should be designed to limit expenditures on retrofitting of historic structures under the Section 404 Hazard Mitigation Grant Program. Moreover, mitigation measures under Section 406 should be clarified.

• *Block grants would improve mitigation outcomes.* There is a strong need for some type of FEMA-approved global mitigation fund or block grant rather than the piecemeal matching program currently in place. Hazard mitigation procedures could be changed from project-by-project federal reviews to block grants that could be spent on the basis of strategies tailored to state needs. States, however, would need to have a certified Section 409 plan in place to be eligible for such a block grant.

• *Explore earthquake insurance.* Insurance policies can also be used to entice mitigation investments. Similar to the National Flood Insurance Program (NFIP), an earthquake insurance program could require individuals and communities to adopt mitigation measures through land use and building code measures. The more successfully a community adopted mitigation measures, the greater would be the reduction in insurance premium costs for individuals and businesses. However, unlike the NFIP, an earthquake insurance program should encourage more extensive applications of land use measures. Some observers maintain that the NFIP actually encourages floodplain development by placing too much emphasis on structural strengthening through building codes rather than encouraging land use measures that lead to avoidance of hazard areas.

Acknowledgments

We appreciate the invaluable assistance of Paula Schulz, the California SHMO, and Jack Eldridge of FEMA Region IX in arranging interviews during our visit and of Leo Levenson of FEMA Region IX in providing data for our report.

Note

1. This chapter is based on interviews with federal, state, and local officials in California conducted by Philip Berke and David R. Godschalk during a case study visit in July 1995, some six years after the Loma Prieta earthquake and a year and a half after the Northridge earthquake.

References

Bauman, C., and M. Green. 1995. *Revision of the Community Safety Element: The San Francisco Experience.* San Francisco: City and County Planning Department.

Buika, J. 1993. "The Federal Emergency Management Agency's Assistance to the San Francisco Bay Area Following the October 17, 1989, Loma Prieta Earthquake, CA: Implications for an Eastern United States Earthquake." Paper presented at the 1993 National Earthquake Conference, "Earthquake Hazard Reduction in the Central and Eastern United States: A Time for Examination and Action," May 2–5, Memphis, Tennessee.

California Seismic Safety Commission. 1991. *California at Risk: Reducing Earthquake Hazards 1992–1996.* Sacramento: California Seismic Safety Commission.

———.1994a. *California at Risk: Reducing Earthquake Hazards 1992–1996.* Sacramento: California Seismic Safety Commission.

———.1994b. *Research and Implementation Plan for Earthquake Risk Reduction in California.* (Blue Report.) Sacramento: California Seismic Safety Commission.

———.1994c. *California at Risk: Reducing Earthquake Hazards 1992–1996: 1994 Status Report.* Sacramento: California Seismic Safety Commission.

———.1995. *Northridge Earthquake: Turning Loss to Gain.* Report to Governor Pete Wilson. Sacramento: California Seismic Safety Commission.

City and County of San Francisco.1990a. *Hazard Mitigation Grant Program.* San Francisco: City and County Planning Department.

———.1990b. *Text of Ordinance Authorizing Bond Election Proposition A.* San Francisco: City and County Planning Department.

———.1995. *San Francisco's Community Safety Element.* San Francisco: City and County Planning Department.

City of Watsonville. 1990. Hazard Mitigation Plan. Watsonville, Calif.: Planning Department.

————.1992. *Community Based Disaster Plan.* Watsonville, Calif.: Planning Department.

————.1994. *Watsonville 2005 General Plan.* Watsonville, Calif.: Planning Department.

FEMA (Federal Emergency Management Agency) and Governor's Office of Emergency Services. 1994. "Joint FEMA/OES Section 406 Hazard Mitigation Policy Statement." San Francisco: FEMA Region IX.

FEMA (Federal Emergency Management Agency). 1997. *Report on Costs and Benefits of Natural Hazard Mitigation.* Washington, D.C.: FEMA.

GAO (General Accounting Office). 1992. *Earthquake Recovery: Staffing and Other Improvements Made Following Loma Prieta Earthquake.* San Francisco: GAO.

Governor's Office of Emergency Services. 1989. *Guidelines for the Development of Local Government Annexes to State Hazard Mitigation Plan.* Sacramento, Calif.: Governor's Office of Emergency Services.

————.1994a. *Flood Hazard Mitigation Plan.* Sacramento, Calif.: Governors Office of Emergency Services.

————.1994b. *Northridge Earthquake, January 17, 1994, Interim Report,* Sacramento, Calif.: Governor's Office of Emergency Services.

————.1994c. *Hazard Mitigation Implementation Strategy: Northridge Earthquake.* Sacramento, Calif.: Governor's Office of Emergency Services.

————.1994d. "Northridge Earthquake: Section 404 Hazard Mitigation Grant Program Strategy." Sacramento, Calif.: Governor's Office of Emergency Services.

————.1995. "Hazard Mitigation Program Strategy." Sacramento, Calif.: Governor's Office of Emergency Services.

State and Federal Hazard Mitigation Survey Team. 1990. *Hazard Mitigation Opportunities for California: The State and Federal Hazard Mitigation Survey Team Report for the October 17, 1989 Loma Prieta Earthquake, California.* Sacramento, Calif.: Governor's Office of Emergency Services.

Persons Interviewed

FEMA Region IX

Jim Buika, regional earthquake specialist

Helen DuBois, senior mitigation specialist

Jack Eldridge, federal hazard mitigation officer and acting chief, Mitigation Division

Michael Hornick, mitigation staff specialist

Jay Jazayeri, mitigation officer, FEMA Field Office, Pasadena, California

Angela Kucherenko, project manager

Leo Levenson, mitigation staff specialist

Gregor Puziss, mitigation staff specialist

Bill Shough, mitigation staff specialist
Frank Wilson, architect

State of California

Paula Schulz, state hazard mitigation officer, Governor's Office of Emergency Services

Local Government and Private Sector

Catherine Bauman, San Francisco City and County Planning Department
Arrietta Chakos, assistant to the city manager, city of Berkeley
Wendy Milligan, assistant director, Office of Emergency Services, Ventura County Sheriff's Department
James Russell, VSP Associates Inc. (consultant to Governor's Office of Emergency Services on update of state earthquake mitigation plan)
John Sucich, Office of the Chief Administrative Officer, city of San Francisco
Yolanda Uribe, program specialist, Office of Emergency Management, city of Los Angeles

CHAPTER 7

Massachusetts After Hurricane Bob and Other Storms

This chapter examines hazard mitigation influences, planning, procedures, and effectiveness following Hurricane Bob (1991) and severe northeast storms in 1991 and 1992 in Massachusetts. The chapter describes the disasters, evaluates the state Section 409 hazard mitigation plan, and reviews Massachusetts's hazard mitigation planning and implementation process as well as the results of the state's mitigation efforts. It identifies key mitigation issues in Massachusetts and offers some conclusions and recommendations.[1]

The Disaster Events

Rather than a single "blockbuster" disaster, Massachusetts was struck by several severe storms in 1991 and 1992. The state's recovery process was affected by these recurring disasters.

Hurricane Bob (FEMA-914-DR-MA)

Hurricane Bob was a strong Category 2 hurricane that passed over most of New England on August 19, 1991. One of the most deadly and intense hurricanes to have struck the northeastern United States, it caused eighteen deaths and $1.5 billion in damage (FEMA 1991). In Massachusetts, rainfall ranged from one to six inches. Damage was most severe in Buzzards Bay, where the storm surge averaged more than six feet and ripped many beachfront houses from their foundations. The state incurred

$42.5 million in losses insured by the National Flood Insurance Program and $35 million in other losses. Nine counties were declared disaster areas.

Northeaster of 1991 (FEMA-920-DR-MA)

Northeast storms, or "northeasters," traditionally pose a bigger threat to Massachusetts and other New England states than do hurricanes because their high surges and winds are of extended duration (ranging from twelve hours to three days, as opposed to six to twelve hours for a typical hurricane), and they occur more frequently. Northeasters typically occur in the winter months and result in flooding, severe coastal erosion, and wave- and erosion-induced damage to coastal structures. An unusually destructive northeaster, formed from the remnants of a hurricane and a low-pressure system, battered the Massachusetts coast on October 30, 1991. Insured losses for the state totaled $80.3 million, with an additional $14 million in other losses (DEM 1993). Hundreds of structures were substantially damaged or destroyed along the northern and southern shores of Massachusetts Bay. President George Bush declared seven counties disaster areas.

Northeaster of 1992 (FEMA-975-DR-MA)

Another major northeaster struck southern New England and the mid-Atlantic states on December 11–14, 1992, causing record snowfall in the inland parts of Massachusetts and serious flooding in all coastal areas of the state. The storm damaged many coastal structures, including roads, docks, piers, and seawalls, along with a water treatment plant in Hull and a sewage treatment plant in Marshfield. There was severe erosion along the entire coast. As much as twenty to twenty-five feet of dunes were lost in coastal towns such as Ipswich and Sandwich. Damage costs of $12.6 million were covered by FEMA's Public Assistance program. More than one-third of this amount was used to pay for debris removal. Private property losses totaled about $12.6 million. The presidential disaster declaration covered eight counties.

1978 Blizzard

The 1993 update to the Section 409 plan and its annex were prepared in response to the above-mentioned storms. In addition to those storms, another significant disaster, the blizzard of 1978, strongly influenced the

development of the state's current hazard mitigation planning and preparedness. The blizzard and coastal flood, which occured on February 6–7, 1978, caused major damage to the entire northeastern United States but most severely affected Massachusetts, Maine, and New Hampshire. Twenty-nine lives were lost in Massachusetts alone. An estimated $300 million (1978 dollars) in damage occurred in Massachusetts and New Hampshire coastal communities, including about $20 million in damage to properties insured by the National Flood Insurance Program (NFIP). Nearly 1,500 homes were substantially damaged or destroyed by high winds and record tides, and more than 10,000 residents were evacuated. Although the Stafford Act was not yet in existence in 1978, most of today's major disaster relief programs were available in some form to compensate victims of the storm. These included SBA home and business loans, NFIP payments, and individual and family grants from the Department of Housing and Urban Development's Federal Disaster Assistance Administration, an agency replaced by the Federal Emergency Management Agency (FEMA) in 1979.

Massachusetts's 1993 Section 409 Plan

Massachusetts has one of the most comprehensive and well-integrated hazard mitigation plans of those that we reviewed.

Content and Methodology

In October 1993, the Division of Resource Conservation (DRC) of the Massachusetts Department of Environmental Management (DEM) prepared the *Commonwealth of Massachusetts 409 Hazard Mitigation Plan* (DEM 1993) in response to two federally declared disasters: FEMA-914-DR-MA (Hurricane Bob, August 1991) and FEMA-920-DR-MA (northeaster, October 1991). An accompanying annex was prepared in response to FEMA-975-DR-MA (northeaster, December 1992). Although numerous state and federal agencies are credited with contributing to the plan, the state hazard mitigation officer (SHMO) and his staff, based in the DRC, were the principal authors. The governor's office and FEMA Region I both approved the plan. The 1993 plan replaces the original plan that was prepared in 1986 after Hurricane Gloria and updated in 1987 and 1989.

The plan covers the entire state and purports to address many different types of hazards: northeast storms, hurricanes and coastal storms, heavy

rainstorms, coastal erosion, tornadoes, urban fires and wildfires, and earthquakes. Only hurricanes and northeast storms receive significant attention, however.

Strengths of the Plan

The Massachusetts Section 409 plan is thorough, clear, internally consistent, and innovative—certainly one of the strongest plans reviewed for this project. Indeed, Massachusetts was selected as a case study site primarily on the strength of its Section 409 plan. All major elements required by federal regulations are present and clearly identified, with the quality of each element generally rating above average. The capability assessment, for example, is an excellent review of relationships among affected agencies, featuring not only textual descriptions of agency actions and responsibilities but also flowcharts illustrating hierarchies and working relationships and detailed appendixes containing relevant federal and state executive orders and state policy memoranda.

Unlike most other Section 409 plans, the Massachusetts plan clearly weaves all required elements together, resulting in a coherent hazard mitigation strategy emphasizing five overarching goals. The bulk of this synthesis appears in the proposed mitigation activities section, in which twenty-eight proposed mitigation initiatives are provided under nine objectives. These objectives in turn are grouped under five goals: improvement of government response capability, postdisaster rebuilding guidance, protection of public health and safety, protection of natural and historic resources, and enhanced protection of property and infrastructure. Several subparts of this section received the highest possible score (3 on a 0–3 scale) from project reviewers, including those dealing with promotion of hazard awareness and knowledge, retrofitting of existing development, and acquisition.

The reviewers noted several model features of the Section 409 plan, including a status report of recommendations from previous Section 409 plans; criteria for hazard mitigation project funding; a detailed table integrating goals, objectives, and recommended mitigation measures; and a description of a sacrificial dune pilot program, in the annex of the plan.

Weaknesses of the Plan

The hazard identification and vulnerability assessment is perhaps the weakest element of the plan, as it is primarily descriptive and relies heavily on references to past events. Although it is clearly written, the section is

brief (four pages) and focuses only on the biggest threats to the state—hurricanes and northeast storms. A September 1994 memo from the SHMO indicated that the Section 409 plan would be revised in fiscal year 1995 to make it more of a multihazard plan, expanding the focus of this section to address other potential hazards, including earthquakes (for which mitigation and planning are the responsibility of a separate agency— the Massachusetts Emergency Management Agencies, or MEMA), urban fires and wildfires, tornadoes, threats to dam safety, and heavy rainstorms. According to a subsequent telephone interview with Richard Thibedeau, the SHMO, an urban fires and wildfires annex had been completed as of October 1996.

A New Plan

A new Section 409 hazard mitigation plan was being developed in the winter of 1997–1998 by the state's hazard mitigation coordinator, a new position funded for the DEM and MEMA by FEMA.

Massachusetts's Hazard Mitigation Planning and Implementation Process

Hazard mitigation in Massachusetts has evolved over time from an initial concern with emergency management.

State Hazard Mitigation Planning

Today, hazard mitigation planning is spearheaded by the state's environmental management agency.

Preparation of Section 409 Plan

In Massachusetts, hazard mitigation planning and implementation are conducted by a partnership between the Massachusetts Emergency Management Agency (MEMA) and the Massachusetts Department of Environmental Management (DEM). MEMA is responsible for traditional post-disaster recovery activities, implementation of hazard mitigation via the Section 406 Public Assistance program, and oversight of the fiscal and contracting components of the Section 404 Hazard Mitigation Grant Program. The DEM is responsible for the state's natural hazard mitigation planning as well as its floodplain management and flood insurance programs. Other agencies, such as the Department of Environmental Protection, MEMA,

and the Massachusetts Coastal Zone Management Program (MCZM) contribute suggestions and information, but DEM staff members are the primary authors of the plans. Institutionally, the offices that prepare today's Section 409 plans are the same ones that prepared the response plans for the blizzard of 1978 and Hurricane Gloria in 1986.

Most members of the current DEM mitigation planning staff assumed their positions in the early 1990s, however. These personnel indicated to the researchers that the early plans were of little help in 1991–1992 when another round of major disasters triggered the preparation of the current Section 409 plan. The early plans, staffers say, were largely descriptive and contained few useful policy suggestions. As a result, the new staff prepared the 1993 Section 409 plan largely from scratch. A DEM intern wrote the first draft, coordinating her interpretation of the federal requirements with input from her supervisors and from other agencies. Unlike the 1986 plan, which focused exclusively on one disaster event (Hurricane Gloria), the new plan attempts to address the problems associated with hurricanes, flooding, and coastal storms using a more overarching, generalized approach. Due to various delays, the plan was not finalized until October 1993, after some Section 404 funds from the 1991–1992 storms had already been awarded. The accompanying annex was approved concurrently with the main plan.

Hazard mitigation planning in general, and the Section 409 and Section 404 programs in particular, are not the sole or even the principal focus of DEM officials. According to estimates provided by the agency, Richard Thibedeau, the current SHMO, spends about 15 percent of his time each week on these issues, principally on management concerns. Richard Zingarelli, the National Flood Insurance Program coordinator, also spends about 15 percent of his time on mitigation. Michele Steinberg, the regional planner who handles most Section 409 issues at the DEM, spends about 30–40 percent of her time on mitigation— mostly on planning and coordination, though this also includes some project involvement. Eric Carlson, a DEM environmental engineer, spends only about 5 percent of his time on mitigation, mainly in reviewing project designs. A part-time intern, Julia Venema, spends fifteen to twenty hours per week, 100 percent of her time, handling various administrative tasks, including Section 404 grant management and project review for closeouts. Additional agencies have personnel devoted to hazard mitigation. The MCZM, for example, has one full-time staff member working on coastal erosion control projects, such as mapping of repetitive loss areas.

State Hazard Mitigation Team and Interagency Hazard Mitigation Team

An important part of the formulation of the state's hazard mitigation goals and policies is the ongoing guidance provided by members of the State Hazard Mitigation Team (SHMT), a standing body whose members are appointed by the agencies they represent, which in turn were identified by the SHMO and his staff. Although the SHMT is identical in concept to the teams required by federal regulations to be assembled following each federally declared disaster, it is different in that it is a standing body that meets even in times of no major disaster. Team members provide regular guidance to DEM staff in articulating the mitigation concerns, preferences, and priorities of individual state agencies. Regular meetings of the SHMT began after a severe localized storm in 1990 and have continued ever since. The arrangement is flexible, and the participation of some agencies is more formal than that of others. Established formal and informal working relationships existed between many of the agencies before the regular SHMT meetings began.

Many agencies wanted to be part of the team simply to help determine how hazard mitigation funds are spent. Other agencies were sought by the DEM as team participants because of their expertise in environmental permitting and housing and community development, as well as their ability to provide independent funding for mitigation projects not eligible under Section 404. For example, the DRC's Office of Waterways helped fund, as a pilot project, a beach dewatering system that helps compact beach materials and thus prevents erosion.

According to DEM staff members, regular, active participation on the part of numerous agencies in the SHMT process has ensured that the reports of the Interagency Hazard Mitigation Team (IHMT) produced after each disaster are active documents with meaningful recommendations to be used as building blocks for Section 409 plan updates. Unlike the situation in some regions, where personnel of the FEMA regional office convene IHMT meetings and write up the recommendations themselves, Massachusetts DEM personnel take pride in writing their own recommendations. DEM staff members want to distinguish Massachusetts as a leader in hazard mitigation and ensure that their state's interests and viewpoints are accurately represented. Key players, both individuals and agencies, in the Massachusetts hazard mitigation process are listed in table 7.1.

Occasionally, IHMT meetings are conducted on a regional basis and include representatives from multiple states affected by a particular disaster. In September 1991, following Hurricane Bob, for example, FEMA Region

Table 7.1. Key Players in the Massachusetts Mitigation Process

Title	Name	Role
FEMA Region I Staff		
Director, Mitigation Division	Al Gammal	Oversees mitigation policy
Federal hazard mitigation officer (FHMO)	Paul White	Coordinates state and federal programs
Massachusetts mitigation specialist	Steven Colman	
Director, Response and Recovery Division	Ed Thomas	(Former director of Mitigation Division, Region I)
Massachusetts Staff		
Governor	William Weld	Policy selection and coordination
Director, Massachusetts Emergency Management Agency (MEMA)	Dave Rodham	Oversight of MEMA mitigation programs (including earthquake mitigation)
Disaster recovery coordinator, MEMA	Cristine Heaune	Coordination of earthquake mitigation programs; fiscal and contract control of Section 404 grants
State hazard mitigation officer (SHMO), Division of Resource Conservation, Massachusetts Department of Environmental Management (DRC/DEM)	Richard Thibedeau	Oversight of state hazard mitigation programs
Regional planner, DRC/DEM	Michele Steinberg	Daily management of Section 409 and Section 404 programs
Program manager, Flood Hazard Management Program, DRC/DEM	Richard Zingarelli	Oversight of state flood hazard mitigation programs; also NFIP Coordinator
Intern, DRC/DEM	Julia Venema	Coordination of Section 404 grants

State Hazard Mitigation Team (Partial List of Participating Agencies)

Massachusetts Coastal Zone Management Program

Massachusetts Department of Environmental Protection

Executive Office of Community Development

Metropolitan District Commission

Office of Waterways

U.S. Army Corps of Engineers (federal agency sitting in advisory role)

FEMA Region I (federal agency sitting in advisory role)

National Resources Conservation Service, U.S. Department of Agriculture (federal agency sitting in advisory role)

I conducted a three-day regional IHMT meeting in New Seabury, Massachusetts, to brief the five participating states on the disaster itself, to prepare a regional hazard mitigation report, and to hold working sessions on improving disaster response, protecting key infrastructure during disasters, protecting boats and harbors, and modifying building codes (FEMA 1991).

Hazard Mitigation Grant Program

The DEM staff attempts to closely align the goals and policies of the current Section 409 plan with those laid out in the administrative plan for the Section 404 Hazard Mitigation Grant Program (HMGP). The HMGP, considered much more important than the Section 409 plan to the state's hazard mitigation efforts, administers federal disaster relief funds in accordance with Section 404 of the regulations implementing the Stafford Act. During our interviews, officials from both FEMA and the state confirmed that the Section 404 program plays a much greater role in determining the state's actual mitigation projects than does the Section 409 plan. Whereas earlier state mitigation policy emphasized structural approaches, current state policy emphasizes nonstructural approaches. This shift in policy has been reflected in priorities for awarding Secton 404 grants, according to the SHMO, who admits that the Section 409 plan provides little discussion of Section 404 funding priorities.

Massachusetts received a total of $1.86 million in Secton 404 funds for the three 1991–1992 disasters (DEM and DRC 1995a). This was a relatively minor amount of assistance compared with that provided to other states, such as California and Florida, which have seen billion-dollar damage totals in recent years in the wake of major natural disasters. The federal funding for Massachusetts came in the form of three grants provided on a 50-50 cost-sharing basis. Although the state received fifty-five HMGP project applications, totaling $7 million, after the storms, it was able to recommend only twenty-five projects with the available funding. The funding breakdown by disaster is shown in table 7.2.

**Table 7.2. Funding Breakdown by Disaster,
Massachusetts, 1991–1992**

DISASTER	HMGP FUNDS OBLIGATED
Hurricane Bob (1991)	$653,291
Northeaster (October 1991)	$733,715
Northeaster (December 1992)	$477,947
Total	$1,864,953

Source: Massachusetts Department of Environmental Management.

Workbook for Local Communities

Another part of the ongoing state-level response to the storms of the early 1990s has been the creation of a workbook to enable communities to prepare hazard mitigation plans without the assistance of outside consultants. State officials hope this workbook and its accompanying model plan, being prepared for the coastal community of Marshfield, will encourage cooperation within communities undertaking mitigation and encourage local officials to think through the priorities identified in the local hazard mitigation plan. The workbook will also show how local governments can comply with multiple sets of regulatory requirements in one document. The workbook will concentrate on repetitive flood losses, identify sources of funding to implement planned measures, and emphasize coordination with other state and local planning efforts. The project was scheduled for completion in late 1996.

According to outlines prepared by the task force in charge of its preparation, the workbook will have five main purposes: (1) to incorporate local participation in state hazard mitigation planning; (2) to assist local governments in developing community hazard mitigation plans (because new NFIP legislation includes funding for developing and implementing mitigation plans and because existing legislation and funding programs favor communities with Hazard Mitigation plans over those that do not); (3) to enable the SHMO to provide technical assistance in developing local mitigation plans; (4) to serve as a model guidance document for other states; and (5) to assist FEMA in implementing its goal in the *National Mitigation Strategy* of reducing disaster assistance by 50 percent over the next twenty-five years (DEM and DRC 1995b).

Federal and FEMA Regional Activities

The staff of FEMA Region I's Mitigation Division consists of fifteen people headquartered in Boston who coordinate the NFIP, the Section 409 and Section 404 disaster mitigation programs, and separate FEMA earthquake and hurricane programs. The regional office has conducted a number of activities in Massachusetts and other New England states aimed at furthering FEMA mitigation policy at the state and local levels. For example, the office has administered workshops on hurricane mitigation planning for state agencies from all northeastern states. It has also participated in the management of a mitigation course offered specifically for state and local planners.

In addition to Paul White, the federal hazard mitigation officer, and other Region I Mitigation Division officials, the researchers met with Ed

Thomas, former head of mitigation for the region and current director of the Response and Recovery Division. Thomas has written several working papers outlining new theoretical approaches to hazard mitigation. One such approach, called the "Patchwork Quilt," uses the analogy of quilt making to clarify the process for communities seeking viable, common sense solutions to mitigation problems. Just as a community might come together to fashion a quilt, so must community members work together toward creative, innovative solutions to the practical problems associated with, for example, relocation and acquisition. There are several key elements to the Patchwork Quilt process. First, a "quilter" must be found—a community leader with vision who can take advantage of the window of opportunity after a disaster to fashion a new vision of the future. Second, a "pattern," or framework, must be chosen to guide the community's mitigation efforts. To this end, technical assistance should be sought from any of a variety of sources, including state and federal mitigation officials, universities, and planning offices. Third, the "fabric" must be chosen—specific programs must be selected to accomplish the community's mitigation objectives. Fourth, it all must be "sewn" together—the community must take action to create a better future. An example of a hypothetical city shows the Patchwork Quilt in action: the community fashions a network of public and private funding and more than twenty federal, state, and local agencies to help it meet the crises brought on by substantial flooding. By putting together the patchwork quilt in this way—synthesizing a mitigation strategy out of many disparate programs and resources—the city is able to balance each individual's needs with the community's long-term objectives (Thomas and Yagerman n.d.).

Thomas presents a similar concept in his paper on "Stone Soup": post-disaster hazard mitigation planning, he writes, is much like the proverbial pot of stone soup, which no individual can create successfully alone but which might instead be the product of a joint effort by an entire community (Thomas n.d.). Each city, region, or disaster area must develop its own package of solutions. Some of the principal programs to include in this package are Sections 404 and 406 of the Stafford Act, technical assistance from FEMA staff, the Disaster Loan Program of the Small Business Administration, the Individual and Family Grant Program, and other programs and organizations that offer aid to disaster victims, such as the Red Cross.

Thomas creatively addresses the practical problems an area faces when trying to make sense of the myriad disaster relief programs and organizations offering some type of assistance. Yet he seems to emphasize certain new procedures and practices, such as the Patchwork Quilt and Stone Soup, to the exclusion of the one program that provides, in theory, perhaps

the best means for states and local governments to map out their hazard mitigation goals and objectives as well as the strategies by which to achieve them. At times, Thomas seems to suggest that the Section 409 planning process needs a major overhaul before receiving any serious attention. It is interesting to query the extent to which such views are prevalent at FEMA's Region I and the other regions and also among state and local officials in Massachusetts. Further, to what extent do concepts such as Patchwork Quilt and Stone Soup accurately describe the hazard mitigation planning being carried out within the various states? Richard Thibedeau, the SHMO for Massachusetts, points out that although Thomas's papers describe the state's overall hazard mitigation efforts in an interesting way, they do not provide a new blueprint for preparing hazard mitigation plans. Thibedeau believes that Thomas's approach emphasizes strategy, not plan preparation, and that perhaps this is the course that should be pursued.

Results

Massachusetts has developed a pratical and straightforward process for implementing hazard mitigation.

Overview

Massachusetts mitigation officials at the state and local levels have pursued a variety of mitigation techniques and programs in an attempt to reduce potential damage from future northeasters, hurricanes, and floods, in sharp contrast to their counterparts in states such as Missouri, who have concentrated on a single mitigation strategy—acquisition of floodplain properties—to the exclusion of most other strategies and programs. Some of these programs have emphasized structural mitigation at the local level—for example, the sacrificial dune construction projects in Scituate and Duxbury, described in the section that follows. Other, more policy-oriented programs have had applicability across the entire state. Examples include new legislation (e.g., the Massachusetts Rivers Bill, which proposes a 200-foot protective zone along every waterway in the state that has water flowing year-round, to be under the jurisdiction of local conservation commissions) and the use of geographic information system (GIS) mapping of coastal erosion to detemine the requirements for a statewide setback program.

Mitigation efforts in the state have focused on a variety of both structural and nonstructural techniques. Among twenty-five projects approved for funding after the three disasters in 1991 and 1992, there were eleven different project types. Those implemented more than once included acquisition of damaged structures, dam studies or improvements, dune restoration, pond or stream improvements, protection of critical facilities, retrofitting of flood-prone residences, and upgrading of culvert or drainage systems. Less frequently implemented project types included an emergency communications link, implementation of a harbor safety plan, development of rebuilding guidelines, and securing of seawall gates. Thirteen of the twenty-five projects had been completed as of August 1995.

Selected Local Communities

The following are descriptions of specific mitigation programs in several communities that the researchers visited.

Town of Duxbury

The researchers met with Tom Broadrick, Duxbury's planning director, to discuss various mitigation projects in the town, including acquisition, retrofitting, and elevation. One project involved the construction of two sacrificial dunes to help protect the town's inner bay. Essentially a beach replenishment program, the project consisted of the deposition of 60,000 cubic yards of sand along the coastline, forming sixteen-foot artificial dunes to protect especially hazard-prone areas. Town officials, including Joe Grady, the conservation administrator, noted that the town was not concerned about losing its investment in the next big storm to hit the area, which could destroy the dunes, since the sand should, it is hoped, remain in the local coastal system. Homeowners, moreover, will have been protected from the most destructive effects of the storm.

City of Quincy

In Quincy, David Greig and Rene Lumaghini were interviewed regarding the city's principal mitigation project, an assistance program to retrofit, floodproof, or elevate residential properties prone to coastal and riverine flooding. The program's genesis was the Section 404 Hazard Mitigation Grant Program (HMGP), and the city was using funds from the HMGP, Quincy's Community Development Block Grant (CDBG) program, and the HOME Investment Partnerships Program to fund the project. The project

aimed to elevate and/or retrofit thirty to sixty homes. The city received a Section 404 grant of $200,000 to cover a maximum of 50 percent of the project cost; this money was made available as grants to applicants selected regardless of income level. Matching funds were to come either from the CDBG program or the HOME program or from the individual property owners themselves if their income exceeded the caps established by the CDBG program.

Town of Scituate

The researchers met with Elinor M. Foley of the Scituate Conservation Commission to discuss the town's various mitigation efforts. Located southeast of Boston, Scituate is a small coastal town with approximately 850 repetitive loss properties (constituting about 20 percent of the town's land area), according to Foley, and most of these have already been retrofitted or elevated. The town's multifaceted responses to the storms of 1991–1992 and earlier storms have emphasized acquisition, retrofitting, elevation, and construction of sacrificial dunes.

Foley stressed that after disasters, conflicts frequently arise between towns such as Scituate and state officials, regarding priorities for mitigation projects. This is due to several factors, primarily poor communication on the part of state officials but also changing state policies regarding structural versus nonstructural mitigation and rules under which substantially storm-damaged homes can be rebuilt, as well as overworked local officials trying to address the various concerns of the town's residents.

On January 31,1992, after Hurricane Bob and the October 1991 northeaster, Scituate submitted an application for HMGP funding to acquire properties from willing sellers on Peggotty Beach, with a goal of restoring the barrier beach to its natural condition. This grant was used in conjunction with funds from the NFIP's acquisition program (Section 1362). Section 1362 funding was used first, with HMGP funds reserved for properties not eligible for Section 1362. Fifteen properties were ultimately acquired on Peggotty Beach. A grant for $300,000 was originally approved under the HMGP, but only $110,000 was actually needed to purchase the two properties not eligible under Section 1362.

After the December 1992 northeaster, Scituate submitted three applications for HMGP funding. Applications to construct stone mounds at Humarock Beach and to reconstruct the Musquashicut Pond Barrier Mound were determined to be of a low priority and thus were denied. The third application, for construction of drainage improvements with a federal share of $375,000, was determined to be of moderate priority and was

put on hold pending available funds. Approximately $96,000 was made available to the town for construction of an outlet drainage pipe.

Conclusions and Recommendations

A number of issues and recommendations emerge from Massachusetts's experience with hazard mitigation.

• *Evolve mitigation policy over time.* Hurricane Bob and the 1991 and 1992 northeasters were severe storms, but they were not the sort of huge-scale catastrophic disasters other states have confronted in recent years. Over the same time period, for example, several states faced the Midwest floods of 1993, Florida was hit by Hurricane Andrew, and California endured two major earthquakes. Each of those disasters resulted in billions of dollars in damage costs, compared with which the Massachusetts damage estimates seem modest. The sheer scale of those other disasters frequently created crisis situations in which a "window of opportunity" developed wherein public officials and private citizens became acutely aware of the need for radical changes in mitigation policy. The crises led to innovations not only in the short-term delivery of disaster relief but also in long-term theories about the most appropriate sorts of mitigation. In contrast, Massachusetts never experienced such a sense of crisis from Hurricane Bob and the coastal storms, and consequently the mitigation infrastructure—the network of state and regional officials charged with implementing mitigation under the Stafford Act as well as carrying out the processes and procedures by which that network regularly functions—was never fundamentally shaken and reconfigured to the extent seen in states that experienced far worse disasters. Regular FEMA disaster relief and mitigation programs and policies have functioned adequately in Massachusetts, and thus no sophisticated new programs have been necessary, such as the complicated "duplication of benefits" program developed in Missouri to facilitate that state's massive buyout of floodplain houses. Nevertheless, the state's mitigation efforts have not remained static; the Massachusetts program has continued a process of slow evolution toward nonstructural mitigation.

• *Develop long-term working relationships.* There is a long history of hazard mitigation planning in Massachusetts. Long before the Stafford Act introduced the current system of Section 409 planning, the state saw numerous public attempts to reduce the consequences of natural hazards,

such as public acquisition in the 1910s of hazardous coastal areas around Duxbury to prevent private development after the Great Storm of 1898. In addition, the state's elected officials have consistently recognized and supported efforts to implement mitigation measures. One recent example was the introduction in 1994 of S.B. 1004, which, if passed, would have established a state program for acquisition of storm-damaged property. Today, the Massachusetts mitigation community is bound together by a healthy network of working relationships among key individuals and agencies involved with administering and implementing mitigation programs. These relationships exist both among employees in different state agencies and between state officials and regional FEMA officials. For example, though the Massachusetts Department of Environmental Management (DEM) and the Massachusetts Emergency Management Agency (MEMA) are separate offices and are responsible for different components of the mitigation process, the two have worked together effectively to integrate MEMA's work on earthquakes into the DEM's larger mitigation strategy and programs. The result is an anticipated earthquake annex to the Section 409 plan. The Massachusetts Coastal Zone Management Program (MCZM) is also an important member of the state's hazard mitigation team. In addition, various state agencies meet regularly under the banner of the State Hazard Mitigation Team (SHMT) to discuss and debate state mitigation policy.

As has been noted in other case studies, the presence of key persons in certain jobs is essential to maintaining a smooth hazard mitigation process. For example, Cristine Heaune at MEMA has served as that agency's primary liaison with the DEM, and her effectiveness in that role seems based not only on her professional competence but also on her cordial relationship and frequent contact with DEM staff members and her willingness to aggressively advance MEMA's interests within DEM programs.

This organizational structure seems to have had the principal effect of keeping mitigation programs running smoothly in Massachusetts. Even though the state mitigation organization has had neither the resources nor the visibility to vigorously pursue the ambitious mitigation agenda set forth in its Section 409 plan, it has functioned adequately and suffered no severe setbacks or internal crises. Indeed, the number of agencies involved in some way in state-level mitigation decision making (principally through the SHMT) has helped to avert many potential turf battles.

One weak link in the mitigation network in Massachusetts seems to be the lack of effective communication between state and local officials. Local officials readily admit to being uninformed about state mitigation goals and objectives and the daily activities and programs of the state offices that

administer mitigation programs. Since these local officials are unaware of how they fit into the state's overall mitigation strategy, they understandably do not try to pursue projects that conform to the Section 409 plan's agenda. The lack of understanding of mitigation itself at the local level also is a problem.

• *Increase the importance of the mitigation plan.* Despite the soundness of Massachusetts's Section 409 plan, the state's Section 404 program appears to be the principal driving force behind most (but not all) hazard mitigation efforts in the states. (As Thibedeau, the SHMO, notes, the DEM and other state agencies accomplish much mitigation without funding assistance, including, for example, the recent passage of a new state septic code and many MCZM projects.) In contrast, the Section 409 plan—in theory the principal policy statement guiding all state mitigation efforts—is not a useful document to anyone at any level. Further, no coherent overall mitigation strategy appears to exist in the state, based on the researchers' interviews with state and local officials. Many solid mitigation projects have been completed; indeed, of the twenty-eight projects mentioned in the plan, only three have not been the focus of some implementation activity. Yet the projects are a somewhat random mixture of techniques, strategies, and programs pursued on an ad hoc basis and selected more on the basis of funding decisions than for their correspondence with the goals and objectives of the Section 409 plan. Flood-prone houses are elevated, vulnerable property is acquired, and earthquake-sensitive areas are mapped, yet there appears to be no overall, focused mitigation program.

As stated earlier, the state's Section 409 plan is strong. Its authors seem to understand the purpose of a hazard mitigation plan, to recognize the potential value of a well-thought-out mitigation strategy, and to have thought about what they ultimately want to achieve with their mitigation program. Yet the plan itself currently has little relevance to the DEM officials who wrote it and who administer state mitigation programs, to the other state agencies whose activities frequently involve hazard mitigation, and especially to the local officials who initiate mitigation funding requests. The situation poses an interesting question: How might the perceived lack of a mitigation strategy in Massachusetts be reconciled with the facts that the state has one of the country's better Section 409 plans (at least according to the criteria developed for this study), the plan recommendations are being implemented, and the plan's suggested Section 404 projects are being funded?

Thibedeau acknowledged the difficulty of the question and noted that funding concerns do appear to dominate Massachusetts mitigation efforts,

if one looks solely at the Section 404 and Section 409 programs. He emphasized, however, that much mitigation is accomplished outside the Section 404 program and that despite the apparent ad hoc nature of the state's efforts, mitigation *is* ultimately being undertaken in the state. He referred to the state's efforts as a kind of "disjointed incrementalism." In other words, although no effective master plan may exist to guide mitigation, there are a number of individual efforts by various people and agencies that, when taken together, add up to effective hazard mitigation. According to Thibedeau, the real problem is that the Section 409 plan "is too narrowly defined; it does not establish any benchmarks to indicate if progress is being made; and, most importantly, it does not lay out a comprehensive mitigation strategy for the state that state/federal agencies and regional and local governments can identify with and find their place/role in the overall hazard mitigation effort." It remains to be seen whether the new plan will deal with these issues.

• *Link the Section 409 plan with Section 404 funding.* One explanation for the ineffectiveness of the Section 409 plan seems to be the confusing relationship between it and the Section 404 program. Despite its other strengths, the Section 409 plan does not provide adequate guidance to state and local officials concerning funding of mitigation projects or prioritization of those projects. Worse, the technical information provided by the DEM does not make clear to local officials that the mitigation projects most likely to be funded are those consistent with the goals, objectives, and strategies laid out in the Section 409 plan. Instead, depending on the sources they track down, local officials may find at least three different lists of priorities for funding Section 404 projects, in various documents: in the 1995 administrative plan for the HMGP, the "project eligibility criteria"; in the Section 409 plan, an "identification of potential hazard mitigation and grant programs projects"; and in the HMGP informational report, a list of "project selection criteria." Although there are no obvious contradictions among the three documents, they are different enough that a local official attempting to navigate the various criteria would understandably become confused.

• *Make local government officials aware of Section 409 planning efforts.* Moreover, even when local officials are able to reconcile the various lists of project eligibility criteria, they frequently remain unaware of the larger Section 409 planning framework for the state, with which their projects are supposed to dovetail. Based on the researchers' interviews at a Duxbury roundtable, there is a distressing lack of familiarity at the local

level with even the concept of a Section 409 plan, much less the specific contents of the Massachusetts plan. It is difficult, if not impossible, for local planners and public officials responsible for obtaining funding to tailor their requests to the goals of a plan of which they are completely unaware. The problem exists at the state level, too: the Section 409 plan appears to be completely unfamiliar to many officials and policy makers outside the DEM and MEMA who nevertheless are responsible for initiating mitigation projects.

The substance of the Section 409 plan must be communicated to local officials in Massachusetts before disasters strike. Those who submit Section 404 grant applications must become aware of the criteria by which their proposals will be evaluated or the plan will be never taken seriously. And if state officials are to communicate the criteria, they must be absolutely clear about what those criteria are and not float different lists in different documents with the obvious potential to confuse and mislead.

The SHMO and other DEM staff members appear to have identified the problem and recognized the leadership role they must assume to fix it. The local hazard mitigation workbook project, beginning in Marshfield, is an excellent first step in this direction, with the potential to make explicit to local officials the direct financial benefits of incorporating the policies in the Section 409 plan into local mitigation programs.

• *Increase respect for the Section 409 plan.* Other state officials may have some knowledge of the Section 409 plan and its goals, but they pay the document little respect or attention. This is understandable, as there are no sanctions or penalties for failing to *follow* the plan. Any overlap between the types of projects suggested in the plan and the projects that, for financial or political reasons, these officials actually pursue may be purely coincidental. The officials most familiar with the plan, its authors at the DEM, are those most likely to work for implementation of the plan's goals, and yet these officials are too low in the state hierarchy to be effective advocates for the plan. Indeed, as one FEMA regional official noted, the SHMO and his office are effectively "trapped in the mid-level of the state bureaucracy" and thus cannot always effectively lobby for the Section 409 plan or for mitigation strategy in general.

Note

1. This chapter documents a case study visit to Boston and Duxbury, Massachusetts, in July 1995 by David J. Brower and R. Matthew Goebel during which they interviewed federal, state, and local mitigation officials.

References

DEM (Massachusetts Department of Environmental Management) 1993. *Commonwealth of Massachusetts 409 Hazard Mitigation Plan.* Boston: DEM.

———. 1995 *Massachusetts Hazard Mitigation Administration Plan—1995 Update.* Draft. Boston: DEM.

DEM and DRC (Massachusetts Department of Environmental Management and Division of Resource Conservation). 1995a. *Hazard Mitigation Grant Program Informational Report.* July. Boston: DEM.

———. 1995b. *Task Report No. 5: Outline—Pre-Flood Hazard Mitigation Planning Workbook.* July. Boston: DEM.

FEMA (Federal Emergency Management Agency). 1991. *Hurricane Bob: Regional Interagency Hazard Mitigation Team Meeting.* Boston: FEMA, Region I.

Thomas, Edward A. n.d. "Stone Soup and Hazard Mitigation." Unpublished manuscript.

Thomas, Edward A., and Barbara Yagerman. n.d. "'The Patchwork Quilt': Creative Strategies for Relocation, Acquisition, and Buy-Out." Unpublished manusript.

Persons Interviewed

FEMA Region I

Ed Thomas, director, Response and Recovery Division
Paul White, federal hazard mitigation officer

State of Massachusetts

Eric Carlson, environmental engineer, Massachusetts Department of Environmental Management (DEM)
Cristine Heaune, disaster recovery coordinator, Massachusetts Emergency Management Agency
Michele Steinberg, regional planner, DEM
Richard Thibedeau, state hazard mitigation officer; director, Bureau of Resource Protection, DEM
Julia Venema, intern, DEM
Richard Zingarelli, National Flood Insurance Program coordinator; manager, Flood Hazard Management Program, DEM

Local Government and Private Sector

Tom Broadrick, planning director, town of Duxbury, Massachusetts
Joe Grady, conservation administrator, town of Duxbury, Massachusetts
David Greig, city of Quincy, Massachusetts

Elinor M. Foley, Conservation Commission, town of Scituate, Massachusetts
Rene Lumaghini, city of Quincy, Massachusetts

CHAPTER 8

Tennessee After a Series of Floods and Storms

The Tennessee case study was conducted to gain a better understanding of state hazard mitigation planning under the Stafford Act in a state that experienced hazard events less catastrophic than those affecting Florida, California, or the Midwest in the 1993 floods.[1] This chapter focuses on how Tennessee's Section 409 hazard mitigation plan was developed and utilized and how Section 404 hazard mitigation projects are identified and implemented in the state.

The Disaster Events

The Section 409 plan in place when the Tennessee case study was conducted (July 1995) was developed in response to a series of five federally declared disasters that occurred between February 1990 and March 1994:

1. FEMA-858-DR-TN (February 1990). Flooding in Copperhill (Polk County) and Chattanooga (Hamilton County), resulting in numerous deaths and thousands of evacuations. Addressed in the original Section 409 plan (1991).

2. FEMA-889-DR-TN (February 1990). Major flooding affecting twenty-two counties, resulting in six deaths and damage costs in excess of $4 million. Addressed in the original Section 409 plan (1991).

3. FEMA-910-DR-TN (February 1991). Flash flooding of several counties throughout Tennessee, resulting in damage costs of millions of dollars. Addressed in a 1991 update to the Section 409 plan.

4. FEMA-1010-DR-TN (February 1994). Severe winter storm that produced more than four inches of ice, resulting in massive tree damage and widespread power outages. In a preliminary damage assessment conducted in seventy-five of the state's ninety-five counties, forty-five utilities in Tennessee reported significant damage. Addressed in the August 1994 update of the Section 409 plan, the focus of this case study.

5. FEMA-1022-DR-TN (March 1994). Flash flooding in Sevier County and Pigeon Forge, affecting fourteen counties. Addressed in the August 1994 update of the Section 409 plan.

In addition to those five disaster events, a tornado in Cumberland County in April 1995 resulted in yet another disaster declaration, FEMA-1057-DR-TN (June 1995). At the time of this case study, FEMA was working with the Tennessee Emergency Management Agency (TEMA) and state and local officials to develop a strategy paper that would pre-identify hazard mitigation projects related to the tornado event. The state hazard mitigation officer (SHMO) also intended to update the Section 409 Plan to reflect the 1995 tornado.

Tennessee's 1994 Section 409 Plan

The August 1994 version of Tennessee's Section 409 Plan is a multihazard plan covering the entire state (TEMA 1994). TEMA developed and updated that plan in response to the 1994 winter storm and spring flood events outlined earlier. Other state government agencies also participated in the planning process. The plan emphasizes floods, which account for all the declared disaster events but the winter storm and the 1995 tornado. The assessment of natural hazards is a combination of historical background, anecdotal excerpts, and, in the earthquake section, scientific research findings. There is no systematic, quantitative analysis of past hazard events or risk assessment detailing the future threat to people and property from natural hazards.

The plan includes a thorough survey of agencies and programs involved in hazard management at the federal and state levels, but it does not assess the effectiveness of the policies, programs, and capabilities identified. The plan includes a specific section devoted to goals and objectives. They are more accurately characterized, however, as proposed actions and strategies, rather than desired outcomes. As was the case for most states, this section was considered weak.

The plan includes seventy-five proposed actions, organized into categories reflecting either a particular hazard (e.g., flooding) or a strategy (e.g., awareness). The proposed actions are quite specific, identifying new or improved legislation, programs, policies, funding sources, supporting and lead agencies, schedules, and background information. The implementation, monitoring, and evaluation section is a concise description of the roles and responsibilities of the SHMO, the proposed Tennessee Hazard Mitigation Council and its advisors, and the Tennessee Mitigation Project Committee (for Section 404 program grants). Absent are specifics on monitoring and evaluation of initiatives. Features of the plan considered exemplary by reviewers include the proposed establishment of the Hazard Mitigation Council and an annual conference. Overall, reviewers considered the plan to be adequate; it is sufficient but not exceptionally good or bad in terms of either content or style.

Tennessee's Hazard Mitigation Planning and Implementation Process

This section includes a chronology of planning and implementation events, a description of Section 409 planning and Section 404 project events, and a discussion of some initiatives by the Tennessee SHMO.

The key players in Tennessee's hazard mitigation planning and implementation process and their roles are listed in table 8.1. TEMA has a small staff that works closely with FEMA Region IV staff and with planners from the Tennessee Department of Economic and Community Development.

Following the February 1994 ice storm (FEMA-1010-DR-TN), Rose Massey became TEMA's full-time state hazard mitigation officer (SHMO). She focused on Section 404 and Section 406 grants and on developing a handbook and a one-page preapplication form ("notice of intent") to guide applicants for Section 404 grants. She also reviewed all Section 406 (Public Assistance program) damage survey reports (DSRs) to identify opportunities to include hazard mitigation projects under the Section 406 program.

While Massey worked on the Section 404 and Section 406 programs, TEMA staff members developed the Section 409 plan as a "boilerplate" combination of the previous Section 409 plan and the Interagency Hazard Mitigation Team's report. Mary Houdac of FEMA's Region IV office provided considerable input. Thus, Massey herself did not draft the 1994 Tennessee plan.

The June 1991 Section 409 plan had led to an executive order establishing the state's emergency services coordinators (ESCs). Building on that

Table 8.1. Key Players in the Tennessee Mitigation Process

TITLE	NAME	ROLE
FEMA Staff		
Chief, Hazard Identification and Risk Assessment Branch, Mitigation Division Region IV	Robert E. McBeth	Oversaw Region IV hazard mitigation staff
Federal hazard mitigation officer (FHMO), Region IV	Lee Stubbs	Responsible for hazard mitigation efforts in TN, MS, and FL; focused on incorporating the Section 409 planning process into the Section 404 grant program; involved in rewriting FEMA's Section 404 requirements
FHMO, Region IV	Ernest Hunter	Previously FHMO for TN; assigned to AL and KY
Hazard mitigation specialist, Region IV	Lawrence Frank	Provided technical assistance to states and localities on Section 409 plan preparation; reviewed Section 409 plans submitted
Staff Member, Region IV	Mary Houdac	Provided technical assistance in preparation of August 1994 Section 409 Plan
Staff Member, Region IV	Belle Marquez	Provided engineering assistance on floodplain aspects of hazard mitigation
Headquarters senior staff	Lacey Suiter	Formerly Director of TEMA
Tennessee Staff		
Director, Tennessee Emergency Management Agency (TEMA)	John D. White, Jr.	Took active administrative role; "ran interference" with FEMA Region IV and headquarters; Served as direct link to governor
State hazard mitigation officer (SHMO), TEMA	Rose Massey	Oversaw all hazard mitigation activities statewide (Section 409 planning and workshops, Section 404 projects); acted as intermediary between locals and FEMA Region IV
Disaster assistance public manager, TEMA	Kevin Lawrence	Oversaw HMGP and PA, IA, and Disaster Preparedness and Improvement Grant programs; served as the PA officer and prepared Section 406 disaster survey reports
Hazard mitigation advisors, Tennessee Hazard Mitigation Council		Panel of twenty-one advisors, primarily state agency directors but also FEMA and Red Cross officials, who provided input on all hazard mitigation initiatives; reviewed and commented on Section 409 plans and amendments; and reviewed and approved Section 404 projects
Emergency services coordinators (ESCs)		Established by executive order of the governor; each state department designates one primary and one alternate person to act as an emergency services coordinator
Planners, Department of Economic and Community Development		Assisted localities with broad range of environmental, land use, economic, and community development planning, including grant writing; often acted as *the* local planners for communities with no full-time planner; department also oversaw the NFIP.
Other		
Staff members, Tennessee Valley Authority (TVA)		Served as a major source of engineering assistance (department has since been eliminated); wrote the pending Section 404 project application for Oakdale
U.S. Army Corps of Engineers		Provided technical reports, studies, mapping and related assistance to communities that was often used in Section 404 project applications

idea, the August 1994 Section 409 plan led to the creation of the Tennessee Hazard Mitigation Council (THMC) within the framework of the ESCs. No separate executive order was issued to create the council. Both groups played significant roles in the Tennessee mitigation story.

In June and July 1994, TEMA routed the Section 409 plan to all Tennessee state agencies and the American Red Cross for review and comment. In August, TEMA and the governor's office informally approved the plan and TEMA submitted it to FEMA's Region IV office in Atlanta. FEMA issued an official letter accepting the plan shortly thereafter.

Implementation of the Hazard Mitigation Grant Program

After a disaster, Tennessee's SHMO holds application briefings in the affected regions, inviting representatives of local, regional, and state agencies and utilities to attend. Federal assistance programs are explained and the Hazard Mitigation Grant Program Application Handbook (TEMA n.d.) are distributed. Agency and utility representatives identify potential projects and submit a "notice of intent" (NOI) to TEMA for the proposed project. The NOI is intended to provide sufficient information for TEMA to evaluate the proposal without subjecting the applicant to the cost, time, and effort of making a full-fledged application. TEMA reviews NOIs with *informal* consultation from FEMA's Region IV's federal hazard mitigation officer (FHMO). Based on that review, the SHMO determines which projects merit completed applications.

For projects deemed eligible to apply, the Section 404 applications are most often developed by state agencies (e.g., Southwest Tennessee Development District, Tennessee Department of Economic and Community Development, Local Planning Assistance Program) on behalf of the local municipal applicant. The SHMO, the FHMO, and a representative of the Department of Economic and Community Development visit each site and provide additional guidance and suggestions on preparing project applications.

The completed applications are reviewed first by the SHMO and an emergency services coordinator from the relevant state agency (each state agency identifies a primary and an alternate coordinator). Applications are then given to all members of the Tennessee Hazard Mitigation Council for review over a two-week period. The TCMC, not the SHMO, issues final approval or denial of projects. Approved projects are submitted to FEMA's regional office.

The SHMO acts as an advocate for local applications submitted to FEMA and as an ongoing liaison between the FHMO and the local applicant. The SHMO tracks the progress of the application, suggests modifications to applications to address FEMA's concerns, and identifies specific additional information requested by FEMA.

Tennessee SHMO Initiatives

In addition to her collaboration with the THMC in processing Section 404 applications, Tennessee's SHMO, has established the following hazard mitigation initiatives:

1. In support of TEMA's local hazard mitigation planning mandate, the SHMO is organized a series of workshops to be held throughout the state. A statewide workshop was held in April 1995, and regional workshops were scheduled to begin in Knoxville the following summer.

2. The SHMO's review (and authorship) of "hundreds" of Section 406 DSRs has led to the inclusion of mitigation in many of those reports. Inclusion of mitigation projects under the Section 406 program has lessened the need to finance the same projects with more limited Section 404 funds. Furthermore, since the gross amount of Section 404 funding is, in part, calculated as a percentage of Section 406 expenditures, there has also been an increase in the total amount of Section 404 funding.

3. The SHMO coordinates the activities of regional, state, and federal agencies in providing local community assistance so as to prevent conflicts of interest; for example, agencies that help prepare applications and plans are not involved in reviewing and sanctioning the results.

4. Through workshops, an application handbook, and the NOI preapplication process, the SHMO seeks to demystify hazard mitigation planning and the Section 404 project application process as much as possible. Examples in the application handbook are consistently used as templates by those preparing applications for local communities.

5. The SHMO issues a weekly status report on all applications and projects in order to identify bottlenecks and expedite the process.

FEMA Region IV Perspectives

At FEMA's Region IV headquarters in Atlanta, the research team inter-viewed two staff members: Lee Stubbs, the federal hazard mitigation officer (FHMO) responsible for Tennessee, and Robert E. McBeth, chief of the Mitigation Division's Hazard Identification and Risk Assessment Branch. At the time of our interviews, Stubbs, who holds an M.S. degree in chemical engineering and business management and communications, had been with FEMA for five years. He viewed his role in the organization as a "true manager" of people, resources, and information whose job is to educate and help prepare state and local officials to do hazard mitigation. Stubbs said that his ultimate goal is to "work himself out of a job"—to make the states fully self-reliant with respect to hazard mitigation.

Tennessee's Section 409 Planning

In 1994, when Tennessee was updating its Section 409 plan, Stubbs was not the FHMO assigned to Tennessee. Stubbs's understanding was that the plan at that time was rather "skeletal," bolstered by reports of the Intera-gency Hazard Mitigation Team from the five declared disasters between 1990 and 1994. FEMA's input was limited to reviewing and commenting on the completed draft of the Section 409 plan, as was common practice in Region IV. (The exception to this practice was in Florida, where FEMA's regional office provided more direct input.) Building of the knowledge base required for developing Section 409 plans was left to the states, as were the setting of priorities and selection of Section 404 projects to submit.

In Stubbs's opinion, the states viewed the Section 409 plan simply as a hurdle they must cross in order to obtain federal funding. Stubbs himself placed more emphasis on the Section 404 administrative plan, which he saw as better suited to helping states set priorities for specific hazards, iden-tify key players, and assign responsibilities within the state. At the time of our interviews, the FHMO was promoting the development of "strategy papers" in lieu of full-blown Section 409 plan updates in the aftermath of disasters in Region IV. Strategy papers are envisioned as more succinct doc-uments addressing specific problems identified by local officials, who are encouraged to think in terms of "what happens where, when, and to what degree." The goal of a strategy paper is to preidentify projects to be funded when a disaster occurs.

Section 404 Projects

The FHMO does not attempt to influence the state's priorities and proce-dures for Section 409 plans or Section 404 projects other than to discourage

projects involving generators and early warning systems and to encourage property acquisition as a mitigation strategy.

Tennessee, like many states, commonly fails to use all available Section 404 funds because it is difficult for the state and particularly the local communities to provide matching funds. This was particularly true before the federal share of hazard mitigation projects was increased from 50 percent to 75 percent of the total project cost (effective June 10, 1993). The FHMO verified that FEMA regarded the 15 percent formula for determining the total amount of federal funding available for Section 404 projects as a minimum, not a maximum. He also verified that Section 404 funds do not exist until Congress "obligates" them; that is, they are appropriated by Congress not at the time the 15 percent share is calculated but only after applications have been prepared and reviewed at the state, regional, and federal levels. This was a commonly held misconception among many state and local officials.

The application process was a source of frustration for both state and FEMA officials. The primary reason for projects becoming "suspended" in the FEMA review process was FEMA's need for more information than was provided in many applications. Inadequate provision of information persisted despite the fact that the Region IV office, at the urging of Tennessee's SHMO, had developed a checklist of required information. This was due to the complex, technical nature of many projects and a lack of good information about potential negative externalities.

The FHMO provided us with the "Project Routing/Tracking Sheet" being used by Region IV to identify individuals within FEMA and their areas of expertise. Stubbs indicated that the regional office's goal for completing an application review is thirty days. However, he acknowledged that this time period was the *minimum*, not the *maximum*, actually required. There was no set sequence of review procedures and no timetable for completing portions of the review or the entire evaluation. McBeth stated that speeding up the application review process was a priority, but it had proved difficult to achieve because FEMA review personnel also have extensive fieldwork responsibilities that take them out of the office on a frequent and often unpredictable basis.

FEMA was attempting to improve the application review process by realigning staff along "functional lines," which would result in staff members being dedicated to the areas of "project eligibility," "administrative and financial" activities, and "coordination of plans, teams, and contracts." This was to have been accomplished in all FEMA regions by October 1995. The realignment would constitute yet another shuffling of roles and responsibilities in an agency in which previous redefinitions and reassignments had

been identified as an obstacle by both FEMA staff and the Tennessee SHMO.

When the regional office completes its review, applications are sent to FEMA's headquarters in Washington, D.C., where the Office of General Counsel (OGC) performs a further review. This headquarters review adds further delay and uncertainty to the process. The process had taken even longer when environmental assessments (EAs) were performed at headquarters; EAs are now performed by regional FEMA staff.

Tennessee Strengths

As is true for any state, the presence of a strong, full-time SHMO was considered crucial to Tennessee's ability to accomplish hazard mitigation. The Tennessee Hazard Mitigation Council was viewed as a definite plus, helping to prescreen applications (unlike the situation in Mississippi, for example, where all applications were submitted and any weeding out was viewed as FEMA's responsibility). Establishment of the THMC was recommended in the report of the spring 1994 report of the DR-1010 winter storm hazard mitigation team, but it would not have been created without the political clout provided by the governor's executive order, further reinforced by the federal-state agreement.

Other strengths of the Tennessee program identified by Region IV personnel include the use of a preapplication (NOI) form; the SHMO's auditing of Section 406 public assistance DSRs to incorporate hazard mitigation; a shift from being reactive to being increasingly proactive in state hazard mitigation efforts; and the existence of a good working relationship between the Region IV FHMO and the Tennessee SHMO.

Results

Tennessee has worked effectively with its local governments to operate a practical hazard mitigation program.

Use of the Section 409 Plan in the Hazard Mitigation Process

The strategy of establishing a state hazard mitigation council and advisors set forth in the Section 409 Plan has been accomplished. The THMC is assembled monthly by the SHMO for informational sessions, and it periodically reviews and votes on completed Section 404 project applications. The THMC's approval authority serves to insulate the SHMO from political

fallout and helps maintain the SHMO's status as an impartial advocate and counsel for local and regional HMGP applicants.

There has been no systematic implementation or monitoring of the list of mitigation recommendations contained in the plan. The plan is viewed as a broadly written source of strategy and goals, not as a blueprint for implementing hazard mitigation.

Section 404 Projects

As of June 27, 1995 (one year and four months after the 1994 winter storm disaster), a total of $375,588 had been obligated under FEMA-1010-DR-TN (the Section 404 federal share plus the grantee-subgrantee administrative funds for all projects). These funds consisted of one acquisition project in Carthage involving eight residential structures ($256,000) and a share of TEMA's management cost for the disaster recovery and mitigation ($119,588).

At the time of our case study, applications for an additional $2,546,600 in grants (a $2 million relocation project and two drainage projects) had been submitted by Tennessee and were pending FEMA's approval. Additional applications were being prepared by the Memphis Light, Gas & Water utility company and the city of Bartlett for seismic retrofitting of groundwater wells. As of June 27, 1995, no projects had been submitted as a result of the March 1994 flood (FEMA-1022-DR-TN), for which funds available for hazard mitigation were more limited. Table 8.2, reproduced from FEMA Region IV's regional project status report, summarizes the status of Tennessee's Section 404 projects as of June 27, 1995.

Property Acquisition, City of Carthage

FEMA had obligated $256,000 for a project to acquire and demolish eight residential structures exposed to repetitive flooding in the city of Carthage, Tennessee. This was a problem the city had been attempting to address since the occurrence of floods in the 1970s. The U.S. Army Corps of Engineers had proposed the construction of dikes, but these were deemed too expensive and would not have solved the residential area's problems. The city had also applied for assistance under FEMA's Section 1362 program, but the application was denied on a technicality. Carthage's mayor learned of the Section 404 program at a public hearing held by TEMA in Cookeville following the February 1994 winter storm, and a planner from the Cookeville regional office of the state's Department of Economic and Community Development, working with the mayor, prepared an application and submitted it shortly thereafter (City of Carthage 1995). (Note:

Table 8.2. Tennessee Hazard Mitigation Grant Program—Project Status as of June 27, 1995

PROJECT	SUBGRANTEE	DESCRIPTION	APPLICANT'S ESTIMATED COSTS	TOTAL APPROVED COSTS	FEDERAL SHARE OBLIGATED	ADMINISTRATIVE COSTS
858-TN-1	Signal Mountain	Generator	$130,000	$130,000	$0	
		858 Total pending	$130,000			
889-TN-1	Fayetteville	Flood warning system	$28,000	$28,000	$14,000	
889-TN-2	Rhea County	Land acquisition	$42,854	$42,854	$0	
889-TN-3	Morgan	Elevation of homes	$196,000	$170,000	$85,00	
		889 Total eligible	$266,854	$266,854	$120,427	$10,065
889-TN-4	Lincoln County	Computer warning system	$5,500	$0	$0	
		889 Total suspended	$5,500			
910-TN-1	Centerville	Removal of gas line	$190,000	$0	$0	
		910 Total pending	$190,000			
1010-TN-2	Carthage	Acquisition	$185,000	$256,000	$256,000	$13,103
		1010 Total eligible	$185,000			
1010-TN-1	Gibson County	Relocation	$2,060,000	$0		
1010-TN-4	Brownsville	Drainage	$282,000	$0		
1010-TN-5	Clarksville	Drainage	$204,600	$0		
		1010 Total pending	$2,546,600			
1010-TN-M	Tennessee Emergency Management Agency	Management costs	$159,450	$159,450	$119,588	$3,392
		Total eligible	$159,450			

Source: Federal Emergency Management Agency, Region IV.

Consistent with other Tennessee projects, although the project clearly addressed a flood-related problem, the application was submitted and approved as a result of the February 1994 winter storm, *not* the March 1994 flood.) Although the project had been approved by TEMA and FEMA, work had not actually begun when this case study was completed because FEMA had not transferred the obligated funds to TEMA, and TEMA would not enter into agreements with localities until funds were literally in the bank.

Applicants in Carthage believed that TEMA had been responsive and helpful throughout the process. After reviewing the application, the SHMO had recommended deleting drainage aspects from it in order to improve chances of FEMA approval. The information required by FEMA was unclear to both the local preparers of the proposal and the state (e.g., the number of required appraisals appeared to change from one to two at some point after the project application was submitted), and after receiving the application, FEMA requested more information. FEMA's slow response was distressing to the mayor of Carthage, who had promoted the acquisition concept to property owners. Some of the property owners had been renting out their properties prior to the application and had already forgone more than a year's worth of rental income during the review process. Even the eventual letter from FEMA announcing approval of the application appeared to send mixed messages to the town, using vague language such as "reasonable assurance" of FEMA's funding. As of the summer of 1995, more than a year after submission of the application, Carthage still had not been able to begin the acquisition and clearance of the properties, and the eight vacant structures and overgrown lots remained.

Drainage and Channel Improvement, City of Brownsville

FEMA was considering a $282,000 application for an engineering study and drainage improvements to protect a low-income neighborhood and adjacent farmland from repeated flooding. According to the application, families had been evacuated from the area four times between 1988 and the summer of 1995. Over the previous eight years, flood damage had averaged $35,047 per year. Properties to be protected by the proposed improvements included four single-family homes, two duplexes, and 75–100 acres of farmland.

In the spring of 1993, Brownsville's flooding problem had been discussed at a meeting of the Madison County Commission devoted to final work on the region's Overall Economic Development Program (Southwest Tennessee Development District 1993). The meeting was attended by Barry Matthews, executive director of the Southwest Tennessee Development

District (SWTDD), a regional association of local governments. In the spring of 1994, Matthews discussed the problem with Dan Bonn of TEMA's Jackson office, who was working on a similar project, and Bonn suggested that Matthews contact the SHMO. Lara Jarrett, an environmental planner with the SWTDD, contacted the SHMO, who then made a site visit. Jarrett also contacted local officials and Brownsville's mayor, who visited the neighborhood and encouraged skeptical residents to cooperate with the SWTDD and the SHMO as they developed the application. This was especially important because there was poor documentation of the extent of property damage and losses from past flooding in the neighborhood, and residents were in the best position to document the cost of past damage. Additional assistance was provided by a local contractor who volunteered to visit homes and estimate damage. The affected homes were not covered by flood insurance, largely because of the low incomes of most residents. Jarrett developed the application under the auspices of the SWTDD.

TEMA and FEMA both promoted acquisition as an option, but this was ultimately deemed excessively expensive and would not have relieved the threat of flooding to the larger neighborhood and the adjacent farmland. The SWTDD submitted the application to TEMA in October 1994. TEMA approved the application and submitted it to FEMA's Region IV office by December 1994. FEMA awarded "conceptual approval" for a new engineering study in June 1995, but TEMA and Brownsville were still awaiting actual funding when this case study was completed.

SWTDD officials believed that existing studies by the U.S. Army Corps of Engineers, a private engineering study, and the use of public meetings to piece together damage history (including photographs and articles from local media sources) were all very useful in preparing the application. TEMA staff were perceived as having been very good front-line contacts between local citizens and FEMA. The application preparer made extensive use of TEMA's Section 404 application handbook, which identified key information to be included within a flexible format. Success in preparing the application and obtaining approval also hinged on the willingness of county and city officials to work together closely and share matching funds. Although the applicants expressed an appreciation of the time required for administrative processing of applications, they believed that the time lag from submission of the application to FEMA to receipt of conceptual approval was excessive.

Drainage Improvements, City of Selmer

Although the city of Selmer's drainage improvement project was not visited by the researchers and had not yet been approved by FEMA, the

SWTDD did provide some information about it. The knowledge and experience gained by SWTDD personnel in preparing this application contributed directly to preparation of an application for the city of Selmer to address repetitive flooding of a residential area involving twenty-eight homes occupied by approximately sixty residents. The area had been plagued by flooding for some forty years, with as many as five to seven flood incidents annually. Although the application identified inadequate drainage as the primary problem, FEMA's and TEMA's preferred mitigation strategy was acquisition, which would have proved costly given the number of homes affected. SWTDD personnel noted that the Selmer application was developed much more quickly at the local level and approved more quickly at TEMA. The application was submitted to TEMA in May 1995 and to FEMA in June.

Seismic Retrofitting of Wells, Memphis Light, Gas & Water

The researchers met with Kevin Poe, an engineer involved in a Section 404 application for retrofitting several wells with seismic fittings operated by Memphis Light, Gas & Water (MLGW). After commissioning two major earthquake studies, including one by Princeton University in 1989, the utility had retrofitted four wells with seismic fittings and generators at a cost of approximately $5 million. The company operated approximately 170 wells and was focusing on protecting key groundwater sources. The Section 404 application requested funds for seismic fittings (not generators) for some 40 of the wells. The utility also benefited from information provided by the Center for Earthquake Research and Information at the University of Memphis. This facility has conducted extensive studies on the New Madrid Fault, which affects Tennessee.

The previous studies commissioned by MLGW; the utility's experience with investigating, pricing, and installing equipment; and a large staff allowed the company to develop its application swiftly, with a goal of submitting the document to TEMA by July 1, 1995. The company was prepared to install the equipment within one month of approval.

As with other applications, this one was the result of a chance discovery of the HMGP program by the applicant. Although the project would mitigate problems resulting from seismic activity, funding, if granted, would be awarded on the basis of the winter storm of 1994. Unlike other applications, no municipalities were involved, and 75 percent of the funding would come from FEMA and 25 percent from MLGW.

Other Projects

The researchers met briefly with William J. Kilp, director of public works for the city of Bartlett, who was preparing an application for retrofitting of

wells that supply the city's drinking water. The application proposed the use of seismic resilient fittings, which are designed to resist breakage and damage during earthquakes. This project was being developed in cooperation with, and as a result of, an identical project at Memphis Light, Gas & Water.

As a result of the March 1994 floods (FEMA-1022-DR-TN), two additional acquisition projects were competing for limited funds in the summer of 1995. For the first time, the Tennessee Hazard Mitigation Council was forced to choose between projects. One project involved repetitive flooding of a residential area (Oakdale), and the other involved a school (Pittman Center) to be purchased, demolished, and rebuilt outside the floodplain. The Tennessee Valley Authority prepared the application for Oakdale.

Conclusions and Recommendations

The Tennessee case suggests a number of useful conclusions about the way the Stafford Act was operating in one state and FEMA region for "garden variety" disasters, situations much less severe than the disasters in Florida and California or the Midwest floods of 1993. Tennessee's experience and the lessons to be learned from it seem quite different from the experiences and conclusions in states affected by more damaging disasters. Understandably, the recommendations drawn from the Tennessee case study are also different.

Conclusions

The Section 409 plan itself was not a direct factor in hazard mitigation proposals or decisions in Tennessee. The certification that Section 404 grant applications are consistent with the Section 409 plan is pro forma at both the state and FEMA regional levels; all Section 404 applications are routinely so certified. No key player considered the Section 409 plan a stimulus, an influence on the choice of options, or a factor in determining priorities among projects. Several key players believed that the Section 404 administrative plan was potentially more useful in prioritizing projects. The strategy paper approach, advocated by the FHMO, was used for this purpose.

Instead, Section 404 projects were the result of a combination of the following factors:

• *A disaster declaration making funds available for mitigation projects that may or may not be directly related to the disaster event.* For example, the Brownsville storm drainage proposal, intended to solve a perennial flooding problem caused by poor storm water drainage, and the Memphis

Light, Gas & Water pump retrofitting proposal were both unrelated to the winter storm that made Section 404 funds available.

• *An informal information network* that includes someone who is aware of Section 404 grants talking with someone who has a mitigation problem and, in some cases, already has the solution but has been unable to get it funded, as exemplified by the Carthage and Brownsville applications.

• *An able entrepreneurial person with the skills to assemble an application and a facilitator or catalyst.* In Tennessee, SHMO Rose Massey became an advocate for the solutions proposed by local and regional officials. In the absence of a local entrepreneurial person and a helpful SHMO, local officials saw the Section 404 application process as intimidating and complex. It overwhelmed them unless they could enlist the expertise of professionals in state and regional agencies.

The number and location of Section 404–funded mitigation projects were determined, and limited, not so much by the level of funding available to FEMA as by the state and local governments' ability to formulate an application, their capacity to provide matching funds, and FEMA's policies about what was fundable. Thus, the total monies requested by a state such as Tennessee were likely to be much lower than what was technically available through FEMA.

Because the total cost of all projects identified was often less than the total amount of available FEMA funds, the state did not have to apply priorities. Tennessee screened projects only for conformity with FEMA guidelines and cost-effectiveness. Projects did receive close review by FEMA and by the state in that regard, however, and applications tended to be for mitigation solutions that had received prior study as the best options but lacked local, state, or alternative federal sources of funding (in some cases the projects had been turned down by other programs).

Mitigation, in the absence of a clear and powerful state-FEMA mitigation strategy or competition among projects for limited funds, was project oriented and piecemeal. The mitigation approach was not comprehensive; nor was it technically sophisticated. Both state and FEMA approvals were issued on a project-by-project basis wherein each project was evaluated on its own merits and to some degree on political merits, although within broad FEMA policy guidelines (e.g., acquisition and relocation were preferred over engineering solutions such as drainage projects, and early warning devices and generators were not favored).

Although Region IV downplayed its influence over state priorities and

procedures, FEMA policies concerning project preferences definitely influenced the types of projects proposed. For example, Region IV clearly preferred acquisition, following national FEMA policy. It also disliked early warning and other equipment projects (i.e., "things you can plug in") and training projects. State SHMOs reflected those preferences in their advice to applicants and in their anticipatory review of projects before sending them on to the FEMA regional office. In Tennessee's case, the FHMO also participated informally in the SHMO's preapplication review of projects.

All parties expressed dissatisfaction with the time and effort required to obtain a Section 404 grant. The status of projects, the application evaluation process, and the timetable for reviews in FEMA's regional and national offices were a mystery to the SHMO and the applicants, who received answers in stages and were confused about the meaning of terms such as "substantial assurance" of approval. Applicants were also frustrated by the lag between FEMA's approval of a project and their receipt of funds from the state. (Part of the answer is that the state waited for the money from FEMA actually to be deposited with the state before entering into a contract with the local community.)

State and local interviewees referred to the FEMA regional office as a "black hole" for several reasons: there was no explicit sequence of steps or roster of people with whom to interact during FEMA's review process; the location and status of the project in the review process were hard to determine; the adjustments the state or community applicant was asked to make and the questions the applicant was expected to answer seemed to vary from project to project and were communicated to the state piecemeal and often only in response to state or local probing; and FEMA review was likely to be interrupted at any time by a disaster event in another state that required the regional staff to halt reviews while performing fieldwork.

FEMA's regional office similarly regarded headquarters as a "black hole" because of the time it took (as long as four months) to review applications, which had already been reviewed at the regional level. Apparently, the review was delayed by both the Office of General Counsel and the requirement for an environmental assessment. Because of the long time lag, the state and local governments worried about desertion of local participants and about continued exposure to the risk of another natural disaster. The dissatisfaction was exacerbated with smaller projects, often entailing funds of much less than $250,000, for which the application effort and time lag seemed particularly excessive given the ratio of the amount requested to the total amount of FEMA funds available for a particular disaster. The

frequent shifts in personnel and responsibilities in FEMA regional offices also exacerbated the situation.

Historically, mitigation has been a relatively low priority at FEMA, but it is rising in importance. Mitigation is not normally a consideration in public assistance or individual assistance funding, for example, although the Section 406 program specifically allows inclusion of related mitigation projects. Implementation of mitigation (e.g., review of Section 404 projects) is regularly put aside to enable FEMA personnel to meet other responsibilities, such as going into the field immediately after disaster events to assist in recovery operations. On the other hand, mitigation is no longer just a report made and filed as part of the disaster declaration process. Furthermore, changes in matching requirements have encouraged an increasing number of mitigation projects and, in the case of Tennessee, prompted a new emphasis on local hazard mitigation planning.

The potential for inclusion of mitigation projects under the Section 406 program is underrealized. Unless the SHMO reviews the Section 406 DSRs for inclusion of reasonable mitigation precautions during rebuilding, mitigation is not included in the recovery process. Inclusion of mitigation in the Section 406 projects would lessen the need to include identical projects later as Section 404 projects, and it would indirectly increase the amount of money available for Section 404 projects by increasing the total amount spent on Section 406 projects.

As with other case studies, the Tennessee case points out that there are several definitional concepts that determine the amount of money *said* to be devoted to Section 404 mitigation grants. The *gross allowable* amount for Section 404 grants is determined as 15 percent of the total of individual assistance, public assistance, and administrative monies allocated by federal sources for the disaster. But Section 404 total spending is also limited to the amount requested in the applications submitted by states. Except in large disasters, such as Hurricane Andrew in Florida, the Northridge earthquake in California, and the Midwest floods of 1993, the applications forwarded by states for Section 404 monies often add up to less than that gross allowable 15 percent. This was particularly true when 50-50 matching was required. It is less true now, but the absence of matching monies and of local capacity to formulate Section 404 applications still minimizes the number of applications submitted. Finally, only some of the applications are funded, and commitment is made by FEMA and the state only in stages, over many months. Thus, the estimates of actual projects funded by Section 404 monies will be considerably smaller than both what is technically allowed by the Stafford Act (gross allowable) and what has been asked for by states (total of the applications submitted).

State agencies with direct ties to local government are an important source of entrepreneurial imagination and expertise in the preparation of applications, which are not likely to be present in smaller municipalities and rural counties. In Tennessee, for example, the regional offices of the state's Department of Economic and Community Development employ professional planners who work regularly with communities over a long time period. These are people who know the communities' problems, and have the knowledge, data, expertise, and experience to formulate compelling applications. Tennessee also has regional economic development districts with staff expertise, experience, and strong entrepreneurial skills.

A hazard mitigation council or hazard mitigation team at the state level is a useful organizational device. It should have the tangible support of the governor and should represent state agencies with relevant expertise, responsibility, and authority. It does not seem vital that it include local representation. It should be involved in drafting the Interagency Hazard Mitigation Team report, revising the Section 409 plan, and assessing, screening, and prioritizing Section 404 project proposals, all of which provide important political insulation for the SHMO.

Conclusions and Recommendations

Several recommendations can be drawn from our review of the Tennessee case.

• *FEMA should allow funding for more comprehensive state and local mitigation planning and implementation.* This should extend beyond the present concept of the Section 409 plan and beyond the concept of Section 404 projects being directly linked to declared disasters. It should permit a wide range of state coordinative action to qualify for financial assistance. Hazards in Tennessee typically have widespread impacts; for example, eighty-five of the state's ninety-five counties were included in the pair of disaster declarations that triggered the revision of the Section 409 plan. Thus, Tennessee could benefit from a strategy that requires local governments to have mitigation plans in place that predetermine mitigation actions to be taken during or after a disaster recovery period—or, better, even before disaster strikes. This approach would both lessen the damage during disasters and improve response to mitigation opportunities afterward.

• *FEMA and the states should provide clearer guidelines for preparation of Section 404 applications and more flexibility in the application.* The Section 404 application process should strike a balance between explicitness about what is needed and flexibility in the way information is to be

provided. For example, Tennessee now has a *Hazard Mitigation Grant Program Application Handbook* that explains how to complete an application and provides samples, (TEMA n.d.) and FEMA's Region IV has a "Hazard Mitigation Grant Program Application Checklist" (FEMA 1995) that includes both general guidelines and specific checklists for each type of project (e.g., acquisition and relocation projects, retrofitting of structures, structural hazard controls, drainage improvements, public outreach and services, and warning and communication projects).

• *FEMA and the states should expedite decisions up and down the ladder of application preparation and approval.* Tennessee's practice of requiring one-page preapplications (notices of intent) seems to work when it is used to screen out proposed projects unlikely to be successful (but it is not useful when prescreening is not required).

FEMA needs to implement a more systematic review process with ongoing staff responsibilities to protect reviews from interruption. FEMA also needs to provide more authority to regional offices, with less oversight by headquarters in Washington, D.C. Finally, FEMA needs to design a simpler application format and an accelerated review process for smaller projects, say, those requiring less than $1 million, and to consider a shift toward a block grant approach.

1997 Update

In December 1997, follow-up calls were made to the Tennessee SHMO and FEMA's Region IV FHMO to update the results of this case study. All projects that were awaiting approval when the case study was conducted have since been approved and are under way, with the exception of the Selmer project, which has been held up for reasons not related to FEMA.

Section 409 Planning

The state Section 409 plan has not been rewritten since the case study was conducted, but the SHMO has agreed with FEMA to rewrite the plan by November 1998. The SHMO has collected Section 409 plans from more than forty-two counties (which include municipal plans within them) and has made those plans an addendum to the state Section 409 plan. These were sent to FEMA's regional office and received approval in April 1997, so all participating counties and municipalities now have FEMA-approved Section 409 plans. The SHMO's goal is to have 75 percent of Tennessee's counties submit plans by the end of 1997.

The SHMO's local planning initiative is supported in two ways: (1) county and city contract funding for emergency management is contingent on the existence of a Section 409 plan, and (2) the state agreement to provide postdisaster public assistance is contingent on the existence of a local Section 409 plan. The SHMO gave each community a diskette with a template for a Section 409 plan but has let each community design its plan according to its own project priorities (TEMA, Hazard Mitigation Planning Guidance for Local Governments, n.d.).

Mitigation Players

The SHMO is still the only full-time staff person involved with hazard mitigation in Tennessee. Rose Massey, who still holds that position, is assisted by the Tennessee Hazard Mitigation Council (THMC), which continues to play a strong role in hazard mitigation planning and grant projects. The THMC's greatest strength is that the many agendas of its members are all included in discussions about hazard mitigation, so every issue is thoroughly discussed. The THMC processes all HMGP proposals before passing them on to FEMA; any decisions made about grants can therefore be easily defended against criticism by legislators or the public. The THMC has standard operating procedures in place now, and during the most recent disaster all requests for funding were made in time and no request was denied by FEMA. The SHMO believes it is very effective and efficient for FEMA to receive only those projects that have received previous approval by the THMC, so that prioritization can be done at the local and state levels and FEMA does not have to make such decisions.

Mitigation Priorities

Local workshops are held every year to update local agencies on the HMGP. Every other year, these workshops provide a full course on hazard mitigation planning. Tennessee is still emphasizing buyout (acquisition) for flood mitigation. The state did fund one elevation project that was very unsuccessful, reinforcing the SHMO's belief that elevation is neither cost-effective nor reliable.

FEMA Approaches

The SHMO believes that FEMA has "come a long way" since the case study was conducted. FEMA has been focusing on local plans and is emphasizing autonomy in local and state hazard mitigation planning. FEMA's Region IV has allowed states to conduct their own benefit-cost analyses on hazard

mitigation projects in order to determine what to pass on to FEMA, and FEMA abides by the states' recommendations for project priority. Region IV has also created a formatted HMGP application for states that will streamline the process.

Note

This chapter is based on a case study conducted in June 1995 by Charles.C. Bohl and Edward J. Kaiser, who interviewed FEMA officials in the Region IV office in Atlanta, Georgia, and state and local government officials in Tennessee.

References

City of Carthage. 1995. *Tennessee Hazard Mitigation Grant Program Application.* January. Addendum, March. Carthage, Tenn.

FEMA (Federal Emergency Management Agency). 1995. *Hazard Mitigation Grant Program Application Checklist.* Atlanta: FEMA, Region IV.

Southwest Tennessee Development District. 1993. *Overall Economic Development Program, July 1993.* Jackson: Southwest Tennessee Development District.

TEMA (Tennessee Emergency Management Agency). 1994. *State of Tennessee Hazard Mitigation Plan.* Nashville: TEMA.

Hazard Mitigation Grant Program Application Handbook. n. d. Nashville: TEMA.

———. n.d. *Hazard Mitigation Planning Guidance for Local Governments.* Draft. Nashville: TEMA.

Persons Interviewed

FEMA Region IV Officials

Robert E. McBeth, chief, Hazard Identification and Risk Assessment Branch, Mitigation Division

Lee Stubbs, federal hazard mitigation officer, Mitigation Division

State of Tennessee

George James, regional director, Tennessee Department of Economic and Community Development

Rose Massey, state hazard mitigation officer, Tennessee Emergency Management Agency

James Mills, principal planner, Tennessee Department of Economic and Community Development

Local Government and Private Sector

David Bowman, mayor, city of Carthage, Tennessee

Lara Jarrett, environmental planner, Southwest Tennessee Development District

William J. Kilp, director, Department of Public Works, city of Bartlett, Tennessee

Barry Matthews, executive director, Southwest Tennessee Development District

Kevin Poe, engineer, Memphis Light, Gas & Water

PART III

Assessing the National Mitigation System

This part of the book describes our assessment of the national mitigation system—the complex institutional grouping of FEMA, state, and local mitigation agencies charged with preparing mitigation plans and carrying out mitigation projects directed toward implementing national disaster policy. We evaluate both the key tools of this system—its plans and projects—and the linkages among the tools, the agencies, and the overall commitment and capacity of the actors.

Our findings reveal a number of weaknesses, most of them foreshadowed by the results of our case studies. As a whole, the plans are typically weak and ineffectual; the projects are typically uncoordinated and slow to get off the ground; and the system has a number of gaps between its components and a lack of consistent capacity and commitment. There are some heartening exceptions, but many obstacles hindered the achievement of effective mitigation through the system as it operated between 1988, when the Stafford Act was enacted, and 1995, when the case studies were carried out.

Chapter 9 reports on our analysis of state Section 409 hazard mitigation plans. Ours was the first national assessment of these plans, and across the country we found that they fell far short of their potential to guide mitigation. On average, the plans were mediocre. Some did not even meet the minimal requirements of the Stafford Act, and most did not meet the standards of good mitigation practice. Rather than functioning as the linchpins of the system, the plans were weak links in the channeling of national mitigation policy goals into day-to-day activities. In chapter 9, we lay out the problems found in our systematic reading and grading of the plans and recommend guidelines for turning them into effective mitigation tools.

Chapter 10 reports on our analysis of state Section 404 hazard mitigation projects funded under the Hazard Mitigation Grant Program. Again, ours was the first comprehensive review of the record of expenditures under this program since its inception. And again, we found its performance disappointing in a number of respects. Although substantial resources have been made available under the Section 404 program, only about a fifth of the available funding has been committed to projects. Many of the projects are single-shot efforts rather than elements of an integrated hazard mitigation strategy aimed at concentrating resources on high-priority needs. The time lag between a disaster declaration and the completion of projects averages some three and a half years, and many projects take much longer to complete. Rather than serving as a powerful tool for carrying out mitigation policy on the ground, the Hazard Mitigation Grant Program often results in scattered spending on a potpourri of

projects. In chapter 10, we suggest a strategy for pulling together this scattered spending in focused mitigation actions.

Chapter 11 analyzes the system that produces mitigation plans and projects, its key components, and its internal linkages. This also is the first attempt to model this institutional structure and its products using empirical data. We found a system with troubling gaps and disappointing outputs. Connections between mitigation plans and projects were missing. Commitment and capacity to carry out mitigation were not consistent across the system. Despite the logic of the laws that created the mitigation policy system, its operation leaves much to be desired.

CHAPTER 9

State Hazard Mitigation Plans: Falling Short of Their Potential

This chapter reports on our systematic content analysis of the state mitigation plans required by Section 409 of the 1988 Robert T. Stafford Disaster Relief and Emergency Assistance Act. Generally referred to as Section 409 plans, they must be prepared by states to establish eligibility for
mitigation grants following natural disasters. In theory, state mitigation
plans should be the linchpins of state mitigation actions. In practice, we
found them falling far short of their potential.

We asked two main questions about the Section 409 plans in existence
in 1995: (1) Are the requirements of the Stafford Act being met? and
(2) What are the strengths and weaknesses of the plans? We answered
those questions by collecting, reading, and evaluating all the available
state Section 409 plans.

We found that although the state plans met many of the pro forma
requirements of the Stafford Act, their quality was not high. A very few
plans were good and a few more had some good elements, but unfortunately, most plans were mediocre. In many plans, important elements
were missing and much of the content was descriptive and general rather
than analytic and specific. It is clear that most of the Section 409 plans
were not intended for implementation in the usual sense but were created
merely to qualify the state for postdisaster mitigation grants under Section
404 of the Stafford Act.

We used the Stafford Act requirements, along with accepted plan-
making principles and best mitigation practice, as the basis for evaluating
the state plans. This chapter describes our findings. First, we lay out the
methodology used in collecting and assessing the hazard mitigation plans.
We then report the results of our exhaustive content analyses of the plans,

done to find out whether they met Stafford Act requirements and what their strengths and weaknesses were. At the end of the chapter, we make recommendations to guide state hazard mitigation officers in preparing Section 409 plans that avoid common pitfalls and create more effective mitigation strategies.

Collecting and Evaluating the Plans: Study Methodology

To start our analysis, we collected state Section 409 plans from thirty-nine states and territories in 1995. Simply collecting the plans was a difficult task. We discovered that the Federal Emergency Management Agency maintained no centralized collection of Section 409 plans, either at national FEMA headquarters or at most of the ten regional offices. Further, no national database tracked the existence of such plans. Consequently, FEMA national officials were uncertain of exactly what Section 409 plans were in effect across the states. The lack of a systematic collection of required plans and of a database describing their existence suggests the low regard in which FEMA officials and staff held the Section 409 plans as an element of hazard mitigation strategy at the time of the study.

Thus, the state Section 409 plans had to be collected from scratch. From May 1994 through August 1995, we contacted each state hazard mitigation officer (SHMO) individually to request copies of all currently applicable plans for the three major, recurrent types of natural hazards: earthquakes, flooding, and hurricanes and severe coastal storms. Even making these contacts was difficult because no current list of SHMOs could be obtained from FEMA. Many of the officials listed as SHMOs either no longer served in that capacity or no longer worked for the state at all. Many state employees, when initially contacted by us, were unsure of who the SHMO was for their state. This is not surprising, since in many states the SHMO often wears more than one hat, performing hazard mitigation on a part-time basis.

Another factor complicating the process of collecting plans was the reluctance of many SHMOs to release copies of their plans to us. The reasons given mostly had to do with the perceived poor quality of the plans by the authors themselves. Some SHMOs feared adverse publicity, and others considered their plans still to be in draft stage and unfit for wide circulation. Still others simply did not want their plans held up to the strict scrutiny of an academic research study.

In August 1995, at the conclusion of the plan collection process, we had

assembled a collection of forty-four state hazard mitigation plans from thirty-nine states and territories (see appendix 9.A for the list of states and plan titles). Of the forty-four plans obtained, forty-one address flooding (inland and/or coastal), twenty-four address earthquakes, and eighteen address hurricanes and severe coastal storms. Thirty-two of the plans cover the entire state; the remaining twelve address only the part or parts of the state affected by the hazards at issue. The plans generally are quite broad in scope, and thirty-four of them address multiple hazards, in keeping with current FEMA recommendations. The other ten plans deal specifically with certain types of hazards; for example, the Alaska and Arizona plans both deal exclusively with flooding. Of the multihazard plans, twenty-one address multiple hazards more or less independently and the other twelve combine hazards in a more or less comprehensive, coordinated approach. Eighteen of the plans were written in response to specific disaster events, and seventeen plans include an update or an annex in response to a specific disaster; there is some overlap between these two categories.

Devising an Evaluation Instrument

We based our evaluation on requirements stated in the Stafford Act, guidelines contained in FEMA's *Post-Disaster Hazard Mitigation Planning Guidance for State and Local Governments*, also referred to as DAP-12 (FEMA 1990), and the knowledge of members of the research team about plan-making best practices. Our evaluation instrument asked whether and how well the state's Section 409 plan addressed specific elements that are required by the Stafford Act or FEMA guidelines or generally recommended in good plans of any type. (The evaluation instrument, titled "Guide for Describing and Evaluating Section 409 Plans," is included as appendix 9.B.)

The evaluation instrument was pretested and revised several times before being applied to the state mitigation plans. The testing process included pairing up members of the research team to apply the instrument to a sample of plans; evaluations were then compared and discussed by the two-person teams and by the entire research group. That process helped us revise the instrument and train ourselves to evaluate plans in a consistent manner, from plan to plan and from evaluator to evaluator.

Devising a Scoring System

We evaluated the plans with a three-part scoring system covering plan breadth, quality, and a total of breadth and quality. The *breadth score* simply measures how frequently basic issues were addressed in the plans—the

proportion of plans that included the issue. The *quality score* measures how well a plan addressed each of its issues. Finally, the *total score* is the sum of the breadth and quality scores. Total scores tend to reflect primarily breadth scores because there was more variation in breadth than in quality (see table 9.1.).

We applied this scoring system—breadth, quality, and total scores—to the collection of Section 409 plans in two different ways. First, we scored *individual issues;* for example, within the hazard assessment component, did the plan assess the value of property exposed to hazards, and if so, how well? Second, we scored the major *required components;* for example, did the plan have a hazard assessment component, and if so, how good was it? This scoring relies on assessing whole groups of individual elements and issues in a plan component.

In evaluating whether and how well individual issues were addressed, questions were scored across the entire collection of fourty-four plans. The *issue breadth score* is the proportion of the plans that addressed a particular issue. It ranges from 0 (no plan addressed the issue or contained that element) to 1 (every plan addressed the issue).

The *issue quality score* is the total score of all plans that addressed a particular issue, divided by the number of plans that addressed the issue. The quality score for any question ranged from 0 (not addressed) to 3 (addressed very well, on the basis of specific indicators indicated in the evaluation instrument). This quality score was then divided by 3 to place it on the same scale as the breadth score.

The breadth score and the quality score were summed to provide an *issue total score,* with a possible range of 0 to 2. For example, 21 percent of the plans assessed the number of people exposed to natural hazards, generating a value of 0.21 on that measure. The quality score for that element was 0.53 on a scale of 0 to 1. The combined total score was then 0.74.

In addition to evaluating how well the plans addressed individual issues, we evaluated each of a plan's four main components: (1) its fact basis (including its hazards assessment and its capability assessment); (2) its goals and objectives; (3) its proposed programs and actions; and (4) its approach to plan implementation, monitoring, evaluation, and updating. These were used to generate a plan component breadth, quality, and total score for each plan.

The *plan component breadth score* was calculated by dividing the number of issues a plan addressed by the number of possible issues identified in the evaluation instrument. The result was a percentage of possible issues addressed, with scores ranging from 0 to 1. For example, a hazard assessment

Table 9.1. Section 409 Plan Scoring and Evaluation System

	Breadth	Quality	Total	Calculated For:
Issue scores	Proportion of plans that addressed the issue (range 0–1)	For plans that did address the issue, strength with which they did so (range 0–3, converted to 0–1 for total calculation)	Sum of breadth and quality scores (range 0–2)	Entire collection of 44 plans
Plan component scores	Number of issues addressed divided by number of issues in section (range 0–1)	Sum score of questions addressed divided by number of questions addressed (range 0–3, converted to 0–1 for total calculation)	Sum of breadth and quality scores (range 0–2)	Individual plans (also averaged for all plans)

section might address five of a possible fifteen issues identified by the evaluation instrument for that component. That plan would receive a breadth score of 0.33.

The *plan component quality score* was obtained by dividing the quality score of issues addressed in the component by the number of issues addressed, with a resulting range from 0 to 3. As with issue quality scores, this number was converted to a range of 0 to 1.

The quality and breadth scores were summed to obtain the *plan component total score* for each plan, with a possible range of 0 to 2. The plan component scores were averaged across the entire collection of plans to provide an average of the breadth and quality of each plan component.

Question One: Are the Requirements of the Stafford Act Being Met?

Each state must have an approved Section 409 plan if it expects to receive federal grants for hazard mitigation following a declared disaster. The Stafford Act provides states with a solid mitigation planning framework, requiring each Section 409 plan to contain specific components:

- Assessment of natural hazards

- Analysis of existing policies and state and local capabilities to mitigate hazards

- Hazard mitigation goals and objectives

- Proposed strategies, programs, and actions

- Proposed approach to implementation

- Proposed approach to monitoring of implementation and hazard conditions

- Proposed approach to updating the plan

- Proposed approach to evaluating the plan and its implementation

In addition, the act also requires that each Section 409 plan:

- Identify projects to be funded under the Hazard Mitigation Grant Program

- Be oriented to developing state and local capability and programs as part of normal government functions

- Be prepared ahead of time and be updated to reflect specific disasters

- Involve key state agencies, local governments, and other public and private bodies that influence hazard management or development policies

- Be coordinated with other hazard evaluation and mitigation planning efforts

The first two issues we address are whether the states all had the required plans and whether the plans all had the required components.

Do the States Have Mitigation Plans?

We estimate that of the fifty-three eligible jurisdictions (fifty states plus the District of Columbia, Puerto Rico, and the Virgin Islands), forty-nine had mitigation plans as of August 1995. We obtained hazard mitigation plans from thirty-nine states and territories. Four states (Colorado, Georgia, Indiana, and Kansas) declined to provide their plans, citing the need to revise the plans before making them available for public scrutiny. Four other states and two territories (Mississippi, New Hampshire, Montana, Wyoming, Puerto Rico, and the Virgin Islands) apparently had plans, but we were unable to obtain them. Four states—Idaho, Maryland, Michigan, and Minnesota—claimed not to have Section 409 plans in 1995. Of these four, Maryland, Michigan, and Minnesota had experienced presidentially declared disasters; Idaho had not.

Thus, all but four of the fifty-three states and territories had mitigation plans at some stage of completion, and one of those four jurisdictions had experienced no declared disaster and therefore was not required to have a plan. So in answer to the question of whether states had Section 409 plans as required by the Stafford Act, we would say: Yes, almost all states did have mitigation plans.

Do the Plans Have the Required Elements?

The Stafford Act requires that state Section 409 mitigation plans contain the elements listed in table 9.2, which shows the number and percentage of plans having each required element.[1] All the plans had hazard assessments and proposed mitigation strategies, programs, and actions. Almost all plans (forty-two of forty-four) had capability assessments. These were usually weak, however, only describing existing programs, with little analysis and no assessment of state and local capabilities to change policies and programs. Eighty-six percent of the plans addressed implementation usually not in a separate component but integrated into proposed programs and actions. Only two-thirds had explicitly stated goals and

Table 9.2. Plans Containing Elements Required by the Stafford Act

ELEMENT	NUMBER OF PLANS CONTAINING ELEMENT (N=44)	% OF PLANS CONTAINING ELEMENT
Assessment of natural hazards	44	100
Analysis of existing policies and state and local capabilities to mitigate hazards	42	95
Hazard mitigation goals and objectives	29	66
Proposed strategies, programs, actions	44	100
Proposed approach to implementation	38	86
Proposed approach to monitoring of implementation and hazard conditions	24	55
Proposed approach to updating the plan	26	59
Proposed approach to evaluation of plan and implementation	21	48

objectives, and often these were very brief, general statements incorporated into the introduction and not derived from a participatory process. Fewer than 60 percent proposed an approach to updating the plans regularly or in response to disaster events, and few showed any evidence of following such an approach (i.e., most had not been updated, except in response to a disaster event). Only about half included proposals for monitoring and evaluating the plan, the implementation process, or changes in hazardous conditions.

Thus, although most of the plans had some of the required elements, a number did not even meet this minimal requirement. So in answer to the question of whether the plans contained the required elements, we would say: No, many of the state mitigation plans failed to do so.

Do the Plans Meet Other Requirements of the Stafford Act?

We also evaluated the plans to see whether they met other Stafford Act requirements, including the requirements that the state mitigation plan identify projects to be funded under the Hazard Mitigation Grant Program (Section 404 and Section 406 grants); that it be oriented to developing state and local capability and programs as part of normal government functions; and that it be prepared ahead of time and be updated to reflect spe-

cific disasters. Plans are also required to involve key state agencies, local governments, and other public and private bodies that influence hazard management or development policies, and they are to be coordinated with other hazard evaluation and mitigation planning efforts.

Almost all plans listed types of projects that could be funded under Section 404 and Section 406 grants should a disaster occur, but very few included a specific listing of particular projects. Such a specific listing is not usually practical in a state plan, however, given that it is comprehensive, statewide, and covers multiple hazards. It would be a more appropriate requirement for a local or regional hazard plan, in which specific projects and priorities can be more readily identified.

Plans did not explicitly develop hazard mitigation programs to be integrated into normal government functions, although many programs could be interpreted in that way. For example, proposed actions often were to be implemented by existing agencies rather than by newly created agencies, or proposals were defined as modifications to existing functions and programs.

Coordination with other hazard evaluation and mitigation planning efforts was explicitly addressed in many plans. For example, coordination was included as a goal in more than half of the plans and was addressed in more than half of the capability assessments (especially state-local coordination, which was included in two-thirds of the plans). Furthermore, intergovernmental coordination was proposed as a strategy in more than half of the plans: 77 percent proposed procedures for state-local coordination, 63 percent proposed procedures for coordination among state agencies, and many plans proposed coordination with preparedness, response, and recovery plans.

Regarding participation in developing the plan, most (thirty-one of the forty-four) plans made little or no mention of participation. As table 9.3 shows, the only significant levels of participation at the state level were by the emergency management agencies, which participated in the development of thirty-six of the plans, and the natural resources/environmental agencies, which participated in the development of about half of the plans. Thirteen plans discussed participation by various stakeholders in their preparation, but only two of those showed evidence that input from participants helped determine the plan's proposals. At the local level, eighteen plans provided evidence of participation by local general-purpose governments (e.g., cities, towns, counties), and eight plans showed participation by local special-purpose governments. Only seven of the forty-four plans demonstrated evidence of private-sector involvement in the making of the plan.

Table 9.3. State Agencies Participating in Development of Section 409 Plans Collected

AGENCY	NUMBER OF STATES IN WHICH AGENCY PARTICIPATED
Emergency management	36
Natural resources/environment	21
Transportation	18
Health	11
Housing/community development	10
Coastal planning/management	6
Education	3
Other	21

The record in meeting these other Stafford Act requirements is mixed, and it is particularly weak in participation in plan development. So in answer to the question of whether the plans met other requirements of the Stafford Act, we would answer: To some extent they did, with relatively good attention to promoting intergovernmental coordination in hazard mitigation, but with relatively poor participation among local governments and other stakeholders outside state emergency management and natural resource/environmental agencies.

In addition to checking for compliance with actual requirements of the Stafford Act, we checked to see whether plans included any indication of having been formally approved, either by reference in the text or by reproduction of some letter of approval. Only eight plans showed evidence of formal approval by the FEMA regional office, and only nine plans indicated approval by the governor. Formal approval by the governor is not technically required, but it would be considered evidence of commitment to the plan on the part of the state executive branch. Another nine plans indicated approval by state officials or agencies other than the governor.

Thirty-three of the plans included a definition of mitigation. Twenty-five of these simply repeated, without elaboration, the Stafford Act definition that "hazard mitigation means any action taken to reduce or eliminate the long-term risk to human life and property from natural hazards" (44 C.F.R. 206.401).

Summary: Meeting the Requirements of the Stafford Act

An estimated forty-nine of an eligible fifty-three states and territories had formulated hazard mitigation plans. Of states that had experienced a dis-

aster, only Maryland, Michigan, and Minnesota had no plan. The Section 409 plans almost always included four of the most important elements of a plan—assessment of hazards, assessment of existing policy, proposals for mitigation programs and actions, and implementation specifications. However, many of the plans failed to include explicitly derived goals and objectives, procedures for monitoring and evaluating the plan and its effects, or procedures for appropriate updating. In fact, Section 409 plans were seldom updated except in response to disaster events.

The plans rarely identified in advance those projects to be funded by Section 404 and Section 406 grants in the event of a disaster, but their action proposals did identify recommended types of projects. This information can be useful in assessing applications for Section 404 and Section 406 grants.

The state mitigation plans did not explicitly identify programs that would become part of normal government functions. On the other hand, implementation of most proposed programs was assigned to existing agencies or involved modifications to existing programs. What was not stressed was the mitigation aspect of ongoing programs existing primarily within other local functions, such as land use and environmental management.

Coordination with other hazard evaluation efforts and other mitigation planning efforts was explicitly addressed in many plans. Plans often involved participation by state emergency management agencies, but fewer than half involved other state agencies or local governments, and fewer than one in five involved the private sector.

Thus far, we have discussed only whether plans were created and whether they contained the major components called for in the Stafford Act. Next, we evaluate the content of the plan elements: the types of projects proposed; the analyses included in hazard and capability assessments; the most common goals; and the proposed implementation, monitoring, evaluation, and updating approaches. We examine both the nature and the quality of each of these main plan elements.

Question Two: What Are the Strengths and Weaknesses of the Plans?

We answer this question for one plan component at a time and then present an overall assessment of the plans. We begin with an assessment of the fact basis of the state plans—the assessment of hazards, analysis of current policy, and estimate of goverment capabilities to address hazard mitigation. Second, we assess the value basis—the goals and objectives

component. Third, we assess the proposed strategies, programs, and actions for mitigation, examining the extent to which the plans emphasized particular approaches to mitigation. Fourth, we assess how the plans implemented their proposals, how they monitored and evaluated implementation and changes in hazardous conditions, and how they proposed that updating be performed.

Fact Basis

Good plans are based on a solid foundation of information about existing and emerging conditions. The first two required sections—a hazard assessment and a capabilities assessment—establish such a fact basis for the remainder of the plan. Together, they should provide an understanding of existing and emerging conditions related to hazards; a description of existing and emerging federal, state, and local policies and programs; and an assessment of state and local government capability to forge mitigation policy and programs.

Hazard Assessment

Stafford Act regulations require all Section 409 plans to contain an "evaluation of the natural hazards in the designated area" (44 C.F.R. 206. 405[a][1]). We examine three aspects of hazard assessment: assessment of *hazard characteristics* (e.g., magnitude, likelihood of occurrence); assessment of *vulnerability* to those hazards (e.g., number of people at risk, value of property); and assessment of *risk* (i.e., combining the likelihood of disaster events of various magnitudes with the likely harm associated therewith).

Our evaluation of the hazard assessment components of the plans is summarized in figure 9.1. Overall, hazard assessment was performed more often and better than vulnerability assessment, which in turn was performed more often, though not better, than risk assessment. This is not surprising, considering that describing the physical characteristics of a hazard is easier than assessing the associated vulnerability of, and risk to, society. In many plans, hazard assessment consisted of little more than a presentation of general meteorological, geographic, and historical data drawn from other reports. Vulnerability assessment, on the other hand, required the plans' authors to analyze hazard data together with demographic and building data, which are difficult to obtain in a form that is compatible with hazard data. Risk assessment is even more daunting because it requires that probabilities of various levels of hazardous events be combined with the likely extent of harm they would cause.

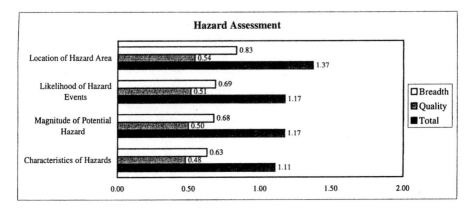

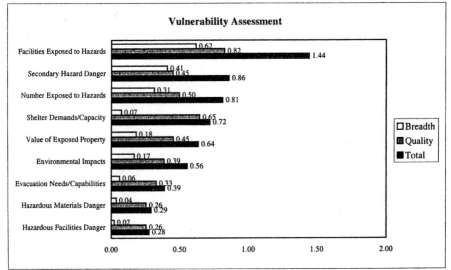

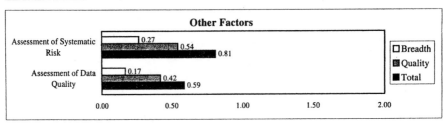

Figure 9.1. Hazard Assessment Scores.

In assessing the hazards as physical phenomena, plans were more likely to describe the locations and boundaries of hazardous areas than to describe the hazards' probability of occurrence, potential magnitude, or particular characteristics (such as separating flash flooding from slower-rise flooding). The quality of descriptions of hazard location, however, was not superior to the quality of descriptions of other hazard dimensions.

Fewer than 50 percent of the plans addressed aspects of vulnerability to the hazard being assessed, other than facilities exposed to hazards. Plans scored higher on assessing whether facilities and people were exposed, assessing shelter demands and capacity, and assessing danger from secondary hazards than they did on assessing environmental impact, property value at risk, evacuation needs and capabilities, and danger from hazardous materials and facilities.

Although only 27 percent of the plans addressed risk assessment, they generally did as good a job on that issue as plans generally did on the more common hazard assessment dimensions.

The research team also evaluated the hazard assessment component of each plan in a more qualitative manner by generally describing its approach or style, strengths and weaknesses, and overall quality. Our qualitative assessments of the plans' hazard assessment components most often described them it in the following ways:

- Very general

- Perfunctory, superficial, and cursory, with little technical information

- Covering historical events but not anticipatory

- Descriptive, not analytic

- Describing the hazard physically but not assessing vulnerability or risk

In search of positive role models, we also selected certain plans that did especially well on the components being assessed. Kentucky's hazard mitigation plan, for example, contained a good hazard assessment. It focused on four types of hazards—flooding, earthquakes, tornadoes, and drought—after explaining why these hazards were selected for detailed analyses. The plan not only offered detailed descriptions of past significant hazard events, but also applied statistics from those earlier disasters in a forward–looking analysis. For each major hazard type, the plan examined history, vulnerability, and current and future exposure. Detailed estimates were provided of the numbers of people and types of populations at risk. Many useful graphic and tabular aids, such as maps of disaster-prone areas, supplemented the text. Kentucky's plan demonstrated

the inclusion of all three elements of a model hazard assessment—description of the physical hazard, vulnerability assessment, and risk assessment; anticipation of potential future situations as well as analysis of past events; and effective use of graphics and tables to make the information more accessible to users. All these qualities are recommended in drafting future Section 409 plans.

Capability Analysis

The second fact–basis component required by the Stafford Act is a capability analysis: "a description and analysis of the State and local hazard management policies, programs, and capabilities to mitigate the hazards in the area" (44 C.F.R. 206.405[a][1]). Our evaluation instrument measured the existence and quality of nineteen possible elements of a capability analysis. See figure 9.2 for the scores on these elements, organized in five categories.

In the first category, three questions in the evaluation instrument examined the plans' assessment of existing hazard mitigation programs, policies, laws, and actions at the federal, state or regional, and local levels, respectively. The plans commonly included an assessment at all three government levels but particularly at the state or regional level and the federal level. The high score for description of state programs makes sense given that the plans were authored by state employees who were especially familiar with the hazard programs with which they dealt on a regular basis.

In the second category of capability analysis, three questions in the evaluation instrument reviewed the plans' assessment of mitigation programs, policies, laws, and actions under consideration or in the process of being put into place, again at all three government levels. These elements of emerging policy were addressed much less often than were programs already in place; whereas the quality scores were again roughly in the middle range, the breadth scores were much lower, indicating that the plans' authors typically were not reviewing emerging developments in hazard mitigation policy. As shown in figure 9.2, 50 percent of the plans addressed state- or regional-level programs under consideration, whereas only 27 percent addressed local-level programs and a mere 16 percent addressed federal-level programs (this despite major mitigation initiatives at the federal level, such as the Performance Partnership Agreements). The plans' overall failure to discuss programs under consideration suggests that their authors either did not know of such programs or did not believe the Section 409 plan to be the appropriate venue for addressing them.

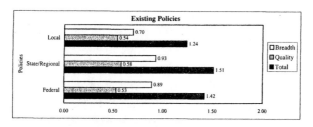

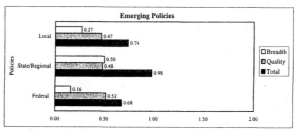

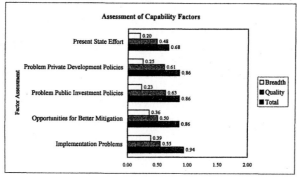

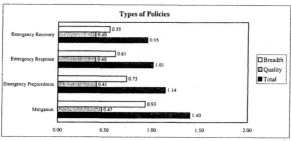

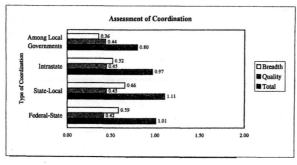

Figure 9.2. Capability Assessment Scores.

A third category of questions in the evaluation instrument examined the extent to which the plans reviewed policy and government capability in each of the four phases of emergency management: mitigation, preparedness, response, and recovery. More than half the plans addressed all four phases of emergency management: 93 percent of the plans reviewed mitigation policy and capability, followed by preparedness (73 percent), response (61 percent), and recovery (55 percent). Despite the comprehensive treatment, however, the coverage itself was not strong, as evidenced by the relatively low quality scores.

A fourth category of questions addressed five factors focusing directly on an assessment of government capability, which extended beyond an examination of existing and emerging policies. This assessment examined the plans' attention to obstacles, opportunities, and capability to forge new policy. Capability in this sense is a dimension of the fact basis that the Stafford Act urges states to address, according to DAP-12, FEMA's Section 409 plan preparation handbook (FEMA 1990, pp. 93–97).

Overall, the plans scored poorly on attention to these capability elements. Only 25 percent identified development policies that created mitigation problems by perversely promoting private development in hazard areas, though the quality score was a moderate 61 percent (we classified scores of 60 percent or higher as "moderately strong"). Similarly, only about one in four plans identified policies that placed public investments at risk in hazard areas, and only one in five assessed the effort (e.g., money or staff) the state devoted to mitigation. The plans scored slightly higher on their assessments of opportunities for increasing mitigation capability (36 percent) and their assessments of problems in implementing mitigation measures (39 percent). The quality of analysis was moderately strong only in identifying problems with urban development policies that place private property or public investment at risk.

The fifth and final category of questions in the capability analysis addressed the assessment of intergovernmental coordination. Federal-state coordination, coordination among state agencies, and state-local coordination were assessed in more than 50 percent of the plans. In fact, state-local coordination was assessed in 66 percent of the plans. Assessment of coordination among local governments, however, appeared in just 36 percent of the plans, indicating a lack of emphasis on interlocal coordination of hazard mitigation efforts. As discussed later in this chapter, few plans proposed improving coordination among local jurisdictions.

Our qualitative descriptions of the plans'capability assessment components most often characterized them in one of the following ways:

- A list of existing agencies and programs, lacking analysis, assessment or critique, and a discussion of capability

- Covers federal and state policy and programs but not local programs

- Brief, cursory, and superficial; missing altogether; or scattered among other components of the plan

- Does not include attention to interrelationships and coordination

Although none of the plans received a high score for capability analysis, some did better than others. Connecticut's Section 409 plan contained one of the better such analyses, with solid, well-written descriptions of effective and innovative programs in the state; the descriptions of flood warning systems and the state's Flood Audit Program were especially noteworthy. Reviewers commented that the level of detail in the analysis was unusual—even going so far as to note the flood height at which water will enter individual houses, identified by owner's name. Another strong aspect of the analysis was its candid discussion of weaknesses in the state's mitigation planning and implementation system.

Conclusions

The fact-basis assessments of natural hazards facing the states were typically stronger than the assessments of government capability to mitigate the hazards, and they were on average the strongest components of the state mitigation plans. Within the hazard analysis components, the elements describing and assessing physical hazards were much stronger than the elements assessing the states' vulnerability to the hazards. Plans were weaker yet in making risk assessments.

Within the capability assessment components, the plans were strongest in describing existing policies and programs but weak in assessing those programs or policies still being put in place. Plans were also weak in assessing the capability of state and local governments to forge new policies or adjust to existing policies and programs.

Value Basis

Goals and objectives should guide the implementation of mitigation programs. The Stafford Act requires the inclusion of goals and objectives in Section 409 plans, along with proposed mitigation strategies and actions (44 C.F.R. 206.405[a][3]). Goals are defined as "long-term and general" in nature—for example, protecting the public safety or reducing property losses. Objectives, in contrast, are "specific and achievable in a finite time period" (FEMA 1990, p. 75).

Figure 9.3 lists the goals stated in the Section 409 plans, ranked in order from those appearing most often to those appearing least often. By far the two most commonly stated goals were protecting human safety and reducing loss to private property. These goals were stated in at least 70 percent of the plans and are consistent with the national goals of FEMA. About half the plans also included the goal of coordinating with other hazard mitigation efforts. Thirty to 40 percent of the plans had goals associated with improving preparedness, improving response, incorporating mitigation into recovery programs, reducing vulnerability of public property, and achieving cost-effectiveness. Approximately 20 percent included goals related to minimizing disruption of a community's economy or social network, minimizing fiscal effects on government, reducing vulnerability of

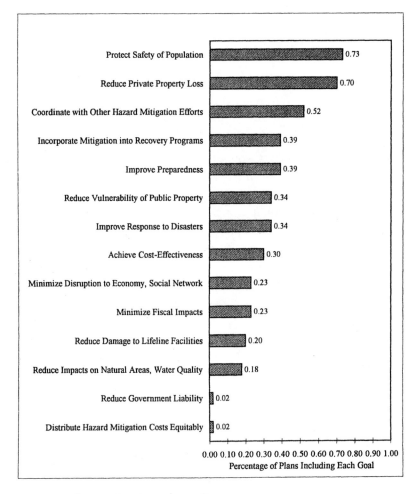

Figure 9.3. Goals Stated in Section 409 Plans

lifeline facilities such as hospitals and power plants, and reducing impacts on natural areas and water quality. Only one plan had the goal of reducing government liability, and one plan had the goal of distributing the costs of hazard mitigation equitably.

Our qualitative analysis of the plans' goals and objectives components recognized the following weaknesses:

- Often there was no separate goals component; goals were stated either in the introduction to the plan or at the beginning of the section on proposed strategies, programs, and actions.

- The discussion was almost always very brief, from one sentence or a few lines to less than one page.

- There was usually no discussion of the rationale for the goals

- Objectives often were not "achievement milestones" so much as "action milestones" (i.e., they referred to the completion of some activity, establishment of a policy, revision of the plan, or determination of vulnerability by a specific date).

- The goals sometimes described the purpose of having a plan document (e.g., to increase awareness, to coordinate actions, or to complete the components required by the Stafford Act) rather than discussing the ultimate ends of hazard mitigation.

- Priorities among goals were seldom discussed.

- Goals seldom included the concept of risk or of establishing an acceptable level of risk.

Although many plans failed to discuss goals and objectives for hazard mitigation in any fashion, and many of the plans that did mention them did so in an offhand manner, perhaps tucking them away in a single paragraph in the introductory section, we found a few plans to be noteworthy in their treatment of goals. For example, Oregon's plan contained four goals that were clearly and simply stated, along with objectives intended to serve as "measuring sticks" for evaluating the success of proposed projects. The goals were ranked by priority: first was protection of life, followed by protection of emergency response capability, protection of developed property, and, finally, protection of natural resources and the environment. Goals were acknowledged as the "first stage in Oregon's overall mitigation planning process" and were to be used as criteria for evaluating Section 404 projects.

Proposed Strategies, Programs, and Actions

The most vital part of any mitigation plan is its proposed strategies, programs, and actions to reduce long-term vulnerability to hazards, simply

referred to as actions in our analysis. We examined plans first for the inclusion of forty-five different types of actions, organized into ten categories. Those combinations of actions and categories most commonly included in plans were interpreted as indicators of the most common state mitigation strategies, representing best mitigation practice.

We also measured how well the plans specified each proposed type of action—that is, whether (1) an action was proposed but few or no specifics were provided; or, better, (2) the proposal included some specifics about what was to be done; or, better yet, (3) the proposal included cost estimates where relevant, or model legislation, or legal analysis, or otherwise represented what an ideal plan would contain. In the analysis that follows, we first identify the types of actions most often proposed and we then discuss the quality of the proposals.

Ten General Categories of Actions

Actions proposed in the plans were organized in ten categories, each category constituting a fundamentally different approach to mitigation. The ten categories, ranked by the frequency with which actions of that type were proposed, are listed in table 9.4.

Plans were most likely to recommend acquisition of land or structures by state government and actions that promote awareness of natural hazards among citizens, property owners, developers, and local officials.

Table 9.4. Categories of Proposed Actions in Section 409 Plans

Category of Action	Number of Specific Types of Actions Included	Average % of Plans Recommending Each Type of Action in Category
Acquisition of property by state	1	66
Promoting awareness of hazards	8	65
Intergovernmental coordination	5	53
Physical control of hazards	3	52
Protecting public infrastructure	4	51
Retrofitting existing development	2	40
Emergency preparedness/ response	4	39
Financial assistance to local governments	5	35
Controlling new development	8	32
Recovery measures	5	22

Those types of actions were recommended by about two-thirds of the plans. Approximately half the plans recommended actions that promote intergovernmental coordination, physical control of the hazard itself, and protection of public facilities and infrastructure. Other types of actions, recommended on average by only 40 percent or fewer of the plans, included those that promote retrofitting, emergency preparedness and response, financial assistance to local governments, control of new development, and recovery measures after a disaster event.

Individual Types of Actions Within the Ten General Categories

Some specific types of actions were proposed more often than others in the same category. Further, some actions in less common categories were proposed more often than less popular actions in more popular categories. In this section, we sort out the specific types of actions most commonly proposed within each category. We discuss the categories in the order of their general popularity, as established earlier, and focus on those actions proposed in at least two-thirds of the plans.

1. Acquisition of property by the state. This category contains only one type of action—acquisition of land or structures by state government. That action was recommended by 66 percent of the state plans. The plan quality score was 0.52, and the total score was 1.18.

2. Promotion of awareness of and knowledge about hazards. This category contained eight types of actions. Of these, the most commonly recommended were:

- Promoting educational awareness (providing information to the public regarding hazard risks and methods of mitigation) (93 percent)

- Providing technical assistance (e.g., workshops) for local officials (91 percent)

- Conducting research to improve knowledge, develop standards, and identify and map hazards (89 percent)

- Implementing disaster warning and response programs (providing information regarding emergency planning) (73 percent)

- Encouraging the purchase of flood or earthquake insurance (68 percent)

Other actions to promote awareness, such as providing technical assistance to property owners (as opposed to officials), requiring disclosure about hazards during real estate transactions, and posting signs to indicate hazardous areas, were recommended less often. The overall plan quality scores for approaches to promote awareness and knowledge are shown in figure 9.4.

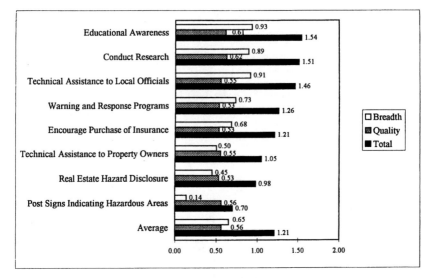

Figure 9.4. Scores for Programs and Actions That Promote Awareness and Knowledge

3. Intergovernmental coordination. This category contains five types of actions. The most commonly recommended were:

- Mechanisms for state-local coordination (77 percent)
- Mechanisms for coordination among state agencies (68 percent)

Recommended less often were actions to promote federal-state coordination and local intergovernmental coordination and actions involving mediation processes to resolve conflicts. The scores for approaches to promote intergovernmental coordination are shown in figure 9.5.

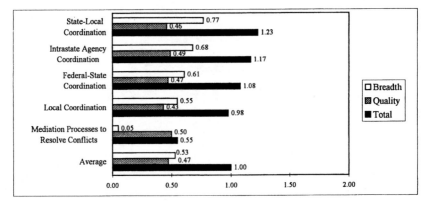

Figure 9.5. Scores for Programs and Actions That Promote Intergovernmental Coordination

4. **Physical control of hazards.** Of the three types of actions in this category, the following two were the most commonly recommended:

- Storm water controls such as drainage systems, channelization, culverts, and detention or retention basins (75 percent)

- Physical structures to lessen the impacts of hazards, such as seawalls, levees, bulkheads, and causeways (64 percent)

The scores for approaches to promote the control of hazards are shown in Figure 9.6.

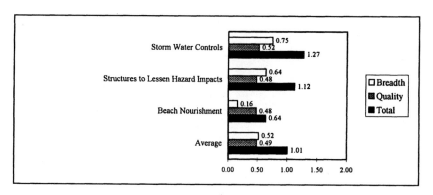

Figure 9.6. Scores for Programs and Actions That Promote Control of Hazards

5. **Protection of public facilities and infrastructure.** Only two of the four types of actions in this category were mentioned in more than 60 percent of the plans: adjusting infrastructure timing, location, and design (70 percents), and retrofitting of community facilities (64 percent). The scores for approaches to protect public facilities and infrastructure are shown in figure 9.7.

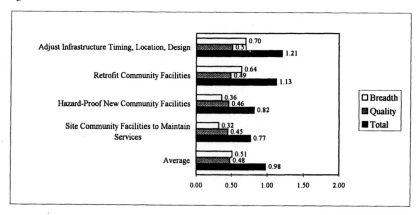

Figure 9.7. Scores for Programs and Actions That Protect Public Facilities and Infrastructure

6. ***Retrofitting of existing private development.*** Neither of the two types of retrofitting in this category, retrofitting of private structures or retrofitting of private infrastructure, was proposed by a majority of plans. Scores are shown in figure 9.8.

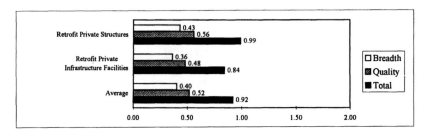

Figure 9.8. Scores for Programs and Actions That Promote Retrofitting of Existing Development

7. ***Emergency preparedness and response.*** Only one of the four types of mitigation actions to promote emergency preparedness and response was proposed by two-thirds of the plans: creation of a preparedness plan or program (66 percent). The scores for that and other actions in this category are shown in figure 9.9.

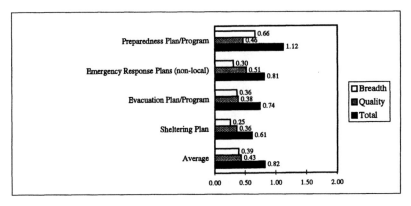

Figure 9.9. Scores for Programs and Actions That Promote Emergency Preparedness and Response

8. Financial assistance for local governments. None of the five types of financial assistance for local governments was proposed by two-thirds or more of the plans. However, 59 percent of the plans did propose financial assistance through FEMA Section 404 or Section 406 grants. Other actions were proposed in fewer plans. The scores for actions to promote financial assistance are shown in figure 9.10.

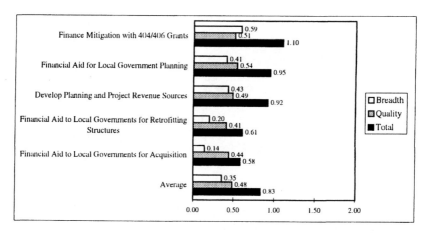

Figure 9.10. Scores for Programs and Actions That Promote Financial Assistance for Local Governments

9. Control of new development. Of the eight types of actions in this category, only two were proposed by two-thirds or more of the Section 409 plans:

- Use of site and building design standards to make new structures less susceptible to hazardous forces (75 percent)

- Control of the type and arrangement of land use in hazardous areas (68 percent)

Half or fewer of the plans recommended the use of subdivision regulations and other standards governing the design of new development, laws to protect natural features that contribute to mitigation (e.g., dunes, wetlands), setbacks or buffer zones around hazardous areas, and tax abatement for the use of mitigation methods. Fewer than three plans recommended density transfers or density bonuses for setting aside hazardous lands from development. The scores for actions to control new development are shown in figure 9.11.

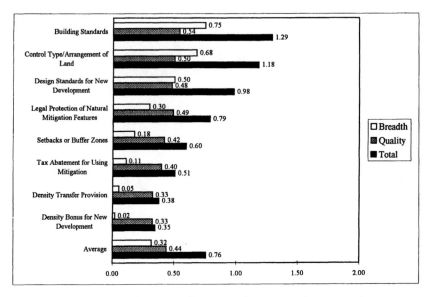

Figure 9.11. Scores for Programs and Actions That Control New Development

10. Recovery measures. Of the five approaches to promoting recovery, the one proposed most often was postdisaster adjustments to infrastructure. None of these mitigation-oriented recovery-type actions, however, was proposed in more than one-third of the plans. The scores for this category are shown in figure 9.12.

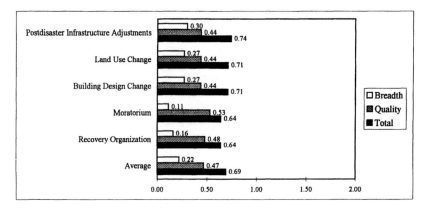

Figure 9.12. Scores for Programs and Actions That Promote Recovery Measures

Considering Individual Actions Apart from General Categories

It is also instructive to examine the pattern of individual types of actions that were recommended without reference to the general categories to which they belong. Figure 9.13 shows the scores for the individual types of proposed actions independent of category and ranked according to total score. Fifteen types of actions were recommended by about two-thirds or more of the plans. Among these, three types were recommended by approximately 90 percent of the plans:

- Providing information to the public regarding risks of hazards and methods of mitigation (e.g., pamphlets, lectures, radio and television announcements, billboards) (93 percent)

- Providing technical assistance (e.g., workshops) for local officials (91 percent)

- Conducting research to improve knowledge, develop standards, and identify and map hazards (89 percent)

These actions are all low in cost, require little political commitment, and require no direct government intervention in urban development processes.

Four actions were recommended by about three-quarters of the plans:

- Establishing mechanisms and procedures for state-local government coordination (77 percent)

- Establishing standards for site design and building design or construction to make new private structures less susceptible to hazardous forces (75 percent)

- Constructing storm water control structures, including drainage systems, channelization, culverts, and detention or retention basins (75 percent)

- Establishing disaster warning and response programs, including public education regarding emergency planning, what to expect when hazardous events occur, and procedures and time frames necessary for evacuation (73 percent)

Of these four, the first and last involve little cost or direct intervention of government.

Eight types of actions were recommended by about two-thirds of the plans:

- Adjusting the location and design of public infrastructure, such as water, and sewage systems and roads, to limit damage from hazards (70 percent)

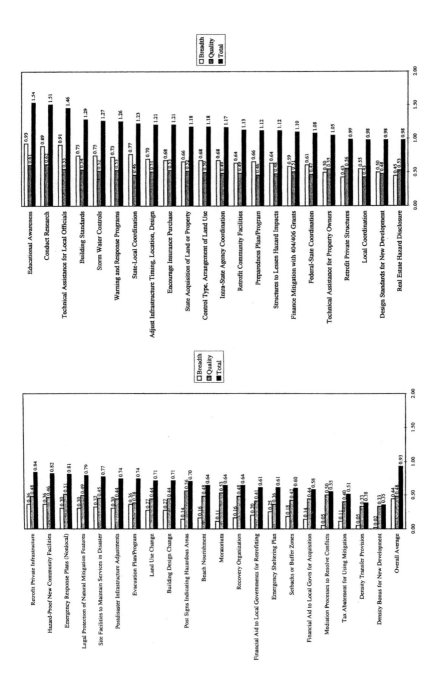

Left chart (Breadth / Quality / Total):

Policy	Breadth	Quality	Total
Retrofit Private Infrastructure	0.36	0.48	0.84
Hazard-Proof New Community Facilities	0.36	0.46	0.82
Emergency Response Plans (Nonlocal)	0.30	0.51	0.81
Legal Protection of Natural Mitigation Features	0.30	0.49	0.79
Site Facilities to Maintain Services in Disaster	0.32	0.45	0.77
Postdisaster Infrastructure Adjustments	0.30	0.44	0.74
Evacuation Plan/Program	0.36	0.38	0.74
Land Use Change	0.27	0.44	0.71
Building Design Change	0.27	0.44	0.71
Post Signs Indicating Hazardous Areas	0.14	0.56	0.70
Beach Nourishment	0.16	0.48	0.64
Moratorium	0.11	0.53	0.64
Recovery Organization	0.16	0.48	0.64
Financial Aid to Local Governments for Retrofitting	0.20	0.41	0.61
Emergency Sheltering Plan	0.25	0.36	0.61
Setbacks or Buffer Zones	0.18	0.42	0.60
Financial Aid to Local Govts for Acquisition	0.14	0.44	0.58
Mediation Processes to Resolve Conflicts	0.05	0.50	0.55
Tax Abatement for Using Mitigation	0.11	0.40	0.51
Density Transfer Provision	0.05	0.33	0.38
Density Bonus for New Development	0.02	0.33	0.35
Overall Average	0.45	0.48	0.93

Right chart (Breadth / Quality / Total):

Policy	Breadth	Quality	Total
Educational Awareness	0.61	0.93	1.54
Conduct Research	0.62	0.89	1.51
Technical Assistance for Local Officials	0.55	0.91	1.46
Building Standards	0.54	0.75	1.29
Storm Water Controls	0.52	0.75	1.27
Warning and Response Programs	0.53	0.73	1.26
State-Local Coordination	0.46	0.77	1.23
Adjust Infrastructure Timing, Location, Design	0.51	0.70	1.21
Encourage Insurance Purchase	0.53	0.68	1.21
State Acquisition of Land or Property	0.52	0.66	1.18
Control Type, Arrangement of Land Use	0.50	0.68	1.18
Intra-State Agency Coordination	0.49	0.68	1.17
Retrofit Community Facilities	0.49	0.64	1.13
Preparedness Plan/Program	0.46	0.66	1.12
Structures to Lessen Hazard Impacts	0.48	0.64	1.12
Finance Mitigation with 404/406 Grants	0.51	0.59	1.10
Federal-State Coordination	0.47	0.61	1.08
Technical Assistance for Property Owners	0.50	0.55	1.05
Retrofit Private Structures	0.43	0.56	0.99
Local Coordination	0.43	0.55	0.98
Design Standards for New Development	0.48	0.50	0.98
Real Estate Hazard Disclosure	0.45	0.53	0.98

- Encouraging property owners to purchase flood or earthquake insurance (68 percent)

- Controlling the type and arrangement of land use in hazardous areas (68 percent)

- Establishing mechanisms and procedures for coordination of state agencies (68 percent)

- Acquiring land or structures in hazardous areas through the state (66 percent)

- Creating an emergency preparedness plan or program (66 percent)

- Retrofitting community facilities (64 percent)

- Building hazard control structures such as levees, seawalls, bulkheads, and causeways to lessen the impact of hazardous events (64 percent)

Of these eight proposals, five involve more significant commitment and intervention, including adjusting the location and design of public infrastructure, controlling the pattern of land use, acquiring land and structures in hazardous areas, retrofitting community facilities, and building hazard control structures such as levees. Thus, about two-thirds of the state Section 409 plans recommended significant government action in the form of these five proposals for regulations and public investments.

Overall Quality

In general, the quality of the plans' recommendations was mediocre. The types of actions presented best (though there was little variation overall) were the same ones recommended most often. However, even for the types of actions having the highest average quality and level of specification, the clear majority of plans included few specifics about the recommendations being made. Plans that included some specifics or went further to include cost estimates, model legislation, legal analysis, or other relevant specifics were in a clear minority.

Conclusions

All of the state Section 409 plans we reviewed (100 percent) contained policy and action recommendations, which are the heart of any mitigation plan. At least two-thirds included recommendations for significant government action in the form of land use and construction regulations, acquisition of land and structures, construction of hazard control structures, and/or relocation or protection of public infrastructure. An even greater number recommended ways to improve general awareness of and

knowledge about hazards and to encourage private and local public mitigation actions, all of which are desirable but do not involve much political commitment, funding, or intervention in the urban development market. Most plans included few or no specifics about the recommendations being made; only a minority of plans included some specifics or went further to include cost estimates, model legislation, legal analysis, or other relevant specifics.

We found much more variation in style and quality in the proposed programs, actions, and strategies component than in the other components of the plans. In general, we characterize this component in the following ways:

- Most plans included few specifics about the proposals or how to accomplish them.

- Many plans' proposals were stated in weak imperative language, indicating little commitment to follow through on proposals. For example, they used language such as "should do" rather than indicating intent to carry something out, or they listed programs and actions already under way, projects approved as result of the most recent disaster event, or possible options for strategies, programs, and actions, or they just described state agencies and their responsibilities.

- Although a significant number of plans did organize proposed actions into strategies (categories), many simply listed unrelated individual projects, actions, and work elements.

- Some plans were stated very much in terms of Section 404–type projects, but usually these listed the projects already initiated in response to the most recent disaster event and described the status of those projects.

Of the plans examined, Massachusetts's Section 409 plan was one of the strongest in outlining proposed mitigation actions, programs, and policies. It was clearly organized, with careful attention to the interrelationships among elements. The recommendations were linked to, and grouped by, the goals and objectives introduced in an earlier section. Proposed actions were presented in two ways: a two-page summary chart and a detailed table providing more complete information about each program, including lead agencies, sources of funding, estimated dates of completion, and general comments. A helpful feature was a status report on recommendations proposed in past plans. Additional recommendations were provided in the postdisaster annex attached to the main plan, and a list of criteria for the funding of Section 404 projects was included. One weakness of the Massachusetts plan's proposed actions section was a lack of specific cost figures.

Other strong plans, such as California's Section 409 plan for earthquakes, did include such figures.

Approaches to Implementation, Monitoring, Evaluation, and Updating

For plans to be effective, they must influence future actions of state and local governments. Thus, an important dimension of any plan is the extent to which it addresses plan implementation, updating, and monitoring and evaluation of the extent to which recommendations are carried out and their effect on vulnerability to hazards.

The Stafford Act specifies that a Section 409 plan should describe "a method of implementing, monitoring, evaluating, and updating the mitigation plan. Such evaluation is to occur at least on an annual basis to ensure that implementation occurs as planned and to ensure that the plan remains current" (44 C.F.R. 206.405[a][4]). DAP–12, FEMA's Section 409 plan preparation handbook, suggests that the implementation section should describe how the proposed policies, programs, and activities, including monitoring and evaluation, will be initiated, modified, and continued (FEMA 1990). The monitoring and evaluation section should describe how the state will identify and evaluate changes in hazardous conditions, implementation of provisions of the plan, and effectiveness of the plan.

We divide our assessment of these dimensions into two parts, addressing implementation first and then discussing monitoring, evaluation, and updating.

Implementation

We measured fifteen dimensions of how the plans addressed implementation. Figure 9.14 shows the proportion of Section 409 plans that addressed each dimension and a quality score indicating how well that dimension was addressed. These two scores were summed to produce an overall assessment score for each of the fifteen dimensions. The dimensions are presented in rank order in the figure, from highest to lowest total score.

Most Section 409 plans did not include a separate section on implementation. Instead, they addressed implementation in other sections of the plan, usually the section on recommended strategies and actions, and included nothing about monitoring and evaluation. When a plan did devote a specific section to implementation, monitoring, and evaluation, it was almost always very brief (one-half page to three pages in length) and

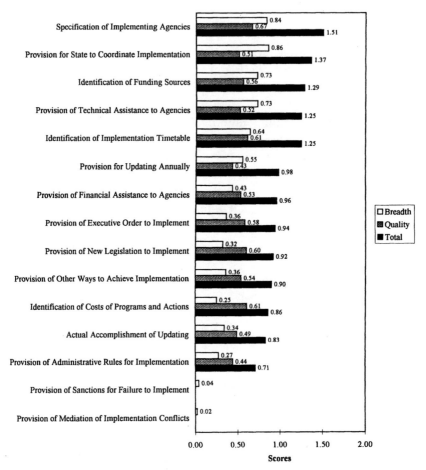

Figure 9.14. Scores for Implementation Elements. Note: Average quality indexes are not calculated for "provision of sanctions" and "provision of mediation implementation conflicts" because of the small number of plans proposing these actions (two plans and one plan, respectively).

very general. The emphasis usually was on the roles and responsibilities of the state hazard mitigation officer.

At least 80 percent of the plans did specify the agencies that were to implement the recommended actions and did provide for state coordination of implementation. Almost three-fourths of the plans identified funding sources and directed that technical assistance be provided to agencies responsible for implementation, and nearly two-thirds of them specified a timetable for implementing recommended actions.

More than 50 percent of the plans did not provide for financial assistance to those agencies responsible for implementation, nor did they provide new implementation authority in the form of executive orders, legislation, administrative rules, or other methods. And only one-quarter of the plans actually identified the costs of the programs and actions recommended. Only one plan provided for mediation to resolve conflicts that arise during implementation, and only two plans specified sanctions for failure to implement. Although more then half of the plans provided for annual updating, only 36 percent had actually been doing so. Other plans were updated only in response to a disaster event.

According to the quality scores for implementation, plans did better at some of the elements that were left out by most plans. For example, in the few instances in which these elements were included, plans did a better job of identifying costs of programs and actions recommended, specifying implementation authority such as executive orders and new state legislation, and outlining sanctions for failure to implement. Of course, these same plans also did well in specifying implementing agencies, funding sources, and timetables for implementation.

On the other hand, although more than half the plans addressed state coordination of implementation, technical assistance for agencies responsible for implementation, and regular annual updating, these elements of plans tended to be weaker than other elements.

We conclude that implementation was among the weaker elements of the Section 409 plans. In most plans, there was no explicit section on implementation; instead, it was integrated into discussions of recommended strategies and actions. The plans tended to address only three elements of implementation often *and* well: specification of implementing agencies, identification of funding sources, and setting of timetables for implementation. Although they also often provided for state coordination of implementation, technical assistance for implementation agencies, and regular annual updating of the plan, they did not do so good a job at those elements. The plans were weakest at actual accomplishment of the annual updating and at specification of sanctions for failure to implement provisions of the plan. And although some plans did well at specifying the costs of programs and actions and at outlining new executive orders or new legislation required, few plans even addressed those issues.

Monitoring and Evaluation

Figure 9.15 shows the results of our assessment of provisions for monitoring and evaluation. The Section 409 plans tended to be even weaker in monitoring and evaluation than in implementation, which itself was not

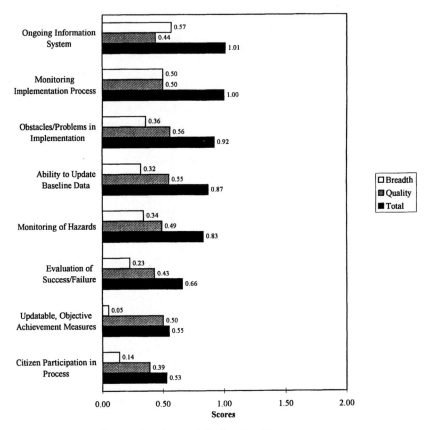

Figure 9.15. Scores for Monitoring and Evaluation Elements

strong. In fact, most plans did not even address most elements of monitoring and evaluation. Only about half the plans specified the monitoring of implementation progress or the development of an ongoing information system, organization, and process for monitoring and evaluation. Only one-third of the plans provided for assessment of obstacles and problems in implementation. More specific elements such as updating baseline data, measuring attainment of objectives, monitoring hazards, evaluating success or failure of measures, and involving citizens were included even less often.

In other words, whereas about half the plans provided in a general way for some ongoing system of monitoring and evaluation, one-third or fewer actually provided for updating of baseline data (32 percent), monitoring of hazards (34 percent), evaluation of success or failure (23 percent), or objective measurement achievement (5 percent).

Conclusions

Monitoring and evaluation were seldom addressed in the state Section 409 plans we reviewed. Regular updating was proposed in most plans but actually evident in few plans. That is, among those states that had a previous plan, only one-third indicated that the previous plan had been updated on a regular basis. Overall, implementation, monitoring, evaluation, and updating were the weakest components of almost all plans. These findings support the interpretation that the Section 409 plans were not intended by their authors—the states—to be implemented in the usual sense of the word. Instead, the plans were intended to qualify the state for Section 404 mitigation project grants or to help in assessing and prioritizing Section 404 project applications from local governments and other agencies.

We did find plans worth emulating, however. California had two active Section 409 plans, one for flooding and another for earthquakes. We consider the state's earthquake plan to be one of the strongest Section 409 plans reviewed for this project; several of its sections may be considered model elements. As was the case with the entire document, the section on monitoring, evaluation, and implementation was exceptionally well organized and was integrally tied to the sections on goals and proposed actions. Individual implementing initiatives were presented in two ways for easy reference—by year and by proposed legislation. The section was supplemented with many useful, easy-to-read tables. Lead agencies were specified for individual initiatives, and cost estimates were provided for selected initiatives. There were annual action plans for implementation. The plan itself is completely updated every five years, and one-year updates are issued in each intervening year.

Other Aspects and Attributes of Plans

We also assessed several general characteristics of state Section 409 plans, including readability, internal consistency, comprehensiveness, and integration with related nonhazard issues.

Only a few of the plans were easily readable, comprehensive, and internally consistent. Of the forty-four plans evaluated, we found twelve to be well illustrated and with clearly written text. The other thirty-two plans were not clearly written for the lay public and were poorly illustrated (e.g., they contained no maps or photographs). Internal consistency was evident in thirteen of the plans and was presumed to be present in twenty-six additional plans (no inconsistencies were found). However, five of the plans demonstrated substantive inconsistencies between parts of the plans.

Thirty-four of the plans responded to only single hazards or specific

disasters or proposed uncoordinated separate actions; the remaining ten were comprehensive in identifying hazards and proposing programs and actions. Nonhazard issues were explicitly integrated with hazard issues in only three plans, and sixteen additional plans mentioned such integration vaguely. Thus, twenty-five of the plans attempted no integration with other issues, such as protecting wetlands while providing for flood mitigation.

Summary of Problems with Most State Hazard Mitigation Plans

States were meeting many of the Stafford Act's basic requirements. We estimate that forty-nine of the fifty-three eligible states and territories had completed hazard mitigation plans to qualify for postdisaster Section 404 grants. Only three states that had experienced natural disasters since 1988 had no plan. The plans typically included four of the components required by the Stafford Act: assessment of hazards, assessment of existing policy, proposals for mitigation, and specifications for implementation. Many plans, however, failed to include formally derived goals and objectives, assessments of state and local mitigation capability, postplan monitoring and evaluation procedures, or procedures for appropriate updating of plans. State emergency management agencies usually participated in making the Section 409 plans, but other state agencies were involved less than half the time, and local governments or private-sector representatives were rarely involved.

Although all plans had a section that assessed physical characteristics of hazards, most merely described the locations and magnitudes of past events, their frequency, and the dangers from separate characteristics of the hazard (e.g., winds, high water, and wave action for hurricanes). They were not likely to assess vulnerability on the basis of analyses of the population, property, and natural environmental processes exposed to the hazard or on the basis of an assessment of the danger from secondary hazards (e.g., dams breaking or hazardous materials being released in the wake of a hazardous event). They seldom made risk assessments combining probabilities of hazardous events with the likely degree of harm from those events. Thus, assessments of natural hazards tended to be general and descriptive rather than analytic or interpretive.

Capability assessments were often included, but most plans simply described existing federal and state programs in mitigation, emergency preparedness, emergency response, and recovery as well as existing

intergovernmental coordination efforts. Less attention was given to revisions in policies and programs being implemented or to more fundamental factors, such as implementation obstacles and opportunities, inadvertent problems posed by other public and private practices, and level of state effort in hazard mitigation.

Goals tended to be perfunctory or absent. Only two-thirds of the plans had a separate goal statement. Goals tended to repeat FEMA goals—protecting the safety of the population, reducing property damage, and coordinating with other emergency management and mitigation efforts. Seldom did the plans discuss the balancing of risks with other goals, priorities among goals, or rationales behind the goals. Seldom did this component of the plan exceed one page, and often it was limited to one or two sentences or a paragraph. Plans that did include objectives often stated them not as achievement milestones but as action milestones; that is, they referred to the completion of an activity rather than to the attainment of an end purpose.

Although all plans contained proposed programs and actions, the proposals were often tentative and stated in generalities. About two-thirds of the plans did recommend land use and construction regulations, acquisition of land and structures, construction of hazard control structures, and/or ways to protect public infrastructure. However, they more commonly recommended measures that imply much less government commitment, funding, or intervention in the land development market—for example, improving awareness of and knowledge about hazards and encouraging mitigation efforts by the private sector and local government. Plans rarely emphasized linkages to Section 404 and Section 406 program grants, and they seldom stressed the integration of mitigation into normal government functions, although they did address coordination with other emergency management and mitigation strategies. Many plans listed actions without organizing them into coordinated strategies.

Implementation was usually integrated into the discussion of proposed actions and programs rather than developed as a separate component of the plan. Implementation tended to focus on specifying implementation agencies, identifying funding sources and setting timetables, and perhaps outlining procedures for coordination among agencies. Plans less often estimated costs of programs or outlined sanctions for failure to implement their provisions. Monitoring and evaluation of implementation also were weak, when they were addressed at all. Updating procedures, although often proposed, were actually evident in few of the plans. Thus, we judge implementation, monitoring, evaluation, and updating to be the weakest components in almost all plans.

Again, on the basis of our content analysis of forty-four state mitigation plans, we would judge the overall quality of most Section 409 plans to be mediocre. A very few plans were good, and a few more had some good elements. Important elements were missing in most plans, however, and much content was descriptive and superficial. It is clear that most of the plans were not intended for implementation in the usual sense but were merely intended to meet requirements necessary to qualify states for FEMA postdisaster mitigation grants.

Recommendations for Making Better State Hazard Mitigation Plans

We conclude this chapter with a set of recommendations for making better state hazard mitigation plans. Whereas the foregoing summary of problems with current plans and examples of effective plan components suggest necessary improvements, we now turn these findings into positive planning guidelines. The recommendations are designed to produce Section 409 plans that are not exercises in bureaucracy but comprehensive, meaningful evaluations of hazard threats and compelling proposals of steps communities can take to mitigate those threats. The recommendations are organized by the components required or suggested to be in plans by the Stafford Act, but they are not intended to replace FEMA regulations or the general guidelines in DAP-12 (FEMA 1990), which should be the principal guide for state and local officials.

Introductory Section

The initial portion of a Section 409 plan should include basic information allowing the reader to identify the plan (author, title, date, state, contact person, and association with specific hazard events); determine its purpose and scope (hazards addressed, components included, geographic jurisdiction covered, and whether it includes an update or annex); identify the participants involved in preparing the plan (local general-purpose and special-purpose governments, state agencies, other organizations, and private-sector involvement); and determine whether the plan has been formally approved or adopted and by whom. A definition of mitigation should be included near the beginning of the plan, not just repeating the FEMA definition but also connecting the definition with the concept of environmental quality and sustainable communities.

Mitigation Goals and Objectives

A clear statement of goals forms the "value basis" of the Section 409 plan. Goals should be articulated clearly at the start of the hazard mitigation planning process so that they may inform the selection of proposed hazard mitigation policies, programs, and actions. Figure 9.3 provides a good initial list of goals to be considered when making the plan. Mitigation goals are best presented separately early in the plan, even before the hazard assessment, to lay the groundwork for the analyses and recommendations to follow. But in any case, goals should be clearly identified for easy reference. Goals should also be explicitly prioritized so that the most important ones can be easily identified and recommendations can be assessed with relation to them. Goals should include a discussion of the level of acceptable risk for the community and the kinds of risks that are or are not acceptable. The goals should pertain to the ultimate ends of hazard mitigation, not the purposes of having a planning document. Objectives should be achievement milestones rather than action milestones; that is, they should measure progress toward achieving a goal rather than completion of some activity or policy. Oregon's plan provided a good example of a goals section, as discussed earlier in this chapter.

Assessment of Natural Hazards

An ideal hazard assessment component of a Section 409 plan should focus on three principal issues: (1) identifying the hazard threat or threats facing the state, (2) assessing the vulnerability to the hazard of people, property, and other community resources, and (3) assessing the most severe threats associated with the hazard on the basis of their likely degree of harm. Figure 9.1 suggests the dimensions of hazards and associated risks that should be considered. This section of the plan should be illustrated with maps, tables, and other graphic elements and should be geared toward anticipating future conditions rather than merely describing past events or describing existing conditions.

Capability Analysis

The capability analysis section should identify and assess the problems with, and effectiveness of, both existing and proposed programs. In addition to providing specific information about current policies and programs, including information about current difficulties in implementation, it should address obstacles to implementation of new programs. A summary chart identifying key legislation, programs, and agencies is a useful feature.

The section should assess government capabilities for implementing mitigation programs at all levels of government and for coordinating mitigation among multiple levels of government (including relevant federal programs, though this is not required by FEMA). Overall, the capability analysis should enable the state to evaluate its political will and update its administrative system for dealing with natural hazards. Connecticut's plan, discussed earlier, contained a solid capability analysis.

Proposed Mitigation Measures

The recommendations of the mitigation plan should be clearly organized, with proposals grouped into coherent strategies. The plan should state priorities for action, reflecting the relative importance and feasibility of each initiative. The strategies and actions should be linked to the goals and objectives and to specific hazard threats, perhaps with a restatement of relevant goals alongside each initiative. The proposals should be forward-looking rather than merely addressing the last disaster. Proposals should be regionally coordinated or statewide, rather than piecemeal, and oriented toward integrating hazard mitigation into normal functions rather than requiring new and cumbersome programs. A summary table should be included showing the relationships of the proposed actions to one another and to the goals and objectives. The plan should present the state's list of criteria for funding Section 404 projects. For each proposed initiative, the plan should indicate the lead agencies charged with implementation, sources of funding, a timetable for implementation, and general comments and policy principles behind the proposal. Useful supplemental information might include model legislation or a legal analysis or budget analysis. Pilot programs might also be proposed and discussed. Massachusetts's Section 409 plan, discussed earlier, was exemplary in outlining proposed mitigation measures.

Proposed Approach to Implementation, Monitoring, Evaluation, and Updating

The implementation, monitoring, and evaluation section should describe a schedule of priorities, timing of actions, responsibilities of agencies or officials, financing mechanisms for proposals, and monitoring and evaluation mechanisms both for general implementation of the Section 409 plan and for specific mitigation proposals. The section should identify the kinds of future state financial resources committed in the plan and the amount of future state commitment in the form of agency staff, budget,

and technical assistance. The state's authority to implement the plan should be clearly evident in the plan in the form of copies of executive orders, new state legislation, administrative rules, and possible incentives for implementation by state and local agencies and sanctions for failure to implement. The plan should also specify a systematic procedure for monitoring and evaluating the implementation of mitigation and for tracking the success or failure of each measure in reducing vulnerability to hazards.

The plan should not be a static document, to be looked at only after a new disaster. Rather, there should be provisions for updating the plan at regular intervals as well as in response to significant events, such as declared disasters. Updating should include reevaluation of goals and priorities and adjustment of strategies and actions. California's Section 409 plan provides a good example of a model implementation, monitoring, and evaluation section.

Additional Recommendations

The Section 409 plan should be internally consistent—that is, all sections should complement one another and contain no contradictions. For example, the goal statements and the analyses of hazards and capabilities should provide the rationale for proposed mitigation strategies and programs.

Again, the Section 409 plan should not be considered an isolated document that is relevant only in emergency management situations. Rather, it should be folded into the state's larger land use, environmental, and capital improvement frameworks. The plan should consider solutions proposed in other planning contexts that might also address hazard problems, and it should consider the extent to which its mitigation proposals might coordinate with and address state issues beyond mitigation, such as wetlands protection. Ideally, integration with other state and local issues would be explicit in either the goals section or the proposed mitigation strategies, programs, and actions section.

Usually, the Section 409 plan should be comprehensive in its coverage, taking a broad approach to identifying hazards and proposing mitigation programs and actions. Occasionally, a narrow focus may be appropriate in a state's particular circumstances, but normally a big-picture, multihazard approach provides the greatest insight into the way policies and strategies interact with one another and with other state policies and programs.

Although the content analyses reported in this chapter and the guidelines we derived from our study speak to preparing a mitigation plan under Section Section 409 of the Stafford Act, it is important to remember that the Section 409 plan should not constitute the state's entire effort to miti-

gate hazards. Rather, FEMA, state, and local officials should be encouraged to formulate mitigation strategies in which the Section 409 plan is but one part of a comprehensive intergovernmental effort that tackles the problem of reducing vulnerability to natural hazards.

Note

1. We counted a component as included if it appeared anywhere in the plan, not just in a section titled with that component's name.

Reference

FEMA (Federal Emergency Management Agency). 1990. *Post-Disaster Hazard Mitigation Planning Guidance for State and Local Governments.* DAP-12. Washington, D.C.: FEMA.

Appendix 9.A: Section 409 Plan Collection

STATE OR TERRITORY	TITLE	DATE	HURRICANE	FLOOD	EARTHQUAKE
1. Alabama	*Hazard Mitigation Plan*	1994	•	•	•
2. Alaska	*State of Alaska Flood Hazard Mitigation Plan*	1993		•	
3. Arizona	*State of Arizona Flood Hazard Mitigation Plan*	1992		•	
4. Arkansas	*Arkansas Hazard Mitigation Plan*	1995		•	•
5. California (earthquake)	*California at Risk: Reducing Earthquake Hazards 1992–1996*	1991			•
6. California (flood)	*Flood Hazard Mitigation Plan*	1994	•	•	
7. Colorado	Under revision; unable to obtain				
8. Connecticut	*Hazard Mitigation Implementation Measures for 1994*	1994	•	•	•
9. Delaware	*State of Delaware Hazard Mitigation Plan (Draft)*	1994	•	•	•
10. District of Columbia	*Hazard Mitigation Plan, June 1994*	1994	•	•	
11. Florida	*State of Florida Hazard Mitigation Plan*	1994	•	•	•
12. Georgia	Under revision; unable to obtain				
13. Hawaii	*State of Hawaii Earthquake Preparedness Plan* (includes hurricane and lava plans)	1993	•		•
14. Idaho	No plan				
15. Illinois	*Illinois Hazard Mitigation Plan of 1993 (Draft)*	1993		•	•
16. Indiana	Under revision; unable to obtain	1995			
17. Iowa	*1994 Iowa Hazard Mitigation Plan*	1994		•	•
18. Kansas	Under revision; unable to obtain	1995			
19. Kentucky	*Hazard Mitigation Plan*	1995		•	•
20. Louisiana	*State of Louisiana Hazard Mitigation Plan*	1991	•	•	•
21. Maine	*State of Maine Hazard Mitigation Plan, 1993 Update*	1993	•	•	•
22. Maryland	No plan				
23. Massachusetts	*Commonwealth of Massachusetts 409 Hazard Mitigation Plan*	1993	•	•	
24. Michigan	No plan				
25. Minnesota	No plan				
26. Mississippi	Unable to obtain	1995			
27. Missouri	*State of Missouri Hazard Mitigation Plan*	1994		•	•

Appendix 9.A (continued)

STATE OR TERRITORY	TITLE	DATE	HURRICANE	FLOOD	EARTHQUAKE
28. Montana	Unable to obtain				
29. Nebraska	*Hazard Mitigation Plan*	1994		•	
30. Nevada	*Nevada's Earthquake Risk Reduction Plan:1993–1997*	1995		•	•
31. New Hampshire	Unable to obtain	1994 Updated			
32. New Jersey	*Hazard Mitigation Plan, DR-973-NJ*	1993	•	•	
33. New Mexico	*Section 409 Hazard Mitigation Plan for FEMA-992-DR-NM*	1993		•	
34. New York	*New York State Hazard Mitigation Plan*	1993	•	•	•
35. North Carolina	*North Carolina Hazard Mitigation Plan*	1995	•	•	
36. North Dakota	*1989 North Dakota Hazard Mitigation Plan, FEMA-825-DR-ND*	1994		•	
37. Ohio	*Flood Hazard Mitigation Plan (Draft); May–July 1990 Flood Disaster*	1991		•	
38. Oklahoma	*Oklahoma Flood Hazard Mitigation Plan and Annex*	1993		•	
39. Oregon (I)	*Natural Hazards Mitigation Plan*	1992		•	•
40. Oregon (II)	*Action Plan to Mitigate Flood and Wind Hazards in Clatsop and Tillamook Counties*	1994		•	
41. Pennsylvania	*Commonwealth of Pennsylvania Hazard Mitigation Plan*	1994–1995 update		•	•
42. Puerto Rico	Unable to obtain				
43. Rhode Island	*State of Rhode Island and Providence Plantations: Hazard Mitigation Plan 1993–94*	1994	•	•	
44. South Carolina	*State of South Carolina Hazard Mitigation Plan*	1992	•	•	•
45. South Dakota	*State of South Dakota Multi-Hazard Mitigation Plan and Annex*	1994		•	•
46. Tennessee	*State of Tennessee Hazard Mitigation Plan*	1994		•	•
47. Texas (I)	*Hazard Mitigation Plan for Areas Affected by Severe Storms and Flooding, 1989*	1995	•	•	
48. Texas (II)	*Hazard Mitigation Plan for Areas Affected by Severe Storms and Flooding, 1990*	1990		•	

continues

Appendix 9.A (continued)

State or Territory	Title	Date	Hurricane	Flood	Earthquake
49. Texas (III)	*Hazard Mitigation Plan for Areas Affected by Severe Storms and Flooding, 1991*	1991		•	
50. Texas (IV)	*Hazard Mitigation Plan for Areas Affected by Severe Storms and Flooding, 1992*	1992		•	
51. Utah	*Hazard Mitigation Plan*	1989		•	•
52. Vermont	*State of Vermont Hazard Mitigation Plan*	1994		•	•
53. Virginia	*Hazard Mitigation Management Plan*	1995	•	•	•
54. Virgin Islands	Unable to obtain				
55. Washington	*Washington State Flood Damage Reduction Plan (Revised)*	1993		•	
56. West Virginia	*State of West Virginia Hazard Mitigation Plan*	1994		•	•
57. Wisconsin	*State of Wisconsin Flood Hazard Mitigation Plan*	1992	•	•	
58. Wyoming	Unable to obtain	1994			

Appendix 9.B. Guide for Describing and Evaluating Section 409 Plans

This appendix contains the protocol used by the research team to systematically describe and evaluate the state hazard mitigation plans. This introduction briefly describes the guide, how it was prepared, and how it was applied. It also contains a copy of the guide. Chapter 9 presents our analysis of the data we obtained by applying the guide to forty-four state mitigation plans.

Description of the Guide

This guide provides a protocol for describing and assessing state hazard mitigation plans (Section 409 plans). The protocol is based on statutory requirements of the Stafford Act; guidelines contained in *Post-Disaster Hazard Mitigation Planning Guidance for State and Local Governments* (Washington, D.C.: Federal Emergency Management Agency, 1990), also know as DAP-12; and generic planning principles. It also draws from the experience of the research team in developing and applying a previous evaluation guide for hazard mitigation elements of local comprehensive land use plans.

The guide contains several sections, which generally represent the components of a plan recommended or required by the Stafford Act and Section 409 guidelines. The first portion of the guide, titled "Identification and Classification Information," requests information about the identity of the plan (title of the plan, author, date of preparation, state, etc.), the scope of the plan (hazards addressed, components included, etc.), the participants involved in preparing the plan, whether the plan was formally approved or adopted, the definition of mitigation employed, and whether any of the plan's features might serve as an example for a model Section 409 plan, among other information.

Part I, "Assessment of Natural Hazards," describes and assesses how well the plan evaluates the natural hazards in the designated area, often the entire state. Questions address the plan's hazard assessment, vulnerability assessment, risk assessment, and data assessment.

Part II, "Capability Analysis of State and Local Hazard Management Policies, Programs, and Capabilities," evaluates how well the plan analyzes existing policies and programs, including problems caused by current policies; opportunities for and obstacles to creating mitigation initiatives; the level of present effort devoted to mitigation; and intergovernmental coordination of programs.

Part III, "Goals and Objectives," determines which, if any, of fourteen different mitigation goals are stated in the plan.

Part IV, "Description and Evaluation of Proposed Strategies, Programs, and Actions," assesses the extent to which each of fifty-four different types of programs and actions is proposed in the plan to reduce long-term vulnerability to hazards. It also evaluates the plan's innovativeness, connection to hazard assessments, whether it is forward-looking, whether its proposals are directed toward the appropriate hazard characteristics (e.g., wind, flooding, or wave action for hurricanes), whether they are regionally coordinated, whether priorities are indicated, and other related issues.

Part V, "Description and Evaluation of Proposed Approach to Implementation, Monitoring, and Evaluation," assesses the plan's proposals for implementing, monitoring, evaluating, and updating the mitigation plan.

Part VI, "Other Aspects and Attributes of the Plan," assesses the integration of the plan with other state and local issues, its readability, its comprehensiveness, its provisions for updating and for participation by various stakeholders, its internal consistency, and the level of future state financial and other resources committed in the plan.

Each of these parts also contains questions asking the plan appraiser to characterize the corresponding section of the plan in a few phrases or sentences and to identify any elements that are noteworthy and could serve as models for other Section 409 plans.

How the Guide Was Created and Applied

The research team examined the Stafford Act and the DAP-12 guidelines to glean criteria for the contents of a mitigation plan. We also incorporated planning principles developed in an earlier study of state-mandated local planning for hazard mitigation. Instructions to the plan appraiser were incorporated into the instrument itself; there is no separate user's guide.

The instrument development process involved the creation of numerous drafts. We used teamwide discussions and applications of draft versions to sample plans to determine the concepts to be assessed and the scales to be used in measuring the quality of specific plan elements. Then, working independently, each member of a two-person team applied the protocol to the same plan and compared their results. We went through several rounds of trial applications, each time pairing different researchers and applying the instrument to different plans in order to refine the protocol and standardize our interpretations of criteria. When we settled on the final version of the protocol, we continued to apply it in teams of two,

resolving differences in interpretation of each plan as we went along, until we were satisfied that we all were interpreting the questions and criteria in a consistent manner. After that, individual researchers assessed the remaining plans.

The results of most of the assessment questions were coded into a database that allowed statistical analysis. Open-ended questions were read directly from the questionnaires as a basis for part of the analysis. Nominations for model elements of plans were collected in a loose-leaf notebook for reference in recommending improvements in state mitigation planning.

The remainder of this appendix consists of a copy of the "Guide for Describing and Evaluating Section 409 Plans," which was completed for each Section 409 plan evalutated in our study.

Guide for Describing and Evaluating Section 409 Plans

Identification and Classification Information

I. Identification

Assigned ID (Two-digit state abbreviation and single-digit number assigned to plan within state; e.g., Alaska = 011):

Evaluators: _____   Dates of Evaluation: _____

Title of Plan (include any report number): _____

Date of Plan (include date of revisions or addendums): _____

Author/Preparer (agency and/or person): _____

Contact Person: _____

Telephone:_____   Fax: _____

Address: _____

II. Scope of the Plan

Hazards Covered (circle all that apply):

Riverine flooding	Fires	Exotic pests/diseases
Flash flooding	Tornadoes	Sinkholes, subsidence
Hurricanes and coastal storms	Dam safety	Radon
Earthquakes	Winter storms	Other (please specify):
Beach erosion	Drought	

Which hazards are emphasized?_____

Does the plan cover (circle one): Whole state   Part of state
If part, what part? _____

Does the plan (check all that apply):

☐ Address a single hazard only?

☐ Address multiple hazards more or less independently?

☐ Address multiple hazards more or less in a comprehensive,coordinated approach?

☐ Respond to a specific disaster (i.e., the basic plan, not the update/annex)?

☐ Include an update/annex in response to a specific disaster?

(Give the name and FEMA identification number of disasters responded to and date of disaster declaration.)

Y N Does the plan contain evidence that evaluation and updating have been performed, "at least on an annual basis to ensure that implementation occurs as planned, and to ensure that the plan remains current" (C.F.R. 206.405[a][4])? (Circle Y for Yes, N for No.)

Y N Is this plan specifically and explicitly a Section 409 plan in response to the Stafford Act (i.e., not a plan that was actually prepared under another process or under other law but is being used as the state's Section 409 plan)? (If the plan was not explicitly prepared as a Section 409 plan in response to the Stafford Act, please explain.)

Does the plan contain the following elements required by the act (C.F.R. 206.405[a])?

Y N (1) An evaluation of the natural hazards in the designated area

Y N (2) A description and analysis of state and local hazard management policies, programs, and capabilities to mitigate the hazards in the area

Y N (3) Hazard mitigation goals and objectives

Y N and proposed strategies, programs, and actions to reduce or avoid long-term vulnerability to hazards

Y N (4) A method of implementing,

Y N monitoring,

Y N evaluating,

Y N and updating the mitigation plan

Y N (updating at least once on an annual basis)

What other main elements does it have that are not listed here?_____

III. Participation in Developing and Implementing the Plan

Y   N   Is there evidence that local general-purpose governments (e.g., cities and towns, counties) participated in developing the Section 409 plan? In what ways were they involved?

Y   N   Is there evidence that local special-purpose governments (e.g., district-level) participated in developing the Section 409 plan?

Identify the types of organizations. _____

In what ways were they involved? _____

Y   N   Is there evidence of private-sector involvement in development of the Section 409 plan? If so, what type of organizations (e.g., insurance associations, trade associations, professional associations) participated? What state agencies participated in developing the Section 409 plan?

Y   N   Coastal planning/management

Y   N   Natural resources/environment

Y   N   Transportation

Y   N   Emergency management

Y   N   Housing/community development

Y   N   Education

Y   N   Health

Y   N   Other (please specify)

Is there evidence of formal approval and/or adoption of the plan by any of the following?

	No	Approved	Date
FEMA regional office	☐	☐	_____
Governor	☐	☐	_____
Other state officials/agencies	☐	☐	_____

(Name the official or agency.) _____

IV. Other Features and Characteristics of the Plan

Y   N   Is mitigation defined in the plan?

Y   N   If yes, does it correspond to the following definition in the Stafford Act? "Hazard mitigation means any action taken to reduce or eliminate the long-term risk to human life and property from natural hazards" (44 C.F.R. 206.401).

If no, write down the definition (and the page number where it can be found).

What components, features, or characteristics, if any, does this plan have that might serve as an example for a model Section 409 plan? (For example, does it have a strong implementation section or some innovative strategies? Include page numbers for reference.) Compile from parts I–V of this instrument.

Part I. Assessment of Natural Hazards

This part of the plan is supposed to be "an evaluation of the natural hazards in the designated area" (C.F.R. 206.405[a][1]). According to the DAP-12 guidelines, this section should identify hazards, their location, and society's vulnerability to them in terms of probability and magnitude. Our purpose is to assess whether and how well the plan does those things. We also want to assess the relevance of this section to the goals and policies sections of the plan; the professionalism of the report (the extent to which sources and limitations are identified and methods are explained); and the inclusion of future conditions as well as existing situations and past events.

Coding ranges from 0 to 3. Code "0" if the type of information or analysis is not addressed or is barely mentioned without presenting any useful information. Code "1" if that type of information is mentioned and discussed in general terms. Code "2" if quantitative information is presented on past experience at least, and for all or most of the relevant parts of the state. Code "3" if the information includes maps, presents future vulnerability in addition to reporting past experience, and generally reflects what an ideal plan would contain.

Code for three types of hazards: earthquakes, riverine and inland flooding, and hurricanes and coastal storms. Record comments and page numbers for reference. Enter codes in blanks after each item number.

Hazard Assessment

1.1 _____ Delineation of location and boundaries of hazardous areas

1.2 _____ Delineation of magnitude of potential hazard

1.3 _____ Delineation of likelihood of occurrence of hazardous event

1.4 _____ Description/analysis of separate characteristics of the hazards (e.g., for hurricanes, wind, high water, and wave action)

Vulnerability Assessment

1.5 _____ Assessment of number of people exposed to hazards, including special populations (elderly, hospitalized, handicapped)

1.6 _____ Assessment of value of property exposed to hazards

1.7 _____ Assessment of number of critical facilities, such as hospitals, bridges, sewage treatment plants, water treatment plants, schools, power plants, and police and fire stations, exposed to hazardous forces

1.8 _____ Assessment of danger from secondary hazards, such as a dam breaking

1.9 _____ Assessment of danger from hazardous facilities (e.g. nuclear or chemical plants) in hazard areas

1.10 _____ Assessment of danger from exposure to hazardous materials in the wake of a natural disaster

1.11 _____ Assessments of shelter demand (number of people requiring shelter) and capacity (number of people who can be sheltered)

1.12 _____ Assessment of evacuation needs and capabilities

1.13 _____ Assessment of environmental impacts of a disaster

Risk Assessment

1.14 _____ Systematic risk assessment, combining probabilities of hazardous events with the likely degree of harm from those events

Other

1.15 _____ Assessment of quality of data about hazards (reliability, validity, spatial specificity, relevance)

1.16 Y N Should any element of this part of the plan be considered as a model Section 409 plan element? If yes, what specific element do you suggest, and on what pages does it appear?

1.17 In a few sentences, characterize the assessment of natural hazards— the approach or style used, strengths and weaknesses, and the overall quality of the assessment.

Part II. Capability Analysis of State and Local Hazard Management Policies, Programs, and Capabilities

This part of the plan is supposed to be "a description and analysis of the State and local hazard management policies, programs, and capabilities to mitigate the hazards in the area" (C.F.R. 206.405 [a][2]). DAP-12 suggests that this section include programs and policies that increase as well as reduce vulnerability to hazards and that it assess government capabilities to address hazard mitigation.

Coding ranges from 0 to 3. Code "0" if the type of capability information is not addressed or is barely mentioned without presenting any useful information. Code "1" if that type of information is mentioned and discussed, with a general description of what governments are doing or an overall list of legislation, programs, or involved agencies. Code "2" if specifics about current policies and programs are presented, with some quantitative information about expenditures or other aspects of the programs. Code "3" if the plan identifies and assesses problems with, obstacles to, or effectiveness of existing programs or if it assesses government capabilities or otherwise represents what an ideal plan would contain. Record comments and page numbers for reference. Enter codes in blanks after each item number.

Hazard Mitigation Programs, Policies, Laws, and Actions in Place

2.1 _____ Federal

2.2 _____ State/regional

2.3 _____ Local

Hazard Mitigation Programs, Policies, Laws, and Actions Being Put in Place or Under Consideration

2.4 _____ Federal

2.5 _____ State/regional

2.6 _____ Local

Which Policies and Capabilities Are Reviewed?

2.7 _____ Emergency preparedness

2.8 _____ Emergency response

2.9 _____ Emergency recovery

2.10 _____ Mitigation

2.11 _____ Identifies problematic development policies that promote private development in hazard areas

2.12 _____ Identifies problematic policies that place public invest- ments at risk in hazard areas

2.13 _____ Assesses special opportunities for increasing mitigation capability

2.14 _____ Assesses obstacles/problems in implementation of mitiga- tion measures

2.15 _____ Assesses present effort (e.g., monetary investment, staffing) by state

Assessment of Coordination

2.16 _____ Federal-state coordination

2.17 _____ Coordination among state agencies

2.18 _____ State-local coordination

2.19 _____ Coordination among local governments

2.20   Y   N   Should any feature of this section be considered a model Section 409 plan element? If yes, which features? (Include page numbers for reference.)

2.21 In a few sentences, characterize the assessment of government capa- bility to address mitigation of natural hazards—the approach or style used, its strengths and weaknesses, and the overall quality of the assessment.

Part III. Goals and Objectives

This part of the plan should contain "hazard mitigation goals and objec- tives." It may be included in the section with "proposed strategies, pro- grams, and actions" because the Stafford Act lists them together. DAP-12 suggests that goals are long-term ends and that objectives are more spe- cific, measurable intermediate ends, which are achievable and mark progress toward goals. Code "0" if not mentioned, "1" if included as a goal. Record comments and page numbers for reference. Enter codes in blanks after each item number.

3.1 _____ A goal to protect the safety of the population

3.2 _____ A goal to reduce loss of private property

3.3 _____ A goal to reduce damage to or vulnerability of public property

3.4 _____ A goal to reduce damage to or vulnerability of lifeline facilities (hospitals, bridges, power plants, etc.)

3.5 _____ A goal to minimize fiscal impacts of disasters

3.6 _____ A goal to distribute hazard management costs equitably

3.7 _____ A goal to reduce government liability

3.8 _____ A goal to improve preparedness

3.9 _____ A goal to improve response to disasters

3.10 _____ A goal to incorporate mitigation into recovery programs

3.11 _____ A goal to coordinate with other hazard mitigation efforts of state and local governments

3.12 _____ A goal to reduce hazard impacts that also works to preserve natural areas, water quality, and open space

3.13 _____ A goal to minimize disruption of economy, social network, and socioeconomic continuity

3.14 _____ A goal of cost-effectiveness

3.15 Other goals (describe): _____

3.16   Y   N   Are priorities among goals and objectives stated (e.g., by ranking) so that some goals are specified as being more important than others? If yes, which are the more important goals?

3.17   Y   N   Are the concepts of "level of risk" and "acceptable risk" discussed (e.g., is it made clear what kinds and levels of risk are and are not acceptable)? If yes, please record the page numbers of the discussion.

3.18   Y   N   Should any feature of this section be considered a model Section 409 plan element? If yes, which features? (Include page numbers for reference.)

3.19 In a few sentences, characterize the goals component of the plan—approach or style used, strengths and weaknesses, and overall quality.

Part IV. Description and Evaluation of Proposed Strategies, Programs, and Actions

This section of the plan should contain "proposed strategies, programs, and actions to reduce or avoid long term vulnerability to hazards" (C.F.R. 206.405 [a][3]). Coding ranges from 0 to 3. Code "0" if the particular type of program is not proposed. Code "1" if the type of action or program is proposed but few specifics are provided. Code "2" if the proposal includes some specifics about what is to be done. Code "3" if the proposal includes cost estimates, where relevant, or model legislation or legal analysis, or if it otherwise represents what an ideal plan would contain. Give a grade of 0, 1, 2, or 3 to the overall categories of measures (e.g., "A. Promote Awareness/Knowledge") as well as to individual measures (e.g., "4.1 Educational Awareness"). Record comments and page numbers for reference. Enter codes in blanks after each item number.

A. Promotion of Awareness/Knowledge

4.1 _____ Educational awareness: provide public information regarding hazard risks and methods of hazard mitigation (e.g., pamphlets, lectures, radio and television ads, billboards)

4.2 _____ Technical assistance (e.g., hazard workshops) for local officials

4.3 _____ Technical assistance (e.g., workshops) for developers or property owners

4.4 _____ Real estate hazard disclosure—voluntary or mandatory: inform real estate consumers (buyers and renters) about the nature and extent of hazard risks to new and existing structures

4.5 _____ Disaster warning and response program: provide public information regarding emergency planning (e.g., what to expect when hazardous events occur, evacuation procedures and time frames)

4.6 _____ Post signs indicating hazardous areas: inform the public of the potential presence of a hazard at particular sites

4.7 _____ Encourage purchase of flood or earthquake insurance

4.8 _____ Conduct research to improve knowledge, develop standards, and identify and map hazards

B. Control of New Development

4.9 _____ Control type and arrangement of land use in hazardous areas

4.10 _____ Subdivision regulations, storm water management, and other standards governing design of new development

4.11 _____ Density transfer provision (e.g., transfer of development rights, cluster development)

4.12 _____ Setbacks or buffer zones near hazard areas

4.13 _____ Laws to protect natural mitigation features (e.g., dunes, wetlands) while also mitigating hazards

4.14 _____ Density bonus for new development: higher development density offered in return for dedication or donation of land in areas subject to hazards

4.15 _____ Building standards: site/building design or construction standards designed to make new private structures less susceptible to hazardous forces

4.16 _____ Tax abatement for using mitigation: tax breaks and incentives to property owners and developers who use mitigation methods for new development

C. Promotion of Retrofitting of Existing Development

4.17 _____ Retrofit private structures: bring privately owned structures into compliance with building standards designed to mitigate hazard impacts

4.18 _____ Retrofit private infrastructure facilities: bring private facilities, such as storm water management systems, into compliance with mitigation standards

D. Acquisition

4.19 _____ Land or structure acquisitions by state: remove private property from the market by fee-simple or less-than-fee-simple acquisition

E. Financial Assistance

4.20 _____ Develop revenue sources for mitigation planning and projects

4.21 _____ Finance mitigation through Section 404 and Section 406 grants

4.22 _____ Provide financial aid to local governments for mitigation planning

4.23 _____ Provide financial aid to local governments for retrofitting of public structures

4.24 _____ Provide financial aid to local governments for acquisition

F. Control of Hazards

4.25 _____ Physical structures to lessen the impacts of hazards (e.g., seawalls, levees, bulkheads, causeways)

4.26 _____ Storm water controls: drainage systems, channelization, culverts, detention/retention basins

4.27 _____ Beach replenishment

G. Protection of Public Facilities and Infrastructure

4.28 _____ Adjust the timing, location, and design of public infrastructure (e.g., water and sewer systems, roads) to limit hazard damage

4.29 _____ Retrofit community facilities

4.30 _____ Hazardproof new community facilities to minimize damage

4.31 _____ Site community facilities (e.g., schools, hospitals, fire stations) to maintain critical services during hazard events

H. Recovery Measures

4.32 _____ Land use change: redefine the allowable use of lands after a disaster

4.33 _____ Building design change: change in predisaster building practices during postdisaster rebuilding

4.34 _____ Moratorium: temporary freeze on rebuilding and other postdisaster construction

4.35 _____ Recovery organization: special task force or other group to manage recovery process in the community

4.36 _____ Postdisaster adjustments to community facilities and public infrastructure (e.g., water and sewer systems, roads).

I. Emergency Preparedness and Response

4.37 _____ Preparedness plan/program

4.38 _____ Evacuation plan/program

4.39 _____ Emergency sheltering plan: provision of safe sheltering to residents of hazardous zones (e.g., specifying schools to serve as shelters, ensuring adequate shelter space for new development)

4.40 _____ Emergency response plans for organizations other than local government (e.g., hospitals, nursing homes, marinas)

J. Promotion of Intergovernmental Coordination.

4.41 _____ Federal-state intergovernmental coordination

4.42 _____ State-local intergovernmental coordination

4.43 _____ Local intergovernmental coordination

4.44 _____ Coordination among state agencies

4.45 _____ Mediation processes to resolve conflicts

K. Other Measures

4.46 _____ Model local hazard mitigation (HM) program

4.47 _____ Identify/appoint local HM officers

4.48 _____ Inspection and maintenance programs for public facilities and infrastructure

4.49 _____ Inspection and maintenance programs for private facilities

4.50 _____ Inspection and maintenance programs for disaster pre-paredness equipment

4.51 _____ Encourage/develop local HM planning

4.52 _____ Encourage public-private cooperation

4.53 _____ Strengthen tracking of HM proposals

4.54 _____ Encourage community participation in the National Flood Insurance Program

4.55 _____ Other Measures (Please describe.)

L. More General Characterization of the Plan's Proposals (Answer yes or no, with comments if useful.)

Are the proposals:

4.56 Y N innovative (original, in contrast to listing familiar and easy measures somewhat unrelated to the specifics of the situation)? If yes, specify innovative features.

4.57 Y N connected to assessment of hazards, to assessment of policies and capabilities, and to the goals and objectives of the plan?

4.58 Y N forward-looking instead of or in addition to addressing the last disaster?

4.59 Y N directed toward the appropriate array of specific hazard characteristics (wind, storm surge, waves, flood level, erosion, liquefaction, secondary impacts such as dam failure, and at specific locations) rather than general hazard types (e.g., hurricanes)?

Do the proposals:

4.60 Y N incorporate regionally coordinated or statewide strategies (instead of a single locality, the boundaries of a single hazardous area, or the area of the last disaster)?

4.61 Y N incorporate dispute resolution processes?

4.62 Y N include an experimental component such as a pilot program or a program to monitor the success of proposals?

4.63 Y N state action priorities that reflect relative importance or feasibility?

4.64 Y N help government agencies integrate hazard mitigation into normal government functions?

What type of plan is it (i.e., how would you characterize the plan)?

4.65 _____ Does it rely more on *police power* (0) or on *incentives* and information (1)? (Enter code.)

4.66 _____ Does it specify *actions* (0), or state *general policy* (principles) to be followed (1)? (Enter code.)

4.67 _____ Is it *output oriented* focusing on accomplishing a strategy or having an effect (0), or *input oriented*, focusing on actions to be taken or policies to be adopted (1)? (Enter code.)

4.68   Y   N   Is it *contingency based?* That is, does it suggest alternative responses, depending on "triggers"?

4.69   Y   N   Does the plan organize measures into coherent strategies?

4.70   Y   N   Should any feature of this section be considered a model Section 409 plan element? If yes, which feature? (Include page numbers for reference.)

4.71 In a few sentences, characterize the "strategies, programs, and actions" component of the plan—what approach or style is used, what are its strengths and weaknesses, and what is the overall quality of this part of the plan?

Part V. Description and Evaluation of Proposed Approach to Implementation, Monitoring, and Evaluation

This section of the plan is supposed to describe "a method of implementing, monitoring, evaluating, and updating the mitigation plan. Such evaluation is to occur at least on an annual basis to ensure that implementation occurs as planned, and to ensure that the plan remains current" (C.F.R. 206.405[a][4]). DAP-12 suggests that implementation should describe how the proposed policies, programs, and activities, including monitoring and evaluation, will be initiated, modified, and continued. Monitoring and evaluation describes how the state will identify and evaluate changes in hazardous conditions, implementation of provisions of the plan, and effectiveness of the plan. Some of these features may be part of the "proposed strategies, programs, and actions" section covered in part IV of this instrument.

Coding ranges from 0 to 3. Code "0" if the type of implementation action is not mentioned, either as part of a separate section on implementation, monitoring and evaluation or integrated into the section proposing the mitigation programs and actions. Code "1" if it is proposed but few specifics are provided. Code "2" if the proposal includes some specifics about who is responsible, target dates by which time action should be taken, and/or how the action is to be financed. Code "3" if the plan rather completely describes a schedule of priorities, timing of actions, responsible agencies or officials, and/or financing proposals and monitoring/evaluation programs or if the plan otherwise represents what an ideal plan would contain as a strategy of implementation, monitoring, and evaluation. Record for comments and page numbers for reference. Enter codes in blanks after each item number.

Implementation

5.1 _____ Provision for the state to coordinate implementation

5.2 _____ Provision for updating the plan annually

5.3 Y N Has updating been accomplished?

5.4 _____ Mediation to resolve conflicts that arise during implementation

5.5 _____ Technical assistance to agencies/governments responsible for implementation

5.6 _____ Financial assistance to agencies/governments responsible for implementation

State Implementing Authority Provided:

5.7 _____ Executive order

5.8 _____ New state legislation

5.9 _____ Sanctions

5.10 _____ Administrative rules

5.11 _____ Other ways to achieve implementation

5.12 Y N Are implementing agencies specified?

5.13 Y N Are costs of programs and actions identified?

5.14 Y N Are funding sources identified?

5.15 Y N Is a timetable identified for implementation?

Monitoring and Evaluation

5.16 _____ Provision for monitoring of hazards

5.17 _____ Provision for monitoring of implementation progress

5.18 _____ Provision for evaluation of success/failure of measures

5.19 _____ Citizen participation in the process

5.20 _____ Provision for updating baseline data

5.21 _____ Provision for updating data that measure criteria implied by objectives

5.22 _____ Assessment of obstacles/problems in implementation

5.23 _____ Development of an ongoing information system, organization, and process for monitoring and evaluation

5.24   Y   N   Should any feature of this section be considered a model Section 409 plan element? If yes, which feature? (Include page numbers for reference.)

5.25 _____ In a few sentences, characterize the implementation, monitoring, and evaluation component of the plan. What approach or style is used, what are its strengths and weaknesses, and what is the overall quality of this part of the plan?

Part VI. Other Aspects and Attributes of the Plan

Coding ranges from 0 to 2. Code "0" if the aspect or attribute is not present in the plan. Code "1" if it is present but only to a limited degree. Code "2" if it is present to a strong degree. (See the individual questions for more complete definitions of codes.) Record comments and page numbers for reference. Enter codes in blanks after each item number.

6.1 _____ **Integration with other state and local issues.** Solutions that address other problems may also address hazard problems. For example, policies that provide wetland protection also enhance flood mitigation.

   1 = Mention is made of integration with nonhazard issues, but integration is vague.

   2 = Nonhazard issues are explicitly integrated with hazard issues in goals and/or policies and programs of action.

6.2 _____ **Readability/legibility.** Is the plan clear, easily understood, and well illustrated?

   1 = Plan is not well illustrated (e.g., it contains no maps or photographs), and the text is not clearly written for the lay public.

   2 = Plan is well illustrated, and text is clearly written and understandable.

6.3 _____ **Comprehensiveness.** How comprehensive is the plan?

   1= Plan is responsive only to single hazards or specific disasters, or it proposes simple, separate actions.

   2 = Approach is comprehensive in identifying hazards and proposing programs and actions.

6.4 _____ **Responsiveness.** Is there provision for updating the plan through reevaluation and adjustment of strategies and actions to respond to specific hazard events and other changes in situation?

1 = Discussion is very general, perhaps even vague.

2 = Specific procedures are proposed.

6.5 _____ **Participation.** Is there provision for participation by all stakeholders through notification, opportunity for active participation or written comment, and public hearings, and is there evidence of consideration of input from participants?

1 = Participation is discussed in a general fashion.

2 = Participation is discussed in detail.

6.6 _____ **Overall internal consistency** of the plan, within and among parts. For example, do the analyses of hazards and capability and the goals relate to and provide rationale for the proposals made in the recommendations section (in contrast to pages of journalistic descriptions of past disasters, collections of unprocessed data, boilerplate/background information, etc.)? Are the same data used when relevant to several elements of the plan?

1 = Cross-references are provided, and no inconsistencies are apparent.

2 = Consistency is demonstrated and is very evident.

Financial resources

6.7 _____ How much and what kind of future state financial resources are committed in the plan?

6.8 _____ How much future effort by state government agencies is committed in the form of staffing, budget, technical assistance, and other resources?

CHAPTER 10

The Hazard Mitigation Grant Program: Scattered Spending

This chapter examines some key implementation results, or "outcomes," of state hazard mitigation efforts that our study found. Specifically, we looked at the types of local and state hazard mitigation projects that had been proposed, funded, and implemented under the Stafford Act. Our study represents the first comprehensive review of these national expenditure patterns for the Federal Emergency Management Agency's (FEMA's) Hazard Mitigation Grant Program (HMGP), also referred to as the Section 404 program. The study covers all ten FEMA regions from 1988, when the HMGP was established, through 1995.

The Hazard Mitigation Grant Program (HMGP)

One analyst has estimated that between 1995 and 2010, natural disasters will cost nearly $90 billion and could claim as many as 5,000 lives in the United States. (Engi 1995). Although many federal programs involve some aspect of disaster relief or natural hazard relief, the HMGP is the one most clearly aimed at reducing such disastrous losses through the solicitation and funding of hazard mitigation projects.

The HMGP was created in November 1988 by Section 404 of the Robert T. Stafford Disaster Relief and Emergency Assistance Act (FEMA 1993). The purpose of the Section 404 program is to assist states and local communities in implementing long-term hazard mitigation measures following a presidential disaster declaration. The key terms from the HMGP mission statement are *assist*, *long-term*, and *following*. The goal is to help

build awareness and capacity at the local and state levels that will lead to long-term results in reducing losses from natural hazards. During the period of our study, however, HMGP funds became available only "following" a major disaster declaration. These goals and limitations must be kept in mind when evaluating the effectiveness of the program.

In response to the Midwest floods of 1993, federal funding for the Hazard Mitigation Grant Program was significantly enhanced by the Hazard Mitigation and Relocation Assistance Act, also known as the Volkmer Act (44 C.F.R. 206, Subpart N), a 1993 revision of the Stafford Act's provisions. Originally, HMGP funding was limited to 10 percent of the estimated federal assistance provided under the Public Assistance (PA) program (Section 406 program) and as much as 50 percent of a project's total eligible costs. Since the Volkmer Act went into effect, on June 9, 1993, the total amount of HMGP funding for a disaster has been based on 15 percent of the estimated federal assistance provided under both the Public Assistance *and* Individual Assistance programs (minus administrative expenses) for each disaster. In addition, the maximum amount of federal funding was increased to cover as much as 75 percent of a project's total eligible costs. Federal funds require state or local matching funds, which can be in the form of cash, in-kind services, or materials.

Eligible applicants include state and local governments, some private nonprofit organizations, and Indian tribes. The types of projects that can be funded cover a broad range of categories, from structural improvements to land acquisitions and education and training. The states are responsible for administering the Section 404 program, and applicants must apply through their state hazard mitigation officer (SHMO).

Although program guidelines state that new project proposals must be submitted for approval within ninety days after FEMA approves the state's hazard mitigation plan for the disaster, it is not clear how strictly this deadline is enforced. FEMA representatives in more than one region have spoken of the need to "close out" disasters (i.e., stop accepting HMGP grant applications) that are several years old. In most cases, it appears that applications continue to be reviewed as long as money is still available.

Building a Hazard Mitigation Grant Program Funding Database

At the time this study was conducted, FEMA did not maintain a central repository of information on projects funded through the Section 404 program—a surprising gap in knowledge about spending under a major fed-

eral policy. Thus, to track and analyze expenditure patterns on a national basis, we had to build our own database of HMGP allocations made since enactment of the Stafford Act in 1988.

We collected data directly from FEMA's ten regional offices and one satellite office (Miami) for all disasters declared under the Stafford Act. Our final database represents HMGP projects for all fifty states and all United States territories. Data arrived in the summer and fall of 1995, with the final updates received and processed in the spring of 1996.[1]

Information on a total of 1,967 project applications was assembled, including approximately $215 million in Section 404 program funds obligated during this period in relation to 178 declared disasters. The expenditure data were summarized and analyzed in terms of disaster type (e.g., earthquake, flood), specific disaster (e.g., Hurricane Andrew), project type, annual trends (by declaration and obligation dates), state and regional variations, and project status. A subset of the data was also used to examine the average length of time between disaster declaration dates and dates when project funds were obligated. Appendix 10.A provides an overview of HMGP applications and funds for all declared disasters during the study period.

Section 404 Program
Expenditure Patterns, 1988–1995

In order to understand the Section 404 program's seven-year spending patterns, we sorted the data by several categories. Looking at the total amounts of FEMA *funding by disaster type* showed that almost 80 percent of both total available FEMA funds and total available Section 404 funds were allocated to the "big three" disaster types—earthquakes, hurricanes, and floods. A look at the disasters for which *no Section 404 funds had been allocated* showed that some $580 million in potential hazard mitigation project funding was not being used.

An examination of the *timing of funding* showed the often long lags between disaster dates and dates of mitigation projects. Research into the *types and dates of hazard mitigation projects funded* showed the high priority given to structural and drainage projects and to acquisition and relocation projects and showed how this priority changed over the seven years of the study.

A look at *state and regional variations in hazard mitigation grant funding* (obligated and pending) showed concentrations in FEMA's Regions IV (Atlanta), IX (San Francisco), VII (Kansas City), and V (Chicago) as well

as the states of California, Illinois, and Missouri. A review of the *top ten disasters* (from the total of 230) showed that they accounted for some 77 percent of total available FEMA funding between 1988 and 1995. An examination of *Section 404 project application processing times* showed an average of two years between disaster declaration date and project obligation date.

These expenditure patterns reveal some disturbing information about the efficiency and effectiveness of the Hazard Mitigation Grant Program. After presenting a review of the data, this chapter identifies these policy implications and suggests a way to reinvent the Section 404 program to overcome its past problems.

Disaster Totals for the Study Period

Information was collected for all declared disasters and HMGP project applications since the Stafford Act took effect, on November 24, 1988, beginning with declaration FEMA-818-DR-NC on December 2, 1988, and ending with declaration FEMA-1047-DR-AL on April 21, 1995, the most recent disaster for which project information was available. Notable disasters that occured during this period include Hurricane Hugo (1989); the Loma Prieta earthquake (1989); Hurricane Bob (1991); Hurricane Andrew (1992); Hurricane Iniki (1992); the Midwest floods (1993); the Northridge earthquake (1994); and Tropical Storm Alberto (1994).

Table 10.1 provides a summary of disasters occurring during this time period.[2] We identified 230 declared disasters that occurred during the study period, accounting for nearly $11.5 billion in total FEMA funding available for the Individual Assistance (IA) program, the Public Assistance (PA) program, and the Hazard Mitigation Grant Program combined. When types of disasters are ranked by total FEMA funding, earthquakes, hurricanes, and floods represent the three categories with the highest funding.[3] Nearly 80 percent of all FEMA funding during the study period went toward earthquakes, hurricanes, and floods.

The number of declarations for a particular disaster type is of less importance than the destructive force of each particular event, which explains the wide variations in the FEMA funding available for different types of disasters. Although floods, with eighty-two events, were clearly the most frequent type of disaster to occur, representing more than one-third of all declarations, they accounted for only slightly more than 16 percent of the FEMA funding available during the time period. In contrast, the six earthquakes that occurred represented only 2.6 percent of all declarations but accounted for more than one-third of FEMA funding. Similarly, the fifteen hurricanes that occurred represented only 6.5 percent of all declarations

Table 10.1. Summary of Declared Disasters, 11/24/88–4/21/95 (FEMA-818-DR-NC–FEMA-1047-DR-AL) (Sorted by Total FEMA Funding)

	Disasters		Total FEMA Funding			Number of Areas Affected		
Type	Number	% Total	Amount Available (IA, PA, HMGP)[a]	% Total Available	Average Funding per Disaster	FEMA Regions	States and Territories	Counties
Earthquake	6	2.6	$4,118,292,700	35.8	$686,382,117	2	2	23
Hurricane	15	6.5	$3,073,326,147	26.7	$204,888,410	5	13	200
Flood	82	35.7	$1,868,183,605	16.3	$22,782,727	9	35	1,402
Severe storm	30	13.0	$854,834,667	7.4	$28,494,489	8	23	519
Flood & Tornado	31	13.5	$522,216,063	4.5	$16,845,679	5	16	876
Typhoon	12	5.2	$350,021,651	3.0	$29,168,471	2	8	47
Fire	6	2.6	$334,054,048	2.9	$55,675,675	2	2	20
Snow/Ice storm	18	7.8	$251,498,872	2.2	$13,972,160	10	17	405
Tornado	19	8.3	$54,745,402	0.5	$2,881,337	5	11	113
Coastal storm	5	2.2	$38,067,314	0.3	$7,613,463	2	4	23
Volcano	1	0.4	$12,454,712	0.1	$12,454,712	1	1	1
Fishing losses	3	1.3	$10,863,000	0.1	$3,621,000	2	3	18
Human cause	1	0.4	$4,167,716	0.0	$4,167,716	1	1	1
Other	1	0.4	$2,303,463	0.0	$2,303,463	1	1	1
Totals[b]	230	100.0	$11,495,029,360	100.0	$49,978,389			

Source: Federal Emergency Management Agency headquarters, Washington D.C.

Note: These are disasters that occurred from the enactment of the Stafford Act through the most recent disaster for which Section 404 program data were available.

[a]IA = Individual Assistance program, PA = Public Assistance program, HMGP = Hazard Mitigation Grant Program.

[b]Totals rounded to 100.0%.

yet accounted for nearly 27 percent of FEMA funding. The differences are clearly revealed by the "Average Funding per Disaster" figures: $686 million per earthquake, $205 million per hurricane, and $23 million per flood.

Floods had the most extensive geographic impact, affecting nine of the ten FEMA regions, including 35 states and more than 1,400 counties. Snowstorms, ice storms, and the "flood and tornado" category (a hybrid category used by FEMA) also had wide geographic impacts. Earthquakes had the most concentrated impact, affecting only two FEMA regions, including 2 states and 23 counties.

Section 404 Expenditures by Disaster Type

Table 10.2 summarizes information on Section 404 program applications and funding by disaster type between enactment of the Stafford Act in 1988 and mid-1995. During this period, a total of 1,967 applications were submitted for consideration, involving 178 declared disasters. The estimated combined federal, state, and local cost for all applications submitted was approximately $939 million. Of all applications submitted, 876 (45 percent) were approved or completed at the time of the study, representing $473 million in total project costs and nearly $215 million in Section 404 program funds.[4]

Types of disasters were also ranked by total Section 404 program funding available for each category. Because the amount of Section 404 funding available is calculated on the basis of IA, PA, and administrative funding, the order of disaster types and variations in both number of disasters and Section 404 funding available closely mirrors the findings for total FEMA funding summarized in table 10.1.

As table 10.2 shows, hurricanes produced the greatest number of project applications (677, or more than one-third of all projects submitted) but accounted for only about 10 percent of the total Section 404 program funds obligated. Floods, which produced 28 percent of all projects submitted (559 project applications), accounted for nearly half of all Section 404 program funds obligated. Earthquakes, with only 7.4 percent of the projects submitted, accounted for about 15 percent of the total obligated. Since the Northridge earthquake resulted in the submittal of only two projects as of the spring of 1995—neither of which had funds obligated—these percentages were expected to change dramatically when the Northridge applications began to be processed.

The pie chart in figure 10.1 shows the percentage of Section 404 funding that went to each disaster category from 1988 through 1995. The

Table 10.2. Summary of Section 404 Projects by Disaster Type, December 1988–April 1995 (Sorted by Section 404 Funds Available)

Type of Disaster	Disasters with Section 404 Projects	Section 404 Funds Available[a] Amount	% Total	Section 404 HGMP Projects[b] Submitted	Approved[b]	Section 404 HMGP Funds Obligated	% Total
Earthquake	5	$503,392,707	47.1	145	83	$31,929,930	14.9
Flood	70	$197,711,651	18.5	559	337	$106,550,855	49.6
Hurricane	15	$129,296,304	12.1	677	159	$21,116,723	9.8
Severe storm	19	$110,233,140	10.3	104	37	$9,604,178	4.5
Flood or tornado	29	$44,980,271	4.2	234	107	$28,055,202	13.1
Fire	5	$31,157,187	2.9	63	55	$6,177,347	2.9
Snow or ice storm	11	$24,548,674	2.3	77	42	$3,739,154	1.7
Typhoon	10	$16,831,811	1.6	45	22	$5,983,402	2.8
Tornado	8	$4,139,356	0.4	25	17	$486,049	0.2
Coastal storm	5	$2,699,088	0.3	28	16	$1,056,484	0.5
Fishing losses	0	$1,416,913	0.1	0	0	$0	0.0
Volcano	1	$1,091,308	0.1	10	1	$70,000	0.0
Human cause	0	$416,937	0.0	0	0	$0	0.0
Other	0	$300,452	0.0	0	0	$0	0.0
Total[c]	178	$1,068,215,799	100.0	1,967	876	$214,769,324	100.0

Source: FEMA regional offices.

[a]Estimates based on 10% of the total Section 406 program funding for disasters occurring in 1988–1993 and 15% of the combined total of Section 406, Individual Assistance, and administrative funding for disasters occurring after June 7, 1993.

[b]Includes projects approved, obligated, and completed.

[c]Totals rounded to 100.0%.

percentage shares of Section 404 funds *received* contrast sharply with the percentage shares of Section 404 funds *available* (see table 10.2). For example, although earthquakes represented nearly half of the total amount of Section 404 funds available, they received only about 15 percent of the funds actually distributed during this time period. Floods, which represented 18.5 percent of available funds, received close to half.

The differences in percentage shares of applications, amounts of Section 404 funds available, and amounts distributed by disaster type are the result of several underlying factors, including the chronological order in which disaster events occurred; the magnitude of disasters; the quality and appropriateness of Section 404 applications submitted; and local, state, and federal policies affecting which applications get submitted and funded. Floods, for example, led all disaster types, capturing nearly 50 percent of Section 404 funding, largely as a result of the Midwest floods of 1993. Had the Northridge earthquake occurred earlier, the shares for earthquakes and floods probably would have been reversed.

Table 10.2 also includes an estimate of $1.07 billion available for hazard mitigation projects through the Section 404 program during the study period. This means that the $215 million in Section 404 funds distributed represents just *20 percent* of the estimated Section 404 funding available for hazard mitigation from 1988 through 1995. Even after subtracting the nearly $433 million in potential Section 404 funding for the Northridge earthquake—which was relatively recent and as of April 1995 had produced only two applications and no grants—we are left with nearly $421 million (39 percent) in potential Section 404 funding that had not been committed to hazard mitigation projects.

The pie chart in figure 10.2 breaks down the status of project applications for the study period. As the chart indicates, 45 percent (876) of the 1,967 HMGP project applications submitted under the Stafford Act had been approved, 37 percent (735) remained pending, and 17 percent (338) had been either denied or withdrawn. Applications categorized as approved include projects that had been approved or completed or for which Section 404 funds had been obligated.

The 37 percent (735) of Section 404 project applications categorized as pending include projects that had been appealed or outsourced to other agencies or were in various stages of the review process. These projects represent an additional $271 million in HMGP grant applications. Even if *all* these pending projects were ultimately approved and the Northridge case was excluded, nearly $150 million in hazard mitigation funds would remain unencumbered and with *no applications pending.* One possible

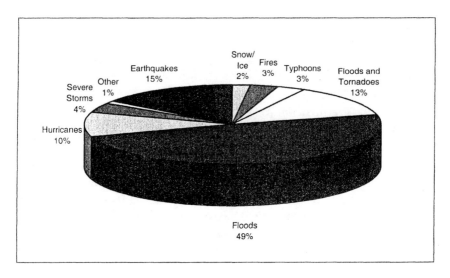

Figure 10.1. Section 404 Funding by Disaster Type, December 1988–April 1995. *Source:* FEMA regional offices.

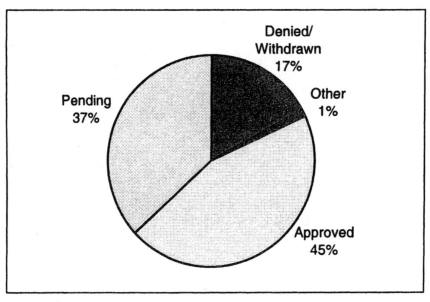

Figure 10.2. Status of Section 404 Applications, December 1988–April 1995. *Source:* FEMA regional offices.

explanation for the 55 percent of projects (1,073) that either had been rejected or remained pending is that many HMGP applications were a poor fit with hazard mitigation purposes and were more consistent with preparedness, response, and recovery objectives.

The average HMGP grant was approximately $245,000, ranging from about $133,000 for hurricane-related projects to $385,000 for earthquake-related projects. Flood-related projects averaged $316,000.

In terms of total project costs, for every $1.00 in Section 404 program funds distributed, an average of $1.20 in additional funds was leveraged from other sources. This figure is largely a reflection of the grant matching requirements of the Section 404 program that limited federal funding to 50 percent of a project's total *eligible* costs prior to June 9, 1993, and 75 percent for all subsequent disasters. For example, for a disaster prior to June 1993, a $100,000 project with $80,000 in *eligible* costs could receive a maximum of $40,000 from the federal government. The ratio of HMGP funds to total project costs is also skewed by the fact that HMGP funds are often distributed in installments. Matching grants come from a wide variety of state, local, and private sources but can also come from other federal programs, such as the Community Development Block Grant (CDBG) program.

Disasters Without Section 404 Program Applications or Funds Obligated

Of the 216 declared disasters with hazard mitigation funding available during the study period, 178 resulted in at least one Section 404 project application. (Fourteen of the 230 declared disasters had no HMGP funding available and are not included in this analysis.) This means that no applications were submitted for 38 declared disasters during this period. Based on the IA and Section 406 PA funding identified, the remaining 38 disasters with no Section 404 applications submitted had an estimated $76 million in potential Section 404 funding available.

In addition, there were 32 disasters that resulted in only one application and 70 that resulted in two to five applications (table 10.3). This means that only about one-third of disasters declared during this time period (76 disasters) resulted in more than five Section 404 program applications. For disasters with only one application submitted, only $2.6 million of a potential $13.8 million had been obligated or set aside for specific projects. For the 140 disasters with fewer than six applications, a total of nearly $553 million in potential Section 404 funding was uncommitted.

Table 10.4 provides a breakdown of disasters by amount of Section 404

program funds obligated for approved or completed projects (excluding the fourteen disasters for which no HMGP funds were available). Surprisingly, 77 disasters (36 percent) had not received any Section 404 funds as a result of project applications. These 77 disasters include 38 that resulted in no applications and 39 that resulted in at least one application. Another 43 (20 percent) disasters had received less than $100,000 in Section 404 funds. Although nearly $215 million in Section 404 funds had been distributed, only 25 disasters (11 percent) had received $1 million or more in Section 404 funds. The five disasters (2 percent) that had received $10 million or more included three associated with the Midwest floods as well as the Loma Prieta earthquake and a July 1993 flood and tornado in Wisconsin. The 77 disasters with no funds obligated had a total of about $580 million in HMGP funding potentially available based on IA, Section 406 PA, and administrative funding levels, including $433 million from the Northridge earthquake alone.

Table 10.3. Disasters by Section 404 Applications Submitted, December 1988–April 1995

NUMBER OF APPLICATIONS	NUMBER OF DISASTERS	% TOTAL
None	38	18
1	32	15
2–5	70	32
6 or more	76	35
Total	216	100

Source: FEMA regional offices.

Table 10.4. Disasters by Section 404 Funds Obligated, December 1988–April 1995

AMOUNT OF FUNDS OBLIGATED	NUMBER OF DISASTERS	% TOTAL
No funds obligated	77	36
$1 to $100,000	43	20
$100,000 to $1 million	71	33
$1 million to $10 million	20	9
$10 million or more	5	2
Total	216	100

Source: FEMA regional offices.

Why have so many disasters produced few or no HMGP project applications? Eighteen of the disasters with no applications submitted (and 34 of the disasters with fewer than six applications) were declared after January 1, 1994, which may have been too soon for applications to have been submitted when our data were being collected, given the time lag between disaster occurrence and project submissions. This still leaves 20 disasters with no applications submitted and 106 with fewer than six applications submitted that were at least eighteen months old when data were collected.

A second possible explanation for the relatively large number of disasters with few or no Section 404 applications and little or no funding is that certain types of disasters are less likely to generate interest in the HMGP. Table 10.5 shows that unusual disaster types, such as disasters resulting from fishing losses, human causes, and other causes produced no applications and thus received no Section 404 funding. One volcano disaster was also declared during the study period, producing very little HMGP activity. These four categories are excluded from the remainder of the analysis.

Tornadoes (43 percent with no applications), severe storms (34 percent), and snow or ice storms (31 percent) were the most likely to result in no Section 404 applications. Except for hurricanes, floods, and the "flood or tornado" category, at least half of the disasters in each category produced three or fewer Section 404 applications. Tornadoes led this group, with 13 of 14 events (93 percent) producing three or fewer applications, followed by 67 percent of typhoons (8 of 12), 60 percent of coastal storms (3 of 5), and 59 percent of severe storms (17 of 29).

Of disasters that did not receive any Section 404 funds, tornadoes led, with 11 of 14 events (79 percent) receiving no Section 404 funds, followed by severe storms, with 17 of 29 events (59 percent); snow or ice storms, with 9 of 16 events (56 percent); and earthquakes, with 3 of 6 events (50 percent). The last column in table 10.5 ranks disaster types in terms of the percentage of events that received less than $100,000 in Section 404 funding. In addition to unusual types of disasters, tornadoes, severe storms, earthquakes, fires, and snow or ice storms were the least likely to receive $100,000 or more in Section 404 funding. Floods and tornadoes, hurricanes, coastal storms, typhoons, and floods were the disaster types most likely to receive $100,000 or more in Section 404 funding. This may be due to the increased likelihood of destruction to public property from these disaster types and to the fact that mitigation measures are more apparent in the wake of these events. The one exception involves earthquakes. Although earthquakes are highly likely to result in destruction to public property and reveal clear opportunities for hazard mitigation, 4 of 6

Table 105. Disasters with Few or No Section 404 Applications and/or Funds, December 1988–April 1995 (Sorted by Percentage of Disasters with less than $100,000 in Section 404 Funds)

Type of Disaster	Total Disasters	Disasters with No Applications		Disasters with 0–3 Applications		Disasters with No Funds		Disasters with <$100,000 in Funds	
		Number	%	Number	%	Number	%	Number	%
Fishing losses	3	3	100	3	100	3	100	3	100
Human cause	1	1	100	1	100	1	100	1	100
Other	1	1	100	1	100	1	100	1	100
Volcano	1	0	0	0	0	0	0	1	100
Tornado	14	6	43	13	93	11	79	11	79
Severe storm	29	10	34	17	59	17	59	23	79
Earthquake	6	1	17	3	50	3	50	4	67
Fire	6	1	17	3	50	1	17	4	67
Snow or ice storm	16	5	31	8	50	9	56	10	63
Flood	76	6	8	36	47	19	25	36	47
Typhoon	12	2	17	8	67	2	17	5	42
Coastal storm	5	0	0	3	60	1	20	2	40
Hurricane	15	0	0	3	20	3	20	6	40
Flood or tornado	31	2	6	10	32	6	19	12	39
Total	216	38	18	109	50	77	36	119	55

Source: FEMA regional offices.

events received less than $100,000 in Section 404 funds. The low funding level for earthquakes is probably due more to administrative delays and the magnitude of the events than to the connection between hazard mitigation and disaster type per se.

A third possible reason for the lack of applications is that 79 of the disasters that resulted in fewer than 6 applications occurred when the maximum federal funding was limited to 50 percent of total eligible project costs (the maximum federal share increased to 75 percent in June 1993). The requirement that 50 percent of Section 404 project funding must come from the state or locality undoubtedly discouraged some potential applicants. A comparison of disasters from the 50 percent era and disasters from the 75 percent era, however, reveals that more than one-quarter of the Section 404 funds available prior to June 1993 were distributed, compared with only 17 percent of Section 404 funds available since then. If the Northridge earthquake is excluded, however, we find that more than 41 percent of all Section 404 funds available during the 75 percent era were obligated. This lends strong support to the notion that the 50 percent matching requirement prior to June 1993 was an obstacle to participation in the Section 404 program.

A fourth probable reason for the lack of project applications after many disasters is that the administrative process moves very slowly, involving many layers of local, state, and federal agencies and organizations. In some cases, officials and agencies are simply unprepared to accept applications and administer a review process for some time after a disaster. In others, such as the Northridge earthquake, the magnitude of the event overwhelms the capacity of hazard mitigation and emergency management staff to solicit and screen applications in a timely manner. States that experience a steady stream of disaster events, such as California, Florida, and flood-prone states along the Mississippi River, inevitably develop a backlog of disasters and projects that cannot all be attended to simultaneously.

A final possibility is that disasters with few if any Section 404 project applications represent missed opportunities by the states and localities where the Section 404 program, or hazard mitigation in general, is not well known or understood. In fact, it can be argued that the lack of applications and large amounts of unused funds represent missed opportunities regardless of the other reasons discussed here.

Significant disasters resulting in fewer than 6 applications include the Northridge earthquake of January 1994 ($432,597,873 in potential HMGP funding) and the Louisiana portion of Hurricane Andrew of August 1992 ($7,039,353 in HMGP funds available). The largest disasters for which no applications were submitted were severe storms in California

Table 10.6. Section 404 Funds Available and Obligated by Disaster Type, December 1988– April 1995

Type of Disaster	Funds Available (Millions)[a]	Funds Obligated (Millions)	% Obligated
Earthquake	$503.4	$31.9	6
Flood	$197.7	$21.1	11
Hurricane	$129.3	$106.6	82
Severe storm	$110.2	$9.6	9
Flood or tornado	$45.0	$28.1	62
Fire	$31.2	$6.2	20
Snow or ice storm	$24.5	$6.0	24
Typhoon	$16.8	$3.7	22
Tornado	$4.1	$0.5	12
Coastal storm	$2.7	$1.1	41
Other	$3.2	$0.1	3
Total	$1,068.1	$214.9	20

Source: FEMA regional offices.
[a]Individual Assistance program and Section 406 Public Assistance program.

in January 1995 ($23,372,528), severe storms in California in March 1995 ($11,446,426), fires associated with the Los Angeles riots, which followed the Rodney King verdict in May 1992 ($10,636,019), and severe storms in Pennsylvania in March 1994 ($9,699,797).

Table 10.6 compares the amount of Section 404 funds available with the amount of Section 404 funds obligated (committed) for each disaster type. The hurricane and "flood or tornado" categories led all disaster types, with 82 percent and 62 percent, respectively, of all available HMGP funds distributed for projects at the time data were collected. Coastal storms followed, with 41 percent of available Section 404 funds obligated. Earthquakes, which accounted for 47 percent of HMGP funds available for all disaster types, had obligated only 6 percent.

Trends in Section 404 Expenditures

The bar graph in figure 10.3 provides a snapshot of overall trends in Section 404 program expenditures by disaster declaration date. It shows the amount of HMGP funding that had been spent on projects for disasters that occurred in each year. As of April 1995, disasters declared in 1989 had received $43.1 million in Section 404 funds, whereas disasters declared in 1993 had received $121 million. Trends by declaration date generally indicate the magnitude of disasters occurring in any particular year. The impacts of large disasters, such as the Loma Prieta earthquake in

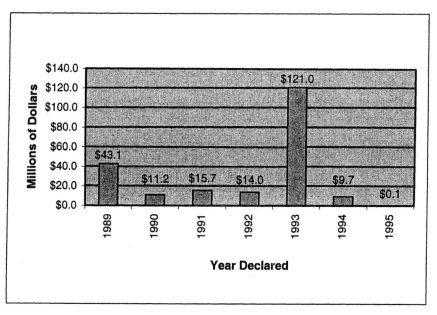

Figure 10.3. Section 404 Grants by Disaster Declaration Date, December 1988–April 1995. *Source:* FEMA regional offices.

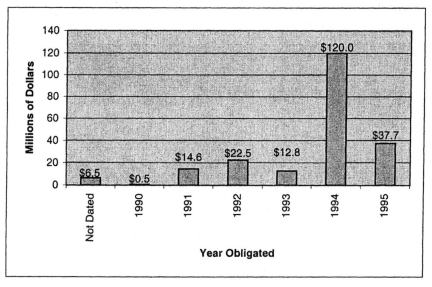

Figure 10.4. Section 404 Grants by Date Obligated, December 1988–April 1995. *Source:* FEMA regional offices.

1989 and the Midwest floods of 1993, are clearly visible in the height of the bars in the graph. The low figures for 1994 and 1995 are due largely to the time lag between disaster occurrence and approval and funding of projects.

The bar graph in figure 10.4 tracks the dates when Section 404 funds were actually expended. The graph reveals the initial lag between the first disasters, in late 1988 and early 1989, and program obligations, which did not appear in any quantity until 1991. The jump in program obligations for 1994 reflects the quick turnaround for projects stemming from the Midwest floods of 1993, and the obligations through April of 1995 suggest an acceleration or a growing accumulation of project applications being processed.

Section 404 Expenditures by Project Type

The next series of figures and tables explores HMGP expenditures by the types of hazard mitigation projects funded. The categories used to classify hazard mitigation projects were drawn from a survey of expenditures conducted by FEMA (1992). Since projects are not classified consistently from one FEMA region to the next (if they are classified at all), the analysis necessitated the assignment of standardized project codes. The following is a summary list of the project categories used (see appendix 10.B for the full list):

1. *Drainage projects,* such as replacement of culverts, replacement of drainage ditches, construction of detention ponds, stabilization of levees and dikes, and construction of ring levees

2. *Acquisition/relocation* of structures and buildings, purchase of single-family homes and mobile homes, and purchase of land in flood or seismic zones or mudslide areas.

3. *Education/training* workshops, development of videotapes, and production of informational pamphlets

4. *Equipment purchases,* such as warning systems, radios, flood gauges, power generators, and computers

5. *Structural improvements,* including seismic retrofitting, floodproofing of sewage treatment complexes and pumps, upgrading of piers and wharves, and repair or reconstruction of fuel storage tanks

6. *Planning programs,* including beach management plans, design of

storm drainage systems, studies of dam and engineering reports, development of zoning and building code ordinances, and development of hazard mitigation plans

7. *Land improvements,* including beach replenishment, and stabilization of sand dunes, bulkheads, and piers

To these seven project categories were added a category for applications to recover administrative costs and a category for unclassified applications. Because administrative and unclassified projects account for a very small percentage of projects and total HMGP funds, they are sometimes grouped together in tables and figures as "other" project types.

Section 404 Applications and Approval Rates for Project Categories

Table 10.7 summarizes the number of Section 404 applications submitted and approved, by project type. The categories with the most projects approved were structural improvements to public and private facilities (234 projects), drainage projects (186), and acquisitions and relocations (171). Categories with the highest *percentages* of applications approved were the education and training and the acquisitions and relocations categories; FEMA approved some three out of four applications for these two categories. In contrast, fewer than half of drainage project applications and fewer than one-third of structural improvement project applications were approved. Overall, fewer than half (45 percent) of all HMGP applications received were approved during the study period.

Table 10.7. Section 404 Project Applications and Approvals by Project Type, December 1988–April 1995

Type of Project	Projects Submitted	Projects Approved[a]	% Approved
Structural improvements	757	234	31
Drainage projects	397	186	47
Equipment purchases	245	96	39
Acquisition/relocation	233	171	73
Planning	100	54	54
Land improvements	91	46	51
Education/training	75	57	76
Other	69	32	46
Total	1,967	876	45

Source: FEMA Regional Offices
[a]Includes projects approved, obligated, and completed.

A comparison of the percentage shares of projects submitted and approved for each of the project types reveals only one significant variation. Whereas structural projects represented 38 percent (757) of all Section 404 applications, they constituted only 31 percent (234) of the projects approved. In contrast, acquisition and relocation projects represented only 12 percent (233) of all applications received but—with a 73 percent approval rating—constituted 20 percent (171) of all projects approved. Although several factors may contribute to these variations, a clear preference is shown for acquisition and relocation projects, which were strongly recommended by FEMA following the 1993 Midwest floods.

Section 404 Expenditures by Project Category

The HMGP awarded approximately $215 million in matching grants during the period 1988–1995. Table 10.8 shows the amounts of Section 404 funds obligated for the nine categories used to classify Section 404 applications. The percentage breakdown for these dollar amounts is depicted graphically in figure 10.5.

Although acquisition and relocation projects constituted just 20 percent of approved Section 404 projects, they accounted for more than half of all Section 404 program funds obligated during this period, representing a total of $123 million. Structural improvements, which accounted for just more than a quarter of all approved projects, received the second largest share of funding, at nearly $54 million. Nearly half of all funds committed to structural improvements ($26 million) went for seismic retrofitting of buildings. Other significant subcategories of structural improvements

Table 10.8. Section 404 Grants by Project Type, December 1988–April 1995

TYPE OF PROJECT	SECTION 404 GRANTS	% TOTAL
Acquisition/relocation	$123,410,320	57.5
Structural improvements	$53,898,116	25.1
Drainage projects	$15,705,830	7.3
Equipment purchases	$7,476,348	3.5
Planning	$6,517,949	3.0
Land improvements	$4,311,516	2.0
Education/training	$1,614,131	0.8
Administration	$1,569,175	0.7
Unclassified	$265,939	0.1
Total	$214,769,324	100.0

Source: FEMA regional offices.

included building improvements ($7.8 million for walls, rooms, etc.); utility improvements ($5.4 million); improvements to storm water and water treatment facilities and pumping stations ($5.3 million); flood-proofing ($2.4 million); and storm shutters ($1.1 million).

Drainage projects received a little more than 7 percent of all Section 404 program funding, representing about $15 million. Equipment purchases represented 3.5 percent of all grants (approximately $7.5 million); nearly two-thirds of this went toward the purchase of power generators, which FEMA no longer considers a proper use of HMGP funds. All other categories received 3 percent or less of funds obligated.

Funding for education and training ($1.6 million) was concentrated on workshops and miscellaneous education and training programs for public employees and the general public (about $1.3 million). Approximately $250,000 of the funds for education and training was spent on pamphlets, brochures, literature, and videotapes. Within the planning and research category, about one-quarter ($1.7 million) of the funds went for preparedness, response, and recovery planning, which are not generally considered hazard mitigation activities. Other significant subcategories of planning and research included loan subsidy or grant programs ($964,000), vulnerability and risk analyses and studies ($880,000), and formation of hazard planning and mitigation programs ($851,000). The most significant subcategory within the land improvements category was

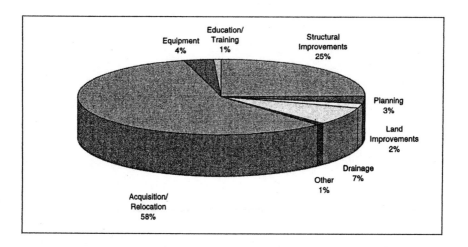

Figure 10.5. Section 404 Grants by Project Type, December 1988–April 1995. *Source:* FEMA regional offices.

brush clearing, controlled burns, and fuel breaks, which accounted for more than one-quarter ($1.2 million) of the category's total.

Trends in Section 404 Expenditures by Project Category

Acquisition and relocation projects led all categories of hazard mitigation projects, with nearly 58 percent of all HMGP funds obligated. A closer examination reveals that more than 81 percent of these funds (nearly $100 million) was obligated in 1994 alone as a result of the Midwest floods of 1993. This level of funding for acquisitions and relocations was unprecedented for any project category. Figure 10.6 chronicles the variations in level of funding for acquisition and relocation projects from 1988 through 1995 and highlights the funding surge in 1994 following the Midwest floods.

Figure 10.7 shows the trends in Section 404 program grants for all project types other than acquisitions and relocations from 1988 through 1995, based on the date funds were obligated. When acquisitions and relocations

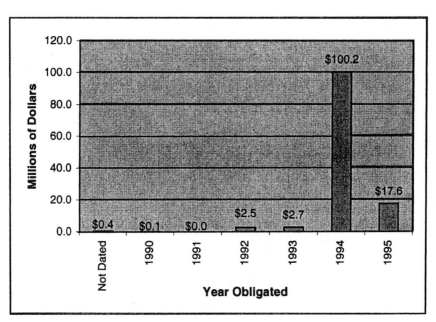

Figure 10.6. Section 404 Grants for Acquisition and Relocation Projects, December 1988–April 1995. *Source:* FEMA regional offices.

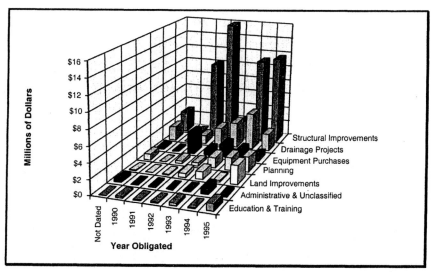

Figure 10.7. Section 404 Grants by Project Type and Year, December 1988–April 1995. *Source:* FEMA regional offices.

are excluded, funding for structural improvements shows up as dominating the program for most years since 1991. Funding of drainage projects grew rapidly from 1991 through 1994 and then declined sharply in 1995. Purchases of equipment, such as radios, generators, weather instruments, and warning systems, peaked in 1991 and then declined, reflecting FEMA's policy of discouraging the funding of many types of equipment (e.g., generators) as hazard mitigation initiatives. Funding for other project categories remained relatively flat, with the exception of planning and research, which grew at a slow, steady pace, reaching nearly $2 million in 1995. Funding of land improvements, which was relatively flat throughout the study period, rose sharply in 1995, reaching $2 million.

Regional and State Variations in Section 404 Program Participation

FEMA operations are organized into ten multistate geographic regions. These regional groupings are as follows, with locations of regional offices in parentheses:

- *Region I* (Boston)—Maine, New Hampshire, Vermont, Massachusetts, Connecticut, and Rhode Island

- *Region II* (New York)—New York, New Jersey, Puerto Rico, and the Virgin Islands of the United States

- *Region III* (Philadelphia)—Pennsylvania, Delaware, Maryland, West Virginia, Virginia, and the District of Columbia

- *Region IV* (Atlanta)—Kentucky, Tennessee, North Carolina, South Carolina, Georgia, Alabama, Mississippi, and Florida

- *Region V* (Chicago)—Minnesota, Wisconsin, Illinois, Indiana, Michigan, and Ohio

- *Region VI* (Denton, Texas)—New Mexico, Texas, Oklahoma, Arkansas, and Louisiana

- *Region VII* (Kansas City, Missouri)—Iowa, Nebraska, Kansas, and Missouri

- *Region VIII* (Denver)—Colorado, Utah, Montana, North Dakota, South Dakota, and Wyoming

- *Region IX* (San Francisco)—California, Nevada, Arizona, Hawaii, the Territory of Guam, the Territory of American Samoa, the Commonwealth of the Northern Mariana Islands, the Republic of the Marshall Islands, the Federated States of Micronesia, and the Republic of Palau

- *Region X* (Seattle)—Oregon, Washington, Idaho, and Alaska

There is considerable regional variation in hazard mitigation activity. Table 10.9 summarizes HMGP activity for FEMA's ten regions from 1988 through 1995. The table identifies the status of Section 404 program applications, the total amount obligated for Section 404 projects, and the total amount of Section 404 funds pending for each region. Regions that participated heavily in the HMGP in terms of number of projects submitted include Region IV (741 applications, the majority from Florida) and Region IX (318 applications, the majority from California). Five other regions each submitted more than 100 applications during the study period.

Region IV accounted for 38 percent of all HMGP applications submitted over the life of the program, followed by Region IX, with just more than 16 percent of the total. No other region contributed more than 10 percent of the 1,967 applications submitted nationwide.

Region IX had the most projects approved (22 percent), followed by Region VII and Region I, each with about 14 percent of all approved projects. Although Region IV represented 38 percent of all applications, it accounted for only 13 percent of all approved projects.

Region IV accounted for two-thirds of all projects listed as pending nationwide, and Region IX held a little more than 10 percent of pending projects. This means that the other eight regions combined held less than one-quarter of the projects listed as pending.

Table 109. Section 404 Program Activity by FEMA Region, December 1988–April 1995

FEMA Region	Status of Projects				Section 404 Funds	
	Submitted[a]	Approved[b]	Pending[c]	Denied or Withdrawn	Obligated	Pending
I	149	122	14	11	$5,223,604	$654,157
II	105	31	57	17	$8,040,357	$34,506,281
III	21	16	0	1	$696,670	$0
IV	741	115	488	135	$7,846,284	$118,454,397
V	155	88	7	60	$53,783,964	$10,080,668
VI	156	93	20	37	$9,437,898	$23,004,704
VII	184	123	54	7	$61,215,848	$24,035,107
VIII	48	30	11	7	$2,740,388	$0
IX	318	189	76	50	$54,087,719	$57,966,492
X	90	69	8	13	$11,696,592	$2,550,008
Total	1,967	876	735	338	$214,769,324	$271,251,813

Source: FEMA regional offices.

[a]Includes some 18 projects not yet classified as Approved, Pending, or Denied or Withdrawn.

[b]Includes projects approved, obligated, and completed.

[c]Includes projects pending, outsourced, suspended, and appealed.

Figure 10.8 summarizes the percentage of applications approved in each of FEMA's ten regions during 1988–1995. Region IV had the highest number of pending projects and the lowest percentage of approved projects, with only 16 percent (115 of the region's 741 applications) approved. This is primarily attributable to the large number of applications associated with Hurricane Andrew that were outsourced to the state of Florida and were still classified as pending (365 of 501 applications submitted by Florida for Hurricane Andrew). Region II was the second lowest, with only 30 percent (31) of its 105 HMGP applications approved, probably due to the fact that all the region's disasters occurred when federal matching grants were limited to a 50 percent maximum.

Regions I and X enjoyed the highest approval rates, with 82 percent (122 of 149) and 77 percent (69 of 90), respectively. Region IX had 59 percent of its applications approved (189 of 318) but had received only two applications for the Northridge earthquake. The midwestern Regions V and VII managed 57 percent and 67 percent approval rates, respectively, significant approval rates given the large number of applications generated by the 1993 Midwest floods, which occurred relatively late in the study period. Regions III and VIII each had fewer than 50 applications.

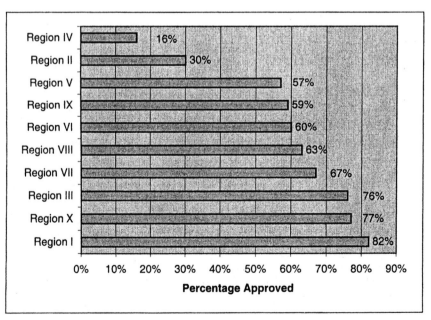

Figure 10.8. Percentage of Section 404 Applications Approved, December 1988–April 1995. *Source:* FEMA regional offices.

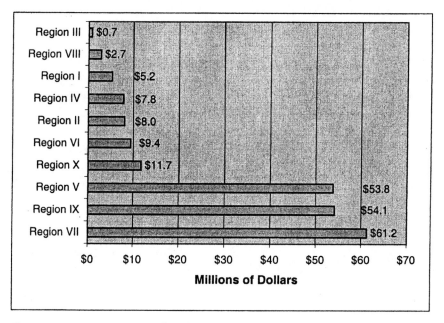

Figure 10.9. Section 404 Funding by FEMA Region, December 1988–April 1995.
Source: FEMA regional offices.

Figure 10.9 summarizes the total amount of HMGP funding received by each FEMA region since the Stafford Act took effect in 1988. Region VII received the largest amount, with $61.2 million (29 percent of all HMGP funds obligated nationwide), followed by Region IX, with $54.1 million (25 percent), and Region V with $53.8 million (25 percent). The remaining seven regions received a combined total of approximately $46 million, or less than one-quarter of all HMGP funds obligated during the study period.

In terms of HMGP funds associated with pending projects (figure 10.10), Region IV represented 44 percent of the total ($118.5 million), followed by Region IX, with a little more than 21 percent ($58 million), and Region II, with about 13 percent ($34.5 million). Region VII, with $24 million, and Region VI, with $23 million, each represented about 9 percent of all pending HMGP funds for applications under review.

The concentration of HMGP funds in certain regions generally reflected high state-level concentrations. Table 10.10 lists the top ten states and territories in terms of HMGP funds received during the study period. California was the top recipient, receiving nearly one of every five dollars in HMGP funds distributed during the period. The four states hardest hit by 1993's Midwest floods—Illinois, Missouri, Iowa, and Kansas—all placed in the top ten and captured a combined share of 41.5 percent of HMGP

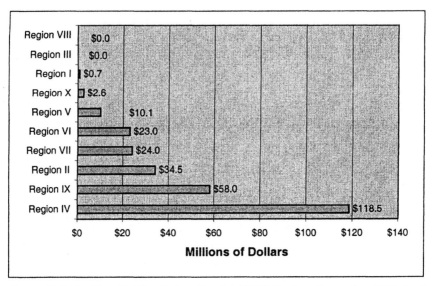

Figure 10.10. Section 404 Funds Pending by FEMA Region, December 1988–April 1995. *Source:* FEMA regional offices.

Table 10.10. States and Territories Receiving Top Ten Shares of Section 404 Funds, December 1988–April 1995

Rank	State or Territory	FEMA Region	Total State Section 404 Grants	% Federal Section 404 Grants
1	CA	IX	$40,023,397	18.6
2	IL	V	$32,703,391	15.2
3	MO	VII	$30,059,085	14.0
4	IA	VII	$17,727,590	8.3
5	WI	V	$11,763,647	5.5
6	KS	VII	$8,616,817	4.0
7	AK	X	$8,010,582	3.7
8	AS[a]	IX	$5,909,500	2.8
9	MN	V	$5,813,910	2.7
10	VI[b]	II	$5,070,460	2.4
Total			$165,698,379	77.2

Source: FEMA regional offices.
[a]American Samoa.
[b]Virgin Islands of the United States.

funds distributed during the period. Two Pacific territories—American Samoa and the Virgin Islands—also placed in the top ten, but they accounted for a combined total of only 5.2 percent of all funds distributed. Together, the top ten recipients accounted for more than three-quarters of all HMGP funds distributed from 1988 through 1995. States with no

HMGP applications or funds included Pennsylvania, West Virginia, Wyoming, Montana, Colorado, Idaho, and Nevada. States with some HMGP applications but no funds included South Carolina and New York.

Selected Disasters

Ultimately, the concentration of HMGP funds in a relatively few regions and states is a function of the number and—more important—the magnitude of disasters involved. Table 10.11 provides background information on the top ten disasters that occurred after the Stafford Act took effect in terms of total FEMA funding available. These ten disasters accounted for an astonishing 77 percent ($8.8 billion) of the total $11.5 billion in funding for all 230 disasters occurring from 1988 through 1995. The table shows that four of the largest ten disasters occurred in California. The $4.5 billion in funding for these four California disasters represents 40 percent of the total for all 230 disasters combined.

Table 10.12 summarizes the status of HMGP applications and funding levels for significant disasters from the study period. These top ten disasters dominated the Section 404 program, accounting for half of all HMGP applications submitted, a little more than one-third of all approved projects, and approximately two-thirds of all HMGP funds obligated from 1988 through 1995. This is despite the fact that four of the disasters (three in California) had yet to receive a single dollar in HMGP funding and three others had received less than 10 percent of the total HMGP funds available. Indeed, for these ten disasters less than 17 percent of the potential HMGP funds available for hazard mitigation projects had been obligated.

As of April 1995, the majority of HMGP funds obligated had gone to the Midwest floods, which accounted for an impressive 82 percent of the Section 404 program funds available for this disaster, and the Loma Prieta earthquake, which had received about half the funds available as a result of the 1989 event. The 82 percent obligation level for the Midwest floods distinguishes them as a truly exceptional case, given the fact that the floods occurred just two years before data for this study were collected. In comparison, it took more than three times as long (six and one-half years) to obligate just 47 percent of the HMGP funds available for the Loma Prieta earthquake. One major difference between the two cases is that when the Loma Prieta earthquake occurred, the maximum federal share for hazard mitigation projects was only 50 percent of total eligible project costs (the "50-50 era"); it was changed retroactively by the Volkmer Act to

Table 10.11. Top Ten Disasters by Total FEMA Funding Available, December 1988–April 1995

Rank	Disaster	Declaration Date	FEMA Region(s)	Areas Affected States and Territories	Counties	Total FEMA Funding Available (IA, PA, HMGP)[a]
1	Northridge earthquake	1/17/94	IX	CA	3	$3,316,583,693
2	Hurricane Andrew	8/24/92	IV, VI	FL, LA	40	$1,635,623,344
3	Hurricane Hugo	9/20/89	II, IV	VI[b], PR[c], SC, NC	113	$1,265,007,425
4	Midwest floods	7/9/93	V, VII, VIII	MO, IA, IL, NE, SD, KS, ND	430	$875,369,897
5	Loma Prieta earthquake	10/18/89	IX	CA	12	$761,545,597
6	Hurricane Iniki	9/12/92	IX	HI	7	$238,165,574
7	Tropical Storm Alberto	7/7/94	IV	GA	55	$197,502,825
8	Floods, CA	2/3/93	IX	CA	27	$196,271,230
9	Severe storms, CA	1/10/95	IX	CA	42	$179,189,379
10	Floods, TX	10/18/94	VI	TX	38	$149,537,479
Total						$8,814,796,443

Source: FEMA regional offices.

[a]IA = Individual Assistance program; PA = Public Assistance program; HMGP = Hazard Mitigation Grant Program.
[b]Virgin Islands of United States.
[c]Puerto Rico.

Table 10.12. Top Ten Disasters by Section 404 Funds Available, December 1998–April 1995

RANK	DISASTER	STATUS OF SECTION 404 PROJECTS				SECTION 404 FUNDS	
		SUBMITTED[a]	APPROVED[b]	PENDING[c]	DENIED[d]	AVAILABLE[e]	OBLIGATED
1	Northridge earthquake	2	1	1	0	$432,597,873	$0
2	Midwest floods	195	145	46	4	$114,178,682	$93,763,476
3	Hurricane Andrew	506	90	365	48	$71,242,198	$5,883,424
4	Loma Prieta earthquake	129	69	35	22	$67,214,303	$31,636,014
5	Hurricane Hugo	101	13	59	29	$48,708,480	$8,108,716
6	Tropical Storm Alberto	17	1	15	1	$25,761,238	$261,951
7	Severe storms, CA (1/95)	0	0	0	0	$23,372,528	$0
8	Floods, TX (10/94)	6	0	6	0	$19,504,889	$0
9	Floods, CA (2/93)	22	5	15	2	$19,309,358	$602,051
10	Severe storms, CA (3/95)	0	0	0	0	$11,446,426	$0
	Total	978	324	542	106	$833,335,975	$140,255,632

Source: FEMA Regional Offices

[a]Includes some projects not yet classified as Approved, Pending, or Denied.
[b]Includes projects approved, obligated, ongoing, and completed.
[c]Includes projects pending, outsourced, suspended, and appealed.
[d]Includes projects denied, withdrawn, ineligible, and voided.
[e]Based on 10% and 15% formulas for determining maximum Section 404 funding available.

75 percent (the "75-25 era") to cover the Midwest floods and subsequent disasters.

The areas affected by the second and third largest disasters from this period, Hurricane Andrew and Hurricane Hugo, respectively, have also failed to effectively tap the potential HMGP funds available. Nearly six years after Hugo hit, less than 17 percent of the hurricane's available HMGP funds had been distributed. Likewise, three years after Andrew occurred, only about 8 percent of available HMGP funds had been obligated for projects. Both disasters occurred while the maximum federal share for hazard mitigation projects was limited to 50 percent of total eligible project costs.

Finally, Table 10.13 summarizes the top ten disasters in terms of the amount of HMGP funds actually obligated. Note that only four disasters from the previous table remain: the Midwest floods, Loma Prieta, Hugo, and Andrew. The other six disasters in the table represent a diverse cross section of disaster types and geographic locations, including two disasters from the Pacific territories. What is most striking about these ten disasters is that they represent only about one-third of all HMGP funds available and 45 percent of approved projects, but they account for an impressive 83 percent of all HMGP funds distributed from 1988 through April 1995. More than half of all HMGP funds available for these disasters had been obligated.

Section 404 Application Processing Time

The data collected on declared disasters and HMGP projects included a variety of dates that allowed us to evaluate the length of time involved in developing, reviewing, and approving hazard mitigation projects under the Stafford Act. Nearly all the approved projects (865 of 876) identified the date on which funds were obligated for an approved project. These projects also represented all ten FEMA regions. In cases in which multiple dates were identified (most likely recording when each installment of funds was distributed), the earliest date was considered the "obligation date."

Obligation dates were compared with their respective disaster declaration dates to gauge how much time typically passed from the time a disaster occurred to the point when projects were funded. The average time from declaration date to obligation date came out to 743 days, or just more

Table 10.13. Top Ten Disasters by Section 404 Funds Obligated, December 1988–April 1995

Rank	Disaster	Declaration Date	Status of Section 404 Projects				Section 404 Funds	
			Submitted[a]	Approved[b]	Pending[c]	Denied[d]	Available[e]	Obligated
1	Midwest floods	6/10/93	195	145	46	4	$114,178,682	$93,763,476
2	Loma Prieta earthquake	10/18/89	129	69	35	22	$67,214,303	$31,636,014
3	Flood and tornado, WI	7/2/93	7	5	0	2	$8,235,263	$11,305,493
4	Hurricane Hugo	9/20/89	101	13	59	29	$48,708,480	$8,108,716
5	Severe storm, AK	9/13/94	4	4	0	0	$7,075,594	$7,618,331
6	Hurricane Andrew	8/24/92	506	90	365	48	$71,242,198	$5,883,424
7	Hurricane, AS[f]	12/14/95	19	17	2	0	$2,673,775	$5,879,500
8	Flood and tornado, MN	6/11/93	19	11	3	5	$9,316,392	$5,567,718
9	Fire, CA	10/28/93	47	41	2	4	$11,059,534	$4,941,836
10	Typhoon, GU[g]	8/28/92	4	2	0	2	$2,279,854	$3,500,000
	Total		1,031	397	512	116	$341,984,075	$178,204,508

Source: FEMA Regional Offices

[a] Includes some projects not yet classified as Approved, Pending, or Denied.
[b] Includes projects approved, obligated, ongoing, and completed.
[c] Includes projects pending, outsourced, suspended, and appealed.
[d] Includes projects denied, withdrawn, ineligible, and voided.
[e] Based on 10% and 15% formulas for determining maximum Section 404 funding available.
[f] American Samoa.
[g] Guam.

than two years. Thus, it typically takes two years to solicit, prepare, collect, review, and fund HMGP projects. This means that if it normally takes six to nine months for applications to be solicited and prepared, another fifteen to eighteen months passes after applications are submitted for review. Typically, state officials review applications before sending them to the FEMA regional office, which may then forward them to FEMA's headquarter branches for specialized reviews.

Five FEMA regions also provided dates when a number of projects were received in their offices. Calculations for these 450 projects yielded an average of 196 days, or just more than six months, from the date an application was received until the date on which funds were obligated. What is not clear is how many other offices an application had to pass through before making its way through FEMA's regional offices.

A small subset of 49 completed projects from two regions also indicated the date when the project was completed. Since the date obligated simply represents the date on which federal funds are made available for a project, we compared the project completion dates with the dates that funds were obligated to gauge how much longer it typically took to carry out a funded project. The average time from the date when funds were obligated to the date when a project was completed was 568 days, or a little more than a year and a half after funds became available. Adding this to the two years typically required to get a HMGP project funded suggests that it could take *three and one-half years,* on average, to complete a hazard mitigation project once a disaster has occurred.

It is important to note that none of these time factors takes into account the 735 projects (37 percent of all Section 404 applications) that were still pending or the time involved for projects that were denied. The figures pertain only to projects that either had HMGP funds obligated or were completed at the time the study was conducted.

Policy Implications

Our analysis of expenditure patterns in the Hazard Mitigation Grant Program highlights several points of interest to hazard mitigation policy makers. These include missed opportunities for carrying out projects, confusion over the use of Section 406 public assistance funds and Section 404 mitigation project funds, long periods of maintaining disaster funding on the books, geographic concentrations of disasters, inconsistent shifts in project priorities, and consequences of bureaucratic red tape and procedural delays.

Missed Opportunities

First among the policy issues is the very large amount of funds available for hazard mitigation that have gone wanting. Between 1988 and April 1995, more than $1 billion in HMGP funding became available, but only about $215 million (20 percent) was actually obligated. Particularly perplexing are the large number of disasters that generated few or no HMGP applications. Although some disasters occurred too recently to have resulted in many applications, projects with small numbers of applications and small amounts of funds obligated are spread throughout the life of the program. The challenge of coming up with a 50 percent match prior to June 1993 provides some explanation, but there remains a great surplus of unused funds from both the 50-50 era and the 75-25 era.

A more likely culprit is the slow administrative process for handling HMGP applications, which involves many layers of local, state, and federal agencies and organizations and a complex, often highly technical, review process that relies on specialists.

Another probable obstacle is the low level of awareness of the HMGP, or of hazard mitigation in general, at the state and local levels. Even where sufficient awareness exists, the demands of the much larger Individual Assistance (IA) and Public Assistance (PA) programs can easily overwhelm emergency management staff, leaving little capacity to pursue hazard mitigation initiatives. Recalling the old adage that "an ounce of prevention is worth a pound of cure," the inevitable focus on disaster relief efforts can lead to costly oversight of hazard mitigation opportunities.

Regardless of the reasons behind apparent low levels of participation in the HMGP, the dearth of applications and the enormous amount of unclaimed funds represent missed opportunities for the communities and states that have not mobilized the resources necessary to leverage federal funds for hazard mitigation. Since HMGP funds can be applied to a wide variety of hazard mitigation activities and are not bound to disaster-specific applications, there are undoubtedly endless opportunities to mitigate future losses of life and property that have been overlooked. Clearly, there is a need to enlist more proactive individuals and agencies in state hazard mitigation, including full-time state hazard mitigation officers, who can identify the opportunities and champion the applications through a sometimes arduous development and review process.

The Section 404/406 Muddle

Muddying the hazard mitigation arena is the umbrella of federal assistance programs that appear to overlap and conflict with one another. Potential

applicants may be unsure which program, if any, is appropriate for various types of hazard projects, and they often get conflicting advice when attempting to navigate through the web of programs. Since those closest to potential projects, often local officials or planners, may not be familiar with the HMGP or even the term *hazard mitigation,* getting potential projects into the HMGP pipeline often depends on a chance encounter with a state or federal official.

A principal area of confusion for applicants and administrators alike appears to involve the relationship between the HMGP (Section 404) and the PA (Section 406) program. The HMGP differs from the PA program in that it can fund mitigation measures to protect public or private property. According to FEMA's HMGP brochure, for public property damaged in the disaster, it is more appropriate to fund mitigation measures under Section 406 before applying to the HMGP. In states where the PA and HMGP administrators work closely together or where they happen to be the same person, funding of some mitigation through the PA program is actively pursued. The data collected for this study, however, revealed that many mitigation projects involving public property continue to be funded through the HMGP.

Funding of public property and infrastructure improvements through the HMGP diminishes hazard mitigation resources in two ways. First, it reduces the amount of money available for supporting other hazard mitigation projects. Second, it reduces the estimated PA program funds, which serve as the basis for calculating the overall amount of HMGP funding available.

The amount of unused HMGP funding available, however, suggests that lack of funding is not the primary problem. Instead, the vague domains of various disaster relief programs combined with the historically lower profile and resources of the HMGP may be inhibiting broader participation in the program.

Never-Ending Disasters

After we identified hundreds of millions of dollars in unclaimed HMGP monies from disasters that occurred as long ago as 1988, another question emerged: When does the application process cease? Some FEMA regional offices are beginning to set horizons for closing out older disasters, most of which date from the 50-50 era of federal matching funds, when it was more challenging to piece together project funding. Scores of disasters with available funds remain open, however, creating an administrative and budgeting quagmire. Since HMGP mitigation projects need not be disaster

specific, there is nothing to prevent a wide variety of hazard mitigation projects from being financed through an older disaster's HMGP funds. Seismic retrofitting of structures, for example, can be (and has been) funded with HMGP monies resulting from a snow and ice storm, consistent with a multihazard mitigation strategy. There have also been cases in which older disasters with remaining HMGP funds suddenly receive an influx of applications. Part of the problem is the political aspect of closing out disasters while funds are, theoretically, still available.

Resource Mismatches

Given the heavy concentration of hazard mitigation funding in a relatively small number of regions and states, it would be rational to allocate the most FEMA resources to regions where the majority of disasters occur. If one were to base such a scheme on the distribution of HMGP funding from 1988 through 1995, about 29 percent of FEMA's staff would be based in Region VII, 25 percent in Region IX, 25 percent in Region V, and the other 21 percent divided up among the remaining seven regions. Although such a scheme may seem unreasonable, it serves to highlight the heavily unbalanced HMGP workload from one region to the next.

The heavy concentration of HMGP funds in three disaster-prone regions brings up an additional concern with mismatched resources. If a primary goal of the HMGP is to act as a catalyst and help states and localities plan for and implement hazard mitigation, then concentrating funds in the states and regions most experienced in disaster events (and perhaps best educated and prepared with respect to hazard mitigation) might result in neglect of less experienced and prepared states and regions. Running contrary to this is the belief that more hazard mitigation funds are needed where more disasters have occurred historically.

Despite the apparent propensity for disasters to occur more often in some states and regions, the location of the next ten largest disasters is at best uncertain. What is certain is that the magnitude of one or more of these events will overwhelm local, state, and federal officials. Perhaps the best that can be done is to maintain permanent, flexible staffing at the federal level that can be focused where the need is greatest. Although this arrangement may be manageable on the national level, it is less realistic on the state and local levels. Thus, federal assistance may be required at both the regional administrative level and the state and local levels, where administrative capacities are more limited.

Shifting Project Priorities

Our review of HMGP funding by project type revealed clear preferences for acquisition and relocation projects, which unquestionably represent a permanent form of mitigation that averts future loss of life or property at specific locations. FEMA's preferences for other types of hazard mitigation projects are less clear. Trends in HMGP funding revealed many types of projects that were inconsistently funded across time and across regions, particularly projects involving equipment such as power generators, warning systems, and radio and communications equipment. Although officials at FEMA's regional offices want to avoid dictating what types of projects get funded, preferences need to be clarified. This will help to prevent undesirable projects from entering the HMGP pipeline and will reduce federal, state, and local tensions concerning project eligibility.

Our examination of funding of project types also revealed what would have to be described as a weak commitment to hazard mitigation education and training (receiving less than 1 percent of all HMGP funds) as well as to planning and research (3 percent of all funds). Funding objectives for hazard mitigation planning and research were also puzzling, as more than a quarter of these funds went for preparedness, response, and recovery planning. Although there is a clear preference for real-world projects over studies and reports in the HMGP, it could be argued that hazard mitigation is best achieved through a well-informed and educated populace. Acquisition of homes in a floodplain can be seen as mitigation only if new homes are not built in hazardous areas elsewhere, where the same mistakes can be repeated.

The large percentage of applications that were denied or withdrawn or that remained pending (more than half of all applications) highlights a larger problem—that of soliciting quality projects with a clear hazard mitigation purpose. States and localities regularly submit HMGP applications that deal with emergency preparedness, response, and recovery but have little to do with mitigating hazards. As FEMA increases its emphasis on hazard mitigation, it will need to continue to educate emergency management staff and officials at the state and local levels if it hopes to encourage the submission of HMGP applications with clear hazard mitigation objectives.

Too Much Process

Our analysis of the time typically required to solicit, develop, review, and act on HMGP applications highlights a common complaint—that it takes far too long for projects to be funded. The most complete information from

the study showed that it takes an average of two years from a disaster's declaration date to the time when a project is funded. This means that many projects take longer than two years to get funded. Add to this another eighteen months typically needed to carry out a project once it has been funded, and applicants are looking at a process that, on average, will require three and a half years to complete. This may not be an inordinate amount of time to carry out the seismic retrofitting of a major public facility, but a large portion of HMGP projects are considerably less ambitious and technical.

The problem is not FEMA's alone. Those regions that tracked the time it took to process HMGP applications averaged about six months for a typical application. Yet the process often involves multiple reviews by administrative and technical staff in agencies at the state, regional, and federal levels. Applicants can easily lose track of an application's progress and become frustrated. Local officials who become advocates for projects can lose credibility when their applications drag on for a number of years. Reducing the red tape associated with HMGP applications should be high on the priority list of any policy changes envisioned for the program.

The Section 404 Program in Context

Given the amount of funds that had not been obligated during the period of our study, the question arises as to whether the HMGP is *over*funded. In comparison with FEMA's total funding for disaster relief programs, this would not appear to be the case. The $1.07 billion available for hazard mitigation efforts represents less than 10 percent of the $11.5 billion in FEMA funding for IA, PA, HMGP, and administrative expenses for the first seven years under the Stafford Act.

It has been argued, however, that the HMGP was intended as a catalyst for local and state hazard mitigation efforts, not as a bottomless money pit to bankroll mitigation on a nationwide basis. Although this study found that the HMGP has considerable amounts of unused funds available for projects, these resources appear meager when compared with the magnitude of losses from natural disasters in the past and projected into the future.

The HMGP spends an average of just $31 million annually. If all the HMGP funds available between 1988 and 1995 had been expended, this figure would jump to an average of $153 million annually. In contrast, the total public and private losses for a single disaster of the magnitude of the Northridge earthquake can reach $20 billion or more. In addition, as mentioned at the beginning of this chapter, between 1995 and 2010 the costs

of natural disasters may approach $90 billion, with the loss of as many as 5,000 lives (Engi 1995). Thus, put in the context of the catastrophic losses it is attempting to mitigate, HMGP funding appears modest at best.

Reinventing the Hazard Mitigation Grant Program

The great need for hazard mitigation combined with the current underutilization of the HMGP suggest a need to consider alternative models for the program. This final section suggests one such alternative, based on the way metropolitan planning organizations currently preidentify and prioritize potential highway improvement projects. The reader should note that the regions discussed in this section are regions *within* states (substate regions), not multistate FEMA regions.

Most policy reviews of the hazard mitigation program emphasize the need for the following:

- Predisaster (proactive) hazard mitigation initiatives (plans and project identification)

- Coordinated, region-wide mitigation planning (again, by this we mean substate regions, not multistate FEMA regions)

- Local hazard mitigation planning and project identification and additional resources (funds, staff, expertise) to carry out these activities

- A stronger connection between state hazard mitigation plans (and planning) and hazard mitigation projects

- Greater local participation in state hazard mitigation planning

- Identification of better applications of hazard mitigation projects

- Accelerated identification, approval, and funding of hazard mitigation projects

One possibility for addressing these needs would be the creation of a regional (substate) procedure for identifying and prioritizing hazard mitigation projects. The model could be based on the process used for identifying highway improvement projects carried out by metropolitan planning organizations (MPOs). Along these lines, an existing regional organization would be designated that would solicit and prioritize hazard mitigation projects from local governments. Clear guidelines would be established for the submission, review, and prioritization of projects. The list of projects

could be updated annually or biannually, serving as an incremental update of the state hazard mitigation plan.

Where a regional organization doesn't currently exist, the MPOs themselves might help initiate the process by bringing together emergency management personnel from state, regional, and local levels. This process should not involve the creation of another level of review or governance. The regional panel would consist of local, regional, and state representatives assembled to collectively rank proposals. No permanent governing body would be required. With preidentified, prioritized projects in hand, a state hazard mitigation council, rather than FEMA's regional office, could then conceivably act as the final approval body, thus eliminating another level of review.

Following a disaster, the list of projects would be supplemented by new projects identified, and the entire list would then be reprioritized. High prioritization would not ensure approval, but low prioritization would act as de facto rejection if available funds have been exhausted by higher-priority projects. Although the MPO priority-setting process for highways does not guarantee funding of projects, it does act as a powerful incentive for local communities and regions to get organized and act cooperatively in developing a list of projects. For hazard mitigation, this incentive would be much greater if predisaster project funds were made available on a regular basis so that project sponsors would not be waiting (indefinitely) for a disaster to occur in order to have any hopes of funding.

Advantages of adopting the regional hazard priority-setting model include the following:

- Projects are preidentified, allowing for greater focus on hazard mitigation priorities during the postdisaster period and less scrambling to solicit, develop, review, and judge applications.

- A regional focus encourages cooperative efforts among state, regional, and local governments. This is particularly important for local governments, which typically lack the staffing, funds, and expertise needed to develop hazard mitigation applications. Currently, local governments must seek out these resources on an ad hoc basis as the need arises, each one stumbling through the process in relative isolation and repeating the mistakes made by others.

- Regional coordination of project identification, application development, and prioritization also allows the state hazard mitigation officer to focus on carrying out high-priority projects (instead of attempting to personally assist individual localities), coordinating planning and projects, and—perhaps most important at the state level—educating

regional organizations about hazard mitigation and best mitigation practices and planning.

- Making preidentification of projects a regular, cooperative, region-wide activity and part of a regular updating of the state Section 409 hazard mitigation plan strengthens the link between HMGP projects and Section 409 hazard mitigation planning and more directly involves local participation. The incentive for preidentifying projects also encourages regions and localities to develop better local hazard assessment information (plans, GIS databases, studies) to support their projects. There could be a requirement that projects selected be consistent with local land use plans.

- More regional-local participation, incentives to preidentify projects on a regular basis, and freeing up of the state hazard mitigation officer for more education activities should increase knowledge of hazard mitigation and lead to more appropriate hazard mitigation projects with better chances of swift approval. A predisaster focus on hazard mitigation projects also minimizes the confusion of multiple programs competing for attention immediately after a disaster.

- The process of soliciting, developing, reviewing, and judging hazard mitigation projects, which currently takes place in the often chaotic wake of disasters, would be more efficient. When projects are preidentified and preevaluated, the postdisaster period is more manageable, enabling officials to focus on identifying new projects and adjusting the prioritization of projects.

Three further aspects need to be considered. First, the regional prioritization of projects can serve as a first round of approval. Although all projects can be sent up to the state level, prioritization provides decision makers with locally validated criteria (through local participation on the regional review panel) for choosing among projects if applications exceed resources. Currently, this occurs at the state level, and the state then passes applications on to FEMA regional offices for final approval.

Second, if (as proposed) HMGP funds were put under state control through some type of block grant arrangement whereby states become certified by FEMA regional offices, this would position both final project approval and funding at the state level. This arrangement could greatly accelerate the obligation of funds once projects are approved.

Third, a variety of specialized reviews currently take place throughout FEMA's system of regional offices and federal departments, such as benefit-cost analysis and environmental impact assessment. Administration of

these reviews is subject to federal legislation and cannot be easily altered, and yet it represents a known bottleneck in the HMGP review process. Although the topic is beyond the scope of this policy recommendation, we strongly recommend that these review processes continue to be decentralized by FEMA to FEMA regional offices and perhaps to the state level—through consultants if feasible—to reduce application review time.

In speaking with HMGP participants and administrators, we found that although there was dissatisfaction with the way the program currently operates, there was unanimous affirmation of its importance. The funding the HMGP provides for hazard mitigation projects is a catalyst without which the vast majority of projects would never move forward. Thus, any efforts to improve the program will have a far-reaching influence on the implementation of hazard mitigation nationwide.

Notes

1. Data for Region IV (the southeastern United States, including Florida) were updated in the fall of 1995; data for Region X (the Pacific Northwest) were received in the fall of 1995; data for Region IX (including California, Arizona, and the Pacific territories) were updated in the spring of 1996.
2. At the time data were collected, no project data were available for any disaster declared after April 21, 1995, including Hurricane Erin, Hurricane Marilyn, and Hurricane Opal.
3. The disaster types listed are taken from FEMA's Disaster Automated Reporting and Information System (DARIS).
4. The amount of Section 404 funds available was estimated on the basis of formulas in the 1988 Stafford Act, as revised by the 1993 Volkmer Act.

References

Engi, Dennis. 1995. *Historical and Projected Costs of Natural Disasters*. Albuquerque, N.M.: Sandia National Laboratories.

FEMA (Federal Emergency Management Agency). 1992. *Project Survey Results, Hazard Mitigation Grant Program*. Washington, D.C.: FEMA.

———. 1993. *Hazard Mitigation Grant Program*. Washington, D.C.: FEMA.

Summary of HMGP Applications and Funds for All Declared Disasters by Disaster Type, 11/24/88–4/21/95 (FEMA-818-DR-NC–FEMA-1047-DR-AL)

Appendix 10.A. Summary of HMGP Applications and Funds for All Declared Disasters by Disaster Type, 11/24/88–4/21/95 (FEMA-818-DR-NC–FEMA-1047-DR-AL)

Disaster Number	FEMA Region	State or Territory	Date Declared	Total FEMA Funding Available (IA, PA, HMGP)[a]	HMGP Applications					HMGP Funds			Counties Affected
					Submitted	Approved[b]	% Approved	Pending[c]	Denied/ Withdrawn	Available[d]	Obligated	% Obligated[e]	
Floods and Tornadoes													
828	VI	TX	5/19/89	$29,224,607	11	8	73	0	3	$1,634,842	$1,249,026	76	87
856	IV	AL	2/17/90	$10,072,347	4	3	75	0	1	$682,454	$254,887	37	27
857	IV	GA	2/23/90	$13,073,527	7	2	29	0	5	$924,198	$796,538	86	38
859	IV	MS	2/28/90	$7,910,599	6	1	17	3	2	$599,747	$235,672	39	35
861	IV	AL	3/21/90	$32,307,125	10	4	40	0	6	$1,891,416	$284,147	15	33
863	VI	TX	5/2/90	$22,406,950	14	9	64	0	5	$1,285,805	$1,050,598	82	64
866	VI	OK	5/18/90	$12,339,285	27	15	56	0	12	$1,025,561	$951,992	93	39
869	V	IN	6/4/90	$8,356,065	1	1	100	0	0	$585,238	$401,000	69	30
870	V	OH	6/6/90	$15,148,638	20	1	5	0	19	$884,480	$653,600	74	25
871	V	IL	6/22/90	$6,503,974	3	3	100	0	0	$541,258	$415,181	77	16
873	VII	NE	7/4/90	$3,992,602	4	4	100	0	0	$317,881	$293,647	92	23
874	V	WI	7/13/90	$6,164,804	11	1	9	1	9	$422,146	$49,980	12	17
888	IV	MS	1/3/91	$2,299,872	2	0	0	1	1	$103,767	$0	0	12
900	VI	TX	4/12/91	$16,468,224	10	5	50	0	4	$254,171	$191,969	76	5
904	VI	LA	5/3/91	$25,464,185	2	2	100	0	0	$1,283,908	$642,180	50	38
906	IV	MS	5/17/91	$8,783,303	5	0	0	4	1	$642,114	$0	0	42
946	V	MN	6/26/92	$5,620,750	6	0	0	0	6	$534,257	$0	0	10
948	VIII	SD	7/2/92	$1,073,825	5	5	100	0	0	$97,494	$58,760	60	8
951	V	OH	8/4/92	$8,991,733	1	1	100	0	0	$648,194	$0	0	24
962	V	IN	9/18/92	$4,936,862	1	1	100	0	0	$474,899	$138,625	29	15
966	IV	FL	10/8/92	$4,491,146	4	2	50	1	1	$321,708	$27,186	8	7
982	IV	FL	3/13/93	$64,788,427	12	2	17	9	1	$3,242,595	$99,234	3	38
991	VI	OK	5/12/93	$16,382,352	16	8	50	1	7	$1,093,245	$819,320	75	44

993	V	MN	6/11/93	$71,425,674	19	11	58	3	5	$9,316,392	60	57
994	V	WI	7/2/93	$63,137,015	7	5	71	0	2	$8,235,263	137	47
999	VIII	SD	7/19/93	$30,340,297	18	9	50	7	2	$3,957,430	55	39
1006	VII	MO	12/1/93	$5,852,013	5	2	40	3	0	$763,306	41	24
1020	IV	GA	3/31/94	$5,206,570	2	1	50	1	0	$679,118	6	12
1042	IV	GA	10/19/94	$14,872,078	0	0		0	0	$1,939,836	0	13
1043	IV	FL	11/28/94	$2,467,474	0	0	0	0	0	$321,844	0	2
1047	IV	AL	4/21/95	$2,113,740	1	1	100	0	0	$275,705	21	5
Floods and Tornadoes Total				$522,216,063	234	107	46	34	92	$44,980,271	62	

Coastal Storms

920	I	MA	11/4/91	$15,976,749	13	8	62	2	3	$914,344	59	7
921	I	ME	11/7/91	$2,338,693	1	1	100	0	0	$190,672	107	5
923	I	NH	11/13/91	$827,668	3	0	0	3	0	$53,998	0	1
975	I	MA	12/21/92	$17,809,703	10	6	60	4	0	$1,434,547	21	9
976	III	DE	1/15/93	$1,114,501	1	1	100	0	0	$105,527	9	1
Coastal Storms Total				$38,067,314	28	16	57	9	3	$2,699,088	39	

Earthquakes

845	IX	CA	10/18/89	$761,545,597	129	69	53	35	22	$67,214,303	47	12
943	IX	CA	5/4/92	$11,473,784	0	0	0	0	0	$1,044,538	0	1
947	IX	CA	7/2/92	$17,806,730	5	4	80	0	1	$1,314,045	18	2
985	X	OR	4/26/93	$8,336,568	1	1	100	0	0	$889,818	0	4
1004	X	OR	10/15/93	$2,546,328	8	8	100	0	0	$332,130	18	1
1008	IX	CA	1/17/94	$3,316,583,693	2	1	50	1	0	$432,597,873	0	3
Earthquakes Total				$4,118,292,700	145	83	57	36	23	$503,392,707	6	

continues

Appendix 10.A. (Continued)

Floods

Disaster Number	FEMA Region	State or Territory	Date Declared	Total FEMA Funding Available (IA, PA, HMGP)[a]	HMGP Applications				HMGP Funds			Counties Affected
					Submitted	Approved[b]	Approved	Pending[c]	Denied/ Withdrawn	Available[d]	Obligated	% Obligated[e]
820	VIII	UT	1/31/89	$1,015,551	2	2	100	0	0	$108,400	$95,048	88	1
821	IV	KY	2/24/89	$9,691,683	19	0	0	5	14	$639,411	$0	0	67
822	X	WA	4/14/89	$2,474,163	3	3	100	0	0	$224,004	$200,840	90	4
823	VI	TX	4/23/89	$2,104,844	3	2	67	0	0	$148,581	$74,748	50	9
824	V	MN	5/8/89	$4,217,041	5	4	80	0	1	$361,053	$255,800	71	8
825	VIII	ND	5/8/89	$2,391,853	7	5	71	0	2	$208,641	$123,089	59	6
829	VI	LA	5/20/89	$4,919,640	2	1	50	0	0	$191,873	$158,521	83	30
830	I	ME	6/7/89	$1,238,563	5	5	100	0	0	$111,415	$112,775	101	4
831	V	OH	6/10/89	$2,669,537	0	0	0	0	0	$0	$0	0	13
832	X	AK	6/10/89	$4,533,125	12	10	83	0	2	$311,555	$183,891	59	3
834	IV	KY	6/30/89	$4,413,108	1	0	0	1	0	$295,287	$0	0	12
835	VI	LA	7/17/89	$4,163,339	3	2	67	0	0	$62,313	$64,397	103	19
836	VI	TX	7/18/89	$7,304,562	3	1	33	0	1	$83,846	$55,000	66	9
840	I	VT	9/11/89	$1,888,753	8	6	75	1	1	$263,188	$135,715	52	5
846	IV	KY	10/30/89	$6,931,145	7	0	0	2	5	$448,641	$0	0	11
847	III	VA	11/8/89	$3,755,207	5	5	100	0	0	$333,753	$144,326	43	1
849	VI	LA	11/22/89	$1,361,958	0	0	0	0	0	$0	$0	0	3
852	X	WA	1/18/90	$13,584,113	13	9	69	1	3	$1,059,715	$663,409	63	7
853	X	OR	1/24/90	$2,111,912	7	2	29	3	2	$194,873	$9,563	5	2
858	IV	TN	2/27/90	$2,150,433	1	0	0	0	1	$143,543	$0	0	3
862	IV	FL	4/3/90	$1,753,143	0	0	0	0	0	$0	$0	0	11
865	VI	AR	5/15/90	$11,837,878	9	6	67	1	2	$924,401	$584,205	63	37
867	VII	MO	5/24/90	$10,412,911	6	4	67	2	0	$715,823	$238,593	33	10
868	VII	IA	5/26/90	$13,229,127	10	7	70	2	1	$801,195	$48,718	6	39

875	I	VT	7/25/90	$3,265,603	9	8	89	0	1	$299,074	$256,642	86	5
876	I	NH	8/29/90	$1,975,838	14	14	100	0	0	$178,872	$172,145	96	8
877	V	WI	8/30/90	$372,108	0	0	0	0	0	$260	$0	0	1
879	VII	IA	9/6/90	$2,184,064	1	1	100	0	0	$126,595	$105,463	83	17
880	IV	GA	10/19/90	$8,189,325	3	1	33	0	2	$558,095	$96,339	17	9
881	IV	SC	10/22/90	$5,810,314	12	0	0	5	7	$429,668	$0	0	13
883	X	WA	11/26/90	$47,431,599	17	13	76	3	1	$3,742,640	$1,936,661	52	19
884	IX	AZ	12/6/90	$6,360,611	3	2	67	1	0	$632,359	$99,460	16	8
885	V	IN	12/6/90	$3,871,702	1	0	0	0	1	$119,965	$0	0	1
889	IV	TN	1/4/91	$6,002,022	4	0	0	3	1	$410,639	$0	0	22
890	IV	AL	1/4/91	$4,335,506	1	1	100	0	0	$228,451	$221,254	97	12
891	V	IN	1/5/91	$6,601,222	1	1	100	0	0	$393,139	$230,873	59	73
893	IV	KY	1/29/91	$3,324,753	8	0	0	4	4	$326,424	$0	0	19
895	IV	MS	3/5/91	$2,688,798	2	1	50	1	0	$204,170	$2,320	1	18
896	X	WA	3/8/91	$3,770,935	2	0	0	1	1	$356,050	$0	0	10
897	IV	GA	3/15/91	$3,120,796	4	1	25	3	0	$240,412	$161,266	67	15
902	VI	LA	4/23/91	$4,092,761	4	3	75	0	1	$103,042	$97,301	94	15
907	VI	AR	5/30/91	$3,047,574	2	1	50	0	1	$274,454	$188,638	69	21
908	VII	NE	5/28/91	$5,125,846	7	4	57	2	1	$510,492	$242,043	47	7
910	IV	TN	6/21/91	$4,716,651	1	0	0	1	0	$462,158	$0	0	9
911	VII	IA	7/12/91	$2,475,208	2	1	50	0	1	$202,379	$842	0	16
930	VI	TX	12/26/91	$22,650,786	13	12	92	0	1	$1,394,238	$1,000,364	72	65
931	II	PR	1/22/92	$63,328,718	1	0	0	0	1	$1,066,075	$0	0	35
932	IX	MN	2/7/92	$2,412,174	0	0	0	0	0	$154,783	$0	0	6
933	III	DE	2/6/92	$2,923,805	7	3	43	0	0	$274,754	$130,632	48	2
935	IX	CA	2/25/92	$63,074,171	9	6	67	0	3	$5,991,851	$1,445,199	24	5
937	VI	TX	3/20/92	$2,560,519	0	0	0	0	0	$0	$0	0	3
938	I	VT	3/18/92	$3,397,589	10	5	50	1	3	$300,349	$216,860	72	5

continues

Appendix 10.A. (Continued)

Disaster Number	FEMA Region	State or Territory	Date Declared	Total FEMA Funding Available (IA, PA, HMGP)[a]	HMGP Applications					HMGP Funds			Counties Affected
					Submitted	Approved[b]	Approved	Pending[c]	Denied/Withdrawn	Available[d]	Obligated	% Obligated[e]	
940	I	ME	3/27/92	$2,912,297	7	6	86	1	0	$263,112	$236,966	90	10
941	V	IL	4/15/92	$23,088,444	2	1	50	0	1	$1,555,478	$304,616	20	1
944	III	VA	4/21/92	$5,715,030	1	1	100	0	0	$438,933	$345,000	79	28
945	VI	NM	6/18/92	$1,233,713	3	2	67	0	0	$49,469	$73,117	148	1
952	IV	FL	8/14/92	$6,640,316	5	3	60	2	0	$617,655	$149,725	24	4
953	V	IN	8/17/92	$3,012,823	0	0	0	0	0	$215,149	$0	0	6
954	VII	NE	8/19/92	$1,905,544	2	1	50	1	0	$193,446	$55,000	28	8
964	V	WI	9/30/92	$2,619,256	2	0	0	0	2	$214,847	$221,457	103	8
965	VII	IA	10/2/92	$2,542,196	0	0	0	0	0	$265,163	$0	0	9
972	I	CT	12/17/92	$6,507,666	6	6	100	0	0	$437,156	$286,328	65	3
973	II	NJ	12/18/92	$47,912,375	28	9	32	15	4	$3,692,659	$74,256	2	12
974	II	NY	12/21/92	$51,827,924	12	1	8	11	0	$3,415,423	$0	0	5
977	IX	AZ	1/19/93	$85,166,278	10	7	70	2	1	$8,390,876	$2,001,960	24	13
978	VI	LA	2/2/93	$1,947,627	0	0	0	0	0	$0	$0	0	9
979	IX	CA	2/3/93	$196,271,230	22	5	23	15	2	$19,309,358	$602,051	3	27
983	VII	NE	4/2/93	$6,597,583	2	2	100	0	0	$753,591	$474,900	63	13
986	VII	IA	4/26/93	$3,533,008	0	0	0	0	0	$245,757	$0	0	15
988	I	ME	5/11/93	$2,871,729	2	2	100	0	0	$263,874	$198,465	75	12
989	VII	MO	5/11/93	$3,650,247	0	0	0	0	0	$0	$0	0	8
990	I	VT	5/12/93	$1,108,739	1	1	100	0	0	$102,554	$76,713	75	4
992	VI	NM	6/7/93	$1,408,085	1	1	100	0	0	$181,183	$23,500	13	4
995	VII	MO	7/9/93	$237,307,814	43	43	100	0	0	$30,953,193	$29,509,102	95	105
996	VII	IA	7/9/93	$229,465,905	59	30	51	28	1	$29,930,335	$17,471,524	58	99
997	V	IL	7/9/93	$219,486,907	36	36	100	0	0	$28,628,727	$31,973,986	112	39

ID	Region	State	Date	Amount									
998	VII	NE	7/19/93	$53,229,345	13	6	46	7	0	$6,942,958	$3,746,766	54	52
1000	VII	KS	7/22/93	$78,910,359	16	13	81	3	0	$10,292,656	$8,616,817	84	57
1001	VIII	ND	7/26/93	$26,629,270	10	8	80	1	1	$3,473,383	$285,867	8	39
1022	IV	TN	4/14/94	$5,212,273	0	0	0	0	0	$679,862	$0	0	17
1029	I	ME	5/13/94	$667,556	1	1	100	0	0	$87,073	$69,799	80	1
1041	VI	TX	10/18/94	$149,537,479	6	0	0	6	0	$19,504,889	$0	0	38
Floods Total				$1,868,183,605	559	337	60	135	77	$197,711,651	$106,550,855	54	

Hurricanes

ID	Region	State	Date	Amount									
841	II	VT^f	9/20/89	$318,119,849	31	9	29	16	6	$12,611,900	$5,070,460	40	3
842	II	PR^g	9/21/89	$520,243,465	4	3	75	0	1	$6,631,747	$2,892,479	44	57
843	IV	SC	9/22/89	$364,827,404	53	0	0	34	19	$23,733,909	$0	0	24
844	IV	NC	9/25/89	$61,816,707	13	1	8	9	3	$5,730,924	$145,777	3	29
855	IX	AS^h	2/9/90	$25,562,578	2	1	50	1	0	$63,896	$30,000	47	5
913	I	RI	8/26/91	$10,373,949	7	7	100	0	0	$993,314	$285,899	29	5
914	I	MA	8/26/91	$29,886,472	19	15	79	2	1	$2,905,061	$489,163	17	11
915	I	ME	8/28/91	$4,469,384	11	10	91	0	1	$414,138	$298,325	72	9
916	I	CT	8/30/91	$6,167,495	4	3	75	0	1	$600,868	$73,085	12	6
917	I	NH	9/9/91	$1,973,102	3	3	100	0	0	$187,903	$68,611	37	4
918	II	NY	9/16/91	$12,686,413	4	0	0	4	0	$1,250,115	$0	0	1
927	IX	AS	12/13/91	$79,609,060	19	17	89	2	0	$2,673,775	$5,879,500	220	5
955	IV	FL	8/24/92	$1,497,444,929	501	85	17	365	48	$64,202,845	$4,206,124	7	4
956	VI	LA	8/26/92	$138,178,415	5	5	100	0	0	$7,039,353	$1,677,300	24	36
1003	IV	NC	9/10/93	$1,966,925	1	0	0	0	1	$256,555	$0	0	1
Hurricanes Total				$3,073,326,147	677	159	23	433	81	$129,296,304	$21,116,723	16	

continues

441

Appendix 10.A. *(Continued)*

DISASTER NUMBER	FEMA REGION	STATE OR TERRITORY	DATE DECLARED	TOTAL FEMA FUNDING AVAILABLE (IA, PA, HMGP)[a]	HMGP APPLICATIONS					HMGP FUNDS			COUNTIES AFFECTED
					SUBMITTED	APPROVED[b]	APPROVED	PENDING[c]	DENIED/ WITHDRAWN	AVAILABLE[d]	OBLIGATED	% OBLIGATED[e]	
Typhoons													
854	IX	MP[i]	2/5/90	$2,142,580	1	1	100	0	0	$181,754	$199,362	110	4
882	IX	PW[j]	11/28/90	$5,561,421	5	5	100	0	0	$71,614	$125,450	175	1
886	IX	FM[k]	12/14/90	$14,430,217	16	7	44	3	6	$206,813	$791,924	383	2
887	IX	GU[l]	12/24/90	$7,805,580	1	1	100	0	0	$260,498	$350,000	134	1
892	IX	FM	1/17/91	$1,192,132	2	1	50	0	1	$23,137	$12,398	54	1
924	IX	GU	12/4/91	$8,271,488	3	1	33	0	2	$398,524	$648,350	163	1
925	IX	MH[m]	12/6/91	$5,112,661	0	0	0	0	0	$174,384	$0	0	8
926	IX	FM	12/10/91	$1,413,930	2	2	100	0	0	$75,338	$230,202	306	5
934	IX	FM	2/7/92	$762,641	2	1	50	0	1	$73,414	$58,216	79	5
957	IX	GU	8/28/92	$62,547,095	4	2	50	0	2	$2,279,854	$3,500,000	154	1
961	IX	HI	9/12/92	$238,165,574	9	1	11	8	0	$13,025,314	$67,500	1	7
971	IV	MN	12/16/92	$2,616,332	0	0	0	0	0	$61,168	$0	0	11
Typhoons Total				$350,021,651	45	22	49	11	12	$16,831,811	$5,983,402	36	
Fishing Losses													
1036	X	OR	8/2/94	$2,635,000	0	0	0	0	0	$343,696	$0	0	8
1037	X	WA	8/2/94	$6,600,000	0	0	0	0	0	$860,870	$0	0	6
1038	IX	CA	9/13/94	$1,628,000	0	0	0	0	0	$212,348	$0	0	4
Fishing losses Total				$10,863,000	0	0	0	0	0	$1,416,913	$0	0	
Fires													
872	IX	CA	6/30/90	$5,575,650	4	3	75	0	1	$330,478	$81,472	25	4
919	IX	CA	10/22/91	$60,021,240	10	9	90	0	1	$5,361,523	$1,052,823	20	1
922	X	WA	11/13/91	$9,394,835	1	1	100	0	0	$894,853	$70,616	8	6

942	IX	CA	5/2/92	$144,219,597	0	0	0	0	0	$10,636,019	$0	0	1
958	IX	CA	8/29/92	$30,052,962	1	1	100	0	0	$2,874,779	$30,600	1	2
1005	IX	CA	10/28/93	$84,789,764	47	41	87	2	4	$11,059,534	$4,941,836	45	6
Fires Total				$334,054,048	63	55	87	2	6	$31,157,187	$6,177,347	20	

Snow/Ice Storms

826	X	AK	5/10/89	$5,567,186	7	4	57	0	3	$524,754	$208,360	40	12
850	VI	TX	1/9/90	$12,157,256	0	0	0	0	0	$0	$0	0	10
851	IV	FL	1/15/90	$8,555,625	0	0	0	0	0	$0	$0	0	32
860	V	IL	3/6/90	$5,815,813	0	0	0	0	0	$581,793	$0	0	10
894	IX	CA	2/11/91	$9,488,558	0	0	0	0	0	$930	$0	0	33
898	II	NY	3/21/91	$55,791,133	11	4	36	6	1	$5,403,445	$0	0	13
899	V	IN	3/29/91	$22,659,280	3	2	67	0	1	$2,087,402	$1,601,240	77	26
901	I	ME	4/19/91	$11,336,543	3	3	100	0	0	$1,045,413	$949,696	91	1
909	X	AK	5/30/91	$2,187,269	1	1	100	0	0	$197,793	$0	0	4
928	VII	IA	12/26/91	$12,145,298	5	5	100	0	0	$1,214,090	$101,043	8	44
929	V	MN	12/26/91	$8,618,574	7	0	0	3	4	$817,879	$0	0	12
1011	VI	AR	2/28/94	$9,623,345	10	5	50	5	0	$1,255,219	$400,643	32	13
1014	III	VA	3/10/94	$20,007,652	0	0	0	0	0	$2,609,694	$0	0	72
1016	III	ND	3/16/94	$9,900,789	0	0	0	0	0	$1,291,407	$0	0	9
1018	IV	KY	3/16/94	$19,694,930	4	1	25	0	3	$2,568,904	$494	0	68
1027	VII	NE	5/9/94	$30,186,452	5	0	0	2	3	$3,937,363	$0	0	15
1028	V	MI	5/10/94	$5,576,307	21	17	81	0	4	$727,344	$477,678	66	10
1045	VIII	SD	3/14/95	$2,186,862	0	0	0	0	0	$285,243	$0	0	21
Snow/Ice storms total				$251,498,872	77	42	55	16	19	$24,548,674	$3,739,154	15	

continues

Appendix 10.A. (Continued)

Tornadoes

Disaster Number	FEMA Region	State or Territory	Date Declared	Total FEMA Funding Available (IA, PA, HMGP)^a	HMGP Applications					HMGP Funds			Counties Affected
					Submitted	Approved^b	% Approved	Pending	Denied/ Withdrawn	Available^d	Obligated	% Obligated^e	
818	IV	NC	12/2/88	$697,906	0	0	0	0	0	$0	$0	0	9
819	V	IL	1/13/89	$1,041,413	1	0	0	0	1	$89,344	$0	0	5
827	IV	NC	5/17/89	$5,655,084	1	0	0	0	1	$516,546	$0	0	13
833	VI	LA	6/16/89	$565,770	0	0	0	0	0	$0	$0	0	9
837	I	CT	7/17/89	$16,292,998	12	12	100	0	0	$1,492,102	$249,933	17	2
848	IV	AL	11/17/89	$2,970,364	2	0	0	1	1	$230,068	$0	0	2
878	V	IL	8/29/90	$5,439,528	2	0	0	0	2	$460,483	$0	0	3
903	VII	KS	4/29/91	$4,266,565	0	0	0	0	0	$213,254	$0	0	6
905	VI	OK	5/8/91	$1,948,707	3	3	100	0	0	$128,827	$108,729	84	6
939	IV	MS	3/20/92	$1,002,623	0	0	0	0	0	$62,502	$0	0	4
949	VI	TX	7/2/92	$670,369	0	0	0	0	0	$0	$0	0	3
959	V	WI	9/2/92	$1,432,835	1	0	0	0	1	$61,354	$0	0	1
963	V	WI	9/18/92	$2,122,119	3	2	67	0	1	$199,118	$127,387	64	1
967	IV	MS	10/17/92	$1,613,138	0	0	0	0	0	$155,012	$0	0	1
968	IV	MS	11/25/92	$3,698,761	0	0	0	0	0	$240,019	$0	0	21
969	IV	GA	12/1/92	$2,208,589	0	0	0	0	0	$174,589	$0	0	14
970	IV	TX	12/4/92	$1,037,691	0	0	0	0	0	$0	$0	0	1
980	IV	GA	3/4/93	$1,378,654	0	0	0	0	0	$116,140	$0	0	8
987	VI	OK	4/26/93	$702,288	0	0	0	0	0	$0	$0	0	4
Tornadoes total				$54,745,402	25	17	68	1	7	$4,139,356	$486,049	12	

Volcanoes

864	IX	HI	5/18/90	$12,454,712	10	1	10	6	3	$1,091,308	6	1
Volcanoes total				$12,454,712	10	1	10	6	3	$1,091,308	6	1

Severe Storms

838	III	DC	8/28/89	$2,849,213	5	5	100	0	0	$281,073	12	1
839	III	MD	8/28/89	$3,441,988	2	1	50	0	1	$343,837	9	1
912	V	WI	8/6/91	$2,579,633	1	1	100	0	0	$251,994	24	5
936	II	NJ	3/3/92	$3,854,325	14	5	36	5	4	$384,027	1	5
950	VI	AR	7/24/92	$731,339	2	2	100	0	0	$70,136	38	5
960	VI	TX	9/9/92	$1,827,173	0	0	0	0	0	$0	0	26
981	X	WA	3/4/93	$16,844,801	14	13	93	0	1	$1,592,569	47	7
1002	V	IN	9/9/93	$1,990,506	0	0	0	0	0	$259,631	0	6
1007	III	VA	12/22/93	$88,764	0	0	0	0	0	$11,578	0	1
1009	IV	MS	2/18/94	$65,073,163	8	1	13	1	6	$8,487,804	4	26
1010	IV	TN	2/28/94	$54,172,187	7	2	29	5	0	$7,065,937	6	71
1012	VI	LA	2/28/94	$6,856,211	1	0	0	1	0	$894,288	0	5
1013	IV	AL	3/3/94	$14,166,725	5	0	0	5	0	$1,847,834	0	10
1015	III	PA	3/10/94	$74,365,112	0	0	0	0	0	$9,699,797	0	44
1017	III	DE	3/16/94	$5,710,191	0	0	0	0	0	$744,808	0	2
1019	IV	AL	3/30/94	$5,013,182	3	0	0	3	0	$653,893	0	7
1021	III	VA	4/11/94	$4,698,274	0	0	0	0	0	$612,818	0	33
1023	VII	MO	4/21/94	$2,855,456	4	0	0	4	0	$372,451	0	18
1024	VI	OK	4/21/94	$507,336	1	0	0	1	0	$66,174	0	1

continues

Appendix 10A. (Continued)

Disaster Number	FEMA Region	State or Territory	Date Declared	Total FEMA Funding Available (IA, PA, HMGP)[a]	HMGP Applications					HMGP Funds			Counties Affected
					Submitted	Approved[b]	Approved	Pending	Denied/ Withdrawn[c]	Available[d]	Obligated	% Obligated[e]	
1025	V	IL	4/26/94	$17,466,208	0	0	0	0	0	$2,278,201	$0	0	16
1026	VI	TX	4/29/94	$1,472,493	5	0	0	5	0	$192,064	$0	0	3
1030	III	DC	6/17/94	$2,405,113	0	0	0	0	0	$313,710	$0	0	1
1031	VIII	SD	6/21/94	$4,265,614	5	1	20	2	2	$556,384	$18,210	3	21
1032	VIII	ND	7/1/94	$3,489,324	1	0	0	1	0	$455,129	$0	0	25
1033	IV	GA	7/7/94	$197,502,825	17	1	6	15	1	$25,761,238	$261,951	1	55
1034	IV	AL	7/8/94	$14,537,978	5	1	20	4	0	$1,896,258	$58,291	3	10
1035	IV	FL	7/10/94	$24,877,996	0	0	0	0	0	$3,244,956	$0	0	12
1039	X	AK	9/13/94	$54,246,224	4	4	100	0	0	$7,075,594	$7,618,331	108	3
1044	IX	CA	1/10/95	$179,189,379	0	0	0	0	0	$23,372,528	$0	0	42
1046	IX	CA	3/12/95	$87,755,934	0	0	0	0	0	$11,446,426	$0	0	57
Severe storms totals				$854,834,667	104	37	36	52	15	$110,233,140	$9,604,178	178	9
Other Disaster Types													
0984	II	NY	4/2/93	$4,167,716	0	0	0	0	0	$416,937	$0	0	1
1040	IX	MN	10/6/94	$2,303,463	0	0	0	0	0	$300,452	$0	0	1
Other total				$6,471,179	0	0	0	0	0	$717,388	$0	0	
Grand Total				$11,495,029,360	1,967	876	45	735	338	$1,068,215,799	$214,769,324	20	

Source: FEMA headquarters and FEMA regional offices.

[a] IA = Individual Assistance program; PA = Public Assistance program; HMGP = Hazard Mitigation Grant Program.

[b] Includes projects approved, obligated, and complete.

[c] Includes projects pending, appealed, eligible, and outsourced.

[d] Estimated as 10% of Section 406 PA funds prior to June 9, 1993, and 15% of all Section 406 PA, IA, and administrative funds thereafter per the Stafford Act and its 1993 amendment.

[e] The percentage obligated exceeds 100 for those disasters in which the actual Section 404 funds obligated for projects exceeded the original estimate for the total amount of Section 404 funds available (see previous note). FEMA commits to a level of Section 404 funding shortly after a disaster declaration on the basis of anticipated IA and PA funding. When IA and PA projects are withdrawn or scaled back after this, the estimated amount of Section 404 funds available is reduced. FEMA, however, honors the original Section 404 commitment.

[f] Virgin Islands of the United States.

[g] Puerto Rico.

[h] American Samoa.

[i] Northern Mariana Islands.

[j] Palau.

[k] Federated States of Micronesia.

[l] Guam.

[m] Marshall Islands.

Selected Disasters by Number:

Loma Prieta earthquake   845
Northridge earthquake   1008
Midwest floods   995, 996, 997, 998, 999, 1000, 1001
Hurricane Hugo   841, 842, 843, 844
Hurricane Bob   913, 914, 915, 916, 917, 918
Hurricane Andrew   955, 956
Hurricane Iniki   961
Los Angeles riots   942

Hazard Mitigation Grant Program Project Categories

The following is an expanded listing of project types encountered in both the Section 404 data submitted and the state hazard mitigation officer surveys. Detailed project types are organized according to the seven broad categories used by the Federal Emergency Management Agency (FEMA) to classify projects in *Project Survey Results, Hazard Mitigation Grant Program* (Washington, D.C.: FEMA, 1992).

Category 1: Drainage Projects (1.0)

1.1 Replacement/improvement of culverts, pipes, mains, storm water lines
1.2 Replacement of drainage ditches; channel improvements
1.3 Construction of detention ponds/basins
1.4 Construction/stabilization of levees
1.5 Stabilization of riverbanks and shorelines (retaining walls and riprap)
1.6 Dikes and dams
1.7 Miscellaneous drainage
1.8 Sewer pipes, backup valves
1.9 Barriers, berms
1.10 Floodgates, flood walls
1.11 Dredging

Category 2: Acquisition/Relocation (2.0)

2.1 Acquisition of structures/buildings
2.2 Purchase of homes in hazard zone
2.3 Purchase of land in hazard zone
2.4 Acquisition and demolition

2.5 Acquisition and floodproofing
2.6 Acquisition and relocation
2.10 Miscellaneous acquisition and relocation

Category 3: Education/Training (3.0)

3.1 Workshops for public employees and personnel of state agencies
3.2 Development of videotapes
3.3 Informational pamphlets, brochures, and other literature
3.4 Workshops and seminars for the general public
3.5 Workshops and seminars for public officials
3.6 Education and training
3.7 Miscellaneous workshops
3.8 Miscellaneous education and training

Category 4: Equipment Purchases (4.0)

4.1 Warning systems, sirens
4.2 Radios and other communication devices
4.3 Flood gauges
4.4 Power generators, emergency power supplies
4.5 Computers/GIS
4.6 Data-sharing systems
4.7 Pumps
4.8 Weather stations
4.9 Equipment anchoring
4.10 Miscellaneous equipment purchases
4.11 Emergency Operations Centers, both stationary and mobile
4.12 Vehicles

Category 5: Structural Improvments (5.0)

5.1 Seismic retrofitting
5.2 Improvements to storm water, wastewater, and water treatment facilities and pumping stations
5.3 Upgrading of piers/wharves
5.4 Repair/reconstruction of fuel storage tanks
5.5 Storm shutters
5.6 Other infrastructure improvements (roads, bridges, etc.)
5.7 Building elevations
5.8 Floodproofing of structures and infrastructure
5.9 Structural engineering studies

5.10 Construction/replacement of entire buildings
5.11 Utility improvements
5.12 Emergency shelters
5.13 Equipment elevations
5.14 Other building improvements (walls, rooms, reinforcements, hardening)
5.15 Roll-up doors
5.16 Windows
5.17 Window film
5.18 Roofs
5.19 Miscellaneous structural improvements and retrofitting

Category 6: Planning (6.0)

6.1 Management plans (e.g., beach management plans)
6.2 Design of storm drainage systems
6.3 Vulnerability/risk analyses, inventories, other studies
6.4 Development/strengthening of zoning and building code ordinances
6.5 Development of hazard mitigation plans
6.6 Formation of planning/hazard management districts
6.7 New hazard mitigation regulation/legislation
6.8 Formation of planning/hazard mitigation programs
6.9 Improved/increased technical assistance
6.10 Improved application process
6.11 Fiscal improvements/accountability
6.12 Loan subsidy or grant programs
6.13 Additional staffing
6.14 Development of, improvements to, or increased involvement in insurance programs
6.15 Formation of hazard mitigation team/committee
6.16 Hazard mapping
6.17 Creation of land improvements plan
6.18 Implementation of hazard mitigation plan
6.19 Preparedness, response, and recovery planning
6.20 Miscellaneous planning, administrative, and legislative activities
6.21 Hazard mitigation coordination
6.22 Creation of harbor management plan

Category 7: Land Improvements (7.0)

7.1 Beach replenishment
7.2 Stabilization/restoration of sand dunes, roadway banks

7.3 Bulkheads and head walls

7.4 Piers

7.5 Elevation of structures

7.6 Vegetation management programs

7.7 Erosion controls

7.8 Slope stabilization

7.9 Brush clearing, controlled burns, fuel breaks

7.10 Miscellaneous land improvements

7.11 Hurricane walls, barriers, gates, tidal valves

7.12 Seawalls

Category 8: Administrative Expenses

Category 9: Not Classified

CHAPTER 11

State Implementation of Natural Disaster Mitigation Policy: A Flawed System

In our case studies, plan evaluations, and surveys of state and federal hazard mitigation officers, we learned that there are relatively weak linkages between state hazard mitigation plans and hazard mitigation projects. In this chapter we use cross-sectional data collected from four different sources to perform a more quantitative analysis of the linkages among key elements in the state system designed to implement the Stafford Act. We focus on hazard mitigation projects funded through the federal Hazard Mitigation Grant Program (HMGP) as these represent the most direct, observable method of implementing hazard mitigation plans and policies.

In order for plans to be meaningful and useful, there must be a means for carrying them out. The Stafford Act requires states to prepare multi-hazard mitigation plans to identify, prioritize, and implement mitigation actions to reduce future natural hazard risks. Federal grants of disaster assistance funds depend on the development of hazard mitigation plans. Ideally, there *should* be a linkage between hazard mitigation plans and projects under the Stafford Act. However, the case studies and surveys suggest that the way hazard mitigation programs have been implemented has allowed a disconnect to occur between plans and implementation. This raises the question of how effective the hazard mitigation system has been in achieving implementation outcomes that advance national policy goals.

Federal hazard mitigation policy, like other federal policies that devolve responsibility to state and local government, is increasingly advancing

strategies and solutions at more decentralized levels. A central feature of this devolution trend is greater attention to linkages among federal policy goals, state plans, and implementation outcomes. Federal planning requirements lay out a planning process but do not specify the means states should use to achieve policy objectives. States have discretion in devising strategies to meet federal performance standards. Emphasis is placed on commitment and capacity building through financial and technical assistance (May et al. 1996).

The Stafford Act Framework

Mitigation under the Stafford Act is carried out through two primary activities: mitigation plans and projects. Section 409 requires each state to adopt a state hazard mitigation plan, subject to approval by the Federal Emergency Management Agency (FEMA). All plans are required to include five major elements addressing (1) hazard identification and evaluation; (2) organizational capability assessment; (3) goals and objectives; (4) proposed mitigation activities; and (5) plan implementation and monitoring (44 C.F.R. 206.405[a]). However, states are given considerable latitude in choosing strategies to achieve mitigation. FEMA does not specify plan content but allows states flexibility in deciding how to address hazards issues in their plans (see chapter 9).

Mitigation is also carried out through the Hazard Mitigation Grant Program (HMGP) under Section 404 of the Stafford Act, which provides federal matching funds for state and local mitigation projects. These grants are tied to presidential disaster declarations, are limited to a percentage of the federal disaster assistance available, and must be consistent with the state hazard mitigation plan (see chapter 10).

The federal government has a big stake in long-term hazard mitigation, as it almost always must pay the lion's share of disaster recovery costs. Yet state governments often are apathetic toward hazard mitigation, given perceptions among citizens and elected officials that their communities are *entitled* to federal disaster recovery assistance and the fact that mitigation investments exact up-front, highly visible political and economic costs, whereas benefits are realized only in the distant future (Berke 1998; May 1993; Olshansky and Kartez 1998). Thus, a crucial issue for our study is whether the hazard mitigation system is able to create the commitment and capacity necessary to produce effective, high-quality plans and mitigation projects that implement those plans.

Conceptual Framework of an Intergovernmental System for Mitigation Planning

Our conceptual framework draws on the literature in policy implementation (cf. Mazmanian and Sabatier 1989; Goggin et al. 1990) and state planning mandates to coordinate local growth (Berke and French 1994; Burby and May et al. 1997; Dalton and Burby 1994; Deyle and Smith 1999; Innes 1993).

As shown in figure 11.1, the framework highlights the crucial role of the intergovernmental system in which federal disaster policy is filtered through the commitment and capacity of federal, state, and local government actors and influenced by the disaster experience and political context of the state. These in turn influence the quality of state hazard mitigation plans and, through them, the resulting hazard mitigation projects aimed at reducing risk and vulnerability.

We expect the commitment and capacity of key federal and state agencies to influence plans, the extent to which states implement hazard mitigation, and actual risk reduction outcomes. Personnel of FEMA's regional offices are charged with providing technical assistance to states in their regions for plan preparation and with reviewing plans and HMGP project applications. The commitment (i.e., willingness to support national disaster policy goals to reduce risk through state planning) and capacity (i.e., resources available to assist states) of FEMA regional staff can be crucial in facilitating plan quality and implementation. Similarly, the commitment

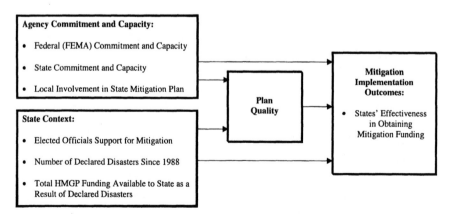

Figure 11.1. Conceptual Framework of Intergovernmental System for Hazard Mitigation.

and capacity of the lead state agency charged with planning can be crucial in promoting the development and implementation of high-quality plans.

In addition, local participation can be important in the development and effective implementation of high-quality state plans. Local governments are key partners because regulation and control of development within hazardous areas normally occur at the local level. Prior research shows that participation by local governments in setting priorities for mitigation can lead to state planning initiatives that are better tailored to local needs and thus more likely to lead to improved implementation outcomes (Deyle and Smith 1998; Innes 1993).

Performance of plans warrants more extensive investigation than is found in the literature (Dalton and Burby 1994; Godschalk, Kaiser, and Berke 1998). Ideally, we would expect expenditures on hazard mitigation to follow the recommendations of well-conceived state plans. However, recent research on planning and implementation has focused predominantly on the influence of the planning process rather than on the plan document, emphasizing different roles for professionals, elected officials, and the affected public in guiding action (Faludi 1987; Healy 1993). Yet the plan document should guide subsequent implementation (Kaiser, Godschalk, and Chapin 1995; Kaiser and Godschalk 1995; Talen 1996). Our study attempts to verify the role of the plan document in guiding implementation.

In our analytical framework, implementation outcomes are gauged by states' use of the federal HMGP, which represents the primary source of funding for hazard mitigation projects. We reasoned that states that are more aggressive in pursuing funding from all eligible disasters, that are more successful in getting HMGP applications approved, and that use the greatest proportions of available HMGP funds will be more active in using mitigation measures.

We recognize that plans may affect other types of outcomes that are not explicitly tied to the HMGP. These outcomes might include plans' influence on educating the public and elected officials, the priority that hazards are given on state action agendas, the level of participation of various interest groups with a stake in hazards policy, and the injection of alternatives that might not have been conceived without the plan. For the purposes of our study, however, we focus on how plans influence the degree of success found in state attempts to obtain FEMA funds for mitigation. While our focus may appear somewhat narrow, our case studies, plan evaluations, and surveys confirmed the key role that the HMGP plays in getting projects implemented that would otherwise go unfunded. In addition, we

maintain that, in theory, states with better plans are better able to educate FEMA officials concerning the need for HMGP in their jurisdictions, propose HMGP applications backed up by sound policy alternatives, and demonstrate how the state is able to fulfill national mitigation goals in the use of HMGP funding.

Federal planning requirements have to recognize the role of key contextual factors, including state political support and prior disaster experience. Attempts to improve state planning should recognize the political context. Previous studies indicate that elected state officials respond favorably to their constituents' demands for hazard mitigation at the state level (Mittler 1989; Rossi, Wright, and Weber-Burdin 1982). Similarly, political support of plans is important to avoid local delays and halfhearted efforts toward achieving plan goals (Alesch and Petak 1986; Burby and French et al. 1985; Dalton and Burby 1994; Mushkatel and Nigg 1987). In addition, prior investigations suggest that the more experience a state government has with disasters, the more likely it will be to give attention to mitigation to prevent future losses (Mittler 1989; Mushkatel and Nigg 1987).

In sum, our conceptual framework highlights the important role of the state mitigation planning and implementation system. Although federal policies are filtered through federal agency staff, they are also affected by state planning agencies, state-initiated local participation programs, and state plans. States' political environments and prior disaster experience also influence the way federal policies are translated into practice. By including all these factors in our analysis, we can evaluate the relative contributions of all factors as well as the linkages among them.

Assessing Linkages: Analytic Methods

Table 11.1 summarizes the coding procedures, measurement construction, and data sources used in this study. The first source of data was the group of hazard mitigation plans that we collected from thirty-nine states.[1] (See chapter 9 for details of the sample.) Plan quality was assessed by coding items for four attributes specified by the Stafford Act for inclusion in state Section 409 mitigation plans: (1) hazard assessment; (2) assessment of organizational capability for implementation; (3) policy recommendations; and (4) monitoring and evaluation of implementation. For each plan, the coding entailed checking the presence or absence of each of a series of items for each attribute. Each item was then rated on the basis of a series of scales.[2]

Table 11.1. Variables and Measurements

FACTOR	SOURCE	MEASUREMENTS	RANGE, [MEAN], (MEDIAN), {STANDARD DEVIATION}
Plan quality (higher scores indicate greater quality)			
Capability assessment	Content analysis	Discrete (0–3)	0.44–1.32 [0.81] (0.81) {0.20}
Hazards assessment	Content analysis	Discrete (0–3)	0.42–1.45 [0.73] (0.78) {0.23}
Monitoring and evaluation	Content analysis	Discrete (0–3)	0.38–1.57 [0.83] (0.87) {0.31}
Mitigation policy recommendations	Content analysis	Discrete (0–3)	0.34–1.66 [0.87] (0.90) {0.28}
Plan quality composite[a]	Content analysis	Continuous (0–3)	0.49–1.29 [0.88] (0.84) {0.21}
State agency commitment and capacity (higher scores indicate greater commitment and capacity)			
Number of emergency management staff	SHMO survey	Continuous	0–220 [48.4] (40) {38.2}
Commitment of emergency management officials	SHMO survey	Ordinal (1–5)	2–5 [3.91] (4) {0.94}
Local involvement (higher scores indicate greater importance)			
Importance of local government in plan preparation	SHMO survey	Ordinal (1–5)	1–5 [3.32] (3) {1.39}
FEMA regional office commitment and capacity (higher scores indicate greater commitment and capacity)			
Capacity of regional FEMA agency	FHMO survey	Ordinal (1–5)	2–4 [3.25] (3) {0.70}
Commitment of senior FEMA regional emergency management officials	FHMO survey	Ordinal (1–5)	3–5 [3.58] (3) {0.63}

State context			
Number of declared disasters (11/88–5/95)	Disaster database[b]	Discrete	0–15 [4.11] (4) {3.25}
Logarithm of total amount of Section 404 funding available[c]	Disaster database[b]	Continuous	5.04–8.77 [6.72] (6.89) {0.69}
Commitment of state elected officials	SHMO survey	Ordinal (1–5)	2–5 [2.93] (3) {0.95}
State implementation results			
Declared disasters with no Section 404 project applications	Section 404 database[d]	Discrete	0–6 [0.79] (0) {1.23}
Percentage of Section 404 project applications approved	Section 404 database[d]	Ratio (0–1)	0–1 [0.67] (0.6) {0.47}

[a]The plan quality composite index is a standardized score composed of four dimensions of plan quality. The four subcomponents were combined and standardized based on 0 to 3, with a Cronbach's alpha of 0.83.

[b]The disaster database was assembled from data provided by FEMA's Washington, D.C., headquarters.

[c]Since the distribution of data for the available Section 404 funding was highly skewed (ranging from $0 to nearly $600 million), the data were logged to transform them into a more normal distribution that could be used in correlation analysis.

[d]The Section 404 database was assembled by the researchers from data provided by FEMA's ten regional offices.

The second data source consisted of data for 1,967 applications received through the HMGP, collected from all ten FEMA regional offices and representing applications from forty-three states. (See chapter 10 for details.) The HMGP data provided two measures of the degree to which states were implementing hazard mitigation (outcomes), including the number of declared disasters with no HMGP project applications and the percentage of HMGP project applications approved or completed.

Two additional data sources were telephone interviews with federal hazard mitigation officers (FHMOs) and state hazard mitigation officers (SHMOs). Types of information collected from the two sets of interviews included assessments of FEMA regional office, state, and local commitment to and capacity for state planning and implementation. FMHOs and SHMOs were selected because they are the most knowledgeable about Section 409 mitigation planning. Interviews were conducted with FMHOs of the ten FEMA regional offices and SHMOs for forty-six of the fifty states.

Each item measuring plan quality was based on a series of three-point scales specified in table 11.1. An index was created to measure overall plan quality. To ensure a reasonable level of measurement reliability, the internal consistency of the summated index was evaluated using Cronbach's alpha, for which summed-rating scales have an average alpha of 0.83. Relevant details about the construction of this index are presented in table 11.1. Items measuring state commitment and capacity and local participation were based on a five-point scale with descriptive anchors for each endpoint.

Finally, we used the Pearson correlation statistic rather than ordinary least squares regression to analyze the data. We dropped the regression models from the analysis because of a problem with empty cells in the databases (i.e., some states were missing interviews, others did not provide plans, and some had no mitigation project applications). That is, the number of observations (i.e., degrees of freedom) was reduced by 30 to 40 percent when we ran regressions using variables from the four databases. This problem limited our ability to examine a range of independent variables simultaneously. We thus decided to use simple correlations to ensure that our findings reflect the population.

Findings

Our findings are organized into two parts. The first part describes independent variables expected to influence the quality of state mitigation plans and hazard mitigation outcomes, including program commitment

and capacity and local involvement and state context. The second part describes plan quality and implementation outcomes and then explains the relationships between the independent variables and both of these factors.

Program Commitment and Capacity

Program commitment and capacity includes several elements. The number of state staff members, the commitment of state officials, and the commitment and capacity of FEMA regional offices will be discussed here.

Table 11.2 indicates the number of full-time emergency management and hazard mitigation staff members employed by lead state emergency management agencies. Almost two-thirds of all emergency management agencies employ forty-nine or fewer emergency management staff members, compared with about one-fifth that employ fifty to seventy-five staff members and about one-sixth that employ more than seventy-five. The lead state agencies employ considerably fewer hazard mitigation staff members than emergency management staff members. Nearly one-half employ one or no mitigation staff member, and only 4 percent employ more than seven. Overall, the median number of full-time emergency management staff members employed by the lead state agencies is thirty-eight, compared with only two mitigation staff members.

Rather than using the number of full-time mitigation staff members, we used the number of full-time emergency management staff in the correlation analysis with plan quality and implementation outcomes. We thought this variable would be a more accurate predictor of staff capacity for mitigation planning and implementation. Our correlation test confirmed this expectation. Moreover, our telephone interviews revealed that emergency management personnel were often active in preparing Section 409 plans and involved with seeking Section 404 project approvals. Thus, sole reliance of use of the number of mitigation staff members as a variable might only partially represent staff capacity for mitigation planning.

Table 11.3 shows how state hazard mitigation officers (SHMOs) evaluated the commitment of state emergency management officials to support mitigation. In general, SHMOs considered these officials to be committed to mitigation efforts. Nearly two-thirds of all respondents rated emergency management officials' commitment as "high" or "very high," whereas more than one-third considered them to have "medium" or "low" commitment. None gave a rating of "very low."

An open-ended follow-up question asked respondents to give reasons for their ratings. The most common reason for assigning a "high" or "very high" level of commitment involved the strong belief on the part of

emergency management officials that mitigation is the most effective long-term deterrent of damage from natural hazards. Other frequently mentioned reasons were high levels of awareness and knowledge of hazard mitigation and extensive work experience by staff members. For those who rated commitment as "medium" or "low," the basic concern was that the staff might increasingly be stretched thin in dealing with FEMA's expanding mandate to promote mitigation.

Table 11.4 shows how federal hazard mitigation officers (FHMOs) evaluated the capacity of their regional offices to carry out hazard mitigation initiatives. Capacity was defined as the overall technical ability of staff

Table 11.2. Full-Time State Staff

NUMBER OF STAFF MEMBERS	PERCENTAGE OF STATES[a] (NUMBER OF STATES)
Emergency management staff (N = 47)	
< 25	28% (13)
25–49	34% (16)
50–75	21% (10)
> 75	17% (8)
Median number of staff members	38
Natural hazard mitigation staff (N = 45)	
0–1	49% (22)
2–4	32% (15)
5–7	13% (6)
> 7	4% (2)
Median number of staff members	2

[a]Percentages may not total 100 because of rounding.

Table 11.3. Commitment of State Emergency Management Officials to Support Natural Hazard Mitigation, as Perceived by SHMOs (N = 46)

RATING	PERCENTAGE	(NUMBER)
Very low	0%	(0)
Low	4%	(2)
Medium	35%	(16)
High	26%	(12)
Very high	35%	(16)

members at the regional office to promote mitigation activities of states within their office's jurisdiction.[3] Regional office capacity was generally viewed as adequate, with 80 percent of respondents rating their regions' capacity as "medium" or "high." Twenty percent of respondents rated their regions' capacity as "low"; none gave a rating of "very low" or "very high."

Another open-ended follow-up question asked respondents to provide reasons for their ratings. The most common reason respondents cited for giving "low" ratings was an inadequate number of staff members to handle the intensive demands placed on regions by the broad mandate given to regional offices by the Stafford Act. Respondents who gave "medium" and "high" ratings echoed these concerns but ranked their regions' capacity higher because of a high level of skill and dedication on the part of staff members.

Table 11.5 indicates FHMOs' ratings of commitment of FEMA regional office staff to supporting mitigation. These evaluations are mixed. One-half of respondents viewed their regions' staff as having a "high" or "very high" level of commitment, and the remaining half viewed commitment as "medium." A follow-up question revealed explanations for these ratings. Among those who gave a "medium" rating, the most frequently cited obstacle to raising commitment dealt with the traditional emphases on crisis response and public assistance. They indicated that many staff members were more supportive of these traditional roles and were reluctant to support FEMA's recent emphasis on mitigation. Respondents who gave high ratings pointed to the strong belief of many staff members that mitigation is a long-range solution to the problems associated with disaster losses and that the traditional crisis-oriented, response mentality cannot effectively deal with these problems.

Table 11.4. Capacity of FEMA Regional Offices to Carry Out Natural Hazard Mitigation, as Perceived by FHMOs (N = 10)

RATING	PERCENTAGE	(NUMBER)
Very low	0%	(0)
Low	20%	(2)
Medium	40%	(4)
High	40%	(4)
Very high	0%	(0)

Table 11.5. Commitment of FEMA Regional Emergency Management Officials to Support Natural Hazard Mitigation, as Perceived by FHMOs (N = 10)

RATING	PERCENTAGE	(NUMBER)
Very low	0%	(0)
Low	0%	(0)
Medium	50%	(5)
High	40%	(4)
Very high	10%	(1)

Local Involvement

Table 11.6 shows how SHMOs rated the importance of local involvement in the preparation of Section 409 hazard mitigation plans. Here again, results were mixed. Nearly one-half rated local involvement as "important" or "very important," whereas nearly one-third considered such involvement "unimportant" or "very unimportant."

When asked to explain their ratings, most of those who rated local involvement as "important" or "very important" indicated that state agencies often need information that only local officials can provide, disasters most directly affect people at the local level, and mitigation measures are generally implemented at the local level. Those who rated local input as "somewhat important" gave several reasons, stating, for example, that local assistance was not solicited by their agency or local input was not high because preparation of the Section 409 plan was a new process and local officials would become more involved in the future. The most common reasons respondents gave for rating local involvement as "unimportant" or "very unimportant" were that local input was not solicited by their agency; the plan was viewed as a state-level rather than a local-level document; local officials did not wish to participate; and the state agency did a poor job at involving local governments.

State Context

The state context includes several elements, including commitment of state elected officials, number of declared disasters, and total amount of HMGP funding.

Table 11.7 indicates how SHMOs evaluated state elected officials' commitment to mitigation as compared with other state priorities. Respondents generally perceived that elected officials provided only limited support for mitigation. Nearly three-fourths of the respondents rated commitment as "low" or "medium," with the remaining respondents rating it as "high" or "very high."

In response to a follow-up question, the SHMO's most often cited the lack of understanding of hazard mitigation as the reason for low commitment on the part of elected officials. Respondents explained that because mitigation was a relatively new concept, many elected officials did not fully comprehend its potential long-term effectiveness. A key concern was that elected officials had not been given sufficient information about mitigation on which to act. In addition, commitment was viewed as low because FEMA does not provide ongoing funds for mitigation. Instead, FEMA provides large amounts of funding in spurts only after a disaster has

Table 11.6. Importance of Local Involvement in Preparation of Mitigation Plans, as Perceived by SHMOs (N = 43)

RATINGS	PERCENTAGE	(NUMBER)
Very unimportant	10%	(4)
Unimportant	21%	(9)
Somewhat important	21%	(9)
Important	19%	(8)
Very important	29%	(13)

Table 11.7. Commitment of State Elected Officials to Support Natural Hazard Mitigation, as Perceived by SHMOs (N = 44)

RATINGS	PERCENTAGE	(NUMBER)
Very low	0%	(0)
Low	43%	(19)
Medium	30%	(13)
High	20%	(9)
Very high	7%	(3)

occurred, a situation that does not lend itself to the development and implementation of a long-range mitigation investment strategy.

Alternatively, a reason frequently cited for perceived high commitment on the part of elected officials was a high level of knowledge concerning hazard mitigation. Respondents asserted that commitment increased as elected officials became more aware of and knowledgeable about the mitigation concept. Other reasons given for increased commitment involved prior disaster experience and FEMA's financial incentives for having a mitigation plan and hazard mitigation team in place.

Two additional "state context" variables were included to account for variations in the disaster experience of states. First, the relative frequency of disaster events was measured in terms of the number of declared disasters states had experienced since the Stafford Act took effect. Six of the fifty states (12 percent) had not experienced a declared disaster during the study period. Approximately one-third of the states (sixteen) had experienced one to three disasters, 28 percent had experienced four to seven events, and another 28 percent had recorded eight or more declared disasters.

Second, the destructiveness of a disaster event was measured in terms of the total amount of HMGP funding that became available during the same time period. Since HMGP funding is calculated as a percentage of the total FEMA funding for a disaster, this provided a good gauge for the severity of disasters states experienced. Roughly one-quarter of the states fell into each of the following categories of available HMGP funds: less than $1 million, $1–$5 million, $5–$10 million, and more than $10 million. Detailed information on the disaster history of states was collected and analyzed as part of our evaluation of the HMGP, which appears in chapter 10.

In sum, several key findings can be derived from our survey of organizational capacity and commitment, local involvement, and state context.

First, the number of state agency staff members available to carry out mitigation was considered to be somewhat low, given the small number of staff members formally assigned to mitigation. Second, the staffs of state emergency management agencies and FEMA's regional offices were viewed as having a fairly strong commitment to advancing mitigation. Third, the technical capacity of FEMA's regional offices was generally viewed as adequate, but there was some concern that current capacity might not be able to meet the growing mandate to advance mitigation.

Fourth, respondents viewed the value of local involvement with mixed results, with nearly one-half rating local involvement as important and nearly one-third considering such involvement as unimportant. Fifth, respondents generally perceived that elected officials in their states provided only limited support for mitigation. Finally, there was wide variation in both the number of declared disasters and the amount of HMGP funding available for states during the study period.

Plan Quality

Our evaluation of the four plan dimensions revealed a generally lackluster quality of state mitigation plans. Table 11.8 shows the scores for each dimension as well as the overall plan quality score. All mean scores for the individual dimensions and the overall plan quality score fall below 1, out of a total possible score of 3. Content analysis of the plans revealed that at least one entire dimension was missing in most plans and that plans were often merely descriptive and superficial. For example, in the hazard assessment dimension, most plans chronicled historical circumstances but did not systematically analyze vulnerability of the population and the built environment, and they seldom made risk assessments in terms of combining probabilities of hazardous events with estimates of loss from those events. (However, these are average scores, and some plans did contain strong components, as described in chapter 9.)

Overall, the average plan quality ratings for the required elements were

Table 11.8. Plan Quality Dimensions

Plan Quality Dimensions	Mean	(Standard Deviation)	Minimum	Maximum
			(Scale of 0 to 3)	
Hazard assessment	0.78	(0.23)	0.42	1.45
Capability assessment	0.81	(0.20)	0.44	1.32
Mitigation policy recommendations	0.90	(0.28)	0.34	1.66
Monitoring and evaluation	0.87	(0.31)	0.38	1.57
Overall plan quality	0.84	(0.21)	0.49	1.29

less than one-half of what they might have been. One can conclude that these poor-quality plans were not useful to the states and were not intended for implementation. Instead, they were prepared merely to meet the requirements necessary to qualify states for federal mitigation grants. A study by FEMA's Office of Inspector General of mitigation planning in thirteen states corroborates our conclusions, indicating that "mitigation planning for most of the states . . . was done to qualify for FEMA mitigation grants, rather than to measure a state's progress in mitigation. States must have FEMA-approved plans to apply for post-disaster funding, so mitigation officials prepared plans . . . to get the 'planning box' checked to qualify for FEMA grants" (FEMA 1994, p. 13).

Associations with Plan Quality

Because we theorized that better plans will produce better mitigation outcomes, the question of which policy variables influence plan quality is crucial. To begin to answer this question, table 11.9 illustrates the results of the correlation analysis investigating the association of state Section 409 plan quality with FEMA regional agency commitment and capacity, state elected official commitment, and local government involvement.[4] Separate analyses were performed for each of the four dimensions of plan quality and for the overall total plan quality. No major distinctions were found in how these factors affect individual dimensions and the overall score. Thus the dependent variable in table 11.9 is the overall score.

Table 11.9. Associations with State Plan Quality

VARIABLE	OVERALL PLAN QUALITY
1. FEMA regional office commitment and capacity	
Regional FEMA commitment ($N = 39$)	0.20
Regional FEMA capacity ($N = 39$)	−0.20
2. State emergency management agency commitment and capacity	
Commitment of state emergency management officials ($N = 37$)	0.22
Number of state emergency management staff ($N = 36$)	0.28[a]
3. Local involvement	
Importance of local government in Section 409 plan preparation ($N = 36$)	0.29[a]
4. State context	
Support of state elected officials ($N = 34$)	−0.10
Number of declared disasters ($N = 39$)	0.14
Amount of prior Section 404 funding available ($N = 37$)	0.30[a]

[a]$p < 0.10$

Three factors were associated with overall plan quality. First, the amount of prior HMGP funding made available to a state had a positive effect on overall plan quality. This finding suggests that as states gain experience using federal mitigation funds, state emergency management agencies are better able to craft policies tailored to their states' needs, generate better fact bases, improve organizational capabilities, and specify benchmarks for monitoring policy performance.

In addition, local participation and the number of state emergency management staff had a positive association with plan quality. A plausible explanation for the positive influence of local participation is that local governments best understand how mitigation policies might apply and be tailored to local political, economic, and hazard conditions. By encouraging their input, plan policies and monitoring of policy performance are likely to be more explicit and of higher quality. For state emergency management staff, it is likely that increased staffing leads to greater capability to craft plans that are more specific and comprehensive in addressing a range of hazard problems. Finally, the remaining five variables (FEMA region commitment and capacity, state agency commitment, support of elected officials, and number of declared disasters) had no effect.

Implementation Outcomes

Table 11.10 summarizes the findings on state variations in implementation outcomes. Two variables are used to represent outcomes. One involves the number of disasters with no project applications, which indicates how efficient and proactive states were in seeking mitigation funds. It also reflects how well states responded to opportunities created by individual disasters. The second variable is the percentage of HMGP applications that had been approved since adoption of a state mitigation plan. It represents how successful states were in preparing mitigation project applications and in pushing them through the arduous Section 404 review process.[5]

Table 11.10 shows that there was also considerable variation in the degree to which states took advantage of available HMGP funds. First, in terms of states' abilities to submit project applications after disasters, only 57 percent of states submitted at least one application for each disaster they experienced, whereas 43 percent had one or more disasters with *no* project applications. Second, in terms of gaining approval for applications submitted, 30 percent of all states succeeded in having more than three-quarters of their applications approved, compared with 37 percent having fewer than one-half approved.

Table 11.10. State Variations in Implementation Outcomes

TYPE OF OUTCOME	NUMBER OF STATES	PERCENTAGE
Number of disasters with no project applications		
0	27	57%
1	11	23%
2	4	9%
> 2	5	11%
Percentage of applications approved		
0–25%	10	22%
26–50%	7	15%
51–75%	15	33%
>75%	14	30%

Associations with Implementation Outcomes

Table 11.11 shows the results of a correlation analysis investigating the association of hazard mitigation outcomes (per the HMGP) with mitigation plan quality, FEMA regional agency commitment and capacity, state planning agency commitment and capacity, local government involvement, and contextual factors (support of state elected officials, number of prior disasters, and amount of prior HMGP funding). To achieve a better understanding of how these factors are associated with hazard mitigation outcomes, correlation analyses were used to examine associations with two outcome measures derived from the HMGP: the number of disasters with no HMGP applications (column 1) and the percentage of HMGP projects approved (column 2).

Several findings emerged from the analysis. As expected, one finding is that plan quality has no association with the two dimensions of the HMGP. Additional analysis revealed no significant differences in either type of implementation outcome between states with higher versus lower quality plans. It could be that plans are of such low quality, in general, that even the better plans have no effect on outcomes. Case study findings (see part II) reveal that Section 409 mitigation plans are typically viewed by state emergency management staffs and elected officials as irrelevant in guiding state mitigation decisions. Emergency management officials consistently viewed the Section 409 plan as an administrative requirement for federal funds. Thus our empirical modeling and case studies consistantly find that HMGP projects are not being managed according to a previously adopted plan.

Table 11.11. Associations with Implementation Outcomes

	CORRELATIONS WITH	
FACTOR	(1) DISASTERS WITH NO SECTION 404 APPLICATIONS	(2) % OF SECTION 404 PROJECTS APPROVED
1. Plan quality		
Plan Quality Index (N = 37, 36)	0.10	−0.26
2. FEMA regional office commitment and capacity		
Regional FEMA staff (N = 47, 46)	0.12	0.05
Regional FEMA commitment (N = 47, 46)	−0.23	0.39[c]
3. State emergency management agency commitment and capacity		
Commitment of state agency officials (N = 42, 41)	0.00	0.06
State planning staff (N = 42, 41)	0.61[c]	−0.28[a]
4. Local involvement and commitment		
Importance of local government in Section 409 plan preparation (N = 41, 40)	0.18	−0.14
5. State context		
Support of state elected officials (N = 43, 42)	−0.03	0.08
Number of declared disasters (N = 47, 46)	0.59[c]	−0.05
Amount of prior Section 404 funding available (N = 47, 46)	0.53[c]	−0.29[b]

[a] $p < 0.10$.
[b] $p < 0.05$.
[c] $p < 0.01$.

A second finding is that commitment of a government agency (i.e., a FEMA regional office) was positively associated with the percentage of HMGP projects approved. It could be that when staff members at FEMA's regional offices are motivated to implement hazard mitigation, the approval rate for HMGP projects increases. It may also be that the more committed FEMA regional staff members are to hazard mitigation, the more effective they are in communicating what appropriate uses of hazard mitigation funds are and, ultimately, soliciting viable mitigation applications from the states.

Two other factors that were significantly related to the percentage of approved HMGP applications deal with disaster experience (i.e., the amount of prior funding) and the number of staff members in the lead state hazard mitigation planning agency. Specifically, as the amount of prior funding and the number of staff members decrease, the percentage of

approved HMGP project applications increases. Intuitively, one might expect just the opposite—that is, less funding would mean less prior experience and ability in dealing with federal mitigation funding opportunities, and smaller staffs would mean lower capacity to seek funds and process such applications. However, given the extensive amount of agency resources required to gain HMGP project approval, states with a significant amount of available HMGP funding have more staff members tied up with seeking project approvals from prior disasters. Even with more staff members, agencies in states with greater amounts of available federal funds are still not able to keep pace with processing HMGP applications. The lengthy process of project approval (which takes an average of three and one-half years) is considered a major obstacle to advancing the HMGP program and retards the achievement of implementation outcomes. For example, as discussed in chapter 6, California's state hazard planning staff expanded in response to the massive 1989 Loma Prieta and 1994 Northridge earthquakes. Yet due to inadequate staffing, the agency fell further behind in processing Section 404 applications with each successive disaster. Thus, applications increasingly became backlogged and tied up large amounts of staff time in the preparation and review process.

Another finding indicates that staffing levels at state planning agencies, number of prior disasters, and amount of prior HMGP funding show strong positive associations with the number of disasters with no HMGP applications. Similar to findings on the percentages of approved projects, greater experience with disasters (e.g., more disasters and available HMGP funding) is likely to be accompanied by an expansion of agency staff to deal with long-term recovery demands and mitigation opportunities from these prior events. Given the overwhelming demands placed on agencies to address these expanding needs, states are less likely to submit additional HMGP applications for multiple disasters, even with increased agency staff resources. A single disaster, such as the Northridge earthquake in southern California or Hurricane Andrew in South Florida, can consume agency resources and divert attention from smaller events. Given limited staff time and resources, states inevitably focus their efforts on those disasters with the most HMGP funds available.

An additional explanation for poor state response in submitting Section 404 applications could be the perceived difficulty of meeting matching fund requirements. This could be worsened when states are facing economic downturns (e.g., California in the early 1990s; see chapter 6) and budgets are austere or when states are still paying large amounts of matching funds from previous disasters.

Implications for Reforming Natural Disaster Mitigation Policy

The study framework suggested that hazard mitigation planning and implementation could be improved by collaborative approaches that promote capacity and commitment and link strong state mitigation plans with prioritized mitigation projects in order to achieve national goals. The analysis described in this chapter provides an empirical test of how federal and state agency implementation efforts are related to the quality of state hazard mitigation plans and to implementation outcomes in the form of hazard mitigation project expenditures.

Several conclusions can be drawn from our findings. First, the two key factors found to enhance overall plan quality were local involvement in plan preparation and state emergency management staffing levels. Our survey findings indicate that, while nearly two-thirds of states have forty-nine or fewer staff members, over three-quarters employed fewer than five hazard mitigation staff and almost half had either one person or no staff member responsible for hazard mitigation. Given the intensive emergency response and preparedness demands placed on state emergency management staffs, and the small or nonexistent staffs committed to hazard mitigation, it is likely that state emergency management staffs are poorly configured to devote time and resources to the relatively new mitigation planning initiative required by federal law. The implication is that the staff assigned to mitigation planning should be expanded. In addition, given that the majority (52 percent) of survey respondents considered local involvement in plan preparation to be unimportant or only somewhat important, more attention must be directed toward getting state and federal officials to appreciate the crucial role that local participation plays in the quality of state hazard mitigation plans.

Prior experience with the HMGP also was an important factor in explaining plan quality. The implication is that more effort should be directed toward evaluating these experiences and documenting lessons learned. Our case study chapters (see part II) shed considerable light on this topic, as they reveal how knowledge gained from prior experiences can be applied to create better plans.

Another clear conclusion is that plans are disconnected from implementation actions. Instead of using plans as frameworks for guiding mitigation decisions, state mitigation policy is disaster driven. Our findings suggest that increased disaster experience (number of declared disasters and level of available federal mitigation funding from prior disasters) is strongly related to a decline in state response in using available federal mitigation funds. The level of staffing is also predicated on prior disasters, as agency

staffs grow in response to increased demand for processing of mitigation applications from prior events. However, the expanded staffs often become overwhelmed with these demands and thus are less able to take advantage of available federal mitigation funds from multiple disasters, at least within the relatively short time period (approximately eight years) of this study. This is most certainly the case with large disasters, such as the Northridge earthquake and Hurricane Andrew, which demand a sustained effort over several years at the local, state, and FEMA regional levels to approve, fund, and complete hazard mitigation projects.

These findings raise important implications for policy makers and for future research and will provide a basis for a more in-depth discussion of recommended reforms to the disaster planning framework operating under the Stafford Act. (See chapter 13 for our recommendations.)

Notes

1. We actually collected forty-four plans from thirty-nine states, since some states had more than one plan (individual plans for different types of hazards). For states with multiple plans, we averaged scores to come up with a single plan quality rating for each state (i.e., single measures for each item in the plan evaluations, which were then used to come up with the plan quality index we used in this linkages analysis).
2. As a check on the face validity of the plan quality ratings, members of the study team reviewed the raw data coding of the resultant ratings for each attribute and made minor revisions in the coding of some plan quality attributes to account for additional items not included in the original plan quality coding. Intercoder reliability checks and computation of scores from such checks were not possible given the procedures followed in data collection. However, a partial check on intercoder reliability was undertaken by comparing ratings from coding by different members of the study team on an initial set of four plans. Rules for resolving disagreements were then devised and subsequently used for coding.
3. The SHMO survey detailed in table 11.3 contained similar questions on capacity, but the results are not reported because of an insufficient number of responses to the staffing question. We thus relied on FMHO perceptions of capacity as a contingent measure of staffing capacity.
4. In one study of state mandates, May (1993) found that the interaction of state agency commitment and capacity has a significant effect on implementation effort. We tested this interaction effect on plan quality and implementation outcomes and found no significant effect.
5. To derive a valid implementation measure, we did not use number of projects approved or dollars spent, since these depend on the size of the disaster. The

larger the disaster, the more money becomes available and the more opportunities there are for submitting Section 404 applications. To level the playing field for states, we used the percentage of projects approved, which reflects how well states did in coming up with good applications. We also used the number of disasters with no applications to reflect how well states responded to new opportunities created by each additional disaster.

References

Alesch, Daniel, and William Petak. 1986. *The Politics and Economics of Earthquake Hazards Mitigation.* Monograph No. 43. Boulder: University of Colorado, Institute of Behavioral Science.

Berke, Philip. 1998. "Reducing Natural Hazard Risk Through State Growth Management." *Journal of the American Planning Association* 64 (1): 76–87.

Berke, Philip, and Steven French. 1994. "The Influence of State Planning Mandates on Local Plan Quality." *Journal of Planning Education and Research* 13 (4): 237–250.

Burby, Raymond, and Steven French, with Beverly Cigler, Edward Kaiser, and David H. Moreau. 1985. *Floodplain Land Use Management: A National Assessment.* Boulder, Colo.: Westview Press.

Burby, Raymond, and Peter May, with Philip Berke, Linda Dalton, Steven French, and Edward Kaiser. 1997. *Making Local Governments Plan.* Baltimore: Johns Hopkins University Press.

Dalton, Linda, and Raymond Burby. 1994. "Mandates, Plans, and Planners: Building Local Commitment to Development Management." *Journal of the American Planning Association* 60 (autumn): 444–462.

Deyle, Robert, and Richard Smith. 1999. "Local Government Compliance with State Planning Mandates: The Effects of State Implementation in Florida" *Journal of the American Planning Association* in press.

Faludi, Andreas. 1987. *A Decision-Centered View of Environmental Planning.* New York: Pergamon Press.

FEMA (Federal Emergency Management Agency). 1994. *Audit of FEMA's Mitigation Programs.* September. Washington, D.C.: FEMA, Office of Inspector General, Audit Division.

Godschalk, David R., Edward J. Kaiser, and Philip Berke. 1998. "Integrating Hazard Mitigation and Local Land-Use Planning." *In Confronting Natural Hazards: Land–Use Planning for Sustainable Communities,* ed. Raymond J. Burby. Washington, D.C.: National Academy Press, Joseph Henry Press.

Goggin, Malcolm, Ann Bowman, James P. Lester, and Laurence J. O'Toole. 1990. *Implementation Theory and Practice: Toward a Third Generation.* Reading, Mass.: Addison-Wesley.

Healy, Patsy. 1993. "The Communicative Work of Development Plans." *Environment and Planning B.,* 20:83–104.

Innes, Judith. 1993. "Implementing State Growth Management in the United States: Strategies for Coordination."pp. 18–43 *in Growth Management: The Planning Challenge of the 1990s,* ed. J. Stein. Newbury Park, Calif.: Sage.

Kaiser, Edward J., and David R. Godschalk. 1995. "Twentieth Century Land Use Planning: A Stalwart Family Tree." *Journal of the American Planning Association* 61 (3) 365–385.

Kaiser, Edward J., David R. Godschalk, and F. Stuart Chapin, Jr. 1995. *Urban Land Use Planning.* 4th edition. Urbana: University of Illinois Press.

May, Peter. 1993. "Mandate Design and Implementation: Enhancing Implementation Efforts and Shaping Regulatory Styles." *Journal of Policy Analysis and Management* 12 (4): 634–663.

May, Peter, Raymond Burby, Jennifer Dixon, Neil Ericksen, John Handmer, Sarah Michaels, and D. Ingle Smith. 1996. *Environmental Management and Governance: Intergovernmental Approaches to Hazards and Sustainability.* London: Routledge.

Mazmanian, Daniel, and Paul Sabatier. 1989. *Implementation and Public Policy, with a New Postscript.* New York: Landham.

Mittler, Elliot. 1989. *Natural Hazard Policy Setting: Identifying Supporters and Opponents of Nonstructural Hazard Mitigation.* Monograph No. 48. Boulder: University of Colorado, Institute of Behavioral Science.

Mushkatel, Alvin, and JoAnn Nigg. 1987. "Opinion Congruence and the Formulation of Seismic Safety Policies." *Policy Studies Review* 4 (6): 20–39.

Olshansky, Robert, and Jack Kartez. 1998. "Managing Land Use to Build Resilience." In *Confronting Natural Hazards: Land-Use Planning for Sustainable Communities,* ed. Raymond J. Burby. Washington, D.C.: National Academy Press, Joseph Henry Press.

Rossi, Peter, James Wright, and E. Weber–Burdin. 1982. *Natural Hazards and Public Choice: The State and Local Politics of Hazard Mitigation.* New York: Academic Press.

Talen, Emily. 1996. "Do Plans Get Implemented? A Review of Evaluation in Planning." *Journal of Planning Literature* 10 (3): 248–259.

Recasting the National Mitigation System

In this final part, we recommend some vital reforms of the national hazard mitigation system. We focus on two key areas—creating a mitigation ethic and creating a mitigation system aimed at achieving sustainable communities.

Chapter 12 lays out a number of ethical dilemmas commonly encountered in mitigation practice. It points out the difficult ethical choices faced by individuals and groups, discussing these in terms of ethical roles and responsibilities, competing values, fairness, and ethical biases underlying mitigation analyses. It tackles the perplexing issue of how responsibility for public safety is diffused and avoided rather than equitably shared. Finally, it recommends a series of guidelines for ethical mitigation, ranging from giving public needs priority over private needs to giving preservation of human life priority over protection of property, from avoiding actions that place disproportionate burdens on the least advantaged to considering the interests of future generations, and from holding those who create a hazard culpable for it to requiring those who benefit from risky behavior to assume mitigation costs.

Chapter 13 poses a new vision for natural hazard mitigation—the creation of sustainable communities. Such communities would be resilient with respect to the natural variability of the environment, developed with a recognition of the predictable hazards that result from building human settlements in areas subject to recurrent floods, earthquakes, and hurricanes. We recommend a series of reforms to convert the mitigation system from a disaster-driven system to a threat-driven system, to change disaster policy from a focus on individual disasters to a focus on living sustainably within an ecological system with foreseeable variations, and to focus mitigation practice on using best mitigation practices aimed at developing resilient communities.

CHAPTER 12

Ethical Guidelines for Hazard Mitigation

Decisions about planning for, responding to, and recovering from natural hazard events and disasters pose serious ethical questions involving choices among different societal values and normative standards. A host of individuals and groups face these ethical choices in each phase of disaster management, from predisaster mitigation and preparedness to response, recovery, and reconstruction.

However, there has been little debate over ethical issues related to natural hazards and disasters. Only a few authors address such ethical dimensions (e.g., Partridge 1988; Beatley 1989), and there is little discussion in the professional literature (e.g., Mucha 1994). The ethical literature of the disciplines involved with natural hazards, such as city and regional planning, does not specifically address natural hazards (e.g., Howe 1980; Howe and Kaufman 1979). This chapter fills the gap left by this failure to confront the crucial ethical issues posed by natural hazard mitigation decision making.

Understanding Mitigation Ethics

Our goal is the creation of more informed, reflective, and ethical mitigation policies and actions. In this chapter, we expose key ethical quandaries in hazard mitigation and clarify their nature. Our findings are drawn from case studies reported in previous chapters as well as interviews and analyses conducted under a related study funded by the National Science Foundation, titled "Ethical Issues in Natural Hazard Management."[1]

There is considerable variation in hazard officials' perceptions about whether ethical issues are important or even present in natural hazards

policy. Many individuals we interviewed said that ethics had little to do with natural hazards and were perplexed at the nature of our inquiries. Others, however, made immediate connections to ethics and perceived the dilemmas and policy issues they confront as fundamentally ethical in nature. Although some variation is a matter of semantics, clearly there were great differences in the ways individuals perceived and framed mitigation policy questions.

Whether or not interviewees acknowledged ethical dimensions, we found ethical and moral concepts and language to be pervasive in mitigation. Professionals and policy makers commonly said things like "We have obligations to do . . . ," "They deserve to have . . . ," "That individual was wrong not to have done . . . " Making mitigation decisions clearly involves extensive value judgments, though they may not always be seen or acknowledged as such by the individuals involved.

Moreover, we found many instances in disaster events in which considerable personal and institutional judgment was exercised. Whether it was a damage inspector determining whether a home was damaged beyond habitability or a program administrator making a determination about eligibility, there were numerous "street-level" mitigation decisions (i.e., the exercising of situation-specific discretion and judgment).

The following sections describe the major categories of ethical questions we encountered during our interviews and case studies. Our typology covers four issue areas: appropriate ethical roles and responsibilities; competing values in mitigation; fairness in mitigation; and ethical aspects of mitigation analyses. We conclude with preliminary ethical guidelines for those involved in mitigation policy, especially mitigation professionals.

Ethical Roles and Responsibilities

Ethical issues regarding mitigation confront individuals in a number of social roles, including planning and design professionals, politicians, mitigation officers and program administrators, among others. It is not always clear who has the ultimate responsibility for public safety.

Who Is Responsible for Safety?

Who holds ultimate responsibility for ensuring the safety of the public and for mitigating natural hazards? Hazard mitigation occurs in a morally diffuse environment—that is, in answering the question of who is responsible

for safety and mitigation, at least in the United States, there is no simple or clear answer. In a sense, everyone is responsible and no one is. Housing consumers expect government to ensure the safety of their homes and the buildings in which they work. Society, on the other hand, places much of the responsibility on builders, design professionals, and the consumer public. In short, precisely who has the moral onus is unclear.

We uncovered many different views about who is or might be responsible and little consensus, since responsibility is not assigned to any one group or profession. There is a strong sense among many that responsibility must be *shared* among a number of groups and actors, including government agencies and regulators (at a number of jurisdictional levels); the private sector (e.g., building owners, corporations, merchants); professionals (e.g., architects, engineers); and individuals (as citizens, consumers, homeowners). We found evidence of efforts to assign responsibility for safety to each of these groups.

Some believe that building owners hold special responsibilities. A recent report by the California Seismic Safety Commission states, for instance, that *building owners* are "primarily responsible" for ensuring the safety and quality of construction of their buildings (though they are often not aware of this requirement) and that they may be held liable "for failure to take reasonable measures to prevent injuries to employees, tenants, and customers" (California Seismic Safety Commission 1995, p. 26). Building owners, however, often opt for least-cost design and construction options, in part because their investment time frame may be relatively short. Subsequent building owners and the larger community and state may ultimately bear the cumulative long-term costs of these decisions.

In recent years, considerable onus has also been placed on building owners to retrofit structures for seismic safety. In California, a number of localities have adopted retrofit ordinances requiring improvements to be made within a certain time frame (e.g., see Berke and Beatley 1992). And although financial assistance has been provided in some cases, retrofitting often involves significant expense to building owners, raising the question of whether they should be held responsible for the safety of their occupants (i.e., tenants, businesses) in the event of an earthquake. Is it unethical for a building owner or merchant to operate a business wherein people frequently enter and leave a structure that is likely to collapse in an earthquake?

Retrofitting is a controversial topic in California. Many building owners object to the costs and question the fairness of their being required to absorb these costs. As the president of the Apartment Owners Association of California recently said (Waxler 1996):

People are already losing their buildings left and right because of foreclosures. They've already been beaten up. To hit them with this—there are people who will lose their building. . . . It may be hard and cruel, but how can apartment owners be asked to save all these lives.

Perhaps it is not the responsibility of building owners to "save all these lives," but ultimately the responsibility of *individuals* to look out for their own safety. Some believe that much greater emphasis must be placed on personal responsibility. Individuals could be expected to assess the structural integrity and seismic vulnerability of homes they purchase. They could also be expected to assess the site on which their home is built, determining whether it is in a floodplain, on a seismic fault, or in an area subject to landslides. They could be expected to actively protect themselves and their property by installing shutters in coastal areas or by bolting structures to the foundation in earthquake country. The Oakland, California, firestorm of 1991 illustrates well the potential role played by personal responsibility. Much of the ferocity of that event was a result of uncontrolled growth of vegetation around homes. Ensuring a vegetation-free fire zone around one's home is a critical action that each landowner can take to reduce the threat of such disasters.

There are clear limits, however, to approaches that rely heavily on individual responsibility. Few individuals without an architectural or engineering background could look at a prospective home in South Florida and assess its likelihood to fail in, say, a Category 4 hurricane. In this sense, *government* must be responsible for ensuring safe buildings, and building codes and construction standards can serve this function. In this way, public mitigation programs are analogous to consumer protection and food and drug laws.

Individuals may also be unwilling to spend their housing budgets on safety features when society doesn't emphasize personal preventive planning for natural disasters. Instead, people seem to be encouraged to spend money on nonstructural housing amenities. One builder recently described the decision dynamic of home buyers in this way (Mayer 1996, p. E4):

My feeling is if you poll home-buying consumers and ask if they would be willing to spend X amount to improve the structure of their homes, they will all say yes. But when it comes time to sign on the dotted line, there will be a lot of conflicting demands. Will they spend their money on stronger connections to the foundation or for a beautiful Corian counter top? The problem for consumers is they can't bring relatives or guests into their homes and say "Look at the beautiful connections to my roof."

For individuals to become as concerned about safety as they are about amenities will require active encouragement by government, with aggressive education programs.

This highlights the tension between the needs, interests, and wants of individuals and those of the broader public. Individual mitigation decisions have public or collective consequences—failure to control vegetation around one's home in a wildfire-prone area (witness the Oakland firestorm) undermines the safety of the entire community and the lives of fire-fighting personnel and rescue workers. Failure to ensure the structural integrity of one's home, by installing shutters and hurricane clips, for example, may mean that in the event of a hurricane or storm resulting debris becomes a battering ram, damaging other homes in the community. Does the individual—or, more appropriately, *should* the individual—take into account these public effects when making mitigation decisions? Most ethicists would say yes, yet the cultural milieu stresses individualism.

Thus, even as calls for heightened individual responsibility increase, there remains a necessary role for government. At a minimum, this includes mandates for disclosure of risks and dissemination of information (such as California's 1972 Alquist–Priolo Earthquake Fault Zoning Act and its statewide seismic mapping program). Other responsibilities include setting and enforcing minimum building codes, such as California's Unified Building Code, and safety standards, such as minimum requirements for sheltering and evacuation (California Seismic Safety Commission 1995, chap. 3). Government also has an obligation to create appropriate incentives, financial and otherwise, to encourage responsible individual action.

One difficult question is whether government has the responsibility (i.e., the moral duty) to keep people from occupying hazardous locations. Some believe that government indeed has an affirmative obligation to prevent such exposure, beyond simply informing individuals of the possible hazards. Especially wherever governments engage in regulating development, such regulation creates an expectation of safety—"If this were not a safe place to live, the government would not have allowed us to build here." The realities are quite different; in many places, governments approve development in risky places.

Other actors with some moral responsibility include *banks and mortgage companies* and *insurance companies*. Each of the disaster events we studied resulted in calls for these actors to assume greater responsibility (e.g., Wright 1996). They could provide incentives for individuals, such as lower mortgage interest rates for better-built homes and lower insurance rates for good design. Perhaps these actors also have a moral obligation to

disallow risky behavior—for example, to disapprove a mortgage for a home to be built in a floodplain.

Performance of the construction and building trades has been an issue in recent disasters, raising questions about their ethical duties. Building contractors exercise daily judgments about what types of materials to use, how much supervision and oversight to exercise, and where to "cut corners" in construction (are workers really putting in the requisite number of nails?). It is not clear that contractors and the construction industry in general feel an ethical obligation to produce a high-quality, and thus safer, product. Shoddy construction was especially implicated in the damage from Hurricane Andrew and the Northridge earthquake (e.g., see California Seismic Safety Commission 1995).

To expect a higher standard of practice requires that builders and contractors be equipped with the necessary knowledge to be more ethical and responsible. Projects such as Blue Sky are positive steps. Funded in part by FEMA, Blue Sky aims to demonstrate how simple building technologies can strengthen homes at modest additional cost (see Mayer 1996). Before builders can begin to understand their ethical duty to use six nails to attach a roof tile rather than the conventional four, they need the training and knowledge to see this as a practice that will substantially strengthen a building in the face of hurricane forces.

Questions about ethical practices within the insurance industry were also raised by interviewees. Especially in California, there was a sense that the insurance industry was engaging in redlining, or curtailing the issuance of homeowners' insurance in certain areas of high risk exposure. The resulting moral indignation comes from a sense that the industry is unfairly taking advantage of circumstances, and that companies are operating opportunistically, raising premiums and dropping customers who have had policies for many years. This "cherry-picking"—insuring only the safest properties—is seen as unfair and inequitable, particularly when the companies are making profits on other types of insurance (e.g., automobile, life) in the same geographic regions. Indeed, this sentiment is behind some of the "coupling" requirements in states such as California and Florida; for example, in California, if a company offers a homeowners' policy, it must also offer earthquake insurance.

There is also a perception that the current state of natural hazards insurance is at least partly a function of the past practices of insurance companies, such as underestimating the chances of major disasters and emphasizing the recruitment of new policyholders over minimizing or mitigating risks. This perception is, however, somewhat at odds with the belief that those who are exposed to risks ought to be paying higher rates.

There are also questions about who is responsible for the impacts of disasters once they have occurred. The case studies raised a number of questions regarding *culpability*, a moral concept suggesting that those who are responsible for causing damage ought to be held accountable, correcting the damage or otherwise compensating affected parties. And indeed, the assignment of *blame* is common after disaster events. Following the Northridge earthquake, for example, the city of Los Angeles was blamed for the collapse of an apartment complex that killed sixteen people, and a lawsuit was instituted by the families seeking damages. Following the Loma Prieta earthquake, Caltrans (the California Department of Transportation) received considerable blame for the collapse of the Cypress Freeway and for failing to design and build it to stronger seismic standards. Many of these conflicts find their way into the courts and are settled there.

Professions and Professional Ethics

Numerous professions influence the safety of people and property. The list of professions involved in designing, planning, and building includes architects and engineers (both structural and civil engineers), geologists and engineering geologists, building code officials, planners, and contractors and developers, though strictly speaking the latter two fields may not be considered professions (see table 12.1).[2]

Each profession could be said to have moral responsibilities that accompany its professional practice, and many professional organizations issue formal professional codes of ethics or codes of professional conduct. Many of those we interviewed believed that building and design professionals have gradually retreated from exercising a strong sense of professional

Table 12.1. Some Professionals and Professional Organizations Influencing Mitigation

	PROFESSIONAL ORGANIZATIONS
Architects	American Institute of Architects
Structural engineers	National Society of Professional Engineers
Consulting engineers	American Society of Civil Engineers
Engineering geologists, geologists	Association of Engineering Geologists
Land use planners	American Planning Association, American Institute of Certified Planners
Building code officials	Council of American Building Officials, International Conference of Building Officials

responsibility. Increasingly, the tendency is for individuals to define their professional roles as narrowly as possible and to avoid taking responsibility for the ultimate safety of a building or site (contrary to many of the codes of ethics). Moreover, there is often little coordination among the different professions involved in designing a structure and no clear line of responsibility among them (California Seismic Safety Commission 1995).

The disasters we examined confirm the retreat from professional responsibility and the limitations of a building and development system in which ultimate responsibility is confused and uncertain. Two grand juries were convened following Hurricane Andrew, for instance, and their reports are a strong indictment of a building system in which responsibility is avoided and shoddy workmanship and unsafe buildings result. The grand juries blame a building system in which inspection and enforcement are lax, construction practices are questionable, and architects and engineers fail to ensure that structures are built according to plan and code. In the words of the first grand jury report, "In short, what has evolved is a building profession that no longer is held to a standard of professionalism. This lackadaisical approach to regulation and professionalism by the industry itself and by the government which regulates it, is no longer tolerable" (Dade County Grand Jury 1992, p. 14).[3]

What are these professional duties and obligations? The interviews and case studies highlighted several areas of agreement and disagreement. Some professionals expressed a strong moral obligation to protect public safety. Indeed, the language of the professional codes of ethics tends to strongly endorse this ethic of public safety. The "Principles of Ethical Behavior" of the Association of Engineering Geologists, for instance, states; "Engineering Geologists have a responsibility to promote the public health, safety and welfare by applying their specialized knowledge to mitigate geologic hazards and geologic constraints" (Association of Engineering Geologists 1985, p. 1). Other codes make similarly strong statements.

The Council of American Building Officials' Code of Ethics speaks of the protection of life, health, and property being "a solemn responsibility of the highest order" and a "trust" bestowed by the public and states that the certified building official shall place the public's welfare above all other interests and recognize that the chief function of government is to serve the best interests of all the people. Building officials shall recognize the continuing need for developing improved safety standards for the protection of life, health, and property, and acknowledge a professional obligation to contribute time and expertise in the development of such improvements (Council of American Building Officials n.d.).

In San Francisco, one recent test of professional ethical standards has been the debate over the city's new URB (unreinforced building) ordinance. Largely as a result of concerns about the effects of the ordinance on Chinatown residents and businesses, a weaker retrofit standard (which is actually lower than standards for a substantial renovation or change of use) was adopted. Although there were concerns that the ordinance might result in raised rents and displacement of low-income residents, what has actually happened, according to San Francisco's chief building inspector, is that buildings are not being retrofitted to current professional standards and building practices are inferior to those in other communities.

One issue involves the active avoidance of responsibility. We heard of engineers who chose not to inspect building sites for fear that doing so would expose them to future liability challenges should a building later fail (and they were advised to follow this path by their insurance companies). Most thoughtful professionals we talked with, though understanding why such liability-limiting actions might be taken, saw it as professionally inappropriate and unethical to actively avoid opportunities to ensure that buildings were actually being constructed according to plan and with appropriate building materials and methods. There is a sense that each profession must begin not just to stop avoiding responsibility but also to proactively assume greater responsibility for ensuring safe buildings and environments.

Another response is that professionals are at least obligated to abide by the law. This often translates into designing and building according to the prevailing code. Many professions (as well as many citizens and politicians) tend to define what is ethically required by what is legally mandated. But as many recent disaster events have shown, building codes are usually minimum standards and do not necessarily protect the public from major disasters. These are not the safety standards to which professionals should aspire. Professionals are required at least to meet the minimum requirements of the law, but some of our interviewees believed that adherence to the law eclipses consideration of broader ethical duties.

Other values that may apply in particular professions may not be explicitly acknowledged in a code of ethics. The engineering field and its subfields, such as civil engineering, have historically reflected a sense that nature and natural forces can be controlled. Historical reliance on levees and flood control structures in riverine environments, and use of seawalls and shore-hardening structures in coastal environments reflect the significance of an "engineering ethic." Such an ethic could be described as arrogant in its belief in the engineering abilities of the human species and in

the superiority of engineering solutions even in the face of high financial and environmental costs.

Substantive ethics of professions, however, change in response to changes in social values. Civil engineering, for instance, is today practiced with much greater attention to environmental concerns than it was previously (though still with not sufficient attention to many such concerns). Interestingly, the July 1996 issue of the magazine of the American Public Works Association is devoted to environmental and sustainable development topics, and the cover features a highway in Hawaii that "lies lightly on the land" (American Public Works Association1996).

Another issue involves professionals taking on design projects for which they are not qualified. State licensing boards deal with this to some degree, but certain professions (e.g., architects and engineers) are legally allowed to design almost any type of building or structure. The commercial end of one's practice may tempt design professionals to take on projects for which they are not fully or adequately prepared.

Designing structures to withstand disaster forces can be complex, and keeping up with changing professional standards and technical knowledge is another responsibility. As the California Seismic Safety Commission notes, "Designers must be accountable not only for the design of individual buildings but also for staying up to date regarding the state-of-the-art in earthquake resistant design" (California Seismic Safety Commission 1995, p. 27).

Professionals involved in design and mitigation may also face conflicting duties. Under the California seismic mapping program, those wishing to develop property that lies within a delineated liquefaction zone must prepare a geotechnical report. These reports explore whether hazardous conditions exist and what mitigation and design actions could be taken to address them. Typically, such reports are prepared by consulting engineers or engineering geologists. Under current California law, the client commissioning the report is not required to submit it if the results are not to his or her liking. The client can have as many reports prepared as he or she can afford, until the desired conclusions are reached. And, apparently, duties to the client forbid the consultant from sharing the findings with the government. The consultant thus may have conflicting obligations— duties to the client and to the safety of the general public.

Much of the debate about professional responsibility centers on disclosure of information to clients and the duty to inform them about options. As a matter of practice, however, this has not always happened. In California, architects and engineers have been accused of failing to explain to clients that designing and constructing to mandated seismic standards will

not ensure an economically viable building after an earthquake. Current seismic standards are intended to ensure safety (i.e., to prevent the buildings from falling down), but many building owners appear not to understand that additional seismic strengthening is required to ensure a usable building. The California legislature is considering mandating that architects and engineers disclose to clients that they are designing buildings "to code" and that in the event of an earthquake the building may not be economically usable. The client would also be given a list of possible technologies and mitigation techniques to make the building stronger. Once given this information, the building owner is left to decide what the appropriate building performance should be.

The professional reward structure may also serve to discourage mitigation. Public acclaim is lavished on aesthetic designs, with architectural journals and magazines tending to focus on visual aspects. Few professional accolades are given to those who design and build a structure that survives a major earthquake (though this is possible: witness Frank Lloyd Wright's Imperial Hotel, which survived a major earthquake in Tokyo). In a climate of cost saving, in which choices must be made between, say, additional seismic reinforcement and a more spectacular building facade, the latter will often prevail. This suggests the importance of modifying the professional reward structure so that mitigative design practices are encouraged or at least not discouraged.

Professionals must also confront the question of how to separate professional from personal judgments about the acceptability of a development proposal. Coastal geologist Orrin Pilkey is sometimes criticized by his geologic and scientific colleagues for failing to disentangle these judgments. For example, it may be his professional opinion that a beach will erode at a certain rate, but it would be his personal judgment that building on that beach is inappropriate or unethical. Sorting out these judgments is difficult, especially in light of the stated duty to protect and advance public safety.

In the design professions, tension exists between the desire to design safe and exemplary buildings and sites and the need to earn a living. In a competitive capitalist system, concern for safety may be secondary to the selling of professional services. A consulting engineer or engineering geologist who develops a reputation for overly stringent assessments of geologic hazards and design recommendations may find relatively little work. Contrary to this concern, a recent article in *Civil Engineering* asks, "Is it necessary to compromise engineering ethics to remain competitive in today's marketplace?" and answers the question in the negative (Mucha 1994, p. 62). Some clients prefer the services of professionals known to have

high ethical standards. In either event, professionals have to balance the demands of earning a living with the demands of upholding high standards of ethical practice.

Politics and Politicians

Our case studies raised questions about the appropriate role of politics and politicians in making mitigation decisions. One example is the conflict over Auburn Dam, a proposed flood control project on the American River, northwest of Sacramento, California. The dam, a 508-foot-high structure, would cost about $1 billion to construct. Opponents of the dam have criticized the tactics of its chief congressional supporter, Representative John Doolittle, who they believe strong-armed local officials into supporting the project by threatening to block funding for any other flood control alternative. Similar accusations of dishonesty and distortion of the truth arose in several of the case studies.

At a fundamental level, these concerns question what ethical standards we expect of our politicians, leaders, and decision makers. Should they be held to high standards of honesty, courage, and integrity in dealing with the public and others? What is their appropriate role relative to mitigation? Is it to simply respond to the immediate expressed demands of the public (and thus, perhaps, to secure reelection) or to exercise leadership in promoting a long-term vision of a safer community in which to live?

Honesty "writ large" came into play in the Auburn Dam conflict. Ron Stork of Friends of the River, a local environmental group opposing the dam, observed that Sacramento is a community "in a state of denial about its basic geohydrological circumstances." In the minds of Stork and others, Sacramento's leaders, though perhaps not lying, have not been honest with their constituents. As Stork argues, honesty is the first ethical obligation—citizens should be told they live in a floodplain and that certain things will happen when the levees break. The presence of an extensive levee system and the infrequency of flooding in the area may cause people to minimize or underappreciate the flood risk. Meanwhile, extensive new development is occurring in the floodplain, especially in the at-risk Notomos community. Are officials being fully honest with constituents? Should elected officials (and perhaps others) be expected to act courageously in attempting to combat local complacency and "community denial"?

Many local politicians see their roles primarily as promoting economic development and growth and only secondarily as minimizing risks from

natural disasters. Indeed, in several of the case studies, we found examples of local mitigation and recovery efforts being aimed essentially at promoting economic development, often with ambivalence toward or disregard for hazard reduction. One city in Iowa had purchased floodplain properties under the buyout program and was reselling them to new businesses, a prospect made possible by an impending certification that a surrounding levee would protect the land from a 100-year flood event. In this case, a hazard reduction program was converted to an economic development strategy that may increase the property and people at risk (see chapter 5). In South Florida after Hurricane Andrew, federal recovery monies were used to finance economic development and growth-related projects, including an ambitious race-track complex. These projects often had little to do with making the community more resilient to hurricanes (see chapter 3).

Partisan politics sometimes gets in the way of public safety. A top state official in California complained that charges from the federal government of waste in the aftermath of the Northridge earthquake were largely politically motivated (i.e., the controversy represented the clash of a Democratic federal administration and a Republican administration at the state level). Specifically, federal officials have claimed that the state had been gouging the federal government in charges for repairing several buildings, such as the University of Southern California hospital. FEMA dispatched auditors to investigate the possibility of fraud, and a "nasty public feud" ensued.

Concerns were also expressed about unfair imbalances in political power and how these translate into differing levels of mitigation or recovery resources. In California, several interviewees pointed to how quickly bridges and highways were rebuilt in Los Angeles following Northridge, as compared with rebuilding in the San Francisco Bay Area after Loma Prieta. Even though the Northridge event had happened some five years later, reconstruction had been progressing faster there, and some Bay Area officials attributed this to the greater political importance of southern California.

Interest-group politics may also interfere with public safety. One interviewee noted that although schools in California are subject to state seismic retrofit requirements, hospitals had managed to remain exempt from this law. The explanation given was that the hospital lobby in California is a powerful one. Interestingly, there have been proposals, so far unsuccessful, in the California legislature to require that patients admitted to hospitals be informed of the seismic risks associated with staying there.

Lack of political courage might also be seen in the efforts of politicians

to avoid raising taxes in election years to pay for disasters. California Governor Pete Wilson's plan to pay for the costs of Northridge through a state bond measure (that did not pass) was seen by many as a clear political tactic to avoid the issue before the fall 1994 elections. Critics of Wilson, such as state senator Tom Hayden, advocated other ways to raise the funds that would have been, in the long run, much less expensive.

Mitigation Officials and Program Administrators

In examining implementation of mitigation programs and policies, the amount of personal interpretation is striking. Program guidance is often sparse, and mitigation officials often must make personal, sometimes on-the-spot, moral judgments about the merits of a particular claim, request, or proposal. How vaguely defined programs are implemented raises serious ethical dilemmas for program administrators and their roles.

Several examples emerged from the case studies. One involved the structuring and implementation of local hazard mitigation programs funded under FEMA's Hazard Mitigation Grant Program (HMGP) (chapter 10). Under this program, unique local mitigation measures are proposed, often with little previous experience about the implementation issues or problems that will be encountered. Many involve distribution of monies to homeowners or others to undertake mitigation measures. For example, eligibility questions arose in a local program established after the Loma Prieta earthquake to provide financial assistance to homeowners undertaking seismic retrofits during rebuilding. Should all residents be eligible, or should there be some form of means testing? (The former was decided.) Should individual grants be unlimited, or should they be capped at a certain maximum? (Eventually a cap was instituted, after large individual requests were submitted.) Should homeowners be eligible for retroactive coverage for retrofit expenditures made before the program was created? (The decision was made to allow this.) And should funding be allowed only for seismic upgrades, not for termite damage, roof repair, and the like? (Specific guidelines were developed to limit expenditures to those related to seismic building or bracing.)

Following the Northridge earthquake, similar judgment calls were made in determining which homes were inhabitable and which were not. Even though a standardized damage assessment methodology was used, some damage assessors made determinations according to whether people would be put out on the street and whether alternative housing was available from the city rather than strictly on whether a structure was considered uninhabitable based on the assessment criteria. Is the official's role

here exclusively one of thinking about the safety and habitability of structures, or should she or he consider other issues, such as balancing safety
against the availability of housing?

Program administrators face the dilemma of whether to interpret a program or program requirement narrowly or to allow (or promote) creativity
in interpretation that allows something positive or appropriate. Should
administrators look to the "letter" of the law or the "spirit" of the law, or
should they go beyond both when the outcome is seen as desirable in some
important way (e.g., improves the quality of someone's life or reduces
long-term hazard exposure)?

We encountered many differing interpretations of federal and state disaster programs. It was reported that after the Northridge earthquake, a
decision was made to allow funding for the bolting of homes to founda-
tions under the minor home repair program because it provided 100 percent coverage (compared with the 25 percent match that would have been
required through the Individual Assistance Hazard Minimization Program), even though, as one FEMA employee critically observed, such an
expenditure was not really a minor home repair. The creative program
administration in this case was the result of a strong push for seismic mitigation following Northridge, certainly an admirable and important public
objective.

The Moral Community

Philosophers and ethicists often refer to the "moral community," defined
as the people to whom moral consideration should be given. Whose interests and welfare should be taken into account when making a particular
mitigation decision or allocating benefits?

Different approaches to defining the moral community were important
after Hurricane Andrew and the Northridge earthquake. In both, controversies arose over the eligibility of illegal residents to receive disaster assistance. In both, FEMA provided aid to illegal residents, and the agency was
criticized by some for doing so. Following Northridge, Congress placed
additional restrictions on such aid through a supplemental funding bill.
Under these new requirements, aid could not be extended beyond ninety
days without "self-certification" of citizenship. The law has since changed
again, leaving it up to states to decide on this question. In California, currently only life-saving medical assistance can be provided to illegal
residents.

There is disagreement about this within the hazard mitigation community. The issue is perhaps the most sensitive in California. One official

with the Governor's Office of Emergency Services (OES) indicated during an interview that he believed it was inappropriate to deny people in need, regardless of their citizenship. He pointed out that we send millions of dollars in foreign assistance to other countries each year, so to deny assistance to individuals in the United States because of lack of citizenship seems arbitrary. The current director of the OES had a different view, indicating that it was inappropriate in the face of federal and state budget deficits to be providing disaster assistance to individuals who were here illegally.

Another way to define the moral community is geographically or spatially. Many mitigation issues involve cross-boundary or interjurisdictional effects. The filling of wetlands, watershed degradation, and construction of flood control projects upstream will have definite effects downstream. Understandably, local officials (and citizens) tend to think first about their own jurisdictions and do not commonly undertake mitigation actions that primarily or in large degree benefit other jurisdictions. These "other" jurisdictions often are not viewed as part of the relevant moral community.

The moral community can also be defined in temporal terms. Historically, public policy (and, indeed, most individual actions) tends to be driven by a very short time frame. Things that might happen in the future and people who might be affected are simply not seen as important, if they are considered at all. But many individual and collective decisions about natural disasters clearly affect the future and the lives of future residents. These ethical duties are frequently described in terms of intergenerational equity, intertemporal justice, or obligations to future generations.

One rationale for the existence of building codes is that even though any particular owner of a building may be willing to accept a low level of safety, the building will probably be occupied by a number of tenants and owners in the future who may not agree with this risk assessment. The chief building inspector for the city of San Francisco has articulated a professional responsibility to ensure the safety of buildings for "future users" and for members of the public who have made no direct personal choice to place themselves at risk. He stated this "building philosophy" in a recent paper on the Kobe earthquake (Kornfield n.d., p. 2):

> As a building official, I am committed to a code of professional behavior which to me is usually clear but which is often puzzling, even absurd, to others. One of the basic precepts I employ when viewing building concerns is that I represent, in absentia, the unknown future user.

Wheras the average mortgage may be for only 30 years, buildings survive and are used for much longer periods, perhaps hundreds of years. Equally true, a 30-year or even 60-year coastal setback for a building may protect it in the short term but may expose future residents to significant erosion and storm risks. Taking safety into account for the full and complete life of a coastal structure would suggest much more stringent setback standards, perhaps on the order of 100 years, 200 years, or longer. Moreover, many individual decisions about buildings or sites can cumulatively affect the long-term patterns of hazards and the safety levels future residents will experience. Although the building of one or two structures in a floodplain may seem insignificant or the building of a road or other public facility in a high-risk area inconsequential, such decisions can set in motion patterns of future development that may significantly influence risk levels for future generations. A report by the National Science and Technology Council (NSTC 1996) states that the current generation must take into account the effects of its actions on the vulnerability of future generations.

Other obligations to the future include environmental and historic preservation actions. Preservation and restoration of a pristine natural river canyon, it can be argued, is required as part of the natural legacy we are duty-bound to pass along to our descendants. Similarly, seismic retrofitting of buildings such as San Francisco's city hall and opera house involves an effort to preserve the cultural capital of society and ensure that this capital is passed along and not lost in an earthquake.

Funding of mitigation programs also raises questions of temporal ethics. Some objected to Governor Wilson's proposal to fund the state costs associated with the Northridge earthquake by floating bonds because it would essentially transfer these costs onto future taxpayers. Where future residents would enjoy the benefits of a mitigation project, such as a levee project with a useful life of fifty years, such a financing scheme might be less troubling, but where the primary objective for such a proposal is to find the least painful way of paying for something, the principle of intertemporal equity may be violated.

Competing Values in Mitigation

Many values compete in mitigation choices. Should the emphasis be on public safety and property protection, environmental preservation, historic preservation, personal freedom, or individual property rights?

Public Safety, Property Protection, and "Acceptable" Risk

Two values frequently involved in mitigation are protection of public health and safety and protection of private property. When we asked mitigation professionals which value should be given priority, the frequent answer was public safety, and there did appear to be considerable consensus on this opinion. A number of mitigation plans can be cited that state the priority of this issue and have presented, at least as official policy, the expression public safety. Furthermore, this appears to be the single most important moral value that motivates and guides many hazard mitigation professionals.

Yet public safety and property protection often conflict. One example in South Florida was the practice at many marinas of requiring boat owners to pick up and trailer out their boats in advance of an oncoming hurricane or coastal storm. Intended to protect private property, this practice adds to evacuation congestion and diminishes people's ability to get quickly out of harm's way. After Hurricane Andrew, Florida issued a legislative pronouncement that protection of property shall not, at least in the case of boat removal, take priority over preservation of human life and safety.

Another potential conflict occurs when emergency response personnel are asked to risk their own lives. The risk that such personnel take is viewed as appropriate, especially where the goal is to save the lives of others. But often such personnel are asked to risk their lives to save a residence or a business. In the Oakland firestorm, for instance, a number of firemen lost their lives essentially fighting property destruction. There is no clear dividing line between these values—public safety and property protection often go hand in hand. The Oakland firestorm was clearly also a major threat to human life. The question is to what extent the protection of property justifies placing people's lives in jeopardy.

The issue of public safety versus property protection is a significant one in California with respect to the seismic safety provided by building codes. Protection of human life has historically been the primary goal behind such codes, which are intended primarily to ensure that buildings are "survivable"—that is, that when an earthquake occurs, people will be able to leave the buildings alive. Yet many, including many building owners, have assumed that seismic codes are intended to protect property as well, believing that if a building is constructed to code, it will survive an earthquake and be economically functional following the event. This is a misunderstanding.

A significant issue for many communities is how much risk from nat-

ural disasters is deemed acceptable. Clearly, choices about acceptable risk are implicit in the adoption of any specific mitigation program or policy (for a discussion of acceptable risk, see Fischhoff 1984). There are a number of different risk standards in use. In floodplain management, for example, the National Flood Insurance Program (NFIP) is heavily focused on the 100-year flood, whereas the U.S. Army Corps of Engineers has historically used the "standard project flood," or 500-year flood. In coastal areas, there is great variation in shoreline setback requirements, ranging from no setback in many coastal states and localities to 30-year and 60-year setbacks in states such as Florida and North Carolina, respectively. In California, certain public buildings, specifically hospitals and schools, must be built to a much higher seismic standard. Retrofit ordinances typically stipulate compliance time lines that assume greater priority for buildings that house many people.

Environmental Values and Ethics

In many natural hazard mitigation efforts, questions arise about ethical duties and responsibilities to the environment. Over the past two decades, there has been an explosion of publications regarding environmental ethics, though few of them address natural hazards or natural disasters directly (e.g., see Nash 1989; Rolston 1988).

The most contentious mitigation cases involve a trade-off between public safety and property protection on the one hand and protection of the natural environment on the other. One case involves protection of the endangered Stephens' kangaroo rat, indigenous to southern California, versus protection of homes and property from wildfires. Protection of this species under the federal Endangered Species Act was blamed for property losses because of restrictions placed on the disking of vegetation around homes, a fire control measure. In 1989, weed abatement standards were issued by the Riverside County Fire Department that prohibited disking around homes, though daylight mowing and other abatement techniques not disturbing the ground were permitted. In late 1993, a fierce wildfire erupted in Riverside County, a result of high winds and dry conditions (it was one of twenty-one wildfires in southern California that year). Twenty-nine homes were lost in the fire, and some homeowners claimed that the prohibition on disking was the cause of the losses. A study by the General Accounting Office (GAO) concluded, however, that weed abatement of any kind probably would not have saved the homes, given the intensity of the blaze (GAO 1994).

Since the fires, disking within 100 feet of homes has been authorized, and representatives of the U.S. Fish and Wildlife Service believe that this action will not threaten the survival of the Stephens' kangroo rat. Interestingly, there was never a question about whether emergency firebreaks in habitat areas would be permitted, as these "would be in the defense of lives and therefore would not violate the ESA [Endangered Species Act]" (GAO 1994, p. 6). The GAO report notes that even though limited disking is now authorized, there remains the perception of a conflict between fire suppression and species protection.

In South Florida, a controversy has long raged over the proposed expansion of a critical segment of Highway 1 (in southern Dade County) that has been a bottleneck for hurricane evacuation from the Florida Keys. The road expansion has been criticized by the environmental community as ecologically destructive and growth inducing. Proponents of the project see it as essential for evacuating people in a timely manner and thus strongly justified on public safety grounds.

Similar value clashes have arisen over the proposed Auburn Dam in northern California. As noted earlier, construction of the dam has been vehemently opposed by environmentalists, who view the project as highly destructive, as it would result in the loss of forty miles of pristine river canyons.

The 1996 wildfires in the western United States further illustrate these conflicts. Allowing such fires to run their course may be necessary to restore the ecological equilibrium of forest ecosystems, given eighty years of fire suppression. Yet firefighters are often placed in the position of having to fight such fires because of nearby development and having to protect private property at the cost of deploying limited resources to protect other important natural resources. One fire specialist with the Bureau of Land Management was recently quoted on the liabilities of allowing large fires to burn: "You can't let a small fire become a 100,000-acre fire because there'll always be a 7-Eleven in the way" (Kenworthy 1996, p. A11).

Many other examples of environmental issues can be cited. Following Hurricane Andrew, disposal of debris was a major concern, and some of it ended up being placed on environmentally sensitive lands (Dade County has now developed a plan for dealing with debris). Hurricane Hugo devastated the Francis Marion National Forest, affecting the endangered red-cockaded woodpecker. The Midwest floods of 1993 flushed toxic chemicals down the Mississippi River. Although many such impacts are natural (e.g., pine forests destroyed by hurricane winds), there is almost always a

human action that exacerbates vulnerability (e.g., habitat destruction endangering the red-cockaded woodpecker). Mitigation ethics suggest it is our duty to limit human-caused increases in vulnerability and environmental destruction.

These conflicts raise questions about the priority of environmental values relative to others. We found considerable variation in the answers to these questions. In the Auburn Dam controversy, proponents of the dam unabashedly put public safety values ahead of protecting the environment. Representative Doolittle, a supporter of the project and representative of the district in which the dam would be constructed, said: "It's just a matter of priorities. We feel life, limb and property have to come ahead of the aesthetic considerations of the canyons. . . . These canyons are not that unique anyway" (Egan 1996). The director of emergency management for Monroe County, Florida (the Florida Keys), expressed a similar sentiment concerning the Highway 1 expansion. Although he was supportive of environmental goals, he had little tolerance for the arguments of environmentalists who oppose the highway. In his mind, the pressing need for public safety easily outweighed the possibility of environmental damage.

Very often, however, there are alternative measures that will protect the environment as well as people and property. Furthermore, protection of the environment is often the most effective strategy for mitigating natural hazards. Conservation of wetlands, for instance, can serve as an effective and economical flood control strategy; coastal dune systems act as natural seawalls. Protection of natural values in watersheds is a preventive, cost-effective strategy for flood mitigation.

Many environmental ethicists argue that to maintain what exists today is simply inadequate, given the level of past destruction and degradation. And there is little question that major environmental destruction characterizes many of the hazardous areas we examined—consider the numerous levees along the Mississippi and Missouri Rivers or the extensive armoring of much of the U.S. coastline. Indeed, the very loss of naturally functioning ecosystems (e.g., the gradual destruction of wetlands in the Mississippi-Missouri watershed) has exacerbated, if not outright caused, many natural disasters.

Thus, one important environmental value is restoration. A restorative ethic acknowledges that substantial damage has been done and that there is a moral obligation to repair this damage. A number of restorative initiatives can be seen in our case studies. Following the Midwest floods, there were calls to return the rivers to their natural function and to restore

important ecological conditions (Wright 1996). Substantial federal funds were expended under the Wetlands Reserve Program to pay farmers to return floodplain land to wetlands. In one agricultural levee district in Iowa, the entire area was purchased and added to the Mark Twain National Wildlife Refuge. Implementing such a restorative ethic is difficult, however. After the 1993 Midwest floods, there was talk of allowing rivers to return to their natural, meandering flows and not rebuilding many levees. However, most damaged levees were repaired, as vested political and economic interests make such proposals difficult and costly to effectuate.

An even broader environmental ethic in natural hazards is "deep ecology," an ethic that sees a fundamental unity between humans and the natural environment. Deep ecology, more Eastern than Western in orientation, views rivers, mountains, fault zones, and coastlines as fundamental extensions of the human species and sees an act of destruction as harm to ourselves. It is difficult for many to imagine a time (at least in the foreseeable future) when this form of deeper connection could be realized, yet many believe we must begin to move in the direction of attaching more intrinsic value to the natural environment and living more lightly on the planet.

The concept of sustainability as related to natural hazards is another important link to environmental ethics. The notion that it is possible to promote sustainable communities and sustainable land use patterns means that it may be possible to both reduce hazard vulnerability and protect the natural environment (see chapters 2 and 13).

Historic Preservation Values

Another important value in discussions of mitigation policy is the preservation of buildings and landscapes of historical value. Sometimes these values complement mitigation, but at other times the two are at odds. Historic buildings are frequently much more vulnerable to natural disasters such as earthquakes, so dilemmas often arise in the aftermath of major events such as Northridge. A building owner may be faced with conflicting values. Preservationists want historic buildings restored, yet to do so frequently means bringing the buildings up to current code, and the costs involved may be exorbitant. Although federal and state historic preservation laws specify procedural requirements, they generally do not prevent owners from demolishing historic buildings if they believe the repair cost is too great.

A potential option is to exempt historic buildings from contemporary

safety standards. In this way, society makes the conscious choice to allow exposure of people and perhaps the community at large to greater risk in exchange for the preservation of historically significant buildings.

Recent disasters provide examples of efforts to preserve important buildings. A number of historic public structures have been deemed of such importance that extensive public monies are being spent to restore and retrofit them (including, for example, San Francisco's city hall and the opera house).

The fairness of asking private owners of historic buildings to spend millions of dollars to repair and upgrade them has also emerged as an issue. St. Joseph's Cathedral in Oakland, California, is a case in point. Renovating and strengthening this church would have cost some $9 million. Administrators of the church believed it could not afford this expenditure and wanted to tear it down, but preservationists wanted to save it. Eventually the building was torn down, and in the eyes of some residents, an important community building was lost. But should private owners be required to spend large amounts of their own money to save a structure for the public good?

An example of the importance of historic preservation values in mitigation was the flood levee project planned to protect the small town of St. Genevieve, Missouri. An important town in the westward expansion of the nation, St. Genevieve contains some impressive eighteenth-century French colonial architecture. The levee, expected to cost approximately $50 million, was found not to be cost-effective (with an estimated benefit-cost ratio of 0.2), but, the project has progressed anyway as a result of the town's historic significance as perceived by a number of individuals and groups. The low benefit-cost ratio is primarily the result of the fact that St. Genevieve is a small town and thus very little property is actually at risk, as well as the fact that the necessary levee system is a relatively complicated one.

Tough choices must often be made about the amount of preservation or restoration that can be afforded. There is a wide range of opinion about the correct balance. For instance, Richard Andrews, head of the Governor's Office of Emergency Services in California, believes that preservationists may sometimes go too far and wonders about the real historic value of buildings that may only be forty or fifty years old. In the debate over restoring the Los Angeles Coliseum following the Northridge earthquake, some preservationists argued for preserving even the urinals, concession stands, and palm trees as historic. Andrews believes that such agruments go too far. He says that rather than always choosing to do battle

over these issues, preservationists should realize that retrofitting of historic buildings is ultimately the most effective long-term preservation strategy, at least in earthquake country.

Personal Freedom, Lifestyle Choices, and Paternalism

Hazard mitigation policy may restrict the freedom of individuals or communities in order to bring about a broader level of public safety. An example of this type of conflict is a government's preventing an individual from building in a high-hazard zone, such as a floodplain or a seismic fault zone. Following Hurricane Hugo, the South Carolina Beachfront Management Act prevented many property owners from rebuilding in the so-called dead zone, twenty feet landward of the dune line. From the perspective of the state, clearing people and property from these risky locations makes great sense, yet such a policy conflicts with the desires of developers to build in these locations and the desires of housing consumers who wish to purchase homes there.

Personal freedom, especially in the United States, is a prized value, and there is concern wherever government restrictions curtail these freedoms. In a host of ways, however, membership in society requires giving up certain personal freedoms in exchange for larger, collective benefits. Individuals consent to abide by traffic laws because without them, there would be little practical value in having the freedom to drive. Many mitigation issues might be seen in a similar light. Restrictions on the amount of development in the Florida Keys (e.g., under the local rate-of-growth ordinance) or on Sanibel Island, Florida, for example, limit development to preserve the community's ability to evacuate when a storm threatens. Regional evacuation plans in Florida and elsewhere work in similar ways.

Even though mitigation programs sometimes take away certain personal freedoms, they give back an assurance of safety that would be difficult to achieve individually. Building codes represent a case in point. Although housing consumers might be expected to know more about the safety of their homes than they usually do, most individuals do not have the technical knowledge to evaluate the safety of a home. In this way, just as we as ordinary citizens do not expect to have to make a safety judgment each time we enter an elevator because we assume that it has been inspected and certified by the government as being safe to ride, so also do we assume that our buildings possess at least a minimum level of safety.

The ethical dilemma is one of finding the right balance, and conflicts emerge where individuals perceive mitigation policies as interfering too much with individual liberties. Some believe that if a person wishes to live

on an isolated barrier island, with no chance of evacuation, he should be allowed to do this. If an individual consents to live in a seismically deficient apartment building, she or he ought to be permitted to make this personal choice. For example, those living along the flooded rivers in the Midwest were seen as seeking a desirable lifestyle choice. And for many of these people and communities, periodic flooding and the resulting cleanup have been normal and endurable. Efforts to relocate them out of the floodplain raise questions about whether such programs interfere with their lifestyle choices.

The charge of *paternalism* sometimes arises—the belief that government is preventing a personal freedom or behavior exclusively or primarily for the benefit or welfare of that individual (e.g., "government knows whether that is an acceptable risk better than you do") (Beatley 1994). Defenders of mitigation, however, are quick to point out the many public costs and implications of individual actions. Individuals may be prevented from placing themselves at risk not for their own benefit but because there are serious public costs associated with these decisions. One implication of such individual actions is that others, namely police and fire personnel, may end up placing their own lives at risk when having to rescue these individuals in the event of a disaster.

Excelsior Springs, Missouri, one of the communities participating in the Midwest buyout program, illustrates these public costs. Here, flash flooding is a serious problem, and the police department has frequently had to rescue occupants of the floodplain. Now that the floodplain has essentially been "cleared out," no dangerous rescues have been required; for this reason, the city's police chief strongly supports the buyout program.

A number of different ways to balance personal freedom and public safety have been identified. One is to permit substantial individual risk taking but to ensure that individuals are well informed about the nature of these risks and the implications of their choices. The individual choosing to live on the remote barrier island may be permitted to do so but would be informed about the storm risks associated with the location and perhaps would be required to watch a videotape showing the force of previous hurricanes.

It may also be possible to assess individuals for the extra financial costs of living in high-risk areas. Some local jurisdictions have begun to establish hazard management zones (special taxing districts) in which a fee is assessed to cover the costs associated with, say, flood cleanup or floodplain maintenance. Interestingly, user fees are increasingly being applied to a wide range of individual actions that create public costs.

Another suggested approach in Excelsior Springs was for the fire department to maintain a list of dilapidated buildings into which it will not send

personnel in the event of a fire (because of the danger of collapse). Perhaps a similar list could be developed for properties in especially risky locations, putting property owners on notice that in the event of a flood, they cannot expect to be rescued.

Making some mitigation programs voluntary is another way to minimize infringement on personal liberty. Many saw the Midwest buyout program as a success because it was completely voluntary; property owners did not have to sell their property if they did not want to. It was an attractive option presented to them, but most floodplain occupants did not perceive that it was being forced on them. Had the program been mandatory, many would not have found it acceptable.

Property Rights and the Takings Issue

In the United States, infringement on private property rights raises special legal and ethical challenges. Under the U.S. Constitution (and most state constitutions), government is prevented from "taking" private land without just compensation. Courts have determined that "takings" can occur through regulation as well as through outright government appropriation, though they have historically been vague about the exact point at which a regulation becomes a taking. Many of the more potent hazard mitigation strategies, such as those set forth in the original South Carolina Beachfront Management Act, raise serious takings challenges. Indeed, the case of *Lucas v. South Carolina* centered on the constitutionality of the act and was taken to the U.S. Supreme Court. The case involved an owner of two small beachfront lots in the community of Isle of Palms, South Carolina. As a result of the act, the owner was unable to build permanent structures on either lot (both lots were seaward of the ideal dune line). The owner, David Lucas, sued the state, claiming that a regulatory taking had occurred, and was awarded $1.2 million. The state supreme court reversed the court's decision on appeal, agreeing with the South Carolina Coastal Council's argument that the act was intended to prevent the creation of a public harm—namely, destruction of the state's public beaches. Lucas appealed to the U.S. Supreme Court, which reversed and remanded the state supreme court's decision, issuing an opinion endorsing the need for public compensation when government regulation takes away all development value or potential.

The past decade has witnessed the emergence of a potent political movement in support of private property rights. New takings legislation has been passed in a number of states, including our case study state of Florida. New legislation has also been proposed and debated in Congress,

including a proposal that would dramatically change takings law by requiring government compensation when regulations devalue property by as little as 10 percent. Almost any form of mitigation involving regulation could be affected.

The takings issue raises a host of ethical questions, and a full examination of them is not possible here (see Beatley 1994 for a more extensive discussion). At a fundamental level are questions about the meaning of private property. Should private property rights be seen as largely absolute and inviolable, or are they necessarily constrained by the broader needs of the community and society? Do landowners have the right to reap the full and complete market value of their land, or are they entitled only to a reasonable economic return? What about cases in which government regulations are intended only to prevent a landowner from creating a public harm, as opposed to securing a public benefit—is compensation required in these cases as well? And if compensation is required after a certain devaluation threshold is reached, is this threshold applied to the entire parcel or simply to the portion of the land affected by the regulation?

Ironically, charges of infringement of private property rights can also be made when government withholds a mitigation or recovery benefit. Following the 1993 Midwest floods, for instance, some private levees were determined to be ineligible for the federal levee repair program. As the Galloway Report notes, some property owners argued that denial of such benefits constituted an "abridgement of their entitlement" and a "violation of their property rights" (Interagency Floodplain Management Review Committee 1994, p. 184).[4]

Questions about the ethical obligations of landowners also emerge. In the spirit of Aldo Leopold, we can wonder whether owners of the land have, in addition to rights to use and benefit from land, affirmative duties to act as stewards of it and to consider the needs of the broader community and public. There is no question that individual decisions about the use of land have broader implications. Flooding along the Mississippi and Missouri Rivers, and in many other watersheds is in large part a function of landowners filling wetlands, creating impervious surfaces, destroying natural vegetation, and otherwise altering the natural environment. Acknowledgment of individual ethical obligations to the land might do much to minimize the effects of certain natural disasters.

Other Values

Other value issues emerged in the case studies. In California and Florida, debate about strengthening public school buildings has been cast in terms of trade-offs in the use of limited educational funds. A school administrator

in Los Angeles saw the mandates for nonstructural seismic retrofitting after the Northridge earthquake as taking away funds that might otherwise be spent on schoolbooks and other school services.

It is not entirely clear, however, that such views are appropriate. In the case of educational expenditures, to many it seems foolhardy to skimp on strengthening school buildings, and the choice between safety and schoolbooks is a false one. Both are worthy public expenditures; ethical governance should find ways to fund both to an adequate level. If ensuring a seismically safe school is ethically required, there may be other viable ways to pay for it. Perhaps users (e.g., families with school-age children) should be assessed a seismic safety surcharge or the property tax rate should be raised. Public resources are clearly limited, but the choice that appears ethical is often a function of the way public trade-offs are structured and presented.

Fairness in Mitigation

Fairness in mitigation involves several related issues. These include issues of fair process and procedure, distributional equity, who pays, entitlement, and "not in my back yard" (NIMBY).

Equal Treatment

In terms of fairness issues, inequities were seen by some of our interviewees when similarly situated individuals were perceived as being treated differently from others. Often, this had to do with mitigation benefits or general disaster assistance received by individuals following a disaster. After the Midwest floods, the buyout program provided the same financial benefits to homeowners who had not bought flood insurance as to those who had. The latter group saw this as inequitable. A similar problem was seen in the NFIP loophole that allowed homeowners to purchase flood insurance at the last minute, essentially as they saw the flooding progress down the basin toward them. This loophole was closed by the National Flood Insurance Reform Act of 1994 (see chapter 2).[5]

Following Hurricane Hugo, under the South Carolina Beachfront Management Act, owners of homes within the high-risk dead zone (an area twenty feet landward of the dune line) that were two-thirds or more damaged were prevented from rebuilding in that zone. However, owners of structures with somewhat lesser damage, say 60 percent, were allowed to rebuild (Beatley 1990). The South Carolina Coastal Council not only

allowed owners of structures less than two-thirds damaged to rebuild but also allowed them to raze the existing structures and erect entirely new ones if they chose to do so. Thus, in some areas, homeowners experiencing very similar damage levels were treated dramatically differently by the permitting system.

Another example involved provision of funds under the minor home repair program following the Loma Prieta earthquake. Under the program, a home must be determined to be uninhabitable to receive funds. Yet to be classified as uninhabitable might require only a broken window or a damaged water heater. Such structures are essentially similar to habitable structures, but as a result of relatively minor damage, they qualify for federal repair monies.

Examples also emerged of programs that have changed over time, whereby similarly situated individuals are treated differently depending on whether they seek benefits (or permits) earlier or later in the recovery process. In Excelsior Springs, Missouri, the assistant city manager noted an inequity affecting property owners whose applications for relocation assistance were processed early in the buyout program. Individuals whose applications were processed toward the end of the program were able to claim additional funds to cover the difference between the fair market value of their homes and local replacement costs. As the so-called gap funding became available, property owners might receive significantly different buyout payments from those received by their neighbors.

Postdisaster permitting requirements may also change over time. For example, those who rebuilt soon after the Oakland, California, firestorm had fewer restrictions to deal with than did those who rebuilt later on. According to the Oakland building department, as more reconstruction was carried out, and more people moved back into the area, public complaints increased and the number of conditions placed on redevelopment grew (e.g., restrictions on allowable hours of construction, aesthetic complaints about homes).

Some rules and requirements have been ignored or inconsistently administered. For instance, in Florida after Hurricane Andrew, the substantial improvement requirements of the NFIP came under fire, especially in the community of Saga Bay. Under the NFIP, structures with more than 50 percent damage are required to be rebuilt according to current elevation standards. For many homeowners, particularly owners of older structures built on-grade, this rule imposes substantial expense. The rule has been enforced by FEMA and localities participating in the NFIP for many years, yet following Hurricane Andrew the interpretation was changed to allow Dade County to use a standard of 50 percent of the *replacement* cost

of a damaged structure; that is, a building would have to be built to the new flood elevation only if the amount of damage exceeded 50 percent of the cost of a replacement structure. This interpretation meant that residents of Saga Bay were relieved of the requirement to comply with the substantial improvement rule, even though many other homeowners before and since Andrew have been required to adhere to it. Similar inconsistencies arose after the Midwest floods.

Another example of inconsistent treatment of individuals occurred following Hurricane Hugo. There was a prohibition on rebuilding structures larger than their prehurricane size, but coastal property owners discovered, and the South Carolina Coastal Council allowed, a way to get around this limitation. Basically, property owners could reconstruct larger homes if they simultaneously requested an approval to rebuild what they had before the storm and an approval to add to their structures (up to a total of 5,000 square feet in size). Ironically, this position was defended on grounds of fairness. Because new homes could be built to a maximun size of 5,000 square feet, it seemed unfair to restrict rebuilding to a lesser size.

Following disaster events, officials are faced with conflicting public sentiments about mitigation rules. Although consistent implementation is one important value, there are also strong pressures to relax standards following a disaster. There is a natural desire to help people who have been devastated by a disaster and to do everything possible to allow them to restore their lives to a state of normalcy.

Mitigation officials may also see some unfair treatment as a necessary evil in exchange for achieving some greater mitigation good. This seems to be the defense of the Midwest buyout program. Proponents say that although it may be unfair to extend buyout benefits to those who have taken no action to protect themselves (and have not purchased flood insurance), the reality is that without the buyout program, these people will rebuild in the floodplain, later costing the federal government millions of dollars. Clearing the midwestern floodplains and creating safer and less costly settlement patterns is seen as a greater good that may supersede concerns about unequal treatment. Of course, it may often be possible to achieve these greater mitigation "goods" without sacrificing fair and equitable treatment. In the case of the Midwest floods, relocation benefits might have been structured in ways that rewarded past participation in the NFIP, providing greater benefits for these individuals.

Process or Procedural Ethics

Mitigation process issues include questions of how to solicit public input and involvement. Mayor Warford of Pattonsburg, Missouri, a community

devastated by the Midwest floods, described his philosophy of involving all members of the community in deciding whether or not to relocate the town. As a result, some 96 percent of the residents were participating in the relocation. He contrasted the democratic, participatory process of Pattonsburg with that Chelsea, Iowa, where the town was split on the relocation issue and the mayor took an advocacy role.

Following the Loma Prieta earthquake, the city of San Francisco took a deliberate, participatory approach to dealing with demolition decisions. Damaged buildings were roped off, and public meetings were held to determine what should be done with the structures. Even though the city holds unusual powers following such a disaster and can legally demolish a structure without a building owner's consent, officials believe that in the long run, fewer disagreements and conflicts (and fewer lawsuits) will result if a somewhat slower approach is taken. In contrast, the city of Santa Cruz quickly demolished buildings following the disaster and was sued as a result.

A question of procedural fairness arises in places such as Pattonsburg, Missouri, and Valmeyer, Illinois—midwestern towns completely relocated to new sites outside the floodplain—where officials had to create a system for distributing home sites in the new locations. Pattonsburg developed a system wherein residents drew for time slots during which to choose a building lot from the new town plan. First priority in drawing was given to those who were moving their homes to the new town; second priority was given to those building new homes there. Third priority was given to those with mobile homes. Last priority was given to individuals from outside the community. Valmeyer developed a similar allocation system. Although citizens questioned some of the priorities (e.g., owners of mobile homes believed that their lifestyle was being looked down on), the town developed what was generally perceived as an equitable arrangement for distributing home sites.

Distributive Equity

Among the ethical issues raised during our interviews concerning fairness in allocating mitigation benefits and burdens was the question of whether low-income and minority group individuals and communities are disproportionately affected by natural disasters. In the Midwest, low-cost housing is frequently located in riverine floodplains, and consequently many low-income residents live in the areas most vulnerable to disasters. Moreover, low-income residents are more likely to live in substandard housing, which is more structurally vulnerable to earthquakes and other natural hazards.

Another dimension involves the negative side effects on low-income and minority citizens as a result of otherwise desirable mitigation programs. Mandatory retrofit ordinances can displace low-income residents. In California, communities are required by law to develop seismic retrofit programs, aimed primarily at retrofitting especially vulnerable unreinforced masonry buildings. Some cities, such as Los Angeles, have instituted mandatory retrofit ordinances, requiring building owners to undertake seismic upgrades by a certain date under threat of condemnation. Although these programs have strengthened and upgraded buildings, they have also resulted in direct displacement due to the razing of some structures and economic displacement due to the raising of rents.

In the Florida Keys, a similar dilemma exists over enforcement of Monroe County's floodplain management ordinance. Under the requirements of the National Flood Insurance Program, new structures must be built at or above the 100-year flood elevation level (the base flood elevation, or BFE), with no habitation allowed below this level. Yet over time, a number of small apartments have been created illegally below the BFE; there are some 2,000 nonconforming units. These apartments constitute a significant number of affordable housing units in a county in which housing is very expensive. What should Monroe County do in this situation—stringently enforce the law, cracking down on these illegal units, or turn a blind eye, recognizing the affordable housing benefits these units provide?

Similar concerns were expressed about the buyout program following the 1993 Midwest floods. Because the floodplain is a major location of affordable housing, concerns were voiced that buying out these structures to reduce exposure to floods would have the unintended consequence of reducing the supply of affordable housing. Concern about this led some communities, such as Cherokee, Iowa, to take proactive steps (including developing a new subdivision) to add new housing opportunities while other units were being destroyed or taken out of commission. Some communities encouraged the moving of homes to new sites and the auctioning of purchased homes when these homes were structurally salvageable.

Another important dimension of the equity question has to do with the fairness of allocating mitigation benefits. Do all citizens have the same access to and ability to benefit from mitigation programs, or do low-income and minority residents and communities receive disproportionately low amounts of these benefits? There is evidence to suggest that following Hurricane Andrew, minority and low-income communities had a difficult time securing recovery benefits (Dash, Peacock, and Morrow 1997).

The issue of distributive equity also involves questions about the criteria

for allocating mitigation or postdisaster benefits. Many benefits are distributed on the basis of a principle of equal benefit regardless of income or wealth. At least for certain mitigation programs, distributive equity may argue for some form of income- or wealth-based limit so that scarce public funds can be targeted to those individuals and communities in greatest need.

Who Should Pay for Mitigation?

Ethical issues arise in determining who should pay for hazard mitigation and for disaster preparedness, response, and recovery. Following the Northridge and Loma Prieta earthquakes, serious questions arose about who should pay the costs of repairs and retrofits. After Northridge, a state bond referendum to pay for California's share of disaster assistance was turned down by voters, raising questions about whether taxpayers recognized a financial obligation to absorb at least a portion of the expense associated with disaster recovery. Similar questions arise over the appropriate federal share of disaster assistance and the extent to which the federal government should pay for flood control projects (see chapter 2).

Who should pay is closely related to who will benefit. In the Auburn Dam case, opponents question why federal taxpayers should be required to pay for flood control and other benefits for the residents of only one state. Opponents argue that if the project is essential, it should be financed locally, calling it "a boondoggle of epic proportions" and pointing out that it would be much cheaper to improve the existing levee system in the Sacramento area and fairer to have residents of the area pay for it themselves (Egan 1996, p. 22). Currently the cost-sharing scheme for the dam would be 75 percent federal and 25 percent nonfederal, and the state of California would apparently pay some 70 percent of the nonfederal share. There is legitimate reason to think that if the project were to be funded locally, there might be a much more serious consideration of whether it (or the particular level of protection it provides) could be afforded.

Proponents of the project argue that the costs are simply too high for local jurisdictions to absorb and that it is in the national interest to prevent a disastrous flood in Sacramento. They say the project makes good economic sense. Although the dam would cost about $1 billion, it would protect the region from flooding that could cause some $10 billion in damage.

One possible approach is to base the distribution of costs on the benefit standard: those who benefit most from mitigation measures should pay the lion's share of their costs. There are, in fact, a number of mitigation programs based on this standard. Benefit assessment districts, based on this

principle, are being used in a number of places around the country; an example is the vegetation management district in Oakland, California. Another variation is the culpability principle discussed earlier, which holds that the burden of paying for mitigation should fall primarily on those individuals and communities responsible for creating the hazardous circumstances in the first place.

Entitlement and Expectations

A significant ethical quandary is the extent to which individuals and communities are entitled to certain disaster assistance or mitigation benefits. Further, if people and communities are morally entitled, what level of benefits are they due?

A number of federal and state officials involved in mitigation policy have commented negatively about the pervasive expectation among the public that if a disaster strikes, government will cover a major portion of the cost. Over time, they have seen the emergence of a "victim" mentality whereby those affected by natural disasters see themselves as victims needing and, indeed, deserving financial assistance. The ethical question is whether it is fair to view affected individuals and communities through such a lens of victimization.

The Midwest floods and the subsequent federal buyout program offer examples of this sense of entitlement. We encountered a sense of frustration and sadness on the part of a number of government employees who worked closely on the buyout. Some characterized participants as selfish and wanting to get as much as they could from the buyout settlement, describing their actions in terms of greed. Because the buyout and disaster assistance monies were federal, they were seen by many local residents as "free money." Especially costly in public funds were the communities relocated to new sites, including Pattonsburg, Missouri, and Valmeyer, Illinois. In these cases, the intent was to allow the entire community to relocate as a unit so that community members could stay together. These relocation efforts raised questions about entitlement. Even if society agrees that individuals are entitled to be bought out or compensated in the aftermath of a flood, is an entire community entitled to be relocated? To many interviewed for this study, the answer was clearly no.

Valmeyer received particularly heavy criticism. One official described the relocation project as "a total waste" of federal funds, noting that the 1993 floods marked the first time the town had been flooded in fifty years. This official believed it would have been much less costly to add to the existing levee system, which in his opinion performed well. The offical

questioned whether the town's legitimate claim to some modest levee improvements qualified it to require that the larger public pay to recreate the town on an entirely new site.

One view is that individuals and communities may not be entitled to aid if they had opportunities to reduce their risks but chose not to take them. Should individuals in the floodplain be bailed out by the federal government in light of the fact that they had opportunities to purchase flood insurance (or to take other forms of preventive action) but chose not to? In theory, under the NFIP, nonparticipating localities are ineligible for federal disaster assistance, a provision clearly reflecting the philosophy that a community and its residents should take actions to reduce their risks.

Missouri officials mentioned several small towns in which officials blatantly disregarded local floodplain management ordinances and allowed development in the floodplain without requiring elevation. Although it may be understandably difficult in a small town to impose regulatory requirements on friends and neighbors, failure to take preventive actions should negate expectations of a bailout.

There is an increasing expectation government should "take care of the disaster problem." Citizens expect government to compensate them for any harm done them, regardless of who is or is not at fault and regardless of their own ability to take preventive and corrective action. Indeed, some mitigation officials acknowledged that they had a hand in creating this expectation. In the case of the Midwest buyout, officials may have been partly responsible for "setting the tone," giving the impression that government intended to "make whole" the affected homeowners. The buyout program is also likely to influence what homeowners and citizens will expect in future disaster events, in the Midwest and elsewhere. As one local planning official put it, "FEMA came in here and was handing out money like it was paper."

In other specific cases, mitigation personnel or agencies have created expectations that certain personal expenditures would be reimbursed or certain program benefits would be made available. In these cases, individuals and communities developed legitimate expectations to receive these benefits. Policy makers and those involved in providing mitigation benefits may have a positive duty to work toward adjusting expectations or counteracting false expectations when they develop.

NIMBY in Mitigation and Recovery

The phenomenon of NIMBY (not in my backyard) raises a number of fairness issues. Even though the objects of "NIMBYism" may be activities that

are hard to support from a community's perspective (e.g., a waste inciner-
ator), they are often activities that address important collective needs.
Those who experience the negative effects of such activities view them as
unfair, even if the benefits to the larger community or to society in general
outweigh the local negatives. ·

Several examples of postdisaster NIMBYism emerged in the disaster case
studies. In the San Francisco Bay Area, a number of freeways and overpass
structures were repaired and strengthened after the Loma Prieta earthquake. A contentious debate centered on the rebuilding of the Central
Freeway in San Francisco. Some neighborhood residents did not want the
highway to be rebuilt at all, though this was probably never a very realistic
option. Others argued for design options that would minimize the effects
of traffic. Although they are a nuisance to neighbors, the noise and traffic
must be balanced against the regional benefits provided by the highway.
City planning officials indicated that the freeway was still a needed part of
the regional road and highway system. Similar debates occurred over the
rebuilding of the Cypress Freeway in Oakland, resulting in significant
modifications in the highway design.

A second example of the NIMBY phenomenon is seen in the redevelopment process following Hurricane Andrew. Neighborhood opposition
developed regarding a planned fifty-seven-home Habitat for Humanity
subdivision in southern Dade County. Neighbors objected to the presence
of low-income residents, claiming that they would create future crack
houses (Noonon 1993). The project was eventually abandoned because of
the opposition.

Ethical questions in such conflicts include whether it is fair and equitable to expect certain individuals and neighborhoods to bear a disproportionate burden in support of a greater public good (e.g., the need for
affordable housing in the aftermath of a hurricane); whether NIMBY
opposition is based on legitimate concerns or unfounded fears and preju-
dices; and what sort of compensation or design changes are ethically
required to address NIMBY concerns.

Ethical Aspects of Mitigation Analyses

Ethical issues also arise in the analysis of hazards and mitigation alternatives. These involve both the assumptions underlying analytical methods
and the ways in which scientific and technical uncertainty is handled.

Assumptions in Methods of Analysis and Choice

The ethical assumptions, underpinnings, and biases of particular tools and methods for making public decisions are becoming clearer (Tong 1986). Decisions about mitigation are guided by tools, methods, and techniques with similar ethical assumptions. Decision makers using these mitigation tools must be honest and forthright about their assumptions and analytic limitations.

One tool frequently used in mitigation decision making is benefit-cost analysis. Although this tool can be useful in guiding societal choices, it relies on a number of implicit assumptions: that all benefits and costs can be quantified and expressed as monetary values; that the future may be severely discounted; and that the principle of maximizing social utility should guide choices about mitigation.

Historically, environmental benefits have been inadequately taken into account in benefit-cost analyses. The Galloway Report criticizes the ways in which national economic development (NED) is calculated for federal water resources projects. It specifically notes the failure to adequately consider values that are not easily quantified in monetary terms (Interagency Floodplain Management Review Committee 1994, p. 85):

> Because of their non-market nature, environmental quality, ecosystem health, the existence of endangered species, and other social effects are not easily quantified in monetary values. This limits formulation and acceptance of projects capable of striking a better balance between flood damage reduction or other water resources development and the environment.

The report goes on to recommend the development of techniques that will better account for these nonquantifiable values.[6]

The utilitarian moral assumption underlying benefit-cost analysis may obscure other equally important moral criteria. Some mitigation projects may be ethically defensible even when they are not cost-effective, or when the calculated benefits do not exceed the costs. The St. Genevieve, Missouri, levee is an example of such a project; here, the benefit-cost ratio is rather low. However, the project protects significant historic values for current and future generations, values not adequately captured in the methodology of benefit-cost analysis. Another example occurs when distributive equity or fairness is a consideration. Even though it may not be cost-effective to seismically retrofit buildings in low-income neighborhoods, this may be the morally correct thing to do.

Issues of Scientific and Technological Uncertainty

Many disputes over natural hazard mitigation policy involve disagreements about the precise nature, magnitude, and geographic extent of hazards. There is limited knowledge about dynamic natural forces such as hurricanes, and the interactions among these physical forces, topography, and landscape are complex. Therefore, there is much uncertainty inherent in mitigation policy and decisions, and major ethical questions arise regarding how to address this uncertainty.

One dilemma is how to present information about hazards and risks to the public. On the one hand, there is concern about unduly alarming the public. On the other hand, there is concern about conveying the false impression that mitigation measures will fully protect citizens from disaster events. Several interviewees expressed misgivings about the perceived precision of hazard maps and mapping programs, worrying that if people find their homes located outside a hazard zone on such a map, they will think (falsely) they need not worry about natural disasters. This raises the question of whether public officials, planners, and others have a duty to make special efforts to convey to the public the inherent uncertainties in such maps.

A report on the Midwest floods of 1993 by the Lincoln Institute of Land Policy points out the problems of "floodplain semantics." Speaking in a seemingly precise and scientific manner about, say, the 100-year floodplain conveys to the public a sense of certainty and exactness that does not exist. "By using this apparently precise language, floodplain maps, levees and flood insurance premiums have all created a false sense of security," the report states. "By trying to quantify the risks of flooding, governments have encouraged taxpayers and landowners to see hard lines and guarantees where nature sees only flexible environments and shifting probabilities" (Faber 1996, p. 9).

Guidelines for Ethical Mitigation

In this section, we suggest guidelines for ethical mitigation as starting points for debate. The guidelines are directed primarily to mitigation officials but will also be relevant to citizens, design professionals, and others in involved in the mitigation process.

Ethical mitigation requires mitigation officials to to the following:

   1. Acknowledge and openly discuss the ethical choices involved in mitigation. Hazard mitigation raises questions of ethical choices. Those

involved in mitigation policy—elected officials, government administrators, and citizens alike—should be encouraged to view mitigation policy through an ethical lens and to attempt to clarify and better understand the ethical dimensions of mitigation.

2. Identify and take into account the full array of moral duties and claims; consider the full range of moral issues. Ethical dilemmas in mitigation concern trade-offs between competing values. In structuring their choices, mitigation officials should avoid relying solely on narrow economic criteria; instead, they should evaluate the full range of ethical claims. Mitigation officials should ask not only "What can we afford?" but also "What is ethically required?"

3. Directly involve affected individuals and groups in mitigation decisions; promote an open and democratic process. Ethical mitigation recognizes the moral obligation to actively involve all members and groups in the community, especially those who will be directly affected by mitigation decisions. Mitigation ethics requires a democratic, participatory process in which people's concerns, ideas, and creative input matter and are taken into account.

4. Give public needs priority over individual wants. There are many mitigation circumstances in which individual actions and desires (e.g., a desire to rebuild on the beach or to gain exemption from a building standard) must be balanced against public needs. Public safety must be given priority. Mitigation programs and policies that benefit only a few individuals, rather than the broader public, are questionable.

5. Be honest and direct with the public about risks; expect honesty and courage from elected officials in confronting the prospects of disaster. Community members have the right to a frank assessment of the risks and hazards they face. Public officials, especially elected officials, should be honest and direct in educating the public about the potential for disasters and measures that can and should be taken to prevent or prepare for such events.

6. Encourage individuals and groups to assume personal responsibility for safety and hazard reduction; acknowledge the special duty of government to ensure public safety. Ethical mitigation requires that responsibility for promoting safety be acknowledged by building owners, merchants, lending institutions, and insurance companies, among others. Individuals also have a significant degree of responsibility to educate themselves and to make informed personal decisions about risks from natural disasters. Government regulations and actions (e.g., through building codes and

construction standards) should ensure the safety of homes and buildings. Where people are allowed to occupy buildings and locations that are not safe, they have the right to be informed of these risks.

7. *Apply mitigation rules, regulations, and standards fairly and consistently.* Mitigation ethics require clear and consistent application of mitigation standards and requirements, both before and after a disaster event. Procedural fairness may require that public officials resist the natural human tendency to suspend or loosen requirements following a disaster to allow a quick return to normalcy.

8. *Treat similarly situated individuals similarly.* Ethical mitigation requires that individuals in similar circumstances be treated similarly. Clear explanations should be given when benefits and treatment differ. Efforts should be made to treat people in accordance with their unique circumstances.

9. *Obey and enforce the law.* Fairness in mitigation implies that administrators have an a priori obligation to enforce mitigation law. Failure to enforce the law amounts to treating unfairly the majority of citizens and property owners who adhere to the law (as in the case of the substantial improvement rule under the NFIP). A more ethical practice would be to seek to change a law if necessary so that all affected parties are treated uniformly and consistently. Unequal treatment may sometimes be defended to achieve a greater mitigation (public) good, such as relocating people and property out of harm's way, but there are often ways to achieve public mitigation goals without sacrificing equity and fairness, and mitigation officials have an obligation to develop such solutions.

10. *Demand professional accountability; ensure that the safety of the public is placed above the profit motive and the selling of services.* Implementation of hazard mitigation relies heavily on individuals in the design and building professions especially architects and engineers. Efforts are required to reinvigorate the stated ethical standards and obligations of these professions and to reinforce the implication that these professional roles carry with them important responsibilities to the public. Individuals in other hazards-related professions also should be encouraged to reflect on their ethical obligations, and their professional organizations should give greater attention to ethical standards and ways in which these standards translate into practice.

11. *Give protection of human life priority over protection of property.* In considering the mitigation priorities of a community, officials should

explicitly confront the relationship between the goal of saving lives and the goal of protecting property. Ideally, mitigation policies and programs will support both goals (building codes are an example), but when a choice between them is necessary, ethical mitigation gives moral priority to protection of human life.

12. Preserve and restore the natural environment. Mitigation strategies and policies that damage the environment should be avoided, and those that respect and restore the environment should be encouraged. Mitigation officials have an ethical obligation to search for mitigation solutions that overcome confrontations between environmental preservation and protection of public safety and/or property. Sustainability offers the promise of a synthesis of mitigation values and environmental preservation and restoration.

13. Protect and preserve historic buildings and resources. Mitigation solutions that simultaneously protect public safety and preserve historically valuable buildings and landscapes should be emphasized.

14. Develop mitigation alternatives that satisfy multiple values. Ethical mitigation favors policies and actions that simultaneously satisfy a number of important public values. Unnecessary conflicts between values can be avoided by diligently seeking out such alternatives.

15. Minimize the negative side effects of mitigation programs on individuals and communities. Ethical mitigation requires sensitivity to negative effects on a neighborhood or community. Where such effects are real, mitigation officials should look for ways to reduce or minimize them. Education and community dialogue may be appropriate when negative effects are more imagined than real. Efforts should be made to ensure that a particular neighborhood or community has not been unfairly burdened with a disproportionate share of uses, projects, or activities that generate negative effects.

16. Avoid mitigation that places disproportionate burdens on the least advantaged in society; strive to improve the conditions of the least advantaged. Mitigation ethics require attention to the distributive effects of programs and policies. Mitigation programs must be designed and implemented in ways that minimize negative effects on the least advantaged members of society. Moreover, mitigation ethics hold that all individuals and communities are entitled to share in a common level of public safety.

17. Ensure equal access to mitigation benefits. In the distribution of mitigation and postdisaster benefits, special care must be exercised to ensure

that all groups have equal access to them. Special efforts may be needed to ensure that groups are not excluded from benefits because of their language or their social or economic circumstances.

18. Consider the interests of future generations in making mitigation decisions; take a long-term view. Ethical mitigation assumes a long moral time frame, entailing a fundamental responsibility to ensure that the people and communities to follow are safe and that their quality of life is high.

19. Consider the negative effects of mitigation actions (or of failure to take them) on neighboring communities; minimize these effects. Many local actions (e.g., filling of wetlands, paving of open space) and mitigation efforts (e.g., construction of levees) have negative effects on neighboring communities. These effects should be taken into account and minimized. Mitigation alternatives that also benefit other communities and the larger region should be favored.

20. Provide mitigation benefits and disaster assistance based on need, not citizenship. The needs and circumstances of individuals and groups after a disaster should govern decisions about their eligibility for disaster assistance.

21. Respect the personal freedom and life choices of individuals. Values of freedom and personal choice are important and should be protected wherever possible. Government and society may, however, have legitimate reason to curtail certain personal freedoms and to place restrictions on life choices when they interfere with the freedoms of others or when individuals are not fully able to assess or comprehend (or cannot reasonably be expected to assess or comprehend) the serious risks involved. Those mitigation programs and policies that interfere least with personal freedom and choice (e.g., hazard disclosure, voluntary relocation) should be given full consideration first.

22. Respect private property; restrict its use where necessary to prevent disasters or where other important public values are jeopardized. Mitigation programs and policies sometimes involve restrictions on ways in which property owners can use their land. If important public interests are served by mitigation programs and policies, government has the right—indeed, the duty—to control private use of land, especially where this serves to prevent or reduce public harm. There is no ethical basis in modern society for landowners to expect to reap the maximum economic profit from their land. The point at which a regulatory "taking" occurs remains ambiguous, but compensation is ethically required (and even this

is debatable) only when there is essentially no remaining economic use for the land.

23. Encourage landowners and property owners to acknowledge their ethical duties to minimize the creation of hazards and to protect important public values; promote a hazards-based land ethic. Owners of land should recognize that along with rights of use, certain duties attach to landownership. Owners of private land should not take actions that create significant harm or hazard for others or for the broader public or that degrade or destroy the land and its natural ability to reduce or mitigate natural hazards.

24. Hold those individuals or entities that create or cause a hazard (or disaster) culpable for it; those who cause or contribute to a disaster should bear responsibility for it. Under ethical mitigation, those culpable can be asked to compensate, repair, or otherwise rectify the circumstances.

25. Require those who benefit from risky behavior to assume (a portion of) the costs of mitigation. Ethical mitigation supports shifting much of the financial burden of mitigation to those states, communities, and individuals that benefit from risk-taking behavior. There is little ethical basis for expecting the larger public (e.g., federal or state government) to cover the costs of mitigation projects that benefit primarily the constituents of one locality or region. Need and the ability to pay should also be considered in determining a fair distribution of costs.

26. Work to modify expectations about public disaster assistance. Ethical mitigation suggests that some amount of disaster assistance is reasonable but that individuals and communities should bear some or all of the risk associated with living in a dangerous location or under dangerous conditions, particularly where personal opportunities to protect and mitigate are available. Ethical mitigation also recognizes that government may have created or helped to create these expectations. Mitigation officials have a moral duty to strive to actively correct or adjust such expectations.

27. Clarify the ethical assumptions of analytic tools used in mitigation decisions. All analytic and decision-making tools used in mitigation involve ethical assumptions. Those who use these tools have an obligation to understand and be sensitive to these assumptions and to be honest and forthright about them when conveying findings and recommendations to the public and to decision makers. Benefit-cost and cost-effectiveness analyses in particular raise questions concerning moral bias, and the outputs of such techniques must be tempered by a consideration of the full array of ethical concepts and obligations.

28. *Convey the inherent uncertainties of science where they exist.* There is an ethical obligation to convey the nature of risks to the public in as clear and understandable a way as possible and in a way that avoids giving a false impression of the accuracy and certainty of scientific predictions.

Notes

1. NSF Grant No. SBR-9312161, "Ethical Issues in Natural Hazard Management" (Timothy Beatley and David Brower, principal investigators), funded by the Ethics and Values Program, was an exploratory study of the types and nature of ethical issues and quandaries that arise with respect to natural hazards and disasters. The primary research method was the conduct of case studies of recent disaster events, especially Hurricane Andrew (1992), the Midwest floods (1993), and the Northridge earthquake (1994). Each offered opportunities to understand the major ethical quandaries that faced a variety of individuals, groups, and institutions. In addition to extensive interviews, a literature review and extensive analyses of media and newspaper coverage were undertaken. To a lesser extent several other disaster events and hazard controversies were examined. These include the Loma Prieta earthquake (1989), Hurricane Hugo (1989), the Oakland, California, firestorm (1991), and the Auburn Dam and American River flood control debate. Together, these events illustrate a rich mosaic of moral and policy dilemmas that arise in mitigation.
2. Other professions and professional organizations are involved in one way or another with community building and development and hazard mitigation, including the Association of State Floodplain Managers, the Association of State Wetlands Managers, the National Association of Homebuilders, and the International City/County Managers Association, among many others.
3. The grand jury reports are especially harsh in their criticism of the system of inspection and code enforcement. In the words of the first report:

   > The effectiveness of this community's building inspection process has been questionable for decades. The process has remained vulnerable to innuendoes of corruption, at worst, and apathy at best. . . . Essentially, we have been a community dependent upon the building industry to police itself. . . . Lack of code enforcement contributed greatly to the property destruction and damage this community suffered. The evidence was abundantly clear as the rubble and remains of construction were observed. The opened guts of thousands of homes exposed countless violations of the SFBC and sound construction practices. No one, including the present staff of Dade County's largest inspection department, denies this blatantly unconscionable truth. . . . Historically, the Dade County Building and Zoning Department has had a high turnover of leadership and has lacked adequate, qualified staff, particularly during the boom years of construction. The Department's staff has traditionally lacked adequate training and suffered from an ineffective inspection per inspector ratio. Shamefully, prior to 1991, no roofing systems expert existed for roofing inspections. (Dade County Grand Jury 1992, pp. 10–11)

4. Another property rights complaint heard by the committee involved possible restrictions placed on "flood fighting" by individuals and groups (Interagency Floodplain Management Review Committee 1994, p. 184).
5. Under the National Flood Insurance Reform Act of 1994, a waiting period of thirty days is imposed before insurance coverage becomes effective.
6. Specifically, the report recommends the development and use of a "system-of-accounts analysis" (Interagency Floodplain Management Review Committee 1994, p. 86).

References

American Public Works Association. 1996. *APWA Reporter* (Kansas City, Mo.), 63 (6) July, theme issue on environmental topics.

Association of Engineering Geologists. 1985. *Principles of Ethical Behavior.* Sudbury, Mass.: Association of Engineering Geologists.

Beatley, Timothy. 1989. "Towards a Moral Philosophy of Natural Disaster Mitigation." *International Journal of Mass Emergencies and Disasters* 7 (1): 5–32.

———. 1990. *Managing Reconstruction Along the South Carolina Coast: Preliminary Observations on the Implementation of the Beachfront Management Act.* Quick Response Research Report No. 38. Boulder: University of Colorado, Natural Hazards Research and Applications Information Center.

———. 1994. *Ethical Land Use: Principles of Policy and Planning.* Baltimore: Johns Hopkins University Press.

Becker, William S. 1994. "The Case for Sustainable Redevelopment." *Environment and Development* (American Planning Association), November, 1–4.

Berke, Philip, and Timothy Beatley. 1992. *Planning for Earthquakes: Risk, Politics, and Policy.* Baltimore: Johns Hopkins University Press.

California Seismic Safety Commission. 1995. *Northridge Earthquake: Turning Loss to Grain.* Report to Govenor Pete Wilson. Sacramento: California Seismic Saftey Commission.

Council of American Building Officials. n.d. *Code of Ethics.* Falls Church, Va.: Council of American Building Officials.

Dade County Grand Jury. 1992. *Final Report of the Dade County Grand Jury, Circuit Court of the Eleventh Judicial Circuit of Florida in and for the County of Dade, Spring Term A.D. 1992.* December 14.

Dash, Nicole, Walter Gillis Peacock, and Betty Hearn Morrow. 1997. "And the Poor Get Poorer: A Neglected Black Community." In *Reshaping of Miami: Ethnicity, Gender, and the Sociology of Disasters,* ed. Walter Gillis Peacock, Betty Hearn Morrow, and Hugh Gladwin. New York: Routledge.

Egan, Timothy. 1996. "Great Dam: Life Saver, or a Big Boondoggle?" *New York Times,* June 9, 22.

Faber, Scott. 1996. *On Borrowed Land: Public Policies for Floodplains.* Cambridge, Mass.: Lincoln Institute of Land Policy.

FEMA (Federal Emergency Management Agency). 1995. *National Mitigation Strategy.* January. Washington, D.C.: FEMA.

Fischhoff, Baruch. 1984. *Acceptable Risk.* Cambridge: Cambridge University Press.

Frankena, William. 1973. *Ethics.* Englewood Cliffs, N.J.: Prentice Hall.

GAO (General Accounting Office). 1994. *Impact of Species Protection Efforts on the 1993 California Fire.* GAO/RCED-94-224. July. Washington, D.C.: GAO.

Habitat for Humanity. n.d. *Jordan Commons: A Homestead Habitat for Humanity Neighborhood.* Homestead, Fla.: Habitat for Humanity.

Howe, Elizabeth. 1980. "Role Choices for Urban Planners." *Journal of the American Planning Association* 46:398–409.

Howe, Elizabeth, and Jerome Kaufman. 1979. "The Ethics of Contemporary American Planners." *Journal of the American Planning Association,* 45:243–255.

Interagency Floodplain Management Review Committee. 1994. *Sharing the Challenge: Floodplain Management into the Twenty-First Century.* (Galloway Report.) Washington, D.C.: Government Printing Office.

Kenworthy, Tom. 1996. "Wildfires Rekindle Debate on What's Best for Forests." *Washington Post,* September 2.

Kornfield, Laurence. n.d. *"Catfishing in Japan."* San Francisco: Department of Public Works.

Mayer, Caroline E. 1996. "Withstanding a Huff and a Puff: Outer Banks Officials Spearhead U.S. Campaign for Stronger Homes." *Washington Post,* August 31, E1, E4.

Mucha, D. Michael. 1994. "Is It Necessary to Compromise Engineering Ethics to Remain Competitive in Today's Marketplace?" *Civil Engineering,* May, 62–63.

Nash, Roderick. 1989. *The Rights of Nature: A History of Environmental Ethics.* Madison: University of Wisconsin Press.

Noonon, Maggie. 1993. "Habitat Effort Provokes Opposition." *Planning,* January, 13.

NSTC (National Science and Technology Council). 1996. *Natural Disaster Reduction: A Plan for the Nation.* Washington, D.C.: NSTC.

Partridge, Ernest. 1988. "Ethical Issues in Emergency Management." In *Managing Disaster: Strategies and Policy,* ed. Louise Comfort. Durham, N.C.: Duke University Press.

President's Council on Sustainable Development. 1996. *Sustainable America: A New Consensus for Prosperity, Opportunity, and a Healthy Environment for the Future.* Washington, D.C.: President's Council on Sustainable Development.

Rolston, Holmes, III. 1988. *Environmental Ethics: Duties to and Values in the Natural World.* Philadelphia: Temple University Press.

Tong, Rosemarie. 1986. *Ethics in Policy Analysis.* Englewood Cliffs, N.J.: Prentice Hall.

U.S. House. 1994. *Report of the Bipartisan Task Force on Disasters.* 103rd Congress. December 14 (not printed).

Waxler, Kathryn. 1996. "Northridge Quake's Costly Legacy: Price Is Major Obstacle to Proposal for Reinforcing L.A. Structures." *Washington Post,* January 18, A12.

Wright, James M. 1996. "Effects of the Flood on National Policy: Some Achievements; Major Challenges Remain." In *The Great Flood of 1993: Causes, Impacts and Responses,* ed. Stanley A. Changnon. Boulder, Colo.: Westview Press.

CHAPTER 13

Natural Hazard Mitigation: Planning for Sustainable Communities

This chapter recommends actions to make mitigation work to produce *sustainable communities*—communities that are able to withstand natural hazard stresses and keep on functioning. We first describe the new vision of sustainable communities in the context of natural hazards. We then recommend reforms to overcome obstacles to future sustainable communities that we have discovered in the operations of the U.S. hazard mitigation system and in mitigation policy and practice. Our goal is to create a favorable climate for mitigation in the United States in order to make the national mitigation system strong enough to counter future threats of catastrophe from natural hazards.

Sustainable Communities: The New Vision for Natural Hazard Mitigation

The concept of sustainable development has created a new popular understanding of the need for society to plan future actions rather than simply respond to each crisis that may arise. Planning for sustainable development links concerns for social, economic, and environmental well-being in a participatory process aimed at meeting present needs while preserving the ability of future generations to meet their needs (see chapter 2). Sustainable development envisions a planet where people live in harmony

with the natural environment, acknowledging its variability as well as harvesting its resources. On such a planet, human settlements are located and built through a planned process so as to become sustainable communities. Originally associated with environmental policy, the goal of sustainability has now also become a centerpost of natural disaster policy (United Nations 1992).

The Sustainable Development Vision Applied to Natural Hazard Mitigation

When natural hazard mitigation is added to the sustainability vision, the goal becomes the creation of development that reduces the vulnerability of populations to natural disasters while reducing poverty, providing jobs and promoting economic activity, and improving people's living conditions (Munasinghe and Clarke 1995). To sustainability's economic, environmental protection, and social criteria is added a fourth criterion—sustainable development must be *resilient* to the natural variability of the earth and the solar system (NSTC 1996). A slightly different way of stating this same criterion is that development must be then *disaster resistant* (FEMA 1997; Institute for Business and Home Safety 1997). A resilient community is one that lives in harmony with nature's varying cycles and processes.

The Goal: Resilient Communities

One goal of sustainable development is to build resilient communities. Such planning ensures that the development market and government decision makers operate with full awareness of the risks natural hazards pose to people and property. It provides them with proven community development solutions to cope with natural hazard risks.

Resilient communities may bend before the extreme stresses of natural hazards, but they do not break. They are consciously constructed to be strong and flexible rather than brittle and fragile. This means that their lifeline systems of roads, utilities, and other support facilities are designed to continue functioning in the face of rising water, high winds, and shaking ground. It means that their neighborhoods and businesses, their hospitals and public safety centers are located in safe areas rather than in known high-hazard areas. It means that their buildings are constructed or retrofitted to meet building code standards based on the threats of natural hazards faced. It means that their natural environmental protective systems, such as dunes and wetlands, are conserved to protect their hazard mitigation functions as well as their more traditional purposes.

We know how to build resilient communities. The techniques are not complicated or mysterious; many are simply common sense. Others are proven planning and engineering practices. But we do not use them often in practice. What is needed to achieve sustainable development and resilient communities?

The Means: Mitigation Commitment and Capacity

In our assessment of mitigation policy implementation in the United States, we identified two crucial, but often lacking, system characteristics:

- *Commitment is the dedication of policy makers to mitigate hazard impacts before disasters strike*, as indicated by their concern for mitigation, their willingness to budget human and fiscal resources for mitigation, and the priorities they give to mitigation programs relative to other emergency management actions. To what extent are planners and decision makers *willing* to act on the belief that mitigation is important?

- *Capacity is the ability to plan and implement mitigation programs*, as indicated by the human, legal, and fiscal resources in place, the effectiveness of intergovernmental communication and motivation, the knowledge and tools at hand to analyze and cope with hazard risks, and the outcomes of mitigation planning and expenditures. To what extent are planners and decision makers *able* to carry out effective mitigation programs?

We found troubling gaps in both commitment and capacity throughout the mitigation implementation system. Although it is improving, commitment on the part of decision makers remains weak at the state and local levels, where mitigation programs do not receive serious attention until a major disaster has occurred. Capacity, though also improving, remains problematic throughout the intergovernmental system, partly as a consequence of the historical dominance of relief and recovery, rather than mitigation, within the emergency management field.

Our recommendations for reform are aimed at building stronger hazard mitigation commitment and capacity in three arenas: (1) the intergovernmental system within which mitigation actions are taken, (2) the disaster policy framework that guides mitigation actions, and (3) the practice approaches that implement disaster policy. Because these recommendations depart from the way hazard mitigation has been done during the past decade, we see them as breaking through the status quo's built-up layers of agency relationships, bureaucratic procedures, and decision-making techniques in order to reach a higher level of sustainability.

Breaking Through to Sustainability: Summary of Recommendations

Despite the problems with the Stafford Act, its basic legislative structure appears to be sound. We believe that an effective mitigation system can be put in place through reforms that build on the framework of the act but change the way it is implemented.

The basic challenge for reform is to convert the original Stafford Act approach from a disaster-driven system to a policy- and threat-driven system so that it becomes proactive rather than reactive. The Federal Emergency Management Agency has taken some promising actions in this direction, including preparation of the *National Mitigation Strategy* (FEMA 1995b) and creation of the Performance Partnership Agreements (PPAs) funding process in 1995. Our recommendations are intended to complement and extend the proposals of FEMA's Mitigation Directorate.

On the basis of our research, we see additional possibilities for strengthening mitigation implementation in three main areas—the institutional system, the policy framework, and the practice tools. Our reasoning for these recommendations is discussed in the following sections. First, however, we present a summary of our main recommendations:

1. *System reform.* Convert the mitigation approach of the Stafford Act from a disaster-driven system to a policy- and threat-driven system so that it becomes proactive rather than reactive.

2. *Policy reform.* Change the disaster policy framework from a focus on reacting to individual disasters to a focus on living sustainably within an ecological system with foreseeable variations.

3. *Practice reform.* Institute best mitigation practices aimed at developing resilient communities.

Reforming the Intergovernmental Mitigation System

The Stafford Act's institutional framework can be thought of as a "system" of laws, regulations, programs, incentives, and people that produces certain "products"—state hazard mitigation plans and projects intended to reduce vulnerability to future natural hazards. The conceptual framework for our study assumes a linked set of components organized in a top-down policy system in which federal laws, regulations, and priorities are transmitted through FEMA regional offices to state mitigation agencies, affecting their mitigation plans and projects.

As shown in figure 1.1 in chapter 1, within this policy system federal mitigation policy directly affects FEMA regional implementation, which in turn directly influences state commitment and capacity, state Section 409 plan quality, and state implementation results, including Section 404 projects, which then lead to risk reduction outcomes. Finally, risk reduction outcomes feed back into the next round of federal policy as the system "learns" what types of mitigation work best.

The Reactive, Disaster-Centered Mitigation System of the Past

In practice, we found that the system assumed in our conceptual framework did not work as originally conceived. Our revised conceptual framework, shown in figure 13.1, contains several differences from our initial assumed framework. It remains a top-down system, but it is more situational, complex, and loosely coupled than initially envisioned. And because of these differences, it is not nearly as effective as a mitigation system should be.

First, the main driving factor influencing state mitigation action is the most recent *presidentially declared disaster*. That is, the system is reactive rather than proactive. State commitment and capacity wax and wane with the latest disaster. State Section 409 plans respond to the latest disaster (chapter 9). State implementation actions, in the form of Section 404 projects, are derived from the effects of the latest disaster (chapter 10). Thus, the latest disaster event intervenes in and strongly affects the system's performance (chapter 11).

Second, the *local level,* including local governments, private industry, and individuals, intervenes between state attitudes and actions and

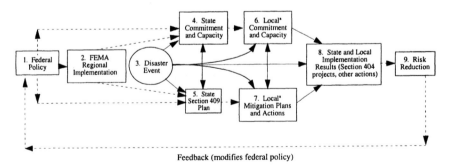

Feedback (modifies federal policy)

*Includes local governments, private industry, and individuals.

Figure 13.1. Intergovernmental Policy System for Natural Hazard Mitigation in Practice.

implementation results. Unfortunately, the system does not provide well for local mitigation. The *National Mitigation Strategy* asserts that all mitigation is local, but the Stafford Act focuses on state governments. Our new system view includes local commitment and capacity and local mitigation plans and actions as important influences on implementation results, as well as targets for state influence and action. In fact, the most direct influences on implementation results are the most recent disaster and state and local mitigation commitment and capacity, as illustrated by our case studies in chapters 3–8.

Third, there is little *implementation connection* between the state Section 409 hazard mitigation plan and state and local Section 404 hazard mitigation projects. The project proposals are generated either before or concurrently with the preparation of the Section 409 plan, both *following* the disaster. The bulk of Section 404 project applications are generated by local governments on the basis of their experience with the most recent disaster and bear little if any connection to state Section 409 plans. Thus, the linkage between state plans and implementation results is indirect and weak.

Fourth, *state and local mitigation commitment and capacity* are weak. The federal hazard mitigation officers we surveyed rated the mitigation capacity and commitment of about two-thirds of the states in their regions as medium or below (chapter 11). The majority of these respondents emphasized that staff and funding limitations restricted their ability to engage in commitment and capacity building as well as in overall hazard mitigation. More than two-thirds of the state hazard mitigation officers surveyed also rated their state's mitigation capacity as medium or below. This is borne out in their reports that the median number of emergency management staff members devoted to natural hazard mitigation per state is only *two,* with just fewer than half the states reporting a full-time mitigation staff of *zero to one.* For mitigation commitment, more than two-thirds rated their state elected officials as medium or below, and 84 percent rated their local emergency management officials as medium or below. However, they rated their state emergency management officials' commitment higher, with only 37 percent at medium or below.

Fifth, the *implementation contribution* of state Section 404 hazard mitigation projects to long-term risk reduction is not evident. This is a result of the long time lags in approving projects, the tendency of projects to respond to the last disaster rather than to be forward-looking, the failure to obligate much of the available mitigation funding, and the scattershot nature of the projects proposed in many cases (chapter 10). It is also the

result of failure to implement the objectives of state Section 409 plans through coordinated mitigation project priorities (chapter 9). Finally, it results from a lack of clear and consistent national hazard mitigation implementation priorities to guide state and local mitigation plans and project proposals. Although FEMA did declare acquisition and relocation projects as the highest priority during recovery from the 1993 Midwest floods in Missouri and Iowa (chapters 4 and 5), this has not been followed up with similar implementation guidance for subsequent disasters, and thus the lists of approved Section 404 projects tend to be mixed bags. Taken together, these factors, along with a lack of systematic evidence collection and monitoring to validate the contribution of Section 404 expenditures to risk reduction outcomes, make it difficult to know exactly how much hazard risks have actually been reduced through Section 404 implementation efforts.

The Proactive, Sustainable Mitigation System of the Future

To create a mitigation system that will result in sustainable communities, the indirect linkages among mitigation actors at various levels, their commitment and capacity, and the "tools" of mitigation—plans and projects—need to become more direct and effective. In the process, the system needs to become more of a partnership than a top-down system in order to make state and local actors responsible for mitigating the risks they face.

The sustainable mitigation system that we envision looks very different from the past system (see figure 13.2). At the *federal level*, FEMA no longer acts alone but joins with other federal agencies within a national sustainable communities policy team, building on the efforts of the President's Council on Sustainable Development (1996a, 1996b). Hazard mitigation policy is one element of a broader national policy on sustainable communities. FEMA is responsible for assembling and publishing a regular

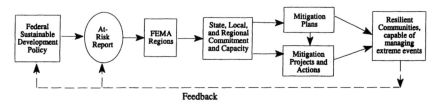

Figure 13.2. A Sustainable Mitigation Policy System.

"at-risk" report to Congress and the American people documenting the risks we face from potential future catastrophes, what is being done to mitigate them, and the economic, social, and environmental benefits of mitigation. National mitigation policy is derived from the hazard threats identified in the at-risk reports and communicated to FEMA regions and states, which make plans and implement projects to counteract the identified threats.

FEMA regions operate mitigation teams, whose mission is to build mitigation capacity and commitment at state, substate regional, and local levels. These teams are made up of skilled and experienced hazard risk analysts, mitigation planners, project designers, and implementation specialists. They travel to the states in each FEMA region to work with mitigation agencies and to assist them in educating elected officials and citizens about the hazard risks they face and the mitigation actions they can undertake. They also cooperate with the comprehensive planning staffs in the states, substate regions, and localities to assist in integrating mitigation objectives with other goals of comprehensive plans and growth management programs. Mitigation teams collaborate with states in establishing benchmarks for measuring progress toward resilient communities and are evaluated according to the progress their client agencies make toward reaching the capacity and commitment benchmarks.

States, substate regions, and local governments maintain hazard mitigation staffs, prepare and update hazard mitigation plans, and operate mitigation implementation programs made up of coordinated and prioritized mitigation projects. Resilient community plans resulting from these planning processes are reviewed and approved by the top decision makers at that level of government and represent action commitments rather than simply advisory documents. Effective mitigation is the product of many actions by individuals, businesses, utility companies, nongovernmental organizations, local governments, regional planning agencies, and state agencies, which must be coordinated by consistent mitigation plans. States are reviewed annually according to their benchmark targets, and those that achieve the target standards are certified as "mitigation managing" states. Certified states become eligible for higher funding levels and additional procedural flexibility.

Resilient communities are the goal of the system. Standard risk and vulnerability data are made available through geographic information systems and computer models to assist in guiding new development to safe locations and identifying existing development in need of retrofitting. Data collected on the performance of communities in meeting disaster challenges are used to inform future mitigation policy. For example, follow-up measurements are made of various past mitigation projects to see how much protection they afford in subsequent disasters.

To achieve the desired future sustainable mitigation system, we offer recommendations aimed at filling gaps in the current unsustainable system.

Regular "At-Risk" Report

Issue a regular "at-risk" report to Congress and the American people to increase national commitment to hazard mitigation by educating the public and elected officials about both the individual and cumulative risk magnitudes of potential disasters, what is being done to mitigate them, and the economic, social, and environmental benefits of mitigation.

The accelerating risks of natural hazards have not been granted the national attention they deserve. Each new disaster brings a flurry of attention, which then dies down as federal disaster funds are disbursed, the stricken communities start to recover, and the media highlight other "news." Disaster professionals are aware of the geometrically progressing risks, but citizens and decision makers do not identify growing and accumulating hazard risks as a genuinely serious policy problem.

Public safety is an undeniable core responsibility of the federal government. Whereas other public safety threats, such as crime and drugs, are well publicized, natural hazard threats are not. Elected officials clamor for postdisaster assistance but neglect spending for predisaster mitigation, which might have a greater long-term effect on public safety in many urban areas.

In order to move natural hazard risks onto the national action agenda, we recommend that FEMA make a regular natural hazards report to Congress documenting the risk magnitudes of potential disasters faced by the country. If there were one common approach for the hazard and vulnerability assessment elements of state Section 409 plans, this reporting process could be started relatively simply by compiling the state assessments into a cumulative "at-risk" report by state, FEMA region, and the nation as a whole. Such publication and national attention also might raise the quality of individual state hazard assessments. It could include other available indicators, such as annual hazard losses and dollars spent for mitigation by geographic area.

The report could be expanded later to include scenarios of major metropolitan area disasters (damage, injury, cost) under present conditions and projected growth estimates and disaster probabilities. This risk assessment might report standard measures such as the National Hazard Exposure (NHE) for various types of individual hazards (e.g., floods, earthquakes, hurricanes) as well as cumulative measures of the likely current and projected costs and damages on a nationwide basis.

The report should also describe the status of federal, state, and local mitigation plans and programs. It could start from our analysis of the content and quality of current Section 409 plans and an analysis of the type, amount, and anticipated effectiveness of current Section 404 and other mitigation projects and actions. It could include the status of FEMA's recommended mitigation strategies by type of hazard and by geographic area. It could estimate the effectiveness of these mitigation strategies in reducing projected hazard risks.

This system change would be aimed at reducing the national tendency to ignore potential disasters until they have occurred. By assessing and reporting on the risks faced in comparison with the mitigation actions taken, it would make information about risks and mitigation widely available and understandable. Although information provision alone will not guarantee the necessary commitment to mitigation, it is a necessary part of a sustainable national system and one that has been conspicuous in its absence to date.

Broader Mitigation Responsibility

Broaden the institutional structure for mitigation by extending responsibility for achieving resilient communities to include not only states but also localities, private and nongovernmental organizations, and individuals.

The existing mitigation policy implementation system concentrates on federal and state government agencies dealing with emergency management. Yet implementation of mitigation programs also depends on active local governments as well as nongovernmental and private organizations and individual households. Unless the responsibility of these entities is explicitly recognized, they may fall through the cracks in mitigation planning and implementation. Current planning regulations allow for approval of local Section 409 plans as well as plans credited through the Community Rating System. But most states do not require local mitigation plans to be consistent with state plans or even with state standards.

Such a requirement could be added to the certification standards for state hazard mitigation plans. Thus, certified states would have to establish procedures for assisting local governments in preparing local mitigation strategies, for extending the scope of mitigation actions to organizations and households, and for reviewing the adequacy, consistency, and implementation of the lower-level strategies. Alternatively, this objective could be achieved by giving additional pass-through funding to supplemental local mitigation project funding for those states that develop local mitigation planning programs or by making some types of local postdisaster funding contingent on approved local plans.

Local mitigation strategies could be elements of local comprehensive plans, elements of emergency management plans, or free-standing mitigation plans. Some states, such as California, Florida, and North Carolina, already require hazard elements in their mandatory local comprehensive plans (Godschalk, Kaiser, and Berke 1998). Other states may require that mitigation strategies be included as annexes to emergency management plans. Massachusetts is assisting one of its communities in preparing a local hazard mitigation plan that can serve as a model for other jurisdictions (Chapter 7). In whatever way these local mitigation strategies are implemented, they should be integrated with other local programs for land use control and public facility provision.

Mitigation should not be seen as only a government responsibility. The design and building professions, through their professional organizations, can play a major role in making mitigation work. Architects, engineers, builders, and developers must conduct their practice in accordance with the safety principles in their professional codes of ethics. Individuals also can contribute to mitigation by demanding hazard information to enable them to make informed housing choices and by incorporating safety features into the buildings in which they live and work (chapter 12).

Development of State and Local Mitigation Capability

Charge FEMA with the tasks of developing state and local mitigation capacity and commitment, give it the resources needed for these tasks, and grade its performance in carrying them out.

Considerable effort will be required to close the existing gaps in state and local capacity and commitment if effective mitigation plans are to be developed and carried out. We recommend that FEMA take a leadership role in building state capacity and commitment through mitigation teams, using training programs targeted to mitigation planning and implementation. States, in turn, could assume responsibility for building local mitigation capacity and commitment.

We believe that FEMA's national and regional offices will need to refocus staff resources to accomplish these tasks, creating mitigation planners and implementation specialists, as well as regional mitigation teams to certify state mitigation plans and strategies. Selection of these staff members will be critical to success in building state and local commitment and capacity. If permanent staff positions are not available, perhaps these planning, training, and organizational development tasks could initially be handled by FEMA reservists.

We recognize that this type of organizational development does not reflect the traditional roles of FEMA and state emergency management

programs. Training projects rank among the lowest expenditures of Hazard Mitigation Grant Program funds. However, new staff members and budget resources devoted to improving commitment and capacity should have important long-term payoffs in more effective mitigation. The progress of efforts to develop capacity and commitment should be carefully evaluated to ensure that the learning objectives are being achieved.

Required State Mitigation Planning and Implementation

> Require states to maintain hazard mitigation staffs, plans, and implementation programs, and base federal disaster funding and project approvals on demonstrated state commitment and capacity.

Every state should be expected to maintain an adequate ongoing hazard mitigation planning program if it is to receive federal disaster funding. This planning effort should include a full-time hazard mitigation staff adequate to deal with the state's hazard situation. For states that face few natural hazards, the staff might be small, consisting of a state hazard mitigation officer and support personnel. For states facing greater disaster threats, the staff should be correspondingly larger to ensure adequate capacity to meet the state's particular mitigation needs.

The state mitigation plans should be reviewed and approved by top state officials, preferably governors or cabinet officers, to ensure that the plans are taken seriously as state policy and resource commitments rather than simply being seen as paper exercises to satisfy a federal funding requirement.

Federal approvals of disaster funding and mitigation projects should be based on demonstrated state mitigation commitment and capacity. States that elect not to invest in such commitment and capacity should be prepared to receive only minimal federal disaster assistance.

Reforming Mitigation Policy

If mitigation policy is to become effective enough to meet the challenge of creating resilient communities that can withstand future disasters, gaps in implementation policy must be closed and the orientation of the policy framework must be changed from reactive to proactive.

Reactive Past Mitigation Policy

The original Stafford Act and its implementing regulations have been interpreted in practice to assume a reactive, postdisaster approach to miti-

gation planning and implementation, with a single-disaster focus rather than a cumulative hazard risk perspective. Little national attention has been paid to the content or broader implications of mitigation plans and programs, which have been conceived as stand-alone products unrelated to other state and local plans and programs.

Under these circumstances, it is not surprising that state mitigation plans have been of low quality and that expenditures under the Hazard Mitigation Grant Program have been piecemeal and of limited long-term effectiveness. This may have been acceptable under previous expectations of major disasters as low-cost, relatively infrequent events. However, it will not be acceptable under future catastrophe scenarios, in which failure to carry out predisaster mitigation may result in multistate or even national crises.

The linkages between hazard mitigation and other public policies related to sustainability have not been made clear and persuasive enough to generate demand for coordinated actions. The multistate Midwest floods of 1993 demonstrated that the effectiveness of the mitigation strategies of individual states and localities was inextricably linked to river basin conservation and development policies, to agricultural support policies, to infrastructure subsidy policies, to housing policies, and to economic development policies (chapters 4 and 5). Yet there is no comprehensive federal program that recognizes these linkages. Instead, each individual policy is separately administered.

Proactive Future Mitigation Policy

To achieve sustainability, future mitigation policy must be comprehensive in scope, not only in terms of its geographic coverage but also in terms of its content. The policy must have a clear goal—sustainable communities—and clear means of achieving this goal—all-hazards mitigation plans and projects. Our reform recommendations flow from these features.

Sustainable Communities Strategy

Make hazard mitigation a high priority of the national "Sustainable Communities" strategy proposed by the President's Council on Sustainable Development, in order to bring hazard mitigation into the state and local planning family and to connect all levels of government in a comprehensive effort to integrate hazard mitigation into community planning, economic development, and preservation of environmental capital.

To reduce the isolation of mitigation from other, more widely accepted public programs, it needs to be marketed to citizens and decision makers as

part of a "package" of actions aimed at developing sustainable communities. Mitigation can and should be integrated with planning for community economic development, land use, growth management, transportation, and environmental protection (Godschalk, Kaiser, and Berke 1998).

Hazard mitigation planning should play a prominent role in the programs being developed by the President's Council on Sustainable Development (1996a). The council's draft report on sustainable communities contains recommendations on natural disaster prevention and mitigation; however, these are very general and do not reflect the full importance and complexity of the topic (1996b). The national sustainability policy initiative represents an opportunity to promote mitigation goals and practice. We suggest a new mitigation vision rooted in the principles of sustainable development.

· The importance of hazard mitigation to a sustainable community is apparent to most professional planners. However, it has not been made clear to elected officials and citizens. To help bring this connection to the public's attention, a standard of community resiliency—a community's ability to avoid destruction through planning and development management strategies for avoiding, resisting, and recovering from the impacts of natural hazard forces—should be included as one of the criteria for sustainability. Economic development in sustainable communities should be planned so as not to be "unacceptably brittle and fragile" (NSTC 1996, p. 2).

Some postdisaster efforts to integrate mitigation and sustainable community development have been relatively successful. For example, during the recovery from the Midwest floods, development was removed from some hazard areas, which were then converted to public open space (Becker 1994). During the recovery from Hurricane Andrew, Habitat for Humanity developed the forty-acre Jordan Commons project using sustainable community principles, making the houses more resilient through use of steel frame designs, minimizing resource and energy consumption, recycling water, and using solar energy (chapter 3). These are promising, but limited, applications.

By far the more significant opportunities for application of sustainability principles occur during the predisaster period, when they can be incorporated into new and retrofitted development through state and local policies, plans, and standards. The objective is to build resiliency criteria not just into mitigation plans but also into state and local public construction programs, metropolitan transportation improvement plans, building and development codes, comprehensive community plans, and all the guidance systems for managing community development and redevelopment. For example, the *Strategic Regional Policy Plan for South Florida* links sustain-

ability goals with measurable benchmarks and indicators and recommends specific policies to achieve the goals (chapter 3).

We believe that a national Sustainable Communities strategy would be an effective way of initiating the task forces, research, and policy changes necessary to achieve this objective. Such an effort should be guided by the work of the President's Council on Sustainable Development and should include top officials from FEMA, the Department of Housing and Urban Development, the Department of Transportation, and the Environmental Protection Agency, who can carry it to the state and local levels. On the FEMA side, for example, the Performance Partnership Agreements could include resiliency standards against which state and local mitigation programs are evaluated. Such standards might include building code provisions for structural strength relative to hazards faced; environmental provisions to maintain natural features such as beaches, dunes, and marshes that protect property from hazard forces; and similar standards for sustainable communities.

Certified Predisaster, All-Hazards Mitigation Plans

> Convert the present focus on postdisaster state Section 409 plans to a focus on predisaster, all-hazards, comprehensive mitigation planning at both the state and local levels, coupled with pre- and postdisaster implementation programs and subject to annual certification reviews.

Following a presidentially declared disaster, each state currently is required under Section 409 of the Stafford Act to prepare, and submit to FEMA for approval, a hazard mitigation plan in order to qualify for federal mitigation grants. If prepared during the calm before the storm, *predisaster* mitigation plans allow for comprehensive evaluation of hazards faced, vulnerability of people and property in hazardous areas, and capability of state and local governments to guide future development away from hazardous areas and strengthen structures exposed to hazards. They offer a process for setting goals and objectives in which all stakeholders can be educated about hazard risks and involved in setting mitigation priorities. They provide a framework for designing mitigation activities, including Section 404 projects as well as other actions, to achieve measurable mitigation objectives over time. Finally, they support ongoing monitoring and evaluation of mitigation progress according to explicit benchmarks as well as regular plan updating to account for implementation experience.

Following a disaster, *postdisaster* hazard mitigation plans can build on the lessons learned as a result of the damage sustained to increase resilience

before the next disaster. Mitigation professionals can benefit from increased public concern about hazards and increased federal funding and technical assistance in rethinking their mitigation strategies and in carrying out larger mitigation projects. They should update adopted plans, incorporating the lessons learned from the disaster.

Our assessment of plans found a number of serious problems. Had we given the plans letter grades, the average would have been about a C minus (see chapter 9). Despite the poor overall average, we found several stronger plans and a number of commendable individual plan elements. This is heartening evidence that mitigation planning can work; the task is not impossible.

If mitigation is to be widely effective, the present production of postdisaster state mitigation plans simply to meet a requirement for grant funding must be converted to serious ongoing, preventive mitigation planning. This will require each state to have a full-time state hazard mitigation officer qualified in hazard mitigation planning, charged not only with producing the state mitigation plan but also with coordinating state efforts with local mitigation planning and carrying out mitigation projects.

A working group convened by FEMA in 1994 to revise mitigation regulations recommended that Section 409 of the Stafford Act be amended to require predisaster, all-hazards comprehensive planning and multiagency involvement at the state level (FEMA 1996). We agree that these elements must be made part of future state hazard mitigation planning, along with a concerted effort to involve local governments and private-sector stakeholders.

FEMA's establishment of Performance Partnership Agreements (PPAs) is a promising move toward ongoing mitigation planning. We recommend that this be complemented with a procedure for annual review and certification of state Section 409 hazard mitigation plans and planning programs. States with certified plans and planning programs would then be eligible for regular annual mitigation funding as well as special postdisaster mitigation grants. Mitigation planning certification requirements would include the following:

- A state mitigation plan submitted by the governor, approved by the FEMA regional director, and reviewed annually under the PPA

- An approved hazard mitigation grant administrative plan to implement the state mitigation strategy, including actions, funding, and responsible officials and also updated annually

- A full-time, permanent (year-round) mitigation officer who is qualified in mitigation planning

- Staff members who are qualified to provide technical assistance on sound mitigation techniques and grant programs, conduct benefit-cost analyses, and prepare documentation required under the National Environmental Policy Act of 1969 (NEPA)

- A mitigation coordinating council made up of representatives from relevant state and local government agencies and the private sector to advise on proposals and priorities of the plan, mitigation strategy, and implementation program

- A process for developing local mitigation plans and strategies that are integrated into local comprehensive plans and development regulations and that are approved by the state as consistent with the state mitigation plan and state mitigation standards

Our analysis of current state hazard mitigation plans spells out the weaknesses of the plans as currently prepared relative to standards for effective plans (see chapter 9). The standards of best mitigation practice that we created to review the plans could be used by FEMA to certify plans and their annual updates. Although each state should have flexibility in creating its plan, FEMA should guide state mitigation planning with clear performance criteria and mitigation policy guidance. In return for states' meeting certification standards, FEMA programs could be required to be consistent with approved state plans, similar to the consistency standard applied in the national Coastal Zone Management Act.

Pre- and Postdisaster Mitigation Funding

Change the focus of federal Section 404 hazard mitigation grants from postdisaster reconstruction projects to pre- and postdisaster preventive mitigation funding for states carrying out certified hazard mitigation programs and localities seeking to become sustainable communities.

Following a presidentially declared disaster, affected state and local governments are eligible to receive grants under the Hazard Mitigation Grant Program created by Section 404 of the Stafford Act. The Section 404 program funds projects that protect either public or private property, unlike the Section 406 Public Assistance program, which funds only public projects. Types of projects that can be funded under the Section 404 program range from structural improvements to education and training.

States administer their own Section 404 programs under FEMA oversight, and applicants apply through the state, with approval by FEMA.

Problems with past Section 404 programs include the following:

• The large difference between available funds and funds actually used for hazard mitigation projects represents a substantial missed mitigation opportunity—only about 20 percent ($215 million of $1,068 billion) of the Section 404 funds available between 1988 and mid-1995 were obligated by 1995 (chapter 10).

• The imbalance between disaster locations and FEMA regional staff resources adds to administrative difficulties—Regions V (headquartered in Chicago), VII (headquartered in Kansas City, Missouri), and IX (headquartered in San Francisco) administered about 75 percent of the obligated Section 404 funding and, along with Region IV (headquartered in Atlanta), about 80 percent of the total (obligated plus pending) Section 404 funding from 1988 through 1995 (chapter 10). (FEMA has begun to address this problem by forming regional teams to help close out past disasters.)

• The average length of time between a disaster declaration and project funding is two years, and then it typically takes eighteen months to carry out a funded project, resulting in a lag of three and a half years from disaster to project completion.

• Bureaucratic tie-ups and confusion about what constitutes mitigation result in a failure to focus mitigation actions on priority needs and make it difficult to assess the effectiveness of mitigation strategies.

Clearly, an important way to improve future mitigation is to strengthen and tighten the process for funding hazard mitigation implementation projects. The present Section 404 Hazard Mitigation Grant Program is triggered by a declared disaster and anchored in the postdisaster period. This hampers predisaster mitigation implementation and divorces it from the comprehensive predisaster mitigation plan. Stated simply, the only way states have been able to get federal mitigation funding is to suffer a disaster, in contrast to having funding available beforehand to enable them to mitigate the effects of future disasters.

The present Section 404 program is designed primarily to support individual projects rather than more comprehensive programs or strategies. Because the funding is tied to individual projects, each of which must be individually evaluated on a number of criteria, from benefit-cost ratio to

environmental impact, the funding process is complicated, slow, and ineffective.

We recommend an ongoing predisaster mitigation funding program for state and local governments that seriously pursues the goal of resilient communities. In the long run, this would save the taxpayers money as communities became more resilient. It would also get the attention of state and local government officials and increase the priority of their predisaster mitigation activities. Finally, it would allow states to plan multiyear mitigation programs based on a predictable funding source.

Mitigation funding should be based on equitable cost sharing whereby all those who are affected contribute (chapter 12). There should be one consistent federal-state cost-sharing arrangement rather than the current arrangement, which politicizes disaster relief and encourages states to vie for higher percentages of federal funding on the (sometimes questionable) grounds of their inability to cope with a disaster. States should follow the example of Florida in creating a "rainy day" fund to increase their financial self-sufficiency for dealing with likely disasters (chapter 3). Local governments should budget funds to carry out their mitigation strategies. (See chapter 5 for the example of Davenport, Iowa, which has been buying out floodplain properties with revenues from a special sales tax since 1990.) Individuals who elect to develop or hold property in hazardous areas should contribute to mitigation costs, and state and federal incentives that subsidize such development should be discontinued.

Such a mitigation funding program could be based on the history and anticipated risk of each state's disasters and funded by insurance surcharges and/or low-interest federal loans. It should include specific performance criteria and be subject to careful auditing and oversight reviews. Mitigation programs could be required to incorporate national hazard mitigation priorities but would be tailored to meet the specific hazards and fit the particular institutional contexts of individual states, substate regions, and localities.

The process used by metropolitan planning organizations for generating highway improvement projects suggests a possible predisaster model for identifying and prioritizing hazard mitigation projects at the substate level. Each state would be divided into a series of hazard planning regions, ideally using existing regional organizations. (See the Iowa case study in chapter 5 for an example of a state mitigation strategy that relies on regional organizations.) These regions would solicit and prioritize hazard mitigation projects from local governments on a regular basis, linking them to implementation of their mitigation strategies and the objectives of

the state hazard mitigation plan. The state would then award mitigation grants based on the basis of the regional priorities. This would avoid the confusion and delays of initiating planning and decision making in the wake of a disaster by preidentifying the priority projects.

There is a precedent for block grant funding in the new rules of the Flood Mitigation Assistance Program (FMAP). Funds are allocated to FEMA regions on the basis of the number of states in the region, flood insurance policies in force, and the number of repetitive loss structures present. FEMA's regional offices approve grants for technical assistance, planning assistance, and project implementation using specified criteria for project evaluation. Thus, FMAP funding for both mitigation planning and implementation is ongoing rather than disaster specific.

Reforming Mitigation Practice

We see the need for a number of changes in mitigation practice. In many ways, practice changes can be more important than policy changes, since they have a more direct effect on the "nitty-gritty" daily mitigation decisions. They may also be easier to carry out than the more sweeping policy changes. The practice changes recommended here focus on mitigation tools and the ways they are used.

Reactive Past Mitigation Practice

The Stafford Act and its implementing regulations have been interpreted in practice as assuming that the major tools for hazard mitigation are after-the-fact state postdisaster plans and state and local postdisaster expenditures on mitigation projects (even though the regulations clearly state that Section 409 plans should be prepared ahead of time and updated to reflect specific disasters). As employed, these tools have been shown to result in slow, piecemeal, and ineffective outcomes. The quality of the products, which are prepared during the stress of disaster recovery, is low, and FEMA has accepted mediocre "paper" mitigation plans with little risk analysis or weak substantive strategies (chapter 9) and individual mitigation projects with little long-term coordination (chapter 10).

Local government officials, who must submit most of the mitigation grant proposals, are typically left out of the state mitigation planning loop and do not have the technical capacity to perform basic risk analysis. Local government mitigation plans, when they exist, are too often unrelated to comprehensive or land use plans that might be used to implement mitiga-

tion recommendations. Rarely do they envision a role for the nongovernmental actors who may have to carry out mitigation actions, such as private businesses and individual households.

Historically, during the hectic postdisaster decision-making process, FEMA has been cast in the role of a recovery funding agency and judged (particularly by politicians) by its performance in getting recovery funding "out the door" rather than as an agency strongly concerned with development of longer-term and less tangible mitigation capacity and commitment. Thus, FEMA staffing has been oriented toward the highly visible emergency response and recovery functions rather than toward mitigation planning aimed at producing and implementing coordinated predisaster state-local and public-private mitigation strategies.

Proactive Future Mitigation Practice

Mitigation practice could be strengthened through "accountable devolution" of responsibility and authority to states and localities. Under this approach, FEMA's role would be to create incentives and tools for effective performance, to assist state and local mitigation agencies in planning and carrying out mitigation strategies, and to evaluate the outcomes in light of national standards. FEMA would no longer be involved in detailed and time-consuming reviews of each individual postdisaster mitigation project proposal. Instead, it would focus on helping to reduce cumulative vulnerability to risk through implementation of comprehensive federal, state, and local pre- and postdisaster mitigation plans and strategies. Its regional teams would play a vital role in building state and local mitigation commitment and capacity.

Three practice changes could make a lot of difference. Provision of hazard information for state and local mitigation planning would help to overcome this Achilles' heel of present practice. Requiring regional-scale mitigation plans would extend the vision of planners and decision makers beyond their jurisdictions to include the complete natural system that spawns the hazard risks. And issuing best mitigation practice manuals would help inspire and educate mitigation planners in large and small agencies across the country as well as save them time and money.

Hazard Assessment Information
for State and Local Mitigation Planning

Make hazard assessment information accessible to state and local planners to assist mitigation planning and decision making, using GIS databases and computer models to map vulnerable areas.

Prominently missing from the present practice of hazard mitigation planning is solid hazard assessment information (chapter 9; Deyle et al. 1998; Godschalk et al. 1998). Most state hazard mitigation plans do rudimentary *hazard identification*, defining the magnitude (intensity) and probability (likelihood) of natural hazards in geographic areas. A much smaller number do *vulnerability assessment*, characterizing the populations and property at risk in a given area and estimating the damage that might result from a hazard at various intensities. Almost none do the more advanced *risk analysis*, estimating the probable degree of injury and damage that might result from exposure of people and property to a hazard in a given area over a specified time period.

Most hazard identification is presented on maps, such as the familiar flood and hurricane storm surge maps. The Flood Insurance Rate Maps (FIRMs) produced by the National Flood Insurance Program show the floodways and floodplains for 100-year floods. Hurricane storm surge maps show the areas subject to flooding at different storm intensities. Earthquake hazard mapping, which is more complex than flood mapping, is just now being conducted; California, for example, released its first preliminary seismic hazard zone maps in 1996. Hazard identification maps such as these show the extent of hazard areas, but they do not show the current or future projected populations or property at risk, information that is necessary in order to estimate vulnerability. Lack of vulnerability information in turn handicaps mitigation planning, priority setting, and implementation.

Earthquake hazard maps developed for the Portland metropolitan area illustrate the use of hazard identification maps in regional land use planning and administration of building permits (Spangle Associates 1996). Funded by the U.S. Geological Survey and FEMA, these color maps portray seismic hazards from landslides, liquefaction, and ground amplification at a scale of 1:24,000. They give hazard information to assist in planning for the distribution of land uses and in creating structural designs for construction. Land uses are classified into eight groups, ranging from those with potentially catastrophic consequences if damaged and, hence, requiring the most protection from earthquake damage to those with low occupancy and hence requiring minimal protection. These catagories are related to four mapped zones of relative earthquake hazards ranging from most to least hazardous on the basis of slope instability, ground motion amplification, and liquefaction susceptibility. Metro, the regional government serving the Greater Portland metropolitan area, is also compiling a nonresidential building database on a geographic information

system (GIS), which can be used with the hazard maps to assess vulnerability of existing structures to earthquake damage. Once the maps and building assessments are complete, Metro will conduct a damage and loss estimate using models developed by FEMA and Portland State University.

The advent of GIS and digitized land use data has opened new possibilities for improving hazard assessment information, as illustrated by Metro's earthquake hazard maps. New hazard assessment tools could allow mitigation planners to predict the impacts of natural hazards and assess the costs and benefits of alternative plans and mitigation strategies (Deyle et al. 1998). However, the development and diffusion of these new hazard assessment tools are constrained by uneven knowledge about occurrence of some hazards, limited data on structures within hazard areas, and difficulties in designing hazard assessment programs that are user-friendly enough to be handled by most mitigation planners.

We recommend that the federal government invest in the creation of a comprehensive suite of computerized hazard assessment tools for use in mitigation planning and implementation by state and local governments. The technology is available, using GIS databases and scientific studies to identify hazards and assess and map vulnerability. The first applications should aim at developing the capability to create standardized vulnerability maps, such as Metro's seismic maps. Availability of such maps for all types of natural hazards would greatly improve the quality of state and local hazard mitigation planning.

A longer-range application would be to provide mitigation planners with damage estimation software to enable them to assess the effectiveness of various mitigation options. Work is under way on two earthquake modeling programs: HAZUS (Hazards U.S.) has been developed by FEMA to run on desktop personal computers under its project on Standardized Earthquake Loss Estimation Methodology, and RAMP (Regional Assessment of Mitigation Priorities) is being developed by a consultant under contract with the Governor's Office of Emergency Services in California. FEMA is also planning to extend its methodology to hurricanes. However, most hazard modeling systems, such as Sea, Lake, and Overland Surge from Hurricanes (SLOSH), are operated by technical specialists rather than by the state and local planners who rely on the hazard maps produced by these systems. Future generations of hazard modeling systems should be designed for use by generalist mitigation planners in preparing impact analyses of proposed development projects and comprehensive plan alternatives.

Regional-Scale Mitigation Plans

> Institute regional-scale mitigation plans covering natural systems, such as river basins, earthquake faults, and coastal areas, to ensure resilient regions as well as resilient communities.

Natural systems have their own geography and do not necessarily respect boundaries of government jurisdiction. The Midwest floods of 1993, for example, affected nine states. Although each state prepared its own mitigation plan, there was no master regional mitigation plan that coordinated actions on the scale of the river basin. Yet flooding in downstream jurisdictions was a direct consequence of actions taken in upstream jurisdictions. These consequences resulted not only from emergency sandbagging and other disaster preparedness actions but also from long-term wetland reclamation and other measures affecting the river's ecological system and its ability to respond naturally to, and contain, flood conditions. Similar regional considerations apply to mitigation planning for earthquakes and hurricanes.

Current mitigation planning is limited by government jurisdictions to states and local governments. Regional mitigation planning would require intergovernmental agreements in the form of interstate compacts, as were used in planning the Lake Tahoe region, or memorandums of agreement among local governments and substate regional planning agencies. These agreements could specify means of coordinating risk and vulnerability analyses, plans for mitigation, and emergency evacuation and sheltering. FEMA could assist the agencies involved in initiating regional mitigation planning processes. In a number of cases, regional institutions, such as river basin planning agencies, already exist. In other cases, new institutions would have to be created.

Not every area of the country will need a regional hazard mitigation plan. In many cases, the state and local plans will be adequate. However, in some regions, a broader view of hazard mitigation will provide the best way to coordinate mitigation planning and implementation across jurisdictional boundaries.

Best Mitigation Practice Manuals

> Publish manuals of best mitigation practices for resilient communities describing successes, identifying ethical principles, and recommending practical techniques for planning and implementing mitigation at the state, substate regional, and local levels.

Mitigation planners need guidance in reorienting their practice to achieve resilient communities. Because this is a radically new approach,

there are many published arguments for undertaking sustainable development but few down-to-earth examples of success. The literature identifies the need to integrate hazard mitigation into plans for economic development, environmental conservation, and social equity, but it fails to provide ethical principles and practical techniques to carry out this type of boundary-spanning planning.

One way to help reorient mitigation planning toward more sustainable practice is to publish manuals of best mitigation practices. Such manuals have proven very helpful in other fields, such as urban development (Ewing 1996) and urban stream protection (Schueler 1995). They include principles of best practice and techniques, along with detailed descriptions of effective applications, including background information. Because mitigation practice differs depending on the institutional and geographic setting, it would be useful to have manuals for each scale of planning—state, substate regional, and local.

Conclusion: Creating a Supportive Climate for Mitigation

In the course of our study, we encountered a number of competent and hardworking people devoted to the cause of effective natural hazard mitigation, particularly during our on-site case studies. Many of them were concerned that publishing our accounts of the problems they faced and the imperfections of the solutions they proposed might damage the mitigation cause. Our response is that identification and analysis of these problems and imperfections, even when painful, are necessary first steps to understanding and strengthening the national mitigation system. Our analysis is dedicated to creating a supportive institutional climate for mitigation planning in order to achieve sustainable communities.

Past mitigation planning operated in a boom-or-bust setting. After a declared disaster, the boom is on. Federal money pours in, state and local staffs are built up, elected officials at all levels are deeply concerned, and a variety of agencies and organizations are eager to cooperate. However, not only do the compressed recovery time schedules make it difficult to carry out effective mitigation, but once the recovery is complete, the climate turns to bust. Budgets are cut, staffs shrink, decision makers lose interest, and other agencies and organizations return to normal business. This kind of crisis-driven planning is understandably prone to mistakes and inefficiency.

We want to help make mitigation work, not simply to criticize its shortcomings. It is critical to create an institutional climate that supports

mitigation both before and after disasters. In such a climate, mitigation is a *valued, ongoing activity*. It has a stable budget, funded not only by the federal government but also by state and local governments. It has a qualified staff, with opportunities for continued development and advancement. It has the interest and respect of elected officials, who include it in their policy formulation. And it has a working team of agency and organization representatives who seek to further its goals within their programs and plans.

Our vision is one in which the parts of the intergovernmental mitigation system work together for sustainable, resilient communities. Decision makers at all levels insist on effective mitigation policy and practice. Bureaucratic red tape and tensions are cut back. Responsibility and participation are dispersed across all government levels. Training and development are major system activities. Hazard assessment tools are state of the art. Hazard mitigation plans are carried out through prioritized mitigation projects. And all the actors are committed to learning from experience how to more effectively reduce future hazard risks. Although these goals are too idealistic to serve as a short-term strategy for reinventing mitigation today, they are a useful starting point and vision for longer-term reform of the mitigation system.

We believe that our recommendations, if put into practice, will help achieve a supportive climate for mitigation. Other actions also will be necessary, including changes to public and private hazard insurance, disaster relief funding formulas and cost-sharing arrangements, and disaster-specific programs. However, mitigation should work much better if the changes put forth here are carried out.

Implementing our recommendations will require changing the current national hazard mitigation system, its policies, and its practices. Making these changes will not be cheap or easy, especially in the short run. Doing what is necessary to make mitigation work will require strong leadership and political backbone, particularly in terms of reorienting citizens and public officials from the notion of maximum federal disaster relief as an *entitlement* to the notion of shared hazard mitigation as a *responsibility*. However, the potential for significant long-term payoffs—in terms of reduced suffering, damage, and disaster relief payments and increased community sustainability and resiliency—should outweigh the immediate costs.

Postscript

Since our study was completed, FEMA has prepared the *National Pre-Disaster Mitigation Plan* (FEMA 1998), in response to a directive contained

in the report of the Conference Committee (Report 105-297) of the HUD, VA and Independent Agencies Joint Subcommittee on Appropriations. The vision of the plan is a future in which all communities in the United States that are vulnerable to natural hazards have in place the practices, policies, and capabilities to minimize the negative impacts of such hazards on the private and public sectors. The goals are to implement natural hazard loss reduction practices and policies and to improve the performance of facilities and systems in natural hazard events. The plan lays out a series of principles and objectives for implementation. This attention to predisaster mitigation is heartening evidence that the concerns identified in our study are being taken seriously at the national level.

References

Becker, William S. 1994. "The Case for Sustainable Redevelopment." *Environment and Development* (American Planning Association), November, 1–4.

Deyle, Robert E., Steven P. French, Robert B. Olshansky, and Robert G. Paterson. 1998. "Hazard Assessment: The Factual Basis for Planning and Mitigation." In *Confronting Natural Hazards: Land-Use Planning for Sustainable Communities,* ed. Raymond J. Burby. Washington, D.C.: National Academy Press, Joseph Henry Press.

Ewing, Reid. 1996. *Best Development Practices.* Chicago: Planners Press.

FEMA (Federal Emergency Management Agency). 1995a. *Mitigation: Cornerstone for Building Safer Communities.* Washington, D.C.: FEMA.

———. 1995b. *National Mitigation Strategy: Partnerships for Building Safer Communities.* Washington, D.C.: FEMA.

———. 1996. *Draft Proposed Rule for Disaster Assistance: Hazard Mitigation.* Amendment to 44 C.F.R. Part 206. Washington, D.C.: FEMA.

———. 1997. *Partnership for a Safer Future.* Strategic Plan, Fiscal Year 1998–Fiscal Year 2007. Washington, D.C.: FEMA.

———. 1998. *National Pre-Disaster Mitigation Plan.* Washington, D.C.: FEMA.

Godschalk, David R., Edward J. Kaiser, and Philip Berke. 1998. "Integrating Hazard Mitigation and Local Land-Use Planning." In *Confronting Natural Hazards: Land-Use Planning for Sustainable Communities,* ed. Raymond J. Burby. Washington, D.C.: National Academy Press, Joseph Henry Press.

Godschalk, David R., Richard Norton, Craig Richardson, David Salvesen, and Junko Peterson. 1998. *Coastal Hazards Mitigation: Public Notification, Expenditure Limitations, and Hazard Areas Acquisition.* Report for North Carolina Division of Coastal Management. Chapel Hill: University of North Carolina. Center for Urban and Regional Studies.

Institute for Business and Home Safety. 1997. *Natural Disaster Initiatives of the Insurance Sector.* Boston: Institute for Business and Home Safety.

Munasinghe, Mohan, and Caroline Clarke, eds. 1995. *Disaster Prevention for Sustainable Development.* Washington, D.C.: International Decade for Natural Disaster Reduction and World Bank.

NAPA (National Academy of Public Administration). 1993. *Coping with Catastrophe: Building an Emergency Management System to Meet People's Needs.* Washington, D.C.: NAPA.

NSTC (National Science and Technology Council). 1996. *Natural Disaster Reduction: A Plan for the Nation.* Washington, D.C.: NSTC.

President's Council on Sustainable Development. 1996a. *Sustainable America: A New Consensus for Prosperity, Opportunity, and a Healthy Environment for the Future.* Washington, D.C.: President's Council on Sustainable Development.

———. 1996b. *Sustainable Communities: Task Force Report.* Final Review Draft. Washington, D.C.: President's Council on Sustainable Development.

Schueler, Thomas R. 1995. *Site Planning for Urban Stream Protection.* Washington, D.C.: Metropolitan Washington Council of Governments.

Spangle Associates. 1996. *Using Earthquake Hazard Maps for Land Use Planning and Building Permit Administration.* Report of the Metro Advisory Committee for Mitigating Earthquake Damage, prepared for Metro Portland, Oregon.

United Nations. 1992. *Agenda 21.* New York: United Nations.

U.S. Army Corps of Engineers. 1995. *Interim Technical Data Report: Metro New York Hurricane Transportation Study.* Wilmington, N.C.: U.S. Army Corps of Engineers, Wilmington District.

About the Authors

David R. Godschalk

Dr. David R. Godschalk is Stephen Baxter Professor of City and Regional Planning at the University of North Carolina at Chapel Hill. He holds a Ph.D. degree and a master's degree in City and Regional Planning from the University of North Carolina as well as a Bachelor of Architecture degree from the University of Florida and a B.A. degree from Dartmouth College. In addition to conducting hazards research, he has served as a consultant on coastal development management and hazard mitigation and has been chair of the Mitigation Committee of the National Hurricane Conference. A former chair of his department, he has also been an elected member of the Chapel Hill Town Council and editor of the *Journal of the American Institute of Planners.*

Timothy Beatley

Dr. Timothy Beatley is Associate Professor in the Department of Urban and Environmental Planning of the School of Architecture at the University of Virginia. He holds a Ph.D. degree in City and Regional Planning and a Master of Arts degree in Political Science from the University of North Carolina at Chapel Hill, as well as a Master of Urban Planning degree from the University of Oregon and a Bachelor of City Planning degree from the University of Virginia. A former chair of his department, he has participated in national studies on mitigation policy and has completed a study for the Office of Technology Assessment on risk allocation policy in the coastal zone. His recent work centers on sustainable development and environmental ethics. He is a fellow of the Urban Land Institute.

Philip Berke

Dr. Philip Berke is Associate Professor in the Department of City and Regional Planning at the University of North Carolina at Chapel Hill. He holds a Ph.D. degree in Urban and Regional Science from Texas A&M Uni-

versity, an M.S. degree in Natural Resources Planning from the University of Vermont, and a B.A. degree in Economics and Environmental Science from Empire State College. He is a Faculty Fellow of the Lincoln Institute of Land Policy and a Fulbright Scholar Research Fellow at the Center for Environmental and Resource Studies at the University of Waikato, New Zealand, where his work involves natural hazard risk assessment, sustainable development, and land use planning. He is a consultant to the United Nations on hazard mitigation and environmental management and a former Associate Director of the Hazard Reduction and Recovery Center at Texas A&M University.

David J. Brower

David J. Brower is Research Professor in the Department of City and Regional Planning at the University of North Carolina at Chapel Hill. He holds a B.A. degree in Political Science from the University of Michigan and a J.D. degree from the University of Michigan Law School. He has directed a national evaluation of the Coastal Zone Management Act and served as Associate Director of the Center for Urban and Regional Studies at the University of North Carolina. He has participated in the formulation of mitigation policy at the local, state, and national levels. Much of his recent work addresses sustainable development and environmental ethics.

Edward J. Kaiser

Dr. Edward J. Kaiser is Professor and former Chairman of the Department of City and Regional Planning at the University of North Carolina at Chapel Hill. He holds a Ph.D. degree in City and Regional Planning from the University of North Carolina at Chapel Hill and a Bachelor of Architecture degree from the Illinois Institute of Technology. He has researched land use approaches to flood and hurricane hazard mitigation, including the effects of state planning mandates on local hazard mitigation planning and implementation. He has served as coeditor of the *Journal of the American Planning Association* and is the lead author of *Urban Land Use Planning,* with David R. Godschalk and F. Stuart Chapin Jr. (Urbana: University of Illinois Press, 1995).

Charles C. Bohl

Charles C. Bohl is a doctoral student in the Department of City and Regional Planning at the University of North Carolina at Chapel Hill, where he is completing a dissertation on mixed-use centers. He holds a master's degree in planning from the State University of New York at Albany and a B.A. degree from New York University. Prior to entering the

graduate program at the University of North Carolina, he was Economic Development Specialist for Niagara Mohawk Power Corporation in Albany, New York. He also served on the board of the New York State Economic Development Council and the Capitol Regional Economic Development Corporation.

R. Matthew Goebel

R. Matthew Goebel is an Associate with Clarion Associates, planning consultants in Denver, Colorado. A graduate of the joint Law and Planning degree program at the University of North Carolina at Chapel Hill, he earned his master's degree in Regional Planning and his J.D. degree in 1997. He also holds a B.A. degree from the University of Texas at Austin. He formerly has worked with Blayney Dyett, urban and regional planners in San Francisco, and with Hardy-Heck-Moore, historic preservation consultants in Austin, Texas.

Index